"general...
— read about
correlation

# Introduction to Psychological Measurement

# Introduction to Psychological Measurement

## Jum C. Nunnally, Jr.

professor of psychology
vanderbilt university

mcgraw-hill book company

new york     st. louis     san francisco     düsseldorf     london
mexico     panama     sydney     toronto

# Introduction to Psychological Measurement

*Library of Congress Catalog Card Number*
77-100850
ISBN 07047559-8

567890 KPKP 798765432

This book was set in Electra by Monotype Composition Company, Inc., and printed on permanent paper and bound by The Maple Press Company. The designer was Paula Tuerk; the drawings were done by John Cordes, J. & R. Technical Services, Inc. The editors were Walter Maytham and Cynthia Newby. Sally R. Ellyson supervised the production.

# Dedication

To the two persons who influenced
me most in my early training
Professor B. Orman McDonald
Professor William Stephenson

This book is intended to serve as a comprehensive text for undergraduate courses in psychological measurement. Some historical perspectives regarding the author's writings on psychological measurement should help indicate the nature and purpose of this book. The author's first book on psychological measurement was *Tests and Measurements: Assessment and Prediction* (McGraw-Hill, 1959), which was intended as a comprehensive text for undergraduate courses in psychological measurement and educational measurement. In addition, the book covered and discussed some matters that ordinarily would be reserved for graduate courses, e.g., some technical matters regarding multivariate analysis.

In order to present this material in depth, however, three books on measurement were needed: (1) an undergraduate text on educational measurement, (2) a graduate-level text on psychological measurement, and (3) an undergraduate text on psychological measurement. The first appeared in 1964: *Educational Measurement and Evaluation* (McGraw-Hill). The second appeared in 1967: *Psychometric Theory* (McGraw-Hill). The reader has in his hands the third book of the trio.

In essence, this is not a revision of *Tests and Measurements* (1959); rather, it is a new book. Consequently, it would be a waste of time to make comparisons between this book and the 1959 book, and that would only serve to demean an old friend.

There are a number of salient features of this book, the first of which is an emphasis on measurement in the science of psychology generally rather than on applied problems of psychological measurement. Up until recent years there was a tendency to link the term psychological measurement with applied problems of testing in schools, clinics, industry, and governmental agencies. Such applied problems of measurement are important, and some principles relating to such problems are discussed in this book; but much more emphasis is placed on principles which relate to psychology as a burgeoning science. Thus issues concerning reliability, validity, psychological scaling, test construction, and many others are discussed in a way that is equally as relevant for basic research in psychology as for applied uses of tests.

A second feature of this book is that it concerns both measurement in controlled experiments and measurement in studies of individual differences. The topic of psychological measurement has been identified frequently with studies of the ways in which people differ from one another, perhaps because problems of measurement are so obvious there (e.g., in the measurement of intelligence) and because so much usable hardware has been developed in that connection. But problems of psychological measurement are equally important in controlled experiments on learning, perception, physiological processes, behavior in group situations, and other topics of experimentation. For this reason, the book discusses many parallels between problems of psychological measurement in studies of individual differences and in controlled experiments. In addition, Chapters 15 and 16 are devoted to discussions of principles of psychological measurement that relate to many types of controlled experiments.

A third feature of the book relates to the emphasis on general principles of measurement rather than on applied problems. This is not a catalog of available tests or a how-to-do-it manual for the use of tests. If one is interested in these important matters, there are much better books than this one. General sources for these purposes are listed in the suggested additional readings; sources with respect to the use of particular instruments are generously referenced. While there is no attempt to be encyclopedic with respect to tests, many examples of available instruments are used to illustrate principles of measurement. Also, Appendix C provides brief descriptions of many commercially distributed tests.

A fourth feature of this book is that statistics are discussed only where necessary. There is an unfortunate tendency of some writers on psychological measurement to enter every discussion with a flight into statistics. Such pedantry allows one to avoid the thin ice of controversy that covers so many important issues in psychological measurement. Wherever possible, quantitative issues in this book are talked out rather than mathematized. For example, Chapter 5 sticks mainly to a discussion of principles relating to reliability of measurement. More technical issues and statistics are presented in detail in Appendix D. It is felt that an emphasis on verbal description rather than on mathematical equations is particularly appropriate for an audience of undergraduate students. The book should be understandable to students who have no prior knowledge of statistics.

At this point in the preface, it is traditional to thank people for their help and encouragement. I had thought of thanking my colleagues who have helped me in numerous ways, but there are far too many of them. Consequently, I will mention only Dr. Richard Gorsuch, whose careful, astute criticisms of the manuscript were invaluable. I had thought of mentioning how much my family had suffered because of the long hours that I worked on this book, but looking at their smiling faces, they do not appear to have suffered so much. The constant attention of three capable, gracious ladies made the book a pleasure to write. The ladies are Mrs. Nancy Ator, Mrs. Jacqueline Caldwell, and Miss Dorothy Timberlake.

Jum C. Nunnally, Jr.

# Contents

# PART 1:

## Historical and Theoretical Foundations of Psychological Measurements

# CHAPTER 1

# The foundations of psychological measurement

Psychological measurement is a close and important concern to all of us. The student who reads these pages for a course assignment is very much interested in one type of psychological measurement: the method of grading used by the instructor. The person who aspires to higher education needs the best possible measurement of his capabilities before wagering his future. A successful marriage depends on the personalities of the partners, and it would be worth a great deal to a young couple to have their compatibility measured in advance. Many millions of dollars are spent in measuring public reaction to political candidates, new brands of soap, and television programs. In these and many other ways, psychological measurement is a part of everyday living.

In addition to being important in everyday life, psychological measurement methods are also crucially important for basic research in psychology. A typical experiment concerns the effects of different levels of sound intensity on pupil size in the eye, for which it is necessary to measure fine changes in pupil size as sound levels are alternately increased and decreased. Another typical experiment concerns the effects of different types of communications on attitudes toward racial integration, for which it is necessary to measure attitudes adequately. A third typical experiment concerns the tendency for some types of group situations to induce anxiety in the group members, for which it is necessary to measure anxiety.

It can be argued persuasively that obtaining adequate measurement methods is *the* major problem in the science of psychology. Psychological theories are filled with variables that either cannot be measured at all at the present time or can be measured only approximately, e.g., anxiety, creativity, dogmatism, achievement motivation, attention, and frustration, to mention only a few. How to obtain better measurement methods in psychology is the major topic of this book.

In spite of the many needs for psychological measurement methods, few had been developed up to the turn of this century. It is surprising that men learned so much about the world around them without learning more about themselves. A technique was developed for measuring the circumference of the earth 2,000 years before psychological tests came into general use. There are still many weak spots in the storehouse of psychological measurement methods. Important decisions must often be made about people on the basis of very crude "yardsticks." The results of many controlled experiments are difficult to interpret because of inadequacies in measurement methods. The slowness with which psychological measurement has developed is due, in part, to the complexity of the individual human being. Some mistaken ideas about the purpose and substance of psychology have also retarded the development of measurement methods. These will be discussed in the following sections.

### The nature of psychological data

The development of psychological measurement and of psychology as a whole was delayed, in part, by some misunderstandings about the nature of the subject matter. The philosopher Kant once said that it would not be possible to have a science of psychology because the basic data could not be observed and measured. Modern psychologists would agree with Kant to the extent that only certain kinds of psychological phenomena are open to observation and measurement.

Psychological science concerns itself with the study of human behavior, with the actions, judgments, words, and preferences of individuals. The study of such tangible behavior complies with the requirements of scientific research. However, other phenomena that are spoken of as being "psychological" cannot be the subject of *direct* scientific study. Some of these are sensations, feelings, and images.

Throughout the history of philosophic thought there has been a tendency to divide psychological phenomena into those which are "physical" and those which are "mental." This division of phenomena is referred to as *psychophysical dualism*, the belief in separate mental and physical processes. Because of this unfortunate logical standpoint, scholars have been drawn into many needless arguments about the "connections" between the mental and the physical.

By adopting a set of simple rules, the seemingly difficult problem of psychophysical dualism can be circumvented. The purpose of scientific effort is to test statements about the world of events—all those events which can be seen, heard, touched, or otherwise experienced in common. The phenomenon being studied might itself be impalpable, such as magnetism, atomic action, or the transfer of heat. But our knowledge of the phenomenon must always come from publicly observable events: the changing direction of a compass needle, the action of a Geiger counter, the reading on a thermometer, or the score on a test.

Before a statement can be accepted as either true or false, there must be a demonstration of evidence in the world of observable events. Only then can the statement be tested. The evidence must be such that it can be examined by others. The procedures for obtaining the evidence should be sufficiently clear to allow independent investigators to gather new evidence with respect to the problem. These are some of the major rules that have been adopted by scientists, and the worth of the rules is demonstrated by the progress that science has made during the last several hundred years.

Rather than trying to pass judgment on the whole field of psychology as to whether it is "mental" or "physical," it is more logical to examine particular kinds of statements in psychology to see whether they meet the requirements of scientific inquiry. In this way we shall find many statements that are testable, as well as many statements that we shall want to avoid because they are untestable.

Some testable and untestable statements in psychology can be illustrated if the reader will imagine that he has in his hand a large, red, juicy-looking apple. Take a bite of this make-believe apple. Does it taste good? If you had a friend there with you, would it taste "better" to him than to you? How much more pleasant would his sensation be—twice as pleasant or three times as pleasant? This is an issue that cannot be studied directly. There is no way to measure your sensations directly. They are uniquely yours in a way that exempts them from direct observation by others. Lift the apple in your hand. Do you have a feeling of "weightiness" in response to the apple? How "large" is your feeling? This is another phenomenon that cannot be observed by others or measured directly.

There are some issues that could be studied with respect to the apple. Which would you rather have—an apple, an orange, or a pear? The way in which you respond to the question will demonstrate your preferences, and your preferences can be compared with those of other persons. How much do you think the apple weighs—7, 8, or 9 ounces? Your judgment can be compared with the weight of the apple, and a measure of your accuracy can be obtained.

Your subjective experiences—your feelings, sensations, and desires—cannot be observed by others and thus cannot be subjected to measurement. Once you *do* something with respect to your feelings—make a judgment, state a preference, or even talk to others about the experience—your behavior meets the requirements of scientific inquiry, and measurement becomes possible.

It may seem trivial to say that an individual's sensation of pleasantness is not open to scientific study but that his report of pleasantness is a legitimate scientific datum.   However, failure to make this distinction forces the scientist into some knotty problems about the nature of his data.   If it is claimed that the individual's sensation of pleasantness is being measured, one can always inquire as to the proof that the individual really enjoys the apple.   The answer is, of course, that there is no way to prove that he enjoys the apple or, for that matter, to prove that there is any sensation at all related to the apple.   We have only the individual's word as to whether he likes the apple or not, and the verbal report, in this instance, is the basic datum with which the scientist must deal.

The fact that we are restricted to what the individual does or says does not foreshadow defeat in psychological work.   There is much that can be learned about human behavior, and there are many ways in which one human action can be predicted from others.   For example, the individual's stated preferences for fruits would probably be predictive of what he would purchase or what he would choose to eat.   More importantly, the scores that a person makes on psychological tests can predict approximately how well he will perform in many real-life situations.   Also, many regularities are found in experiments on learning, perception, and other topics in psychology.

## Emotional barriers to psychological measurement

Psychological measurement efforts are often reacted to as if they were "nosy" activities, in which people are asked personal questions and embarrassed with their shortcomings, and in which investigators experiment with emotionally laden matters.   Most of us feel a twinge of anxiety when we see ourselves portrayed as a set of statistics or when our abilities are compared with those of others.   We like to think of ourselves as being unique in a way that exempts us from study.

Psychology has been held in disfavor by persons who think of it as a denial of "free will."   Their argument is that if a person's behavior is predictable, he has no choice in his actions, no freedom of will.   Psychology starts with no a priori viewpoints about the nature of man, but looks instead for the regularities that occur in human behavior.   When such regularities are sought, they are found in abundance.   For example, a white object will nearly always be regarded as larger than a black one of the same size.   Persons who make low scores on intelligence tests seldom manage to complete college training.   If you are like most of us, you are consistent to some degree about the kinds of clothes that you buy, the types of people that you choose as friends, the place where you like to sit in a theater, and many other things that can be measured and studied.

Some people think of psychology as an attempt to intrude on religious and ethical beliefs.   Psychology's behavioristic approach automatically prevents it from directly investigating the individual's experimental world.   Psychology can study the differences in ethical and moral practice among people, but cannot reach decisions about which beliefs are more real or more correct.

## measurement in science

Of course, measurement is an important issue in all science, not just in psychology. Scientific theories concern predicted relationships between measured variables, e.g., between the temperature of metal and the degree of molecular motion or between heart rate and blood pressure. Obviously, the variables with which science is concerned must be adequately measured before relations between them can be studied in detail.

Although tomes have been written on the nature of measurement, in the end it boils down to something rather simple: *Measurement consists of rules for assigning numbers to objects in such a way as to represent quantities of attributes.* The term "rules" indicates that the procedures for assigning numbers must be explicitly formulated. In some instances the rules are so obvious that detailed formulations are not required. This is the case when a yardstick is employed to measure lengths of lumber. What should be done is intuitively obvious, and consequently it is not necessary to study a thick manual of rules before undertaking the measurement. Such examples are, however, the exception rather than the rule in science. For instance, measuring the amounts of various components in chemical compounds often requires complex procedures that are not intuitively obvious. Certainly the rules for measuring most psychological attributes are not intuitively obvious, for example, the intelligence of schoolchildren, the amount of retention in a study of paired-associate learning, "drive level" in a study of rats, and attitudes toward Negroes.

Frequently in this book reference will be made to the "standardization" of measures of psychological attributes. Essentially, a measure is said to be "well standardized" if different people employ the measure and obtain very similar results. Thus a measure of the surface temperature of planets in the solar system is well standardized if different astronomers who employ the methods obtain very similar numerical results for particular planets on particular occasions. Similarly, an intelligence test is well standardized if different examiners give approximately the same scores to the same children. Formulating explicit rules for the assignment of numbers is a major aspect of the standardization of measures. Other aspects of standardization will be discussed throughout this book.

In the definition of measurement given above, the term "attribute" indicates that measurement always concerns some particular feature of objects. Strictly speaking, one does not measure objects—one measures their attributes. Thus one measures not the child, but rather the intelligence of the child. Although the distinction may sound like mere hairsplitting, it is important. First, it demonstrates that measurement requires a process of abstraction. An attribute concerns relations between objects on a particular dimension, e.g., weight and intelligence. A red rock and a white rock may weigh the same, and two white rocks may have different weights. Thus the attribute of weight is an abstraction which must not be confounded with all the particular features of objects. The point will be quite obvious to the sophisticated reader of this book, but it is not obvious, for example, to children or to adults in many primitive societies. With the latter there is sometimes confusion between a particular attribute of objects and all the recognizable attributes of objects. The failure to abstract a particular attribute makes concepts of measurement difficult to grasp. To some extent this confusion resides in the minds of civilized adults. For example, it is difficult for some people to understand that a criminal and a well-behaved member of society can have the same level of intelligence (as measured by intelligence tests).

A second reason for emphasizing that measurement always concerns a particular attribute is that it forces us to consider carefully the nature of the attribute before attempting to measure it. One possibility is that the attribute does not exist. For example, the many negative results obtained in the efforts to measure an attribute of "rigidity" in people make it doubtful that there is such an attribute. It is not necessarily the case that all the terms used to describe people are matched by measurable attributes, e.g., ego strength, extrasensory perception, and dogmatism. Another possibility is that a measure may concern a mixture of attributes rather than only one attribute. This frequently occurs in questionnaire measures of "adjustment," which tend to contain items relating to a number of separable attributes. Although such conglomerate measures are sometimes partly justifiable on practical grounds, their use offers a poor foundation for psychological science. As this book will show in detail, each measure should concern some one *thing*, some isolatable, unitary attribute. To the extent that unitary attributes should be combined to form an overall appraisal, e.g., of adjustment, they should be rationally combined from different measures rather than haphazardly combined within one measure.

Still looking at the definition of measurement, it is emphasized that *numbers* are used to represent *quantities*. Quantification concerns *how much* of an attribute is present in an object; numbers are used to communicate the amount. Quantification is so intimately interwoven with the concept of measurement that the two terms are often used interchangeably.

Measurement is closely related to counting. Essentially what one does in any measurement method is to count similar units. Length is measured by counting equal units of extension (inches or centimeters). Weight is measured by counting equal units in the form of ounces, pounds, or grams. The amount of gasoline placed in an automobile is determined by counting the number of gallon units. The physical characteristics of the measuring instruments are valuable in that they do the counting for the observer.

Psychological measures are also intimately related to counting. Thus a clock serves as a counter for the fractions of a second used to measure reaction time. By counting the number of word pairs correctly remembered in a study of paired-associate learning, one arrives at a measure of the amount learned. Similarly, by counting the number of items correctly answered on a test of ability, one arrives at a measure of ability. By counting the number of answers indicative of personal adjustment, one arrives at a measure of adjustment.

Measurement is legitimately derived from counting operations only if the units counted are qualitatively and quantitatively the same. Regarding the former consideration, a count of 12 does not constitute a legitimate measure if six units are inches and six units are pounds or if six items relate to intelligence and six items relate to adjustment. Regarding the latter consideration, a count of 14 is not a legitimate measure of length unless all 14 units are quantitatively equal, in the form of equal inches, feet, centimeters, meters, or other units. Similarly, if one interprets the interval between an IQ of 100 and an IQ of 110 as equal to that between an IQ of 110 and an IQ of 120, he is assuming that the 20 units of IQ between 100 and 120 are quantitatively equal to one another. Later in this chapter, a more extensive discussion will be presented of the nature of units on psychological measures.

In the definition given earlier, it is said that numbers are assigned to *objects*. The objects in psychology are usually people or lower animals. In some instances, however, they are material objects. For example, when people rate the pleasantness of each word in a list, the words are measured, and the people act as part of the measurement process.

Although the definition emphasizes that *rules* for quantification are at the heart of measurement, it does not specify the nature of such rules or place any limit on the "allowable" kinds of rules. This is so because a clear distinction should be made between the standards of measurement, qua the measurement process, and standards for validating measures, or determining their usefulness, once they are in existence. Initially, any particular set of rules, or any class of rules, is only a hypothesis. The hypothesis must be tested with respect to standards that are external to the measurement process per se. In other words, the proof of the usefulness of any measure is determined by the extent to which it enhances scientific explanation. Thus one psychologist might establish a set of rules for the measurement of dogmatism which seems quite illogical to his colleagues, but the usefulness of the measure could not be dismissed a priori. The usefulness of the measure would be determined by empirical investigations, where it would be determined to what extent the measure had functional relationships with important variables.

In establishing rules for the employment of a particular measure, the crucial consideration is that there must be a set of unambiguous rules. The rules may be developed from an elaborate deductive model, they may be based on much previous experience, they may flow from common sense, or they may spring from only hunches, but the proof of the pudding is in how well the measure serves to explain important phenomena. Consequently *any* set of rules that unambiguously quantifies properties of objects constitutes a *legitimate* measure and has a right to compete with other measures for scientific usefulness. (How scientific usefulness is determined will be discussed in Chapter 6.)

## advantages of standardized measures

Although the reader probably has a healthy respect for the importance of measurement in science, it might be useful to look at some of the particular advantages which measurement provides. To examine the advantages of standardized measures, it is necessary to consider what would be left if they were not available—for example, if there were no measures of temperature or intelligence. What would be left would be subjective appraisals, personal judgments, or whatever one would want to call the inituitive processes involved. Some of the advantages of standardized measures over personal judgments are discussed below.

### Objectivity

The major advantage of measurement is that it takes the guesswork out of scientific observation. A key principle of science is that any statement of fact made by one scientist should be independently verifiable by other scientists. The principle is violated if there is room for disagreement among scientists about the observation of empirical events. For example, since we have no standardized measure of "ego strength," two psychologists could disagree widely about the ego strength of a particular person. Obviously, then, it is not possible to make scientific tests of theories concerning ego strength. Thus theories concerning atomic particles, temperature of stars, intelligence of children, drive level in rats, and so on, are testable to the extent to which there are unambiguous procedures for documenting empirical events. Standardized measures provide such procedures.

A case could be made for the argument that the major problem in psychology is that of measurement. There is no end of theories, but the theories are populated with terms (hypothesized attributes) which presently cannot be adequately measured; consequently the theories go untested. This is the problem with Freudian theory. There are no agreed-upon procedures for observing and quantifying such attributes as ego strength, libidinal energy, narcissism, and others. In fact it seems that major advances in psychology, and probably in all sciences, are preceded by breakthroughs in measurement methods. This is attested to by the flood of research following the development of intelligence tests. Recent advances in techniques for measuring the electrical activity of individual nerve cells provide another example of how the development of measurement methods spurs research.  Scientific results are inevitably reported in terms of functional relations between measured variables, and the science of psychology will progress neither slower nor faster than it becomes possible to measure important variables.

## Quantification

The numerical results provided by standardized measures have two advantages.  First, numerical indices make it possible to report results in finer detail than would be the case with personal judgments.  Thus the availability of thermometers makes it possible to report the exact increase in temperature when two chemicals are mixed, rather than only the fact that the temperature increases.  Similarly, whereas teachers may be able to reliably assign children to broad categories of intelligence such as "bright," "average," and "below normal," intelligence tests provide finer differentiations.

A second advantage of quantification is that it permits the use of powerful methods of mathematical analysis.  This is essential in the elaboration of theories and in the analysis of experiments.  Although it may be a long time off for psychology, it is reasonable to believe that all theories will eventually be expressed in mathematical form.  Only when theories are in mathematical form is it possible to make precise deductions for experimental investigation.  Without powerful methods of analysis, such as factor analysis and analysis of variance, it would be all but impossible to assess the results of research.

## Communication

Science is a highly public enterprise in which efficient communication between scientists is essential.  Each scientist builds on what has been learned in the past, and day by day he must compare his findings with those of other scientists working on the same types of problems.  Communication is greatly facilitated when standardized measures are available.  Suppose, for example, that in an experiment concerning the effects of stress on anxiety reaction, it is reported that a particular treatment made the subjects appear anxious.  This would leave many questions as to what the experimenter meant by "appear anxious," and consequently it would be very difficult for other experimenters to investigate the same effects.  Much better communication would be achieved if standardized measures of anxiety were available.  If the means and standard deviations of scores for the different treatment groups were reported, very efficient and precise communication with other scientists would be possible.  Even if subjective evaluations of experimental results are very carefully done, they are much more difficult to communicate than statistical analyses of standardized measures.  The rate of scientific progress in a particular area is limited by the efficiency and fidelity with which scientists can communicate their results to one another.

Economy

Although it frequently requires a great deal of work to develop standardized measures, once developed they are usually much more economical of time and money than subjective evaluations.  For example, even if a teacher were a good judge of intelligence, he would probably need to observe a child for some months to make a sound judgment.  A better appraisal could usually be obtained from one of the group measures of intelligence, which would take no more than an hour to administer and might cost less than 25 cents per child. Rather than have clinical psychologists individually interview each recruit for the armed services, a large group of recruits can be administered a printed test. In a study of the effect of a particular drug on amount of activity of white rats, it would be far more economical to employ standardized measures (e.g., the activity wheel) than to have trained observers sit for hours noting the amount of activity.

Besides saving time and money, standardized measures often free highly trained professionals for more important work.  Physicists, psychologists, and many other types of professional people are in short supply, and the shortages will apparently grow worse in the years ahead.  Consequently, a great saving is obtained in many instances when time-consuming observations by professionals are replaced by standardized measures.  Of course, sometimes it is difficult to disentangle the scientist from the measurement process, which, for example, is the case in employing individually administered tests of intelligence.  Although some individual tests of intelligence are highly standardized, they still require much time for administration and scoring.  The direction of progress, however, is always toward developing measures that either require very little effort to employ or are so simple to administer and score that semiskilled workers can do the job.  Standardized measures are in most cases, although not all, more economical of the scientist's time than subjective observation, thus freeing him to devote more time to the scholarly and creative aspects of his work.

## measurement and mathematics

It is important to make a clear distinction between measurement, which is directly concerned with the real world, and mathematics, which is purely an abstract enterprise that need have nothing to do with the real world.  Perhaps the two would not be so readily confused if they did not both frequently involve quantification.  Mathematical systems are purely deductive, being sets of rules for the manipulation of symbols.  Symbols for quantities constitute only one type of symbol found in mathematics, and much of modern mathematics concerns deductive systems whose symbols do not relate to numbers.  Any set of rules for manipulating a group of symbols can be a legitimate branch of mathematics as long as the rules are internally consistent. Thus the statement *"iggle wug drang flous"* could be a legitimate mathematical statement in a set of rules stating that when any *iggle* is *wugged*, it *drang* a *flous*. An elaborate mathematical system could be constructed in which both the objects and the operations were symbolized by nonsense words. Of course, the system might not be of any use, but its legitimacy would depend entirely on the internal consistency of the rules. Thus if the system of rules left it in doubt whether the *iggle drang* a *flous* or *drang* a *squiegle*, there would be a flaw in it.

In contrast to mathematics, measurement always concerns numbers, and the legitimacy of any system of measurement is determined by empirical data. Measurement always concerns *how much* of an attribute is present, which requires a numerical statement of the amount. At the lowest level of quantification, measurement concerns the presence or absence of an attribute, such as the presence of brain damage, blue eyes versus brown eyes, smokers versus nonsmokers, males versus females, and hospitalized mental patients versus persons on the outside.

Measurement concerns the real world in terms of purposes, operations, and validity. The purpose is to quantify the attributes of real objects and persons; the operations concern doing something (according to a set of rules) to obtain measurements. The validity, or usefulness, of a measure always depends on the character of empirical data. If a measure is intended to fit a set of axioms for measurement (a model), the closeness of the fit can be determined only by the extent to which relations in empirical data meet the requirements of the model. Regardless of the character of the model or even if there is no formal model, the eventual and crucial test of any measure is the extent to which it has explanatory power in its relations with other variables.

Scientists *develop* measures by stating rules for the quantification of attributes of real objects; they *borrow* mathematical systems for examining the internal relations of the data obtained with a measure and for relating different measures to one another. Although past experience, common sense, and rational argument may make a good case for one method of measurement or mathematical analysis over another, the final justification requires finding a rich set of lawful relations between variables in the real world.

## Measurement and statistics

Because the term "statistics" is used so broadly, one could argue that the theory of psychological measurement has either a great deal or little to do with statistics. First, it is important to make a distinction between *inferential statistics* and other mathematical methods of analysis. Inferential statistics concern probability statements relating observed sample values to population parameters. Thus obtaining the arithmetic mean of the scores on one test or the correlation between scores on two tests would constitute a mathematical analysis which would not have to involve inferential statistics. One such additional step would consist in employing inferential statistics to determine the statistical significance of the difference in average test scores of women and men. Even though a difference might be found in a particular study of men as compared with women, this leaves open the larger question of whether or not a difference would be found if all the men and women in the country were investigated. Inferential statistics would allow one to determine the odds that a real difference would persist from the particular persons investigated to the parent population of persons involved. Since the purpose of performing mathematical analyses of central tendency, dispersion, and correlation is to describe various aspects of empirical data, these and related methods of analysis are said to form *descriptive statistics*, in contrast to inferential statistics. Employment of inferential statistics, as in setting confidence zones or in "testing for significance," would constitute additional steps.

Because very little will be said in this book about probability statements relating sample values to population parameters, the quantitative methods would be better spoken of as methods of analysis or descriptive statistics rather than as inferential statistics. Thus correlational analysis, factor analysis, discriminatory analysis, and others can be discussed and employed without necessarily resorting to inferential statistics, which is not meant to imply that inferential statistics per se are not useful adjuncts to the development and use of psychological measures.

A second important distinction is that between statistics concerning the sampling of people and statistics concerning the sampling of content (test items). After measures have been developed and then employed in empirical investigations, it is important to employ inferential statistics concerning the sampling of people. Before measures are developed, however, the theory that guides such measurement is much more related to the sampling of content than to the sampling of people. As will be described in detail later, it is useful to think of the items on a particular test as being a sample from a hypothetical infinite population or universe of items measuring the same trait. Thus a spelling test for fourth-grade students can be thought of as a sample of all possible words that would be appropriate. Measurement theory would then concern statistical relations between the scores actually made on the test and the hypothetical scores that would have been made if all items in the universe had been administered.

Thus there is a two-way sampling problem in psychology, one concerned with the sampling of people and the other with the sampling of content. The former concerns the generality of findings over populations of persons, and the latter concerns the generality of findings over populations of test items. It proves all but impossible to take account simultaneously of both dimensions of sampling when performing statistical analyses. One dimension of sampling is difficult enough to consider in any particular analysis. What is typically done in practice is explicitly to take account of one dimension of sampling and simply keep the other dimension in mind as a possible influence on the results of the experiment. Thus in a study of the influence of a particular type of training on achievement in mathematics, explicit account would be taken of the sampling of subjects, but it would be kept in mind that somewhat different results might have been obtained with a different measure of achievement. Similarly, in a study of reliability, where the major concern would be with the sampling of content, it would be kept in mind that the results might have been somewhat different in a larger sample of persons or in a sample drawn from another source.

The practical necessity in particular studies of making explicit statistical analyses of only one of two dimensions of sampling does not spoil the game. What is required is that the generality of findings, either over people or over content, be investigated in subsequent studies. An even safer approach, if feasible, is to sample so extensively on one dimension that only sampling error with respect to the other dimension need be a serious concern. This is the recommended approach in the development of psychological measures. Enough subjects should be used in developing psychological measures so that sampling error with respect to persons is a minor consideration. At least hundreds, and where possible thousands, of subjects should be used in the development of a new measure. In the remainder of this book it will be assumed that all mathematical analyses are based on large numbers of subjects; consequently in the text we shall be left free to consider only the sampling of content. Even if it were feasible to work with statistics that considered both dimensions of sampling simultaneously, studies conducted on relatively small numbers of subjects would not be sufficient. For example, in a study of the reliability of a new measure, the need is to determine what the reliability *is*; a statement only that the reliability coefficient is significantly different from zero is nearly worthless.

Apparently it is difficult for some persons to comprehend that in the development of psychological measures the major concern is with the sampling of content rather than with the sampling of people. For example, students in psychology frequently fall into the trap of assuming that the reliability of a test increases with the number of people used in the study of reliability. Any reader who does not already know will learn later that the reliability estimate obtained in any particular study is independent of the number of persons in the study but that in any study the reliability is related to the number of items on the test.

## measurement scales

During recent years there has been much talk in psychology about the different possible types of measurement scales, and there has been much soul-searching about the types of scales characterized by different types of psychological measures. Although these discussions represent a healthy self-consciousness about scientific methods, they have, the author thinks, led to some unfortunate confusions. Essentially the issues concern what sorts of "interpretations" can be made of the numbers obtained from psychological measures. More precisely, the issues concern the legitimacy of employing particular classes of mathematical procedures with measures of psychological attributes. Does a measure of intelligence have the same mathematical status as a yardstick? Does a measure of learning rate in paired-associate learning have the same mathematical status as a measure of electrical resistance?

Different types of measurement scales concern different uses made of numbers. Some of these uses are classified in the following sections.

### Labels

Numbers are frequently used to keep track of things, without any suggestion that the numbers can be subjected to mathematical analyses. For example, a geologist working in the field might choose to number his specimens of rocks 1, 2, 3, etc., in which case the numbers would be used purely as labels and would have no implications for mathematical analyses. It would make no sense to add the numbers representing the first and second rocks and equate that sum in any way with the 3 relating to the third rock. Other examples of numbers used as labels are the numbers on football players' backs, numbers on highway signs, and the numbers of atomic elements.

It must be emphasized that any measurement scale concerns an *intended use* of numbers. One intended use of numbers is for labeling. In this instance there is no intention of performing mathematical analyses of the numbers, and the numbers are not considered to represent quantities of attributes. It may be the case, however, that numbers as labels happen to correlate with quantities of attributes. Thus in the example of the geologist and his rocks it may be that, as his sack of rocks grows heavier, he discerningly picks smaller and smaller specimens; consequently the numbers used as labels would incidentally relate to the weights of the rocks. Similarly, high-numbered highways may in some way be quantitatively different from low-numbered highways, and atomic elements further along in the numbering scheme may be quantitatively different from earlier-positioned elements. The crucial point is that, in discussing the nature of measurement scales in particular instances, one must justify the *use* of the numbers. Whether or not there are incidental quantitative correlates of a particular set of numbers is not relevant to a discussion of the legitimacy of the intended use of the numbers. Since labels are not intended to imply quantities of attributes, no justification is required for the employment of numbers as labels.

## Categories

Closely related to the use of numbers as labels is their use to represent groups of objects.   For example, the geologist might classify each of his rocks into one of the categories of sedimentary, igneous, or metamorphic and refer to these categories as 1, 2, and 3.   Other classification schemes include different professions, the two sexes, and brain-damaged and normal people.   The only differences between employing numbers as labels and employing them to represent categories are that in the latter case (1) more than one object goes with each number, and (2) all the objects assigned to the same number are alike with respect to some attribute.   As is true of numbers used as labels, numbers used to represent categories in a classification scheme have no quantitative implications.   Similarly, numbers used to represent categories may have many incidental correlates with quantities of attributes.   Thus, on the average, males and females differ in height, athletic ability, and a host of other attributes, but that is entirely unrelated to justifying the use of the numbers "1" and "2" to stand for males and females, respectively.   Since numbers used to represent categories are not intended to have quantitative implications, no justification is required for the use of numbers for that purpose.

In discussing categorization, a distinction should be made between using numbers to represent categories and using them to signify the frequency with which objects appear in different categories.   Thus the geologist might categorize 22 of his specimens as igneous rocks.   In such instances it is sometimes said that one "measures" the number of cases in different categories, but according to the definition of "measurement" given earlier, this would be an improper use of the term.   It would be more proper to say that one enumerates, or counts, the objects in categories.

## Ordinal scales

An ordinal scale is one in which (1) a set of objects or people is ordered from "most" to "least" with respect to an attribute, (2) there is no indication of "how much" in an absolute sense any of the objects possess of the attribute, and (3) there is no indication of how far apart the objectives are with respect to the attribute.   Rank ordering is the most primitive form of measurement (excluding labels and categories as constituting measurement).   It is primitive in that it is basic to all higher forms of measurement, and it conveys only meager information.

An ordinal scale is obtained, for example, when a group of boys is ordered from tallest to shortest.   This scale would give no indication of the average height: as a group the boys might be relatively tall or relatively short.   The scale would supply no information about how much the boys varied in terms of height.   With respect to methods of analysis, it is meaningless to compute the mean and the standard deviation of a set of ranks. These indices are the cornerstones of most of the powerful methods of mathematics and statistics needed in psychology, methods without which it would be all but impossible to advance the science.

What is frequently not understood is that the numbers employed with ordinal scales provide only a convenient shorthand for designating relative positions of objects. A rank-order scale is obtained when, for any N persons (Ss), it is known that $S_i > S_j > S_k > S_n$ with respect to an attribute.

Some have claimed that most psychological scales, e.g., intelligence tests, should be considered to provide only a rank ordering of people rather than any higher form of measurement. In a later section, issue will be taken with that point of view.

## Interval scales

An interval scale is one in which (1) the rank ordering of objects is known with respect to an attribute, (2) it is known how far apart the objects are from one another with respect to the attribute, but (3) no information is available about the *absolute* magnitude of the attribute for any object. An interval scale would be obtained for the heights of a group of boys if, instead of being measured directly, the height of each boy were measured with respect to the shortest boy in the group. Thus the shortest boy would obtain a score of 0, a boy 2 inches taller than the shortest boy would obtain a score of 2, a boy 3 inches taller would obtain a score of 3, and so on. More directly related to what is done with most psychological measures would be the specification of intervals in terms of the distance of each boy from the arithmetic mean of heights of the boys. Thus a boy whose height is 2 inches above the mean would receive a score of +2, and a boy who is 2 inches below the mean would receive a score of −2. Intervals about the mean height, or such intervals for any other attribute, can be calculated without actually knowing how far any of the persons are from the zero point (for example, zero height or zero intelligence).

A potentially important item of information not supplied by interval scales is the absolute magnitude of the attribute for any particular person or object. Thus even though the tallest boy may have an interval score above the mean of +6 (6 inches above the average), this would not tell us how tall he is in an absolute sense. He might be the tallest boy in a group of Pygmies.

Because interval scales are sometimes spoken of as "equal-interval" scales, it is easy to make the mistake of assuming that such scales require an equal number of persons or objects at each point on the continuum—a rectangular distribution of scores. What actually is meant by "equal" is that intervals on the scale are equal regardless of the number of persons or objects at different points on the scale. Thus on an interval scale for the measurement of intelligence, the *difference* between IQs of 100 and 105 would be assumed equal to the *difference* between IQs of 120 and 125. Of course, the practical implications of such equal differences on the scale might be most unequal, but strictly speaking that has nothing to do with the interval character of the scale. Similarly, if three automobiles are traveling 30, 60, and 90 miles per hour, respectively, the interval between the first two is equal to the interval between the second and third, but of course these two intervals might have very different implications for traffic safety, gas mileage, and wear and tear on the automobiles. Thus it is necessary to draw a careful distinction between the character of a measurement scale, interval scale or otherwise, and the practical implications of the scale points.

### Ratio scales

A ratio scale is obtained when (1) the rank order of persons with respect to an attribute is known, (2) the intervals between persons are known, and (3) in addition, the distance from a rational zero is known for each person. In other words, a ratio scale is a particular type of interval scale in which distances are stated with respect to a rational zero rather than with respect to, for example, the height of the tallest boy or the shortest boy or the mean height. Obviously, if an interval scale of height is available and in addition the absolute height (distance from zero) of any boy in the group is known, the absolute heights of all the other boys can be calculated.

### Other scales

Ordinal, interval, and ratio scales are the basic scales of measurement. There are, however, many possible variants and combinations of these (see Coombs, 1960, for a discussion of some of the possibilities).* For example, one could have an *ordered metric* scale in which (1) the rank order of persons is known and (2) the rank order of intervals is known but (3) the magnitudes of the intervals are not known. In such a scale it would be possible to say that the largest interval is between persons A and B and the smallest interval is between persons C and D, but it would not be possible to say that the former interval is twice as large as the latter.

Stevens (1958) has proposed a *logarithmic interval scale*, where if the successive points on the scale are designated $a$, $b$, $c$, etc., the successive ratios of magnitudes corresponding to those points would be $a/b = b/c = c/d$, etc. Then

$$\log a - \log b = \log b - \log c = \log c - \log d$$

* In addition to employing the usual form of bibliographic citations to reference particular statements, suggested additional readings are listed at the ends of chapters. The latter concern readings that amplify the discussions in each chapter. A complete bibliography appears on pages 511–20.

etc.  Many other variants of the three basic types of measurement scales can be postulated, but they have been of little importance in psychometric theory or application.


## measurement scales in psychology

If the considerations in the foregoing paragraphs about measurement scales are important, it is proper to inquire about the types of scales developed with respect to psychological measurements.  Psychological investigations are concerned with all the types of scales discussed previously.  Some investigations are concerned with categorical data, such as the numbers of mental patients of different kinds, comparisons of brain-damaged people with normal people, and the comparison of smokers and nonsmokers.

In some cases psychological data are expressed in the form of ranks.  This would be the case when subjects rank-order 10 patches of gray paper from darkest to lightest.  This would also be the case when subjects rank-order the names of 20 national groups from those which are liked most to those which are liked least.  When data such as these are clearly in the form of ranks, one should be cautious in applying mathematical analyses that assume interval or ratio scales.

Leaving aside for a moment considerations of interval scales, there are some forms of psychological data that are rightfully considered ratio scales.  This is the case, for example, with some forms of data that are expressed in terms of time, such as the length of time required for a rat to traverse a maze or reaction time in human subjects.  In such cases, zero amount of time is a meaningful concept, and it is also meaningful, for example, to speak of one subject taking twice as much time as another subject.  Another instance in which psychological data are reportable in terms of ratio scales is found in certain types of studies of learning.  If, for example, there are 20 pairs of words to be remembered, it makes sense to speak of zero amount of learning, and it also makes sense to form ratios among the numbers of pairs learned by the same subject at different stages of learning.

The above examples are the exception rather than the rule—most psychological data are legitimately expressible only as interval scales rather than ratio scales.  It makes no sense, for example, to speak of zero intelligence or zero self-esteem, and it makes no sense to say that one person is twice as anxious as another or that one person has 1½ times as much reasoning ability as another.  Having only interval scales rather than ratio scales for most attributes does not present a serious problem.  Most of the methods of mathematical and statistical analysis needed in psychological research require only interval scales, e.g., correlational analysis and analysis of variance.

There are some who would challenge the assumption of interval scales for most psychological measures, although the number of people who would do so apparently decreases each year. If that challenge could not be met, psychology would have to foresake many of its more powerful methods of mathematical and statistical analysis, which would have an extremely bad effect on the field. It has been found that these powerful methods of analysis produce essentially the same results when the intervals on measurement scales are altered to a considerable extent, as would be the case, for example, when working with the square roots of scores on an intelligence test rather than with the scores themselves. Thus even those purists who chastise psychologists for the assumption of interval scales will have to admit that deviations from those assumptions usually have scant effects on the analyses which are performed. Also, a good argument can be made that there are no "real" or "correct" intervals for any measurement scale, but rather that the intervals are established as a matter of convention. Thus if scientists find a particular calibration of intervals to make sense and to be scientifically useful, those calibrations of intervals are accepted as a measurement convention. This is the case, for example, with measurements of the hardness of rocks and the intensities of earthquakes. Other measurement methods could be used which would produce different intervals of measurement. Both the old and the new calibrations of intervals would be scientifically acceptable. Which should be used in the long run would be determined by which calibration led to neater mathematical relationships with other variables, but there would be nothing wrong with taking the intervals seriously on either type of measure when performing mathematical analyses.

The real issue does not concern whether or not to use the intervals on measurement scales in mathematical analyses—if they are there, why not use them? The issue is one of which calibration of intervals will prove more useful in the long run. Consequently, there is nothing wrong with performing mathematical operations that take seriously the intervals of measurement when investigating intelligence tests, personality tests, and other measurement methods employed in psychology. With the foregoing considerations in mind, it would be foolish of psychologists not to employ those powerful methods of mathematical and statistical analysis which assume interval scales, unless the data were originally obtained from ranking methods.

## measurement in psychology

There are a number of special fields in psychology, among them clinical, social, physiological, and differential psychology. Research in all areas of psychology is dependent on adequate measurement methods. The measurement problems have proved more difficult in some areas than in others. For example, the clinical psychologist finds it difficult to measure things like the improvement of patients in psychotherapy and the severity of emotional disorders. One of the most difficult problems for psychologists is to find ways to measure important human attributes.

## Experiments and individual differences

Psychologists study two interrelated types of data about human beings and lower animals. First, they perform experiments to determine effects on behavior of different types of treatments. For example, investigations are made of the effects of magnitude of reward on the rate at which rats learn a maze. One group of rats is rewarded at the end of the maze with one food pellet, another group of rats is rewarded with three pellets, and a third group is rewarded with nine pellets. The larger the reward for reaching the goal box of the maze, the faster rats learn the maze, which tells us something about the effects of rewards on learning rate. As another example of experimental treatments, investigations are made of the thresholds for perceiving words that differ in terms of frequency of usage in printed material. Each word is shown on a screen for a fraction of a second, and the subject must report the word. Some of the words appear very frequently in printed material, others appear with moderate frequency, and still others are very rare in printed material. It is found that more frequently used words are more easily identified than less frequently used words, which tells us something about the influence of familiarity on perceptual recognition. It is customary to speak of psychological experiments as being concerned with stimulus-response (S-R) relationships. The experimenter does something to the subject (which constitutes the stimulus), and then he observes the subject's response. In this way, we try to establish laws of behavior for mice and men.

In addition to being interested in S-R laws, psychologists are also interested in individual differences in both mice and men. Studies of individual differences are frequently said to concern response-response (R-R) laws because they relate to the different responses made by subjects. For example, a group of subjects is administered an intelligence test and a test of memory. Statistical measures of correlation are made to see whether people who are high in intelligence are also high in the test of memory, and vice versa for people who are low in intelligence. As another example of studies of individual differences, 10 tests of different types of reasoning are administered to a large group of persons, and statistical analyses are made to determine the number of different types of abilities involved in the tests.

Although there has been a tendency to think of the search for S-R laws as being a basically different enterprise from the search for R-R laws, the two are closely related. In nearly all experiments, the average differences between treatment groups tend to be small in comparison with the individual differences between subjects. Although as a group rats that are given nine pellets tend to learn more rapidly than rats that are given only one pellet, some rats in the one-pellet group learn more rapidly than some rats in the nine-pellet group. In an experiment on perceptual recognition, it is found that there are individual differences between people in terms of recognition thresholds for words of all kinds. Such individual differences tend to obscure S-R laws, and only by learning to measure such individual differences, or to control them, can we finely document S-R laws.

Not only are individual differences important to consider in the results of psychological experiments, but also some of the most important types of individual differences occur in those circumstances. Most studies of individual differences have occurred outside the context of psychological experiments, for example, in the investigation of the abilities involved in tests of reasoning. In such studies there is no experimental treatment, in the stricter meaning of the term; rather, responses to different types of test items are sampled. Some of the more important studies of individual differences, however, do occur in the context of psychological experiments. As was mentioned previously, there are large individual differences between people in terms of recognition thresholds for words, regardless of what types of words are employed. Individual differences are also found in experiments concerning different types of rehearsal of memory tasks, in which it is found that some people consistently perform better than others.

It will be necessary to have a wedding of S-R and R-R laws before a more complete science of psychology can be established. Those who are concerned with psychological experiments eventually will have to take account of the wide individual differences that hamper the pursuit of S-R laws, and those who investigate individual differences will need to take advantage of the rich theory and firm methodology that inhere in psychological experiments.

## Measurement in differential psychology

Differential psychology concerns two kinds of problems: (1) the logic and methods of measuring individual differences and (2) the study of how individual differences arise and how they relate to one another. The first concerns the tools for measuring individual differences; the second concerns the facts that have been established by applying the tools.

Although the major emphasis in this book is on the study of individual differences, we should not overemphasize the conclusions that can be obtained from studies of this kind. There are limits to what can be learned about human behavior from individual differences alone. Although studies of individual differences have proved very useful, it should be remembered that psychology is more extensively concerned with controlled experiments. Efforts will be made in this book to clarify some of the major issues regarding measurement in controlled experiments.

The study of individual differences has a wide appeal in the United States.

Not only has much of the work in this field been done by persons in our country, but the subject of individual differences has a particular appeal for the American public. Perhaps in no other country can a person attract so much attention by being different or doing something unusual.

One of the major reasons why we are interested in differences between people is that this is a "land of opportunity," as the well-worn phrase puts it. Here an individual has more opportunity to use his ability to attain fame and fortune than in countries where, as a result of either the class structure or the lower standard of living, he has less chance of getting ahead. If a person is better-looking, can sing better, is more intelligent, or is a better athlete, he may be on the road to great personal gain. Consequently, people are usually eager to find some way in which they are superior to others, even if it is in so trivial an ability as being able to hold their breath longer.

As evidence of our interest in individual differences, American magazines are replete with short, and usually inadequate, tests of vocabulary, popularity, marital happiness, and so on. The mother is eager to see that little Johnny learns to walk before the neighbor's child. She wants to have his IQ measured and hopes that he is a budding genius.

The study of individual differences has been given considerable attention during the last 70 years. One reason for the interest of psychologists in this type of work is the success that the testing movement has encountered. Some areas of psychology can be more properly regarded as sciences of the future. The groundwork is being laid, but the present storehouse of facts is not large. There is also a great deal still to be learned about the measurement of individual differences. The measurement of personality characteristics has proved a particularly onerous stumbling block. Even considering the uncharted regions in the measurement of human behavior, the testing movement in America has reached an advanced stage of technical sophistication and proved practical importance.

## examples of psychological measures

The emphasis in this book will be on discussing principles that apply to psychological measurement in all types of investigations. Although the book is not intended to be a catalog of existing measurement techniques, in later chapters some of the most prominent techniques (e.g., intelligence tests) will be discussed and illustrated. Before those particular measurement techniques can be discussed in a meaningful way, it will be necessary to consider many principles that apply to all measures in psychology. While these principles are being discussed, however, it would be good for the reader to have in mind some concrete examples of typical measurement techniques, which will be discussed and illustrated below.

### Discrimination learning

An important type of investigation is that concerning the rate at which subjects learn successfully to discriminate cues for reaching some type of goal, for example, an investigation involving a rat in a T maze, which, as the name implies, is in the shape of a T. The rat runs from the start box at the bottom of the T to the choice point and then turns either left or right. For half of the rats in a group, food is on the left on all trials but never on the right, and vice versa for the other half of the rats in a group. If the rat makes an incorrect turn, he is lifted out of the T maze and thus is not permitted to eat on that trial. A typical study concerns the effects of different levels of food deprivation on learning in different groups. One group of rats is placed in the maze after four hours of food deprivation, another group after 24 hours, and a third group after 48 hours. The T maze is used to investigate the effects of many variables on discrimination learning.

### Perceptual recognition

Many investigations are made of the ease with which objects are recognized visually when they are presented for only a fraction of a second. An instrument used for this purpose is called a *tachistoscope*. The subject looks into a box, at the other end of which there is a screen. The experimenter controls which object is presented on the screen and for what lengths of time. An interesting type of experiment with this measurement procedure concerns *backward masking*. The subject is shown two words in rapid succession, and he is told to report only the first word. It is found that the second word tends to "mask," or interfere with, the accurate reporting of the first word, and the degree of masking varies in interesting ways with the length of time each word is presented, the interval between presentations, and other aspects of the experimental treatment.

### Perceptual vigilance

Important investigations are made of the perceptual alertness (vigilance) of subjects in monitoring visual displays. In a typical measurement method, the subject watches a clocklike mechanism in which a pointer jumps at regular intervals from point to point, much like the second hand on a watch. At random intervals, the pointer jumps two points rather than one, which the subject indicates by pressing a button. If he is not alert, he will fail to detect the double jump. The subject's vigilance is affected by the nature of the visual display, distracting stimuli (e.g., randomly occurring tones), fatigue, and other variables. Such investigations are important in designing optimal mechanical equipment, e.g., for astronauts in our space program.

## Short-term memory

One way to measure short-term memory is to present visually or orally a list of randomly ordered numerals (e.g., 6-4-7-9-5-2-8) and require the subject to repeat them in precisely the order in which they were given. The ability to remember such lists depends on the number of digits, the temporal spacing between presentation of digits, the length of time between presentation of the last digit and the effort to recall, the activity of the subject during this interval, and other factors. Short-term memory is also measured with complex geometrical designs. After a short exposure to a design, the subject is required either to reconstruct it or to select it from among a number of similar designs.

## Conformity

Social conformity can be measured in group situations in which members of the group are required to estimate the length of lines presented on a screen. In a group of four persons, only one is actually a subject. The subject does not know that the other three persons are actors who are making an effort to influence his responses. When asked to judge which of three lines is longer, all three actors choose a line that is slightly shorter than the longest line. They do this over a series of 10 or more trials. The measure of conformity consists of the number of times that the subject is "pressured" into choosing the incorrect line.

## Verbal reports of emotions

Verbal reports are widely used in many studies of human beings. Although in some types of experiments it is much more difficult to investigate human behavior than to investigate that of lower animals (e.g., effects of severe punishment on learning rates), one of the major advantages of performing research on human subjects is that it allows one to employ measures based on verbal reports. An example is the study of the effects of different types of stressful situations on amount of anxiety. Persons who typically have extreme stage fright are randomly divided into four groups. One group is given no treatment; a second group is taught some techniques of muscle relaxation; a third group is given conventional psychotherapy; and a fourth group is given a *placebo*, an inert pill which is described to the subjects as a cure for nervousness. A verbal-report measure of anxiety is administered shortly before the subjects are required to make a speech to an audience of 40 persons. In the verbal-report measure, each subject indicates the extent to which he is anxious by marking seven-step scales concerning feelings of nervousness, dryness of the throat, pounding of the heart, fear of giving the speech, and other characteristics.

### Reading comprehension

In achievement tests for elementary schools, it is important to measure how well students understand written material. A typical test consists of having students read paragraphs and then answer questions regarding the content. The following two multiple-choice questions would be asked after fifth-grade students read a paragraph concerning the United States Congress:

1. The major purpose of the Congress is to
a. pass laws
b. direct foreign policy
c. command the armed forces
d. supervise law enforcement

2. One way in which the Senate is different from the House of Representatives is that the Senate
a. controls the spending of government money
b. votes on new tax laws
c. gives advice to the President
d. approves treaties with other countries

### Intelligence

Because of the importance of measuring individual differences in intelligence, a later chapter will be devoted to that topic, and the measurement of intelligence will be mentioned at numerous other places in the book. As will be seen later, intelligence tests measure a mixture of abilities that are important for many roles in life, particularly for successful performance in schools of all kinds.

Intelligence tests are heavily populated with items concerning the understanding and use of words. Two typical items are as follows:

1. *Severe* means most nearly the same as
a. lenient
b. harsh
c. frightening
d. unpleasant

2. *Boat* is to *sail* as *automobile* is to
a. road
b. driver
c. tire
d. motor

In addition to employing items concerning verbal comprehension, intelligence tests usually employ items concerning numerical concepts.  Two typical items are as follows:

1. Which one of the following numbers is most nearly the same as the square root of 24.5?
  *a.* 16
  *b.* 4
  *c.* 5
  *d.* 640

2. Which one of the following numbers is closest to 9?
  *a.* 9.1
  *b.* 9.09
  *c.* 8.905
  *d.* 8.9

Intelligence tests also employ items concerning memory, spatial and perceptual judgment, and various types of reasoning.  As will be discussed more fully in Chapter 10, intelligence tests differ somewhat from one another in terms of the types of items that are combined to obtain a measure of general ability.

## Summary

Whether or not it is recognized and designated as such, psychological measurement is an important ingredient of everyday life.  Also, standardized measures are crucially important for basic research in psychology.  Systematic measurement methods were rather late in coming, and only during the last 100 years has the problem been carefully studied.  A major drawback to the development of measurement methods has been the failure to distinguish the kinds of psychological phenomena that can and cannot be measured.  Psychological science is concerned with human behavior, with the actions, words, judgments, and preferences of people—all of which are open to measurement.  Psychological science is not concerned with purely subjective phenomena; until the individual *does* something about his feelings, there is nothing to measure.

We are so accustomed to measuring physical objects and assigning numbers to them on the basis of ratio scales that it is easy to assume that all measurements are of that kind.  However, many measurements must be made on a cruder basis.  Consequently, it is important to specify the type of measurement scale which is in use.  This will indicate the kinds of mathematical procedures that can be legitimately employed.  Some types of psychological data are obviously in the form of ranks, and at the other extreme it is reasonable to consider that some types of psychological data constitute ratio scales.  Most types of psychological data, however, are most reasonably interpreted as constituting interval scales.  This assumption permits the use of powerful methods of mathematical and statistical analysis, without which the science of psychology would be in a very weak position.

Measurement is an important issue in all areas of science, not just in psychology.  Some of the major advantages of standardized measures over informal observations are objectivity, economy, facilitation of communication between scientists, and the availability of powerful methods of mathematical analysis.

Although we should be impressed with the need for measurement methods, this should not dim the importance of simple human observation and thought in the search for scientific lawfulness.  Measurements are helpful to the scientist in explaining and exploring theories, but only the human observer can invent theories.  No amount of elaborate measurement can make up for a lack of ideas on the part of the experimenter.

## Suggested additional readings

Lorge, I.  The fundamental nature of measurement.  In E. F. Lindquist (Ed.), *Educational measurement*.  Washington: American Council on Education, 1951.  Ch. 14.

Nunnally, J. C. *Psychometric theory*.  New York: McGraw-Hill, 1967.  Ch. 1.

Stevens, S. S.  Problems and methods of psychophysics.  *Psychological Bulletin*, 1958, 55, 177–196.

Torgerson, W.  *Theory and methods of scaling*.  New York: Wiley, 1958.  Chs. 1, 2.

# CHAPTER 2

# Historical perspectives on psychological measurement

People have always been interested in the measurement of human attributes, and embryonic studies can be traced even to ancient China. However, it was only approximately one hundred years ago that the first systematic attacks were made on problems of psychological measurement. During the nineteenth century, the field of psychological measurement was nourished by two major influences. First, psychological measurement borrowed heavily from the concepts and tools that had been applied so successfully in physics, chemistry, and astronomy. The nineteenth century was a period of great progress in the physical sciences, and men of that day reasoned that the methods of physical science could be applied to the human mind. It was during this period that *psychophysics* was born: the precise and quantitative study of how human judgments are made. Psychophysics has a proud tradition, and it has had a wholesome influence on measurement methods in all areas of psychology.

The second major influence on the development of psychological measurement methods was the clinical tradition growing out of medicine, psychiatry, and social welfare research. In these efforts there was an urgent need for methods of measuring emotional stability and intelligence. The first practical mental tests grew out of this tradition and were applied to the problem of classifying mental deficients in public schools.

It has been only during the last several decades that these two traditions have merged. The union of scientific technology and mathematics with the clinician's intuitive approach and his concern for people produced the modern methodology of psychological measurement.

In addition to the two major influences described above, a number of other historical trends had a prominent influence on the development of psychological measurement methods. There are many needs for psychological tests in education, and measurement methods have grown at the same rate as educational facilities. Because of the many direct uses for statistical methods in the development and use of psychological tests, the early developments in the discipline of statistics were prominent influences on the growth of psychological measurement.

The theory of evolution had a very important influence on psychology as a whole and particularly on the field of psychological measurement. Although the theory of evolution developed in biology and had its most important influence there, it helped foster new concepts of human behavior and interested psychologists in measuring human adjustment and the inheritance of psychological traits.

More recently, the two great wars of this century had very important impacts on psychological measurement. In both conflicts psychological tests were needed for the selection and classification of armed forces personnel. Never before had psychological tests been used in such wholesale quantities, and they proved their worth so well that psychological testing received wide public acceptance.

The growth of measurement methods for use in controlled experiments has paralleled the growth of measurement methods for the study of individual differences. During the last 100 years, methods have gradually been developed for the measurement of results in studies of learning, perception, physiological processes, and other types of behavioral variables.

During the last thirty years or so, a methodology has grown concerning the development and use of measurement in all aspects of psychology. This methodology is called *psychometric theory*. It concerns the issues relating to the basic principles of measurement which were discussed in the previous chapter as well as the principles to be discussed in later chapters.

Each of the major trends mentioned above will be discussed in some detail in this chapter. Only by understanding these historical roots can the modern methodology and practice of psychological measurement be seen in their proper perspectives.

## psychophysics

### The personal equation

Considerable progress was made during the eighteenth century in the development of scientific instruments: chronographs, telescopes, compasses, microscopes, and many others. Although scant attention was given to the place of the human observer in the use of these instruments, a fortunate mishap stirred interest in the problem. In 1796 at the observatory at Greenwich, England, an astronomer's assistant, named Kinneybrook, found himself consistently at odds with his superior about astronomical observations.  It was Kinneybrook's job to observe the time of transit for certain stars (this consisted, essentially, in noting the time that a star passed one of the cross wires on a telescope).  It was found that Kinneybrook differed with his superior on the average by more than one-half second.  Although such an amount of time might seem trivial for practical purposes, it was sufficient to introduce serious error into astronomical calculations.  The astronomer encouraged Kinneybrook to be more accurate in his observations, but in spite of his efforts, Kinneybrook retained his characteristic difference in observation time.

Astronomers as well as other scientists became interested in Kinneybrook's difficulties.  Astronomers began to compare their measurements with one another and found that there were consistent differences between them.  It became necessary, then, to determine an individual's "personal equation," his characteristic tendency to overestimate or underestimate observations by a certain amount.  This brought a recognition that people differ in their judgments and that such individual differences can be measured and accounted for in scientific work.

## The limen of sensation

Soon after interest had been focused on the personal equation, philosophers and the early psychologists began to speculate about the threshold of awareness, the *limen*.  The limen is the point at which a visual object, or stimulus of any kind, comes into awareness.  If you sit looking at the sky during the late afternoon and wait long enough, stars will become visible.  One minute you do not see them, and the next minute you do.  It is interesting to speculate about the precise moment at which the stars come into awareness, the absolute limen. The absolute limen can also be illustrated using a watch.  If you hold a watch at arm's length, you will not be able to hear the ticking (unless you have an unusually noisy watch).  As you draw the watch closer, you reach a point at which you can hear the ticking, which is the absolute limen.

In addition to the absolute limen, there is a *difference limen*, the difference in stimulation which makes the individual aware of a difference.  The difference limen can be illustrated with a hypothetical experiment.  Assume that you have two light bulbs, which we shall refer to as $S_t$ and $S_1$.  The brightness of $S_t$ is fixed at a particular level and is not changed throughout the experiment. Let the current be adjustible on $S_1$ so that the intensity of light can be varied, and then make $S_1$ the same brightness as $S_t$.  If you increase the intensity of $S_1$, making it gradually brighter, there will be a point at which the subject will become aware of the difference between $S_t$ and $S_1$.  The difference in intensity of the two lights at that point is the difference limen, or, as it is sometimes referred to, the JND, the just noticeable difference.  Another kind of difference limen can be obtained by making $S_t$ and $S_1$ very different in intensity at the beginning of the experiment.  Then $S_1$ can be made gradually dimmer until the subject can no longer see a difference between $S_1$ and $S_t$.  When the difference limen is obtained in this way, it is referred to as the JNND, the just noticeable *not* difference.  The JND and the JNND are usually not quite the same in experimental findings; therefore, the experimenter often averages these to obtain a better estimate of the difference limen.

During the first half of the nineteenth century, considerable study was made of the limen: studies of the sensitivity of touch, hearing, vision, and other sense modalities.  One of the prominent persons in this work was Ernst Weber, a German physiologist.  One of Weber's principal findings concerns the size of the difference limen at various levels of stimulation.  If, in the judgment of weights, a weight of 6 pounds is just noticeably different from a weight of 5 pounds, would a weight of 11 pounds be just noticeably different from a weight of 10 pounds?  To carry the question further, would a weight of 101 pounds be just noticeably different from a weight of 100 pounds?  Your everyday experience tells you that this is not the case, that the difference limen is dependent on the level of intensity of $S_t$.

Weber found that the JND tends to be a constant ratio of the intensity of $S_t$.  If, in terms of the example above, a weight of 6 pounds is just noticeably different from a weight of 5 pounds (the JND is 1 pound at this level of intensity for $S_t$), the ratio would be 1.2.  Then we would predict that the JND for an $S_t$ of 10 pounds would be 2 pounds (a weight of 12 pounds would be just noticeably different).  The JND can then be expressed in the form of an equation as

$$JND = cS_t$$

The above equation, which is referred to as *Weber's law*, is approximately true for many different situations involving judgments.  It has even been applied analogously to such situations as the willingness of an individual to invest money.  For example, an individual might be willing to invest $100 in a radio for a $3,000 car but not be willing to spend that much on a radio for a $2,000 car—the willingness to invest more money tending to be a function of the amount of money already invested.

## Gustav Fechner

In the hands of Gustav Fechner, the rising interest in human judgment became the cornerstone for modern psychological measurement.  Fechner went to the University of Leipzig when he was sixteen years old and remained there —studying, then teaching and doing research—until his death 70 years later.  He took his university degree in medicine, but his subsequent livelihood and reputation were based on his work in physics.  He sought accomplishment as a philosopher, and almost in spite of himself he became a great psychologist. Fechner was what we might refer to today as an "oddball." His philosophic speculations concerned the presence of consciousness in all things, even imputing consciousness to plants and inanimate objects. He wrote numerous pamphlets under the pen name of Dr. Mises. In a heraldic tone the pamphlets called on the sleeping world to arise to the new philosophy.

Fechner tried to support his metaphysical beliefs with scientific experiments. He seized on the studies of human judgment, and particularly the JND, as the starting point for his work. His research was based on the postulate that sensation cannot be measured directly but that it is legitimate to ask an individual whether a sensation is present or not and whether one sensation is more intense than another. This is still the logical foundation of psychophysics. Fechner set out on a long program of research on human judgment, and in the course of this he invented the major methods of measurement and many of the procedures of analysis which are used today. He performed the now classical studies on lifted weights, visual brightness, and the sense of touch. Although he never proved his philosophic points, he demonstrated how the logic and methods of science could be used in psychological measurement.

Fechner's contributions in the middle of the previous century earned him the title "father of psychophysics." Psychophysics concerns relations between psychological responses and events in the outside world. Thus in studies of lifted weights, the weights are measurable stimuli in the world of real events. Covert responses to such stimuli are not directly open to psychological investigation, but overt responses are. This distinction was discussed in the previous chapter.

The investigation of overt responses to physical stimuli requires precise methods for presenting the stimuli and precise methods for eliciting responses to them. Each method for presenting stimuli and eliciting responses is referred to as a *psychophysical method*. Fechner's major contribution was the development of a number of psychophysical methods and the application of these to a variety of types of human judgment. For example, in studies of lifted weights, he employed the method of *pair comparisons*. With that method, the subject compares weights two at a time and states which is heavier. The weights are lifted either in succession or simultaneously, one with the left hand and the other with the right hand. The method of pair comparisons and other psychophysical methods developed by Fechner are still in wide use. Many of his findings regarding the application of these psychophysical methods to lifted weights, loudness of tones, brightness of lights, and other forms of physical stimulation remain valid today.

In the 100 years that have passed since Fechner made his major contributions, psychophysics has pushed far ahead in terms of developing many new psychophysical methods, refinements of experimental procedures, and mathematical methods for analyzing results. Whereas psychophysical methods were originally employed with stimuli whose dimensions could be directly measured (e.g., amounts of weight and lengths of lines), psychophysical methods are now applied also to numerous types of stimuli for which the attribute of interest cannot be measured directly. For example, the method of pair comparisons can be used to obtain preferences of people for different foods. The subject is asked which he likes better—apples or oranges, apples or pears, oranges or pears, and so on, for all two-choice comparisons in a set of food names. Of course, there is no way to measure the tastiness of fruits directly, in the same way that one measures amount of weight. Psychophysical methods are employed these days not only with respect to judgments of physically measurable dimensions but also with respect to preferences, interests, attitudes, and almost all types of responses that men and lower animals are capable of making.

It is important to note that psychophysics was not originally concerned with individual differences, and most current work in psychophysics also is not concerned with individual differences. As originally conceived, psychophysics concerned lawful relations that hold for all people. It was for this reason that, in much of his research, Fechner used himself as his only subject.

Although psychophysics is important in its own right, its wider contribution has been to a general psychometric theory, which concerns principles that apply in all studies of individual differences and in all studies of experimental treatments. As an example of psychophysical methods in studies of individual differences, multiple-choice items on tests of ability are direct counterparts of a psychophysical method employed with judgments of lifted weights. Psychophysical methods are employed with respect to results in numerous types of controlled experiments, particularly the results of experiments on learning, motivation, and perception. As a separate enterprise, psychophysics is now considered to represent only one type of experimental treatment. For example, investigations are made of relations between the perceived loudness of tones and physical measurements of the loudness of tones.

Chapter 7 will provide an elementary survey of psychophysical measurement methods and related methods of analysis. There it will be shown how psychophysical methods provide principles and techniques for all psychological measurement. The important points to understand from this historical introduction to psychophysics are (1) psychophysics represents a bridge between the exact measurement methods developed in the physical sciences and measurement methods developed in psychology, and (2) psychophysical measurement methods are important in many studies of individual differences and in many types of psychological experiments, as well as in the more strictly psychophysical types of studies of simple judgment with which Fechner was concerned.

## the growth of statistics

The construction and use of psychological measures are intimately connected with statistical concepts and statistical techniques. Therefore, it would be helpful to discuss some of the foundations of statistical methods before they are applied to measurement problems in subsequent chapters.

The impetus for the development of statistical methods came initially not from the budding scientific disciplines but from the needs of gamblers. Gamblers needed some principles for the setting of betting odds in roulette, dice, and card games. Men such as Bernoulli, de Moivre, Laplace, and Gauss laid the foundation for our modern systems of mathematical statistics between the middle of the seventeenth century and the middle of the eighteenth century.

The central notion in the discipline of statistics is that of *probability*. Before the development of statistics, scientific laws were expressed in a way that allowed no room for errors in prediction. The law of falling bodies, the predictions of celestial movements, and the laws of heat exchange were intended to predict events in nature exactly. However, in actual experiments the results seldom come out exactly as predicted. Such inconsistencies were explained in terms of the inability to achieve purified laboratory conditions, which require complete vacuums, noncompressible fluids, completely constant temperature, and other ideal circumstances. Later it came to be realized that such ideal conditions could never be obtained and that consequently the results of experiments could be only approximately predicted. In some fields of research we have seen a succession of laws, each of which came closer to explaining a scientific problem. Scientists have come more and more to look on all laws as approximations, approximations that fit the real world so closely as to be "true" for all practical purposes.

The need for a consideration of probability is more necessary when dealing with some phenomena than when dealing with others. Even relatively crude scientific principles will serve us in everyday life, in problems such as constructing a canoe to hold a certain amount of weight, setting up a system of gears to lift tree stumps, and determining the amount of water that will be needed to fill a swimming pool. But we can see why gamblers were in great need of the statistics of probability. The individual flip of a coin or throw of dice will obey not even an approximate lawfulness. With events like these, it can be said only that one outcome is more likely, or more probable, than another. Because of the randomness of the individual event, statistical laws are true only on the average. For example, if we flipped a coin 1,000 times, we would expect to obtain approximately 500 "heads" (although a "biased" coin might fool us here).

In many scientific situations, predictions can be made only about averages or total effects rather than about individual events. For example, the laws of gases are true only on the average. It can be predicted how a gaseous body will behave under changes in temperature, but it cannot be predicted how the individual molecule will behave. As the temperature is increased, the molecular movement increases, on the average. However, some of the molecules might slow up for a time because of collisions with others, and some of them might accelerate beyond the average. But when the behavior of nearly countless molecules is averaged out, predictions become very accurate for all practical purposes.

The social sciences are particularly dependent on concepts of probability. For example, a principle about the behavior of "mobs" might hold only for the action of the group as a whole. It might be predicted that the amount of shouting for the group as a whole would increase. However, assuming some credence for this hypothetical principle, it is quite likely that some of the group members would actually become quieter as the general noise level increased.

In addition to predicting the average performance for a number of events or for a number of persons, it is equally important to learn about the amount of error which such predictions entail. Thinking back to the problems confronting the seventeenth-century gamblers, the errors involved in the prediction of coin tosses can serve to illustrate the problem. If an individual tossed 10 coins on a table, what are the odds that 8 of them would be heads? If the 10 coins were tossed 1,000 times, how many times would all 10 of them be tails? The expected occurrences for 10 coins tossed 1,024 times are shown in Table 2-1. We would expect to get 10 heads, and consequently no tails, in 1 toss out of 1,024 tosses. As would be expected, the most frequently occurring pattern is 5 heads and 5 tails.

The distribution of heads and tails is pictured in graph form in Figure 2-1. If the number of coins in each toss is increased from 10 to 100, the curve will begin to smooth out to resemble that in Figure 2-2.

Curves similar to the bell-shaped curve in Figure 2-2 are encountered very often in practical work. Such a curve is referred to as the *normal distribution*, or it is variously called the *normal curve* and the *normal curve of error*. Much of the early development of statistics was concerned with the properties of the normal distribution.

### Quetelet and the normal distribution

During the last 100 years numerous efforts have been made to apply statistical principles to the human behavior. In the coming chapters we shall see the key role that statistical methods play in the development and use of tests.

**TABLE 2-1**   Expected occurrences of heads and tails for 10 coins which are tossed 1,024 times

| FREQUENCY | 1 | 10 | 45 | 120 | 210 | 252 | 210 | 120 | 45 | 10 | 1 |
|---|---|---|---|---|---|---|---|---|---|---|---|
| Heads | 0 | 1 | 2 | 3 | 4 | 5 | 6 | 7 | 8 | 9 | 10 |
| Tails | 10 | 9 | 8 | 7 | 6 | 5 | 4 | 3 | 2 | 1 | 0 |

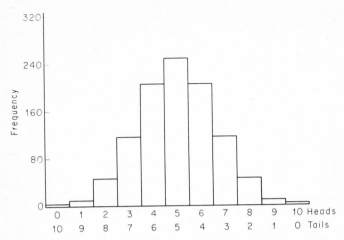

**FIGURE 2-1**    Graph of expected occurrences of heads and tails for 10 coins tossed 1,024 times

During the first half of the nineteenth century, Adolph Quetelet, a Belgian statistician, undertook to gather a considerable amount of information about European populations. He collected information on the number of children in families, the number of children born in different years, and the physical characteristics of people. He found that many of these characteristics distributed themselves in a shape much like that of the normal distribution. For example, he found that the chest measurements of soldiers were distributed like the normal distribution.

Because Quetelet knew that the normal distribution demonstrates the error in many types of predictions, he came to the conclusion that a normal distribution of human traits shows "nature's error" in the composition of human beings. It was his idea that "nature" aims at producing the average man and that the extremes in either direction are "accidents of nature." We remember Quetelet

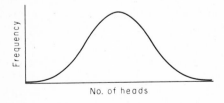

**FIGURE 2-2**    Smoothed curve showing expectancies of heads for a large number of coins tossed many times

not so much for this principle as for the influence he had on men to follow. He was one of the first persons to make systematic studies of individual differences, and he interested others in the application of statistical methods to the study of human behavior.

## the effect of the theory of evolution on psychology

Although the theory of evolution had its most direct influence on the science of biology, it also had an important impact on psychological measurement and psychology as a whole. Before the nineteenth century, the predominant view was that man is a static being, having possessed since the day of creation a uniform and unchanging set of physical and mental attributes. Although Quetelet measured individual differences, he thought of these as nature's mistakes in producing the average man. It had always been noted that men differ from one another, but there had been no systematic attempt to study the part which individual differences play in everyday life.

### Darwin

There were dissenters to the static theory of man and his surroundings, and there were even some, men such as Lyell and Lamarck, who theorized that life changes from generation to generation. It remained for Charles Darwin to amass the evidence to support the theory of evolution. He collected many examples from the animal kingdom showing the changing forms of life that develop in particular environments. He saw that the mechanism of selection, or "survival of the fittest," as he called it, allows some animals to exist and forces others to die off. Therefore, the animals whose particular features make them more suited to an environment survive and pass on their genetic qualities to the next generation.

Darwin's major evidence for evolution was presented in *The Origin of Species,* published in 1859. It brought on several decades of argument among scientists as to the validity of the theory and its implications for scientific work. As the theory came to be accepted, it forced new viewpoints on scientific disciplines. It required biologists and botanists to think of animals and plants as being in a state of change, gradually progressing from one form to another to meet the changing environments. The theory also gave an impetus to the study of individual differences in psychology. It was reasoned that if individual differences in plants and animals make for differential ability to adapt and survive, individual differences in humans would also have a functional significance. Further, if plants and animals inherit ancestral characteristics, some of the individual characteristics of human beings might be accounted for on the same basis.

## early studies of individual differences

### Galton

The several lines of thought that we have traced—psychophysics, statistics, and the theory of evolution—converged in the psychological work of Sir Francis Galton. He was a member of a vanishing breed, the gentleman-scholar, who, without formal university connections, dabbled effectively in a wide range of subjects. His interests ranged from criminology, psychology, biology, and anthropology to the invention of numerous scientific devices. He invented the "supersonic" whistle and delighted himself by calling the dogs of London away from their incredulous masters. He also invented the composite photograph, which is made by superimposing several photographs on one another. He applied the method to the photographs of criminals, trying to obtain a composite of typical criminal features. He once practiced paranoia, going about imagining that everyone was talking about him. After several days he could believe that even horses were plotting against him. In order to understand primitive religions, he built a religion of his own. He placed a comic picture of Punch on the wall and paid it all manner of homage and tribute in order to grasp the meaning of the idol in primitive worship. In addition to his many other activities, Galton also applied his genius to the study of psychological traits.

Galton was Darwin's immediate follower in the field of psychology. He developed an interest in the hereditariness of individual characteristics and made studies of prominent men in England to support his views. In 1869 he reported his findings in *Hereditary Genius,* in which he tried to show that "greatness" runs in families. He came to believe that most important personal characteristics are inherited, not only the prominent physical characteristics, but also abilities and personality characteristics. He believed that criminality and psychological disorders are passed along from father to son by direct inheritance.

Galton founded the study of *eugenics,* the avowed purpose of which is the betterment of the human race through the control of mating. Although Galton never worked out the social problems which his program would involve, he was convinced that a world of superior human beings could be developed by encouraging gifted couples to marry and by discouraging or preventing less gifted individuals from having children.

Galton realized that before his program of eugenics could be undertaken, it would be necessary to learn more about the inheritance of individual characteristics. If it could be shown that a particular attribute—literary ability, for example—is passed from father to son, it should be possible to breed a generation of literary geniuses. However, if the attribute proved not to be inherited, there would be nothing that a program of eugenics could do to improve literary talent. Galton needed first to measure human characteristics before proceeding to study their hereditariness, and it was because of this need to measure individual differences that Galton's contributions are of such importance to us here.

Galton coined the term "mental test" and set about to measure many different human attributes. He recognized the need for standardization in testing, the necessity to present all subjects with the same problems under uniform conditions. Galton's tests bore little resemblance to the ones which are most widely used today. He and his immediate followers in England made much of the philosopher Locke's dictum that all knowledge comes through the senses. From this they reasoned that the person with the most acute "senses" would be the most gifted and most knowledgeable. Most of Galton's tests were measures of simple sensory discrimination: the ability to recognize tones, the acuteness of vision, the ability to differentiate colors, and many other sensory functions. Galton also invented many instruments to use in his research, some of which are used in modified form today.

Galton began the first large-scale testing program at his Anthropometric Laboratory in the South Kensington Museum in 1884. Each visitor was charged threepence for having his measurements taken on a variety of physical and sensory tests, including height, weight, breathing power, strength of pull, hearing, seeing, and the color sense. In order to analyze the data obtained, Galton made use of statistical methods. With these, he determined averages and measures of variation. His particular need was for a measure of association, or correlation, to detect the amount of resemblance between the individual characteristics of fathers and their sons. He made the first attempts to derive the statistics of correlation, the procedures which are now widely used in the study of individual differences.

## Pearson

Galton supported a younger colleague, Karl Pearson, in the development of statistical methods for the study of individual differences. Pearson was the genius in mathematical statistics that Galton was in studies of individual differences. He derived the correlation coefficient, partial correlation, multiple correlation, and factor analysis and laid the foundation for most of the multivariate statistics which are in use in psychology today (some of which will be discussed in the chapters ahead).

Following the work of Galton, the last two decades of the nineteenth century saw a considerable expansion of studies of individual differences in England and the United States. Prominent in this work was James McKeen Cattell, who studied with Galton and then undertook investigations in this country. The tests continued to be largely of a sensory and motor type, measuring sensory speed and reaction time. Toward the end of the century, it came to be realized that these tests were not measuring intelligence. Scores on the tests bore almost no relationship to measures of intellectual achievement, such as school grades, refuting the hypothesis that sensory ability is closely related to intelligence.

## the first practical mental tests

A brief summary will be given of the major developments in psychological testing during this century. Each type of test which is mentioned will be discussed in detail in later chapters.

At the turn of the twentieth century, some notable events in the history of psychological measurement occurred in France. It was there that the humanist tradition and the interest in medicine and social welfare were centered. After the French Revolution, terms such as "equality" and "the rights of man" reflected the new interest in helping the downtrodden, the sick, and also the psychologically maladjusted. Medicine developed rapidly during the first part of the nineteenth century, partly because of the Napoleonic Wars and the need to treat wounded soldiers. Pinel released the insane from their dungeons and insisted that they were sick, not possessed by demons. Charcot, Janet, and Ribot founded the field of psychiatry and developed the first plausible theories of psychopathology. Freud drew his early knowledge from these men and went on to be the founder of psychoanalysis.

### Binet

During the last quarter of the nineteenth century, the distinguished line of French investigators was joined by Alfred Binet. His early work was on the use of hypnotism in treating mental disorders; then near the end of the century, he turned to the problem of measuring intelligence. He was commissioned by the Minister of Public Instruction to construct tests for the measurement of intelligence in schoolchildren. The schools had become alarmed by the number of failures and needed some means of distinguishing the lazy or maladjusted children from those who lacked the fundamental capacity to learn.

Binet, working in collaboration with Simon, completed his first test in 1905. The test was not concerned principally with sensory and motor functions, as had been the case with the tests of Galton and his immediate followers. Instead, it concerned the child's ability to understand and reason about the objects in his cultural environment. Consequently, the test items involved such things as the naming of objects, the completion of sentences, and the comprehension of questions.

The first Binet-Simon test had a range of questions from very simple ones, which even the dullest child might answer correctly, to questions which would indicate a superior level of ability. Practical work with the test indicated that some of the items were more difficult than had been anticipated, and some proved to be insensitive to differences in ability. A revision of the test was made in 1908, in which the items were arranged in terms of age levels, with a group of items being designated as representing average intelligence for each particular age. The highest age level at which a child could perform adequately was called his *mental age*. Later, Stern suggested that the child's mental age be divided by his chronological age, which is essentially the IQ as it has come to be known.

The Binet-Simon tests aroused considerable interest in other countries, in England and especially in the United States. Several translations and revisions of the tests were made in this country, including forms by Goddard (1911) and Kuhlmann (1912). The tests became very popular in studying schoolchildren, particularly in the understanding of psychological maladjustment and juvenile delinquency. The most prominent revision of the Binet-Simon test was completed by Terman (1916), the resulting form being referred to as the Stanford-Binet test. For the first time a considerable amount of research was done to select items which would be appropriate for each age level and which would differentiate age levels. Also, the large number of children tested provided norms for the interpretation of test scores.

Terman and Merrill (1937) presented a revision of the Stanford-Binet in 1937. A truly heroic effort was made to construct a standardized measure of general ability. Several thousand children were tested in all parts of the United States to establish norms. This test has been used more frequently than any other comparable instrument, and a later revision is in wide use today.

## the first group tests of ability

The Binet forms and their revisions are all individual tests, requiring an expert examiner to test one child at a time. During World War I it was necessary to classify large numbers of recruits, to weed out men whose level of ability was so low that they would be a handicap to the service, and also to select more intelligent individuals for positions of responsibility. A special committee of the American Psychological Association, with R. M. Yerkes as chairman, began an investigation of testing procedures for the armed services.

Arthur Otis had been working on a group test of intelligence, which he turned over to the committee. With some revisions, it was put to use. This test is referred to as the Army Alpha Test (Otis, 1939a). It is a short form containing questions on arithmetic, reasoning, and general information. The test proved very successful, came into wide use in the armed forces, and is still used to some extent today. A companion test, the Army Beta (Otis, 1939b), was constructed for use with individuals whose knowledge of English is scanty. The test instructions are given in pantomime, and the test items do not require the subject to use or understand English. The test requires the subject to solve geometrical puzzles and to analyze pictures. Although the Beta test was not so successful as the Alpha test, it set the stage for the nonlanguage tests which are in use today.

## standardized classroom examinations

### The essay exam

The standardized classroom examination as we know it today came into wide use only during the last 50 years. Before that time it was customary for the instructor to give grades on the basis of his accumulated impressions of the student or on the basis of oral examinations. Grading in this way can be unfair to the student who is not popular with the teacher or who does not have the verbal facility to impress others. The first standardized examinations were of the "essay" type, in which the student writes about a number of problems or topics. Although grading is still somewhat subjective, the essay examination is standardized to the extent that all students receive the same questions, which provides a uniform basis of comparison.

### The multiple-choice examination

Progress in classroom examinations has moved in two directions, toward the refinement of essay examinations and toward the development of multiple-choice tests. The advent of the multiple-choice test, or "objective" test, as it is sometimes called, ruled out the unreliability of instructors' impressions, and although there are abuses in the use of multiple-choice tests, examinations of this kind are at least uniformly fair to students.

### Standardized achievement tests

A recent trend in classroom testing is the use of achievement tests which are constructed by a group of specialists, instead of the teacher, and are applied to all the children in a school system. This allows comparison of the children in different classes of the same school and comparison between the children in different schools. Now the teacher can use standardized achievement tests for many different subject matters, ranging from reading ability to knowledge of geography.

## the development of personality tests

In line with the sequence in which tests were developed, we have talked so far about tests of ability, which concern how much an individual knows, how rapidly he can work, or how well he can solve problems. Tests of this kind are sometimes referred to as "cognitive" tests, and the attributes they measure have been contrasted with the variety of attributes which are "noncognitive" and do not concern abilities in the obvious sense. Cronbach (1949) has distinguished these two kinds of attributes as being tests of "maximum performance" as opposed to tests of "habitual performance." You can see how these functions would differ if we were considering a test for "friendliness." It would not be a case of how friendly an individual could be if he tried, for most of us *know* how to be friendly. The question would concern how friendly an individual habitually is in his dealings with others. Noncognitive tests or tests of habitual performance are also called "personality tests." Although the term has come to be used far too broadly to cover interests, attitudes, mental health, and many other matters, it is too firmly in use to be avoided.

Tests of ability were developed first and more firmly not because of a lack of interest in personality but because of the difficulty involved in measuring the noncognitive functions. Galton was as interested in the inheritance of personality as he was in the inheritance of abilities. However, the nearest he came to measuring personality characteristics was in a questionnaire study of "imagery," concerning the extent to which individuals can picture objects in memory. Binet was interested in tests of personality before he constructed the first intelligence test, and among other devices he designed a questionnaire test of "morality" for children.

### Self-report inventories

Not only were psychologists busy during World War I developing intelligence tests, but they were also trying to meet the need for tests of neuroticism and emotional instability. There were too many recruits to be seen individually in psychiatric interviews. R. S. Woodworth constructed a questionnaire which asked each recruit essentially the kinds of questions that would be used in an interview. The questions concerned the individual's adjustment in the home, in school, and among friends. It was used primarily to sift out those men who needed further clinical study.

### Projective tests

During World War I, a Swiss psychiatrist named Hermann Rorschach was working on a novel line in the measurement of personality. The Rorschach test (Beck, 1944), as it has come to be known, consists of 10 inkblots which the subject is required to describe and interpret. The test grew out of Freudian and other "depth" psychologies, with their emphasis on unconscious motivation and the importance of symbolism. The purpose of the test is to get beyond what the subject knows about himself, and is willing to relate, to the "deeper" traits and urges which determine his overt behavior. Since Rorschach's pioneer research, numerous other projective techniques have been developed. In spite of the great difficulties involved in standardizing and validating tests of this kind, the Rorschach and its followers have been widely used in clinical psychology.

## test development in the period between the two world wars

The direction of the measurement movement in psychology changed as a result of the two major conflicts of this century. We saw how the practical problems of World War I encouraged the development of the first group tests of intelligence and personality. The products were inexpensive, convenient tests which could be administered to large numbers of people. Consequently, group tests came into vogue during the 1920s and 1930s and, unfortunately, were often applied uncritically to many problems. There was too little concern for testing the test, too little concern for determining the reliability and validity of the measures. Teachers often took the results of intelligence tests at face value and made major decisions about students on the basis of questionable measures. The general public became oversold on tests, and the IQ came to be regarded as an infallible and fixed mark on the individual. Numerous tests of personality purporting to measure "introversion," "marital adjustment," "happiness," and many other complex attributes were constructed and sold with little research foundation. The uncritical overacceptance of tests during that period is not unlike a similar overenthusiasm that has occurred in connection with the development of many other products: we have seen numerous medical discoveries regarded at first as cure-alls and then later put to a more limited and more proper use.

## test development from World War II to the present

A great conflict again created the need for methods of classifying men. However, this time the need was on a much larger scale. Over ten million men and women were called into service, and they had to be assigned to a wide range of positions—jobs in airplane navigation, electronics, and meteorology, which had not existed a decade earlier.

Instead of having to construct only several group tests, as had been the case in the previous conflict, psychologists were called on to construct numerous batteries of tests, some of them complicated beyond the extremes of what the early testers might have imagined. Psychologists were brought into the problem wholesale and spent several years in implementing the largest testing program that had ever been undertaken. In the process, the logic and methods of psychological measurement were considerably extended, and many investigations were undertaken which would not have been possible without government support. The psychology of testing was pushed years ahead by the work which was done in conjunction with the armed forces. Much of the work was methodological, concerning the best way to measure particular functions, in contrast to the pell-mell effort of earlier decades to compose tests without proper research foundation.

Now we find that the people who construct tests and the people who use them are more aware of the limitations of particular measures, more inquisitive about the research findings on an instrument, and more mindful of alternative approaches. A healthy skepticism has grown, and with it have come promising new lines of investigation in the measurement of individual differences. Testing has become a big business, with numerous firms devoting themselves to the development and sale of tests. Hundreds of psychologists and professional educators spend most of their time as measurement specialists. Psychological publications print hundreds of articles each year on specialized problems in measurement. However, there are still abuses in testing—the sale of tests that are not properly researched, and a naïve acceptance by some persons of any scrap of paper which purports to be a test. In spite of the remaining abuses and in spite of the unsolved problems in many kinds of tests, psychological tests can now point to an increased efficiency and marked economy which they have brought to schools, the armed forces, psychological clinics, and, more recently, industry.

## growth of measurement in basic research

In the previous sections we discussed the development of practicable measures of individual differences, starting with the work of Binet and coming through the two world wars to the present. These developments were important mainly for applied psychology, in relation to education, industry, military services, psychological counseling, and psychiatric treatment. During this century there has been a parallel growth of measurement methods in basic research. As was mentioned previously, measurement in relation to basic research in psychology first appeared in the form of Fechner's psychophysics. Psychophysics in turn nourished the development of precise measurement methods for basic research on individual differences and in controlled experiments. Finally, all efforts to develop measurement methods for basic research have contributed to the growth of a general theory of measurement in psychology (psychometric theory), which is the major concern of this book.

### Basic research on individual differences

Although the work of Binet and his followers produced many usable tests of ability, that work did not tell us much about the essential nature of individual differences in abilities. The same is true of the pioneering work on personality tests. The emphasis in applied settings is on finding measurement methods that work well in practice, which is fine for applied work but does not necessarily lead to a science of individual differences. In this connection it is important to stress that whereas measurement is usually a necessary condition for understanding scientific problems, measurement alone is seldom a sufficient condition for achieving that understanding. For example, in an applied setting, if one wanted to measure the quality of wines, his safest bet would be to have ratings made by professional wine tasters. This type of measurement would work well in practice, in the sense that it would probably be predictive of what people in general would like and purchase, but it would tell us almost nothing about how grapes should be grown or how wine should be made. The same is true of the effort to understand the basic nature of individual differences between people; e.g., having practicable tests of intelligence does not necessarily lead to an understanding of subcategories of intelligence or tell us how those subcategories develop.

The first major efforts at basic research on human abilities were made in England at the turn of the century, at about the same time that Binet was working on the first practicable test of intelligence. This basic research was centered in the work of Charles Spearman and his colleagues. Rather than dive directly into the construction of practicable tests for use in applied settings, Spearman developed and investigated a theory of human abilities. (Spearman's work in this regard will be discussed more fully in Chapter 9.) Essentially the theory asserted that all measures of human ability relate to a *general factor*; that is, there is one yardstick of intelligence. Each measure tends to share in that factor to some extent. Spearman also hypothesized *specific factors*, ones that are uncorrelated with the general factor. For example, a test of memory might relate partly to a general factor of intelligence and partly to a specific factor of its own having to do with a particular type of memory. Spearman also had theories about the physiological underpinnings of the general factor, and he had theories concerning the kinds of learning that lead to the growth of specific factors.

Spearman and his colleagues worked for over thirty years on the development of their theory, on the invention of mathematical procedures for testing the theory, and on the gathering of data from thousands of children and adults. Although few tests that received wide use in applied settings grew out of this work, it laid numerous foundation stones in basic research on individual differences. (This research is summarized in Spearman, 1927.)

Spearman's followers in England have maintained a tradition of basic research on the nature of individual differences between people. Since about 1930, however, the major basic research on individual differences has been done in the United States. Up to about 1950, research on human abilities was characterized more by technical elegance and massive gatherings of data than by careful theorizing. It was soon found that Spearman's general-factor theory does not account for the actual correlations between diverse measures of human ability, which spurred a search for the actual number and kinds of abilities that exist. In this search, many, many different kinds of abilities were found, which posed a dilemma. If human abilities are splintered into so many different kinds, how can these be placed in any coherent scheme that will lead to scientific understanding? During recent years there has been much soul-searching about how to conceptualize and investigate human abilities (these will be discussed in later chapters).

Basic research on individual differences in personality characteristics has grown with, and tended to imitate, basic research on human abilities. As has been true of basic research on human abilities, research on personality characteristics has (1) relied mainly on printed, group-administered tests; (2) centered on a search for the number and kinds of personality traits (factors) that exist in wide varieties of tests; and (3) occasioned the gathering and analysis of mammoth amounts of data from human subjects.

As will be discussed more fully in later chapters, the results of studies of individual differences in personality have been different from the results of studies of human abilities. Whereas many types of abilities were measured easily with printed tests, this has proved very difficult with personality characteristics. Whereas numerous different types (factors) of ability have been found to occur rather widely in different types of tests, only several types of personality characteristics have been found to occur in more than very restricted types of test items. Whereas basic research on human abilities has led to many types of tests that are reasonably valid in applied settings, basic research on personality characteristics has led to few instruments with proved validity in applied settings.

## Controlled experiments

The growth of measurement methods in controlled experiments has paralleled the growth of measurement methods for studies of individual differences. Several examples will be given to illustrate the growth of measurement methods in controlled experiments. A simple form of behavior that has been of interest for over a hundred years is reaction time. The study of reaction time requires some careful methods of measurement. In the second half of the last century, German psychologists developed relatively precise methods for this purpose. Subjects were required to press a button as soon as a light was turned on. More complex forms of reaction time were measured with the use of several lights and different instructions regarding responses to different patterns of lights. Clock mechanisms were devised for accurately measuring reaction time.

In his pioneering studies of conditioned reflexes during the last decades of the last century, Pavlov devised numerous methods for measuring different types of responses. For example, to measure the conditioned reflex of salivation in dogs, he used a small tube running from a salivary gland to a small receptacle. In this way he could accurately measure small changes in salivary flow.

During the early years of this century, E. L. Thorndike developed some of the first methods for measuring rate of learning in dogs and cats. A now famous method developed by Thorndike is the puzzle box. A hungry dog is placed in the box, and outside the box is a bowl of food. The dog can release the latch on a door by pressing a lever. Gradually the dog learns to press the lever very soon after he is placed in the box. The time taken to press the lever is the measure of learning.

During the last 30 years, measurement methods for controlled experiments have mushroomed. When visiting a psychological laboratory for the first time, people are usually surprised at the number and complexity of methods for eliciting and measuring responses in many types of investigations. If it were not for the human subjects and lower animals being investigated, one might think he was in a physics laboratory.

Particularly noteworthy has been the growth of precise measurement methods for physiological psychology. Physiological psychology languished for many years because precise measurement methods were not available. The present availability of numerous precise measurement methods has resulted in an immense growth of physiological psychology in the last several decades.

As is true of basic research on individual differences, many measurement methods still need to be developed for controlled experiments. For example, better measurement methods are needed for the study of various aspects of attention, e.g., physiological changes that occur during heightened attention. Both studies of individual differences and controlled experiments will be nourished by the development of new measurement methods. A "breakthrough" in measurement methods typically results in a flood of interesting new investigations.

## Psychometric theory

All the historical developments discussed in this chapter have led to a general theory of measurement in psychology. It is a theory concerning the development and use of psychological measurement methods, but it is not an empirical theory about how people behave or the nature of individual differences. Some aspects of this theory were discussed in the previous chapter. Some classical topics in psychometric theory to be discussed in future chapters are (1) psychophysical methods, (2) measurement reliability, (3) measurement validity, (4) measurement construction, and (5) many mathematical methods for constructing, validating, and investigating psychological measures. In addition to the classical topics in psychometric theory, there are many specific principles, such as those which concern finding the ideal time limit for a test, correcting a multiple-choice test for the effects of guessing, and constructing norms.

Psychometric theory received its first major impetus from Fechner's psychophysics. Although Fechner did not attempt to generalize psychophysics beyond simple studies of human judgment, he strongly believed that exact measurement in psychology is possible and feasible. His success with very simple types of measurement problems has encouraged an effort to obtain precise measurement methods in all psychology.

The next major contributions to psychometric theory after Fechner's were those of Galton and his colleague, Karl Pearson. They developed statistical methods for analyzing the data obtained from measurement methods, and they devised methods for analyzing the correlations between different measurement methods. Following this work, Spearman made many contributions to psychometric theory concerning test construction, reliability theory, and numerous aspects of correlational analysis and factor analysis.

Spearman's followers in England have continued to make outstanding contributions to psychometric theory. As was true of basic research on individual differences, however, psychologists in the United States have gradually taken over the lead in the development of psychometric theory. Now psychometric theory is so many-faceted and complex that it constitutes a special subfield in psychology.

Psychometric theory has been highly mathematized, more so than any other aspect of psychology and so much so that specialization in it requires a high degree of mathematical sophistication. This does not mean, however, that the most important principles are beyond the reader of this book. Many of the complex mathematical developments concern highly special, technical issues that are of direct interest only to specialists. Also, many of the more complex mathematical developments in psychometric theory are largely museum pieces that have few applications in applied work or basic research. An adequate introduction to psychometric theory can be imparted with words, examples, diagrams, and some very simple forms of mathematics. The remainder of this book will lean heavily on these devices.

Although there are many advances still to be made in psychometric theory, that theory far outdistances theories of human behavior and methods for gathering data relating to those theories. For example, the major problems in the measurement of personality characteristics are not with respect to psychometric theory but with respect to unproductive theories of the nature of personality characteristics and/or largely invalid test items for measuring those characteristics. If more productive theories of behavior were available, and if these were accompanied by techniques for gathering important data, present psychometric theory could work with them to make immense strides in the science of psychology.

## Summary

In spite of the importance of psychological measurement, both for basic research and for problems of everyday living, precise measurement methods began to appear only during the middle of the last century. One of the first spurs to the development of psychological measurement methods was the discovery that scientists differed in making simple observations about natural events. This forced scientists to consider a "personal equation" concerning the extent to which there are individual differences in sensory processes.

The second major spur to the development of psychological measurement methods was the monumental research of Gustav Fechner on relationships between magnitudes of simple forms of sensory discrimination and subjective judgments of those intensities. This work led to the development of an essentially new science—psychophysics, which concerns the precise measurement of relations between the dimensions of physical objects and the dimensions of psychological responses to those objects. Particularly important in Fechner's work was the development of many techniques of measurement, which are now used for the measurement of many different psychological attributes in addition to the very simple processes that Fechner studied.

A third spur to the development of psychological measurement methods was the growth of psychiatry and clinical psychology. In these new disciplines it was necessary to measure individual differences in mental abilities and personality characteristics. From this work came many practicable mental tests, many of which are still used in modified form today. Applied work with psychological tests has mushroomed during the present century, and now psychological tests are used very widely in clinical settings, industry, schools, and military activities.

A fourth spur to the development of psychological measurement methods came from the growth of basic research in psychology, which began during the last half of the nineteenth century and has moved at a rapid pace since that time. It has been necessary to develop precise measurement methods both for controlled experiments and for basic research on individual differences between people. Presently psychological theories are populated with variables that are difficult to measure, which is the reason why basic researchers in psychology are keenly concerned about the theory of psychological measurement.

All the above developments have nourished the growth of psychometric theory, which concerns the principles that underlie all psychological measurement. Psychometric theory is important in basic research and in applied psychology, and it is important in controlled experiments and in the study of individual differences. The major purpose of this book is to provide an introduction to psychometric theory.

## Suggested additional readings

Boring, E. G.  A *history of experimental psychology.*  (Rev. ed.)  New York: Appleton-Century-Crofts, 1950.

Jenkins, J. J., & Patterson, D. G.  *Studies in individual differences.*  New York: Appleton-Century-Crofts, 1961.

# PART 2:

## Statistical Methods
## Used with
## Psychological Measures

# CHAPTER 3

## Scores, norms, and related statistics

Test results are usually reported in some numerical form, for example, the total number of questions answered correctly on a true-false test. Such numbers are referred to as *raw scores*. Raw scores are seldom directly meaningful without some qualification as to how well other persons do or the established standards of performance. If Johnny tells his mother that he has made 22 in arithmetic and 48 in spelling, she might say, "That's good work in spelling, but we must do something about your arithmetic." But the 22 in arithmetic might have been the highest score, and if the spelling test consisted of 100 words and the teacher expected the students to know the majority of them, a score of 48 would be an indication of poor performance.

### measures of central tendency

The first thing that we need to learn about Johnny's performance is how well the students as a group performed on the two tests. This will tell us whether Johnny is above or below average. To simplify the problem, let us assume that there are only 11 students in the class and that they made scores on the two tests as follows:

|          | Arithmetic | Spelling |
|----------|------------|----------|
| Johnny   | 22         | 48       |
| Fred     | 12         | 52       |
| Mary     | 14         | 49       |
| Bill     | 12         | 51       |
| Jane     | 14         | 55       |
| Susan    | 14         | 52       |
| Michael  | 17         | 50       |
| Sharon   | 19         | 62       |
| Harry    | 11         | 56       |
| Patricia | 15         | 52       |
| Eric     | 20         | 75       |

By looking at the list of scores, it can be seen that Johnny did very well in arithmetic in comparison to the other students, but relatively poorly in spelling. However, his mother probably would not have an opportunity to look at the list of scores, and it would be a clumsy way to make comparisons if it were necessary to pass around the list to everyone who was interested in the test results.

### Mode

Some index is needed to let the mother know at once whether Johnny did as well as the other children. One such index, called the *mode,* is obtained quite simply by finding the score made most frequently by the students. In the arithmetic test, more students made a score of 14 (Mary, Jane, and Susan) than any other score. The mode is 52 on the spelling test. Although the mode is not as useful as some other measures, it is sometimes used in testing as a measure of central tendency.

### Median

Another measure of central tendency is obtained by seeking the score which has an equal number of students above and below that point, which is called the *median.* In the arithmetic test, the median is 14. Of the 11 students, five made scores higher than 14, and six made scores of 14 or less. The median is 52 on the spelling test, and there are three students whose scores fall exactly at the median. If there is an even number of scores, the median falls between two scores. If Fred had not taken the arithmetic test, the median would have fallen between 14 and 15. The usual practice is to split the difference and say that the median is 14.5. If Johnny's score of 48 were not considered on the spelling test, the median would again lie between two scores, both of which are 52. The median would then still be 52.

The median can be thought of as the score made by the "average person."

This is different, as will be shown shortly, from the average score. One advantage of the median is that it is easy to understand. The teacher would find it relatively easy to explain this index to Johnny's mother, and it would prove useful in discussing his class standing.

The reason that the mode and the median are not used more is that they cannot serve as a basis for the derivation of other statistics which are needed. If we start off with certain statistical measures instead of others, it greatly simplifies the mathematical work to follow, and the mode and the median are poor starting points.

### Mean

A measure of central tendency can be obtained which is easy to understand and can also be used in numerous other mathematical developments. The *mean* is obtained by adding all the scores on a test and dividing the sum by the number of persons tested. Introducing some of the symbolism which will prove useful, let X stand for the raw scores made on a test, N for the number of subjects, and M for the mean. Then the equation for the mean is

$$M = \frac{\Sigma X}{N}$$

The summation sign ($\Sigma$) stands for the process of adding scores—the scores of Johnny, Fred, Mary, and so on—for the 11 students.

The symbolism can be made more specific through the use of subscripts to show the test on which the mean is being obtained. Letting the arithmetic test be referred to as test 1, the equation for the arithmetic mean can be more completely specified as

$$M_1 = \frac{\Sigma X_1}{N_1}$$

Different subscripts can be used to designate other tests, such as the subscript 2 to refer to statistical operations on the spelling test scores and the subscripts 3, 4, 5, and so on, to designate other tests.

Applying the equation to the students' grades, a mean of 15.45 is found for the arithmetic test and a mean of 54.73 for the spelling test. A comparison can be made of the three measures of central tendency on the two tests as follows:

|        | Arithmetic | Spelling |
|--------|------------|----------|
| Mode   | 14         | 52       |
| Median | 14         | 52       |
| Mean   | 15.45      | 54.73    |

The three measures give similar results on both tests. Note that the mean on the spelling test differs by 2.73 from the median and the mode. Looking back at the scores, it can be seen that 7 of the 11 students made less than the mean on spelling. This is due to Eric's performance in spelling, a score so divergent from the others as to affect the mean unduly. It is in situations like this that the mean can cause confusion in the interpretation of test scores.

When either one person or a small group of persons make scores which are markedly higher or lower than those of the rest of the group, the median is often more useful than the mean for interpreting test results. Fortunately, such extreme cases as the example above are not often found in practice.

### Deviation scores

As a first step in transforming raw scores to a more useful form, each score can be expressed in terms of its distance from the mean. The transformed scores are referred to as *deviation scores* and are symbolized by a lowercase $x$:

$$x = X - M_x$$

The equation states that each person's deviation score is obtained by subtracting the mean from his raw score. The class grades can be transformed to deviation scores as follows:

| Arithmetic | Spelling |
|---|---|
| $x_1$ | $x_2$ |
| 6.55 | −6.73 |
| −3.45 | −2.73 |
| −1.45 | −5.73 |
| −3.45 | −3.73 |
| −1.45 | 0.27 |
| −1.45 | −2.73 |
| 1.55 | −4.73 |
| 3.55 | 7.27 |
| −4.45 | 1.27 |
| −0.45 | −2.73 |
| 4.55 | 20.27 |

Deviation scores tell whether an individual is above or below average. Because Johnny's deviation score in arithmetic is positive, we know that he is above the mean; because his deviation score in spelling is negative, we know that he is below the mean.

## measures of dispersion

Before we can interpret a particular deviation score, we must learn how widely the scores are scattered above and below the mean.  A deviation score of 2.00 would represent superior performance if all the scores were closely packed about the mean.  But if there were deviation scores going as high as $+100$ and as low as $-100$, a deviation score of 2.00 would indicate near-average performance. Consequently, we need an index of the spread, or scatter of scores about the mean, in order to interpret particular deviations.

### The range

There are various indices of how widely a group is scattered, or of the dispersion, as it will be called.  One very simple index, the *range*, is obtained by subtracting the lowest score from the highest score.  The highest score on the arithmetic test is 22, and the lowest is 11.  This gives a range of 11.  The range on the spelling test is 27, showing that the dispersion of scores here is greater than on the arithmetic test.  The range is a quickly obtained and often-used index of dispersion.  However, it lacks some of the properties that are needed for an acceptable measure.  It is dependent on only two scores, the highest and the lowest.  If Eric had not taken the spelling test, the range would be only 14 instead of 27.  Also, the range lacks the mathematical properties which can lead to the development of other statistics (a point to which we shall appeal quite often in choosing statistical measures).

### The average deviation

An index of dispersion which is dependent on all the scores instead of just two of them and which indicates the position of an individual in a group is the *average deviation* (AD).  As the name implies, it is obtained by finding how much the scores deviate on the average from the mean, as follows:

$$AD = \frac{\Sigma|x|}{N}$$

where the symbol $|x|$ indicates that we are dealing with absolute deviations, paying no attention to the signs.  For example, using the absolute deviations for the scores on the spelling and arithmetic tests, we have

$$\Sigma|x_1| = 32.35 \qquad \Sigma|x_2| = 58.19$$

$$AD = \frac{32.35}{11} \qquad AD = \frac{58.19}{11}$$

$$AD = 2.94 \qquad AD = 5.29$$

One way to change deviation scores into a more useful form is to divide each of them by the AD. This conversion will give Johnny a score of 2.23 in arithmetic and $-1.27$ in spelling. However, developing this measure further will not be worth the effort. There are more desirable measures of dispersion which can be used; the range and the AD have been discussed to provide a background for the measure now to be developed.

### The standard deviation

The AD has a serious fault: it is based on absolute scores. It is very difficult to work mathematically with absolute scores; consequently, if the AD is used in some of the early statistical work, it severely limits the development of other measures. However, we shall also find ourselves blocked if we seek a measure of dispersion by working with the deviation scores. The sum of these is always zero in any set of scores. Therefore, equations based on the sum of deviation scores "fall apart" and leave nothing with which the mathematician can work.

An alternative to using either $x$ scores or $|x|$ scores is to work with the squared deviations. These will all be positive, and it also happens that they provide an excellent starting place for the derivation of many other statistics. The squared deviations on the two tests are as follows:

| $x_1^2$ | $x_2^2$ |
|---|---|
| 42.90 | 45.26 |
| 11.90 | 7.45 |
| 2.10 | 32.83 |
| 11.90 | 13.91 |
| 2.10 | 0.07 |
| 2.10 | 7.45 |
| 2.40 | 22.37 |
| 12.60 | 52.85 |
| 19.80 | 1.61 |
| 0.20 | 7.45 |
| 20.70 | 410.87 |
| $\Sigma x_1^2 = 128.70$ | $\Sigma x_2^2 = 602.12$ |

The *mean square deviation* can be obtained by summing the squared deviations and dividing by the number of persons who took the test. This statistic is called the *variance* and is symbolized as $\sigma^2$:

$$\sigma^2 = \frac{\Sigma x^2}{N}$$

An even more useful statistic is obtained by taking the square root of the variance, which is then called the *standard deviation*:

$$\sigma = \sqrt{\frac{\Sigma x^2}{N}}$$

Applying the formula to the arithmetic and spelling tests, the following variances and standard deviations are found:

| Arithmetic | Spelling |
|---|---|
| $\sigma^2 = \dfrac{128.70}{11}$ | $\sigma^2 = \dfrac{602.12}{11}$ |
| $\sigma^2 = \phantom{0}11.70$ | $\sigma^2 = \phantom{0}54.74$ |
| $\sigma = \phantom{00}3.42$ | $\sigma = \phantom{00}7.40$ |

Subscripts can be used with the equations for variance and standard deviation to indicate which test is being studied; for example, $\sigma_1$ can refer to the standard deviation of the scores on a particular test.

The standard deviation and variance can be obtained without actually going through the step of converting from raw to deviation scores, as follows:

$$\sigma^2 = \frac{\Sigma(X - M)^2}{N}$$

$$\sigma^2 = \frac{\Sigma X^2}{N} - \left(\frac{\Sigma X}{N}\right)^2$$

Identical results will be obtained with either approach, showing here at an early stage the mathematical maneuverability that is gained by working with squared deviations.

### the effect of linear transformations on the mean and standard deviation

*multiplicative trans.*

If an arbitrary number were added to each of the raw scores in a distribution, how would this change the mean and standard deviation? For example, we could add 5 to each of the arithmetic scores mentioned earlier. The new mean would then be 5 more than the original mean. The proof of this is simple:

$$M_x = \frac{\Sigma X}{N}$$

$$M_{(x+c)} = \frac{\Sigma(X + C)}{N}$$

$$= \frac{\Sigma X + \Sigma C}{N}$$

$$= \frac{\Sigma X}{N} + \frac{\Sigma C}{N}$$

$$= \frac{\Sigma X}{N} + \frac{NC}{N}$$

$$= \frac{\Sigma X}{N} + C$$

$$= M_x + C$$

where $C$ stands for any *constant*, such as 5, and $M_{(x+c)}$ stands for the mean of the scores after the constant is added to each score in turn.

Then if the mean of the original scores is 10 and we add 5 to each of the scores, the new mean is 15. (The student should work out the simple proofs on his own. Not only will this be relatively "painless," but a thorough understanding of the steps in the simple proofs will make it easier to follow more complex statistical developments.)

Next we can determine what happens to the standard deviation when a constant is added to each of the scores. We could derive this from the raw-score equation, but since we know that the standard deviation is the same whether it is determined from raw or deviation scores, it will be simpler to work with the deviation-score equation:

$$\sigma_{(x+c)}^2 = \frac{\Sigma[(x + C) - M_{(x+c)}]^2}{N}$$

The mean of the original deviation scores is zero by definition. Then the mean of the new scores is $C$, so we can rewrite the equation as

$$\sigma_{(x+c)} = \sqrt{\frac{\Sigma(x + C - C)^2}{N}}$$

which reduces to

$$\sigma_{(x+c)} = \sqrt{\frac{\Sigma x^2}{N}}$$

This is the same formula used to obtain the standard deviation of the original scores. We have then proved that the standard deviation is unchanged if we add a constant to, or subtract a constant from, each of the scores. Then if the standard deviation of a set of scores is 2 and we add 5 to each of them, the new standard deviation is also 2.

Next we can see what will happen if each of the scores is multiplied by a constant. The mean would then become

$$M_{(cx)} = \frac{\Sigma(CX)}{N}$$

Because a constant term can always be moved to the left of a summation sign,

$$M_{(cx)} = \frac{C\Sigma X}{N}$$
$$= C\left(\frac{\Sigma X}{N}\right)$$
$$= CM_x$$

We have proved that if each score is multiplied by a constant, the mean of the new scores equals the mean of the old scores times the constant. Then if the mean of the original scores is 10 and we multiply each score by 3, the new mean is 30.

The effect on the standard deviation of multiplying each score by a constant is as follows:

$$\sigma_{(Cx)} = \sqrt{\frac{\Sigma(Cx)^2}{N}}$$
$$= \sqrt{\frac{\Sigma C^2 x^2}{N}}$$
$$= \sqrt{C^2\left(\frac{\Sigma x^2}{N}\right)}$$
$$= C\sqrt{\frac{\Sigma x^2}{N}}$$
$$= C\sigma_x$$

The standard deviation of the new scores will be $C$ times as large as the old standard deviation. Then if the standard deviation of the original scores is 2 and we multiply each score by 3, the new standard deviation is 6. The reader should satisfy himself that the variance will increase by the square of the constant.

We have taken the time to derive these results for several reasons. The mean and the standard deviation will appear many times in the discussion of test results, and it is important to understand their properties. Knowing how these statistics are affected by linear transformations will allow us to make many computational shortcuts without having to recompute the mean and the standard deviation. Also, the simple proofs which are involved here demonstrate some of the manipulations which, when applied to more complex equations, permit us to derive many useful results.

## score distributions

### The normal distribution

The standard deviation is most easily interpreted when working with a normal distribution of scores. The normal distribution, or normal curve, as it is sometimes called, was mentioned in Chapter 2, but no full explanation was given at that time. The normal distribution refers to the way in which the score frequencies fall. Instead of listing test scores, as we did with the arithmetic and spelling tests, the same information could have been given by specifying the number of persons who obtained each score. Using the symbol $f$ to stand for frequency, frequency distributions for the two tests are as follows:

| Arithmetic | | Spelling | |
|---|---|---|---|
| $X_1$ | $f$ | $X_2$ | $f$ |
| 22 | 1 | 75 | 1 |
| 21 | 0 | .. | |
| 20 | 1 | .. | |
| 19 | 1 | 62 | 1 |
| 18 | 0 | .. | |
| 17 | 1 | .. | |
| 16 | 0 | 56 | 1 |
| 15 | 1 | 55 | 1 |
| 14 | 3 | 54 | 0 |
| 13 | 0 | 53 | 0 |
| 12 | 2 | 52 | 3 |
| 11 | 1 | 51 | 1 |
| .. | . | 50 | 1 |
| .. | . | 49 | 1 |
| .. | . | 48 | 1 |

The frequency distributions are presented graphically in Figure 3-1. There are not enough scores to indicate much about the distribution shape for either test. However, when there are many scores instead of just 11, the shape of the distribution begins to become apparent. If we had given the arithmetic test to 200 students, the distribution of scores in arithmetic might have looked like that in Figure 3-2. In Figure 3-2 it can be seen that most of the scores are clustered around 16 and that scores become fewer and fewer as we go either toward high scores or toward low scores.

As the scores in Figure 3-2 are drawn, they resemble the normal distribution. The normal distribution can be thought of as the science-fiction counterpart of the frequency distribution that would be approximated if 1 million students were administered a test containing 1 million arithmetic problems. Although the normal distribution is purely a mathematical abstraction, it frequently provides a reasonably good approximation of the distribution obtained with moderately large numbers of persons and test items, e.g., 200 students who are administered 100 arithmetic problems. Consequently, the statistical properties of the normal distribution frequently hold reasonably well with actual data.

The standard deviation tells the percentages of persons whose scores fall in different regions of the normal curve. Figure 3-3 shows that approximately 68 percent of subjects make scores between plus one and minus one standard deviation and that 95 percent of the scores fall between plus two and minus two standard deviations. A detailed breakdown of the percentages of scores in

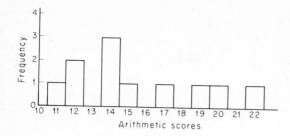

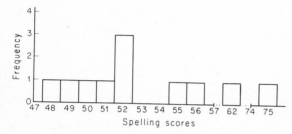

**FIGURE 3-1**    Frequency distributions for arithmetic and spelling tests

various regions of the normal distribution is presented in Appendix B. It will prove useful in interpreting the many statistics based on the normal distribution.

### Standard scores

A very useful type of score can be obtained by dividing an individual's deviation score on a test by the standard deviation of the scores:

$$z = \frac{x}{\sigma_x} \quad \text{or} \quad z = \frac{X - M_x}{\sigma_x}$$

where $z$ symbolizes the standard score.

Applying the formula to Johnny's arithmetic score, we find

$$z = \frac{22 - 15.45}{3.42}$$
$$= \frac{6.55}{3.42}$$
$$= 1.9$$

An individual's standard score indicates his place in the frequency distribution (if the distribution of scores is approximately normal). If a person has a

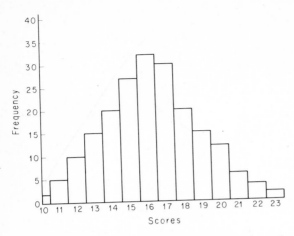

**FIGURE 3-2**    Hypothetical frequency distribution of arithmetic scores for 200 students

standard score of 2.1, this indicates that his score is above two standard deviations and that about 98 percent of the subjects made lower scores. Similarly, a person who makes a standard score of less than $-1.0$ made a lower score than 84 percent of the subjects.

When the raw scores on different tests are converted to standard scores, they have the same mean, which is zero in all cases. What is the standard deviation of a set of standard scores? Because of the way in which standard scores are obtained, the standard deviation of any set of standard scores is 1.00.

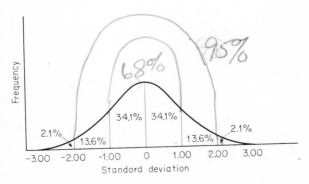

**FIGURE 3-3**    Percentages of subjects in various regions of the normal distribution (The percentages add up to 99.6 instead of 100 because a fraction of 1 percent of the cases lie above and below three standard deviations)

Converting raw scores to standard scores makes results comparable from test to test. If an individual makes a standard score which is positive on two tests, we know that he did better than average on both tests. If he makes standard scores of 1.00 on one test and 1.50 on another, we know that he performed better on the second test.

## Transformed standard scores

For practical purposes, it is often useful to express test scores by a modification of $z$ scores. A teacher might have difficulty in explaining to a student's mother that a standard score of zero means average performance rather than zero performance. Also, the negative values which are obtained with standard scores are difficult for some persons to understand. Starting with a set of standard scores, and knowing what we do about transformations, we can derive a new set of scores with any mean and standard deviation that we like. If we desire to have the scores in such a form that the mean is 100 and the standard deviation is 10, the first step is to multiply all the standard scores by 10. Then 100 is added to each of the resulting scores. If it is desired to compare the scores on two tests which have different means and standard deviations, the mean and standard deviation of one test can be made the same as the mean and standard deviation of the other. It proves much easier to make transformations directly on raw scores than to compute standard scores first.

## Rank-order scores

In Chapter 1 it was said that psychological measures are sometimes expressed in the form of ranks. Ranks are often used to describe test scores when the number of subjects is not large. If a mother is told that her daughter made the fifth highest score in a class of 11, she can easily understand how well her daughter performed in comparison with the other children.

The scores on the arithmetic and spelling tests can be expressed as ranks. Because Johnny made the highest score on the arithmetic test, his score would become rank 1. Eric would have rank 2, Sharon would have rank 3, and so on. When several persons make the same score, they are given the average of their ranks. For example, three persons have scores of 14 in arithmetic. They must share the ranks of 6, 7, and 8. The mean of these three ranks is 7, and consequently all three would be given a rank of 7. Two people have scores of 12, and they must share the ranks of 9 and 10. They are each given a rank of 9.5. The lowest score, that made by Harry, is then given a rank of 11.

## Percentile ranks

When the number of scores is large—say, 200 instead of 11—it proves useful to make a conversion of ranks. One useful conversion is made by expressing each individual's score in terms of the percentage of scores which are lower. If an individual ranks fourth among 200 persons, then 196 persons rank lower. Dividing 196 by 200, we find that the individual has a percentile score of 98. Because several or more persons will usually make the same score, a modification of the basic formula is often used to take account of tied ranks. The formula is to divide the number of people below a particular score, plus half the number of people who make the score, by the total number of subjects. Scores obtained in this way are referred to as *midpoint percentile ranks*.

Percentile scores, like ranks, are useful in explaining test results to individuals who have little background in the statistics of testing. However, they are awkward for other statistical manipulations that might be needed. Percentiles provide no indication of the distance between scores. There might be a wide gap in raw scores between the person who has a percentile score of 70 and the person who has a percentile score of 71, but this would not be seen from the percentile scores alone. Percentile scores underemphasize the differences between scores on the extremes of the distribution. Looking back at Figure 3-3, it can be seen that only about 2 percent of the cases fall between standard scores of 2.00 and 3.00. These standard scores would be equal to percentile ranks of about 97 and 99. Although the scores appear to be separated by only a trivial amount when expressed in terms of percentiles, we can see that in terms of standard scores there is a wide separation.

What is the distribution form of a set of percentile scores? The same percentage of subjects make scores between the 99th and 90th percentiles as between the 89th and 80th percentiles, and so on. Consequently, the frequency distribution is flat, or rectangular, as it is called (see Figure 3-4).

## norms

Although standard scores or percentile scores would give a good indication of where Johnny stands in relation to his 10 classmates, there would still be a question as to how well he performs in relation to students in other schools. It

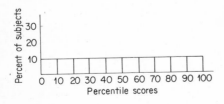

**FIGURE 3-4**    Frequency distribution of percentile scores

may be that Johnny is in a particularly bright class in which average performance means high performance in comparison with that in other classes. It might be that Johnny goes to a school in a "well-to-do" neighborhood where the children as a group are well above the community average. To dramatize the specificity of scores in a particular setting, we can image the problems involved in testing a class made up of geniuses. Because of the mechanics of obtaining standard scores and percentiles, half the students would inevitably come out "below average." But, of course, below-average performance of geniuses would be comparable to superior performance of less gifted children.

## Normative populations

In order to understand how well a child performs on a test, it is often necessary to compare his score with the scores made by children in previous years and the scores made by children in a range of localities. In order to interpret the test score made by an applicant for a particular branch of the armed forces, it would be necessary to compare his score with the scores of many other applicants. The larger group with which an individual is compared is called a *normative population*.

The collection of people who constitute a normative population is determined by the use to which the scores will be put. If achievement test scores are being used to place students in special high school study programs in a particular city, the normative population should contain students from all the grammar schools in that city. If a selection test for the armed forces is being used to select individuals for pilot training, the normative population should contain the individuals who have previously applied for pilot training.

On some occasions, the normative population must be quite large. When selecting students for college, the normative population consists, at least hypothetically, of all the graduating high school students in the United States. Later we shall see that in order to interpret the scores on a particular intelligence test, the test was given to several thousand children in all parts of the country. In other testing situations, the normative population may be quite small. To interpret the results of a course examination, the teacher may need to make comparisons only with the scores made by several previous classes.

## Scoring in respect to norms

It is often more meaningful to compare an individual's test score with the scores obtained from a normative population rather than with those of some smaller and less representative group. In this case, an individual's standard score would be determined by a comparison with the mean and standard deviation of the normative population. Similarly, percentile scores would be determined by the scores found in the normative population. Instead of going through the labor of actually computing such scores for each new individual, it is easier to compose a table which allows a direct conversion of raw scores to standard scores or percentile scores.

## Sampling of scores

The group of persons actually tested is usually small in comparison with the total number of persons in the normative population. Seldom will there be test scores for all the individuals who could conceivably be included. Even a group of several thousand children is small in comparison with the many millions of children in this country. The norms obtained from a sample are then only estimates of the norms which would be obtained from the entire normative population.

## Sampling bias

When choosing a sample for constructing norms, it is important to select a group which is as representative as possible of the normative population. The sample would be biased if all the tests were given at one school because, as we said earlier, the particular school might be above or below average for the community as a whole. If the sample is meant to represent all the children in the United States, it must be ensured that there is a balance of children from all sections of the country, that there is a proportionate representation of urban and rural children, and that all races and ethnic groups are included.

One way of ensuring a representative sample is to choose the subjects randomly from the normative population. This might be feasible in establishing norms for the performance of students in one city. It would be possible to randomly select, say, 500 of the children as a sample. On any larger scale it is not feasible to gather a completely random sample. While it is conceivable that a sample of the children in the United States could be obtained by selecting randomly from among all the millions of children, this would be prohibitively expensive and time-consuming. It might be necessary to travel several hundred miles just to test one subject who, because of the sampling procedure, was chosen from a remote region. When, as is usually the case, it is not feasible to use a completely random sample, there are alternative sampling methods which can be applied. For example, one can obtain norms from children in a representative list of schools, the list being compiled in such a way as to obtain children from localities across the country. Efforts would be made to ensure that the list of schools provided an approximate representation of the country as a whole in terms of geographic regions, urban-rural balance, economic status, and other important variables. A sample obtained in this way could provide a reasonably good approximation of the norms that would be obtained from a purely random sample.

## Sampling error

Regardless of how representative a sample is, results obtained from it can only estimate the true norms in the population. If we find the mean and standard deviation of a test in a sample, it must be considered how much these estimates are likely to be in error. As in all sampling problems, the larger the number of cases (more items in the sampling of content and more persons in the sampling of scores), the less the estimates will be in error.

## The sampling distribution of the mean

In an ideal situation, it is possible to determine the error that will be involved in making estimates from a sample. In such a situation, it would be necessary to know the statistics in advance, here the mean and standard deviation, which would be obtained in the entire population. This would be the case where tests were given to all the subjects in a population. Samples of the tests could be drawn randomly just to see how much the means and standard deviations of the samples would depart from the actual mean and standard deviation which are known to exist in the population. We could draw out samples of different sizes to see how much more error is involved in the ones which have a relatively small number of people.

If we draw 100 samples with 50 test scores in each, the *sample means* could be plotted in a frequency distribution and compared with the *population mean*. We would find a distribution resembling that in Figure 3-5. In Figure 3-5 we see that the distribution of means is like the normal distribution. If the sample is not biased, the mean of the sample means will coincide approximately with the population mean. Figure 3-5 shows that the means obtained from samples cluster about the population mean, and the means which are extremely different from the population mean will be found infrequently.

Another example could be cited in which each of the 100 samples would contain the scores of 200 persons. The 100 means could be obtained and plotted like those in Figure 3-5. Again we would expect to find a near-normal

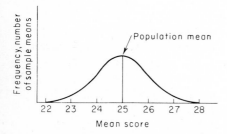

**FIGURE 3-5**    Distribution of sample means about the population mean

distribution, with the mean of the sample means very close to the population mean. However, because each sample now contains 200 instead of 50 persons, we would expect to find the distribution of means clustered more tightly about the population mean. Because of the greater stability obtained from a sampling of 200 persons, it would be surprising to find sample means which deviated by as much as two score points from the population mean.

In the same way that a standard deviation can be computed for any group of scores, a distribution of means can also provide a standard deviation. We would expect the standard deviation of the means for the samples of 50 persons to be larger than the standard deviation of the means for the samples of 200 persons. In fact it would be about twice as large.

If, as in this ideal example, we knew the mean and standard deviation of the population, we could determine what the standard deviation of the means for a particular sample size would be without going to the trouble of drawing samples and computing means. The standard deviation of the means, usually called the *standard error of the mean*, would be very useful in specifying the accuracy of norms. For example, if we know that the population mean is 25 and the standard error of the mean is 1, we can tell how rarely means of a particular size could be obtained from samples. Working backward, if we know the standard error of the mean for a particular sample size and know the mean of one sample, we can state the likelihood that the population mean will differ from the sample mean by any number of score units.

Unfortunately, in nearly all practical work with norms, only the mean and standard deviation can be obtained for one sample. There are statistical techniques for working backward from sample values to the standard error of the mean. A standard error can also be obtained for the standard deviation to determine the extent to which the standard deviation obtained from a sample is likely to be divergent from the population standard deviation. To explain these procedures in detail would take us far afield from the central topics of tests and measurements. The purpose here is to make the reader aware of the existence of sampling error and its influence on norms. There are numerous books devoted primarily to sampling error (see the Suggested Additional Readings at the end of this chapter) in which detailed procedures are given for estimating the accuracy of norms.

### Age norms

We discussed previously how percentile scores and standard scores could be used to express norms. In some situations it is desirable to express norms in terms of children's ages. One such set of norms could be obtained by testing the vocabulary of children at all ages from four to twelve years. For this purpose, a list of 100 words varying in difficulty could be used. The mean score could be obtained for each age group separately. A graphic plot of these might look like that in Figure 3-6. Figure 3-6 shows, for example, that seven-year-old children have a larger vocabulary than five- and six-year-old children, as would be expected. Age norms would prove useful in interpreting the vocabulary score made by a particular child. Suppose that he is seven years old and has a vocabulary score of 25. The mean score for the seven-year-olds in the normative sample is 30. We can then look to find the age group which corresponds to a score of 25. Although there is no age group whose mean falls exactly at this point, we can work as though the curve were continuous throughout all age levels and determine the fractional age group that would correspond to a particular score. Reading from Figure 3-6, it can be seen that an age of approximately 6.5 would correspond to a score of 25. It then can be said that the seven-year-old boy has the vocabulary of a 6½-year-old. Age norms fit in well with the way in which we customarily think about children's progress, and they are therefore very useful in the interpretation of test scores.

### Mental age

Age norms are employed with some of the general intelligence tests, such as the Stanford-Binet. By comparing a child's score with age norms, it can be determined whether he is more or less intelligent than the average child of his age. A score which is compared in this way with age norms is referred to as a *mental age*. If a six-year-old child performs as well as the average seven-year-old, he is said to have a mental age of seven. Similarly, the six-year-old who performs only at the level of the average five-year-old would be said to have a mental age of five.

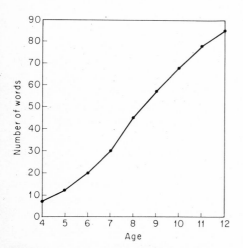

**FIGURE 3-6**     Mean vocabulary scores of children at each age level from four to twelve years

The term "mental age" is somewhat misleading. It gives the impression that the score a child makes on an intelligence test is a direct measure of total ability. Although tests of this kind have worked well in practice, it is not reasonable to believe that they measure all that could be considered intelligence. Even though there is a tendency for children to score much the same on different intelligence tests, especially those which depend heavily on the use and understanding of language, the correspondence is far from perfect. Therefore, a child's mental age is partly a function of the test which is employed.

### Grade norms

A set of norms which are very similar to age norms can be obtained by finding the mean scores for children in various grade levels. If a standard spelling test were given to children in grades 4 to 8, the means could be plotted by grades much as they were plotted by ages in Figure 3-6. A comparison of a pupil's score with grade norms gives the teacher an indication of how well he is progressing.

### Quotient scores as norms

Dividing an individual's mental age by his chronological age gives a score which is called an *intelligence quotient*, or, as it has come to be known, the IQ. If an eight-year-old child does as well on an intelligence test as the average ten-year-old, he would have an IQ of 125. The formula for obtaining the IQ is then

$$IQ = \frac{MA}{CA} \times 100$$

where MA stands for mental age and CA stands for chronological age.

In spite of the wide use and popularity of the IQ, it bears a number of misleading connotations. Because the IQ is a ratio, a ratio of MA to CA, it suggests that a ratio scale is available for intelligence. Not only is it questionable whether the term "intelligence" should be used with the available tests, but it is also certainly unwise to consider IQ scores to constitute a ratio scale. How unwise this is becomes evident when we consider the IQ of a child who got none of the items correct on the test. Such a child would certainly be retarded, but it makes no sense to say that his intelligence is zero.

The IQ is misleading when applied to adults. It has been found that an individual's score on an intelligence test increases until the late teens and then levels off. If a twenty-year-old has an IQ of 150, this cannot be interpreted to mean that he has a level of ability equal to that of the average thirty-year-old. Another problem with obtaining the IQ as a ratio of mental age to chronological age is that the results are misleading unless the standard deviations of IQs are the same at all age levels. It might be found that the standard deviation of IQs for the sixth-year level is 12 and that the standard deviation for the tenth-year level is 18. Then an IQ of 120 would mean something very different for one child at the sixth-year level and for another child at the tenth-year level.

To circumvent the aforementioned difficulties, most modern intelligence tests obtain IQs as a type of transformed standard score within age groups rather than as a ratio of mental age to chronological age. By means of methods discussed previously, standard scores at all age levels are transformed to a distribution having a mean of 100 and a standard deviation of approximately 15. The details of obtaining IQs in this way will be discussed in Chapter 10.

### Perspectives on norms

Before concluding this section on the development and use of norms, a number of important principles should be either reiterated or freshly stated here. First, norms are meaningfully interpretable only with respect to some definable reference group, e.g., a sample of all adults in the country or a sample of fourth-grade children in the schools of a particular city. Second, the reference group which is chosen depends on the types of decisions under consideration. Thus different reference groups would be required for selecting students for college and for selecting students for graduate study. Third, norms are useful mainly in applied work with tests rather than in basic research. In basic research one is typically interested in correlations between measures and/or mean differences relating to treatment conditions. For neither of these are norms very important. Fourth, in applied work with tests, two types of norms are generally regarded as superior to others for most purposes. Standard scores (or transformed standard scores) are very useful for performing statistical manipulations of data. They are not as directly useful for *interpreting* test results, however, as percentile scores are. The only meaningful way to interpret a standard score is to refer it to a table of percentages based on the normal distribution. Since percentiles do that directly, it makes more sense to employ them than to go the long way around of working with standard scores.

### Summary

Test scores cannot be interpreted directly, without reference to some standard. One type of standard consists of evaluative judgments made about the meaning of different scores obtained in some uses of measures that require content validity. The best example is that of a classroom examination containing multiple-choice items. The instructor might notify students in advance of the examination that certain percentages of correct answers will earn grades of A, B, C, D, or F. Then any particular score could be interpreted directly by these standards.

A second type of standard is that which is obtained from validation studies of a predictor test and criterion. If such studies show, for example, that only those persons who score at least as high as 45 on a predictor test have a high probability of succeeding in pilot training, that serves as a standard for selecting or rejecting a particular person for training.

The third, and in many ways the most important, type of standard consists in comparing a particular person's score with scores of persons in some reference group, such standards being referred to as *norms*. One must consider the average score in a group, for which the arithmetic mean is the preferred measure in most cases. Also, one must take account of the variability of scores from individual to individual, for which the standard deviation is the most generally useful measure.

The two most widely used types of norms are those based on standard scores (or transformed standard scores) and those based on percentiles. The former are more useful for statistical analyses; the latter are more useful for interpreting how well individuals perform with respect to a particular group of persons.

Norms are always established with respect to a particular population of persons, which in the extreme might include "everybody," but more typically they are established with respect to subgroups in the population. For example, it is meaningful to compare children's performance with that of other children of the same age, which is facilitated by the use of *age norms*. It is also meaningful to compare children's performance with that of other children in the same school grade, which is facilitated by the use of *grade norms*.

Because most psychological attributes are distributed in such a way as to resemble the normal distribution, the statistical properties of the normal distribution are helpful in the interpretation of norms. In particular, if norms are expressed in terms of standard scores or any linear transformation of standard scores, such scores can be interpreted in terms of percentages of persons who lie in various regions of the normal distribution.

Norms are useful mainly with respect to applied problems concerning uses of predictor tests and achievement tests. Norms are of only incidental value for basic research in psychology.

## Suggested additional readings

Chase, C. I. *Elementary statistical procedures.* New York: McGraw-Hill, 1967.

Games, P. A., & Klare, G. R. *Elementary statistics for the behavioral sciences.* New York: McGraw-Hill, 1967.

Walker, H. M., & Lev, J. *Elementary statistical methods.* New York: Holt, 1958.

# CHAPTER 4

# Correlational analysis of measurement methods

It is not possible fully to understand the logic and method of psychological measurement without first becoming acquainted with some elementary principles of mathematics and statistics. Measures of central tendency and dispersion were discussed in Chapter 3, and measures of correlation will be discussed in this chapter. For readers who already have a good grounding in the mathematical and statistical methods relating to psychological measurement, the discussions of such methods in this book will provide useful reminders. Even for the person who has had no previous training in statistics and who has a scanty knowledge of mathematics in general, the discussions in this and other chapters will provide an understandable and sufficient account of the essential features of the methods involved.

Without correlational analysis (or some substitute methods), it would be impossible to develop psychological measures adequately or to analyze the data obtained from research with such measures. Essentially, correlational analysis concerns the extent to which people are ordered alike or differently on two measures. As will be pointed out in Chapter 6, the validity of a predictor test in a particular situation is the degree to which the test correlates with a criterion, e.g., the degree to which scores on a vocabulary test correlate with average grades in college. If students who made high scores on the vocabulary test subsequently tend to make high grade averages and if students who made low vocabulary scores tend to make low grade averages, the two sets of scores correlate well. This provides evidence that henceforth the vocabulary test could be used to make estimates of which students will or will not perform well in college.

Correlational analysis is useful in measures that require content validity. For example, a professor might want to learn to what extent three tests employed during a semester course in psychology measure the same thing. If there is a strong tendency for students to be ordered alike on the three tests, this would suggest that the course content is rather homogeneous in terms of the abilities required during different parts of the semester.

As another example of the usefulness of correlational analysis with measures that require content validity, it would be informative to correlate reading achievement scores with reading speed scores on an achievement test battery employed with students in elementary schools. If fast readers also have a high degree of understanding of what was read, and slow readers a low degree of understanding, this would represent a high correlation. Whatever the degree of the correlation, the use of correlational analysis in this example would help educators understand the nature of the abilities involved and would provide suggestions about classroom practices.

Besides having many uses in applied research, correlational analysis is also invaluable in many types of basic research in psychology, for example, in a study of the effects of three different drugs on the motor coordination of mental patients. The same patients would be administered the three drugs on different occasions, and following each administration of a drug, the test of motor coordination would be given. The major interest in such a study would be in the average effect of each drug on motor coordination, but it would also be important to determine the consistency with which individuals responded to the drugs. This could be determined by correlating the three sets of scores obtained from the test of motor coordination. If those correlations were not high, it would mean that different patients tend to react differently to the different drugs, which certainly would be an important item of information.

Correlational analysis is absolutely essential for basic research on individual differences between people. A typical study would involve the investigation of six tests of reasoning ability. It is hypothesized that three of the tests concern mainly deductive reasoning and that the other three tests concern mainly inductive reasoning. These hypotheses could be tested by administering the six measures to a large group of persons and applying correlational analyses to the resulting six sets of scores. Support for the hypotheses would be obtained if (1) the three tests supposedly concerning deduction correlated highly and (2) the three tests supposedly concerning induction correlated highly but (3) the tests concerning induction had only low correlations with the tests concerning deduction.

In addition to there being many uses of correlational methods *after* measures are developed, the psychometric theory underlying the initial development of new measures rests heavily on correlational concepts and methods of analysis.

As one prominent example, it will be seen in the next chapter that correlational analysis is necessary to determine the reliability of measurement methods.

It should be clear from all the foregoing reasons and examples that correlational analysis is essential for the psychometric theory that underlies the development of psychological measures and also for performing research with all types of measures after they are developed. The remainder of this chapter will acquaint the reader with the fundamentals of correlational analysis. Although the principles which will be discussed are common to all uses of correlational analysis, they will be illustrated in the simple situation in which a particular predictor test is being used to predict a particular criterion variable.

### Statistical methods in scientific activity

Perhaps it would be wise to consider for a moment why there is need for statistical procedures in scientific enterprise. In classical mathematics, the kind encountered in introductory algebra, simultaneous equations like the following are often found:

|     | x   | y   |
| --- | --- | --- |
| a.  | 2   | 1   |
| b.  | 4   | 2   |
| c.  | 8   | 4   |
| d.  | 10  | 5   |

Each pair of the above numbers forms an equation. Equation *a* says that when *x* is 2, *y* is 1, or, in other words, that *x* is twice as large as *y*. Equation *b* says that when *x* is 4, *y* is 2, which shows again that *x* is twice as large as *y*. Equations *c* and *d* also affirm that *x* is twice as large as *y*. The same relationship would be found by adding the four equations together. When a number of equations all supply the same information, they are said to be *equivalent*.

One of the exercises in elementary algebra is to make a graphic plot of equations like those above. This is done in Figure 4-1. Any set of two-variable equations, called a *bivariate relationship*, can be plotted as in Figure 4-1 by locating the point for each equation in terms of the values on the *x* and *y* axes. In Figure 4-1 all the points lie on a straight line.

Now let us consider some equations that concern real-life things rather than abstract mathematical relations. Turning back to the earlier example of the prediction of college grade averages, imagine that a predictor test is in use. Let us say, in this case, that a vocabulary test was administered to incoming freshmen and that the scores are to be compared with grade averages at graduation.

In order to find out how well the predictor test works, we would want to compare vocabulary scores with grade averages. Comparisons could be made of

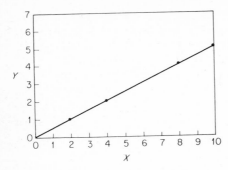

**FIGURE 4-1**  Graphic demonstration of functional relationship between variables x and y

the raw scores on the two variables, but, because the size of raw scores is dependent on the method of test construction used, this would cause some confusion.  The important consideration is whether the students who make high vocabulary scores also make high grade averages and whether the students who make low vocabulary scores also make low grade averages.  Consequently, it is most meaningful to express both vocabulary and grade average in standard-score units.  To simplify the comparison, we shall deal with only nine students.  Means and standard deviations are obtained on vocabulary and grade averages for the nine students only.  Standard scores are determined for the nine students on vocabulary and grade average, with the following results:

| Student | Vocabulary ($z_x$) | Grade average ($z_y$) |
|---------|--------------------|------------------------|
| A | 1.55 | 1.18 |
| B | 1.16 | 1.77 |
| C | 0.77 | 0.59 |
| D | 0.39 | −1.18 |
| E | 0.00 | 0.59 |
| F | −0.39 | −0.59 |
| G | −0.77 | −0.59 |
| H | −1.16 | −0.59 |
| I | −1.55 | −1.18 |

Just as in the earlier example we considered each pair of numbers to constitute an equation, each pair of standard scores above also forms an equation. Student A has a vocabulary standard score ($z_x$) of 1.55 and a grade standard score ($z_y$) of 1.18.  Then, by dividing 1.55 into 1.18, a ratio of .76 is found. In the previous example, only one equation was necessary to determine the overall relationship between two variables. If that were so in the present example, we could say that each student's grade standard score is exactly 0.76 times as large as his vocabulary standard score. Let us go on to see what relationships the other equations specify. The equation for student B indicates that the ratio is 1.53, the equation for student C indicates .77, and that for student D indicates −3.03. It is obvious that these equations provide very different indications of the overall relationship between vocabulary $(z_x)$ and grades $(z_y)$. When, as in this example, simultaneous equations do not agree with one another, they are said to be *nonequivalent*.

### Correlation

Nonequivalent relations are the typical, and not the unusual, scientific finding. Whether the subject matter is physics, chemistry, biology, or psychology, the numerous observations tell different stories about the form of a particular relationship. In some investigations where the variables are simple and easily controlled, the divergence from equivalence is very small. In more complex problems, such as predicting how individuals will perform on a particular job, the divergence from equivalence is usually considerable. Statistical methods were developed as a means of dealing with nonequivalent equations.

A graphic comparison is made of vocabulary and grade standard scores in Figure 4-2 (the "best-fit" line in the figure will be explained shortly). It is obvious that the points do not lie on a straight line, but there is a tendency for the two variables to go together. How would the relationship be summarized? We might use only our impression and say that there is a "strong correspondence" or a "moderate correspondence." A better approach is to use a statistical statement of the degree of relationship between vocabulary and grade averages.

There are a number of ways in which statistics can be developed for this problem. One that might seem reasonable at first thought is to add together all the vocabulary standard scores and divide this sum into the sum of the grade standard scores. This method worked with the equations in the earlier example, but it will not do here. As the reader will remember from Chapter 3, the sum of standard scores on any variable is zero. Consequently, we would get zero equals zero as a summarizing equation, which is certainly true, but does not provide the needed statistic.

Previously it was shown that working with squared scores and squared deviations leads to some very useful results. We shall appeal to that principle again by looking for a summary equation which leads to the smallest sum of squared errors in prediction (the principle of "least squares"). That is, there is a predicted standard score in school grades obtained from the actual standard score in vocabulary. The difference between the predicted score in school grades for any person and his actual score in school grades is the error of

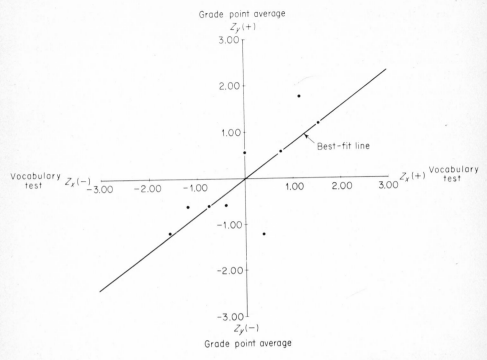

**FIGURE 4-2**     Comparison of standard scores on a vocabulary test with grade-point averages expressed as standard scores

prediction. The square of this quantity constitutes a squared error of prediction. Thus we shall seek a ratio between vocabulary and grade standard scores such that the sum of the squared errors in predicting grades will be at a minimum. This means that we are seeking an equation like the following:

$$z_y' = bz_x$$

such that

$$\Sigma(z_y - z_y')^2 = \text{a minimum}$$

where

    $b$ = a constant
    $z_y$ = a grade standard score
    $z_x$ = a vocabulary standard score
    $z_y'$ = an estimate of a grade standard score

The equation above is referred to as a *linear equation*: no matter what value we choose for $b$, it results in a straight line of relationship. Of the infinite number of values that could be chosen for $b$, there is only one that satisfies the least-squares criterion. The method for determining the correct $b$ value is derived quite easily from elementary calculus. The method which is derived in this way can be applied to the present problem. The first step is to multiply each vocabulary standard score by its corresponding grade standard score, as follows:

$$
\begin{aligned}
1.55 \times \phantom{-}1.18 &= \phantom{-}1.83 \\
1.16 \times \phantom{-}1.77 &= \phantom{-}2.05 \\
0.77 \times \phantom{-}0.59 &= \phantom{-}0.45 \\
0.39 \times -1.18 &= -0.46 \\
0.00 \times \phantom{-}0.59 &= \phantom{-}0.00 \\
-0.39 \times -0.59 &= \phantom{-}0.23 \\
-0.77 \times -0.59 &= \phantom{-}0.45 \\
-1.16 \times -0.59 &= \phantom{-}0.68 \\
-1.55 \times -1.18 &= \phantom{-}1.83
\end{aligned}
$$

$$\Sigma z_x z_y = 7.06$$

$$b = \frac{\Sigma z_x z_y}{N}$$

$$= \frac{7.06}{9}$$

$$= .78$$

The final steps are to sum the standard-score cross products $(\Sigma z_x z_y)$ and divide the result by the number of persons $(N)$. This is all that is necessary to obtain $b$, the value which satisfies the least-squares criterion. In this case $b$ is .78, which means that the best (least-squares) estimate of each grade standard score is obtained as follows:

$$z_y' = .78 z_x$$

Then the estimated grade standard score for student A is

$$z_y' = .78 \times 1.55$$
$$= 1.21$$

Student A actually has a grade standard score of 1.18; consequently, the estimate is in error by 0.03 score points. Although there will be errors in prediction as a result of using $b$ to summarize the relationship, the sum of the squared errors will be less than that obtained from any other linear equation.

Because the prediction equation above is a linear formula, $b$ can be used to draw a best-fit line as is done in Figure 4-2. For every unit the line moves over the vocabulary axis, it moves up 0.78 units on the grade average axis. Those who have studied trigonometry will recognize $b$ as the tangent of the angle formed by the best-fit line and the vocabulary axis.

When the constant term $b$ is sought by the least-squares criterion in respect to standard scores, it is given a special name: the *correlation coefficient*. Also, when dealing with standard scores, the symbol $r$ is usually employed instead of $b$. Then we can rewrite the best-fit equation as follows:

$$z_y' = rz_x$$

Thus, in our example, to obtain the best estimate of the grade standard scores, we multiply each vocabulary standard score by the correlation coefficient.

When the constant term is found for standard scores, it not only serves to place the best-fit line but also has descriptive value of its own. The correlation coefficient $r$ varies in different problems from $+1.00$ through zero to $-1.00$. If the correlation is $+1.00$, it means that there is a perfect correlation. Then the prediction equation becomes

$$z_y' = z_x$$

and the predicted grade standard scores will be exactly the same as the actual grade standard scores. As the correlation coefficient goes downward from $+1.00$, the predictions become poorer and poorer. When the correlation reaches zero, the prediction equation is as follows:

$$
\begin{aligned}
z_y' &= rz_x \\
&= 0z_x \\
&= 0
\end{aligned}
$$

Because the mean of a set of standard scores is zero, a zero correlation leads to the prediction that all scores fall at the mean of the criterion. A negative correlation means that high scores on one variable go with low scores on the other variable, and vice versa.

The foregoing equation for the correlation coefficient $r$ is called the *product-moment* (PM) equation. It is so called because standard scores are sometimes called "moments" and because $r$ equals the average product of such moments on two measures. There are numerous computational equations for obtaining the PM coefficient, all of which lead to exactly the same $r$. These are to be distinguished from other correlational methods, which will be discussed later in this chapter.

Although the equation for the correlation coefficient $r$ above is relatively easy to understand, it is not the easiest approach to computing the correlation. Standardizing scores over several hundred persons, rather than over the nine cases employed above, involves a considerable amount of work. Therefore, it is easier to compute the correlation coefficient from deviation scores or from raw scores. Some manipulations of the basic equation will show how this is done:

$$r = \frac{\Sigma z_x z_y}{N} \tag{4-1}$$

$$r = \frac{\Sigma (x/\sigma_x)(y/\sigma_y)}{N}$$

$$r = \frac{\Sigma xy}{N \sigma_x \sigma_y}$$

$$r = \frac{\Sigma xy}{\sqrt{\Sigma x^2} \sqrt{\Sigma y^2}} \tag{4-2}$$

Equation (4-2) can be used to compute the correlation coefficient from deviation scores. Next we can replace each $x$ value in Equation (4-2) by $X - M_x$ and each $y$ value by $Y - M_y$ and obtain the following raw-score equation:

$$r = \frac{N\Sigma XY - (\Sigma X)(\Sigma Y)}{\sqrt{N\Sigma X^2 - (\Sigma X)^2} \sqrt{N\Sigma Y^2 - (\Sigma Y)^2}} \tag{4-3}$$

It must be remembered that the correlation coefficient specifies the relationship between two sets of standard scores. Either the computations begin with standard scores, as in Equation (4-1), or the standardizing is done in the computations, as in Equations (4-2) and (4-3). The three equations above will give exactly the same correlation coefficient. Although Equation (4-3) looks complicated, it is actually the easiest way to obtain the correlation coefficient if an automatic calculator is available.

Not only is it easier to compute the correlation coefficient from deviation scores and raw scores, but also it is often convenient to form the prediction equation from deviation scores and raw scores. The prediction equation specifies how the best-fit line is drawn.

The standard-score equation

$$z_y' = rz_x \tag{4-4}$$

can be converted to the deviation-score equation

$$y' = r \frac{\sigma_y}{\sigma_x} x \tag{4-5}$$

where

$y'$ = estimated deviation score on criterion (grades)
$x$ = actual deviation score on predictor (vocabulary)
$r$ = correlation between predictor and criterion
$\sigma_y$ = standard deviation of criterion
$\sigma_x$ = standard deviation of predictor

Equation (4-5) could be used to predict students' deviation scores in college grades from their deviation scores on the vocabulary test. Thus, if a student has a vocabulary deviation score of 3 and the correlation is .50 and if the standard deviations for vocabulary and grades are 2 and 1, respectively, the prediction is as follows:

$$y' = .50 \times \frac{1}{2} \times 3$$
$$= .25 \times 3$$
$$= .75$$

The prediction is that he will be 0.75 deviation-score units above the mean of grade averages. Let us say that he actually makes a deviation score of 1.25 in grades and that the prediction is therefore in error by 0.50 deviation-score units.

The prediction equation can also be expressed in raw-score terms:

$$Y' = r \left(\frac{\sigma_y}{\sigma_x}\right) (X - M_x) + M_y \tag{4-6}$$

where

$Y'$ = estimated raw score on criterion (school grades)
$X$ = actual raw score on predictor (vocabulary)
$\sigma_y$ = standard deviation of criterion
$\sigma_x$ = standard deviation of predictor
$M_y$ = mean of raw criterion scores
$M_x$ = mean of raw predictor scores

Although Equation (4-6) looks complicated, it is a straightforward extension of Equations (4-4) and (4-5). Equation (4-6) might predict that a person with a raw vocabulary score of 20 will make a raw grade average of 2.6.

Equations (4-5) and (4-6) can both be used to plot best-fit lines. Equation (4-5) would be used if deviation scores are plotted, and Equation (4-6) would be used if raw scores are plotted. The correlation coefficient and the three prediction equations above are the basic statistical procedures needed for the validation and use of predictor tests.

The correlation coefficient is, of course, not used to predict grade averages that are already known, but to forecast the grade averages of incoming freshmen. If subsequent groups of incoming freshmen are of about the same caliber as their predecessors, the correlation between vocabulary and later grades will be approximately the same. Therefore, it is safe to use the first correlation to forecast the grade averages of incoming freshmen.

### The standard error of estimate

Another way to understand correlational analysis is to think in terms of the errors of prediction. Figure 4-3 shows a typical comparison of raw scores on a test and on a criterion. (Whereas in the earlier example the correlation was .78, here it is .50.) Here we shall assume that the best-fit line is known to begin with, as shown in Figure 4-3, and see how it is used to make predictions.

When a bivariate relationship is pictured as in Figure 4-3, it is referred to as a *scatter diagram*. The points are plotted in terms of intervals instead of discrete scores. That is, all the vocabulary scores from 0 to 9 are plotted in the first column, all the scores from 10 to 19 are plotted in the second column, and so on for all intervals. Each column is referred to as an *array*, and there are as many arrays as there are intervals on the vocabulary axis.

In order to predict any student's grade, simply find his score on the vocabulary axis and then move upward to the best-fit line. Then move parallel to the vocabulary axis to the predicted grade average. If a student makes a vocabulary score of 10, the prediction is that he will make a grade average of approximately 2.92. If a student makes a vocabulary score of 80, the prediction is that he will make a grade average of approximately 4.12. In each case we predict as though all the points lay on the best-fit line, but, in fact, the points in each array scatter above and below the line. This tells us that a prediction from any point on the vocabulary axis about how well an individual will perform in school is likely to be in error in proportion to the scatter of the Y points about the prediction line. If the scatter about the best-fit line is large, prediction will be poor; as the scatter lessens, the prediction becomes better and better.

In Chapter 3, the standard deviation was given as a measure of dispersion. The same kind of measure can be used in the scatter diagram to describe the error in predicting grades from vocabulary scores. A measure of the standard-

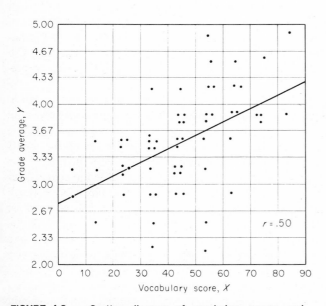

**FIGURE 4-3**    Scatter diagram of vocabulary scores and school grade averages

deviation type could be determined for any one array by subtracting the predicted grade average (at the point of the best-fit line) from each of the grade averages actually found. We could then find the standard deviation of the prediction errors. A like measure could be obtained for each of the arrays, and these could be averaged to determine an overall estimate of the dispersion about the best-fit line. The method used in practice is slightly different from this procedure. Instead of finding the separate dispersions and averaging them, all the deviates are determined about their respective points of prediction, and these are placed in the conventional standard-deviation formula. The resulting value is called the *standard error of estimate* and will be symbolized as $\sigma_{est}$.

The standard error of estimate is an absolute measure of error in predicting Y, but the units in which the criterion is expressed are often arbitrary functions of test construction practices. If, for example, the criterion is a course examination, the range of the grades could be from 1 to 10, 50 to 100, or any other range in accordance with the system of grading used. Consequently, it is necessary to compare the standard error of estimate with the standard deviation of the criterion before the efficiency of prediction can be determined.

As was mentioned previously, if we had no knowledge about the criterion scores of particular people, the best bet would be that they all fell at the mean of Y, which would be in error in accordance with the size of the standard deviation of criterion scores which is actually obtained. The standard deviation of Y would specify the likelihood that predicted scores would fall within certain intervals on the criterion continuum. Then, as would be expected, when the correlation between the test and the criterion is zero, the standard error of estimate will be the same as the standard deviation of Y. As the correlation becomes larger and larger, $\sigma_{est}$ becomes comparatively smaller than $\sigma_y$. The ratio of these two measures of dispersion leads to a very useful index of predictive efficiency.

It is easy to picture what the scatter diagram will look like as the correlation becomes larger and larger; the area of scatter will become progressively more narrow. This progressive narrowing can be seen in Figure 4-4. The three "boxes" shown in Figure 4-4 indicate the areas in which most of the points would lie for three different sizes of correlation. The narrower the box on the vertical axis, the smaller would be the errors in predicting criterion scores from scores on the predictor. With a correlation of only .25, the box is quite "fat," and points in the scatter diagram would scatter nearly as much as possible. With a correlation of .70, the box would be rather "thin," and points would be confined to a comparatively small part of the possible space. In each case, the vertical height of the box is proportional to the $\sigma_{est}$ corresponding to the size of the correlation.

The correlation coefficient concerns the squares of $\sigma_y$ and $\sigma_{est}$. The squares are used because the resulting equation indicates how the best-fit line should be drawn, as well as the degree of relationship between the two variables. As

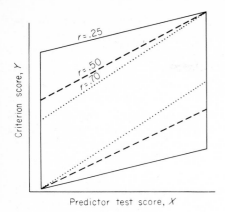

Criterion score, Y

r = .25

r = .50

r = .70

Predictor test score, X

**FIGURE 4-4**    Areas of scatter for different-sized correlations

was noted previously, the square of a standard-deviation type of value is called the *variance*. The ratio of the two squared values is then a variance ratio, a term that will be encountered quite often in testing theory. If this ratio were used as a measure of relationship, it would read "backward": a high ratio would indicate a weak relationship, and a low ratio would represent a strong relationship. This difficulty is overcome by subtracting the ratio from 1, which results in the following equation:

$$r^2 = 1 - \frac{\sigma_{est}^2}{\sigma_y^2} \tag{4-7}$$

$$r = \sqrt{1 - \frac{\sigma_{est}^2}{\sigma_y^2}} \tag{4-8}$$

The letter $r$ stands for the correlation coefficient, $r^2$ is said to be the *percentage of variance explained*, and $1 - r^2$ is spoken of as the *percentage of variance unexplained*. It is perhaps easier to visualize the meaning of $r^2$ than of $r$ itself, but as was shown previously, the correlation coefficient is directly useful in making predictions.

Although $\sigma_{est}$ does not appear directly in Equation (4-1), (4-2), or (4-3), it can easily be derived after the $r$ is obtained. Equation (4-7) can be suitably transformed as follows:

$$\sigma_{est} = \sigma_y \sqrt{1 - r^2} \tag{4-9}$$

The standard error of estimate relates to the normal curve in the same way that the standard deviation does. Consider, for example, all the persons who make exactly the same score on a predictor test. It would be predicted that all such persons would make the same score on a criterion variable, but unless the correlation is 1.00, those persons will vary with respect to criterion scores. The standard error of measurement is a measure of how much dispersion there is in that regard. Assuming that the distribution of criterion scores in that case is approximately normal, the $\sigma_{est}$ could be used to establish probabilities regarding scores on the criterion variable. Because approximately 95 percent of the cases in a normal distribution lie within two standard deviations above and below the mean, one could say that the odds are only 1 in 20 that any person with a particular score on a predictor test will be outside two standard errors of measurement above or below the predicted criterion score. (This logic hinges on the assumption that the best-fit line goes through the mean criterion score corresponding to each score on the predictor test, which is a matter that will be discussed later.)

### Nonlinear relationships

We have spoken so far only about linear relationships. Equations (4-1) to (4-3) indicate the linear correlation between two sets of scores, and Equations (4-4) to (4-6) place the best-fit straight lines in scatter diagrams. Equations (4-7) to (4-9) were used to illustrate the dispersion about the best-fit straight line. A possibility that has not been mentioned so far is that the bivariate relationship might not be linear. A relationship is linear if the points in each array spread equally above and below the best-fit straight line. Technically, the relationship is linear if the mean criterion score for each array falls exactly on the best-fit line.

In any particular scatter diagram, the array means can be plotted and compared with the best-fit straight line. It is expected that the array means will diverge from the line by small amounts, if only because of sampling error. However, in the use of psychological tests it is rare to find that the array means show some systematic trend other than a straight-line function. When this happens, the relationship is called *curvilinear*; a curvilinear relationship is illustrated in Figure 4-5. Figure 4-5 shows that criterion scores increase with predictor test scores up to a point and then start to decline. Then the people who make very high scores on the test do less well, as a group, on the criterion than the people who make only moderately high test scores. Although curvilinear relationships are sometimes found in psychological experiments, such a marked departure from linearity as the one shown in Figure 4-5 is rarely found in using tests.

Equation (4-7) was illustrated with a linear relationship, but it can be applied equally well to curvilinear relationships like that shown in Figure 4-5. The only difference is in the way the standard error of estimate is obtained. Instead of computing the statistic about the best-fit straight line, $\sigma_{est}$ can be obtained about the array means. The mean criterion score in each array is subtracted

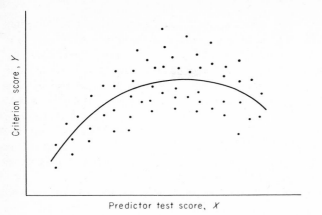

**FIGURE 4-5**    Scatter diagram illustrating a curvilinear relationship

from the criterion scores in each array. The differences are then squared and summed over all arrays. The resulting sum is divided by the number of individuals. This is then the squared standard error of estimate taken about the array means. When this is placed in Equation (4-8), it gives a general index of correlation which is independent of the form of the relationship. Equation (4-8) is a measure of correlation that can be used on relationships of all kinds. When the standard error of estimate is obtained about the best-fit straight line, the resulting statistic is called the *correlation coefficient* and is symbolized as *r*. When the standard error of estimate is obtained about the array means, the resulting statistic is called the *correlation ratio* or *eta*.

It must be kept in mind that the linear correlation equations will place the best-fit straight line in the scatter diagram regardless of whether the relationship is actually linear. Before the linear correlation equations are applied, the scatter diagram should be inspected to see whether the relationship is reasonably linear. If there is only a moderate curve in the relationship, the linear equation will still do an adequate job of describing the trend. However, if there is apparently a marked tendency toward curvilinearity, a test of statistical significance should be made (see McNemar, 1962, pp. 255–262). Then if the departure from linearity is statistically significant, either the correlation ratio should be applied or it should be pointed out that the linear correlation equation was applied to a curvilinear relationship. When correlations are stated in research reports, readers will assume that the relationships are reasonably linear. Among the assumptions which are made in employing the correlation coefficient *r*, linearity of relationship is the most important.

In order to use $\sigma_{est}$ as a measure of error in making predictions, the bivariate relationship should have several characteristics in addition to linearity. Earlier in the chapter a discussion of the errors of prediction in terms of the array dispersions was presented.  A possibility which was not mentioned at that time is that the array dispersions may not be equal.  An example of unequal dispersions is shown in Figure 4-6.  Although relationships similar to the one shown in Figure 4-6 are sometimes found in practice, they are usually considered undesirable.  The $\sigma_{est}$ obtained for this relationship would be an underestimate of the error in predicting from high $x$ scores and an overestimate of the error in predicting from low $x$ scores.  The assumption in using the correlation coefficient is that the dispersion about the best-fit line is the same for all the arrays on the $x$ axis.  The presence of equal array dispersions is referred to by the rather formidable name *homoscedasticity*.

Not only is it desirable to have equal array dispersions, but it is also helpful if the points in each array are normally distributed about the best-fit line.  This means that the points are more numerous where the best-fit line crosses the particular array and progressively less numerous in moving upward or downward from the best-fit line, in accordance with the frequencies expected from the normal distribution.  Normality of array dispersions is necessary if the $\sigma_{est}$ is used as a standard-deviation type of measure.  Only if the distribution is normal will 68 percent of the cases fall between plus and minus one standard error, and so on for all other segments of the distribution.

It is also desirable, but not absolutely necessary, that each of the two variables in the correlation problem have an approximately normal distribution of scores.

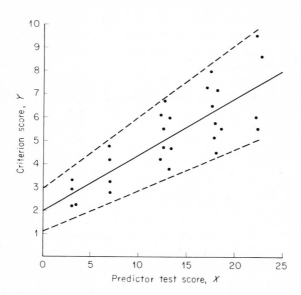

**FIGURE 4-6**    Scatter diagram in which array dispersion increases with test score

In practice it is found that highly skewed variables and other forms that differ markedly from the normal are often accompanied by one or more of the several undesired features in the bivariate relationship, such as nonlinearity.

## Regression

Looking back at Equation (4-4), it can be seen that the best prediction is always that an individual will make a standard score nearer the mean of the criterion than his standard score on the predictor—except in the case of a correlation of 1.00. Also, because each of the standard scores on the predictor is multiplied by a constant $r$, the standard deviation of the predicted scores will always be smaller than the standard deviation of the real criterion standard scores. Because of the need to make bets nearer the mean of Y than $\sigma_y$ would indicate, the best-fit line is often referred to as the *regression line*, and Equations (4-4) to (4-6) as *regression equations*.

The observed tendency for predictions to regress toward the mean was the original stimulus for developing the correlation coefficient. For example, it was noted that the sons of very tall fathers tended to be shorter than their fathers and that the sons of very short fathers tended to be taller than their fathers. There is a simple reason why the regression tendency occurs. The people who make the highest scores on the predictor test can either make the highest criterion scores or vary downward toward the mean. Similarly, the people who make the lowest scores on the predictor test can either make the lowest scores on the criterion or vary upward toward the mean. Consequently, the array means of the extremes on the predictor regress toward the criterion mean. The in-between arrays tend to follow suit, resulting in the general tendency of regression toward the mean.

The slant, or slope, of the best-fit line is evidence of the regression tendency. The slope indicates the number of units of X that are required to advance a unit of Y. When dealing with standard scores, the correlation coefficient is the slope of the best-fit line. For example, when there is a correlation of .50, the best-fit line moves over two units on the predictor axis before going up one unit on the criterion axis.

Correlational analysis can be used to predict the X's from the Y's as well as the Y's from the X's. With linear product-moment correlational analysis, it does not matter which variable is labeled X and placed on the horizontal axis and which is labeled Y and placed on the vertical axis. In the example above, the height of fathers could be predicted from the height of sons. The correlation coefficient will be the same regardless of which variable is labeled X. Also, we could predict test scores from grade-point averages, although no practical purpose would be served. Correlation equations (4-1) to (4-3) would be unchanged, and we would obtain the same coefficient of .78 that was determined earlier. Regression, correlation, and standard-error-of-estimate equations

(4-4) to (4-9) would be altered by substituting $Y$'s for $X$'s and $y$ subscripts for $x$ subscripts, and vice versa.

Linear transformations

One important property of the correlation coefficient is that it is completely insensitive to linear transformations of the predictor and criterion scores. A linear transformation consists of adding a constant amount to each score, subtracting a constant amount, or multiplying or dividing each of the scores by a constant amount. For example, the correlation in Figure 4-3 would remain .50 if the number 10 million were added to each of the scores on the predictor test and each of the assessment scores were multiplied by 20 billion. The reason why the correlation coefficient is insensitive to linear transformations is that it is a measure of the relationship between two sets of standard scores. Either standard scores are used in the correlation equation or the conversion to standard scores is done in the deviation-score and raw-score computational equations.

## the statistical significance of correlations

Before correlation coefficients are used in any way, they should be tested for statistical significance. In undertaking a correlational analysis, the interest is usually in determining the relationship between two variables, here predictor test and criterion scores, in a whole population of people. We are seldom interested in only the relatively small sample of persons whose scores are actually used to compute the correlation. Therefore, we must question the precision with which a correlation coefficient determined from a sample of persons mirrors the real correlation between variables in the whole population of persons.

To illustrate the influence of sampling error on correlation coefficients, imagine that we are trying to learn the correlation between height and weight for British male adults. It would be exceedingly laborious to measure the height and weight of every male over twenty-one in England, and no small amount of work would be required to compute the correlation. If a research worker set out to learn the correlation between height and weight, he would probably work with only a small sample from the population. The sample might be quite large—say, over ten thousand men—or perhaps only a few dozen men would be used instead.

Even if the population correlation is zero, the correlation found for a particular sample probably would not be exactly zero. We might draw a number of different samples of persons—say, all of them with 100 persons—and run the separate correlations. It would be expected that these correlations would range around zero. There would be no reason to expect more positive than negative coefficients, or vice versa. The dispersion of the coefficients about zero would be dependent on the $N$, or sample size. That is, the correlations obtained from successive samples would crowd nearer to zero when the sample size was large—assuming again that the population correlation was exactly zero. The distributions of coefficients that would be obtained for different sample sizes would look like those shown in Figure 4-7. Because the true correlation is zero in Figure 4-7, all the nonzero coefficients are due to chance. On occasion these chance coefficients can be quite large. Notice that with an $N$ of 10, correlations greater than $+.50$ and less than $-.50$ would occur appreciably often purely by chance.

Before any effort is made to interpret a particular correlation, some assurance must be obtained that the coefficient is significantly different from zero. Otherwise the correlation may represent a chance sampling of people from a population in which the true value is zero. One way to gain some confidence in particular correlations is to learn the odds, or the probability, that the correlation could have been obtained by chance alone. If the probability is very low—say, 1 in 100, or at the .01 level, as it will be called—it is relatively safe to assume that the correlation is not merely a chance relationship.

Although it is important in research on psychological measures to consider the statistical significance of correlations, it would be impossible in this book to discuss that topic in detail. The purpose here is to make the reader aware of the need for such inferential statistics. These are discussed in detail in the Suggested Additional Readings at the end of this chapter.

## the influence of the dispersion on correlations

An important property of the correlation coefficient is that its size is directly related to the standard deviation of the variable being estimated. Looking back

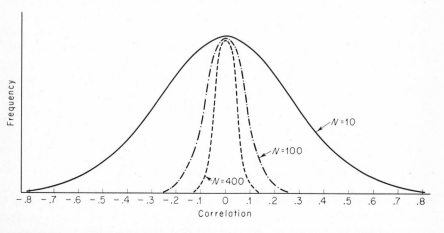

**FIGURE 4-7**    Distributions of sample correlations when the population correlation is .00 (*N* is the sample size)

at Figure 4-3, what would happen to the correlation if only the people with grade averages above 2.67 were considered in the calculation? This would certainly reduce the standard deviation of grades Y, but it would have relatively little influence on $\sigma_{est}$. The reader should remember that the assumption of equal array dispersions requires that $\sigma_{est}$ be the same regardless of the region of predictor scores being considered. If only the people who score above 2.67 in grades were considered in the computations, the correlation would be smaller. Looking back at Equation (4-7), it will be seen that this is the only possible result. Whenever the dispersion of ability is altered, the correlation changes. One must be careful to note that the change in dispersion must be a change in sampling such that the range of "real ability" varies. As the reader will remember, changing the size of the standard deviation by a linear transformation of the criterion scores will have no influence on the correlation. Whereas $\sigma_{est}$ tends to be the same in different samples of persons, the correlation varies with the dispersion of scores.

Because of the influence of the criterion dispersion on validity, the standard deviation of the criterion scores should be compared with that which is generally found in the criterion situation. If the dispersion used in validation work is different from the usual dispersion found, a statistical correction gives an estimate of what the test validity would be with a more representative dispersion of criterion scores (see Thorndike, 1949, pp. 169–176).

The influence of the dispersion on test validity relates to an interesting and often misunderstood observation: Intelligence tests become less successful predictors as higher educational levels are reached. The tests correlate around .70 with grammar school grades, around .60 with high school grades, and around .50 with college grades, and they tend to correlate only slightly with the grades of students in graduate school. The reason for the progressive decline in validity is that the dispersion of intellectual ability is gradually being decreased. The less able students are dropped out year by year. At the graduate school level, there is relatively little dispersion of intellectual ability. Tests can "commit suicide," if, as is often the case, they are used at various stages to determine who should continue in school. Theoretically the stage could be reached where the test correlates zero with the criterion which it has been so successful in predicting over the years. This situation is much like that of the physician who advises his patients so successfully on how to remain well that he finds himself with no ailments to treat.

## other uses of PM correlation

This section will consider three indices of relationship: phi, point-biserial, and rho. There is apparently some confusion in the minds of nonspecialists about these coefficients. It is frequently assumed that they are different from one another and that they are all different from the PM formula. Both assumptions are incorrect. All three of these "other" coefficients are the same, and they are all the same as the "regular" PM coefficient. Such "other" coefficients are sometimes thought to be different because the computations "look" different, but this is due entirely to the type of data to which they are applied rather than a different mathematical rationale. Some shortcut formulas have been developed for cases where one or both of the variables are not continuous, e.g., for correlating two dichotomous variables. These are only special cases of the PM formula, and aside from the convenience of working with such shortcut formulas when computers are not available, the PM formula could be used to obtain exactly the same result that would be obtained from phi, pointbiserial, or rho.

### Phi

When both distributions are dichotomous, a shortcut version of the PM coefficient is available which is called *phi*. Phi can be illustrated in the situation where two test items are being correlated:

*Item 1*

fail    pass

|  | fail | pass |
|---|---|---|
| **pass** | 17 | 30 |
| **fail** | 33 | 20 |

*Item 2*

The above diagram shows the scores for 100 students on two items. It indicates, for example, that 30 students pass both items and 33 fail both items. It is convenient to symbolize the four quadrants as follows:

*Item 1*

*Item 2*

| b | a |
|---|---|
| c | d |

A shortcut version of the PM coefficient is obtained as follows:

$$\text{phi} = \frac{ac - bd}{\sqrt{(a+b)(c+d)(b+c)(a+d)}} \tag{4-10}$$

As was mentioned previously, although the formula for phi looks different from the PM formula, the former is only a special case of the latter. When correlating two dichotomous distributions, exactly the same results as those obtained from phi would be obtained by standardizing scores and placing these in the PM formula.   If half the persons pass one item and passes are scored 1 and failures scored 0, all persons passing would have a standard score of +1, and all those failing would have a standard score of −1.   Such standard scores may look rather strange, but that does not disturb the mathematics of the problem.

Before the advent of high-speed computers, phi was frequently applied to artificially dichotomized variables.   For example, in item analysis, dichotomous item scores can be correlated with artificially dichotomized total scores on the test.   One way to dichotomize total scores is to make all scores below the median zero and all scores at or above the median 1.   Phi could then be used to correlate each item with total test scores.   Unless computational labor is a very important consideration, it is unwise to artificially dichotomize one or both of the variables being investigated.   If both variables are continuous, it is best to apply the regular PM formula.   If one variable is inherently dichotomous (e.g., pass-fail on test items) and one is continuous, it is best to apply point-biserial, which will be discussed in the next section.   Information is always lost when a continuous variable is artificially dichotomized.   As a shortcut version of the PM coefficient, phi is the preferred measure of relationship when variables are inherently dichotomous.

### Point-biserial

When one dichotomous variable is to be correlated with a continuous variable, a shortcut version of the PM formula called *point-biserial* ($r_{pb}$) is available.   This formula is employed most frequently in correlating a dichotomous test item (e.g., pass-fail) with total scores on a test.   The shortcut formula is as follows:

$$r_{pb} = \frac{M_s - M_u}{\sigma} \sqrt{pq} \qquad (4\text{-}11)$$

where

$M_s$ = mean score on continuous variable of "successful" group on dichotomous variable

$M_u$ = mean score on continuous variable of "unsuccessful" group on dichotomous variable

$\sigma$ = standard deviation on continuous variable for total group

$p$ = proportion falling in "successful" group on dichotomous variable

$q = 1 - p$

As is true of phi, $r_{pb}$ was sometimes employed in earlier days where one of two continuous variables was artificially dichotomized.   For example, rather than applying the regular PM formula to the continuous scores on two tests, scores on one of the two tests were dichotomized, the "cut" most frequently being done at the median.   Then the shortcut equation was applied.   This is very poor practice, however.   The saving in computational time is not great, and fuller information would be obtained by correlating the two continuous variables.   Point-biserial is the preferred measure of correlation when one variable is continuous and the other is inherently dichotomous, e.g., pass-fail or male-female.   As mentioned previously, the numerical result obtained by applying the regular PM equation is exactly the same as that which would be obtained with the shortcut version $r_{pb}$.

## Rho

For correlating two sets of ranks, a shortcut version of the PM equation called *rho* is available.   The equation could be used, for example, to correlate the rankings of two judges of the extent to which 20 patients had improved in the course of psychotherapy.   The equation is as follows:

$$\text{rho} = \frac{6\Sigma d^2}{N(N^2 - 1)} \tag{4-12}$$

where $N$ is the number of objects or persons ranked and $d$ is the algebraic difference in ranks for each object or person in two distributions of ranks. Although rho is sometimes spoken of as a "nonparametric" index of relationship, this certainly is not the case.   Rho is only a shortcut version of the regular PM equation.   Results obtained by applying rho are exactly the same as those obtained by applying the regular PM equation to two sets of ranks.

There are three possible reasons for employing rho.   First, two continuous distributions can be converted to ranks and rho applied to save computational labor.   This should not constitute a general reason, however, because the saving in computational time is not great.   In this instance, rho applied to the ranks would usually be very close to the regular PM equation applied to the continuous variables, particularly if both continuous variables are approximately normally distributed.   A second reason for applying rho is to estimate what the PM correlation would be between two distributions which are markedly different in shape if the two were rescaled to have approximately the same shape. If, for example, one distribution is highly skewed to the left and the other is highly skewed to the right, the PM correlation will be less than it would be if both distributions had the same shape.   If both distributions were transformed to have the same shape, say, if both were normalized, the correlation would increase somewhat.   Before going to the labor of transforming the two distributions, it might be useful to estimate how much the variables would correlate after the transformation.   This can be done with rho.   By ranking scores on the two variables and applying rho, one will obtain a correlation that closely approximates the correlation that would be obtained from the two normalized variables.   This is a legitimate reason for applying rho, but the circumstance arises infrequently.

The third, and best, reason for employing rho is to correlate two distributions that are inherently expressed as ranks. This would be the case for the example mentioned earlier where 20 patients are ranked with respect to improvement during the course of therapy. When measurement is in the form of rank order, rho provides a useful index of correlation. Because rho is a PM equation and PM equations are often said to "require" interval scales, some would call this an illegitimate use of rho. It is hard to see much sense in such arguments. Since rho ranges between +1 and −1, it serves to describe the degree of relationship between two sets of ranks. Tests of statistical significance are available (McNemar, 1962) when both variables are inherently in the form of rank order. As a shortcut version of the regular PM equation, rho is the preferred measure of relationship when both variables are inherently in the form of ranks.

## estimates of PM coefficients

Although they are not PM coefficients themselves, two coefficients have been used to estimate results that would, under special circumstances, be obtained from the PM equation. It will be recommended that these coefficients not be used in most cases, but they are spoken of so frequently in the literature relating to measurement theory that a brief discussion of them is required.

### Biserial

When one variable is dichotomous and the other continuous, the biserial correlation $r_{bis}$ can be used in place of the point-biserial correlation. The equation for $r_{bis}$ is as follows:

$$r_{bis} = \frac{M_s - M_u}{\sigma} \left( \frac{pq}{z} \right) \tag{4-13}$$

where

$M_s$ = mean score on continuous variable of "successful" group on dichotomous variable

$M_u$ = mean score on continuous variable of "unsuccessful" group on continuous variable

$\sigma$ = standard deviation on continuous variable for total group

$p$ = proportion falling in "successful" group on dichotomous variable

$q = 1 - p$

$z$ = ordinate of normal curve corresponding to $p$

Biserial can be used to estimate the PM correlation that would be obtained from two continuous distributions if the dichotomized variable were normally distributed. In the past, $r_{bis}$ has been used to save computational time over that required for the PM coefficient. This could be done by "cutting" one distribution at the median and then computing $r_{bis}$ rather than $r$. Another use of $r_{bis}$ is to correlate scores on an inherently dichotomous variable with those on a continuous variable. For example, a preliminary form of a questionnaire might employ dichotomous items, e.g., agree-disagree. If the preliminary form is successful, plans are made to construct a form in which each item will be rated on an 11-point scale of agreement. The success of each item depends on the extent to which it correlates with performance in a learning experiment. The biserial correlation of each dichotomous item with the criterion (success in the learning experiment) would be an estimate of the PM correlation that would be obtained by correlating the 11-point scale with the criterion.

### Tetrachoric correlation

Taking the logic of biserial correlation a step further, the tetrachoric correlation coefficient $r_t$ is used to estimate the PM correlation of two continuous variables from dichotomized versions of those variables. One use of $r_t$ would be with two continuous variables that have been artificially dichotomized, such as two continuous variables each of which has been "cut" at the median. Another use of $r_t$ is with two variables which are inherently dichotomous at the time of the analysis. The purpose here would be to estimate what the PM coefficient would be *if* the two variables were continuous, e.g., the correlation between two questionnaire items scored on 11-point scales rather than in terms of dichotomous responses.

Exact computing equations for $r_t$ are extremely complex, and even some of the approximate equations are rather involved. Instead of employing the equations, it is better to use the computing diagrams available for the purpose (discussed in McNemar, 1962).

### Use of $r_{bis}$ and $r_t$

There are very strong reasons for *not* using $r_{bis}$ and $r_t$ in most of the ways they have been used in the past. If continuous scores are available for both variables, any savings in computational labor over the regular PM coefficient is not worth the dangers involved. First, if one variable or both are inherently dichotomous, it is usually illogical to estimate what the PM coefficient would be if both variables were continuous. Unless subsequent steps are made to turn the dichotomous variables into continuous variables, such estimates serve only to fool one into thinking that his variables have explanatory power beyond that which they actually have. It is tempting to employ $r_{bis}$ and $r_t$ rather than phi and $r_{pb}$ because the former are usually larger, but that is not a legitimate reason for doing so.

A second reason for not employing $r_{bis}$ and $r_t$ is that even if it were sensible to make such estimates of the PM coefficient between two continuous variables, they are frequently very poor estimates. Both these coefficients depend very heavily on a strict assumption of the normality of the continuous variables, either of the variables that have been artificially dichotomized or of continuous variables that are to be generated later. When the assumption of normality is not met, the estimates can be off by more than 20 points of correlation. The author once had occasion to compare a biserial correlation between two continuous variables (one of which was dichotomized at the median for the analysis) with the regular PM coefficient applied to the continuous variables. The former was .71, and the latter was .52! The errors of estimate frequently found with these two coefficients show that they should generally not be employed.

There is another important reason for generally avoiding the use of $r_{bis}$ and $r_t$. It was said that one of the great virtues of PM correlation is that it opens the door to many powerful methods of analysis, but this is not true of the two estimates of PM correlation. After one obtains $r_{bis}$ and $r_t$, there is very little that can be done with them mathematically. It should be strongly underscored that these two estimates *cannot* be used in partial correlation, multiple correlation, factor analysis, or *any* other forms of multivariate analysis. There have been instances in the past of the use of $r_t$ in factor analysis. Perhaps no harm was done, but there is no mathematical basis whatsoever for employing $r_{bis}$ and $r_t$ in multivariate analysis.

After this scathing denunciation of $r_{bis}$ and $r_t$, it should be pointed out that there is one important, legitimate use for these coefficients. This is in the development of mathematical models relating to measurement theory. It might be necessary, for example, in one mathematical model concerning test construction to assume that all the items have the same biserial correlation with total test scores or the same tetrachoric correlation with one another. This might permit the development of some useful principles which could be tested in empirical studies. There is nothing wrong with using $r_{bis}$ and $r_t$ in mathematical models, but they definitely should not be used to determine the correlation between sets of empirical data.

## other measures of correlation

In addition to the measures of correlation discussed above, many other measures of the degree of relationship between two variables have been developed. None of these has achieved the prominence of the PM coefficient because none fit as neatly into the mathematical developments required for multivariate analysis, e.g., factor analysis.

In this discussion of the value of different approaches to correlational analysis, it should become clear why it was stated in Chapter 1 that it is essential to employ methods of analysis appropriate to interval scales. It was shown that the PM coefficient is a function of the ratio of two variances, the variance of the errors of estimate divided by the variance of the dependent measure (Equation [4-7]). The variance is a sensible index of dispersion only when the intervals of the scale are taken seriously. (A set of ranks has no variance.) To forsake the interval would be to forsake the variance, and to forsake the variance would be to forsake all the powerful methods of analysis that are needed.

What is lost when the assumption of an interval scale is forsaken is illustrated by the attempt to develop nonparametric correlation coefficients for ranked data. (Previously it was pointed out that rho is not a nonparametric index of relationship.) The only index that has achieved prominence is Kendall's tau (Kendall, 1948). Although tau is an index of the extent to which persons or objects are ordered alike on two variables and although the sampling distribution of the index is known, it has been used very little in research. The reason is that, as in the case of so many other non-PM measures, it is very difficult to extend tau to problems of multivariate analysis.

## Summary

Essentially, correlational analysis concerns the extent to which persons are ordered alike on two variables. Such forms of analysis are highly important for the development and investigation of psychological measures. Predictive validity depends directly on the extent to which scores on a predictor test bear strong relations with scores on a criterion variable, and correlational analysis is essential for determining the strength of such relations. Construct validity is concerned with correlations between measures that all purport to measure the same thing, e.g., anxiety or intelligence. Although content validity depends primarily on rational considerations rather than statistical evidence, correlational analysis provides useful information, such as in correlating one item in a spelling test with scores on the total test or correlating one achievement test in spelling with another achievement test in spelling.

Although potentially there are many approaches to correlational analysis, one has proved to be by far the most useful—the product-moment (PM) approach. The PM coefficient is the average product of standard scores on two measures. Many different computational methods are available for arriving at the same correlation coefficient. These differ in terms of appearances and in terms of ease of computation, but in essence they are all the same method.

Because the PM correlation ranges between 1.00 and minus 1.00, it provides a directly meaningful indication of the direction and extent of the relationship between scores on two measures. In addition, the PM coefficient relates to a number of other informative aspects of the relationship between two sets of scores. Equations are available for determining the statistical significance of an obtained correlation or the statistical significance of the difference between two obtained correlations. Such tests of statistical significance provide one with some confidence in the "reality" of correlational results. The standard error of estimate, which concerns the amount of error in predicting scores on one variable from knowledge of scores on another variable, can be derived from the PM correlation. Equations are available for estimating how much different a correlation would be if it were obtained from a sample of persons that had either larger or smaller standard deviations than those in the original sample (the effects of dispersion).

One of the most important virtues of PM correlation is that it serves as a very useful foundation for more complex methods of analysis needed in the development and investigation of psychological measures, e.g., multiple correlation and factor analysis. This cannot be said of some of the non-PM estimates of the PM coefficient (e.g., tetrachoric) or of some of the non-PM coefficients that are not intended to estimate the PM coefficient (e.g., tau). The principles of correlational analysis discussed in this chapter will prove invaluable for an understanding of the remaining chapters of this book.

### Suggested additional readings

Dixon, W. J., & Massey, F. J.  *Introduction to statistical analysis.*  New York: McGraw-Hill, 1951.

Lindquist, E. F.  *A first course in statistics.*  (Rev. ed.) Boston: Houghton Mifflin, 1942.

McNemar, Q.  *Psychological statistics.*  New York: Wiley, 1962.

Thorndike, R. L.  *Personnel selection: Test and measurement techniques.*  New York: Wiley, 1949.

Walker, H. M., & Lev, J.  *Elementary statistical methods.*  New York: Holt, 1958.

# PART 3:

## Methods for Determining the Scientific Usefulness of Psychological Measures

# CHAPTER 5

# Reliability of measurements

Reliability concerns the *precision* of measurement regardless of *what* is measured. Some random error is involved in all scientific measurements. For example, a metal ruler expands and contracts with changing temperatures. This introduces some error into measurements and consequently lowers the precision of measurements made with this ruler. Measurement error of this kind tends to obscure scientific lawfulness. For example, if there is a close relationship between electrical resistance and length of a wire, the relationship would be somewhat obscured if the wire were measured with the unstable metal ruler. This is why precise measurements can be made only by holding temperature constant or by using a measuring instrument that does not vary with temperature. Psychological measures also contain a portion of random error analogous to that of the metal ruler. In this chapter we shall discuss some of the ways of detecting measurement error and eliminating it from tests. (Computing formulas and other technical matters regarding test reliability are discussed in Appendix D.)

A careful distinction should be made between test validity and test reliability. A test can have high reliability and not be valid for any particular purpose. For example, we might use the weight of individuals to predict college grades. Whereas weight may be measured very precisely and thus be highly reliable, it would be invalid as a predictor of college grades. As will be shown in the pages ahead, the opposite is not true. In order for a test to be highly valid, it must be highly reliable also. High reliability is a *necessary* but not *sufficient* condition for high validity.

In Chapter 6 it will be pointed out that, essentially, the validity of measurements concerns *generalizability*. The validity of measures requiring content validity depends upon the extent to which one can generalize the results obtained from one set of items to other items of the same kind, e.g., the extent to which the items on one test of spelling reflect the results that would be obtained from tests containing different items relating to spelling. With instruments requiring predictive validity, the question of generalizability is a simple one, that of the extent to which one can generalize from scores on the predictor test to scores on a particular criterion variable. With measures that require construct validity (e.g., measures of anxiety and intelligence), issues relating to generalizability are rather complex, but in essence they concern the extent to which research results obtained with one supposed measure of a construct are much the same as those obtained with other supposed measures of the construct.

Reliability of measures can also be considered an issue relating to generalizability. Essentially, reliability concerns the extent to which measurements of particular traits are *repeatable* under the same conditions. Repeatability of measurement is a fundamental necessity in all areas of science. If a chemist found that two thermometers measured the temperature of a particular liquid differently, he could not trust either instrument. If two foremen in a factory rated the effectiveness of a particular worker differently, the actual effectiveness of the worker would be in doubt. If two forms of an intelligence test produced very different results, one would regard the results from both tests with suspicion.

Reliability concerns the extent to which one can safely generalize from the results obtained by applying a measurement method to people in one situation at one point in time to the application of the same, or a supposedly comparable, measure of the same trait to the same people in a similar situation at another point in time. If one can safely generalize in these ways, it can be said that a measure is highly reliable; if not, it must be admitted that there is considerable *measurement error* in some way related to the nature of the measuring instrument or the way in which it is used.

Later it will be shown that it is meaningful to speak of reliability in percentage terms, with the reliability ranging from 100 to 0 percent for different measurement methods. Thus if a particular measure is 80 percent reliable, it can also be said that it is 20 percent unreliable, or that measurement error dominates 20 percent of the variance of scores. As a basic step in any scientific problem, it is necessary to determine the extent to which measures are dominated by reliable variance or by measurement error. Before moving to a direct discussion of how reliability is measured, it would be useful to give a concrete example of the effects on research results when the reliability of a measure is reduced (measurement error increased).

Measurement error, or unreliability, always works to obscure or, as we say, *attenuate* any type of scientific lawfulness. Whatever "real" lawfulness there is in nature will appear blurred if relatively unreliable measures are used to

chart that lawfulness.   When dealing with predictor tests, this means that to
the extent to which the test has much measurement error, it cannot do a good
job of predicting a criterion.   Measurement error tends to attenuate correlations; i.e., it makes them closer to zero.   An example may help to show how
this works.

Figure 5-1 shows a hypothetical relationship between a predictor test and its
criterion.   As would be the case only in hypothetical circumstances, the test
predicts its criterion perfectly, and all the scores lie on a straight line.   Let us
see what happens when some measurement error is introduced into the test
scores.   What we shall do is flip a coin for each score in turn.   If it turns up
heads, we shall add three points to the score, and if it is tails, the score will be
left as it is.   Flipping the coin for each of the test scores in turn, we find the
following:

| Original score | Coin flip | New score |
|---|---|---|
| 0 | H | 3 |
| 1 | T | 1 |
| 2 | H | 5 |
| 3 | H | 6 |
| 4 | H | 7 |
| 5 | T | 5 |
| 6 | T | 6 |
| 7 | H | 10 |
| 8 | H | 11 |
| 9 | H | 12 |
| 10 | T | 10 |
| 11 | T | 11 |
| 12 | H | 15 |
| 13 | T | 13 |

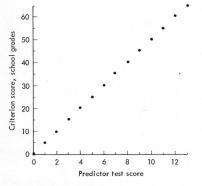

FIGURE 5-1    Relationship between a
predictor test and its criterion before
measurement error is added

In Figure 5-2 the new scores, with the included error component, are plotted against the criterion. The criterion scores have not, of course, been changed by the random additions to the predictor test scores. In Figure 5-2 it can be seen that there is no longer a perfect correlation. The effect of adding error to the scores is to lower the correlation. Starting off with a perfect relationship, there is no way for the relationship to change except to a lower correlation. The important point is that the addition of random error will tend to lower the correlation, no matter what it was originally. If we had pictured a scatter plot with a correlation of .50, the random addition of score points would have tended to make the correlation nearer zero. Likewise, if we had had a correlation of −.50, the random addition of score points would have tended to make the correlation nearer zero.

Random error works to make an observed relationship less regular than it would be if the randomness were not present. This is why we speak of error, or unreliability, as attenuating, i.e., lessening, a correlation. With as few scores as those in the example above, it is possible that the random changes in scores either would leave a correlation unchanged or could, in a very rare circumstance, make the correlation larger. However, the odds are against anything but a lowering of the correlation, and if the number of subjects is as large as it is in most testing situations (over 100 persons), it can be predicted not only that the correlation will be lower but, with fair accuracy, just how much it will be altered.

The basic issues in the discussion of measurement error are illustrated in Figure 5-3. It is assumed that each person has a *true score*, one that would be obtained if there were no errors of measurement. In the figure, person A has a relatively high true score, and person B has a relatively low true score. Since there is some random error in the score obtained for a person on a par-

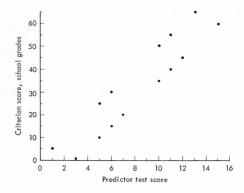

**FIGURE 5-2**     Relationship between a predictor test and its criterion after measurement error is added

ticular occasion, obtained scores would differ from true scores on a random basis. If it were possible to give many alternative forms of a test, e.g., many different spelling tests constructed by the same procedures, the average score on the tests would closely approximate true scores. Scores obtained from the alternative forms would be distributed symmetrically above and below the true scores. Since such random errors are expected to be normally distributed, it is expected that distributions of obtained scores will be normally distributed about true scores.

The wider the spread of obtained scores about true scores, the more error is involved in employing the instrument in question. The standard deviation of the distribution of errors for each person would be an index of the amount of error. If the standard deviation of errors were much the same for all persons, which is usually assumed to be the case, one standard deviation of errors could typify the amount of error to be expected. This typical standard deviation of errors is called the *standard error of measurement* and is symbolized as $\sigma_{meas}$. The size of $\sigma_{meas}$ is a direct indication of the amount of error involved in using a particular type of instrument.

## The reliability coefficient

A very useful measure of reliability is obtained by correlating the scores on alternative forms of a measure. Alternative forms of a spelling test could be composed by selecting 60 spelling words from fourth-grade readers and randomly dividing them into two 30-item tests of spelling ability. An alternative form for an existing measure of achievement in arithmetic could be constructed by composing a collection of items that were similar to items in the existing test.

If alternative forms of a test exist, the two tests can be administered to a group of subjects. Each subject will then have a score on each test, and it is a straightforward matter to correlate the two tests with the regular PM equation (discussed in Chapter 4). The resulting correlation is called the *reliability coefficient*, and it is given the special symbol $r_{11}$. This symbolism is used because, in terms of the theory of reliability, one is correlating a test with itself (the alternative form intended to be a second version of the first test).

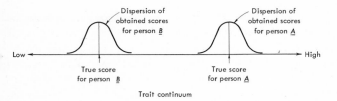

**FIGURE 5-3**    True scores and distributions of obtained scores for two persons

If $r_{11}$ is 1.00, there is no measurement error at all in either of the alternative forms. People are ordered exactly alike on the two forms, scores are entirely repeatable, and one can generalize with perfect accuracy from one test to the other. At the other extreme, if $r_{11}$ is zero, the theory of reliability (discussed in detail in Appendix D) leads to the conclusion that both measures are entirely unreliable, in which case the distributions of scores are distributions of pure errors. This would be like the situation in which the score for each person on each test was obtained from a toss of dice. Then we would expect to find a zero correlation between the "alternative forms."

Of course the reliability is usually somewhere between 1.00 and zero. The size of $r_{11}$ is a direct indication of the amount of reliability. The better, commercially distributed tests typically have reliability coefficients ranging between .80 and .95. (More detailed standards will be discussed later.)

For reasons which are discussed in detail in Appendix D, the correlation between alternative forms of a test $(r_{11})$ is an estimate of the *squared correlation* of either test with hypothetical true scores. The correlation of one test with true scores is symbolized as $r_{1t}$, and the correlation of the alternative form is symbolized as $r_{2t}$. Then the theory of reliability indicates that $r_{11}$ equals $r_{1t}^2$ and that $r_{11}$ equals $r_{2t}^2$.

Because the square of a positive correlation is always smaller than the correlation itself (unless the correlation is 1.00), the theory of reliability leads to the conclusion that the correlation of a test with true scores is larger than the correlation of that test with an alternative form. A moment's reflection will make it clear that this is a reasonable conclusion. If one could actually correlate scores on a test with the underlying true scores, there would be measurement error from only one source. There would probably be some measurement error in the test, but by definition, there would be no measurement error in the true scores. In contrast, when one correlates scores on alternative forms of a test, there are *two* sources of error. Consequently, $r_{11}$ is less than either of the hypothetical correlations $r_{1t}$ and $r_{2t}$.

To estimate how much more $r_{1t}$ and $r_{2t}$ are than $r_{11}$ requires one to make an assumption, which is that the amount of error in the two tests is approximately the same. (This is usually a reasonable assumption.) Then the theory of reliability (discussed in more detail in Appendix D) leads to the conclusion that $r_{11}$ equals the square of either $r_{1t}$ or $r_{2t}$.

In Chapter 4 it was shown that the square of any correlation equals the *percentage of variance* that one test explains in another. Then, since $r_{11}$ equals the square of either $r_{1t}$ or $r_{2t}$, it equals the percentage of true-score variance explainable by either of the alternative forms. If, for example, the correlation between alternative forms $(r_{11})$ is .80, one can say that each measure is 80 percent reliable. In that case, it would be equally meaningful to say that 20 percent of the variance in each test consists of measurement error. For the foregoing reasons, the reliability coefficient is such an important statistic that it should be determined for all new measures in psychology as well as in all areas of science.

## Estimation of true scores

The scores on a particular test are often spoken of as *fallible scores* because there is a degree of measurement error involved. In contrast, true scores are, in that sense, infallible. One can visualize a scatter diagram showing the relationship between the fallible scores on any test and true scores. This is illustrated in Figure 5-4.

According to the principles of correlational analysis discussed in Chapter 4, estimates of true scores in terms of deviation scores can be obtained as follows:

$$t' = r_{11}x_1 \qquad\qquad (5\text{-}1)$$

where

$t'$ = estimated true deviation scores
$x_1$ = deviation scores obtained on test 1
$r_{11}$ = reliability coefficient

## Standard error of measurement

Equation (5-1) provides only an estimate of true scores. The precision of the estimate is dependent on how well the reliability coefficient is determined.

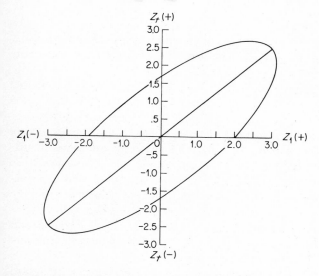

**FIGURE 5-4**    Regression line and scatter contour for hypothetical relationship between obtained scores and true scores

Some methods of estimating the reliability coefficient will be discussed in the following sections. Even if the reliability coefficient is determined in the most rigorous manner, there is still an element of error in the estimation of true scores.

Looking back at Equation (5-1), it can be seen that true scores are estimated from the reliability coefficient, which is a special kind of correlation coefficient. In Chapter 4 it was shown that the correlation coefficient not only provides a way of estimating one set of scores from another but also indicates the amount of error involved in the estimation: the standard error of estimate. The reliability coefficient can be used in a similar way to estimate the error dispersion of sample scores about true scores:

$$\sigma_{meas} = \sigma_1\sqrt{1 - r_{11}} \tag{5-2}$$

where

$\quad \sigma_{meas}$ = standard error of measurement
$\quad\quad \sigma_1$ = standard deviation of test 1
$\quad\quad r_{11}$ = reliability coefficient

Using the example above of a test with a standard deviation of 10 and a reliability coefficient of .90, the standard error of measurement would be obtained as follows:

$$
\begin{aligned}
\sigma_{meas} &= 10\sqrt{1 - .90} \\
&= 10\sqrt{.10} \\
&= 10 \times .333 \\
&= 3.33
\end{aligned}
$$

It must be kept in mind that the standard error of measurement ranges about the estimated true score for an individual, not, as is often mistakenly assumed, about the obtained score.

The score that a person makes on a test should never be taken as an exact point. First, it is necessary to recognize that measurement error tends to push scores out in both directions from the mean. High scores are usually overestimates of ability, and low scores are underestimates. Second, measurement error introduces a zone of uncertainty about each estimated true score, the size of which is indicated by the standard error of measurement. Consequently, an individual's score should be considered to lie somewhere in a band along the score continuum. The width of the band which is used depends on the precision with which scores will be interpreted. If we set the odds at 1 in 100 that the individual's score will not be overestimated or underestimated, the individual can be considered to lie in a band stretching 2.56 standard errors of measurement above and below his estimated true score.

If, as is reasonable to assume, measurement errors are normally distributed, statistics relating to the normal distribution (see Appendix B) can be used to establish odds in connection with the standard error of measurement. In

Appendix B it is shown that approximately 99 percent of the cases lie between plus 2.56 and minus 2.56 standard deviations about the mean. For this reason, we expect the odds to be that less than 1 score in a 100 will be more than 2.56 or less than 2.56 standard errors of measurement removed from the respective true scores.

The use of the standard error of measurement to set confidence intervals can be illustrated with the example above in which true scores for two persons are estimated to be 9 and −18, respectively, and the standard error of measurement is 3.33. The .01 confidence level would then lie 8.52 (2.56 times 3.33) score units above and below each estimated true score. For a person with an obtained score of 10 and an estimated true score of 9, the confidence band would stretch from .48 to 17.52. In other words, if the individual were given 100 sample tests which met the assumptions given earlier, we would expect to find only 1 of the 100 scores to be either less than .48 or greater than 17.52. Because most test scores are reported as integers, the confidence-zone limits could be rounded to the nearest whole numbers of 0 and 18. The .01 confidence band for a person with an obtained score of −20 and an estimated true score of −18 would extend from −26.52 to −9.48.

The measurement-error confidence band is often indicated by stating the individual's score as so much plus or minus 2.56 standard errors of measurement. For example, an IQ might be reported as 120 plus or minus 10. However, a common mistake is to space the confidence zone symmetrically about the obtained score rather than about the estimated true score. The correct procedure is to space the confidence zone either symmetrically about the estimated true score or asymmetrically about the obtained score. Illustrating the former, the scores in the example above could be phrased as 9 plus or minus 8.52 and −18 plus or minus 8.52. Using the latter approach, we would say that the scores are 10 plus 7.52 or minus 9.52 and −20 plus 10.52 or minus 6.52. Only if an individual's obtained score is exactly at the mean, and consequently the deviation score is zero, would the confidence zone be symmetrical. Then with a standard error of measurement of 3.33 in the example above, the score would be stated as zero plus or minus 8.52.

## The correction for attenuation

It was said earlier that unreliability tends to attenuate, or lower, the correlation of a test with any other variable. The theory of measurement error (see Appendix D) allows us to estimate how much the unreliability influences the predictive power of a test. For example, if we have correlated the scores on two tests and have made an estimate of the test reliability, we can predict what the correlation would be if one test were made perfectly reliable:

$$\bar{r}_{12} = \frac{r_{12}}{\sqrt{r_{11}}} \qquad (5\text{-}3)$$

where

$r_{11}$ = reliability estimate for test 1
$r_{12}$ = correlation of tests 1 and 2
$\bar{r}_{12}$ = estimate of how much test 1 would correlate with test 2 if test 1 were made perfectly reliable

Equation (5-3) can be illustrated in the situation where a test correlates .50 with a criterion and the test reliability is estimated as being .81:

$$\bar{r}_{12} = \frac{.50}{\sqrt{.81}}$$
$$= \frac{.50}{.9}$$
$$= .56$$

We would expect then that, as the test is made more and more reliable, its predictive validity will move toward .56.

The correction for attenuation is often said to estimate the "true" relationship between a test variable and a criterion; however, because of the assumptions which must be made, such estimates should always be taken with a "grain of salt." The correction can be inaccurate if an improper measure of reliability is made and/or if not enough subjects are employed to provide a stable estimate of the reliability. That such corrections are sometimes erroneous is dramatized by the fact that some corrected coefficients are greater than 1.00!

The correction for attenuation is helpful in indicating the improvement in predictive validity that might follow from an improvement in test reliability. In the early stages of a research program, it is often necessary to compose short and relatively unreliable tests. The correction for attenuation provides a helpful suggestion as to how well particular tests will work if they are lengthened and more highly standardized.

Whereas it is important to consider the measurement error in predictor tests, it is equally important to consider the measurement error in the criteria they are meant to forecast. In many situations, the criterion is less reliable than the predictor test. This is particularly true when the criterion consists of impressionistic ratings by foremen and supervisors. The reliability of the criterion can be used in the correction for attenuation as follows:

$$\bar{r}_{12} = \frac{r_{12}}{\sqrt{r_{22}}} \tag{5-4}$$

where

$\bar{r}_{12}$ = estimated correlation of a test with a completely reliable criterion
$r_{12}$ = correlation of a test with obtained criterion scores
$r_{22}$ = reliability of the criterion

If a predictor test correlates .32 with a criterion and the reliability of the criterion is .64, the correction for attenuation would be as follows:

$$\bar{r}_{12} = \frac{.32}{\sqrt{.64}}$$

$$= \frac{.32}{.8}$$

$$= .40$$

Whereas the correction for attenuation due to the unreliability of the predictor test is only an indication of the increased validity that might result from improving the predictor, the correction due to the unreliability of the criterion indicates how well the test "really" works at present. Predictor tests often work much better than the test-criterion correlations indicate. If, as is often the case, criteria are relatively unreliable, the predictors actually do a much better job than the correlations show. It is then quite sensible to correct for attenuation due to the criterion unreliability, as shown in Equation (5-4), to estimate the "real" test validity.

Finally, a double correction for attenuation can be made which considers the unreliability in both the predictor and the criterion:

$$\bar{r}_{12} = \frac{r_{12}}{\sqrt{r_{11}}\sqrt{r_{22}}} \tag{5-5}$$

where $r_{12}$ is the estimated correlation between a perfectly reliable predictor and a perfectly reliable criterion, and other symbols retain the meanings given above. For example, if a test correlates .36 with a criterion and if the reliabilities of the predictor and the criterion are .81 and .64, respectively, the correction would be as follows:

$$\bar{r}_{12} = \frac{.36}{\sqrt{.81}\sqrt{.64}}$$

$$= \frac{.36}{.9 \times .8}$$

$$= \frac{.36}{.72}$$

$$= .50$$

Not only can the correction for attenuation be made to estimate what a correlation would be if the test were made perfectly reliable, but it can also be used to estimate how much the predictive validity will rise if the reliability is raised by any particular amount (see Appendix D).

Although corrections for attenuation were illustrated with applied problems concerning relations between predictor tests and the criteria they are used to predict, such corrections are equally useful in basic research in psychology. In the early stages of basic research, it is frequently economical to work with short, modestly reliable instruments. The correlations are then attenuated by the modest reliability, and it is important to estimate the size of the "real" relationships that exist in nature. This can be done using the double correction for attenuation (Equation [5-5]). Also, it is useful to employ corrections for attenuation that estimate how much correlations will increase if reliabilities are increased by particular amounts (see Appendix D).

## sources of unreliability

It was stated that any random influence on test scores will cause unreliability. There are many ways in which this can happen in practice. Some of the most prominent sources of unreliability are discussed in the following sections.

### Poorly standardized instructions

If parts of the test instructions are given orally by the tester, there is always the possibility that testers will vary the instructions to the extent that measurement error will be introduced into the scores. The tester who gives inadequate instructions, failing, for example, to mention that the subjects can go back later to questions which are left blank initially, will penalize his group. If the tester is too lenient in setting the time limit for a test, the group will make higher scores than they would have with a strict adherence to time. If the test instructions vary in any way from group to group, the results of the test will tend to be unreliable.

When test instructions are not written as part of the examination booklet, a standard set of instructions should be made for all testers to read to their groups. In addition, all testers should adhere strictly to time limits and other standardized procedures.

### Errors in scoring tests

On multiple-choice tests, the errors in scoring are purely mechanical. If the test is scored "by hand," it is possible accidentally to score some correct answers as incorrect, and vice versa. Also, errors can be made in counting up the number of correct and incorrect answers for each person. If tests are machine-scored, an improperly functioning machine can add a considerable amount of measurement error to test scores.

The errors in scoring an essay examination are more subtle in character, but they also make for unreliability. One of the prime sources of unreliability in scoring essay examinations is the fact that different instructors use different grading standards. If three instructors teach different sections of the same course, they will probably have at least slightly different ideas about what kinds of answers merit good and bad marks. If each instructor grades his own examinations, the grade that a person gets is partly dependent on the instructor he happens to have.

Measurement error is also "built into" the individual instructor. If an instructor regrades a set of essay examinations after a period of time and there are no identifying marks to indicate what the earlier grades were, the grades will be somewhat different the second time. Measurement error also occurs when the instructor changes his standards as he grades a set of essay examinations. He might have strict standards at first, but as he goes through the papers and sees that none of them measure up, he is likely to become more lenient. Consequently, the grade a student receives is dependent on the chance appearance of his test in the order in which the tests were graded.

### Errors due to subjectivity of measurement

Closely related in kind to measurement error that occurs in the scoring of essay examinations are many other sources of measurement error due to the subjectivity of measurement. This is the case, for example, when foremen rate the effectiveness of workers, e.g., on an eight-step scale ranging from highly effective to highly ineffective. If a foreman rated the same men twice, without receiving any additional information about the men during the time between the two rating sessions, he would probably give somewhat different ratings on the two occasions. Also, if two foremen rate the same men, they are likely to disagree about some of the ratings. Thus the rating that a man receives is somewhat capriciously dependent on the time at which he is rated and/or on the person who performs the rating. These are obvious sources of measurement error.

An example from basic research is that in which trained observers make ratings of the amount of anxiety shown by subjects in an experiment concerning different kinds of psychological stress. Somewhat different ratings of the same subjects might be obtained from different observers, and there would be an element of guesswork in the ratings made by each observer.

Subjectivity of measurement does not necessarily mean that the results are unreliable. There are instances in which subjective measures are highly reliable, but this tends to be the case when the actions being measured are very obvious, e.g., when an examiner notes the number of times a rat looks to the left or right in a learning task. When complex traits are being measured by subjective ratings, however, measurement error is a very serious problem. This would be the case in the aforementioned examples concerning the rating of workers by foremen and the rating of anxiety by observers.

### Errors due to testing environment

An effort should be made to test subjects under uniform conditions. Carried to extremes, this rule becomes impossible to follow. However, gross differences in testing environment can be eliminated, such as those involving a lighting, noise level, and comfort of surroundings.

### Errors due to guessing

Many test items require the subject to identify a correct response rather than supply one. These are referred to as *identification items*, the simplest example of which is the true-false item. Other examples are items that require the subject to choose the best answer from among four alternatives and those which involve matching the answers in one list to questions in another list. Whenever the item requires identification of one or more correct responses, guessing plays a part in determining test scores. This can be illustrated in the situation in which two persons know the answers to half of the questions on a true-false test. They both correctly mark half of the items, and then they randomly guess (mentally flip a coin) on the remaining ones. Such guessing has two important effects on test scores. First, unless some type of correction for guessing is employed, guessing tends to raise scores. For example, even if true-false items were written in a foreign language with which the subject was totally unfamiliar, he could get approximately half of them right sheerly by random guessing. Also, since the persons who know the least tend to guess the most, guessing tends to increase the scores of less knowledgeable individuals more than the scores of more knowledgeable individuals. Second, and more important for the discussion here, guessing on identification items adds to other sources of measurement error since people differ with respect to the luck that will attend guessing on a particular test administration. For example, one person who guesses on half of the items on a true-false test might get 70 percent of the guessed items correct, whereas another person who guessed on exactly the same items would get only 30 percent of them correct. Obviously, such differences in obtained scores would obscure the fact that both persons have the same true score, which is another way of saying that such fortuitous differences add measurement error. (Effects of guessing on the psychometric properties of measuring instruments are considered in detail in Nunnally, 1967, Ch. 15.)

Effects of guessing on measurement error are inversely related to the number of alternative answers for items. At one extreme is the true-false test, where there is a 50-50 chance of getting items correct purely by guessing. At the other extreme, in a hypothetical multiple-choice test with 100 alternative answers for each item, very few answers would be correctly identified by guessing alone, and the variance over people in amount of luck would be quite small.

A free-response test, one in which the subject supplies the correct answer, is theoretically more reliable than a multiple-choice form. However, there are few subject matters which can be cast in the free-response form, the requirement being that there be only one word or term which represents the correct answer. The point to consider is that multiple-choice tests become more reliable as the number of alternative answers is increased. If the subject matter permits, a test will be more reliable if five or six alternatives are used for each item instead of only two or three.

### Errors due to sampling of content

If the object is to estimate an individual's score on a domain of content, the sampling of content for a particular test will introduce some unreliability.

Every student has had the feeling that he was "lucky" on a particular test, that of the many points covered in the course, the instructor happened to ask about those which he knew. Another student, with the same level of understanding about the course material as a whole, may have been "unlucky" in that he happened not to know the answers to the particular questions asked.

As in all sampling problems, the more items there are, the less unreliability will come from the sampling of items. Generally speaking, longer tests are more reliable than shorter ones. In order to reduce the unreliability due to sampling error, as many items as possible should be used (and also the items should range broadly over the subject matter). However, this is somewhat in opposition to reducing the unreliability due to guessing by providing as many alternatives for each item as possible. Because of the difficulties involved in constructing tests and the limited amount of time available for testing, some compromise must be reached between the need to have both many items and many alternative answers for each item. That is why many constructors of standard tests have sought a compromise solution in using about four or five alternatives, with as many items as time will permit.

In all objective tests (ones in which only negligible errors are due to scoring or subjectivity of measurement), the major source of measurement error is due to the sampling of content. If the sampling is either biased or not sufficiently extensive, resulting scores will not be highly reliable. For example, bias would be present in a test of spelling ability that was slanted toward items in athletics rather than toward words in general. An example of an insufficiently extensive sample would be an intelligence test that contained only 10 items, in which case scores would depend fortuitously on the individual's capability with respect to the particular small set of items employed. A larger number of items would result in more reliable (repeatable) scores.

## Errors due to fluctuations in the individual

A large portion of the measurement error in most tests is due to "chance" fluctuations in the individual which raise or lower his score. A fly lighting on the student's test, a broken pencil, a momentary distraction, a concern about the next school dance, a mistake in marking the answer sheet, and many more such chance events can influence test scores. Although such chance influences tend to average out over a long, well-standardized test, there always remains a component of unreliability due to fluctuations in the individual.

## Errors due to instability of scores

In most testing situations, an individual's score is expected to represent not only his immediate standing but also his standing for some time to come. The stability which is expected of scores is relative to the type of test. If students are given the same examination or a similar examination several weeks after the first testing, it is expected that the two sets of scores will correlate highly. Scores on intelligence tests are expected to remain relatively stable over long periods of time.   If a child's IQ goes up or down by as much as 10 points over a period of two years, it makes the test very difficult to use.   On the other hand, there are measures which are expected to change in relatively short periods of time.   If an experiment is being conducted to alter the attitudes of a group of students toward a political issue, it is expected that results of a test of attitudes given after the experiment will be different from those of a test given before the experiment.   Whenever individuals participate in an experiment, it is expected that changes of some kind will occur.   If measures remain absolutely stable during the study, there are no research findings to report, except that nothing has changed.

Instability of test scores acts much like the other sources of error to reduce the reliability.   If intelligence test scores obtained in the fourth grade are used to place children in special classes in the eighth grade and if the scores have fluctuated markedly during that time, the test scores will do a poor job of classifying the children.   If a child is being placed in a special class because the earlier testing showed he had an IQ of 125 and if a test given four years later shows he has an actual IQ of only 110, the original test score would give a faulty picture of the child's ability.   It is theoretically possible that a person's earlier scores will be more predictive than scores obtained at the time decisions are made about him, but this is almost never found in practice.   The safest assumption is that if scores are used over a period of time as an indication of an individual's standing and the scores are found to be unstable, the instability makes for unreliability.

## estimating the reliability coefficient

What has been said so far about the sources of measurement error and the influence of measurement error on test scores depends on the theory of reliability, the conditions of which were given earlier.   However, the theory is an idealization of the practical circumstances in which tests are used, and consequently we can only estimate the reliability coefficient rather than determine it directly.   There are a number of ways of estimating the reliability coefficient, each of which has its own advantages and disadvantages and each of which is concerned with a different kind of error.

### Retest method

The simplest approach to determining the reliability coefficient is to give the same test on two occasions.   The correlation between the two sets of scores will be an estimate of the reliability coefficient $r_{11}$, as it was denoted earlier.

There are two important disadvantages to using the retest method. The first is that the obtained reliability coefficient will reflect little of the error due to the sampling of content. The second is that the individual's memory of the answers he gave on the first test administration is quite likely to influence the answers he gives on the second. Such influences should diminish as the time between the two test administrations is lengthened, and therefore it is wise to wait at least several weeks before retesting. However, it is possible that memory will affect the second administration to some extent even if several years elapse between testings. Memory works to make the two sets of test scores correlate highly, and consequently the reliability coefficient is usually an overestimate when determined by the retest method.

There are three major instances in which the use of the retest method of estimating reliability is justified. The first is when time and/or funds are not available to construct two forms of the test. In that case the retest correlation will indicate the upper bound of the reliability. If the correlation is low, all is lost, because the reliability estimated by other methods will tend to be even lower. The second instance is that in which there is little reason to believe that memory has a significant effect in making scores on the two administrations similar. This would be the case when (1) there are many test items, say, over 100; (2) the items are difficult to remember; and (3) the retesting is done after a considerable period of time, say, after at least two months. These circumstances would exist in the case of a test consisting of ratings of the pleasantness of simple and complex geometric forms, where a total score concerning liking for complexity is obtained by summing the ratings of 200 geometric forms. A retest would then be made three months later. Because of the large number of ratings and the difficulty of remembering geometric forms, the retest correlation would provide a sensible estimate of the reliability coefficient. The third instance in which the retest method is justifiable is that in which content sampling is not at issue, but rather the need is to measure the repeatability of scores on a particular measuring instrument. This would be the case with many measures employed in controlled experiments, e.g., measures of reliability of reaction time with a particular apparatus. In such instances one is not interested primarily in the reliability as measured by alternative measuring instruments, but rather in the sheer repeatability of scores from the one instrument over different periods of time. Other than in the case of these three justifiable uses of the retest method, however, the methods of estimating the reliability coefficient discussed in the following sections are usually more defensible.

## Alternative-form method

Instead of using the same test on two occasions, it is better to use two *alternative* forms (also called *equivalent* forms and *parallel* forms). That is, instead of making up only one test form, two forms can be constructed which are very much alike. If, in constructing a test, explicit sampling procedures have been used (test items have been sampled from a large collection of relevant items), an alternative form can be obtained by the random selection of new items. However, in the construction of most tests, the sampling is not so exact: the items are simply collected across a broad range of the hypothetical domain of content without an explicit sampling. Then, to obtain an alternative form, the test constructor must try to make up a test that "looks" as much like the first form as possible. Sometimes this is a fairly easy task, for example, where the test contains spelling items, vocabulary items, or arithmetic items. However, it is difficult to compose alternative forms of some of the other tests of ability and many of the personality tests.

When the reliability coefficient is obtained from alternative forms, it will manifest more of the sources of measurement error, and more accurately, than any other method. It will contain all the sources of measurement error found in the retest method and, in addition, will give an indication of the amount of error due to the sampling of content. It is usually wise to separate the administrations of the equivalent forms by about two weeks, which will permit an assessment of the error caused by short-term fluctuations in psychological traits. Long-range stability can be investigated by employing much larger time intervals between test administrations. Although his memory of one test form may give the individual a slight advantage when taking the equivalent form, the effect of memory on the alternative-form reliability coefficient is slight. Were it not for the expense and the difficulties of making up and administering alternative forms, this method of reliability estimation would almost always be preferable to the retest method.

### Subdivided-test method

Instead of making up alternative forms, a compromise procedure has been to obtain "part scores" for different sections within the same test. The most popular of such procedures, referred to as the *split-half method*, consists in giving the individual one score on all the even-numbered questions in the examination and another score on the odd-numbered items. The two halves of the same test can then be correlated to obtain an estimate of the reliability coefficient. A statistical correction then must be made to estimate the reliability of the whole test, not just of the half tests (the correction is given and discussed in Appendix D).

Practical considerations have caused the subdivided-test method to be used as extensively as it has been. In many situations either it is too expensive to compose equivalent forms or it is not possible to obtain the same subjects for a second test administration. However, there are some serious flaws in the use of the subdivided-test method. Although the method determines some of the error due to the sampling of content, it does not do this as well as the alternative-form method. The subdivided test shows none of the error due to instability over time because both halves of the test are given at the same time. For these reasons, the subdivided-test method usually gives an overestimate of the reliability.

It is particularly misleading to use the subdivided-test method on a highly "speeded" test. Such a test would be, for example, one in which the subjects are asked to complete as many simple arithmetic problems as possible in a short period of time. If the problems are very simple, it is a test of how fast the individual can work. Then each person is likely to get nearly all the items correct as far as he goes, and individuals will differ mainly in terms of how many items they have completed when time is called. This works to make the individual's scores very much alike on the split halves. The odd and even scores will be alike on most of the items up to the point at which time is called because most of them will be correct. Also, the odd and even items will be alike beyond that point because they would all be incorrect. The split-half reliability estimate obtained on a purely speeded test, such as the one discussed here, would be meaningless. Fortunately, very few tests are concerned purely with speed. Most tests have some time limit simply as a practical way of getting the test completed, but time, as such, might have only a trivial influence on the scores. However, we should always be wary of split-half reliability estimates obtained on highly speeded tests.

## Methods concerning internal consistency

The individual who works in the field of testing will encounter special methods of reliability estimation based on homogeneity, or amount of correlation between the item responses within one test. The logic for measuring reliability in terms of the correlations between items within a test and equations for practical applications are discussed in Appendix D.

What the equations concerning homogeneity (or internal consistency) do is to estimate the correlation between an existing test and a hypothetical equivalent form, one that may never actually be constructed. To do this requires two major assumptions. The first is that the average correlation between the items within the existing test would be the same as the average correlation between the items in the hypothetical equivalent form. For example, if the average correlation between items in the existing test is .30, it must be assumed that the average correlation between items in the hypothetical equivalent form would also be .30. Second, it must be assumed that the average correlation *between* items in the two forms would be the same as the average correlation *within* the existing form. If the equivalent form actually existed, one could correlate each item on the first form with each item on the second form. Then, with respect to the foregoing example, if the average of those correlations is .30, the assumption is met.

Methods of estimating reliability based on internal consistency sometimes fail to take full account of two major sources of measurement error. Most importantly, the methods do not consider measurement error due to changes in scores over time. This would be a serious problem with measures that are thought to change markedly over time, such as a measure of daily moods. A less important problem is that methods based on internal consistency do not always take full account of the measurement error due to the sampling of content. This is so because there are subtle factors working to make the items within a test correlate more highly with one another than they would correlate with the items on an equivalent form. For example, one frequently uses up most of the "good" items that he can think of in constructing the first test, and consequently items on the second test are frequently of a slightly different kind, e.g., slightly different kinds of spelling words or statements relating to anxiety. In spite of the aforementioned potential dangers of employing methods of reliability estimation based on item correlations, it is surprising how well these methods tend to work in practice. Even if some other method of estimating the reliability coefficient is employed, valuable information is always obtained from methods based on item correlations.

The most generally useful equation for estimating reliability on the basis of internal consistency is called *coefficient alpha*. A shortcut version of the equation that is useful with dichotomously scored items (e.g., multiple-choice items) is *Kuder-Richardson formula 20*, referred to as KR-20. These equations usually provide good estimates of the reliability obtained from correlating alternative forms. They are straightforwardly computed from item statistics, requiring one to know only the variance of scores on each item and the variance of total test scores. The formulas are presented, illustrated, and discussed in detail in Appendix D.

Methods based on item correlations are superior to methods based on subdivided tests because there are so many different ways of subdividing a test. The reliability estimates obtained from these different approaches frequently differ appreciably from one another. Essentially, the methods based on item correlations estimate the average of the reliability coefficients that would be obtained from all possible ways of subdividing the items on a test, which obviously means that the methods based on item correlations are superior to any particular method based on subdivided tests.

### Measurement of stability

Most psychologists prefer to consider the measurement of stability of scores over time a separate problem from the measurement of the other sources of error variance. As was said previously, stability is expected of some instruments and not of others.   Also, whether or not it is necessary for test scores to remain stable depends on the way in which the test is used.   If an instrument is used over a number of years to make predictions, then stability of scores is essential.

It should be obvious that stability can be measured only by the retest and the alternative-form techniques and not by the subdivided-test techniques and methods concerning internal consistency.   Stability can be measured either by retesting or, preferably, by administering equivalent forms over the range of time in which the test is used to make predictions.   The measurement of stability is of more theoretical interest than practical importance.   It is usually unsafe to use test scores obtained at one time to make predictions or counsel individuals at a much later time.   It is better to give tests at the time decisions must be made about individuals.   The measurement of stability is primarily important in helping us understand how human attributes develop and change.

In using either the retest or the alternative-form technique for measuring reliability, it is customary to space the test administrations several days to a month or more apart.   This is done not so much to measure stability over time as to measure errors due to "chance" fluctuations in the individual.   It is reasonable to expect day-to-day fluctuations in moods and physical conditions to influence test scores.   If the two test administrations occurred on the same day or only several days apart, there would be an insufficient basis for measuring the errors due to fluctuating moods and physical conditions.   Also, if the time span between administrations is very short, individuals will remember the first test and will tend to repeat their work habits, guessing behavior, and characteristic mistakes on the second test.

## the reduction of measurement error

Because of the tendency for errors of measurement to lower test validity regardless of the sense in which validity is determined, unreliability is "bad" in any measurement situation.   No definite rule can be stated as to how high the reliability coefficient should be for a test, but in general one is suspicious of a test that has a coefficient under .80.   Some of the better-standardized instruments have reliability coefficients over .90.

What constitutes "good" reliability depends very much on the way an instrument is used.   Paradoxical as it may seem, it is usually more important to have high reliability for measures used in applied psychology than for measures used in basic research.   In basic research, corrections can be made for attenuation of correlation coefficients, and, as was illustrated earlier in this chapter, such corrections frequently do not grossly change the obtained correlations. For example, if two measures correlate .40 and they both have reliabilities of .80, the corrected correlation is only .50.   Thus in basic research one typically does not lose a great deal because of moderate amounts of measurement error.

When working in applied psychology, one must be concerned about the fate of each individual; therefore, one must take account of the standard error of measurement, discussed earlier in this chapter. When, for example, the reliability of a test is no higher than .80, $\sigma_{est}$ is approximately one-third as large as the standard deviation of the criterion variable. Imagine, then, the gross mistakes that would be made in selecting students for college, making decisions about patients in mental hospitals, and assigning men to training programs in the armed forces. When important decisions must be made about people on the basis of psychological tests, even reliabilities of .90 are not high enough.

It must be remembered that measurement error is important only because it attenuates test validity. If a predictor test has a high correlation with its criterion, reliability is no problem. The test constructor is concerned with measurement error when a test fails to predict its criterion. It is sometimes found that the low predictive power of the test is due to unreliability from one or more of the error sources described previously. By removing some of the sources of measurement error, the predictive power of the test can be increased.

### Increased standardization

Rather than worry about unreliability after it has occurred, it is primarily important to remove as many sources of measurement error as possible when the test is being constructed. Anything that works to standardize the test instructions and procedures of administration, to prevent errors in scoring, to equate testing environments, and to lower the influence of guessing will make a test more reliable. Errors in the sampling of content can be reduced to some extent by either an actual sampling of items or a careful effort to range the items across a defined domain of materials. However, even with the best sampling of items, there will be some sampling error because of the limited number of items in any test.

It is often erroneously assumed that the need for test standardization requires that tests be given under the most comfortable conditions possible. The requirement is that all subjects be treated in the *same* way. A particular test may be most valid if the subjects are told little about the instrument or if they are purposely confused. It may also promote test validity if the subjects are purposely distracted and harassed while the test is being administered.

### Increasing the number of items

After all efforts have been made to increase test standardization, the reliability can be raised by making the test longer. The increased length will act to reduce the errors due to "guessing," the errors due to the sampling of content, and the errors due to fluctuations in the individual. If we make several reasonable assumptions about the effect of lengthening a test, we can predict how much the reliability will be raised by increasing the number of items (the equation is presented and explained in Appendix D).

## Residual errors

In spite of the tester's best efforts, some measurement error will remain, and there will be considerably more in some tests than in others. In some of the personality inventories where the individual is asked value questions, the scores will inevitably be unreliable. Similarly, nothing can be done to remove errors due to instability over time, which are errors only in the sense that they hinder predictions. If the trait being measured fluctuates over short periods of time, the test will be of little use in predicting behavior. For example, it is relatively meaningless to give interest tests to grammar school students for the purpose of planning future training. Children change their minds markedly in relatively short periods of time concerning what they want to study and work at professionally in the future.

## Interpretation of reliability coefficients

All commercial tests should report complete reliability data (see APA, 1954). If the test manual either gives no reliability information or states a reliability coefficient without saying how it was determined, the test should be viewed with suspicion. In particular, the manual should tell the standard deviation of scores for the group on which the reliability estimate was made. The reliability estimate is a correlation coefficient, and as is true of all correlations, its size is directly dependent on the dispersion, or standard deviation, of scores. The reliability coefficient is directly meaningful only when the standard deviation of test scores is the same as the standard deviation for the group with which the test will be used. It was said in Chapter 4 that the standard error of estimate tends to remain unchanged with changes in test dispersion but that the correlation coefficient tends to change with the dispersion. Similarly, the standard error of measurement tends to remain the same with changes in the dispersion of test scores, and the reliability coefficient becomes larger as more diverse groups are studied.

If a test is being constructed to predict success for college applicants and a reliability study is being made of the test, the group used in the reliability study should have a standard deviation of test scores which is very nearly the same as that of the total group of applicants. If the reliability study is made on a group of freshmen, the individuals who were refused admission will not be included, and consequently the standard deviation of scores in the reliability study will be too small. The reliability coefficient will then be an underestimate. If the standard deviations are known both for the whole group and the subgroup which is used in the reliability study, statistical correlations can be made (see Thorndike, 1949).

There have been cases where the erroneously high reliability coefficients which have been reported in test manuals were obtained by computing the coefficients on groups of subjects more diverse than those in which the tests were actually to be used. This has been done most frequently in determining the reliability of raw scores or mental ages on intelligence tests by using groups of children ranging in age from, say, nine through twelve years. This makes the standard deviation of scores much larger than would be the case if a representative sample had been obtained at one age level only.

If a test is to be used consistently, and especially if it is a commercially published instrument, thorough reliability studies should be made. The results should then be fully reported, including (1) the method used to estimate the reliability coefficient, (2) the standard deviations of scores, (3) the standard error of measurement, and (4) a description of the sample of persons used in the reliability study.

## Summary

The reliability of measurement methods concerns essentially the repeatability (or generalizability) from (1) one version of a measuring instrument to equivalent versions, (2) one user of a measuring instrument to another user, and (3) one time and circumstance to other times and circumstances. To the extent to which repeatability is not obtained in those ways, measurement error is at work. Measurement error is always "bad," in the sense that it obscures lawful relations in nature, e.g., produces an uneven curve of relationship between two variables when errorless measurement would have shown a smooth curve or produces a lower correlation between two tests than would have been obtained from highly reliable forms.

The major factors producing measurement error are (1) inadequate sampling of content; (2) relatedly, insufficient number of test items; (3) subjectivity of scoring items; (4) poor standardization of instructions and other circumstances surrounding the testing; and (5) changes over short periods of time in the traits of persons being measured. The ideal method of estimating the reliability coefficient is one that takes account of as many of the foregoing sources of measurement error as possible. The alternative-form method accomplishes this, the forms being administered two weeks to a month or so apart. When subjectivity of scoring is an issue, the forms should be scored by different persons.

In some circumstances, other methods of estimating the reliability coefficient may be used in place of, or in addition to, the method of alternative forms.

Under the conditions discussed in this chapter, the retest method is sometimes either the logical method to employ or a defensible way to circumvent the expense of constructing an alternative form for an existing instrument. Even if the alternative-form method is used, it is also wise to apply one of the equations based on internal consistency (Appendix D). In most cases the obtained reliability coefficients are very similar; any major differences would provide valuable information.

A good estimate of the reliability coefficient serves two major functions. First, it leads to many statistical equations for estimating effects of measurement error and relations that would exist if less measurement error were present. Second, and generally more importantly, it provides a useful index of the extent to which results of an instrument can be trusted in applied work or basic research in psychology.

Finally, the reader should be reminded that reliability is a necessary but not sufficient condition for validity. A totally unreliable measurement method cannot possibly produce meaningful scientific findings, but there are enumerable, highly reliable measurement methods that do not explain anything of importance in the domain of science.

## Suggested additional readings

American Psychological Association. *Technical recommendations for psychological tests and diagnostic techniques.* Washington: Author, 1954.

Guilford, J. P. *Psychometric methods.* (2nd ed.) New York: McGraw-Hill, 1954. Ch. 14.

Gulliksen, H. *Theory of mental tests.* New York: Wiley, 1950. Chs. 10, 15, 16.

Nunnally, J. C. *Psychometric theory.* New York: McGraw-Hill, 1967. Chs. 6, 7.

Thorndike, R. L. Reliability. In E. F. Lindquist (Ed.), *Educational measurement.* Washington: American Council on Education, 1951. Pp. 560–620.

# CHAPTER 6

# Validity of measurement methods

As was said in Chapter 5, a test may be highly reliable and yet not be a valid measure of anything. A crucially important phase in the development of a measuring instrument concerns learning whether or not the instrument is useful for any purpose. This phase is usually spoken of as determining the *validity* of an instrument. The term has some misleading connotations, but it is too well ingrained in the literature to permit an easy transition to terms that more properly denote the processes involved; consequently, the term is used in this book, although efforts are made to distinguish sharply between the different meanings which "validity" can have.

In a very general sense, a measuring instrument is valid if it does what it is intended to do. Proper performance of some instruments is rather easily verified, e.g., of the yardstick as a measure of length. It takes very little "research" with this instrument to find that resulting measurements (1) fit in perfectly with axiomatic concepts of the nature of length and (2) relate to many other variables. If all measures so perfectly met these standards, there would be little need to consider the validation of measuring instruments, but such is not the case. For example, whereas it might seem highly sensible to develop measures of emotions from physiological indices such as heart rate, muscle tone, and palmar sweat, it has proved very difficult to find combinations of such indices to measure various emotions. So it is with many proposed measures in the physical, biological, and behavioral sciences: what seem to be good approaches to measurement on an intuitive basis fail to produce the desired empirical results.

Validation always requires empirical investigations, the nature of the evidence required depending on the type of validity. Validity is a matter of degree rather than an all-or-none property, and validation is an unending process. Whereas measures of length and of some other simple physical attributes may have proved their merits so well that no one seriously considers changing to other measures, most measures should be kept under constant surveillance to make sure they are behaving as they should. New evidence may suggest modifications of an existing measure or the development of a new and better approach to measuring the attribute in question, e.g., anxiety, intelligence, or the temperature of stars.

Strictly speaking, one validates not a measuring instrument but rather some use to which the instrument is put. For example, a test used to select college freshmen must be valid for that purpose, but it would not necessarily be valid for other purposes, such as measuring how well students have mastered the curriculum in high school. Whereas an achievement test in spelling might be valid for that purpose, it might be nearly worthless for other purposes, such as forecasting success in high school. Similarly, a valid measure of the response to stressful experimental treatments would not necessarily be a valid measure of neuroticism or anything else. Although a measure may be valid for many different purposes, as intelligence tests are, the validity with which each purpose is served must be supported by evidence.

Psychological measures serve three major purposes: (1) establishment of a functional relationship with a particular variable, (2) representation of a specified universe of content, and (3) measurement of psychological traits. Corresponding to these are three types of validity: (1) predictive validity, (2) content validity, and (3) construct validity. Examples of measures intended to serve those purposes are a test for selecting college freshmen, a test for measuring spelling ability in the fifth grade, and a measure of anxiety. Each of these three types of validity will be discussed in turn.

## predictive validity

Predictive validity is at issue when the purpose is to use an instrument to estimate some important form of behavior, the latter being referred to as the *criterion*. The example given above was that of a test employed to select college freshmen. The test, whatever it is like, is useful in that situation only if it accurately estimates successful performance in college. The criterion in this case would probably be grade-point average obtained over four years of college. After the criterion is obtained, the validity of a prediction function is straightforwardly, and rather easily, determined. Primarily it consists of correlating scores on the predictor test with scores on the criterion variable. The size of the correlation is a direct indication of the amount of validity.

The term "prediction" will be used in a general (and ungrammatical) sense to refer to functional relations between an instrument and events occurring before, during, and after the instrument is applied. Thus a test administered to adults could be used to make "predictions" about events that occurred in their childhood. A test intended to predict brain damage is, of course, intended not to forecast who will suffer brain damage at some time in the future but rather to predict who does and who does not have brain damage at the time the test is administered. When a test is used to predict success in college, "prediction" properly means "forecasting." Others have referred to predictive validity at those three points in time as "postdiction," "concurrent validity," and "prediction," respectively. The fact that different terms are used, however, suggests that the logic and procedures of validation are different, which is not true. In each case a predictor measure is related to a criterion measure, and after the data are available, it does not matter when they were obtained. The nature of the problem dictates when the two sets of measurements are obtained. Thus to forecast success in college, it is necessary to administer the predictor instrument before students go to college, and to obtain the criterion of success in college, it is necessary to wait four years.

Predictive validity is determined by, and only by, the degree of correspondence between the two measures involved. If the correlation is high, no other standards are necessary. Thus if it were found that accuracy in horseshoe pitching correlated highly with success in college, horseshoe pitching would be a valid measure for predicting success in college. This is not meant to imply that sound theory and common sense are not useful in selecting predictor instruments for investigation, but after the investigations are done, the entire proof of the pudding is in the correlations.

Perhaps because of the simplicity of the ideas and the related methods of research, up to about 1950 it was frequently said that the validity of a measure was indicated by the correlation between the measure and its criterion. Actually, predictive validity is seldom the important issue in psychological science; concepts of validity which will be discussed later are of much more importance. Predictive validity is the major issue only in certain types of applied problems in psychology and education, e.g., in using tests to select office clerks, civil service workers, and officer candidates for the armed forces and in making decisions about the hospitalization and treatment of mental patients.

In no other area is predictive validity as important as it is in using tests to help make decisions about schooling. In schools, predictive validity is at issue in measures of "readiness." Thus, for underage children, a test of readiness for the first grade is valid only to the extent that it predicts how well children

will perform in the first grade.   A test used to divide children into different
ability levels is valid only to the extent that it predicts how well children will
do in their different levels of instruction.   A test used to select students for
special programs of study in high school is valid only to the extent that it
actually predicts performance in those programs.   And so it is with all other
tests used for the selection and placement of students—they are valid only to
the extent that they serve predictive functions well.

Clear as the difference may seem, some people confuse predictor instruments
with the criteria they are meant to predict.   A story (a true one) will help to
illustrate this confusion.   A college graduate applied for entrance to a graduate
training program to work toward a master's degree.   He failed to score sufficiently high on an entrance examination (a predictor test), but was given
special permission to enter on a trial basis.   Once in training, he performed
very well, doing better than most of his fellow students.   Near the end of this
student's training, the dean of the college insisted that he would need to retake
the entrance examination and make a satisfactory grade before his degree could
be granted!   Many other equally foolish examples could be given to show how
predictor tests are confused with the criteria they are meant to predict.

Whereas it is easy to talk about correlating a predictor test with its criterion,
in actuality obtaining a good criterion may be more difficult than obtaining a
predictor test.   In many cases either no criterion is available or the criteria that
are available suffer from various faults.

## content validity

For some instruments, validity depends primarily on the adequacy with which
a specified domain of content is sampled.   A prime example would be a final
examination for a course in American history.   Obviously, the test could not
be validated in terms of predictive validity because the purpose of the test is
not to predict something else but to *directly measure* performance in a unit of
instruction.   The test must stand by itself as an adequate measure of what it
is supposed to measure.   Validity cannot be determined by correlating the
test with a criterion because the test itself *is* the criterion of performance.

Even if one argued that course examinations should be validated in terms of
correlations with other behaviors, what behaviors would serve as adequate criteria?   A student might, by any standard, deserve an A in the course but never
take another course in history or ever work in a position where knowledge
gained in the course would be evidenced.   Of course, one would expect a test
to correlate with some other variables, and the size of such correlations would
provide hints about the adequacy of the test.   For example, one would expect
to find a substantial correlation between scores on the final examination in
introductory psychology and scores on the final examination in abnormal psy-

chology (for those students who took both courses). If the correlation was zero, it would make us suspect that something was wrong with one or both of the examinations (or with one or both of the units of instruction). However, such correlations would offer only hints about the validity of the examinations, the final proof resting on the adequacy with which content had been sampled.

There are many other examples of measures that require content validity. Such is the case with all course examinations, in all types of training programs, and at all levels of training. All achievement tests require content validity, as would be the case, for example, with a comprehensive measure of progress in school up to the end of the fourth grade or a comprehensive measure of the extent to which men had performed well in a school for electronics technicians in the armed forces.

Rather than test the validity of measures such as those discussed above after they are constructed, one should *ensure* validity by the plan and procedures of construction. To take a very simple example, an achievement test in spelling for fourth-grade students could obtain its content from a random sampling of words occurring in widely used readers. The plan is to randomly sample from a specified domain of content, and most potential users of the test should agree that this procedure ensures a reasonably representative collection of words. In addition, a sensible procedure would be required for transforming the words into a test. It might, for example, be decided to compose items by putting each correctly spelled word in with three misspellings and requiring the student to circle the correct one. Other decisions would need to be made about ordering the items in the test and about the oral or written instructions to students. These and other details are part of the plan for selecting content and for test construction. The validity of the measure is judged by the character of the plan and by the apparent skill with which the plan has been carried out. If most potential users of the test, or at least most persons in positions of responsibility, agree that the plan was sound and well carried out, the test has a high degree of content validity.

The simple example above illustrates the two major standards for ensuring content validity: (1) a representative collection of items and (2) "sensible" methods of test construction. Of course, in most instances these standards are not so easy to judge as was the case with the spelling test. Often it is logically impossible or unfeasible actually to sample content. For example, how would one sample (in a strict sense of the word) items for an achievement test in geography? Neither the sampling unit nor the domain is well specified. One could sample sentences from textbooks and turn them into true-false items, but for obvious reasons such a test would not be adequate. Rather, what is done in such instances is to *formulate* a collection of items that broadly represents the unit of instruction. To ensure that the items actually represent the unit of instruction, it is necessary to have a detailed outline, or blueprint, of the kinds of questions and problems that will be included. (How such outlines are developed and used is explained in a number of introductory texts on educational and psychological measurement, e.g., Cronbach, 1960; Nunnally, 1964; Thorndike & Hagen, 1961.)   In such cases, judging the quality of the outline is an important part of assessing content validity.

The simple example of a random sampling of content is unrealistic in most situations for a second reason: The selection of content usually involves questions of values.   Thus, for the spelling test, one might decide that it is more important to measure performance on nouns, adjectives, and verbs than performance on other parts of speech; consequently one would restrict sampling to those types of words.   In an achievement test for arithmetic, one might decide that it is more important to stress questions concerning quantitative concepts than those on numerical computations.   And so it is with nearly all measures based on content validity: values determine the relative stress on different types of content.   Of course, where values are important, there are differences in values between people; consequently, there is usually some disagreement about the proper content coverage of particular tests.   Also, since values sometimes change, it can be expected that a test which is viewed today as having high content validity may not be considered so well in that regard later.   The values behind the construction of a measure should be made explicit, e.g., in test manuals, and it should be indicated how those values guided formulation of the test outline and the construction of items.

Content validity also becomes somewhat complex when trying to ensure that "sensible" methods of test construction are employed.   This is not much of a problem with spelling tests because it is relatively easy to construct items that most people will agree are satisfactory.   It requires much more skill, however, to construct items in some other domains of content, e.g., geography, history, and salesmanship training, and there is often controversy about the employment of different types of items (the word "item" referring broadly to questions, problems, worksamples, and other evidence of accomplishment).

Even though there are often problems involved in ensuring content validity, inevitably content validity rests mainly on appeals to reason regarding the adequacy with which important content has been sampled and on the adequacy with which the content has been cast in the form of test items.   In addition there are various methods of analyzing data obtained from the test which will provide important circumstantial evidence.   For example, at least a moderate level of internal consistency among the items within a test would be expected; i.e., the items should tend to measure something in common.   (Methods for performing such analyses will be described in Chapter 8.)   This is not an infallible guide, however, because with some subject matters it is reasonable to include materials that tap somewhat different abilities.   For example, abilities for numerical computation are not entirely the same as those for grasping some of the essential ideas about quantification, but a good argument could be made for mixing these two types of content to measure overall progress in arithmetic.

Another type of circumstantial evidence for content validity is obtained by comparing performance on a test before and after a period of training. If the test is intended to measure progress in training, scores should increase from before to after, and the improvement in scores on individual items can be considered evidence for the validity of those items. There are, however, numerous flaws in this line of reasoning. An item can be obviously trivial and yet show marked changes from the beginning to the end of the course, e.g., spelling of the teacher's name. Many students would not be able to spell the teacher's name correctly on the first day of school, but nearly all would be able to do so on the last day. Conversely, on some very important items there may be little change over time, but that may be due to inadequacy of texts, lack of skill on the part of teachers, or the students' laziness.

Another type of evidence for content validity is obtained from correlating scores on different tests purporting to measure much the same thing, e.g., two tests published by different commercial firms for the measurement of achievement in reading. It is comforting to find high correlations in such instances, but this does not guarantee content validity. Both tests may measure the same wrong things.

In spite of efforts on the part of some to settle every issue about psychological measurement by a flight into statistics, content validity is settled mainly in other ways. Although helpful hints are obtained from analyses of empirical findings, content validity rests mainly upon an appeal to the propriety of content and the way that it is presented.

## construct validity

Whereas up to 1950 most textbooks on measurement spoke only of predictive validity and content validity, actually those two types of validity are important mainly in only certain types of measurement problems in applied psychology. Predictive validity is important in selecting students for college, placing soldiers in special courses of training, making decisions about the treatment of mental patients, and placing people on jobs. Content validity is important for examining progress in elementary school, studying the effectiveness of different methods for training accountants, and assigning grades to college students. Whereas these and other measurement problems are of vast practical importance, such applied problems are not close to the measurement problems that occur in the basic science of psychology.

Like all basic science, psychological science is concerned with establishing functional relations between important variables. (What is an "important" variable is determined either by intuition or by the content of psychological theories.) Of course, variables must be measured before they can be related to one another in experiments, and for statements of relationship to have any meaning, each measure must, in some sense, validly index what it is purported to measure. Examples of important variables in psychology are reaction time, habit strength, intelligence, anxiety, drive level, and degree of frustration. How does one validate measures of such variables? Take, for example, an experiment in which a particular treatment is hypothesized to increase anxiety. Can the measure of anxiety be validated as a predictor of some specific variable? No, it cannot, because the purpose is to measure the amount of anxiety then and there, not to estimate scores on any other variable obtained in the past, present, or future. Also, the measure cannot be validated purely in terms of content validity. There is no obvious body of "content" (behaviors) corresponding to anxiety reactions, and if there were, how to measure such content would be far more of a puzzle that it is with performance in arithmetic.

The degree to which it is necessary and difficult to validate measures of psychological variables is proportional to the degree to which the variable is concrete or abstract. A highly concrete variable would be reaction time, which would be measured, say, by the length of time taken to press a button on a given signal. How quickly subjects press the button *is* the variable of interest, and how to measure the variable is rather obvious. Specialists in studies of reaction time might quibble over microscopically fine differences in measurement techniques, but such slight differences in measurement methods would have scant effects on experimental results. In this case the operations of measurement are of direct interest, and there is no need to "validate" the measure; consequently, the researcher can go about the business of finding interesting relations between that measure and other variables. However, very few variables are so obviously manifested in simple operations. In most instances the particular operations are meant to measure a variable which extends well beyond the operations in question. Consider the use of an activity wheel for investigations with rats. How rapidly the rat treads the wheel is really of little interest in itself, except to the extent that it represents a general level of activity that logically should be manifested in many ways, e.g., in the amount of movement around the floor of a box. Thus the intention is to measure a somewhat abstract variable of activity level, and consequently the validity of any particular measure is open to question. So it is with most measures: they represent efforts to measure relatively abstract variables, ones that are thought to be evidenced in a variety of forms of behavior and not perfectly so in any one of them.

To the extent that a variable is abstract rather than concrete, we speak of it as being a *construct*. Such a variable is literally a construct in that it is something that the scientist puts together from his own imagination, something that does not exist as an isolated, observable dimension of behavior. A construct represents a hypothesis (usually only half formed) that a variety of behaviors will correlate with one another in studies of individual differences and/or will be similarly affected by experimental treatments.

It is important to realize that all theories in science concern mainly statements about constructs rather than about specific, observable variables. A prime example of confusion in this regard concerns the final oral examination of a Ph.D. candidate who had investigated the effects of different drugs on the speed with which mice would swim through a water maze filled with cold water. The dependent measure was time taken to traverse the maze. The candidate spoke of the dependent measure as representing "reaction to stress," the cold water supposedly being stressful to the mice. A member of the examining committee objected to speaking of the dependent measure as representing reaction to stress and took the student to task for not sticking to a description of the experimental results purely in terms of the observables, i.e., mice swimming in cold water. Both the student and the committee member were partly right and partly wrong. By speaking of the dependent measure as representing reaction to stress, the student assumed that the measure had a generality far beyond the actual observables. By suggesting that science is concerned only with the particular observables in an experiment, the committee member was painting a very faulty picture. No one really cares how rapidly mice swim in cold water. The particular measure is of interest only to the extent that it partly mirrors performance in a variety of situations that all concern "stress" or some other construct.

Scientists cannot do without constructs. Their theories are populated with them, and even in informal conversation scientists find it all but impossible to discuss their work without using words relating to constructs. It is important to keep in mind not only that proposed measures of constructs need to be validated for that purpose but also that science is concerned primarily with developing measures of constructs and finding functional relations between measures of different constructs.

Constructs vary widely in the extent to which the domain of related observable variables is (1) large or small and (2) tightly or loosely defined. Regarding point 1, in some cases the domain of related variables is so small that any one of the few observable variables in the domain will suffice to measure the construct. This is true of reaction time, where, as mentioned previously, the alternative methods of measuring are so few and so closely related that any one of them can be spoken of as measuring reaction time without doing much injustice to the "construct." At a higher level of complexity, activity level in the rat should logically be manifested in at least a score of observables, and as it turns out, some of these do not correlate well with others. At the extreme of complexity are constructs like anxiety and intelligence, where the domains of related observables are vast indeed.

Considerations in point 1 above tend to correlate with considerations in point 2: The larger the domain of observables related to a construct, the more difficult it tends to be to define which variables do or do not belong in the domain. Thus it might be relatively easy to get psychologists to agree about whether or not a particular observable should be related to activity level, e.g., a measure of muscle tone. The boundaries of this domain are relatively well prescribed. In contrast, for many constructs the domain of related observables has "fuzzy edges," and the scientist is not sure of the full meanings of his own constructs. Typically, the scientist holds a firm belief about some of the more prominent observables related to the construct, but beyond that he can only guess how far the construct extends. In measuring the construct of intelligence, for example, all would agree that the construct should be evidenced to some extent in various types of problems involving reasoning abilities, but the extent to which some measures of perceptual and memory abilities should be considered part of the construct is a matter of dispute. Such is the case with most constructs: the boundaries of the domain of related observables are not clear.

Because constructs concern domains of observables, logically a better measure of any construct would be obtained by combining the results from a number of measures of such observables than by taking any one of them individually. Since, however, the work is often tedious enough with one measure, let alone a handful, it is sometimes asking too much of the scientist to expect him to employ more than one measure in a particular investigation. Thus any particular measure can be thought of as having a degree of construct validity depending on the extent to which results obtained from using the measure would be much the same if some other measure—or, hypothetically, all the measures —in the domain had been employed in the experiment. Similarly, the combined scores from a number of measures of observables in the domain can be thought of as having a degree of construct validity for the domain as a whole.

The logical status of constructs concerning individual differences is the same as that of constructs concerning the results of controlled experiments. Thus whereas the construct of intelligence is more frequently discussed with respect to studies of individual differences and the construct of habit strength is more frequently discussed with respect to controlled experiments, problems of construct validity are essentially the same for both. (Of course, in different studies a construct may be investigated as the dependent variable in a controlled experiment or in terms of correlations between sources of individual differences, but most measures are used predominantly in one or the other of the two types of studies.)

If the measurement of constructs is a vital part of scientific activity, how then are such measures developed and validated? There are three major aspects of the process: (1) specifying the domain of observables; (2) determining to what extent all, or some, of those observables correlate with one another or are affected alike by experimental treatments; and (3) determining whether or not one, some, or all measures of such variables *act* as though they measured the construct. Aspect 3 consists of determining whether or not a supposed measure of a construct correlates in expected ways with measures of other constructs or is affected in expected ways by particular experimental treatments.  These steps are seldom, if ever, purposefully planned and undertaken by any investigator or group of investigators.  Also, although it could be argued that the aspects should be undertaken in the order 1, 2, 3, this order is seldom, if ever, followed.  More likely, a psychologist will develop a particular measure that is thought to partake of a construct, and then he will leap directly to aspect 3 and perform a study relating the supposed measure of the construct to measures of other constructs, e.g., correlating a particular measure of anxiety with a particular measure of response to frustration.  Typically, other investigators will develop other particular measures of the same construct, and skipping aspects 1 and 2, they will move directly to aspect 3 and try to find interesting relations between their measures and measures of other constructs.  As the number of proposed measures of the same construct grows and as suspicion that they might not all measure the same thing increases, one or more investigators seek to outline in writing the domain of observables related to the construct, which is aspect 1.  All or parts of one or more such outlines of the domain are subjected to investigation to determine the extent to which variables in the domain tend to measure the same thing, which is aspect 2.  The impact of theorizing with respect to aspect 1 and the research results from aspect 2 tend to influence which particular variables are studied in aspect 3.

Since most scientists work as individuals rather than being tied to some overall plan of attack on a problem, each scientist does much what he pleases, and consequently there is seldom a planned, concentrated effort to develop valid measures of constructs according to a step-by-step procedure.  Instead of the domain of observables for any construct being tightly defined initially (aspect 1), more likely the nature of the domain will be *suggested* by numerous attempts to develop particular measures relating to the construct, and subsequently some investigators will attempt more explicitly to outline the domain of content.  Instead of the planned frontal attack on the empirical investigations required in aspects 2 and 3, more likely evidence will *accrue* from many studies of different proposed measures of the construct, and subsequently the available evidence will be accumulated and evaluated.  The investigator hopes that the end product of this complex process will be a construct (1) that is well defined in terms of a variety of observables, (2) for which there are one or several variables that well represent the domain of observables, and (3) that eventually proves to relate strongly with other constructs of interest.  Some of the methods required to reach those goals are described in the following sections.

## Domain of observables

Although on the face of it, one might think that the scientist should outline the domain of observables before assuming that any one observable relates to a construct, this is seldom done.  More frequently, scientists investigate only one observable and assume that it is related to the construct, at least for the time being. For example, there have been many studies relating the Taylor Manifest Anxiety Scale (J. A. Taylor, 1953) to supposed measures of other constructs. The test is intended to relate strongly to other variables in a domain of behaviors constituting anxiety. Many studies have been done in spite of the fact that the domain of the construct has not been well outlined, and it is probably true that if different investigators in this area attempted to outline the domain, there would be some disagreement among them.

Scientists should not be criticized for assuming that particular observables relate to a construct even though the domain of the construct is only vaguely understood. In his lifetime each scientist can perform only a relatively small number of studies (100 might be the average even for very busy scientists), and consequently he does not have time to do all that is required to specify the domain of a construct, develop measures of the construct, and relate those measures to other variables of interest. As the evidence accrues from the work of different scientists interested in a particular construct, however, it is fruitful to attempt a specification of the domain of related variables.

No precise method can be stated for properly outlining the domain of variables for a construct. Essentially the outline constitutes a theory regarding how variables will relate to one another, and though theories themselves should be objectively testable, the theorizing process is necessarily intuitive. Outlining a construct consists essentially in stating what one means by particular words— words such as "anxiety," "habit strength," and "intelligence." In the early attempts to outline a domain, the "outline" usually consists of only a definition in which the word denoting the construct is related to words at a lower level of abstraction. An example is the early attempt by Binet and Simon (1905) to define intelligence: "The tendency to take and maintain a definite direction; the capacity to make adaptations for the purpose of attaining a desired end; and the power of auto-criticism." Brave as such attempts are, when they define a construct with words that are far removed from specific observable variables, they do little to specify the domain in question. An example of a more clearly specified domain is that of Hull (1952) for the construct of "net reaction potential," where the specification is in terms of the observables of probability of response, latency of response, amplitude of response, and number of responses to extinction. Further specifications are made of the observables in each of the four classes of observables.

Whether or not a well-specified domain for a construct actually leads to adequate measurement of the construct is a matter for empirical investigation, but until there is a well-specified domain, there is no way to know exactly what studies should be done to test the adequacy with which a construct is measured. In other words, the major importance of aspect 1 (outlining the domain) is that it tells the experimenter what to do in aspect 2 (investigating relations between different proposed measures of a construct).

### Relations between observables

The way to test the adequacy of the outline of a domain relating to a construct is to determine how well the measures of observables "go together" in empirical investigations. In studies of individual differences, the first step is to obtain scores for a sample of individuals on some of the measures; next, each measure is correlated with all other measures. An analysis of the resulting correlations provides evidence about the extent to which all the measures tend to measure the same thing.

In investigations of construct validity in controlled experiments, the logic is much the same as that in studies of individual differences. One investigates the extent to which treatment conditions have similar effects on some of the measures of observables in the domain. A hypothetical example is given in Figure 6-1, which shows the effects of five levels of stress (the independent variable) on four supposed measures of the construct of fear. Measures A and B are monotonically related to levels of stress, which means that they are affected in much the same way by the experimental treatments. Measure C is monotonically related to treatment levels up to level 4, but falls off sharply at level 5, and consequently it measures something that is not entirely the same as that measured in A and B. Measure D is not related in any systematic manner to the treatment levels, and consequently it could not logically measure the same thing that is measured by A, B, and C. To determine fully the extent to which these and other measures of fear "go together," it would be necessary to see how similarly they behaved with respect to other experimental treatments, e.g., different levels of electrical stimulation of "fear areas" in the brains of rats.

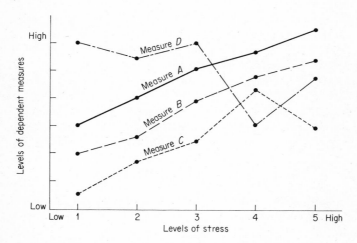

**FIGURE 6-1**    Effects of five levels of stress on four dependent measures

The test of how well different supposed measures of a construct go together is the extent to which they have similar curves of relationship with a variety of treatment variables. It does not matter what the form of the relationship is with a particular treatment variable as long as the supposed measures of the construct behave similarly. Thus, for two supposed measures of a construct, the relationship with one treatment variable could be monotonically increasing; the relationship with another, curvilinear; and the relationship with another, a flat line. In all three instances, however, the two measures of the construct would be affected in much the same way. If two measures were affected in exactly the same way by all possible experimental treatments, it would not matter which one was used in a particular experiment, and consequently one could speak of them as measuring the same thing. To the *degree* to which two measures are affected similarly by a variety of experimental treatments, they can be spoken of as measuring much the same thing. When a variety of measures behave similarly in this way over a variety of experimental treatments, it becomes meaningful to speak of them as measuring a construct. The measures that most consistently behave as the majority of measures do can be said to have the most construct validity.

Methods of investigating construct validity both in studies of individual differences and in controlled experiments involve correlations. Actual correlations are computed between measures of individual differences. A comparison of two curves is, in essence, a correlation of two curves, even though correlational methods might not be applied. Regardless of whether correlations are over individual differences or over levels of treatment effects, they provide evidence about the structure of a domain of observables relating to a construct.

The results of investigations like those described above would lead to one of three conclusions. If all the proposed measures correlate highly with one another, it can be concluded that they all measure much the same thing. If the measures tend to split up into clusters such that the members of a cluster correlate highly with one another and correlate much less with the members of other clusters, it can be concluded that a number of *different* things are being measured. For example, in studying different supposed measures of anxiety, one might find that measures concerning bodily harm tend to go together and that those concerning social embarrassment tend to go together. As a third possibility, if correlations between the measures are all near zero, they measure different things. Of course, the evidence is seldom so clear-cut as to enable one unequivocally to reach one of these three conclusions; rather, there is usually room for dispute as to which conclusion should be reached.

Evidence of the kind described above should affect subsequent efforts to specify the domain of observables for a construct and should also affect theories relating the construct to other constructs. If all the measures supposedly related to a construct correlate highly, this should encourage investigators to keep working with the specified domain of observables and also encourage continued investigation of theories relating that construct to others. If the evidence is that more than one thing is being measured, the old construct should be abandoned for two or more new ones, and theories which assume only one construct should be modified to take account of the multiplicity of constructs. If none of the variables correlate substantially with the others, this is an unhappy state of affairs for the scientist. Of course, it is possible that one of the measures is highly related to the construct and that the others are unrelated to the construct, but it is much more likely that none of them relate well to it. The investigator must postulate an entirely new domain of observables for a construct, or else he will have to abandon it altogether.

### Relations between constructs

In the previous section, means were discussed for studying construct validity in terms of the *internal consistency* with which different measures in a domain tend to supply the same information (tend to correlate highly with one another and be similarly affected by experimental treatments). To the extent that the elements of such a domain show this consistency, it can be said that *some* construct may be employed to account for the data, but it is by no means necessarily legitimate to employ the construct name which motivated the research. In other words, consistency is a *necessary* but not *sufficient* condition for construct validity. A discussion of how one can, if ever, obtain sufficient evidence that a domain of observables relates to a construct requires an analysis of some of the deepest innards of scientific explanation.

Sufficient evidence for construct validity is the fact that the supposed measures of the construct (either a single measure of observables or a combination of such measures) *behave as expected*. If, for example, a particular measure is thought to relate to the construct of anxiety, common sense would suggest many findings that should be obtained with the measure. Higher scores (higher anxiety) should be found for (1) patients classified as anxiety neurotics than for unselected nonpatients, (2) subjects in an experiment who are kept threatened with a painful electric shock than for subjects not so threatened, and (3) graduate students waiting to undergo a final oral examination for their doctorates than for the same students after passing the examination. As another example, if a particular measure is thought to relate to the construct of intelligence, one would expect it to correlate at least moderately with grades in school, teachers' ratings of intelligence, and levels of professional attainment. So it is with all constructs: there are expected correlations with other variables and expected effects in controlled experiments.

First would come the test of internal consistency of elements in the domain; then there would need to be many correlational studies and many controlled experiments. To the extent to which the measures met expectations in those regards, there would be evidence of construct validity.

Obviously, the logic and method of construct validation are complex (see Nunnally, 1967, Ch. 3, for a discussion of some of the details). It is more important for the reader of this book to understand several general principles regarding construct validation than to become acquainted with these complexities. First, construct validation is a vital part of all science, not just psychological science. In the same way that it is necessary to validate measures of anxiety, intelligence, and other psychological attributes, it is also necessary to validate measures of electrical resistance, distance of stars, and chemical properties of animal tissue. Second, construct validity concerns a semantic problem, that of specifying the meanings of terms (e.g., intelligence) with regard to empirical events (e.g., in terms of the example of intelligence, understanding written material and solution of mathematical problems). Third, construct validation requires that the different empirical referents for constructs act alike in studies of individual differences and controlled experiments. Fourth, after that is accomplished, construct validation requires that supposed measures of a construct meet fundamental assumptions about the nature of the trait in question, e.g., that, on the average, more intelligent students do better schoolwork than less intelligent students. Fifth, evidence of construct validity is always circumstantial rather than direct. The more evidence is obtained in that regard, the more confident one can feel in using a particular instrument, or group of instruments, to represent a construct. When that type of confidence has been gained, the construct measures can be used to test theories about natural events.

## generalizability

There is another important concept that is useful in understanding the validation of measures, that of *generalizability*. Science differs from casual observation in that it attempts to make very general statements about natural events. The essence of science is an attempt to explain all natural events in terms of a relatively small set of principles. For example, in terms of casual observation, one witnesses many instances of moving objects—a baseball in flight, a wagon rolling down a hill, and an automobile coming to a halt at a signal light. Physics is concerned with explaining the direction and velocity of all such moving objects in terms of a small set of general principles. Such principles are highly generalizable; i.e., they work regardless of the nature of the object, the nature of the force propelling the object, and other particularities of the situation. The same search for generality of explanation exists in psychological science.

Construct validation consists essentially of determining the generality of findings regarding a particular measuring instrument. For example, by naming a particular instrument a measure of intelligence, one is assuming a generality of findings with that instrument to other instruments. But if scores on different supposed measures of intelligence did not correlate highly (fortunately, they do), any investigations with a particular instrument would be quite limited in generality. It then would not be correct to use the evidence derived from one such test to make general statements regarding the nature of intelligence or relations between intelligence and other attributes.

Another example of how construct validation relates to tests of generalizability is in terms of measures of activity levels in rats. Investigators would like to make very general statements regarding effects of different drugs on activity levels. Such general statements are proper, however, only if the results obtained with one measure of activity are also reflected in other measures of activity. This requires that effects of drugs be tested on a number of different measures of activity, which is a form of construct validation.

Generalizability is also at issue in the validation of predictor tests and tests that require content validity. With predictor tests, the nature of the required generalization is very simple, that of generalizing from scores on the predictor tests to scores on the criterion variable. Thus if scores on a test of scholastic aptitude correlate well with grades in college, one can generalize from the aptitude test to actual performance in college.

Statements concerning generalizability over empirical findings are at issue with both predictor tests and measures of constructs, very narrow generalizations in the case of the former, and broader ones in the case of the latter. In both cases, however, generalizability is tested by experiments. With measures that require content validity (e.g., classroom examinations and standardized achievement tests), generalizability concerns the appropriateness and broadness with which the instrument covers the content in question. For example, if one test in an achievement test battery is intended to measure ability in spelling, the test should measure spelling in a very general way, such that a test score is generalizable to all types of words occurring in readers and school exercises for the particular age group. Thus in measures that require content validity, one is also concerned with generalizability. With such measures, however, the generality (or representativeness) of the content coverage is determined mainly by expert opinions rather than (as with predictor tests and construct measures) by experimentation. Later in this book it will be shown how other issues in psychometric theory can be considered issues relating to generalizability.

## other issues concerning validity

### Other names

Other authors have used different names for the three types of validity discussed in this chapter. Predictive validity has been referred to as "empirical validity" and "statistical validity"; content validity has been called "intrinsic validity," "circular validity," "relevance," and "representativeness"; and construct validity has been spoken of as "trait validity" and "factorial validity."

One frequently encounters the term "face validity," which concerns the extent to which an instrument "looks as if" it measures what it is intended to measure. For example, an achievement test for fourth-grade arithmetic would be said to have face validity if potential users of the test liked the types of items which were employed. Any instrument that is intended to have content validity should meet that standard, but the standard is far from complete. Face validity concerns judgments about an instrument *after* it has been constructed. As was discussed previously, content validity is more properly ensured by the plan of content and the plan for constructing items. Thus face validity can be considered one aspect of content validity, which concerns an inspection of the final product to make sure that nothing went wrong in transforming plans into a completed instrument.

When an instrument is intended to perform a prediction function, validity depends entirely on how well the instrument correlates with what it is intended to predict (a criterion), and consequently face validity is irrelevant. There are many instances in which an instrument looks as though it should correlate well with a criterion even though the correlation is close to zero. Also, there are many instruments that bear no obvious relationship to a criterion but actually correlate well with the criterion. With prediction functions, face validity is important only in formulating hypotheses about instruments that will correlate well with their criteria. Thus even though the correlations tell the full story, it is not wise to select predictors at random. Before research is done on a prediction problem, there must be some hope that a particular instrument will work. Such hope is fostered when the instrument looks as if it should predict the criterion. Also, tests are usually more predictive of a criterion if their item content is phrased in the language and the terms of the objects actually encountered in the particular type of performance. For example, if an arithmetic test is being constructed for the prediction of performance in the operation of particular types of machines, it will probably be more predictive if problems are phrased in terms of numbers of nuts and bolts than in terms of numbers of apples and oranges. For these two reasons, face validity plays a part in decisions about types of tests to be used as predictors and in the construction of items for those tests.

In applied settings, face validity is to some extent related to public relations. For example, teachers would be reluctant to use an achievement test unless the items "looked good." Less logical is the reluctance of some administrators in applied settings, e.g., industry, to permit the use of predictor instruments which lack face validity. Conceivably, a good predictor of a particular criterion might consist of preferences among drawings of differently shaped and differently colored butterflies, but it would be difficult to convince administrators that such a test could actually do a good job of selecting employees.

Although one could make a case for the involvement of face validity in the measurement of constructs, to do so would probably serve only to confuse the issues.  It would be better to think directly in terms of the principles stated in the previous section.

### Place of factor analysis

Methods of factor analysis and their use in the development of measures will be discussed later in this book, but since factor analysis is intimately involved with questions of validity, it would be helpful to place some of the related issues in perspective.  For those who are not already familiar with factor analysis, it should be noted that essentially it consists of methods for finding clusters of related variables.  Each such cluster, or factor, is denoted by a group of variables whose members correlate more highly among themselves than they do with variables not included in the cluster.  Each factor is thought of as a unitary attribute (a yardstick) which is measured to greater and lesser degrees by particular instruments, depending on the extent to which they correlate with the factor.  Such correlations have been spoken of as representing the *factorial validity* of measures.  It would be better to speak of them as representing the *factorial composition* of measures because the word "validity" is somewhat misleading.

The following example can serve to illustrate what is meant by the term "factorial composition."  It might be found that one test correlates highly with other tests which concern the understanding of words and written material, such tests serving to define a factor of verbal comprehension.  It might also be found that the same test correlates very little with tests concerning numerical computations and concepts, such tests serving to define a factor of quantitative aptitude.  A second test might be just the reverse, correlating highly with a factor of quantitative aptitude but not with a factor of verbal comprehension.  A third test might correlate substantially with both factors, and thus would be said to have a mixed composition of factors.

The factorial composition of measures plays a part in all three types of validity discussed in this chapter.  Factor analysis is important in the selection of instruments to be tried as predictors.  Instead of constructing a new test for each applied problem as it arises, one selects a predictor instrument from a "storehouse" of available instruments.  Factor analysis can serve to construct such a storehouse of measures with known factorial composition.  It is then much easier to formulate hypotheses about the possible predictive power in particular instances of particular factors than to formulate hypotheses about the predictive power of instruments developed ad hoc for the problem.

Factor analysis provides helpful circumstantial evidence regarding measures that are intended to have content validity.  For example, a factor analysis of a battery of achievement tests might show that a test intended to measure mathematics correlates rather highly with a factor of verbal comprehension. This would suggest that the words and sentences used to phrase problems were sufficiently difficult to introduce an unwanted factor in the test, which would lead to revisions of the test for mathematics.

Factor analysis is at the heart of the measurement of psychological constructs. As was said previously, the explication of constructs consists mainly in determining (1) the internal statistical structure of a set of variables said to measure a construct and (2) the statistical cross-structures between the different measures of one construct and those of other constructs. Factor analysis is used directly to determine item 1, and procedures related to factor analysis are important in determining item 2.

Factor analysis plays important parts with respect to all three types of validity, but it plays somewhat different parts with each. Regarding predictive validity, factor analysis is important mainly in suggesting predictors that will work well in practice. With content validity, factor analysis is important mainly in suggesting ways to revise instruments for the better. With construct validity, factor analysis provides some of the tools that are most useful for determining internal structures and cross-structures for sets of variables.

## Summary

"Validation" is a catchall name for the procedures for determining the usefulness of measures. In psychology, measures serve three major purposes: (1) prediction of a particular criterion, (2) representation of a specified area of content, and (3) measurement of psychological traits (constructs). Corresponding to each of these functions are three methods of validation: (1) correlating a particular test with a criterion variable, (2) demonstrating the representativeness of a collection of items for an area of content, and (3) showing by experimentation that particular measures fit a construct name.

Predictive validity is the simplest of the three types of validity to understand and the simplest to determine in practice. Predictive ability, however, is limited to only a comparatively small part of the total domain of uses of psychological measures, that of prediction problems in applied situations. Such predictor instruments have proved very useful in school settings and, usually to a lesser extent, in industrial, clinical, governmental, and military settings.

Measures requiring content validity are used very widely, particularly in school settings. It is unsettling to some people that content validity does not rest primarily on empirical findings and on statistical analyses of the results. Content validity necessarily rests mainly on expert judgments about the appropriateness of the content coverage in a particular instrument, but there are some forms of empirical evidence that aid those judgments.

Construct validation is a more complex matter than the aforementioned two types of validation, and the procedures involved are in dispute. Whatever one wants to call the process involved, and however one wants to specify the logic, in all science there is a perennial problem of translating theoretical terms (constructs) into observable, measurable events. Essentially this requires determining (1) whether some or all of the proposed measures of the construct provide much the same information and (2) whether some or all of those measures meet fundamental assumptions about the nature of the construct. All three types of validation can be considered different types of issues relating to generalizability.

### Suggested additional readings

Bechtoldt, H. P.   Construct validity: A critique.   *American Psychologist*, 1959, 14, 619–629.

Campbell, D. T.   Recommendations for APA test standards regarding construct, trait, and discriminant validity.   *American Psychologist*, 1960, 15, 546–553.

Cronbach, L. J., & Meehl, P. E.   Construct validity in psychological tests. *Psychological Bulletin*, 1955, 52, 281–302.

Lennon, R. T.   Assumptions underlying the use of content validity.   *Educational and Psychological Measurement*, 1956, 16, 294–304.

Loevinger, J.   Objective tests as instruments of psychological theory.   *Psychological Reports*, 1957, 3, 635–694.

# PART 4:

Theory and Method
for Constructing
Psychological Measures

# CHAPTER 7

# Psychophysical methods and theories

In the first chapter it was said that measurement concerns the assignment of numbers to objects to represent quantities of attributes. Although any system of operations that will so assign numbers can be spoken of as measurement, it helps to have some internally consistent plan for the development of a new measure. The plan is spoken of as a *scaling model,* and the measure which results from exercising the plan is spoken of as a *scale* ("scale" being another word for "measure"). The simplest example is that of the ruler as a scale of length. The methods for constructing and applying rulers constitute the scaling model in that case. The purpose of any scaling model is to generate a continuum on which persons or objects are located. In the following example, persons $P_1$, $P_2$, $P_3$, and $P_4$ are located on such a continuum:

$$\text{Lower} \longleftarrow \underset{\substack{P_4 \qquad\qquad\quad P_3 \quad P_2 \qquad P_1}}{\rule{0pt}{0pt}} \longrightarrow \text{Higher}$$

*Attribute*

The attribute could be anxiety or spelling ability, for example. Because it is an interval scale, the distances between persons are taken seriously. Thus $P_1$ is considerably higher in the attribute than the other persons, $P_2$ and $P_3$ are close together, and $P_4$ is far below the others.

In any particular measurement problem, scaling potentially concerns a data matrix (table) such as that shown in Figure 7-1. On the front face of the

**155**

cube, rows represent stimuli, and columns represent responses to the stimuli. The "slices" of the cube going from front to back represent the responses of each person to each of the stimuli. The words "stimuli" and "responses" represent anything that the experimenter does to the subject and anything the subject does in return. Typical things (stimuli) the experimenter does to the subject include having him lift weights, presenting him with spelling words, and showing him a list of foods. Typical responses required for these types of stimuli would be judging which of two weights is heavier, indicating whether or not each word is correctly spelled, or rating how much each food is liked.

The data matrix illustrated in Figure 7-1 presents a very complex problem for scaling. The problem is much simpler when there is only a two-dimensional table, as when only one person is studied at a time. This would also be the case if only one type of response were made to each stimulus, e.g., agreeing or disagreeing with each statement on a list. Also, there would be a two-dimensional table of data if each person made a number of different types of responses to the same stimulus, e.g., rating the United Nations on different rating scales anchored by pairs of adjectives such as effective-ineffective, valuable-worthless, and strong-weak. If in the problem there is more than one person, more than one stimulus, and more than one type of response required for each stimulus, there are many, many ways in which any of the three could be scaled. Usually an effort is made to simplify the problem by making the elements in one dimension "replicates" of one another, or at least assuming them to be such.

Some methods of scaling assume that persons are replicates of one another. For example, the percentage of persons in a *group* who say that one weight is heavier than another is assumed to be the same as the percentage of times an ideal

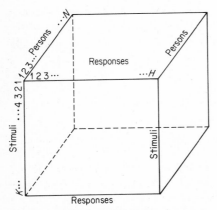

**FIGURE 7-1**    A data matrix for *h* responses of *N* persons to *k* stimuli

*modal individual* would say that one weight is heavier than another on different occasions. The assumption that individuals are replicates is frequently made in scaling stimuli. In scaling persons, it is frequently assumed that responses are replicates of one another. Thus in the previous example of rating stimuli on scales anchored by bipolar adjectives, an overall "favorableness" rating can be obtained by adding responses over the separate rating scales.

When one looks carefully at the different methods for scaling, he will see that in most cases either one of the dimensions of the data matrix is not present (e.g., only one person, one stimulus, or one type of response made to each stimulus) or an assumption is made that allows him to do away with at least one of the dimensions. When the latter is the case, there are usually ways of testing the correctness of the assumption. For example, if a different scale concerning the judgment of weights is constructed for each person and it is found that there are systematic differences in those scales, this would violate the assumption that persons are replicates in that particular situation. If it is found that the bipolar rating scales either do not correlate with one another or evolve into a number of different factors, it would be wrong to assume that the scales are replicates. When such assumptions are found to be incorrect, however, it often makes the problem of measurement very messy indeed.

Although potentially all scaling problems must consider the possibility of a three-dimensional data table like that shown in Figure 7-1, most conventional methods of developing a measurement scale can operate on only a two-dimensional matrix. Consequently, one either gathers data in such a way that only two dimensions of the table are present (by having only one person, one stimulus, or one response) or makes some assumption which allows him to collapse one of the three dimensions (e.g., by averaging responses to stimuli over persons). The next step in deriving a measurement scale is to employ a set of rules (a *model*) that allows one to collapse one of the two remaining dimensions of the data matrix. This would be done, for example, in an experiment in which each individual has been required to rank a number of weights from heaviest to lightest. The data matrix would then consist of the ranks of weights for each person—a two-dimensional table of data. One way to collapse the person dimension would be to average the ranks over persons, which would provide a scaling of the weights. The average ranking would provide an ordering of the weights. This would also be done in an experiment in which individuals either agree or disagree with statements concerning the United Nations. Agreement with a statement is thought to represent a positive atttitude, and disagreement a negative attitude. Since there is only one object being rated, a two-dimensional table of data is obtained. By summing the number of agreements for each person, one collapses the response dimension of the table. Then sums of agreements would constitute an ordering of the persons with respect to their attitudes, and one might want to take the intervals between persons seriously.

Before one turns a two-dimensional table of data into a measurement scale, he should first state a set of assumptions regarding how the attribute in question is manifested in actual data. Then he must test how well the assumptions hold in the data. Each set of assumptions is a model. This chapter is concerned primarily with the models that are most frequently employed for turning two-dimensional tables of data into unidimensional scales. If the data do not fit the assumptions of a particular model for unidimensional scaling, the investigator has three choices: he can (1) try one of the other models for unidimensional scaling, (2) try methods of multivariate analysis, or (3) try some other problem. If methods of multivariate analysis are applied, it might be found that more than one unidimensional scale is required to account for the data. For example, with statements concerning attitudes toward the United Nations, factor analysis might indicate that the statements relate to two different dimensions of attitude. It might be found that some statements relate to a factor concerning the effectiveness of the United Nations in settling diplomatic disputes between nations and that other statements relate to a factor concerning activities of the United Nations in economic matters. Then two scales of attitudes rather than only one would be developed. Such methods of multivariate analysis are discussed by Nunnally (1967) and Torgerson (1958). This chapter will be concerned only with models that are used for developing unidimensional scales.

### Evaluation of models

There are usually different models that can be used for the development of particular scales, and sometimes the models lead to different conclusions about the scale properties of the data. One model might lead to a scale that failed to have a linear relationship with a scale derived from another model applied to the same data. One model might reject the data as conforming to an ordinal scale, whereas another model would accept the data as conforming to an interval scale. How, then, does one know which model is appropriate for a particular problem? There is no sure way to know this in advance. The ultimate test is how well the scales which are derived fit in a nexus of lawful relations with other variables. Before time and effort are expended on such investigations, however, some criteria of "good sense" can be applied.

Part of good sense concerns the intuitive appeal of a scaling model. Although the data of science must be objective, the scientist must rely on his intuition for research ideas. Looked at in one way, a scaling model is nothing more than an explicitly defined hunch, a hunch that particular operations on data will lead to an important measure. If the author's observations are correct, psychologists tend to find intuitively appealing those models which relate to the measurement of simple physical attributes such as length and weight.

Another aspect of good sense in selecting scaling models concerns the evaluation of assumptions in the models in terms of what is already known about the type of data involved. For example, one of the models that will be discussed later assumes that responses to individual test items are highly reliable, and yet there is a wealth of evidence to show that such items usually are not highly reliable.

After a model is used to derive a scale and before strenuous efforts are made to find lawful relations with other variables, some preliminary forms of evidence regarding the usefulness of the scale must be obtained. If the scale values for objects or persons are markedly affected by slightly different ways of gathering data, the scale probably will not work well in practice. There are, for example, numerous ways in which one can have subjects make judgments of weights. If two approaches that seem much the same lead to very different intervals of judged weight, one would be quite suspicious of the interval scales obtained by both approaches. An even more important type of preliminary evidence concerns the amount of measurement error involved in using a particular type of scale, a matter which was discussed in detail in Chapter 5. A scale that occasions a great deal of measurement error cannot possibly be useful for any purpose. Beyond the standards of good sense, however, the ultimate test of any model is the extent to which it produces scales with a high degree of explanatory power for natural phenomena.

## Stimuli and people

Previously it was said that scaling problems potentially concern a three-dimensional matrix of persons, stimuli, and types of responses. In unidimensional scaling, usually each person makes only one type of response to each stimulus, or if he makes more than one type of response, it is sensible to combine responses in some manner. (If there is doubt about the sensibility of combining responses, methods of multivariate analysis can be employed.) In either situation, a scaling model is applied to a two-dimensional matrix of data. What has not been made explicit so far is that methods of scaling employed for scaling stimuli are usually different from those employed for scaling people. Also, which of the two is to be scaled has a strong influence on the way responses are obtained.

It is probably easier to think of measurement problems in terms of the scaling of people. In a simple example, the data matrix is bordered by spelling words on the side and by people on the top. The required response is to indicate whether or not each word is correctly spelled (a single response to each stimulus). Using a 1 for correct spellings and a zero for incorrect spellings, the data matrix would be filled with 1s and zeros. The dimension concerning stimuli (spelling words) would be collapsed by summing the number of 1s for each person.  If it were not thought necessary to apply a more elaborate model to the data, the simple sums of correct responses would serve to scale people on the attribute of spelling ability.

Something more subtle is at issue when the object is to scale stimuli rather than people.  For example, when subjects are asked to judge the loudness of tones by one method or another, the object is to generate a continuum of perceived loudness.  In this instance the tones are quantified with respect to the attribute, and people are part of the measurement process.  In another example of scaling stimuli, preferences for foods can be scaled by having a group of people rate each food on a like-dislike rating scale.  One method of scaling in this instance would be to let the average rating of each food be its scale value.

When one seeks a unidimensional scale of stimuli, the hope is to find a scale that fits the average individual.  Thus a scale developed in this way would be typical of persons as a group, even though it might not perfectly represent the scale that would be obtained by an intensive investigation of any one person. The long-range research purpose in scaling stimuli (rather than persons) is to relate scalings of the same stimuli with respect to different attributes.  Thus after a unidimensional scale has been developed for the perceived loudness of tones, another scaling of the same tones could be made against a background of noise.  Another scaling could be made when each tone is accompanied by a light whose intensity is correlated with the intensity of the tone.  Scaling of the tones could be made in various applied problems, such as in employing the tones as communication signals.  At issue would be mathematical relations between the different scalings of the tones.  The same would be true of scaling foods in terms of preferences.  Rated preferences could be compared with what men in the armed forces chose to eat or with what housewives would purchase. In each instance the object is to relate a scaling of stimuli on one attribute with the scaling of stimuli on another attribute.

Important as it is to scale stimuli, this is not nearly so large an issue in psychology as the scaling of people with respect to attributes.  It is probably true that if one searched through numerous journal articles and textbooks on psychology, one would find that most of the studies are concerned primarily with variables involving the scaling of people (or lower animals) rather than the scaling of stimuli.  Prominently appearing in the literature are studies of learning rate, anxiety, decision time, intelligence, and strength of conditioned responses—all definitely concerned with the scaling of people.  The issue is the same, regardless of whether the scaling of people is for studies of individual differences or for controlled experiments.  Although, for example, approaches to measurement employed for studies of individual differences concerning typical levels of anxiety might be different from those for controlled experiments on anxiety, it would be necessary in both types of studies to scale persons with respect to the attribute of anxiety.

It is important to make a distinction between the scaling of stimuli and the scaling of persons because there are more severe problems with the former. In the scaling of stimuli, research issues frequently concern the exact nature of functional relations between scalings of the stimuli in different circumstances. Thus in the scaling of tones under different conditions, a careful study would be made of the exact "curves" between different scalings. Then it would make quite a difference if a particular relation was linear rather than logarithmic. As was stated in Chapter 1, in most studies concerning the scaling of people, exact forms of relationship between different scalings are not important—at least not at the present stage of development of psychological science. The major requirement is that different scalings of people be monotonically related to one another, i.e., that they rank-order people in the same way. A relationship between two scales is monotonic if higher scores on one scale correspond to higher scores on the other scale, regardless of the exact shape of the curve which would be found on a graph. Thus if there are two different methods for scaling people for the attribute of anxiety and the two are monotonically related, research results will be much the same, regardless of which scale is employed.

Because there are more serious problems with the scaling of stimuli than with the scaling of persons, most of the issues concerning scaling, and most of the models for scaling, have arisen in the context of problems concerning the scaling of stimuli. This can be seen, for example, in the comprehensive treatments of scaling methods by Guilford (1954) and Torgerson (1958). In both books, most of the scaling models are illustrated with the scaling of stimuli (tones, weights, foods), and most of the models are more appropriate for the scaling of stimuli than for the scaling of persons. This difference has had an influence on the language used to describe psychological research. When one speaks of "scaling" and "scaling methods," he is usually discussing a problem concerning the scaling of stimuli. When one is discussing a problem concerning the scaling of persons with respect to an attribute, he is more likely to use terms like "measurement" and "test construction."

## types of responses required of subjects

Before scaling models are discussed, it is necessary to review some of the different types of responses required of subjects. The type of response tends to correlate with the type of stimuli being studied; e.g., one would require that types of responses to tones and to the names of foods be different. Different types of responses are usually required for the scaling of stimuli and for the scaling of persons. Also, different scaling models often require different types of responses. There is no end to the distinctions that one could make regarding all the kinds of responses that are possible in different studies. The three most important types of distinctions are discussed in the following sections.

## Judgments and sentiments

Although there are no two words that perfectly symbolize the distinction, one of the most important distinctions in measurement theory is that between responses concerning *judgments* and those concerning *sentiments*. The word "judgment" is used to cover all those types of responses where there is a *correct* response. This would be the case, for example, when a child is asked, "How much is 2 plus 2?" This would also be the case when subjects are required to judge which of two tones is louder or which of two weights is heavier. In all these instances there is some *veridical comparison* for the subject's response, and it is possible to determine whether each response is correct or incorrect. With some types of judgments, it is also possible to determine the degree of correctness and thus the relative accuracy. For example, when a subject is required to adjust one light to the apparent brightness of another light, it is possible to measure how accurate he is in units of illumination.

The word "sentiment" is used to cover all responses concerning personal reactions, preferences, interests, attitudes, and likes and dislikes. An individual makes responses concerning sentiments when he (1) rates boiled cabbage on a seven-step like-dislike rating scale; (2) answers the question, "Which would you rather do, organize a club or work on a stamp collection?" and (3) rank-orders 10 actors in terms of his preferences. The important difference between judgments and sentiments is that with sentiments no veridical comparison is possible. Thus if an individual says, "I like chocolate ice cream better than vanilla ice cream," it makes no sense to tell him, "You are incorrect." We may abhor another person's tastes for food or sentiments in any other sphere, but sentiments do not require veridical justification. Of course, it may be that the subject is incorrect in the sense that he lies or that he actually behaves in daily life in a manner different from that implied by his stated sentiments. The important point, however, concerns *what the subject is asked to do* in the experimental setting. When expressing a sentiment, the subject is asked to give a personal reaction to a stimulus, and there is no external standard of "accuracy" that makes sense.

In the study of judgments, an important problem is to relate the *perceived* intensity of some attribute to the *physical* intensity of the attribute. For example, in a study where subjects are asked to adjust one light so that it appears twice as bright as another light, the ratio of perceived brightness can be compared with the ratio of physical magnitudes of illumination. Whenever subjects make judgments, there is a veridical comparison either actually available or at least potentially so. The latter possibility is illustrated in the problem where astronomers are asked to estimate the temperature of a number of stars. At present there might be considerable controversy about the correct answers, but *conceivably* there are correct answers that one day can be used to determine the accuracy of present judgments. Such veridical comparisons are not conceivable with sentiments.

In the scaling of stimuli, the logic for validating models for the scaling of judgments is clearer than that for the scaling of sentiments. This is so because the scale of judgments, after it is developed, can be compared with the scale of physical magnitudes. Then, intuitively, one would expect certain types of relations between the scale of judgments and the scale of physical magnitudes. If, for example, an interval scale of the judged loudness of tones does not have a smooth, monotonic relationship with the scale of physical magnitudes, one would probably reject the model used for developing the scale. One would probably expect not a straight line of relationship but some type of smooth, monotonic curve. If this expectation is borne out, it provides no guarantee that the model is correct, but it does provide intuitive support for continued use of the model. Since with sentiments there is no physical scale, there is no way of comparing a scale of sentiments with "actuality." What is typically done is to explore new scaling models on data concerning judgments and, if they apparently work well there, to extend them to studies of sentiments. It is even more apparent with sentiments than with judgments that the usefulness of any scale is determined in the long run by how well it fits in a system of lawful relations with other variables in a particular area of scientific interest.

In the scaling of people, all tests of ability concern judgments, in a broad sense of the term. This is true in tests of mathematics, vocabulary, and reasoning ability. Either the subject exercises his judgment in supplying a correct answer for each item or he judges which of a number of alternative responses is most correct. Tests of interests concern sentiments: the subject indicates the activities he likes and those he dislikes. Measures of attitudes and personality can require either judgments or expressions of sentiment, and it is with these types of measures that the distinction is frequently obscure. On a personality inventory, when responding to the item, "Do you like to be the center of attention at parties?" the subject is asked to express a sentiment. When responding to the item, "Do you usually lead the discussion in group situations?" the subject is asked to make a judgment about his actual behavior in group situations. When responding to the item, "Do most people like you?" he is asked to make a judgment about other peoples' sentiments. Of course, with such items subjects frequently get sentiments mixed up with judgments, whether by intention or out of sheer confusion, and this is one reason why it is difficult to develop valid inventories for measuring personality.

### Comparative and absolute responses

Another important distinction concerns whether the subject is required to make an absolute response to each stimulus separately or to make comparative judgments or expressions of sentiment among the stimuli. The question, "How long is this line in inches?" for example, would elicit an absolute response. An absolute response is also necessary when the subject is required to rate boiled cabbage on a seven-step like-dislike scale. In both instances the subject responds to each stimulus separately, and he indicates the amount of the attribute in an absolute sense.

With comparative judgments and sentiments, stimuli are presented in groups of two or more, and the subject responds to the "more" and "less" of some property. A comparative response is required when the subject is asked to indicate which he likes more, boiled cabbage or boiled turnips, or when he is asked to indicate which of two weights is heavier.

There are few instances in which it makes sense to require absolute responses of subjects. For example, there is little of interest in having people judge the physical magnitude of stimuli, e.g., asking them, "How long is this line in inches?" People are notoriously poor at making absolute judgments of length, weight, and other physical properties of stimuli. In many cases the subject has no way of communicating his absolute judgment of such physical properties. How would the subject respond if he were asked simply, "How bright is this light?" or "How loud is this tone?"

People are simply not accustomed to making absolute judgments in daily life, since most judgments are inherently comparative. Thus subjects can respond with a high degree of confidence when asked which of two lights is brighter or which of two tones is louder. Whereas people are notoriously inaccurate when judging the absolute magnitudes of stimuli, e.g., the length of a line in inches, they are highly accurate in making comparative judgments. If the subject is within 20 feet of two lines and is asked to judge which is longer, he will be accurate almost every time unless the lines differ by less than ½ inch.

As is true of most judgments in daily life, most sentiments are inherently comparative. The individual has some feeling regarding his absolute liking for an object or activity, but such sentiments are strongly influenced by the range of objects or activities available. Thus an individual required to rate boiled cabbage on a like-dislike rating scale (supposedly an absolute response) must surely say to himself, "What else would there be to eat?" If girls are required to rate the photograph of a man on a rating scale anchored by the adjectives "handsome" and "ugly," how can they make such responses unless they subjectively compare the features of the man with those of the many men that they have seen previously?

Even when subjects are requested to make absolute responses to each stimulus in a set, there is considerable evidence that their responses are largely comparative. This would be found when weights are to be rated on a scale ranging from "very heavy" to "very light." If subjects were actually responding to each weight separately, the rating given any weight would remain the same regardless of the sizes of the other weights in the set. But, as anyone would guess, the rating of a particular weight shifts markedly when it is placed in the context of heavier or lighter weights. The same is true of sentiments. If girls are asked to make ratings of the handsomeness of men shown in 20 photographs, the rating of the man in any particular photograph can be shifted markedly by placing it in the context of all relatively ugly men.   When giving absolute judgments and expressions of sentiment, subjects tend to anchor their responses in terms of (1) stimuli of the same kinds that they have experienced in the past and (2) the range of stimuli in the set which is presented.

Potentially, the major advantage of absolute responses is with sentiments rather than with judgments.  The comparative methods are sufficient for most studies of judgments, but in some studies of sentiments it is important to learn the absolute level of responses to stimuli.  This is the case in most studies of attitudes, e.g., in studies of attitudes toward different national groups.  This information could not be obtained from comparative responses, as where the subject is required to rank the names of 10 national groups from "most prefer" to "least prefer."  The individual may dislike all the national groups or like them all, but there would be no hint of that from the rankings (comparative responses).  Absolute responses are important in those studies of sentiments in which it is necessary to obtain an approximate indication of the "neutral" point either for the scaling of persons or for the scaling of stimuli.  For example, in studies of attitudes, it has been hypothesized that people near the neutral point (e.g., of attitudes toward the United Nations) are more susceptible to change than people who are far from the neutral point in either direction.  By requiring absolute responses from subjects, one would be able to determine the neutral point approximately.

Even when absolute responses are required of subjects, the experimenter usually makes comparative analyses and interpretations of those responses.  This is done because absolute responses are frequently obtained much more quickly and easily than comparative responses.  For example, in a study of preferences among 50 foods, the investigator would probably be interested mainly in which foods are liked more and which are liked less.  A direct way to obtain this information would be to have each subject rank all the foods from "most prefer" to "least prefer," but that would probably take each subject an hour or more.  Approximately the same information could be obtained in a much shorter time from absolute responses.  Each subject would rate each food on a like-dislike scale.  An average rating of each food over subjects would be obtained.  Then the experimenter could rank the foods in terms of average ratings, and some of the comparative models for scaling could be used to estimate intervals between foods on the continuum of sentiment.  Thus in many cases where subjects are asked to make absolute responses, the experimenter takes seriously only the comparative information in those responses.

To summarize, absolute responses are useful in some situations for (1) providing shortcut methods of obtaining comparative information and/or (2) obtaining an approximate indication of the neutral point on a continuum of sentiment.   In all other situations, comparative methods are clearly more appropriate.

### scale for response

Another important distinction between types of responses concerns the scale on which the subject is required to respond. In most types of responses, subjects are required to respond to stimuli in terms of an ordinal, interval, or ratio scale; that is, each subject is required to generate a scale having the properties of one of these three basic types of scales. There are many ways in which responses can be obtained with respect to the three types of scales, each way being referred to as a *psychophysical method*.

Most frequently, subjects are required to operate on an ordinal scale. All the particular methods that can be applied for that purpose are called methods of *ordinal estimation*. The most straightforward way to do this is by the method of *rank order*, which, as the name implies, requires the subject to rank stimuli from "most" to "least" with respect to some attribute of judgment or sentiment. A more thorough approach is with the method of *pair comparisons*, in which the subject is required to rank stimuli two at a time in all possible pairs. For example, eight weights would be presented two at a time in all possible pairs, and for each comparison the subject would be required to indicate which is heavier. Even though on each response a comparison is made between only two stimuli, in essence the subject is required to rank the stimuli "1" and "2" on each comparison. From these responses, the experimenter deduces ordinal and interval scales for the full set of stimuli, by methods which will be described in a later section.

Another ordinal method is that of *constant stimuli*. This method is similar to pair comparisons, except that a standard stimulus is successively paired with each member of a constant set of stimuli. It would be used, for example, in a study of lifted weights where the standard stimulus is a weight of 200 grams and the six constant comparisons are weights of 185, 190, 195, 205, 210, and 215 grams, respectively. Constant stimuli would be paired in a random order with the standard stimulus, and on each comparison the subject would be required to indicate which is heavier. (Of course, on each comparison only the experimenter would know which is the standard stimulus.) To obtain reliable data, it is usually necessary to present numerous random orderings of the constant stimuli in comparison with the standard stimulus. Typical results obtained from applying the method of constant stimuli are shown in Figure 7-2.

Another ordinal method is that of *successive categories*, in which the subject is asked to sort a collection of stimuli into a number of distinct "piles," or categories, which are ordered with respect to a specified attribute. For example, subjects could be required to sort 100 statements concerning their favorableness toward the United Nations. The subjects would be given 10 categories, with the first category defined as "very favorable," the tenth category defined as "very unfavorable," and categories between anchored with verbal labels representing intermediate levels of favorableness. There are many variants of the

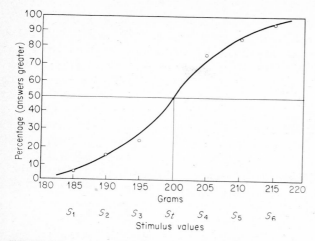

**FIGURE 7-2**    Psychometric function for the application of the method of constant stimuli to a study of lifted weights

method of successive categories, depending on the type of information that the experimenter hopes to obtain. When the experimenter is seeking only ordinal information, the subject is usually allowed to operate in any way he chooses in assigning stimuli to categories. A variant is to require subjects to place an equal number of stimuli in each category, e.g., the top 10 stimuli in category 1 and the bottom 10 stimuli in category 10. Another variant is to require subjects to sort the stimuli into an approximate normal distribution, with its being specified how many stimuli are to be placed in each category (this variant is called the Q sort).

These three approaches to the method of successive categories can be used to obtain ordinal information about the stimuli. The method can be thought of as requiring the subject to rank a set of stimuli in a situation where tied ranks are mandatory. Thus if it is required to place 10 stimuli in each of 10 categories, those placed in category 1 can be thought of as tied for the top rank, and those placed in category 10 as tied for the bottom rank. Then, by averaging the tied ranks over subjects, one can obtain a rather complete ranking of the stimuli, in which there would be few tied ranks. Although there are numerous variants of these methods, the basic approaches to obtaining ordinal judgments and expressions of sentiment are with rank order, pair comparisons, constant stimuli, and successive categories.

One of the most frequently used methods for obtaining *interval* responses from subjects is that of *equal-appearing intervals*. Superficially, the method is very similar to that of successive categories—in both, a set of stimuli must be sorted into a number of ordered categories. The difference is in the instructions.  In the method of equal-appearing intervals, the subject is instructed to sort the stimuli in such a way as to make the intervals between categories subjectively equal.  Thus if the individual is sorting 100 shades of gray paper from darkest to lightest, he would be instructed to work so that the perceived differences between adjacent categories are equal.  Although it is rather difficult to instruct subjects in this task and hard to know how well the experimenter's intention is communicated, the method seeks to obtain equal-appearing intervals.

In addition to the method of equal-appearing intervals for obtaining interval responses, there is a broad category of methods which will be referred to as methods of *interval estimation*.  The most frequently used particular method in this group is that of *bisection*.  For example, the subject is shown two lights of different intensity and is asked to adjust a third light to the point where it is halfway between the other two in terms of apparent brightness, or he is given two statements differing in favorableness toward the United Nations and is asked to select another statement that is halfway between the two in terms of favorableness.  Rather than having the distance between two stimuli bisected, another approach has intervals in terms of some other ratio.  For example, with two fixed stimuli, the subject can be asked to select a third stimulus such that the interval between one of the fixed stimuli and the third is twice as great as the distance between the other fixed stimulus and the third.  In another approach, the subject is presented with two stimuli that are extreme with respect to the attribute and is asked to judge the ratio of intervals formed when each of a number of stimuli is inserted between.

It must be kept in mind that with all the methods of interval estimation, the subject responds in terms of *intervals* of judgment or sentiment.  Though the subject may be forming ratios, e.g., a 1:1 ratio in the method of bisection, responses are with respect to intervals between the stimuli and not with respect to the absolute intensities of the stimuli.  The experimenter might seek to deduce absolute intensities for the stimuli according to a model, but it is important to make a clear distinction between what the subject is required to do and interpretations that the experimenter makes of what is done.  With the interval-estimation methods, the subject is required to estimate the comparative sizes of intervals between stimuli.

The *ratio-estimation* methods require subjects to respond to the absolute magnitudes of stimuli.  As is true of the interval-estimation methods, there are numerous particular forms of ratio estimation.  In a simple example, the subject is shown a light at one intensity and asked to adjust another light until it appears twice as bright as the first, or he is given the name of a food that is thought to be liked moderately well by most persons and asked to rate each of the foods on a list on a scale ranging from "like only one-tenth as much" to "like ten times as much."

Superficially, some of the methods of interval estimation appear similar to those of the methods of ratio estimation.  For example, choosing a stimulus that is halfway between two others is apparently similar to choosing a stimulus that is twice as great as another with respect to some attribute. There are, however, very important differences between methods of interval estimation and methods of ratio estimation. In both the examples above, the subject forms two equal-appearing intervals. When a stimulus halfway between two others is chosen, two equal-appearing intervals are formed. When a stimulus that is twice as intense as another with respect to an attribute is chosen, again two equal-appearing intervals are formed. The important difference is that in the latter case the lower interval is bounded by a *phenomenal zero*. In that case the subject is essentially required to form an interval between two stimuli that is equal to the interval between the less intense stimulus and zero. Whether or not the subject can perform the task, this must be what the experimenter wants the subject to do. In other words, in methods of ratio estimation, the experimenter seeks to obtain responses from subjects with respect to a ratio scale of judgment or sentiment.

The purpose of this section has been to discuss three broad methods for gathering responses from subjects: ordinal estimation, interval estimation, and ratio estimation. There are numerous variants of each of these, many of which have their own names and many of which are called by different names. These are the so-called psychophysical methods, and if one wants to give a different name to each shade and hue of difference in procedure, there are literally hundreds of psychophysical methods. The reader who has a special interest in these methods should consult the excellent books by Guilford (1954) and Torgerson (1958). More important for most readers, however, is an understanding of the three major classes of psychophysical methods described in this section.

## Specification of an attribute

With all the methods discussed so far in this section, judgments or sentiments are expressed with respect to a *stated attribute*. Thus weights are judged with respect to heaviness, and men are rated with respect to handsomeness. In most studies it is possible for the experimenter to specify the attribute involved, but in some studies this is not the case, as when it is known in advance, or suspected, that the stimuli differ with respect to more than one dimension or attribute. This would be the case where responses are made to colored chips that vary in terms of hue, saturation, and brightness. It would occur when subjects respond to the names of United States senators, the senators varying on a number of dimensions of political belief and practice. When the attribute cannot be stated in advance and/or the stimuli vary with respect to a number of attributes, the methods discussed so far cannot be used. The experimenter must obtain *similarity estimates* from the subjects. A frequently used method is to present the subject with three stimuli at a time and ask him which two are more similar.  In this way, the experimenter does not have to specify the attribute(s), but relies instead on the rather global notion of similarity.  Although similarity estimates can be used in place of some of the methods discussed in this chapter for obtaining unidimensional scales, they are useful mainly in multidimensional scaling, which is discussed in Nunnally (1967) and Torgerson (1958).

## methods for scaling stimuli

After responses have been obtained by one of the methods discussed above, the next step is to generate an ordinal, interval, or ratio scale.  In the scaling of stimuli, complex models usually are not required for deriving ordinal scales, and the different models used for that purpose usually arrive at the same ordering of stimuli.  Some examples will serve to show how ordinal scales are obtained.  With the method of rank order, the average ranks would be obtained over subjects, and these would be converted to one overall set of ranks.  The final set of ranks would constitute an ordinal scaling of the stimuli for the typical subject.  In a study where men in photographs are rated for handsomeness, the average ratings would be obtained over subjects, and these would be converted to ranks.  So it is with all the psychophysical methods discussed above—methods for obtaining ordinal scales are usually intuitively obvious.

Scaling models become important when the effort is to construct either an interval or a ratio scale for stimuli.  Usually the effort is to construct an interval scale; in only a few special cases are efforts made to construct ratio scales.  The remainder of this section will consider models that are used for these purposes.  Computational procedures are described by Guilford (1954) and Torgerson (1958).

### Scales based on subjective estimates

In the previous section psychophysical methods were discussed in terms of the *scale of responses*.  It was said that each method requires the subject to respond in terms of an ordinal, interval, or ratio scale.  Even though the subject might be instructed to respond in terms of one type of scale, the experimenter might take the responses as representing another type of scale; e.g., although the subject responded in terms of interval estimates, the experimenter might take seriously only the ordinal information obtained.

With some models for scaling stimuli, the experimenter *does* take seriously the scaling task required of the subject.  In those instances it is easy to obtain ratio or interval scales.  Some examples of how this is done follow.  The subject is required to sort 100 shades of gray paper into 10 categories ranging from "darkest" to "lightest."  Either the more general method of successive categories is employed or the special instructions are used that result in the method of equal-appearing intervals. The experimenter assumes that the subjective processes of the individual are capable of generating an interval scale of perceived brightness. It is admitted that there is some error in the judgments made by one person on one occasion, but efforts are made to reduce the error by averaging judgments over subjects. Thus if a particular shade of gray is rated 9, 9, 8, and 8 by four subjects, the average rating of 8.5 is considered the measurement of that shade of gray on an interval scale. In the same way, measurements would be obtained for all the shades of gray. The scale then would be used in other investigations concerning discrimination of shades of gray.

In another example of a scale based on subjective estimates, methods of interval estimation are applied to statements concerning attitudes toward the United Nations. First, a number of subjects would be employed to determine the most positive and the most negative statements in the set. If there were good agreement at this stage, approximately one hundred subjects would then be asked to select a statement that is halfway between the two extreme statements. The statement receiving the most choices would constitute the center of the scale. Next, subjects would be required to select a statement that is halfway between the most negative statement and the center statement. Continued fractionation in this way would result in an interval scale for the stimuli.

The example above concerning attitude statements can be extended to demonstrate how subjective estimates can be used to approximate a ratio scale. Let us assume that an interval scale of 20 items has been obtained by the method described above. Next, methods of ratio estimation would be required of subjects. To obtain a preliminary indication of the zero (neutral) point, each statement would be rated on a seven-step scale anchored by the terms "highly favorable" for a rating of 7, "highly unfavorable" for a rating of 1, and "neutral" for a rating of 4. The statement having an average rating (over subjects) closest to 4.0 could be used to represent the neutral point on the interval scale, or more refined methods could be employed.

One refinement would be to choose three statements that are rated as moderately favorable, say, with average ratings on the seven-step scale from 5.0 to 6.0. For each of these, each subject would be required to pick an unfavorable statement that is as unfavorable as the other is favorable. In other words, for each favorable statement, the subject would be asked to go across the neutral point an equal distance on the unfavorable side of the continuum. With this information, one could derive a zero (neutral) point for the interval scale which was obtained from the method of interval estimation (the scale discussed in the previous paragraph, not the seven-step scale used to obtain preliminary information about the zero point). Some simple arithmetic could be used to locate the zero point. For example, if the average score on the interval scale for the three negative statements is 2.6 and the average score for the positive statements is 7.4, the zero point should be halfway between, which is 5.0. Then, by subtracting 5.0 from each of the scores of the 20 stimuli on the interval scale, one would arrive at a ratio scale for the stimuli.

There are numerous other models for developing interval and ratio scales based on subjective estimates. The essence of them all is that subjects are assumed capable of producing such scales directly. After this fundamental assumption is made and appropriate methods of gathering responses (particularly those of interval estimation and ratio estimation) are employed, special sets of additional assumptions allow the derivation of interval scales and sometimes ratio scales. The actual models and computational procedures for this purpose tend to be simpler than models based on other fundamental assumptions.

### Scales based on confusions

The second major class of methods for scaling stimuli (there are only two that have achieved prominence so far) differs in a number of important ways from the class based on subjective estimates. Scales based on confusions are derived from *discriminant models,* which are so called because the models are concerned with the extent to which stimuli are discriminated from one another or, conversely, with the extent to which stimuli are confused with one another. In the development of scales based on confusions, one does not take very seriously the subject's ability to generate interval and ratio scales directly; rather, one assumes that this is something the scientist has to do after the data are collected. Primary emphasis is placed on the variability of response to each stimulus—the variability of responses by different persons to the same stimulus and the potential variability of responses by the same person to the same stimulus on different occasions. Although with scales based on subjective estimates it is admitted that such variability is present, most models take no formal account of the variability. Whereas scaling methods based on subjective estimates typically require responses by various methods of interval estimation and ratio estimation, scaling methods based on confusions typically require responses by methods of ordinal estimation, e.g., rank order and pair comparisons.

All scaling methods based on confusions assume that intervals between stimuli are related to the extent to which comparative judgments or expressions of sentiments are agreed on by the subjects. Thus if 95 percent of the subjects judge one weight to be heavier than another, it is assumed that the interval between the two is large in terms of subjective responses to the two weights. In contrast, if only 55 percent of the subjects say that one weight is heavier than another, it is assumed that the interval on a scale of subjective response is much smaller than in the previous case. What the discriminant models do is to state rules for transforming such percentages into interval scales of measurement. It is not the purpose here to present the mathematical details of such models because to do so would be beyond the scope of this book; rather, the purpose is to make the reader aware of the logic underlying such methods.  (The methods are discussed in detail in Guilford, 1954, and Torgerson, 1958.)

The first major assumption in discriminant models is that percentages of comparative judgments and sentiments are indicative of subjective errors in differentiating between stimuli.  For example, an individual may compare two weights on many different occasions.  On 75 percent of the occasions he may say that one weight is heavier, and then on 25 percent of the occasions he may say that the other weight is heavier.  These percentages are thought to mirror the confusion in the subject's mind—now this one feels heavier, and now that one.  The second major assumption in most discriminant models is that the subjective reaction to a stimulus varies from occasion to occasion on a hypothetical yardstick in the mind of the subject.  Thus any particular weight would feel heavier on some occasions than on others.  If one could measure these reactions "in the head," a frequency distribution of the different reactions could be plotted showing the positions on an interval scale.  Of course one cannot measure such reactions; rather, one can only learn percentages of comparative judgments and sentiments.  The third major assumption is that subjective reactions on different occasions are normally distributed.  Thus there is a typical reaction to any stimulus (the mean reaction), and frequencies of reactions that are different from the mean reaction trail off in both directions in a manner that resembles the normal curve.  Since so many types of errors tend to be normally distributed, it makes sense to propose a scaling model which assumes that errors of judgment and sentiment are normally distributed.  It should be understood that the foregoing three assumptions concern hypothetical covert processes that cannot be measured directly.  Only overt responses concerning "more" or "less" with respect to an attribute can be measured directly.  To the extent to which the three assumptions make sense, however, they lead to mathematical techniques for recovering interval scales of covert response.

Scaling with respect to confusions is accomplished by taking advantage of known properties of normal distributions.  A complete description of how this is done would be beyond the scope of this book, but the basic principles involved can be outlined.  (The complete procedures are discussed in Torgerson, 1958.)  In Chapter 2 the normal distribution was illustrated in terms of the percentages of people lying above and below the average value.  The normal distribution applies equally well to the percentage of *responses* made in psychophysical studies, e.g., to the percentage of occasions on which one weight is judged to be heavier than another.  In a normal distribution, percentages of people or percentages of responses correspond to scores on an interval scale.  Thus if one person is taller than 65 percent of the people and another person is taller than 90 percent of the people, the properties of the normal distribution allow one to calculate a score corresponding to the interval between the two persons.  Similarly, if one weight is judged heavier than another weight 70 percent of the time, the properties of the normal distribution permit one to deduce a score corresponding to the interval between the responses to the two weights. The important point to grasp in this connection is that percentage scores can be converted to scores on an interval scale if it is safe to assume that the objects or persons involved are normally distributed with respect to the attribute in question. Such transformations can be made with the table presented in Appendix B.

Because methods of ordinal estimation result in percentages with which stimuli are judged greater than one another with respect to a particular attribute, the results of applying such methods provide fuel for the discriminant models. Although ideally the discriminant models apply to numerous responses to the same stimuli by the same person on different occasions, this approach is unfeasible in practice. It would be difficult to arrange for subjects to participate in numerous experimental sessions. Also, with some types of stimuli, subjects would remember their responses from occasion to occasion, which would prevent judgments or expressions of sentiments from being independent of one another. For these reasons, the discriminant models are usually applied to percentages of people in a group who state on one occasion that one stimulus is greater than another with respect to an attribute, e.g., the percentage of people who say that one weight is heavier than another or the percentage of people who say that they prefer apples to oranges.

An example of a scale developed from a discriminant model is shown in Table 7-1. The first column of the table shows the percentages of people who stated that they preferred each vegetable below to the neighboring vegetable above. Thus 82 percent of the people stated that they preferred cabbage to turnips, 60 percent preferred beets to cabbage, and so on for the other comparisons. The second column of the table shows the interval scale deduced from these percentages, scores on the interval scales being obtained by converting the percentages to scores on a normal distribution. (The complete computational procedures for this example are presented in Guilford, 1954, Ch. 7.)

In Table 7-1, corn is the most preferred vegetable, and turnips are the least preferred. Examples of small intervals are those between peas and stringbeans and between beets and cabbage. Examples of large intervals are those between cabbage and turnips and between stringbeans and spinach. Because half of the subjects preferred spinach to carrots, the interval between the two vegetables is zero, and consequently they receive the same scale score of 1.13. Because scores are on an interval scale, the absolute sizes of the scores are arbitrary. One could add the same number to all the scores and/or multiply all the scores by the same number, but this would not change the relative sizes of the intervals.

To summarize, discriminatory models are based on a number of principles and practices. First, they do not trust subjects to generate interval scales directly, as models based on subjective estimates do. Second, they elicit re-

**TABLE 7-1**    Scale of preferences for vegetables

|  | PERCENT PREFERENCES | SCALE SCORES |
|---|---|---|
| Turnips | . . . | 0.00 |
| Cabbage | 82 | 0.52 |
| Beets | 60 | 0.66 |
| Asparagus | 56 | 0.98 |
| Carrots | 56 | 1.13 |
| Spinach | 50 | 1.13 |
| Stringbeans | 63 | 1.40 |
| Peas | 53 | 1.44 |
| Corn | 63 | 1.63 |

sponses by one of the psychophysical methods relating to ordinal estimates, e.g., the method of pair comparisons. Third, they assume that the response to any stimulus is not some fixed value, but rather that there is some variability in response to each stimulus. This variability may be conceptualized in terms of numerous responses by one individual to the same stimuli on different occasions or, more frequently, in terms of the variability among individuals in a group in response to the stimuli. Fourth, by making assumptions about the distributions of covert responses to each stimulus, percentages of comparative responses are translatable into intervals between the stimuli. Fifth, it is most frequently assumed that covert errors in response to stimuli are normally distributed, which leads to rather direct computations of interval scales in accordance with the mathematical properties of the normal distribution.

## Checks and balances

So far in this section numerous assumptions have been made in employing different models. How does one know whether the assumptions are correct? First, for any model, there are standards of *internal consistency* that the data must meet. (See Torgerson, 1958, for a detailed discussion of these standards.) Some examples will serve to show how such standards are applied. If a rank-order scale is developed by averaging the ranks given to the same stimuli by different people, the data are internally consistent to the extent that subjects give much the same ranks to the stimuli. Internal consistency for the method of bisection can be tested as follows. First, the subject is required to adjust a light to the point where it is halfway between two others in perceived brightness. Second, the subject obtains two intensities that bisect the two intervals obtained in the first step. Finally, the subject bisects the intensities obtained in the second step. If the data are internally consistent, the subject should arrive back at the first intensity used to bisect the first two stimuli. Data obtained from pair comparisons can be tested for internal consistency by examining the transitivity of scale values. If, for example, stimulus $j$ is found to be 1.0 greater than stimulus $k$ and stimulus $k$ is 0.5 greater than stimulus $i$, and if the data are internally consistent, stimulus $j$ should be 1.5 greater than stimulus $i$. For all the scaling models, there are standards of internal consistency that apply. If the internal consistency is low, one would be very suspicious of the scale.

In addition to internal consistency, another important standard concerns the extent to which scale values can be replicated in studies that differ slightly in procedure. This applies when a new study is undertaken using only some of the stimuli employed in an earlier study. If, for example, the study of vegetables illustrated in Table 7-1 were redone and five new vegetables were added, the relative sizes of the intervals between turnips, cabbage, and beets should remain much the same. If the relative sizes of these intervals changed markedly, one would have little confidence in that method of scaling of vegetables. Previously it was described how an approximate zero point on a scale regarding attitudes could be developed by having subjects balance positive statements with negative statements equidistant across the zero point. In that case there would be a choice as to whether the experimenter would give the subject negative or positive statements to be balanced across the zero point. Also, there would be some choice as to which statements would be used in either case. To the extent that such different approaches would lead to *different* zero points, the method would be suspect with regard to the particular problem of scaling. In all other uses of scaling models, it is expected to find essentially the same rank order, intervals, and ratios when methods of gathering responses or methods of analysis are slightly different.

## models for scaling people

Early in the chapter it was stated that problems of scaling potentially concern a three-dimensional table of data, with the dimensions representing persons, stimuli, and responses. (This was illustrated in Figure 7-1.) In the development of unidimensional scales for either persons or stimuli, it is usually possible to "collapse" the dimension concerning different types of responses. Either it is known from previous studies that all the types of responses concern the same attribute, e.g., by a factor analysis of rating scales bounded by different pairs of adjectives, or only one type of response to each stimulus is required. The latter would be the case, for example, if the subject were required only to agree or disagree with each statement in a list or to indicate whether each statement in a list was correct or incorrect. After the three-dimensional table is reduced to a two-dimensional table, models for developing unidimensional scales concern ways for collapsing one of the two remaining dimensions. The previous section discussed ways of collapsing the person dimension to scale stimuli. This section will treat ways of collapsing the stimulus dimension to scale persons.

### Multi-item measures

Before discussing models for collapsing the stimulus dimension of a two-dimensional table of data, it might be wise to reflect on the need for more than one stimulus in psychological measures. The word "items" will be used in a broad sense to stand for any stimuli used in measurement methods. Thus items may be words on a spelling test, comparisons between weights, statements concerning attitudes toward the United Nations, correct choices of a rat in a maze, and reactions in a study of reaction time. What is presented to the subject is the item (stimulus), and in each of the examples above the subject is required to make only one type of response to each item.

There are a number of important reasons for requiring more than one item in nearly all measures of psychological attributes. First, individual items usually have considerable *specificity*. That is, each item tends to have only a low correlation with the attribute being measured and tends to relate to other attributes. On a spelling test, for example, whether or not a child could correctly spell "umpire" would depend in part on his interest in baseball. A boy who spent much time reading baseball stories might correctly spell the word even though he was a poor speller in general. The specificity of individual items is also illustrated by the rating of the following statement on a seven-step scale of agreement-disagreement: "We give more to the United Nations than we get in return." Supposedly that is a negative statement about the United Nations, and people who agree with it *tend* to have negative attitudes. Even though a person might have an overall positive attitude, however, he might agree with the statement because he is not happy with the share of financing borne by this country.

In both examples above, it can be seen that each item relates in only a statistical sense to the attribute being measured. Each item tends to correlate with the attribute in question, but also correlates with attributes other than the one being measured.

Even if individual items had no specificity, measures would still require more than one item, one reason being that most items attempt to categorize people into either two groups or only a relatively small number of groups. Thus an item requiring dichotomous responses (e.g., pass or fail) can at most distinguish between two levels of the attribute. A seven-step rating scale can at most distinguish between seven levels of an attribute. In most measurement problems it is desirable to make fine differentiations between people, and this can seldom be done with a one-item measure.

Even if there were no specificity in items and items were capable of making very fine distinctions between people, there still would be an important reason why one-item measures would not suffice. Individual items have considerable measurement error; in other words, they are unreliable. Each item, in addition to its specificity, occasions a considerable amount of random error. This is seen when people are required to repeat a set of ratings after a period of time.

The person who gave a rating of 3 on one occasion is likely to give a rating of 5 on another, and many other changes of this kind are expected. Another example would be the solving of arithmetic problems on two occasions. The child who got the correct answer on one occasion might not get the correct answer to the same problem on another occasion, and vice versa. Thus there is some randomness related to any item, and consequently the individual item cannot be trusted to give reliable measurement of an attribute.

All three difficulties that have been discussed can be diminished by the use of multi-item measures. The specificity of items can be averaged out when they are combined. By combining items, one can make relatively fine distinctions between people. As was discussed in Chapter 5, the reliability tends to increase (measurement error reduces) as the number of items in a combination increases. Thus nearly all measures of psychological attributes are multi-item measures. This is true both for measures used in studies of individual differences and for measures used in controlled experiments. The problem of scaling people with respect to attributes is then one of collapsing responses to a number of items so as to obtain one score (measurement) for each person.

Later in this chapter a very simple model that is used most frequently for the scaling of people will be discussed. The model results in the familiar summing of item responses to obtain a total score. Thus the score on a spelling test consists of the number of correct answers, and the score on a measure of attitudes toward the United Nations consists of the number of agreements to favorable statements. Before discussing that model, however, it is necessary to discuss the theoretical foundations from which that model grew. Also, it is necessary to understand the competing models that are available.

### The trace line

Nearly all models for scaling people can be depicted by different types of curves relating an attribute to the probability of responding in one way rather than another to items. Four different types of trace lines are shown in Figures 7-3 to 7-6. Dichotomous items are depicted in these figures. For each item, it will be said that there are two types of responses, alpha and beta. Alpha would variously consist of passing rather than failing an item, agreeing rather than disagreeing with a statement, or a rat making the correct rather than the incorrect turn in a maze.

The meaning of item trace lines can be illustrated with a spelling item that might fit the curve in Figure 7-4. The item is the word "decadent," which is read by a teacher to fifth-grade students. As the curve in Figure 7-4 shows, students who are at the highest level of the attribute of spelling ability would have a probability close to 1.0 of correctly spelling the word. At the other extreme of the attribute, even students who are very low in spelling ability would still have a slight chance of spelling the word correctly. Students with

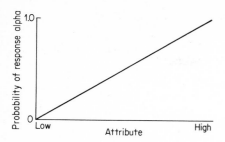

**FIGURE 7-3**     An ascending linear trace line for an item

average spelling ability would have approximately a 50–50 chance of correctly spelling the word.   The curve is relatively flat over both the high and the low extremes of the attribute, which means that the particular item would not distinguish very well between persons who are very high in spelling ability or between students who are very low in spelling ability.   Because the curve tends to be rather steep over the middle range of the attribute, the item would distinguish relatively well between moderately good spellers and moderately poor spellers.

In Figures 7-3 to 7-6, the attribute is the particular thing being measured. In this connection, it is important to make a distinction between the particular attribute being measured and some more general attribute of interest.   Thus the responses of a rat in a maze constitute a particular attribute.   It is hoped that this attribute relates to the more general attribute of habit strength.   On vocabulary tests, identifying correct synonyms for words is a particular attribute, and it is hoped that this particular attribute relates to the general attribute (construct) of intelligence.   The measurement problem itself concerns the relations between particular attributes and the probability of responding in one

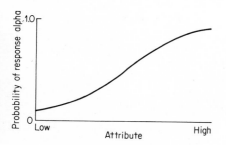

**FIGURE 7-4**     An ascending   monotonic trace line for an item

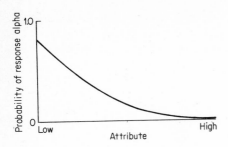

**FIGURE 7-5**    A    descending    monotonic
trace line for an item

way rather than another.   It is only after measures of particular attributes have been constructed that they can be combined to measure more general attributes (constructs).

In the remainder of this chapter, the abscissa for models concerning trace lines will concern particular attributes.   Attributes are defined in a circular sense in terms of whatever a number of items tend to measure in common.   Thus a list of spelling words would tend to measure spelling ability, and the number of correct turns of a rat in a maze would tend to measure amount learned.   The word "tend" is used because it must be recognized that no attribute is perfectly mirrored in any set of items.   Perfect measurement would be possible, for example, if children were administered a spelling test containing all words in the English language or if rats were capable of running an infinitely long maze.   When there is a limited number of items, as there always is, there is some unreliability involved in the measurement of the particular attribute. Completely reliable measures of an attribute are called *true scores*, and the approximations to true scores obtained from any collection of items are called *fallible scores*.   In all the figures showing item trace lines, the abscissa concerns true scores on the particular attribute.   Of course, one does not know exactly

**FIGURE 7-6**    A nonmonotonic trace line
for an item

what the true scores are, but they can be approximated by scores obtained from some combination of the available items. For this reason, after some way has been formulated for combining items, an approximate test can be made for the actual trace line of any particular item; e.g., the trace line for a spelling item can be computed as a function of the number of words correctly spelled on the test.

The concept of trace lines also applies to multipoint items (items that are scorable on more than two points), an example of which is shown in Figure 7-7. Instead of depicting the probability of response alpha, the ordinate depicts the average score on the item. Figure 7-7 shows the average scores on a seven-step rating scale for persons at different levels of an attribute. Other multipoint items whose trace lines could be depicted in that way are scores on essay questions in a classroom examination, number of words correctly recalled in a study of memory, and amount of time taken to respond to a signal in studies of reaction time. An average score is an *expected score*, and consequently Figure 7-7 depicts the expected score as a function of levels of an attribute.

In discussing trace lines, it is useful to think of the attribute as being completely continuous; i.e., it is theoretically possible to make infinitely fine discriminations between people. Also, it is useful to think of there being a large number of persons at each of the infinite number of points on the attribute. In this hypothetical circumstance, the trace line shows the expected response for people at each level of the attribute, the expectation being expressed either as a probability of response alpha for dichotomous items or as an average score for multipoint items. By their nature, expectations are accompanied by some error. On dichotomous items, there is a probability of response alpha at each point, but there is no certainty as to *which* persons at a point will make response alpha and which persons will make response beta. On multipoint items, there is a band of error surrounding the expected average score. Thus although the expected score for a particular point on an attribute might be 3.0, the actual scores of people at that point might range from 1.5 to 4.5.

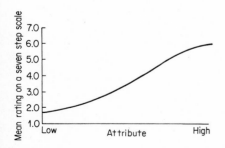

**FIGURE 7-7**   Trace   line   of   average scores on a seven-step rating scale

## deterministic models for scaling people

Deterministic models are so called because they assume that there is *no error* in item trace lines. For dichotomous items, at each point of the attribute it is assumed that the probability of response alpha is either 1.0 or zero. The particular deterministic model employed most frequently is one which assumes that up to a point on the attribute, the probability of response alpha is zero (probability of response beta is 1.0) and beyond that point the probability of response alpha is 1.0. An item of this type is shown in Figure 7-8, and a family of such items is shown in Figure 7-9. Each item has a biserial correlation of 1.0 with the attribute, and consequently each item perfectly discriminates at a particular point of the attribute. Intuitively, this is a very appealing model because it is exactly what one expects to obtain in measurements of length. Thus one would expect to obtain a family of trace lines like that shown in Figure 7-9 for the following items:

|  | Yes | No |
|---|---|---|
| 1. Are you above 6 feet 6 inches in height? | _____ | _____ |
| 2. Are you above 6 feet 3 inches in height? | _____ | _____ |
| 3. Are you above 6 feet in height? | _____ | _____ |
| 4. Are you above 5 feet 9 inches in height? | _____ | _____ |
| 5. Are you above 5 feet 6 inches in height? | _____ | _____ |

Answering "yes" can be considered response alpha. Any person who answered "yes" to item 1 would answer yes to the others. Any person who did not answer yes to item 1 but did answer yes to item 2 would also answer "yes" to items 3 to 5. For five people with different patterns of responses, a triangular pattern of data would be found like that in Table 7-2. An "X" symbolizes an answer of "yes" (response alpha).

### Guttman scale

Although the exact nature of trace lines is never known, one can look at data and see whether they evolve into a triangular pattern like that in Table 7-2.

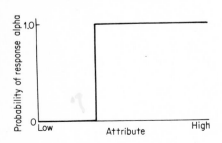

**FIGURE 7-8**    Trace line of an item that discriminates perfectly at one point of an attribute

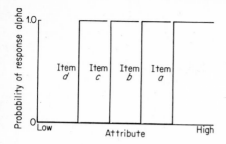

**FIGURE 7-9**    Family of trace lines for four items that meet the requirements of a monotone deterministic model

(In so doing, however, one is making a subtle logical assumption—a point which will be discussed later.)    Some types of items tend to produce a pattern of data like that in Table 7-2.   The following is an example:

|     |  | Yes | No |
|-----|--|-----|----|
| 1. | The United Nations is the savior of mankind. | _____ | _____ |
| 2. | The United Nations is our best hope for peace. | _____ | _____ |
| 3. | The United Nations is a constructive force in the world. | _____ | _____ |
| 4. | We should continue to participate in the United Nations. | _____ | _____ |

There is a high probability that any person who answers "yes" to item 1 will answer "yes" to the other items.   Any person who does not answer "yes" to item 1 but does answer "yes" to item 2 has a high probability of answering "yes" to the other items.

**TABLE 7-2**    Triangular pattern of responses that would fit requirements of a monotone deterministic scaling model

| ITEM | PERSON | | | | |
|------|----|----|----|----|----|
|      | 1 | 2 | 3 | 4 | 5 |
| a | X |   |   |   |   |
| b | X | X |   |   |   |
| c | X | X | X |   |   |
| d | X | X | X | X |   |
| e | X | X | X | X | X |

Any set of items that produces a pattern of responses approximately like that in Table 7-2 is called a *Guttman scale*. In developing such a scale, one administers a collection of items to a group of people and then attempts to arrange the responses so as to produce the required triangular pattern. (Since in actual data there would be more than one person at each level of the attribute, the data would appear in the form of a solid staircase, with the width of each step being proportional to the number of persons at each level.) There are numerous cut-and-try methods for doing this (see Torgerson, 1958). Of course, obtaining the triangular pattern exactly is very unlikely, and therefore it is necessary (1) to discard some items and (2) to find the best possible ordering of items and people. Regarding the latter consideration, of primary concern is the *reproducibility* of score patterns. If the triangular pattern is perfectly obtained, a knowledge of the *number* of responses of "yes" allows one to reproduce all the person's responses. When the triangular pattern is approximately obtained, a knowledge of the number of "yes" responses a person makes allows one approximately to reproduce all that person's responses. For all people and all items, one can investigate the percentage of reproducibility, and it is this percentage which is all-important in the development of Guttman scales.

Conceivably, Guttman scales could be developed for all types of items requiring dichotomous responses. This can be illustrated with a spelling test consisting of 40 items. For each item, the subject indicates whether or not the word is correctly spelled. If the items had trace lines like those in Figure 7-9, a triangular pattern of data would be obtained. In this instance, an X would stand for a correct response to the spelling of the word. If one person has a score of 35 and another a score of 34, this would necessarily mean that the former person got the *same* 34 items correct as the latter person, plus one additional item. If one knew how many words an individual passed, he would know exactly which items that person passed.

### Evaluation of the Guttman scale

In spite of the intuitive appeal of the Guttman scale, it is highly impractical. First, it is highly unrealistic to think that items could have trace lines like those in Figure 7-9, because no item correlates perfectly with any attribute. Although there is no way to obtain the trace lines directly, some good approximations are available. For example, with items concerning spelling, the number of words correctly spelled can be used as an approximation of the attribute (true scores in spelling). When the trace line is obtained in such instances, not only is it not perpendicular at a point, but it also typically tends to have a relatively flat, approximately linear form. Typically, individual items correlate no higher than .40 with total scores. Consequently, it is very unreasonable to work with a model that assumes perfect biserial correlations between items and an attribute.

Second, having the triangular pattern of data is no guarantee that items have trace lines like those in Figure 7-9.  If items are spaced far enough apart in difficulty (popularity on nonability items), the triangular pattern can be obtained even if the trace lines are very flat rather than vertical.  This is illustrated with the following four items:

1. Solve for $x$: $x^2 + 6x + 12 = 3$.
2. What is the meaning of the word "severe"?
3. How much is $10 \times 38$?
4. When do you use an umbrella? (Given orally.)

Although the author has not performed the experiment, the above four items administered to persons ranging in age from six to sixteen would probably form an excellent Guttman scale.  Any person who got the first item correct could probably get the others correct.  Any person who failed the first item but got the second correct would probably get the other two correct.  Those four items would produce the required triangular pattern of data even though there is good evidence that they do not all belong to the same attribute ("factor," in the language of factor analysis).  The reason they apparently fit the model for a unidimensional scale is that they are administered to an extremely diverse population.  They would not fit the model if they were investigated within one age group only.  Consequently, as was suggested earlier, it is not entirely logical to assume that having a triangular pattern of data like that in Table 7-2 is *sufficient* evidence for the presence of a unidimensional scale.

Because the triangular pattern of data can be approximated in any study where items vary greatly in difficulty, in practice this results in scales with very few items (seldom more than eight).  To take an extreme case, if there are three items that are passed by 10 percent, 50 percent, and 90 percent of the people, respectively, the triangular pattern will be obtained almost perfectly, regardless of what the items concern.  The difficulties of items can be dispersed in this way only if the final scale contains only a small number of items.  This usually is done by starting with a relatively large number of items (say, 20) and discarding all items but a few that vary widely in difficulty.  This is only a way of fooling oneself into believing that a unidimensional scale has been obtained when it really has not.  Also, since such scales seldom have more than eight items, they can make only rather gross distinctions between people.

A third criticism of the Guttman scale is that it seeks to obtain only an ordinal measurement of human attributes.  As was argued in the first chapter, there are good reasons for believing that it is sensible to measure most human attributes on interval scales, if not usually on ratio scales.  If psychology were to settle only for ordinal measurement, it would so limit the usable methods of mathematics that the science would be nearly crippled.

A fourth criticism of the Guttman scale concerns its intuitive appeal.  It would be more appropriate to think of items not as yardsticks being applied to the heights of people but rather as rubber yardsticks applied by half-blind investigators. Also, to complete the analogy, one should think of each item as a different rubber yardstick which has been copied from a real yardstick by a five-year-old boy. On some of the yardsticks, the zero point starts at 4 inches, and the boy has made numerous large random errors in copying intervals (widths of 1 inch). If 20 such rubber yardsticks were applied to a group of people, any yardstick (item) would have only a rather flat trace line with respect to the actual heights. By methods which will be discussed in subsequent sections, one could combine the different measurements for each person to obtain an approximately linear relationship with the real scale of heights, and thus in this way one could obtain an interval scale.

In summary, the deterministic model underlying the Guttman scale is thoroughly illogical for most psychological measurement because (1) almost no items exist that fit the model, (2) the presence of a triangular pattern is a necessary but not sufficient condition for the fit of the model in particular instances, (3) the triangular pattern can be (and usually is) artificially forced by dealing with a small number of items that vary greatly in difficulty, (4) the model aspires to develop only ordinal scales, and (5) there are better intuitive bases for developing models for psychological attributes. Considering this heavy weight of criticism, it is surprising that some people still consider this deterministic model a good basis for developing measures of psychological attributes.

## Nonmonotone deterministic models

There are other deterministic models in addition to the Guttman scale (Torgerson, 1958). One of these makes the following assumptions: Each item is responded to in manner alpha by all the people at one level, and each person responds in manner alpha to only one item. Trace lines for three such items are shown in Figure 7-10. The pattern of data produced by such a model is shown in Table 7-3. In contrast to the Guttman scale, in this deterministic model each item has a nonmonotone trace line; i.e., the line goes up and then comes down. The following four items would fit this model:

|  | Yes | No |
|---|---|---|
| 1. Are you between 6 feet, 3 inches tall and 6 feet, 6 inches? | _____ | _____ |
| 2. Are you between 6 feet tall and 6 feet, 3 inches? | _____ | _____ |
| 3. Are you between 5 feet, 9 inches tall and 6 feet? | _____ | _____ |
| 4. Are you between 5 feet, 6 inches tall and 5 feet, 9 inches? | _____ | _____ |

Using the word "items" in the broadest sense, it would be very rare to find any items on psychological measures that would fit this model. All the criticisms that apply to the Guttman scale apply with added force to this nonmonotone deterministic model.

Deterministic models are of use mainly to specialists in the theory of psychological measurement. Such models frequently represent "limiting cases" of

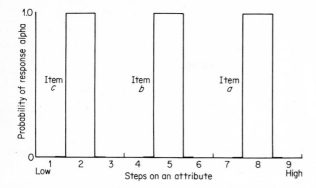

**FIGURE 7-10**    Trace lines for three items that meet the requirements of a nonmonotone deterministic scaling model

models that are actually used to develop measures of psychological attributes. Other than for this use, they are only interesting museum pieces. Only by working with some type of nondeterministic probability model can one develop the measures that are needed in research.

## probability models for scaling people

If trace lines are not assumed to have perpendicular ascents and descents, one is working with some type of probability model. There are numerous types of probability models, depending on the type of curve assumed for the trace lines. The most prominent models are discussed in the following sections.

### Nonmonotone models

Analogous to nonmonotone deterministic models such as the one discussed above are nonmonotone probability models. Any type of curve that changes

**TABLE 7-3**    Pattern of responses to four items that meets requirements of a monotone deterministic scaling model

| ITEM | PERSON | | | |
|---|---|---|---|---|
| | 1 | 2 | 3 | 4 |
| a | X | | | |
| b | | X | | |
| c | | | X | |
| d | | | | X |

slope at some point from positive to negative or vice versa is nonmonotone. Some examples are shown in Figure 7-11. The only nonmonotone model that has been used frequently assumes that (1) the attribute is continuous and (2) each item has a trace line that approximates the normal distribution. The probability of responding in manner alpha is highest at a particular point on the attribute, and from that point the probability of responding in manner alpha falls off in both directions in general resemblance to the normal curve. Three such items are shown in Figure 7-12.

Trace lines need not be exactly normal, and standard deviations of trace lines need not be identical. This model has been used for only one purpose: the development of certain types of attitude scales. Since the scaling procedure was developed by Thurstone, the type of scale is referred to as a *Thurstone scale of attitudes*. Items at three points on such a scale are as follows:

|  | Agree | Disagree |
|---|---|---|
| 1. I believe that the church is the greatest institution in America today. | _____ | _____ |
| 2. When I go to church, I enjoy a fine ritual service with good music. | _____ | _____ |
| 3. The paternal and benevolent attitude of the church is quite distasteful to me. | _____ | _____ |

The first step in obtaining a Thurstone scale is to have a large number of attitude statements rated by about fifty judges (see Edwards, 1957b, for a complete discussion of procedures). Each statement is usually rated on an 11-step scale ranging from "strongly favorable statement" to "strongly unfavorable statement." From 10 to 20 items are selected from the larger collection of items according to the following two standards: (1) items that have small standard deviations of ratings over judges (i.e., agreement is good among judges about where the items belong on the scale) and (2) items that range evenly from one extreme to the other.

The essence of the Thurstone nonmonotone model is that each item should

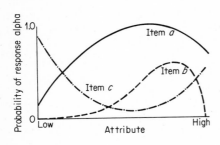

**FIGURE 7-11** Three items with nonmonotone trace lines

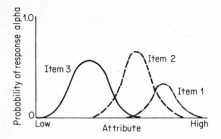

**FIGURE 7-12**    Nonmonotone    normal
trace lines for three items

tend to receive agreement (response alpha) at only one zone of the attribute. To assume an approximately normal distribution for the trace line is to admit that each item occasions some error.

Various methods are used to provide scores on Thurstone scales. If the person agreed with only one item, his score would equal the scale point corresponding to that item. However, it is usually found that a person agrees with at least several of the items, in which case one can obtain a score by averaging the scale points for the items. For example, if a person indicated agreement with three items having scale points of 7, 8, and 9, respectively, his score would be 8.

The major fault of the Thurstone scale and of other nonmonotone probability models is that it is very difficult to find any items that fit. The model obviously would not fit most types of items. For example, how could one find spelling words such that each would be correctly spelled only by persons in a narrow band of the attribute of spelling ability? An item that "peaked" at the lower end of the scale would be one that is spelled correctly only by rather poor spellers. For an item that peaked in the middle of the scale, very few people with superior ability in spelling would give a correct response. This type of scale clearly does not apply to any items requiring judgments.

Even with responses concerning sentiments, the Thurstone model would seem to apply only to certain types of statements relating to attitudes, and even there the model is in logical trouble. Attitude statements tend to fit this model only if they are "double-barreled"—only if they say two things, one of which is good and the other bad. This can be seen by a careful analysis of the three attitude statements given earlier. In item 2, the subject is asked to agree simultaneously with two hidden statements:

I sometimes go to church.
I probably would not go to church except for the fine ritual service and good music.

Item 3 is "triple-barreled." To agree with it, the subject must agree that the church is paternal, benevolent, and distasteful. The three modifiers add up to a moderately negative attitude toward the church. It is possible to construct such items only by subtly building two or more statements into what is ostensibly one statement. This type of item not only is very difficult to construct but also tends to be ambiguous to subjects. Some subjects respond to one of the hidden statements, and some subjects to another. In a more exaggerated form, this ambiguity is evidenced in the following double-barreled statement: "The church is a wonderful, horrible institution."

Another important criticism of nonmonotone probability models is that it is very difficult to think of items for the ends of the scale that would fit. This is illustrated with item 1 in the previous example. Who could have so *positive* an attitude toward the church that he would *disagree* with the statement, "I believe the church is the greatest institution in America today"? Such items are necessarily monotone, continuing to rise as one reaches higher and higher levels of the attribute.

In summary, nonmonotone probability models conceivably apply to only certain types of items for the measurement of attitudes, and there are better ways to construct attitude scales (see Chapter 14). Such better methods are based on the linear model for scaling people, which will be discussed later in this chapter.

### Monotone models with specified distribution forms

In some of the models that assume monotone trace lines, it is assumed that the trace lines fit a particular statistical function. Most frequently it has been assumed that the function is a *normal ogive.* (A normal ogive is a cumulative normal distribution.) Figure 7-13 shows three items having normal-ogive trace lines. The important feature of a normal-ogive trace line is that it is much more discriminating at certain levels of the attribute than it is at neighboring levels. The zone where discrimination is good is that below the steeply ascending part of the curve. The steeper that section of the curve, the higher the biserial correlation of that item with the attribute. If that section were

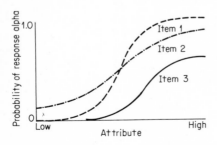

**FIGURE 7-13**    Three items with normal-ogive trace lines

vertical, the "tails" would disappear, the item would correlate perfectly with the attribute, and a collection of such items would form a Guttman scale. As items correlate less and less with the attribute, the S shape tends to flatten toward a straight line, and the slope approaches the horizontal.

The normal-ogive model is appealing for two reasons. First, it makes good sense intuitively. Thus, for each item, one can think of a critical zone on the attribute where there is considerable uncertainty concerning how people will respond. As one moves away from that zone in either direction, the uncertainty is markedly reduced. Persons below that zone will predominantly fail the item, and persons above it will predominantly pass. An increasing slope of the trace line over some zone is more to be expected than, say, a straight line. Other intuitive support for the normal ogive comes from studies concerning the scaling of stimuli. There it is found, for example, that judgments of weights by the method of constant stimuli usually fit a normal ogive (see Figure 7-2).

The second reason for the appeal of this model is that it has very useful mathematical properties that permit the deduction of many important principles (Lord, 1952b). For example, the sum of any number of normal ogives is also a normal ogive, and the exact shape and slope of the latter can be predicted from the ogives which are summed. Then if one obtains a scale by summing scores on individual items (e.g., enumerating the number correct), the average scores or sums of scores form a normal-ogive relationship with the attributes. (The sum of probabilities for any number of normal ogives over a point on an attribute would be the expected sum of scores on the test as a whole for persons at that point.) This means that summing scores on items to obtain total scores (which is the usual approach) produces a scale that is *not* linearly related to the attribute. However, in practice this involves a very slight danger because even if trace lines do form normal ogives, the curves are found to be so flat that they are hard to distinguish from straight lines. Also, when items that vary considerably in difficulty are combined, combined normal ogives look less S-shaped than they would if all items had been equally difficult. For these two reasons, even if one accepts the normal-ogive model, it is reasonable to assume that total test scores have an approximately linear relationship with the attribute.

There are many other interesting deductions that can be made from the normal-ogive model. The most discriminating collection of items for any particular point on the attribute would consist of those items whose sum of ogives is as steep as possible over that point. This fact permits some interesting deductions about the relations between discrimination at a point, difficulty of items, and correlations of items with total scores (Lord, 1952b). Other interesting deductions from this model concern the amount of measurement error (unreliability) for a test corresponding to different points on the attribute.

An important point to grasp in discussing monotone models with specified distribution forms is that these models have not led to ways of scaling persons other than by the conventional approach, which is to sum scores on items. Thus if one is scaling spelling ability, these models do not argue against the conventional method of scaling, which is to count the number of words correctly spelled. The situation is the same with all other attributes. What these models do is to permit some important deductions about the psychometric characteristics of measures that are obtained by summing item scores, and for that purpose they have proved very useful.

### Monotone models with unspecified distribution forms

Finally we arrive at the model that underlies most efforts to scale people (and lower animals). The model makes three major assumptions. First, it is assumed only that each item has a monotonic trace line. It is not assumed that all items have the same type of monotonic curve. Second, it is assumed that the sum of the trace lines for a particular set of items (the trace line for total test scores) is approximately linear. That is, even if items do not all have the same type of monotonic trace line, it is assumed that departures from linearity tend to average out as items are combined. A family of such trace lines is shown in Figure 7-14. The sum of these trace lines is shown in Figure 7-15, which is the trace line of expected scores on a four-item test.

The third assumption is that the items as a whole tend to measure only the attribute in question. This is the same as saying that the items have only one factor in common, a point which will be discussed in detail in later chapters. The implication is that total scores on the particular collection of items summarize all the information about psychological attributes that is inherent in the item scores.

The three assumptions discussed above constitute the *linear model*, or, as it is frequently called, the *summative model*. It is said to be "linear" for two reasons. First, it is assumed that the sum of item scores has an approximately linear relationship with the attribute in question. Second, and more important

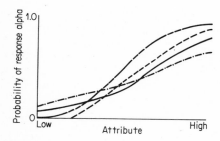

**FIGURE 7-14**     A family of four items with monotone trace lines

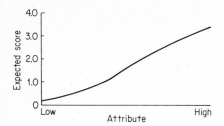

**FIGURE 7-15**    Expected scores on a four-item test—the sum of trace lines in Figure 7-14

for the sake of the name, the model leads to a *linear combination* of items. A simple sum of variables is a linear combination of variables, and a simple sum of item scores is a linear combination of those scores.

If one looks carefully at psychological measures, he will see that in nearly all cases they consist of summing scores over items. Spelling ability is measured by summing scores over items, i.e., by simply counting the number of words correctly spelled. In paired-associate learning, the amount learned by each person is measured by counting the number of pairs recalled. In a study of rat learning in a T maze, the level of learning is measured by the number of correct choices in a block of trials. In a measure of attitudes toward the United Nations, a total score is obtained by summing the number of agreements with positive statements and the number of disagreements with negative statements.

The linear model applies to multipoint items as well as to items which are scored dichotomously. Reaction time in a particular experiment would be determined by averaging the reaction times for a subject in a block of trials. Total scores on an essay examination in history would be obtained by summing scores on individual questions. Attitudes toward the United Nations would be obtained by summing the ratings of 10 statements on a seven-step scale of agreement-disagreement.

It is not difficult to think of psychological measures that fit the linear model —rather, it is difficult to think of measures that do not fit the model. In this chapter we have come a long way around to the conclusion that the most sensible way to measure psychological attributes is to sum scores on items. The essence of the linear model is that it does not take individual items very seriously. It recognizes that the individual item has considerable specificity and measurement error. It does not make stringent assumptions about the trace line. The only assumption made is that each item has some form of monotonic trace line, and even that is not a strict assumption, since some of the items could have slightly curvilinear trace lines and a linear relationship of total scores with the attribute would still be obtainable.

The remainder of this book is based mainly on the linear model. This model makes sense and works well in practice. At the present time there is no other model on the scene that represents a serious challenge in terms of scaling people with respect to psychological attributes.

## Summary

Measurement in psychology potentially concerns a three-dimensional table of data, with the three dimensions concerning persons, stimuli, and responses, respectively. In most investigations, however, the situation is somewhat simpler, in that only two dimensions are present. This would be the case where only one person is investigated, where a number of people make only one response to each stimulus, or where a number of people make numerous responses to only one stimulus.

Assuming either that only two dimensions of the table of data are present initially or that one can employ some assumptions to collapse one of the three dimensions, the problem in generating a psychological measure is to employ a set of rules for collapsing one of the two remaining dimensions. The overall problem is said to be one of *psychological scaling,* and the particular set of rules employed is said to constitute a *scaling model.* Numerous such scaling models are available. Which one is used in a particular investigation is determined by the nature of the data and by the intuitions of the investigator. The wisdom of such decisions hinges on how well the obtained measurement scales help explain psychological phenomena; e.g., a particular model for scaling intelligence might prove to relate strongly with school grades and other forms of success in life.

The selection of a scaling model is influenced by three major characteristics of the research problem. First, it is important to distinguish the scaling of stimuli from the scaling of people. The former would be the case in scaling the perceived loudness of tones, and the latter would be the case in scaling people with respect to spelling ability.

Second, it is important to consider whether the problem concerns *judgments* or *sentiments.* The former would be at issue in a study of lifted weights, and the latter would be at issue in a study of preferences for movie actors. Somewhat different kinds of measurement problems are obtained with the two types of responses. For example, in a study of judgments, it is frequently sensible to assume that individual differences between people are unimportant and thus can be ignored, but that is seldom a safe assumption in studies of sentiments.

Third, it is important to consider whether the problem concerns comparative responses or absolute responses. The former would be the case when subjects rank-order 10 weights in terms of heaviness; the latter would be the case when subjects rate vegetables on a like-dislike rating scale. The two types of responses lend themselves to different scaling models.

There are two major classes of models for the scaling of stimuli: models concerning *subjective estimates* and models concerning *confusions*. In the former class of models, it is assumed that subjects can generate scales directly, and typically what one does is simply to average the scales produced by different subjects. For example, one would average the ratings given of preferences for vegetables and let those average ratings constitute an overall scale. With methods based on confusions, the experimenter does not trust subjects to generate scales directly; rather, he deduces scales from overlapping responses or confusions, e.g., from the percentage of people who prefer each vegetable in a list to each of the other vegetables. Statistical procedures are available for converting such percentages into measurement scales.

In contrast to the aforementioned models for the scaling of stimuli, models for the scaling of persons are intimately concerned with assumptions about shapes of item *trace lines*. An item trace line is a hypothetical curve showing the probability of passing an item, or responding in one way rather than another, as a function of an underlying trait, such as intelligence or aggressiveness. Numerous models can be employed depending upon the assumptions one makes about such hypothetical trace lines. By far the most simple, and in many ways the most sensible, model for scaling people is that which assumes only that trace lines are monotonic, i.e., that higher levels of the trait always correspond to higher probabilities of responding in one way rather than another. This model is referred to as the *linear* or *summative* model because in practice it results in the simple summing of item scores to obtain total scores, e.g., obtaining a score in spelling ability by counting the number of words correctly spelled. The linear model is used much more frequently than any other model for the day-to-day measurement of individual differences in psychological traits and performance in controlled experiments.

## Suggested additional readings

Coombs, C. H.  A theory of data.  *Psychological Review*, 1960, 67, 143–159.

Edwards, A. L.  *Techniques of attitude scale construction.*  New York: Appleton-Century-Crofts, 1957.

Guilford, J. P.  *Psychometric methods.*  (2nd ed.) New York: McGraw-Hill, 1954.  Chs. 2, 10.

Gulliksen, H., & Messick, S. (Eds.)  *Psychological scaling: Theory and applications.*  New York: Wiley, 1960.

Torgerson, W.  *Theory and methods of scaling.*  New York: Wiley, 1958.

# CHAPTER 8

# Test
# construction

Until recent years there was considerable disagreement about proper methods of test construction. Much of the disagreement apparently arose from a failure to state fundamental principles of scaling, validity, and reliability. Without agreement on these principles, different measurement specialists advocated different approaches to test construction. The situation was much like that of three motorists who sit and argue about the best roads to travel when they either do not know where they want to go or plan to go to different places. Now there is apparently more agreement on basic objectives. If the principles discussed in previous chapters are largely correct, it is rather easy to develop satisfactory principles of test construction.

In Chapter 7, the *linear model* was accepted as the most appropriate for the development of most measures of psychological attributes. The model stipulates that test scores are to be obtained by summing scores over items. The items can be either weighted or unweighted, and either they can all have positive signs in the combination or some can have negative signs. All these possibilities are subsumed under the concept of a linear combination of test items. Although there are competing models for special problems of measurement, the linear model has no general competitor. Probably 95 percent of all psychological measures are based on the linear model, and this will probably continue to be the case. For these reasons, it will be assumed that the linear model should be used as a guide in nearly all test construction.

Whereas it will be convenient to speak of "test construction," the principles in this chapter apply to all forms of psychological measurement, e.g., to physiological measures of anxiety, to measures of activity in the rat, and to measures of learning rate in paired-associate learning. The principles apply to any measure that is obtained from a linear combination of individual responses, items on mental tests constituting only a special case. The principles apply to measures of ability, personality, and attitudes, and they apply both to dichotomous items and to items scorable on more than two points.

Previously it was said that, depending on the way tests are used, one of three standards of validity applies—predictive validity, content validity, or construct validity. As will be discussed more fully later in this chapter, the methods of test construction used for measures intended to have predictive validity and for those intended to have construct validity should be the same. Somewhat different methods of test construction are required, however, for instruments that depend primarily on content validity. First, brief mention will be made of principles concerning the construction of measures intended to have content validity, and then the remainder of the chapter will be devoted to principles concerning the construction of measures intended to serve the other two functions.

## construction of achievement tests

As was mentioned in Chapter 6, the achievement test is the most obvious example of a measure that requires content validity. The term "achievement test" will be used in a general sense to refer to (1) examinations in individual courses of instruction in schools of all kinds and at all levels, (2) standardized measures of achievement used routinely by all the instructors in a particular unit of instruction, and (3) commercially distributed tests of achievement used throughout the country. Such measures of achievement are very frequently employed at all levels of education up through graduate school and professional training, in civil service examinations, and in special training programs in military establishments and in industry.

In terms of sheer numbers of tests administered, achievement tests outrank all other tests by far. For three reasons, however, only brief mention will be made here of procedures for the construction of achievement tests. First, the basic principles for constructing achievement tests are rather simple and can be stated quickly. Second, although there are hundreds of special techniques for constructing achievement tests of particular kinds for particular purposes, e.g., achievement tests for grammatical skills and mechanical drawing, these special techniques are of interest mainly to professional educators and specialists in measurement. Since this book is aimed at students in general rather than any special group, a lengthy discussion of such special techniques would be out of place. Third, there are comprehensive books devoted either wholly or in large part to the construction of achievement tests. These are listed in the Suggested Additional Readings at the end of this chapter (see Gerberich, 1956; Nunnally, 1964, Chs. 5, 7; and Wood, 1960).

### The test plan

As was mentioned in Chapter 6, ensuring the content validity of an achievement test by an explicit plan for constructing the test is more appropriate than determining the content validity after the test has been constructed. If representative persons who are to use the test agree in advance on the appropriateness of the plan, arriving at an acceptable instrument is mainly a matter of technical skill and applied research.

The major part of the test plan is an outline of content for the instrument which is to be constructed. Since content validity depends on a rational appeal to an adequate coverage of important content, an explicit outline of content provides a basis for discussing content validity. For example, an outline of content for a comprehensive achievement test for the fourth grade would need to indicate whether or not a section on "study skills" was to be included. If such a section was to be included, it would also be necessary to list the aspects of study skills that would be covered, e.g., use of the dictionary and locating topics in reference books.

In addition to outlining content, the plan should describe the types of items to be employed, state the approximate number of items to be employed in each section and each subsection of the test, and give examples of the types of items to be used. The plan should also state how long the test will take to administer, how it will be administered, how it will be scored, and the types of norms that will be obtained.

When the plan is completed, it is reviewed by numerous persons, including teachers, subject-matter experts, administrative officials (in public schools, industry, the military, and other organizations), and specialists in educational and psychological measurement. Many suggestions might be made for changes, and the revised plan would be resubmitted to reviewers. The hope is that the eventual plan will receive general approval from reviewers.

Of course, such an elaborate plan would be undertaken only for achievement tests that were to be used quite widely, such as commercially distributed tests of overall achievement for elementary school and achievement tests used in large training programs in military establishments. At the other extreme, an instructor probably would not develop an elaborate plan for constructing a course examination (an achievement test) which was to be used only with his students. But even in this case it is wise for the instructor to make an outline of the intended coverage. This will provide a basis for judging the adequacy of coverage, and a discussion of the outline with fellow instructors will help ensure content validity.

## Test items

Of course, a test can be no better than the items of which it is composed. A good plan represents an *intention* to construct a good test, but unless items are skillfully written, the plan never materializes. Most frequently, items are marred by two shortcomings. First, they may be ambiguous because they fail to "aim" students adequately toward the type of response required. A classic example is, "What happened to art during the fifteenth century?" The question is so vague that the student could take many different directions on an essay examination and could legitimately select several different alternatives on a multiple-choice item. A second major fault is that items often concern trivial aspects of the subject matter. It is tempting to populate tests with items concerning dates, names, and simple facts because such items are unambiguous and can be written quickly. Most instructors will agree, however, that memory of simple details is not the important thing to be measured; what is important is to measure various aspects of "reasoning with" the subject matter. But regardless of the type of item employed, it takes considerable skill to write items that adequately measure a true understanding of principles.

There is a choice as to which type of item will be employed, including short-answer essay questions, longer essay questions, and numerous types of objective items. Among objective items, the multiple-choice item is considered the best for most purposes. For three reasons, commercially distributed achievement tests rely almost solely on multiple-choice items. First, they are very easy to administer and score. Second, expert item writers who are highly skilled at composing such items are available. Third, when multiple-choice items are skillfully composed, they can accurately measure almost anything. Time and again it has been shown that a test composed of good multiple-choice items correlates with an essay test of the same topic almost as highly as the reliability of the latter will permit. Since the multiple-choice test is typically much more reliable than the essay test, the conclusion is inescapable that the objective test is more valid. This relationship tends to hold even with material where intuitively it would not seem possible, e.g., in comparison of a multiple-choice test for the pronunciation of a foreign language with scores given on oral exercises.

Although in some instances it logically would be very difficult to employ multiple-choice items to measure achievement (e.g., English composition), most of the major achievement tests have no essay questions.

In practice, though, this is not always a major disadvantage. When essay questions are used in achievement tests, they usually correlate so highly with other sections of the test that they can be omitted. Thus, for example, when essay questions are tried as measures of English composition, they tend to add little new variance to what can be explained by multiple-choice tests of vocabulary, reading comprehension, and grammar. This is due partly to a much higher reliability for the objective sections of the test and partly to a high degree of overlap between abilities required in the objective items and ability in English composition.

In addition to higher reliability and ease of scoring, another advantage of multiple-choice items is that they usually sample the topic much more broadly than would be possible on essay examinations. For example, a 50-minute classroom examination could easily employ 50 multiple-choice items without excessively "speeding" students, but it would be difficult to employ more than 5 one-page essay questions in the same amount of time. How well students performed on the essay questions would depend to some extent on their "luck" regarding which questions were asked, but such luck (measurement error due to the sampling of content) would tend to average out over 50 multiple-choice items. Since there is measurement error due to the sampling of content and an equally large amount of measurement error due to the subjectivity of scoring, the multiple-choice examination is usually much more reliable than the essay examination. A typical finding would be an alternative-form reliability between .60 and .70 for the essay examination and a reliability between .80 and .90 for the multiple-choice examination.

Although the skillful item writer can measure almost anything with multiple-choice items, this is not true of many instructors, particularly those not familiar with principles of measurement and without considerable experience in constructing objective tests. In classes with a large number of students (50 or more), there is usually no choice but to employ an objective examination. To do a careful job of grading that many essay examinations would be a monstrous chore. When there are no more than 15 students in a class, it actually saves time to construct and score an essay examination rather than a multiple-choice examination. Even if the multiple-choice examination is very easy to score, a good one is time-consuming to construct. When there are as many as 30 students, the practical advantage is on the side of the multiple-choice examination. When the class contains between 15 and 30 students, there is no strong practical advantage to using either type of test, and consequently the decision between them should be made on other grounds. If instructors feel more comfortable in constructing one type of test rather than the other, they should probably follow their own intuitions in that regard.

The labors of constructing a multiple-choice test are greatly diminished if the instructor has a pool of items that have been accumulated from previous classes. Once such a pool of items is developed, most of the items for a new test can be drawn from that pool, with the addition of some new items to take into account changing emphases in the unit of instruction. When such a pool of items is available, constructing and scoring a multiple-choice test nearly always takes less time than constructing and scoring an essay test for the same subject matter.

If essay questions are used, it is generally best to employ short-answer questions which can be answered in no more than half a page. Short-answer questions have a number of advantages over long-answer questions. Since more questions can be included, the short-answer examination makes it possible to provide a broader coverage of the content. In short-answer questions, it is easier to "aim" the student toward the intended types of responses. There then will be fewer instances in which a student writes brilliantly on something different from what the instructor intended. Also, short-answer questions are much easier for the instructor to grade. Not only do students get lost while responding to long-answer questions, but instructors also get lost trying to grade them. With short-answer questions, it is much easier for the instructor to formulate a concrete basis for grading and to keep the standards in mind while looking at responses.

After test items are constructed, they should be critically reviewed. Of course, for a classroom examination, the instructor probably would do his own reviewing, but for important achievement tests, a careful review is done by a number of persons. First, the items would be reviewed by experts in test construction. They would consider each item in terms of its appropriateness, apparent difficulty, and clarity. The items that survived that review would then be reviewed by teachers and other potential users of the test.

### Item analysis

Although content validity rests mainly on rational rather than empirical grounds, results from applying an instrument do provide some important types of information. Large-scale investigations are undertaken for important achievement tests. In contrast, the individual instructor may not seek such information at all or may obtain it only incidentally. The first step in obtaining such information is to administer a large collection of items to a large sample of persons who are representative of the individuals with whom the final test will be employed. To have ample room to discard items that work poorly, there should be at least twice as many items as will appear on the final test. All items should be administered to at least 300 persons, preferably to 1,000 or more. Because there are so many opportunities for taking advantage of chance in item analysis, the results may be highly misleading unless there are at least five times as many persons as items.

If computational resources are available for the purpose, the most important type of item analysis of achievement tests is done by correlating each item with the total test score. If the test has different parts for different topics (e.g., reading and science), each item should be correlated with the subscore for its section rather than with scores on the test as a whole. The proper coefficient is point-biserial, which, as was said previously, is the PM formula applied to the relationship between a dichotomous item and a multipoint distribution of scores.

Any item that correlates near zero with test scores should be carefully inspected. In an achievement test, it is possible for an item to correlate near zero with total scores and still be a valid item, but that is rarely the case. It is more likely that the item is excessively difficult or easy, is ambiguous, or actually has little to do with the topic. Unless there are strong grounds for deciding otherwise, such items should generally be discarded. Among the remaining items, those which correlate higher with total scores are generally the better items. They are probably less ambiguous, they cannot be very extreme in difficulty in either direction, and they will tend to make the final test highly reliable.

The next step in item analysis depends on the number of items that have relatively high correlations with total scores. For example, where 100 multiple-choice items are being investigated for a subtest of a large achievement test, correlations with subtest scores are expected to range from zero to about .40. In tests of ability, such correlations are seldom negative, and when they are, it is usually because of sampling error. Correlations above .20 are usually considered good. If there are more than enough items at that level, one can proceed to the next step. If there are barely enough items at that level for the eventual test, there is no choice but to employ those items, and consequently there is no room for further pruning of items. If the number of items at that level is far lower than the number required for the eventual test, the only recourse is to start over with a larger collection of items.

When there are plenty of items that correlate well with total scores, the next step is to investigate the reliability for successive collections of the items. First, the items would be ranked in accordance with their correlations with total scores.

Successive sets of items would be selected, and the internal-consistency reliability would be computed for these sets. The most useful general formula for this purpose is called *coefficient alpha*, which can be applied to collections of items which are scored only on a pass-fail basis or items that are scored on more than two points, e.g., seven-step scales for the measurement of attitudes toward the United Nations. A special version of coefficient alpha, Kuder-Richardson formula 20 (KR-20), saves computing time when items are scored on only a pass-fail basis. The logic for employing such measures of reliability based on internal consistency was briefly discussed in Chapter 5. A more detailed discussion of this logic is presented in Appendix D, along with the formulas themselves. In Chapter 5 it was said that essentially these formulas estimate the correlation between an existing test and a hypothetical alternative form composed of items that are similar to those in the existing test. The formulas provide a very useful, and usually accurate, estimate of the reliability actually found in subsequent investigations of the correlations between alternative tests.

For reasons which will be made clearer in later sections of this chapter, in the item analysis of achievement tests it is best to lay major stress on the correlations of items with total scores rather than on the difficulties ($p$ values) of items. The $p$ value of an item is simply the percentage of persons who pass the item. For example, if 80 percent of the children in a class correctly solve a problem in arithmetic, then the $p$ value of that item is 0.8. After items have passed reviews by measurement experts and other persons, the steps in item analysis are almost identical to those in the item analysis of predictor tests and measures of constructs; consequently, a more complete discussion of methods of item analysis will be reserved for a later section of this chapter.

Again it should be emphasized that item analysis of achievement tests is secondary to content validity. Contrary to what is done with predictor tests and measures of constructs, with achievement tests considerable pains are taken to ensure that all items have content validity *before* they are submitted to item analysis. Thus all items submitted for analysis are assumed to be good, and the analysis provides only additional information. But more important than the information obtained from item analysis is the initial decision to use a particular item in a tryout form of the test. Also, regardless of what is found in item analysis, the final decision to include or to reject an item is based primarily on human judgment. For example, in each section of most achievement tests, the first several items are very easy. These are included to prevent some students from becoming discouraged and to give all students some practice with the particular type of item. Because nearly everyone answers these items correctly, they might appear worthless purely on the basis of an item analysis.

## the criterion-oriented approach to test construction

There are two *incorrect* ways to construct tests: One is to select items according to their correlations with a criterion, and the other is to select items according to their difficulty. Even though both methods are thought to be incorrect, they have been advocated and used so much in the past that it will be necessary to explain them in some detail. The criterion-oriented approach will be discussed in this section. By "criteria" is meant scores relating to some type of performance in daily life, such as school grades, amount of sales made by insurance agents, and ratings of the skill of airplane pilots.

The criterion-oriented approach evolved from the following faulty line of reasoning. First, one asks, "Why construct a test?" Then he answers, "To predict a criterion." If that were so, what would be the best items for the test? Obviously, items that individually correlate well with the criterion would be best. The more each item correlates with the criterion, the more the total test score will correlate with the criterion. According to this line of reasoning, the obvious thing to do is (1) compose a large group of items; (2) administer them to a large sample of individuals in the situation where the test will be used; (3) correlate each item with the criterion, e.g., grades in some course of training; and (4) fashion a test out of those items which correlate most highly with the criterion.

Following this line of reasoning further, there is a way to improve on the foregoing method for the selection of test items. Assuming that one has found a large number of items that correlate well with the criterion, one can further select items in terms of their correlations with one another. Should the items in the final test correlate highly with one another? According to the criterion-oriented approach, the answer is "no." This conclusion follows from the logic of multiple correlation (see Nunnally, 1967, Ch. 5). If a number of variables each correlate positively with a criterion, the multiple correlation is higher when the predictors correlate as little as possible with one another. The maximum multiple correlation would be obtained when the predictors had zero correlations with one another. The same logic would hold for a linear combination of items. When items have low correlations with one another and each correlates positively with the criterion, each item adds information to that provided by the other items, and when scores are summed over items, a relatively high correlation with the criterion will be found.

The average correlation of an item with the other items in a test tends to be proportional to the correlation of the item with total test scores. Then, according to this logic, one would select items that correlated highly with the criterion and had low correlations with total test scores. After these two sets of correlations have been obtained, they can be plotted as shown in Figure 8-1. One then selects items from the indicated region of the figure. If there are enough items in that region, they are used to form the final test.

## What is wrong with the criterion-oriented approach

By now it must be apparent that something is badly wrong with the criterion-oriented approach. Using this method, one would select a polyglot group of items with low internal consistency. Coefficient alpha would be low, and con-

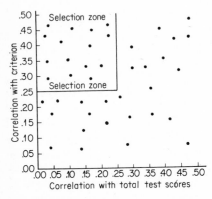

**FIGURE 8-1**    Scatter diagram of item correlations with a criterion and with total test scores

sequently there would be no strong common core (factor) in the items. Since the items would tend to measure different things, there would be no rational basis for the construction of an alternative form. The problem could be approached empirically by selecting another set of items which correlated well with the criterion and for which the internal consistency was low, but the "alternative forms" might not correlate highly.

The major error in the criterion-oriented approach is in the original premise that the purpose of constructing a test is to predict a *particular* criterion. This is seldom the guiding principle in test construction. It is obviously not the reason for constructing measures that require content validity and construct validity. In either case, if one had a criterion (whatever that would be), there would be no need to construct tests. As has been argued previously, with measures that require content validity there is logically no empirical criterion. Although construct validity depends partly on correlations between different proposed measures of a construct, no one of them can be considered *the* criterion. Since most measures used in basic research require construct validity, the criterion-oriented approach clearly does not apply. Since in applied work there are many more uses of achievement tests (measures that require content validity) than of predictor tests, the logic obviously does not hold in most applied work.

The only sphere in which the criterion-oriented approach is not obviously inappropriate is in applied work with predictor tests. It will be shown, however, that the logic does not apply there either. It is almost always poor strategy to *construct* a test to measure a particular criterion; it is better to *select* tests of known factorial composition as potential predictors of a criterion. Instead of forming hypotheses about types of *items* that might be predictive of a criterion, it is better to form hypotheses about types of *whole tests* that might be predictive of a criterion.

Other than for measures that require content validity, the purpose of constructing tests should be to investigate factors of human ability and personality. Each test should follow from a hypothesis about relations between a particular type of item and other types of items. Each test should be homogeneous in content, and consequently the items on each test should correlate substantially with one another. Correlations between different tests should be studied by factor analysis. The resulting factors constitute a standard set of "yardsticks" regarding abilities and personality traits. (The logic of factor analysis and some of the most important factors of human ability that have been found with factor analysis are discussed in Chapter 9.) Gradually, as evidence accrues from factor analysis, the major dimensions of human attributes are determined. In the long run this will result in a catalog of measures for the important dimensions. Then, when one wants to measure a particular factor, the proper measure or combination of measures can be taken from a drawer or off a shelf. This logic applies both to measures of psychological constructs and to predictors of particular criteria. The "shelves and drawers" already contain measures of many important factors, and one can select from among them for the prediction of particular criteria.

The author does not intend to imply that it is wrong to construct new tests with respect to applied problems of prediction, but when they are so constructed, they should not be constructed according to the criterion-oriented approach. Each such test should be homogeneous in content. Of course, one would want to find the correlation of scores with the criterion, and if that were reasonably high, one would want to learn the factor composition of the measure by correlating it with measures of existing factors. Gradually, in this way, tests constructed for prediction problems add to what is known about factors in general.

How, though, can one adequately predict criteria from homogeneous tests? As some will argue, the criterion is usually factorially complex and consequently can be predicted best by a factorially complex predictor test. Instead of building the factorial complexity into a particular test, it is far better to meet the factorial complexity by combining tests in a battery, in which case tests would be selected to measure the different factors that are thought to be important. If items are selected by the criterion-oriented approach, one really does not know *what* factors are being measured. Also, the importance of each factor in the test would be determined by the number of items that happened to be present for the factor and thus would not be rationally related to the importance of the factor in the criterion. The ideal way to combine factors is by multiple regression (see Nunnally, 1967, Ch. 5), and this can be done only by having relatively homogeneous tests relating to each factor. With the criterion-oriented approach, one knows neither what factors are involved in the omnibus test nor what weights are being given to different factors. The fallacy is in assuming that the criterion is to be predicted with *one* test, which to be effective must be heterogeneous in content. It is far better to predict a criterion with a battery of tests, each of which is homogeneous in content.

Even if one accepted the logic of the criterion-oriented approach, it would work poorly in practice. It is very difficult to find items that correlate well with a criterion and have low correlations with one another. Usually the two types of correlations tend to go together, and consequently very few items that met the standards would be found. When the method appears to work, it is usually because only a small sample of subjects is being used, and consequently there is considerable room to take advantage of chance. Subsequent studies would show that the test was not nearly as predictive of the criterion as was suggested by the item analysis. Usually one has a choice between (1) using items that have low correlations *both* with one another and with the criterion and (2) using items that have relatively high correlations with one another and with the criterion. Obviously, then, the homogeneous test would predict the criterion as well as, or better than, the heterogeneous test.

Even if one selects items purely in terms of correlations with a criterion and ignores correlations between items, the criterion-oriented approach is not good. Such a test would usually be factorially complex and would run into the difficulties mentioned previously. Also, such a test would contribute very little to one's understanding of either the applied situation or basic issues concerning human attributes. In the case of the former, since one would not fully understand what factors were involved in the test, no information would be supplied about the factors that make for success in school or on a job. If the factors that lead to success are known, opportunities are provided for training students for success on a particular job, and employees can be trained in that respect. If, in a school situation, it is found that successful perfomance correlates more with memory factors than with other factors, this might suggest changes in the curriculum.

Even if one ignored the weight of argument given so far against the criterion-oriented approach, he would find that the method works poorly in practice. Obviously, it is very wasteful of time and money to construct tests for each new prediction problem. It is much easier to investigate existing measures with known factor compositions. An omnibus test constructed for a particular criterion is often predictive of only that criterion. For example, in an industrial situation, a psychologist involved in the selection of employees for 20 different jobs might need to construct 20 different criterion-oriented tests. In the same situation, a battery of three to seven tests (with different weights for different jobs) might be predictive of all jobs, and usually the battery would be more predictive of success on any particular job than the test constructed specifically for that purpose.

The criterion-oriented test that is predictive of a job in one settting is often not very predictive of an apparently similar job in another setting. Thus a test that successfully selects insurance salesmen might be very poor for selecting magazine salesmen. Also, for any particular job in any particular setting, criteria have a way of changing over time. What people do in particular jobs and the abilities and personality attributes required for successful performance frequently evolve with changes in the organization and developments in technology. Thus the criterion-oriented test that works well now might not work well in five years. One could meet these problems with a battery of tests of known factor composition by investigating different weights required for different jobs and for the same job at different points in time. Also, the evidence might indicate that one or more tests would need to be replaced by more predictive tests.

Because of the obvious bad features of the criterion-oriented approach, it is surprising to find some authors of recent books on psychological measurement flirting with it. Related methods of item analysis clearly are not applicable to measures that require content validity or construct validity. Conceivably they would be appropriate for particular problems in prediction, but it is hoped that sufficient arguments have been made against the use of the criterion-oriented approach there also. In prediction problems, a far better approach is to form a battery of tests from homogeneous measures of known factor composition. How to construct such homogeneous measures will be discussed in a later section.

Before concluding this section it should be made clear that the foregoing criticisms are leveled at methods of test construction based on the correlations of items with *criteria of success in daily life,* such as grades in college, amounts of sales made by insurance salesmen, and ratings of effectiveness of airplane pilots. Criticisms in this section are not leveled at *all* attempts to construct tests wholly or in part by the investigation of correlations of items with some variable external to the items. An example in point is that of selecting items in terms of their correlations with a known factor of human ability or personality. This is a very useful adjunct to the methods for constructing homogeneous tests which will be discussed in a later section.

## constructing tests in terms of item difficulties

For constructing measures of constructs and measures to be used as predictors, a second *incorrect* approach concerns the selection of items in terms of their difficulties. Although the difficulty levels of items do provide important information, this information is secondary to that obtained from correlations between the items. (How to use the latter type of information will be discussed in the next section.)

The difficulty of any dichotomous item ($p$ value) is the fraction of persons tested who receive a score of 1 rather than a score of zero. On tests of ability, a score of 1 means that the individual passes the item; on nonability tests (e.g., a measure of suggestibility), a score of 1 is indicative of a high rather than a low score on the attribute. On a spelling test, a $p$ value of 0.9 would mean that 90 percent of the persons tested passed the item—correctly spelled the spoken word or marked the correct alternative on a printed test.

In test construction, $p$ values are important for two interrelated reasons. First, they influence the characteristics of score distributions. The $p$ values directly determine the mean score, the mean being the sum of the $p$ values. The mean is of only incidental importance, however, in the construction of tests. More importantly, the $p$ values influence the shape and standard deviation of the distribution of total test scores. If the average $p$ value is far removed from 0.5 in either direction, the distribution will tend to be skewed (particularly when the number of items is small, e.g., less than 20), and the standard deviation will tend to be small. Consequently, since it is usually desired to have an approximately symmetrical distribution and to disperse people as much as possible, an argument can be made for having an average $p$ value of 0.5. In addition, even if the average $p$ value is 0.5, the standard deviation of test scores is larger when all the $p$ values are near 0.5 rather than scattered widely above and below that point. Then, to disperse people as much as possible (to discriminate between them), one could argue that it is desirable for all test items to have $p$ values close to 0.5. A test composed of items of that kind is referred to as a *peaked test*.

The other reason why $p$ values are important is that they relate to the reliability. According to coefficient alpha and KR-20, the more highly items correlate with one another, the higher the reliability. The reason that $p$ values are important to consider is that differences in $p$ values for items place mathematical restrictions on the limit to which items can correlate with one another. If two items have different $p$ values (e.g., one has a $p$ value of 0.4, and the other has a $p$ value of 0.5), they cannot correlate perfectly. Also, the more extreme the $p$ values of the two items, the more a particular difference in $p$ value lowers the possible correlation. For example, whereas there would be some restriction where the two $p$ values were 0.4 and 0.5, the restriction would be much greater if the two values were 0.8 and 0.9 or 0.1 and 0.2. Generally, then, it is usually found that if the average $p$ value of a set of items is extreme in either direction, the average correlation between the items is low. For the same reason, coefficient alpha and KR-20 tend to be lower for tests composed of items with extreme average $p$ values than for tests with average $p$ values near the middle of the range. Since coefficient alpha and KR-20 are usually good estimates of the alternative-form reliability, a similar lowering of the reliability is expected when correlating alternative forms of a test if the forms are composed of items whose average $p$ values are extreme in either direction.

Both from the standpoint of the desirable properties of score distributions and from the standpoint of test reliability, one arrives at the conclusion that a peaked test is best. Although no one would take this argument to the extreme of insisting that all items be at the 0.5 level, it could be argued that the items should be selected in the range from 0.4 to 0.6. This is what one would do if he were to construct a test solely in terms of difficulty levels.

## What is wrong with this approach

The faults in selecting items in terms of $p$ values are not nearly so blatant as those in selecting items in terms of the criterion-oriented approach. Also, the point is not that selecting items in terms of $p$ values is incorrect, but rather that there is a much better way to select them. One might end up with a very good instrument purely by selecting items so as to obtain a peaked test. If, after the items were selected, they proved to have a high reliability, it might subsequently be found that the new measure related importantly with other supposed measures of a construct and/or proved effective in predicting particular criteria. If these things happened, the method of test construction worked well in that particular instance. The important point, however, is that, a priori, there are reasons why such pleasant results might not be obtained.

For reasons which were discussed previously, "good" items are ones that correlate well with one another. Since the correlations of items with total scores on a test are directly related to their sums of correlations with one another, it can be said that good items are ones that correlate highly with total test scores. This doctrine will be explained more fully in the next section, but first it will be useful to see what implications it has for the selection of items in terms of $p$ values.

The $p$ values place only *upper limits* on correlations of items with total scores. A $p$ value near 0.5 does not *guarantee* a high correlation with total scores. In a particular analysis, it is possible to find that all the items with $p$ values near 0.5 have correlations near zero with total scores and that items with $p$ values well removed from 0.5 have respectable correlations with total scores. Actually, in addition to the possible advantages of having $p$ values near 0.5, there are reasons for being suspicious of such items. Clearly, one would not consider it good to have true-false items with $p$ values of 0.5 because that would suggest that the items were so difficult that everyone guessed. A test composed of such items would have a reliability near zero. There is reason to be suspicious of items on some nonability tests that have $p$ values near 0.5. For example, on a personality inventory composed of agree-disagree items, any item that is highly ambiguous will tend to have a $p$ value near 0.5. Since subjects are unable to understand the item, they mentally "flip coins" in giving an answer. In a sense, on personality inventories it is comforting to find that an item has a $p$ value somewhat removed from 0.5 (e.g., 0.7) because that at least suggests that the majority of people were able to understand the item well enough to reject or accept it.

An item on a peaked test *may* be a good item, the crucial standard being whether or not it actually correlates well with total scores on the test. It is equally possible, however, that the item might not have a high correlation with total scores either because it is very unreliable or because it reliably measures something different from what the majority of items in the test measure. Since the crucial consideration is how much the item actually correlates with total scores, why not select items mainly in terms of those correlations? That is what will be advocated in the next section. Before that method is discussed, however, some additional comments should be made about selecting items in terms of $p$ values.

Even if one were to admit that $p$ values are all-important in constructing tests, the logic of so doing is clear only for *free-response* items that are *scored dichotomously*. An example of such an item would be one in which students were provided a space to answer the question, "When did Columbus discover America?" For two reasons such items are rare. First, more tests employ multiple-choice items rather than free-response items of any kind. Second, even in those tests which employ free-response items, the items are usually scored on a multipoint basis rather than dichotomously. The former would be the case, for example, in scoring each question in an essay examination on a six-point scale.

On dichotomous items the $p$ value is the mean, and it is directly related to the variance. The variance on these items equals the $p$ value multiplied by 1 minus the $p$ value; 1 minus the $p$ value is symbolized as $q$. Thus the variance equals $pq$, which makes it evident that the variance is directly related to the size of $p$. The closer $p$ is to 0.5, the larger the variance.

When multipoint items are employed, there is no longer a "$p$ value." On multipoint items the mean and variance tend to be related, but they are far from perfectly correlated. For example, on seven-point scales used in measures of attitudes, the nearer the mean is to the middle of the scale, the larger the variance tends to be. In that case, however, should one select items in terms of the mean score or in terms of the variance? One could argue that both should be considered, but there are no obvious principles concerning how these two kinds of information should be combined. It is far better to construct tests concerning multipoint items by methods to be described in the next section.

Considering dichotomously scored multiple-choice items, the selection of items in terms of $p$ values is greatly complicated by the effect of *guessing*. The $p$ value is determined by both the intrinsic difficulty of the item and the effect of guessing. Guessing tends to make $p$ values higher, the amount of "elevation" being inversely related to the number of alternative responses for each item. Where there are only two alternative responses (a true-false test), it would obviously be inappropriate to peak a test at 0.5. Less obviously, it would also be inappropriate when there are four or five alternative responses, as typically found on multiple-choice tests.

One might think that the ideal difficulty for test items could be obtained with a proper correction for the expected effects of guessing (see Nunnally, 1967, Ch. 15), but this would solve only part of the problem. Guessing not only tends to raise $p$ values but also introduces measurement error. Since the less guessing there is, the less measurement error there is, easy items tend to have less measurement error than more difficult ones. Consequently, the most discriminating item would tend to be somewhere between a corrected $p$ value of 0.5 and one of 1.0. There is, however, no certainty as to what the exact value should be. All one can do is generate a model to predict the ideal level and then test how well the model works in practice. Employing one such model, Lord (1952a) deduced that the most discriminating two-choice item would have an *uncorrected* $p$ value of 0.85; a three-choice item, one of 0.77; a four-choice item, one of 0.74; and a five-choice item, one of 0.69. However, not enough research has been conducted to determine whether those deductions, or deductions from other models, hold in the general case.

Even if mountains of research were done to find the "ideal" $p$ values for multiple-choice tests with different numbers of alternatives, the previously described shortcomings of selecting items purely in terms of $p$ values still would be present. At best the $p$ values can only indicate the types of items that are not highly restricted in their possible correlations with total scores. It is far more sensible to construct tests primarily in terms of the actual correlations of items with total scores.

## construction of homogeneous tests

Much of what has been said so far in this book argues for the construction of homogeneous tests. Only some of the most important arguments will be reiterated. Chapter 1 emphasized that measurement always concerns an *attribute*. An attribute is some isolatable characteristic of organisms, some dimension of structure or function along which organisms can be ordered. Items within a measure are useful only to the extent that they share a common core—the attribute which is to be measured. The linear model was accepted as providing a reasonable approach to the construction of most measures in psychology, particularly the construction of measures concerning individual differences between subjects. The model leads to a simple summation of item scores to obtain total scores. In summing scores, it is assumed that each item adds something to the others, and unless the items shared an attribute, it would not be meaningful to sum scores over items.

The major theory of reliability is based on the domain-sampling model, which assumes that each test is a random sample of items from a domain. Although the model holds when the domain contains items from different factors, it makes more sense when items from the domain share only one major factor. Eventually it will be possible to understand the cardinal dimensions of human attributes only when relatively complete factor structures are known for different types of abilities and personality characteristics. The best measures of each factor will be those which correlate highly with one factor and have low correlations with other factors.

Implicit in the considerations above is the premise that tests should be as homogeneous in content as possible. The homogeneity of content in a test is manifested in the average correlation between items and in the pattern of those correlations. If the average correlation between items is very low (and thus the average correlation of items with total scores is low), the items as a group are not homogeneous. This may be because all the correlations are low or because a number of different factors are present in the items. In the latter case there would be a number of item clusters, each cluster being relatively homogeneous, but the clusters would have either correlations near zero with one another or negative correlations. The ideal is to obtain a collection of items which has a high average correlation with total scores and is dominated by one factor only.

## The hypothesis

A new measure should spring from a hypothesis regarding the existence and nature of an attribute. In some cases a formal hypothesis is deduced from a theory regarding a construct. An example would be deducing hypotheses from theories concerning the construct of anxiety. If, as many people assume, anxiety is a form of "generalized drive," many hypotheses follow regarding the attributes of people who are high in the trait (construct) of anxiety. It would be expected that people who are high in anxiety would be characterized by a relatively low ability to solve familiar problems in novel ways, e.g., writing the alphabet from "z" to "a" or solving simple arithmetic problems by a novel approach. On the basis of this hypothesis, one could construct a pool of items. Although in many cases there are no formal hypotheses regarding the existence of attributes, at least the investigator should have an informal hypothesis that can be communicated to others. For example, it might be hypothesized that reliable individual differences exist in the tendency to have common rather than uncommon associations. Although the hypothesis would not be deduced from a formal theory, such individual differences, if they exist, might be important for cognitive and affective processes. The hypothesis suggests a number of types of items that might be used to measure the attribute in question. In one type of item, the subject would be given a stimulus word and two possible response words. One of the response words would be a highly common associate of the stimulus word, and the other would be a less common associate. On each item, the subject would be required to mark the most appropriate associate. Whether the hypothesis follows from a theory or is only a "good idea," it guides the construction of items. Subsequent investigations of the items provide a test of the hypothesis.

## Construction of items

One cannot know for sure how many items should be constructed for a new measure until *after* they are constructed and submitted to item analysis. If the standard is to obtain a test with a coefficient alpha of .80, item analysis might show that the desired reliability can be obtained with as few as 20 items or that as many as 80 items are required. There are some rules of thumb that can be used to determine the number of items to be constructed. Usually 20 or 30 dichotomous items are required to obtain an internal-consistency reliability of .80. Also, usually fewer multipoint items than dichotomous items are required to obtain a particular reliability. For example, it is not unusual to find a coefficient alpha of .80 for 15 agree-disagree attitude statements rated on a seven-point scale. How many more items should be constructed than the minimum required depends on what is known from previous studies about the type of item. If it were known that items of a particular type tend to have high internal consistency (e.g., items on vocabulary tests), at most no more than twice as many items would be constructed as have been found in previous studies to be required for a reliable test. In that case, to obtain a reliability of .80, 30 items would probably suffice for the final test. To provide room for the item analysis to eliminate unsatisfactory items, 60 items would be constructed initially. If very little is known about the homogeneity of items of a particular kind, it is wise to err on the conservative side and to construct more items than would be the case in the previous example. For example, with the previously mentioned measure of the tendency to give common word associations, if it were desired to obtain a test with a reliability of .80, it would be wise to construct 100 items.

A somewhat different strategy for deciding how many items to construct starts by purposefully constructing a smaller number of items than is thought to be adequate, e.g., constructing only 30 items when it is suspected that 30 items will be required to obtain a coefficient alpha of .80. These items are then applied to a relatively small sample of subjects (say, 100), and the results are submitted to item analysis. If either the total collection of items (30) or the most homogeneous subset (say, of 15 items) has a coefficient alpha of at least .50, this indicates that it is worth the effort to construct more items, gather responses from a much larger group of subjects, and perform a more complete item analysis. Ultimately, more labor is required to construct the test in stages rather than in one large step, but this method of construction has the advantage that if the results from the first stage are very discouraging, the project can be abandoned without further loss of time and effort.

### Sample of subjects

After items are constructed and before they are submitted to item analysis, they must, of course, be administered to a sample of people. So that the required types of analyses can be performed, all the items should be administered to all the people. Of course, the sample of people used in this phase of test construction should be reasonably representative of the types of people who will be studied with the eventual test. To take a very bad example, if a test is intended to be used primarily with children from eight to ten years of age, it should not be constructed on the basis of data obtained from college students. Except for such extremes, however, the subjects used in test construction need not be exactly representative of those with whom the final test will be used. Also, often a test is used with many different types of subjects (e.g., some attitude scales), and in such cases it is very difficult to ensure that the group of subjects used in test construction is highly representative of all the different groups with which the test eventually will be used.

As is true of all methods of analysis, it is not possible to say in advance exactly how many subjects should be used to obtain data for item analysis. A good rule of thumb, however, is to have at least ten times as many subjects as items. In some cases this rule is impractical if there are more than about seventy items. For example, if there are 100 items, it might not be possible to obtain 1,000 subjects. In any case, though, five subjects per item should be considered the minimum that can be tolerated.

In gathering data for item analysis, one should administer items under conditions that closely resemble those under which the eventual test will be used. If subjects in the tryout sample are given all the time that they want to complete the items and one intends to place a severe time limit on the eventual test, an item analysis will probably provide very misleading information. If items for a personality inventory are being administered in an atmosphere that encourages frankness and the eventual test is to be administered in an atmosphere where subjects will be reluctant to say bad things about themselves, the item analysis will tell a faulty story.

### Item-total correlations

The remainder of this section will consider methods of item analysis when most of the correlations between items (say, at least 90 percent) are positive. This is almost always the case in measures concerning abilities, i.e., where there is a "correct" response for each item. Some of the correlations may be very close to zero, but if the sample size is large, very few are negative. A later section will consider methods of item analysis when some of the items tend to correlate negatively with the others, as occurs on many personality inventories.

When items correlate predominantly positively with one another, those with the highest average correlations are the best items. Since the average correlations of items with one another are highly related to the correlations of items with total scores, the items that correlate most highly with total scores are the best items. Compared with items with relatively low correlations with total scores, those which have higher correlations with total scores have more variance relating to the common factor among the items, and they add more to the test reliability.

The first step in item analysis, then, is to correlate each item with total scores. Thus if there are 60 items, scores are summed over items, and 60 correlations are obtained. If multipoint items are employed, the regular PM coefficient is the correct measure. If dichotomous items are employed, the correct measure is point-biserial, which, it will be remembered, is only a differently appearing version of the PM formula. The obtained coefficients are then ranked from highest to lowest. If numerous correlations are relatively high (with respect to standards that will be discussed shortly), one is "in business," and a few simple steps can be taken to obtain a final test that has (1) a desired level of reliability and (2) a desired distribution form, this usually being a symmetrical distribution.

There are numerous measures of item-total relationship other than point-biserial. An argument can be made for employing the item-total covariance rather than the correlation because the former takes account of the $p$ values of items as well as the correlation with total scores. The covariance tends to give added weight to items that have $p$ values near 0.5. Correlational methods other than point-biserial have been employed for item analysis. Biserial can be used, and if the continuous total scores are divided at the mean or median, either phi or tetrachoric can be applied.

In addition to the different measures of correlation that can be used in item analysis, numerous other measures of item-total relationship are available. One of the most popular measures is obtained as follows. First, the top and bottom 25 percents of persons in total test scores are found. Second, for each item, the percentages of persons in top and bottom groups who pass the item are determined. Third, the percentage in the bottom group is subtracted from the percentage in the top group. Items that have a large difference in this regard tend to discriminate persons with high total test scores from persons with low total test scores.

Although many different measures of item-total relationship can be employed in item analysis, there is a wealth of data to demonstrate that they all provide much the same information. In a typical study, four different measures of item-total relationship are applied to the same items, and then items are ranked on the different measures. Typically it is found that correlations between the different sets of ranks are .90 or higher, demonstrating that essentially the same set of items would have been selected by any of the methods.

It is recommended that the PM correlation be used in item analysis, which with dichotomous items is point-biserial. Not only does the PM correlation give very much the same information any other measure of item-total relationship would provide, but to the extent that item selection would be slightly different by different measures, the PM correlation is logically better than the other measures.

### Step-by-step procedures

If there are numerous uncorrected item-total correlations above .20, the remaining steps in item analysis are simple. Since about 30 dichotomous items are usually required to reach a reliability of .80, KR-20 would be computed for the 30 items having the highest correlations with total scores. If the reliability is as high as desired, the item analysis is complete. If it is not, one increases the number of items, adding those items which have the next highest correlations with total scores onto the first set of 30 items. When the correlations with total scores are very low (e.g., .05), little can be gained by adding more items. When there are numerous additional items with correlations above .10, how many of them are added depends on how much the reliability needs to be increased. If the reliability of the original group of items is .65 and a reliability of .80 is desired, a good strategy is to add 10 items. Then KR-20 is computed for the 40 items. If the desired reliability is obtained, the item analysis is complete; if not, more items are added. If, for example, the 40-item test had a reliability of .75 rather than .80, a good strategy would be to add the next five items in terms of their correlations with total scores. If this did not achieve the desired reliability, one could add several more items. If at any point the reliability fails to increase or decreases, there is no use in trying out larger numbers of items.

## Successive approximations

A possibility not mentioned in the previous section is that the selection of items in terms of item-total correlations can be improved by successively correlating items with subpools of the items. This can be illustrated where an analysis is being made of 100 items and only 50 of them have nonzero average correlations with the others. In this case, if it were known in advance that there were only 50 items from which to select the final group of items, the other 50 items would be removed from the analysis. If all items were correlated with total scores on the 100 items, the 50 bad items would tend to "water down" the correlations of the 50 good items with total scores. If one has the time and patience and the problem is sufficiently important, a refinement of the basic approach can be made as follows. In the first go-around, all items are correlated with total scores on all items. All items are removed that have item-total correlations which are below some minimum value, e.g., .10. For example, say that 40 items are removed from a total collection of 100. Total scores are then obtained on the remaining 60 items, and each of the 60 items is correlated with those total scores. Then KR-20 is computed for the items that stand highest in those correlations, and if the desired level of reliability is not reached, successive sets of items are added.

One could go through the above steps a number of times, each step leading to a more and more homogeneous group of items. However, it is seldom necessary to work with anything other than the original correlations of items with total scores. Usually the rank order of item-total correlations in successive sets of items refined in that way is much the same as the rank order of the initial item-total correlations. Where such successive refinements are sometimes required is with pools of items where many of the correlations between items are negative, as is sometimes the case with items on personality inventories. This problem will be discussed in a later section.

## The distribution form

One of the supposed advantages of selecting items in terms of $p$ values is that it permits control of the distribution form for total test scores. How can the same control be exercised when one selects items in terms of item-total correlations rather than $p$ values? There is a way to control the distribution form *after* good items have been selected in terms of item correlations. The method will be illustrated in the situation where the first 30 items in terms of item-total correlations produce the desired level of reliability but there are still more items that correlate reasonably well with total scores—say, 20 more such items. The first step would be to plot a frequency distribution for total scores on the first 30 items. If the distribution were symmetrical, the item analysis would be complete. If not, it would be necessary to study the $p$ values of both the 30 items and the remaining 20 good items.

If a distribution is not symmetrical, it is said to be *skewed*. A skewed distribution is one in which the tail on one side of the mode is much longer and thicker than the tail on the other side. Two such skewed distributions are shown in Figure 8-2. If the long tail extends toward the higher end of the continuum, the distribution is said to be skewed to the right (or toward the higher end of the continuum); conversely, if the long tail extends toward the lower end of the continuum, the distribution is said to be skewed to the left (or toward the lower end of the continuum). In the former case the majority of the subjects make low scores, and some subjects make very high scores. In the latter case (skewed to the left), the majority of subjects make high scores, and some subjects make very low scores. Although there are special cases in which such skewed distributions faithfully represent the trait in question (e.g., mental illness or criminal tendency), in most cases they are undesirable because (1) logically the traits are approximately normally distributed, (2) skewed distributions play havoc with some methods of statistical analysis (e.g., they tend to have relatively low correlations with symmetrically distributed distributions), and (3) in skewed distributions, people in the direction of the skew are more reliably differentiated from one another than people near the mode or people on the other side of the mode from the direction of skew.

If the distribution is skewed toward the higher end of the continuum, it means that the test is too difficult. To make the distribution more symmetrical, some of the items in the 30-item test having low $p$ values should be replaced by items from the remaining 20 that have $p$ values above 0.5. If five items having $p$ values between 0.2 and 0.3 are replaced by five items having $p$ values between 0.5 and 0.7, this will tend to make the distribution symmetrical. The distri-

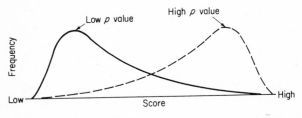

**FIGURE 8-2**    Skewed distributions of scores when the average $p$ value is high and when the average $p$ value is low

bution of the new group of 30 items is then plotted, and if it is symmetrical, the item analysis is complete. If the distribution is still slightly nonsymmetrical, replacement of a few more items will solve the problem. In replacing items in this way, one must recheck the reliability at each step to make sure it is not falling below the desired standard. If it does fall slightly, then at each step in the replacement of items, several more items should be added than are removed. Thus, for example, to achieve both the desired reliability and the desired distribution form, one might end up with a 38-item test rather than a 30-item test.

Actually, though, it is quite unlikely that the distribution of scores will be markedly nonsymmetrical if items are selected purely in terms of correlations with total scores. This method tends to select items in the middle range of $p$ values rather than those at the extremes. Since the restriction on the size of point-biserial is rather severe for items with $p$ values below 0.2 or above 0.8, it is unlikely that items with such extreme $p$ values will be high enough in the rank order of item-total correlations to be included in a test. Since the least restriction in point-biserial is for items having $p$ values at 0.5, items with $p$ values near 0.5 have a greater likelihood of having high correlations with total scores, and consequently such items tend to stand high in the rank order of item-total correlations. (It is important to remember, however, that picking items in terms of item-total correlations favors only those items with $p$ values near 0.5 that actually correlate well with total scores.) Because choosing items in terms of item-total correlations tends to result in the selection of items that are "average" in $p$ value, this method of item analysis almost always produces a symmetrical distribution of scores, and consequently no further refinements are necessary. Also, one seldom seeks anything other than a symmetrical distribution.

Another reason why it is not important in most problems to be highly concerned about the $p$ values of the items which are selected is that the exact shape of the distribution of total scores is seldom a very important issue. This is particularly so in measures of constructs to be used in basic research. For example, with a new measure of introversion, the major concerns are that the reliability be sufficiently high and the distribution be approximately symmetrical. Whether it is slightly skewed in either direction will make very little difference in research. The most the skewness could do is have a very slight effect on the size of correlations with variables which are symmetrically distributed.

## special problems in test construction

In the remainder of the book it will be assumed that the best way to construct most tests is in terms of item-total correlations, as described in the previous section. This section will consider some special problems that arise in employing that method.

## Bipolar domains of items

The discussion in the previous section assumed that most correlations between items are positive, which is usually the case for any test concerning abilities, but is not necessarily the case for measures of personality, attitudes, interests, and other attributes. For example, if an attitude scale regarding the United Nations were being constructed, one approach would be to start by writing 60 statements, half of which were thought to be favorable toward the United Nations and half to be unfavorable. Each item would require dichotomous, agree-disagree responses. If all agreements were scored 1 and all disagreements scored zero, the negative statements would tend to correlate negatively with the positive statements. Then the average correlation of each item with the others would be close to zero, and thus all the items would have item-total correlations close to zero. Obviously, then, it would not be possible to select items in terms of item-total correlations, and the analyses would provide no hints as to what should be done to improve the situation.

If items are selected purely in terms of item-total correlations, the success of this method depends on the investigator's ability to devise a scoring key initially that will make the majority of correlations between items positive. In most cases this is easily done. In the previous example of constructing a measure of attitudes toward the United Nations, the investigator would score agreements with the positive statements as 1 and *disagreements* with the *negative* statements as 1. Then most of the correlations between items would be likely to be positive, and there would be no difficulty in selecting items in terms of item-total correlations. Of course, the investigator might misjudge some of the items, and consequently some items would have negative correlations with total scores. For selecting items in terms of item-total correlations, however, it is not necessary that all the correlations between items be positive, but only most of them. The method will usually work if a scoring key is devised such that 70 percent of the correlations between items are positive. In this case the majority of item-total correlations are positive, and some are probably sufficiently high to encourage further item analysis.

After the first attempt has been made to devise a scoring key that will make most correlations between items positive, the next step is to rank the items in terms of item-total correlations. If at least 70 percent of the correlations are positive and numerous correlations are above .15, one can proceed to the next step, which is to reverse the scoring for all items having statistically significant negative item-total correlations. Thus if an item that correlated minus .15 with total scores had previously been scored 1 for "agree," in the new scoring key it would be scored 1 for "disagree," and vice versa for an item with that same negative correlation which previously had been scored 1 for "disagree." The scoring would not be changed for all items having positive correlations with total scores or nonsignificant negative correlations. Next, a new set of total scores would be obtained with the new scoring key, and each item would be correlated with the new total scores. This time the number of positive item-total correlations would probably increase markedly, and the average size of the correlations would increase. If there are still numerous items having negative item-total correlations, the process can be repeated.

In most bipolar item domains, it is not necessary to go through the iterative procedure described above. Usually the investigator can intuit a scoring scheme that will make most correlations between items positive. This is usually easy to do with attitude scales, interest inventories, and most personality inventories. It might be necessary to go through one rekeying of the items, but seldom would it be necessary to repeat the process a number of times. But, as was said previously, even if the scoring key produces only 70 percent positive item-total correlations between items, the iterative approach will usually produce the needed positive item-total correlations. After these correlations have been obtained, rather than make only one rank order in terms of item-total correlations, it is better to make a different order for items scored "agree" (or "yes") from the order for items scored "disagree" (or "no"). Then one would select an equal number of items from each list to form the first trial test. For example, one would select the top 15 items from both lists and form a 30-item test. If KR-20 is not as high as desired, additional items would be added from both lists. A balanced scoring key of this kind tends to eliminate response styles such as the tendency to agree regardless of the item content.

### Weighting of items

The methods of item analysis discussed in this chapter assume that all items are to be weighted equally in the eventual test, and no mention has been made of the possibility of obtaining differential weights for items. Rather than simply adding the number of correct responses on a test of ability, one could count correct responses on some items 3, correct responses on some other items 2, and correct responses on the remaining items 1. This possibility has not been discussed because it is almost always a waste of time to seek differential weights for items.

A number of different standards could be used for obtaining differential weights for items. If items were being selected in terms of their correlations with an external criterion, they could be weighted by a method that would tend to maximize the correlation of total test scores with the criterion. An approximate method for doing this would be to weight the score on each item by the item-criterion correlation. Since it was strongly recommended that tests not be constructed in terms of item-criterion correlations, it is also strongly recommended that items not be weighted by any function of the item-criterion correlations. A more sensible approach is to obtain differential weights for items by a method that will tend to maximize the reliability of total test scores.

Such a method would fit well with the procedures described previously for selecting items in terms of item-total correlations. An approximate method for obtaining such differential weights is to weight each item by its item-total correlation. To take an overly simplified example, if 10 items all had item-total correlation of .15 and 10 more items had item-total correlations of .3, a higher reliability for the 20 items would be obtained if the former items were weighted 1 and the latter were weighted 2 than if all items were weighted 1.

The crucial question in seeking differential weights for items is that of how much difference the use differential weights makes. It would make a difference if the weighted and unweighted scores on whole tests did not correlate highly and if the reliability of the weighted test was considerably higher than the reliability of the unweighted test. However, there is overwhelming evidence that the use of differential weights seldom makes an important difference. Regardless of how differential weights are determined, typically it is found that on tests containing at least 20 items the weighted test correlates in the high nineties with the unweighted test. Also, the slight increase in reliability obtained by weighting items can be matched in nearly all instances by adding several items to the unweighted test. Since it is much easier to add several items to a test than to go through the labors of determining and using differential weights for items, seeking differential weights is almost never worth the trouble.

Differential weights tend to make a difference when (1) the number of items is relatively small (less than 20) and (2) item-total correlations vary markedly. Seldom do both these conditions occur with dichotomous items, since most such tests contain more than 20 items and the item-total correlations are concentrated in a narrow zone. Some measures composed of multipoint items do have considerably less than 20 items, and the item-total correlations vary more than they typically do on tests composed of dichotomous items. This would be the case in a measure of attitudes which contained 10 seven-point rating scales. In this case an increase in reliability of from 5 to 10 points might be achieved by the differential weighting of items. Even there, however, the same increase in reliability could probably be obtained by adding two or three new items.

For the reasons discussed above, in nearly all cases it is recommended that total scores be obtained by an unweighted summation of item scores. If the reliability is not as high as desired, by far the best approach is to increase the number of items.

## Removal of an unwanted factor

Sometimes it is known in advance that items which are being analyzed to measure one attribute will tend to correlate with an unwanted attribute. This is the case, for example, in tests constructed to measure different factors of human ability, where experience has shown that many types of items concerning human ability tend to correlate with the factor of verbal comprehension. Since no matter what factor is being measured the items will require some understanding of words and sentences, obtaining relatively independent measures of factors other than verbal comprehension is rather difficult.

Another example is in the construction of a measure of anxiety where previous studies have indicated that the type of item being used is likely to produce a test which will correlate substantially with measures of intelligence. This will make it somewhat difficult to perform studies on anxiety, since any results obtained will be confounded with intelligence.

An extension can be made of the method of selecting items in terms of item-total correlations to lessen the effect of an unwanted factor. One would need a larger collection of items initially than is usually required in selecting items in terms of item-total correlations. For example, if the best guess is that a 30-item test will be required to achieve the desired level of reliability, it will be well to start with over 100 items. Each item is then correlated with total scores and with scores on the unwanted factor. To facilitate the selection of items, a scatter diagram should be made of correlations of items with both variables. The desired items are those which have relatively high correlations with total scores and relatively low correlations with the unwanted factor. Although there will tend to be few items in this category, those which correlate highly with total scores and negatively with the unwanted factor are particularly helpful in purifying the test being constructed.

After a set of items has been selected from the scatter diagram, the next steps are to compute KR-20 for the collection of items and to correlate the total scores on those items with scores on the unwanted factor. If the former is high and the latter is low, the item analysis is complete. If that is not the case, new items need to be added, and some compromise might have to be reached between the two considerations. If the overlap between measures of the two attributes is a particularly bothersome problem in research, it will be wise to have the reliability of the new test somewhat lower than desired to prevent the new test from correlating substantially with the unwanted factor.

## Taking advantage of chance

All forms of item analysis tend to capitalize on sampling errors to make the results appear better than they will in subsequent studies. One tends to take advantage of chance in any situation where something is optimized from the data at hand. This occurs in selecting items in terms of item-total correlations, in seeking differential weights for items, and in purifying a test of an unwanted factor. Since the opportunities to take advantage of chance are related positively to the number of variables and negatively to the number of persons, it was recommended that as a bare minimum in item analysis, there should be five persons for each item, and that a safer number is ten persons per item.

When there are at least 10 persons per item, the method of item analysis will take very little advantage of chance. A collection of items found to have a reliability of .84 might in subsequent studies prove to have a reliability of .80, but the drop in reliability is seldom more than a few points. If the exact level of reliability is a crucial issue when items are being selected, a safe procedure is to strive for a reliability at least five points above the crucial level.

The considerable amount of "playing around" with data sometimes required in constructing tests from bipolar domains of items provides more of an opportunity to take advantage of chance than is provided when items are selected in terms of the initial item-total correlations. For this reason, when dealing with such domains of items, one should strive to obtain even more than 10 persons per item if that is feasible.

To investigate the extent to which item analyses (and other forms of analysis that strive to optimize some function of the data) take advantage of chance, it has been recommended that a "holdout" group of subjects be employed. For example, if only 600 subjects are available for testing, one approach would be to base the item analysis on half of the subjects. Then KR-20 (or whatever else was being optimized) would be computed for the first group and for the holdout group. That would certainly provide evidence about the extent to which the analysis had capitalized on sampling errors, but it would be as imprudent an approach as permitting fire prevention to fall to a dangerously low level in order to invest heavily in fire-fighting equipment. If the number of subjects is limited, as it usually is, the far wiser strategy is to use every last subject in the item analysis. This way one tends to ensure in advance that the reliability (or any other function being optimized) will not fall off markedly in subsequent studies.

## speed tests

So far in this chapter it has been assumed that test construction concerns *power tests*, i.e., tests on which subjects are given about as much time as they want. With some types of tests, however, subjects are not given as much time as they want; instead, a highly restrictive time limit is imposed.

In their purest form, speed tests consist of items of *trivial difficulty*. That is, the difficulties would be trivial if subjects were given as much time as they wanted to make responses. By "trivial difficulty" is meant a $p$ value of 0.95 or higher when items are administered under power conditions. One type of item that fulfills this requirement is the simple problem in addition or subtraction. If problems of this type were employed in testing normal adults, all persons would answer almost all the problems correctly if they were given as much time as they wanted. The only way, then, to obtain a reliable dispersion of scores is to employ a highly restrictive time limit, which, for example, would allow the average person to answer only about half the questions.

Items made up of letter groups in a test to measure perceptual speed are also items of trivial difficulty. Each item consists of two pairs of letter groups, each group containing about eight letters of the alphabet mixed with numbers and punctuation marks. In each pair of letter groups, either the groups are identical or one letter in one group is different from the corresponding letter in the other group. The subject is asked to indicate whether each pair of letter groups is identical or not. Obviously, if subjects were given all the time they wanted, all the items would be of trivial difficulty. The only way, then, to obtain a reliable distribution of scores is to employ highly restrictive time limits, e.g., to allow only 10 minutes for responding to 100 items.

The rules that apply to the construction of power tests *do not* apply to the construction of speed tests. Rather, a special set of principles applies to the construction of speed tests.

### Internal structure of speed tests

Previously in this chapter it was shown that the construction of power tests depends very much on the size and patterns of correlations between items. Also, in Chapter 5 it was shown that the theory of reliability relates directly to the size and patterns of correlations between items. Here it will be shown that with speed tests, the size and patterns of correlations between items are artifacts of time limits and of the ordering of items within a test. Consequently, test construction cannot be based on the correlations of items with one another, and the reliability of speed tests cannot be based on internal consistency.

In a speed test, the average correlation between items is directly related to the amount of time allotted for taking the test. If subjects are given all the time they want, the $p$ values of all items will be either 1.0 or close to that, and consequently the correlations between items will be either zero or close to zero. At the other extreme, if subjects are given practically no time for taking the test, the $p$ values will all be zero or close to zero, and consequently the correlations between items will be near zero on the average. Between these two extremes of time limits, the average $p$ values of items range from zero to 1.0. One could, for example, experiment with time limits to obtain an average $p$ value near 0.5, in which case the average correlation between items might be substantial.

In addition to the average correlation between items being related to the time limit, the patterns of correlations between items are determined by the time limit. Let us look at the case where a time limit is employed such that (1) the average $p$ value of items is near the middle of the possible range and (2) by methods to be discussed later, the distribution of total scores is found to be highly reliable. Suppose that one employed the methods discussed previously for constructing a power test. Essentially this consists of selecting those items which correlate highly with total scores, but on speed tests this depends directly on the ordering of items within the test. Items near the beginning of the test would probably have such high $p$ values that they would tend to correlate very little with the other items, and consequently they would correlate very little with total scores. Items near the end of the test would have such low $p$ values that they also would correlate very little with the other items and with total scores. In contrast, items near the middle of the test would tend to have substantial correlations with one another and with total test scores. Since, in a speed test, the ordering of items is arbitrary, the correlations of items with total scores are arbitrary, and it makes no sense to select items on the basis of item-total correlations. The construction of speed tests, then, must be based on principles other than those which apply to the construction of power tests. These principles will be discussed throughout the remainder of this section.

### The item pool

As is true in the construction of all tests, the first step in the construction of a speed test is to develop an item pool. Usually this is rather easily done because the items on speed tests are generally so simple that it is easy to compose them by the dozen. Whereas previously it was possible to give some rules of thumb regarding the number of items required for the item pool for a power test, this is very difficult to do with speed tests because the reliability of speed tests is not as highly related to the number of items as that of power tests. For example, a speed test with 50 arithmetic items might be more reliable than a speed test containing 200 pairs of letter groupings. The reliability of different types of speed tests tends to be intimately related not to the number of items but to the *testing time* required to obtain the most reliable distribution of scores. Thus if the ideal testing times for two different types of speed tests are both 15 minutes, the tests will tend to have roughly the same reliability regardless of the number of items in each. When one constructs the item pool, the number of items should depend on intuitive judgments about how rapidly the items can be answered by the average person. If later it is found that the original item pool was too small, it is usually easy to construct new items.

### Time limits

Constructing a speed test consists almost entirely in finding the *time limit* that will produce the *most reliable distribution of total scores*. The amount of experimentation required to find the ideal time limit depends on previous experience with employing time limits with the particular type of item. Say, for example, that the items consist of simple problems in subtraction and addition and the test is to be used with unselected adults. Previous experience indicates that the average adult can correctly solve such problems at the rate of two per minute. The purpose of test construction is to develop a highly reliable test of numerical computation.   The experimenter thinks that a test of about 80 such items will produce a highly reliable distribution of scores.   He then constructs 80 such items and performs experiments to determine the ideal time limit. Previous experience suggests that the ideal time limit would be somewhere near 40 minutes, but it is safest to perform experiments to make sure.   Consequently, the experimenter administers the items with five different time limits to five different groups, the groups consisting of random selections from a larger sample of subjects.   The experimenter elects to try time limits of 30, 35, 40, 45, and 50 minutes, respectively.

In the experiment above, the ideal time limit is the one that produces the most reliable distribution of scores, the reliability being determined by methods to be discussed later.   Rather than perform studies of reliability at this stage, however, one can use a simpler approach which will usually produce much the same results.   In a speed test the reliabilities produced by different time limits are highly related to the standard deviations of scores produced by those time limits.   Consequently, one selects the time limit that produces the largest standard deviation of scores.   Hypothetical results from the experiment discussed above are shown in Figure 8-3.   As is typically the case, the standard deviation (and thus the reliability) is highest at some point in between the extreme time limits being investigated and tapers off on either side of that point.   In this case, however, the ideal time limit is 45 minutes rather than the 40 minutes originally guessed by the experimenter.

### Measurement of reliability

It is not correct to measure the reliability of a speed test in terms of internal consistency, as is the case with coefficient alpha and KR-20.   The most appropriate measure of reliability is made by correlating alternative forms.   Thus, in

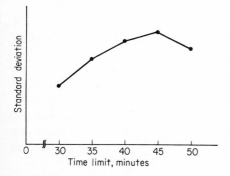

**FIGURE 8-3**    Standard    deviation    of scores on a speed test as a function of different time limits

the previous example, rather than construct only one 80-item test of numerical computation, one would construct two 80-item tests. The correlation between scores on the two tests would be the best estimate of the reliability. A time-saving approximation to the alternative-form reliability can be obtained by correlating separately timed halves of only one test, which will save the labors of constructing an alternative form. In that case, even-numbered items on the test would constitute one form, and odd-numbered items the other form. The first half of the items would be administered with a time limit equal to half that employed with the test as a whole. Immediately after time is called, the second half of the items would be administered with a time limit equal to half that employed with the whole test. The correlation between the separately timed halves would then be corrected by methods discussed in Appendix D to provide an estimate of the alternative-form reliability of the whole test. The estimate is usually rather precise if (1) the trait does not change markedly over the time used for applying alternative forms and (2) performance within a testing session is not markedly influenced by fatigue.

## Summary

The major steps in test construction consist of (1) formulation of a plan, (2) composition of an item pool, and (3) application of statistical methods of item analysis. In the construction of a test that requires content validity (e.g., an achievement test), steps 1 and 2 are most important, but some useful information is also obtained from step 3. With measures that require either predictive validity or construct validity, steps 1 and 2 are important, but in comparison with measures that require content validity, step 3 is more important. Essentially the same methods are used in step 3 (item analysis) with all three types of measures.

There are three basic approaches to item analysis; one is highly recommended, and the other two are not recommended for general use. One method that is not recommended is to select items in terms of correlations with a criterion of successful performance in life, e.g., grades in school or ratings of workers by supervisors. The major faults of this method are (1) it is based on the erroneous assumption that the major purpose in constructing most tests is, and should be, to predict particular criteria; (2) the method can be applied only to predictor tests and not to tests that require either content validity or construct validity; and (3) even if the method rested on firm logical grounds, there are numerous reasons why it would not work well in practice.

A second method that is not recommended for performing item analysis is to select items in terms of their difficulty levels, or $p$ values. The problem with this method is not so much that it is wrong in principle but that it is incomplete. The most that the method can do is to eliminate items that will probably not discriminate well between people with respect to a particular attribute, e.g., spelling ability or reasoning ability. The items that survive such analyses may be good items, but there is no guarantee of that.

The method of item analysis that is recommended for most uses is that which produces homogeneous tests, homogeneous in the sense that the items all tend to measure the same psychological trait. Essentially, then, what one does is to correlate each item with total test scores and select for the test those items which have the highest correlations. If in a particular analysis a collection of items is obtained that has high reliability, the item analysis is complete, and the test can subsequently be used in research.

The selection of test items with respect to homogeneity applies to all "power tests," ones with which a highly restrictive time limit is not employed. Different methods of item analysis are required for the construction of highly speeded tests, e.g., a test of how rapidly one can solve simple problems in addition and subtraction. Items for such tests cannot be selected in terms of correlations with total test scores because the sizes of those correlations depend on where items happen to be placed in the test rather than on their virtues in other respects. Statistical methods for constructing speed tests consist mainly of experimenting to find a time limit that produces the largest standard deviation of scores.

## Suggested additional readings

Davis, F. B. Item analysis in relation to educational and psychological testing. *Psychological Bulletin*, 1952, 49, 97–121.

Gerberich, J. R. *Specimen objective test items: A guide to achievement test construction.* New York: Longmans, 1956.

Gulliksen, H. *Theory of mental tests.* New York: Wiley, 1950. Chs. 9, 18–21.

Nunnally, J. C. *Educational measurement and evaluation.* New York: McGraw-Hill, 1964. Chs. 5, 7.

Wood, D. A. *Test construction: Development and interpretation of achievement tests.* Columbus, Ohio: Merrill, 1960.

# PART 5:

## Examples of Methods for Measuring Abilities

# CHAPTER 9

# Factors of
# ability

Ted Bronson was the smartest student that Miss Brown had ever had in the fourth grade. Now he has moved on to the fifth, and Miss Brown wonders how he is doing in Mrs. Martin's class. At lunch Mrs. Martin says that Ted is indeed bright but not quite as bright as Billy Bernstein. In conversations such as this, we frequently fail to ask an important question: Are they bright in the same ways? We too frequently assume that there is only one factor (dimension or yardstick) of intelligence and that after students have been ordered along it, there is nothing to say about their capabilities.

In contrast to the way in which many teachers are prone to make a simple ordering of students with respect to overall ability, athletic coaches are more discriminating when talking about members of their track teams, for example. If you ask the coach at Woodlawn High whether Russell Husek is a "good athlete," a typical response would be, "Well, he is very good at short-distance running, the 100-yard dash, and other sprints, but he does not do so well on the longer runs; also, he is a pretty good pole-vaulter." Describing another member of the team, the coach might say that he is excellent in all the jumps —broad jump, high jump, and pole vault—but lacks the wind to make a good runner.

In previous chapters the word "intelligence" has been used with some misgivings because it suggests that there is only one general ability, rather than different types of ability. If intelligence is perfectly general, the person who can do one type of intellectual problem well can do all other kinds of problems

**233**

well, and the person who does poorly on one type of problem will do poorly on all others. If abilities are perfectly general, the child who learns to solve arithmetic problems easily will have the same facility in learning spelling, geography, and other subject matters. Another possibility is that human abilities are completely "specific," that there are no correlations between different intellectual tasks. Then, if we know that a particular child is very adept at learning arithmetic, that offers no basis at all for predicting how well he will do in spelling or geography. Taking the case further, if abilities are completely specific and unrelated to one another, the child who can add numbers very quickly might be slower than the average child in doing multiplication.

Human abilities are neither completely general nor completely specific. The real story lies between these two extremes. In this chapter we shall discuss the history of the problem, related research, and some of the different abilities which underlie human intellect.

### Faculty psychology

In the early nineteenth century, the belief was prevalent that human behavior was determined by a large number of separate capacities, or faculties, as they were called. There were proposed faculties of attention, memory, reasoning, willpower, aesthetic appreciation, and many others. It was the early belief that each faculty resided in a particular brain location and that "bumps on the head" were prognostic of the strength of particular faculties. Although the anatomical theories were soon discarded, the belief in a large number of specific human faculties lingered throughout the remainder of the nineteenth century. Faculty psychology represented the extreme of the point of view that human abilities are highly specific.

### Binet and general intelligence

In France at the turn of the century, Alfred Binet (Binet & Simon, 1905) studied the measurement of intelligence. At first he worked in line with the faculty school and sought to measure intelligence through many simple physical and behavioral indices. Some of his "tests" concerned suggestibility, size of the cranium, tactile discrimination, graphology, and even palmistry. Like the others who were trying to measure human abilities, he found that these simple functions do not measure intelligence, as we commonly think of it.

Binet abandoned these efforts and, instead, adopted a "global" conception of intelligence. For practical purposes, he thought that it would not be possible to measure all the simple skills that underlie intelligent behavior. Instead, it would be more feasible to study the end products of intellectual functioning. In other words, rather than go back and try to find out why some people behave more intelligently than others, Binet sought to measure the extent to which individuals could deal intelligently with their present environments. He defined intelligence as "the tendency to take and maintain a definite direction; the capacity to make adaptations for the purpose of obtaining a desired end; and the power of auto-criticism."

Working with Simon, Binet developed the first practical test of general ability (or intelligence, as it is usually called). The first test consisted of 30 items which concerned, variously, following simple directions, defining words, constructing sentences, and making judgments about correct behavior in real-life situations. The Binet-Simon scale has gone through a number of revisions since that time. It set the tone for most measures of intelligence to follow, and even our modern measures of general ability bear many resemblances to those early efforts.

An important point to note about the Binet-Simon scale, and all measures of general ability to follow, is that the child is provided with only one score. Because each child receives only one score, it is succinctly assumed that intelligence is general, or, in other words, that only one factor is involved in the test items. If there are, say, two kinds of intelligence involved in the test, the use of only one score is somewhat misleading. Two children could make the same score, not because they are alike with respect to their abilities, but because one child is high in one of the factors and low in the other, and vice versa for the other child. The same assumption of the generality of human abilities is involved in all the tests of general ability (intelligence tests) which have followed from Binet's early work. Binet's test and all those to follow represent the extreme opposite point of view from that of the faculty school, that intelligence is perfectly general and that one overall index is all that is required to indicate a child's intellectual standing.

### Factor analysis

Rather than argue over whether intelligence is general or is divided up into many specific abilities, we can employ experimental and statistical procedures which will help answer the question. Many different kinds of tests can be given to students, and correlation coefficients can be obtained for all possible pairs of them. As was mentioned in Chapter 4, the correlation coefficient indicates the extent to which two tests measure the same thing. If many different kinds of mental tests were given to a large number of students and the correlations between them were very high, this would be evidence that intelligence is completely general. In other words, all tests tend to measure the same thing. On the other hand, if the correlations between the tests were all zero, it would show that each test measures something different from what is measured by the others, and this would be evidence that intelligence is completely specific to the tasks involved.

A look at some correlation coefficients will show how the question of the generality of intellectual functions is solved. Table 9-1 shows the intercorrelations of six tests. The tests are labeled A through F. The table shows all possible intercorrelations between the tests. For example, the table shows that tests A and B have a low correlation—.19, to be exact. There is a high correlation between tests A and C—.64. Test D correlates only .21 with test A. The highest correlation of test D with any other test is .67, with test F. In the table the blank spaces in parentheses are at points showing the correlations of tests with themselves. Of course, any test correlates perfectly with itself, at least regarding the particular set of scores obtained on any one occasion. What conclusion should be drawn from the correlations presented in Table 9-1? Do the tests all measure the same thing, or do they each measure different traits? Some of the correlations are quite high; for example, there is a correlation of .72 between test A and test E. Other correlations are close to zero.

A rearrangement of the order in which tests appear in the table will help clarify the question regarding the amount of overlap between tests. In Table 9-2, the order of appearance of the tests has been rearranged to show those tests which tend to correlate highly with one another. When the correlations are presented in this way, it can be seen that tests A, E, and C tend to correlate highly with one another, as do tests D, B, and F. Correlations between the two groups of tests are very low. Lines are drawn in the table to demonstrate the tendency of the tests to divide up into two groups. What we have found is that there are two different types of tests, each of which is said to form a *cluster*, or *factor*. Tests A, E, and C relate to one factor, and any student who does very well on one of these tests is likely to do well on all of them. Tests D, B, and F form another factor, and any student who does very well on one of them is likely to do well on the others. However, if a student does well on the tests representative of one cluster, or factor, this provides little information as to how well he will do on the other. In this example, tests A, E, and C all concern verbal comprehension: vocabulary, grades in English, and scores on a reading comprehension test. Tests D, B, and F deal with addition, multiplication, and the solution of algebraic problems, respectively. The second factor concerns the ability to perform arithmetic operations.

Studying correlation tables, such as the two just discussed, allows us to determine how many clusters, or factors, are involved in intellectual tasks. The

**TABLE 9-1      Correlations between six tests**

|   | A | B | C | D | E | F |
|---|---|---|---|---|---|---|
| A | ( ) | .19 | .64 | .21 | .72 | .05 |
| B | .19 | ( ) | .22 | .64 | .12 | .55 |
| C | .64 | .22 | ( ) | .14 | .56 | .28 |
| D | .21 | .64 | .14 | ( ) | .28 | .67 |
| E | .72 | .12 | .56 | .28 | ( ) | .11 |
| F | .05 | .55 | .28 | .67 | .11 | ( ) |

**TABLE 9-2**     Rearrangement of correlations from Table 9-1

|   | A | E | C | D | B | F |
|---|---|---|---|---|---|---|
| A | ( ) | .72 | .64 | .21 | .19 | .05 |
| E | .72 | ( ) | .56 | .28 | .12 | .11 |
| C | .64 | .56 | ( ) | .14 | .22 | .28 |
| D | .21 | .28 | .14 | ( ) | .64 | .67 |
| B | .19 | .12 | .22 | .64 | ( ) | .55 |
| F | .05 | .11 | .28 | .67 | .55 | ( ) |

example presented above is a very simple one: only two factors are involved, and those are quite easily seen by inspecting the correlation table. If the correlational results were always so straightforward and studies contained no more than six tests, it would not be necessary to apply more refined procedures to the results. However, results are seldom as neat as those presented above, and instead of studying only six tests at a time, we often study as many as 50 or more tests in one table. In those instances it is no longer feasible simply to look at the correlation table and rearrange the ordering of the tests in such a way as to show the dominant clusters. Instead it is necessary to apply some mathematical procedures which identify the major factors and indicate the extent to which each test belongs to each factor. The mathematical procedures which are so applied are referred to as *factor analysis*.

For many purposes, the best way of obtaining factors is by simply averaging or summing scores over tests that form a cluster, like the clusters that can be seen in Table 9-2. For example, if a person has standard scores on the three verbal tests of 1.4, 1.1, and 1.5, respectively, these could be summed to provide a score of 4.0 on the verbal factor. The same would be done for the standard scores of each person in the investigation. A second factor could be obtained by summing scores over the three tests in Table 9-2 that concern arithmetic abilities. The factor scores could then be converted to standard scores or to some type of scores that would facilitate interpretations. Also, the factor scores could be used in future correlational studies in basic research or applied work, e.g., correlating scores on the verbal factor with grades in school.

A factor is nothing more than a set of scores obtained by combining scores over individual tests. In the foregoing example, a very simple type of combination of tests was described, that of simply summing scores over three tests. In actual work with factor analysis, it is frequently necessary to employ much more complex combinations of scores. This is necessary because (1) factor analyses frequently concern huge tables showing the correlations between 50 or more tests and (2) the clusters of related tests are not nearly as neatly divisible as they are in Table 9-2. The sheer complexity of the tables of correlations requires the use of some complex methods of mathematical analysis to determine factors and to determine the types of combinations of tests required to measure those factors. However, the basic principles in all forms of factor analysis are the same. Whether by complex or simple means, one first locates groups of tests that tend to measure the same thing, and then one obtains scores on the factors by combining scores on tests that relate to the factors.

In addition to obtaining factors, it is also informative to correlate the scores on each test with the scores of each factor. Because all persons in the investigation have scores on all tests and all factors, it is a simple matter to perform the necessary calculations.

Table 9-3 presents the correlations of the six tests from Table 9-2 with the two factors obtained by summing scores on the two clusters of tests. Such correlations of tests with factors are called *factor loadings*. The loading of test A on factor 1 is .90, and the loading of that test on factor 2 is .17. Factor loadings help one to understand the nature of each factor, and they indicate which tests are better measures of each factor.

During the last half century, many different factor-analytic studies have been performed, not only on tests of human ability, but also on measures of personality, interests, attitudes, and many other kinds of individual differences. Each factor-analytic study represents a very large undertaking. First, it is necessary to compose all the tests that will be used, and as was said previously, these may number more than 50. Then the entire group of tests must be given to a large number of persons, preferably more than 300. After the tests are scored, all possible correlations must be computed between them, resulting in tables of the kind shown above. Then the mathematical procedures of factor analysis must be applied. The end result is a number of factors showing the dominant clusters among the tests. The factors that have been found in each area of individual differences are said to constitute a *structure*, or, as one might say, a map describing the common tendencies among tests.

## Factors of ability

The many factor analyses performed during the last half century have provided the answer to the question of the relative generality or specificity of human abilities. The results show that neither extreme point of view is correct and that a middle ground must be adopted. Arguing for the generality of abilities is the now well-established fact that correlations between tests of ability are almost always positive, even if small in some cases. For example, tests as disparate in appearance as those of vocabulary, memory of digits, and mechanical information all correlate positively, if no higher than .20 or .30. It would be rare indeed to find one type of human ability that correlated negatively with another. If that were found, it would indicate that, statistically speaking, people who performed well on one task would tend to perform poorly on another. Human abilities all tend to go together, even though in some cases the

**TABLE 9-3**    Loadings of six
tests on two factors

| TEST | FACTORS | |
|------|---------|---|
|      | 1 | 2 |
| A | .90 | .17 |
| E | .87 | .20 |
| C | .84 | .25 |
| D | .24 | .89 |
| B | .20 | .85 |
| F | .17 | .86 |

statistical relationships are very weak. These findings offer partial confirmation of the generalist point of view as represented by Binet and those who followed in his footsteps.

Factor-analytic results have also provided confirmation for the multifactor point of view. In addition to the tendency of all tests of human ability to correlate positively with one another, there are definite clusterings of the tests as shown by the correlations which have been obtained. For example, all tests involving the ability to understand words, such as tests of reading comprehension and vocabulary, tend to have high correlations with one another, averaging .60 or more. Similarly, all tests involving numerical computations, such as addition, subtraction, multiplication, and finding square roots, tend to correlate highly with one another and thus form another cluster, or factor. Correlations between the two kinds of tests are positive, typically averaging .30 or higher, but correlations between the members of the two clusters are not nearly so high as the correlations within the clusters. This indicates that the members of each cluster tend to hang together and measure something that is partially separate from what is measured by the other cluster, or factor.

Factor-analytic studies have shown that there are dozens, and perhaps even hundreds, of such clusters, or factors. However, most of these factors are concerned with highly specialized activities. For example, one such highly specialized factor concerns the effect of certain types of visual illusions on perceptual judgment; another concerns the ability to memorize digits presented in serial order. A great deal more research needs to be done before it will be possible to say which of these factors are important and in which situations. Some factors have proved useful in predicting success in school, in industry, and in military settings, but the bulk of them have been used insufficiently to determine their importance. A great deal of research has been done on the factors that make for success in school at all levels, and it has been found that only a few of the factors are very important. The following sections will describe some of the most important factors, including those which are important for schoolwork and for vocational activities.

## verbal factors

The most important factors relating to schoolwork concern the abilities to understand, to use, and to deal with written and spoken language. As is true of all the types of factors which will be discussed, there are many possible verbal factors that can be found by exhaustively analyzing many different types of verbal tests. However, only two of these seem to be very important for schoolwork. They are verbal comprehension and verbal fluency, which will be discussed in turn.

### Verbal comprehension

The most important verbal factor concerns the ability to understand written and spoken language. Verbal comprehension represents most of what we refer to as "reading skill." Although the factor extends far beyond sheer vocabulary, a vocabulary test provides a good measure of verbal comprehension.

Typical items:

1. Which one of the following words means most nearly the same as *salutation?*

a. offering
b. greeting
c. discussion
d. appeasement

2. Which one of the following words is most nearly the opposite of *languid?*

a. unemotional
b. sad
c. energetic
d. healthy

### Verbal fluency

Verbal fluency concerns the ability to produce words and sentences rapidly. It can be thought of as the rate-of-production aspect of verbal ability, in contrast to verbal comprehension, which concerns the depth of understanding of verbal material.

Typical items:

1. Write as many names of foods as you can in the next two minutes.

_____
_____
_____

2. In each of the following rows write three words that mean almost the same as the given word.

**small**    _____    _____    _____
**helpful**  _____    _____    _____
**kind**     _____    _____    _____

Verbal comprehension comes into play when rather complex words, sentences, and paragraphs are being dealt with. Verbal fluency comes into play when the verbal material is relatively simple and when fluidity of expression is at issue. The two types of abilities are somewhat correlated. Correlations of about .40 or .50 are typically found between the tests used to measure verbal comprehension and those used to measure verbal fluency. On the other hand, the two types of abilities are far from perfectly correlated. A child may understand what he reads very well but have difficulty in explaining it because of his lack of verbal fluency. Similarly, the talkative child who produces a torrent of words in ordinary conversation does not always have a depth of comprehension to match. Teachers are sometimes fooled by the child who is quite facile in expression but who does rather poorly when he is required to read and understand material or to analyze poetry or essays.

## numerical facility

One very clear factor of numerical facility has been found in many different studies. It concerns the speed and accuracy of solving arithmetic problems of all kinds—addition, subtraction, multiplication, division, finding square roots, and others.

Typical items:

$$
\begin{array}{cc}
246 & 8,754 \\
+943 & -\ 381
\end{array}
\qquad 16 \times 22 = \underline{\hspace{3cm}} \qquad 284/4 = \underline{\hspace{3cm}}
$$

In addition to items that obviously concern arithmetic computations, the factor also extends to almost any type of task in which quantitative operations are involved, such as the following items, for example:

1. Which one of the following numbers is closest to 8.2?

a. 8.1
b. 8.3
c. 8.18
d. 8.23

2. Which one of the following numbers is most nearly the same as the square root of 15?

a. 225
b.   4
c.   5
d.   1.5

3. Which one of the following would be the largest *positive* amount?

a. $-10 \times -10$
b. $-\ 5 \times -\ 5$
c. $10 \times -10$
d. $9 \times 9$

It should be clearly understood that not all problems containing numbers measure numerical facility. Numbers also appear in many of the reasoning tests, which will be discussed in the next section, but mainly such problems do not concern numerical facility. The numerical facility factor comes into play when some complex (for the age group) numerical solutions must be obtained. If the numbers involved are very simple and they are included only as a way of providing a useful method of expressing the solution to a problem, numerical facility as such may be very unimportant. This distinction will be made clearer in the discussion of reasoning factors.

Tests of numerical facility usually show moderate (about .40) correlations with measures of verbal ability. As was mentioned previously, all measures of human ability tend to correlate positively with one another, but numerical facility has a far from perfect relationship with other factors of ability. Numerical facility is not the same as mathematical reasoning, which is involved in simple algebraic problems. Although algebraic problems require some numerical computations, these are usually relatively simple. Instead, algebraic problems relate more prominently to the reasoning factors, which will be discussed below. The fact that a child is very good in number skills in the elementary grades does not mean that he is likely to be good later in mathematical subject matter, such as algebra, geometry, and trigonometry.

## reasoning factors

Although many different studies of reasoning tests have been performed, the factors involved are still somewhat unclear. Reasoning is a complex domain in which the abilities involved tend to blend in different ways in different tests, making it hard to separate the reasoning factors from one another and to find good measures of any of them. The most clearly determined factors are discussed below.

### General reasoning

The most common and most commonly found factor of reasoning is concerned with the ability to invent solutions to problems. Arithmetical reasoning problems are most characteristic of the factor.

Typical items:

1. If a machine produces bolts at the rate of two each 15 minutes, how many bolts does the machine produce in three hours?
2. How would you get exactly 7 quarts of water from a stream if you had one 5-quart container and one 3-quart container?

As was mentioned previously, even though such simple algebraic problems involve numbers, the main ability being measured is not that of numerical computation.    In order to solve the problems, the student must invent a solution, grasp some principle by which each can be solved.

The general reasoning factor also appears in items concerning serial completion, in which the subject is required to supply the next entry in a patterned series of letters or digits.    Two examples are as follows:

    zzyyxxw_____
    2132435465_____

There is an element of discovery in all the tests that measure the factor of general reasoning, the discovery of some principle whereby a correct solution is obtained.

## Deduction

The deduction factor is concerned with the drawing of conclusions, as in logical syllogisms.    In this type of reasoning there is nothing in particular to be discovered or invented, the ability being concerned with evaluating the implications of an argument.

Typical items:

1. John is younger than Fred. Bill is older than Fred. Therefore, Bill is _____ than John.

2. A student has 10 marbles. No one else in his class has 10 marbles. This means that:

    *a.* No one else in the class has marbles.
    *b.* All the other students have fewer than 10 marbles.
    *c.* Some of the students have fewer than 10 marbles.
    *d.* Some of the students have more than 10 marbles.
    *e.* Only one student has exactly 10 marbles.

Whereas the factor of general reasoning is represented by a very wide variety of items concerning the solution of problems, the deduction factor is more narrowly concerned with only those items pertaining to logical syllogisms.

## Seeing relationships

A third factor of reasoning involves the ability to see the relationship between two things or ideas and to use the relationship to find other things or ideas. This factor is best represented by verbal analogies and design analogies.

Typical items:

*Ship* is to *sail* as *automobile* is to

    *a.* ship
    *b.* seat
    *c.* motor
    *d.* wind
    *e.* driver

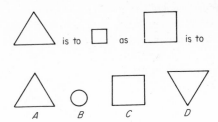

Some items concerning reasoning abilities represent a blend of the factor of seeing relationships and the factor of general reasoning. This is the case, for example, with the series-completion items illustrated previously.

## memory factors

As is true of the other areas of human ability that we have discussed, there is more than one type of memory. Some of the better-established factors of memory are discussed below.

### Rote memory

The best-established factor of memory concerns the ability to remember simple associations where meaning is of little or no importance.

Typical item:

The person is given a list of names, each of which is paired with a number. He is given a minute or so to memorize which number goes with which name. Then he is told to turn the page. The next page contains the list of names without the numbers. He is instructed to write the proper numbers next to the names. Other items which concern rote memory are of the same general kind, involving, for example, pairing colors with words, initials with last names, and letters with geometric forms.

### Meaningful memory

There is substantial evidence to indicate that there is a factor involved in the retention of meaningful relationships which is separable from rote memory. The factor of meaningful memory appears when the student is requested to memorize sentences, meaningfully related words, and lines of poetry.

Typical items:

1. The student is asked to read and to try to remember a list of sentences like the following:

*John repaired the wagon by welding the broken axle.*

The list of sentences is taken away, and the student is then given the same sentences with one or more of the words deleted from each, as in the following:

*John repaired the wagon by welding the broken* _____ .

2. The student is shown a list of meaningfully related pairs of words such as the following:

**dog—bark**
**shoe—leather**
**hard—candy**
**small—box**

The list is taken away, and the student is presented with only one member of each pair, as follows:

**dog**   _____
**shoe**  _____
**hard**  _____
**small** _____

There is evidence for several other memory factors. A number of investigators have reported a memory span factor concerning the ability to recall perfectly for immediate reproduction a series of unrelated items. A typical item would consist of reading a series of five to a dozen digits and giving the digits back in the correct order. There is some evidence for a visual memory factor in which the ability to grasp the relationships within a picture or pattern is important. A typical item would consist of showing the student a picture of a landscape and asking him to remember the details. Then the picture would be taken away, and he would be asked questions like "How many sheep were in the picture?" "What was the boy handing to the man?" "Where was the swing located?" The visual memory factor might be related to the ability to remember faces and witnessed events.

## spatial factors

### Spatial orientation

This factor concerns the ability to detect accurately the spatial arrangement of objects with respect to one's own body. The factor would be necessary in deciphering pictures taken from a maneuvering airplane. If the plane is simultaneously turning and climbing, the landscape looks very different from the normal view. The individual who can accurately detect what maneuver the airplane is going through from looking at only a picture of the landscape from that vantage point has good spatial orientation. The factor appears most prominently when the spatial problems are presented under "speeded" conditions.

Typical items:[1]

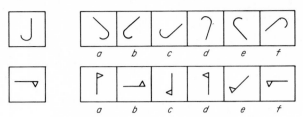

Every alternative that could be obtained
by a rotation of the first figure is to be marked.

### Spatial visualization

This second spatial factor differs in a subtle manner from spatial orientation. It is present when the person is required to imagine or to *visualize* how an object would look if its spatial position were changed. Although there is good statistical support for both of these factors, there has been considerable difficulty in understanding the underlying processes. Spatial orientation seems to require either an actual or an imagined adjustment of one's own body. In spatial visualization the person cannot solve the problem by a bodily adjustment; instead, he must conceive of how an object would look if its spatial position were markedly changed. In contrast to spatial orientation, spatial visualization is best tested under relatively "unspeeded" conditions.

Typical item:

> The subject is shown a folded piece of paper with a number of holes punched in it. He is asked to choose from among a number of unfolded pieces of paper the one that would be the same as the first.

Other examples of items concerning spatial visualization are shown in Figure 9-1.

## perceptual factors

A number of factors have been found which concern the ability to detect visual patterns and to see relationships within and between patterns. Some of these factors are apparently of only limited importance, such as the ability to judge certain types of illusions. Several of the more important factors will be described.

### Perceptual speed

This factor is concerned with the rapid recognition of perceptual details and particularly the recognition of similarities and differences between visual patterns.

[1] Reproduced by permission of Science Research Associates.

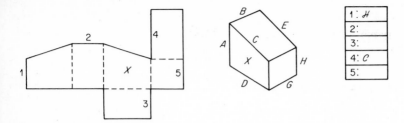

**FIGURE 9-1**    Sample item from the Surface Development Test.   The subject's task is to visualize how a piece of paper will be folded to make an object. He is asked to indicate which lettered edge of the object on the right corresponds to each numbered edge of the piece of paper at the left.   (*Copyright 1962, Educational Testing Service.   Used by permission.*)

Typical items:

1. The person is shown a complex geometric form and is asked to choose from among a number of other forms the one that is the same as the first.
2. The person is told to make a check mark beside each pair of letter groups that are identical and to make no mark beside groups that are different:

x′ # ·Iq_____X′ # ·IQ
a&30(k_____a&3(oK
-ro-/w _____-ro-/w

(Fifty to several hundred pairs would be used, depending on the time allowed.)

### Perceptual closure

This factor concerns the perception of objects from limited cues.   The word "closure" means a sudden awareness of an obscure object or relationship.   Perceptual speed requires only the recognition of a perceptual form.   Perceptual closure requires the "putting together" of a perceptual form when only part of it is presented.
Typical items:[2]

[2] Adapted from L. L. Thurstone, 1944.

In the items on the left, the individual is required to recognize the incomplete words.  In the items on the right, he is required to recognize the number or letter that is partially outlined.

## Flexibility of closure

There is evidence for a flexibility-of-closure factor in problems which require the subject to detect a perceptual pattern which is embedded in a distracting or competing pattern.  This factor is found in such items as the hidden-picture games that are printed in newspapers and some children's magazines.  For example, a picture that looks like a normal landscape at first glance is found, after careful scrutiny, to contain a number of faces hidden in the trees and rocks.  In order to see the faces, it is necessary to resist or "break down" the perception of the object in which the faces are embedded.

Typical items:[3]

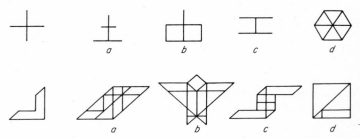

In each of the two items, the figure on the left is embedded in one or more of the four alternative figures on the right.

## present outlooks on studies of human abilities

During the last 30 years, factor-analytic studies of human abilities have pushed far ahead.  In the early 1940s, many psychologists were developing tests for the armed forces.  Tests were developed for so many special types of aptitudes and with respect to so many types of training programs that excellent opportunities were provided to extend what was known about factors of human ability.  Up through 1950, it could be reported that there were over forty well-established factors of ability.  (These are described in detail by French, 1951.)  This was a far cry from the conception of human abilities originally held by Spearman, and it suggested that the Binet type of test was based on very false assumptions about the generality of intellect.

The number of factors of intellect has continued to grow since the survey by French, and now one could argue that there are between 50 and 100 factors,

---

[3] Reproduced by permission of Science Research Associates.

depending on how cautiously one interprets the evidence.   Whereas the purpose of employing factor analysis was to provide an understanding of the nature of human abilities, the results of factor-analytic studies served only to confuse us.   Spearman hoped to show that only one factor of intellect was important, and one gathers that the Thurstones (T. G. Thurstone, 1941) hoped to show that no more than about ten would be required to cover the important ground of human intellect.   Probably no one wanted to find over 50 factors because having found so many, what would one do with them?   Is human intellect really splintered into so many separate dimensions?

In the search for factors, it gradually became apparent that one can artifactually force factors to occur in a number of ways.   One way to do this is to compose several tests that are highly similar in terms of operations and materials.   An example is as follows.   On the first test, the subject is presented with a page of randomized letters and is told to circle as many a's as he can in 60 seconds.   On the next test, he is presented with another page of randomized letters and is told to circle b's.   Then on the third test, he is told to circle c's. The three tests will correlate well with one another, and the correlations between them cannot be accounted for by factors relating to other types of tests.   Then, from a purely mathematical point of view, it must be admitted that the three tests define a factor; but is a factor that is so narrowly defined likely to be of any importance?

Another way to force factors artifactually is to include in the analysis subjects who are heterogeneous in numerous ways and to intercorrelate variables that relate to heterogeneity.   For example, French found an age factor, with the largest loading on chronological age and smaller loadings on tests that change with age.   He reports a sex factor which relates to differences in central tendency between men and women on tests of ability.   Of course, it is important to learn of relations between such vital statistics and human abilities, but should one consider these factors?

There are numerous other ways to force factors to occur artifactually.   One of these is to score the same items in a number of different ways, in which case there will nearly always be high correlations between the different scoring keys.

## judging the importance of factors of ability

Aside from the point that many of the supposed factors that have been found would be better classed as *artifactors* (to coin a word), it is becoming increasingly clear that to prevent utter chaos in the accumulation of factors, some consideration must be given to the *importance* of factors.   Since it is now quite obvious that "laboratory" tests can be constructed so as to produce an endless array of factors, some means must be devised for separating the wheat from the chaff.   How to determine the importance of factors will be discussed in the following sections.

## Mathematical importance of factors

One way in which a factor can be important is in its relations to mathematical models for human abilities. For example, to the extent that a general factor is found in tests of human ability, that factor is important because it goes a long way toward explaining correlations between all tests of ability. The mathematical importance of a factor depends, however, on the nature of the mathematical model. Thus a general factor would be important in a model that concerns a general factor and group factors, but it would not be important, or would be a downright nuisance, in other models. A later section will consider one of the models that has been proposed for explaining human abilities.

## Content generality of factors

A second way in which a factor can be judged important is with respect to the range of test materials involved. Previously it was described how an "artifactor" could be produced by the development of three almost identical tests (the circling of letters). Although there are no concrete standards by which one can gauge the relative breadth of content covered by factors, some of the factors appearing in the literature appear to relate to very narrow domains of content. For example, French reports a factor of *length estimation,* for which some of the tests with highest loadings concern (1) estimating length with a meter stick, (2) estimating length with a meter stick after practice, (3) selecting the shortest of straight lines radiating from a point, and (4) selecting the shortest of crooked lines radiating from a point. This may prove to be an important factor, but from the narrowness of its content one would suspect that it is not. There would be more intuitive support for the factor if it extended to judgments of area and volume and if it related to both regular and irregular figures.

At the other extreme of content generality is the *verbal comprehension factor,* which relates to almost any type of test that directly or indirectly concerns the understanding of words and connected discourse. That factor relates to so many types of intellectual tasks that there is sometimes a problem in reducing its effects in tests that are intended to measure other factors, e.g., effects due to the wording of written or oral instructions and to the verbal material in test items.

There is no way to specify the ideal level of generality for a factor. At the upper extreme of generality, one could argue that a factor is not sufficiently analytic, i.e., that it tends to hide subdimensions of abilities in a particular area. This has often been said about the factor of verbal comprehension, and consequently efforts have been made to break this factor down into several correlated factors. As was mentioned previously, the ideal generality of a factor depends in part on the mathematical model which is used to guide research on human abilities.  At the lower extreme of content generality, however, it is doubtful that some of the highly specialized factors that have been reported will ever prove to be of general importance.  Such is the case with the factor of *length estimation*.  That factor might be important only for predicting success on a job concerned purely with the estimation of the length of things, and if there is such a job, it is probably so unimportant in the total enterprise that predicting success in it would not be worth the labors of employing psychological tests.  Also, aside from the possible use of tests as predictor instruments, it is doubtful that such a narrowly defined factor would prove to be important in the other ways discussed in this chapter.  One gets the impression that this is true of many of the factors which have been reported: they are so narrowly defined in item content that, unless they can be shown to be somewhat more general in that regard, they have little likelihood of becoming important.

In a sense, one can argue that a factor is important partly to the extent that it produces some surprises.  If, for example, one tells a colleague that he has found a factor of length estimation among half a dozen tests all obviously related to the same thing, he is likely to be met with a yawn.  (Of course, in some instances a yawn is undeserved because what frequently appear to be "obviously" similar tasks fail to correlate well with one another.)  At the other extreme of surprise value are some of the perceptual and spatial factors, where moderate-sized loadings are found for some tests that do not obviously concern either perception or spatial relations.  An example is the *gestalt flexibility factor* (French, 1951), which concerns primarily the ability to detect simple geometric configurations within complex configurations.  The surprise value of the factor rests in the fact that a *motor* test (two-hand coordination) has a high loading. Anyone who is interested in the nature of human abilities would not yawn on learning that.  Such surprises stimulate us to think about the more basic factors of ability which underlie test materials that superficially are so different.

## Importance in prediction

One obvious way in which a factor can be important is in the prediction of important criterion variables, such as success in pilot training, grades in college, and improvement during psychotherapy.  In a sense it is unfortunate that so much of the effort to understand human abilities has hinged on applied concerns.  To some extent this has caused us to ignore factors that may be very important for understanding the nature of human abilities but have little predictive validity for the criteria most frequently investigated.  Also, it has led us to deal with factors that probably should be ignored in basic research.  For example, French (1951) reports a factor of pilot interest which concerned biographical data and items of information about aviation.  That factor was useful in predicting success in pilot training during World War II, but since it was so specifically oriented toward one occupation, it is hard to see how it would be important otherwise. (Also, because airplanes have changed so rapidly and the duties of pilots have changed also, the factor is probably no longer very useful for predicting success in pilot training.)

In spite of the many potential uses for factors of ability in predicting performance in real-life situations, most of the uses have been with respect to either (1) success in school at all levels or (2) success in specific occupations. The most outstanding success has been with respect to the former, where it has been found that success in many different types of school settings is reasonably well predicted by factors of verbal comprehension, reasoning, numerical computation, and some of the perceptual and spatial factors. Beyond those, however, other factors tend to have little predictive validity. The validity of factors of human ability for predicting success in particular occupations depends to a considerable extent on the occupation. Much more success has been had with high-level occupations (e.g., engineering) than with low-level occupations (e.g., driving a truck).

Although it is doubtful that studies of predictive validity alone will do all that is required to gain an understanding of the importance of different factors of human ability, there are ways in which such studies could help. It would, for example, be informative to learn more about how factors of ability relate to particular topics in college and to subparts of those topics. In this regard it would be instructive to learn more about how factors of verbal ability relate to the mastery of foreign languages, not only to overall grades in learning languages, but also to the rate of mastering various aspects of the language, e.g., grammar as opposed to vocabulary.

### Ecological importance of factors

Eventually, what will be needed for an understanding of the importance of factors in daily life is a correlation of those factors with individual differences manifested in real-life situations. Presently we do not know to what extent our factors of human ability extend beyond the "laboratory" to the things that people do every day. Are those factors of any importance for making change on a bus, recalling phone numbers, or giving a talk to the PTA? Of course, it is not possible to measure performance in a multitude of real-life situations, but at least it would be possible to conduct informal surveys of what people do in daily life. Persons who are familiar with the known factors of human ability could literally follow people around and watch the things that they do, and any task that possibly concerned one of the known factors could be noted. Also, it would be useful to list important tasks that apparently do not relate to any known factors of ability. Gradually, in this way, a classification scheme could be developed for areas in real life that need to be explained by factors of ability, and studies could be made of the correlations between laboratory tests and daily behavior. It may sound rather farfetched now to talk of such develop-ments, but issues relating to human abilities are sufficiently important to merit the efforts. In this process, we shall certainly find much "chaff" among pres-ently known factors of human abilities, but the remaining "wheat" will stimu-late further basic investigations.

## Importance for psychological constructs

More than anything else, factors need to prove their importance for con-trolled experiments in general psychology. There has always been a great deal of talk about the need to consider measures of individual differences in con-trolled experiments, but not much has been done about it. One can see numerous parallels between factors of human ability and processes that are in-vestigated in controlled experiments. For example, one would expect to find that individual differences in some of the perceptual factors correlate with individual differences in various aspects of visual recognition experiments. As another example, one would expect to find relations between verbal factors, memory factors, and various aspects of studies on verbal learning and verbal behavior. Interesting hypotheses can be generated about relations between various factors of ability and the functions mediated by different parts of the brain.

A suggestion by Ferguson (1954) is illustrative of the many possible links between factors of human ability and basic processes in controlled experiments. He suggested that transfer of training in experiments on learning is governed by factors of human ability. It is well known that practice in one type of learning situation may facilitate learning in new situations, but there has been no way of predicting the amounts and kinds of transfer that would occur. Fer-guson's suggestion is that if a person is given training with respect to one type of problem relating to a particular factor of ability, there will be positive trans-fer to other types of problems relating to the same factor. For example, if an individual is given training with respect to one task concerning a particular factor of reasoning, that might transfer in some degree to different-appearing tasks concerning the same factor. This suggestion offers the possibility of investigating many links between the results of controlled experiments and factors of ability.

Guilford (1961) has pointed out numerous relations between factors of human ability and the processes that are investigated in controlled experiments —concept formation, learning, reinforcement, memory, and others. Fleishman and Hempel (1954) pioneered a type of study which serves to relate factors of ability to controlled experiments; they investigated correlations between factors of ability and progress in different trials of a learning task. They found that the importance of different factors differed with the stage of learning. In learn-ing a psychomotor task, a factor of spatial relations was important in the early trials, but in later trials it correlated much less with performance. On the early trials, factors concerning speed of movement had relatively small correlations with performance, but by the end of training they were the most important factors. There are many other possibilities for investigating relations between factors of ability and learning processes.

## Guilford's concept of the structure of intellect

In threading our way through the history of studies of human abilities, we are brought up to modern times by considering the work of J. P. Guilford (1967) and his colleagues. Guilford has collected mountains of data with respect to factors of intellect, and he has made notable contributions to methods of analysis; more importantly, however, he has done more than anyone else to develop a systematic point of view about the nature of factors of intellect. His work epitomizes the good things that (in the author's opinion) should be done to mesh studies of human abilities with experimental psychology.

One of Guilford's major contributions has been the development of a classification scheme (or taxonomy) for factors of human intelligence. He refers to the classification scheme as the *structure of intellect,* which is depicted in Figure 9-2. The classification scheme implies that all forms of intellectual functioning can be categorized with respect to subdivisions of three major characteristics. The most important characteristic is that of the psychological process that is apparently involved in any test, the process being spoken of as the type of *operation* which subjects perform. One operation is that of cognition, or "knowing," examples of which are knowing the meaning of the word "tangible" and knowing the product of 12 and 12. Memory, as the name implies, involves the operation of retaining information that is briefly presented, such as recalling a phone number heard on the radio or recalling a randomized list of nine letters presented on a screen for four seconds. Divergent production consists of producing a variety of ideas that lead in different directions, such as thinking of unusual uses for common objects and thinking of numerous words that rhyme with "peal." In divergent thinking, there is no one best solution, but rather what is at stake is the production of many clever ideas in some class.

In contrast to divergent production, convergent production concerns finding either the only solution or the best solution to a stated problem. Outstanding examples of items involving convergent production are those concerning arithmetical reasoning, illustrated previously, and those concerning verbal analogies, where the subject must supply the one word that completes the analogy.

As the name implies, the operation of evaluation consists of reaching decisions about the accuracy, goodness, suitability, or workability of proposed solutions to a problem. Any multiple-choice item, for example, involves evaluation. A particular instance is that of items illustrated previously for the factor

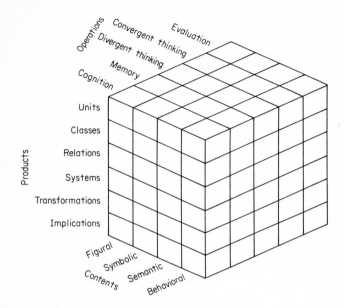

**FIGURE 9-2**    A cubical model representing the structure of intellect (*Adapted from Guilford, 1967.*)

of perceptual speed, in which the subject must judge whether two groups of
letters are the same or different. In everyday life, an example would be that
of evaluating the suitability of a plan for promoting a particular charity.
Whereas in divergent thinking and convergent thinking the subject supplies
his own answers, in evaluative thinking he judges the goodness of ideas posed
by others.

The front face of the cube in Figure 9-2 concerns the nature of test materials
employed. Figural material has been illustrated previously with respect to items
concerning figural analogies, spatial relations, spatial visualization, perceptual
closure, and others. Symbolic content is exemplified in items concerning the
unscrambling of scrambled words and the rapid production of many words that
begin with a particular letter. Items concerning numerical computation also
have symbolic content.

Semantic content is present in items that concern the meaning of verbal
material. Outstanding examples are items in vocabulary tests and in tests concerning verbal analogies. Behavioral content is present in tests in which the
appropriateness of some overt action is at issue, for example, in a typical study
of problem solving in which the subject is presented with a number of objects
and is told to make an instrument that will perform a particular function, such
as holding a lighted candle on a wall.

The third facet of the conceptual scheme in Figure 9-2 concerns the specific task set for the subject.    Units concern the finding or producing of a specified thing, such as correctly unscrambling a scrambled word and naming the objects in items concerning perceptual closure.    Items relating to classes are those which require the subject either to place things in their proper groupings or to recognize proper groupings, as, for example, when a child is shown pictures of a dog and three pieces of furniture and is asked to tell which object does not belong with the others.    Outstanding examples of items concerning relations are those which pertain to the factor of "seeing relations," discussed previously in this chapter.    Items involving verbal analogies and figural analogies are also prime examples.

Items concerning systems are those in which the subject must grasp some principle by which a number of objects are related.    A simple example of such an item is one that involves grasping the principle by which a letter series is constructed and supplying the next letter in the list, as follows:

aabbccdde_____

abacadaea _____

Another example of an item involving systems would be one that required the subject to place eight geometric forms into two groups of four each.    In one such item the only consistent difference might concern the fact that four of the forms are much larger than the others.

Transformations concern appropriate changes of various kinds and would be involved, for example, in items to measure the factor of spatial visualization, discussed earlier in this chapter.    In one item the subject is shown a folded piece of paper with various holes punched in it and is asked to judge how it would look (would be transformed) if it were unfolded.    Another such item relates to the rearrangement of matches to form a particular geometric configuration.    The subject is shown 17 matches placed in such a way as to form six adjacent squares.    He is asked to remove exactly four matches in such a way as to leave only three squares.

Items concerning implications require the subject to extrapolate from the facts given to some conclusion.    Items such as the following, used to measure the factor of deductive reasoning, discussed previously in this chapter, are an outstanding example:

Fred is younger than Bill.

Fred is older than Bob.

Who is older, Bill or Bob?

Another example of such an item is one in which the subject is asked to state what some of the implications would be if the world population were reduced by half during the next 100 years.

## hierarchical models

Although Guilford's classification scheme goes a long way toward establishing a theoretical base for the nature of intellect, it would lead to an appallingly large number of separate factors.  The classification scheme alone leads only to the discovery of more and more factors, and it has nothing to say about possible relations between them.  As Guilford recognizes, what is needed in addition to the classification scheme is a mathematical model for simplifying relations between the many factors following from the scheme.  For this purpose, numerous persons have proposed the use of hierarchical models, which posit increasing levels of generality of factors.  A hypothetical example of factors that would fit such a model was given by Humphreys (1962, p. 476):

> I shall assume that there are four discriminable levels of specificity of tests of mechanical information. These are as follows: (*a*) information about specific tools, e.g., the cross-cut saw or the socket wrench; (*b*) information about groups of tools having a common function, e.g., saws or wrenches; (*c*) information about areas of mechanical interest, e.g., carpentry or automotive; (*d*) general mechanical information, sampling from several areas such as carpentry, automotive, metal work, and plumbing.

A graphic representation of the above hierarchy is shown in Figure 9-3.  At the top is general mechanical information, and immediately below are broad group factors relating to particular areas of mechanical information about different groups of tools.  Further down, specific factors relating to information about particular tools within each group of tools could have been shown.

Another example of a hierarchy given by Guilford (1959) concerns possible relations between different types of factors in his scheme of factors.  The hierarchy is shown in Figure 9-4.  Only the hierarchy for productive thinking is shown in detail.  At the top is overall intellectual ability (like Spearman's general factor), below which is "thinking" as opposed to "memory."  Below "thinking" is "productive thinking," and below that are two types of productive

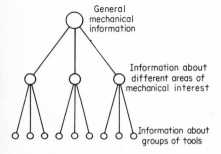

**FIGURE 9-3**    Factor   hierarchy   for   mechanical   information

**TABLE 9-4**    Matrix of factor loadings corresponding to the factor hierarchy shown in Figure 9-3

| TEST | GENERAL FACTOR | GROUP-CENTROID FACTORS | | |
|---|---|---|---|---|
| | A | B | C | D |
| 1 | X | X | | |
| 2 | X | X | | |
| 3 | X | X | | |
| 4 | X | | X | |
| 5 | X | | X | |
| 6 | X | | X | |
| 7 | X | | | X |
| 8 | X | | | X |
| 9 | X | | | X |

thinking. To make the hierarchy for productive thinking complete, one would need to put in additional lines going down to different types of convergent and divergent thinking.

As one can see from Figure 9-4, to propose a complete hierarchical structure for human intellect would result in a very complex system, and it would be extremely difficult to find tests to fit the system. Also, one can always find tests that will not fit the system, e.g., a test that has substantial loadings on more than one group factor at a particular level.

There are several principles that should be heeded in the search for hierarchi-

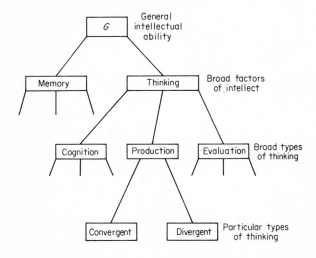

**FIGURE 9-4**    A hierarchical model for factors of intellect (*Adapted from Guilford, 1959.*)

cal arrangements of factors.  First, in the long run it will probably be more fruitful to start near the bottom and work downward rather than start at the top.  For example, rather than start off at the top with "intellect" and look for hierarchical arrangements of factors below it, it would probably be better to start with, say, "productive thinking" and seek a hierarchy below that.  One of the problems in so many studies of human abilities is that they bite off far more than they can chew.  Consequently, factors are poorly defined, and so many factors are found in each analysis that it is hard to make sense of the results.  It would be better to make careful investigations of restricted aspects of intellectual functioning, such as productive thinking.  If hierarchies can be found at a lower level, gradually these can be welded into larger hierarchies at higher levels.

A second principle in searching for hierarchies of factors is that such work has little chance of success without credible theories of human abilities.  The importance of theory is evidenced in the hypotheses about hierarchical relations between factors that follow from Guilford's theories about the structure of intellect.  It is inconceivable that one would find neat hierarchical structures in miscellaneous collections of tests covering a hodgepodge of abilities.

A third principle in searching for hierarchies is that we should abandon the needless assumption that *all* tests in a factor analysis must fit the hierarchy.  As was mentioned previously, it would always be easy to produce a test that did not fit a hierarchy (or any other mathematical model concerning relations between factors of human ability).  What is important is to find tests that *do* form a hierarchy regardless of how many other tests in an analysis do not conform to the hierarchy.  If the tests that do fit the hierarchy explain most of the common variance between all tests in the analysis, the hierarchy offers a sufficient scheme of explanation.  One can then throw away the tests that do not fit the hierarchy and continue to expand the hierarchy upward and downward in new investigations.  The purpose of such studies should be to *impose* lawfulness on nature, not to hope vainly that it will be discovered in anything that anyone wants to call a test.

It may be too much to hope that hierarchies of factors can be found which will meet the mathematical requirements.  Perhaps there are hierarchies at lower levels (e.g., among various tests of divergent thinking), if not more grand hierarchies that encompass all or even larger spheres of human abilities.  To find such hierarchies will require a great deal of work and more careful thought and investigation than have characterized many previous efforts.  If such hierarchies can be found, they will go a long way toward making human abilities understandable.  If they cannot be found, or if some other mathematical model cannot be shown to fit, it will have to be admitted that there are many separate factors of intellect with no logical order among them.  Then the only recourse will be to examine the importance of each separate factor with respect to criteria discussed previously.  Not only would that take a long, long time, but it would also be a rather uninteresting pursuit.

## multifactor test batteries

### The Primary Mental Abilities tests (PMA)

The PMA tests were developed directly out of the factor-analytic work of Thurstone and his colleagues. This was the first comprehensive multifactor battery and marked a milestone in psychological measurement. The first regular edition appeared in 1941. It was called the Chicago PMA Tests for Ages 11 to 17. Three tests were used to represent each of six factors. The following factors were represented: (1) *rote memory*, (2) *verbal comprehension*, (3) *word fluency*, (4) *numerical computation*, (5) *spatial orientation*, and (6) *general reasoning*.

Science Research Associates (SRA) later assumed publication of the PMA series and issued forms for the five- to seven-year and seven- to eleven-year levels as well as for the eleven- to seventeen-year level. The batteries have been considerably shortened, with only one short test being used to measure each factor. Some of the factors are not represented at one or more of the age levels: for example, the rote memory factor is dropped from the eleven- to seventeen-year battery. Figure 9-5 shows typical items which appear in the PMA tests.

In spite of the very important research which preceded the PMA, the current tests fall short of the standards of an efficient multifactor battery. The fact that only one short test is used to measure each of the factors has two unfortunate consequences. First, to have high factorial validity, it is usually necessary to use several tests. By averaging scores, much of the specificity of each test is canceled, and more of the underlying common factor is tapped. Second, either averaging the scores on several tests for each factor or making one longer test for each factor raises the reliability.

In some forms of the SRA PMA, reliability statistics have been either incorrectly computed or inadequately reported. Split-half reliability estimates have been made without regard to the highly speeded nature of some of the tests. In a restudy of the PMA reliability, Anastasi (1954, p. 366) found that when properly computed, some of the reliabilities fell markedly. For example, the word fluency test reliability dropped from a reported .90 to an actual .72, and that of the spatial relations test from .96 to .75. These reliabilities are too low for an adequate multifactor battery.

Along with the insufficient reliability of some of the PMA subtests are mod-

|   |   |   |   |   |   |
|---|---|---|---|---|---|
| J | ∨ | C | ✓ | ? | ( | ∩ |
| | (a) | (b) | (c) | (d) | (e) | (f) |

**FIGURE 9-5**   Sample items from the eleven- to seventeen-year battery of the SRA PMA tests (© 1958, *Thelma Gwinn Thurstone, Reprinted by permission of the publisher, Science Research Associates, Inc.*)

erately high correlations between them.  For the seven- to eleven-year form, intercorrelations were found to range from .41 to .70, and for the five- to seven-year battery, intercorrelations ranged from .51 to .73.  The combination of relatively low reliabilities on some subtests and generally high intercorrelations of subtests considerably weakens the PMA as a multifactor battery.

Although the PMA test manuals make claims for the specific vocational and educational implications of scores, only a small amount of actual research has been done with the battery.  Although norms are given for the battery, very little information has been obtained about the nature of the populations tested.  No information is given on sex differences even for the subtests on which significant sex differences are usually found.

The PMA tests have not kept up with the increasing knowledge about ability factors.  For example, the reasoning test employed in the eleven- to seventeen-year battery, the series-completion type of test, is not the best test to measure general reasoning.  Also, a more modern multifactor battery should include several kinds of reasoning tests in line with more recent factor-analytic findings.  Subsequent research might show that the PMA tests depend excessively on speed.  Some of the tests, such as the word fluency test, should be speeded, but it is doubtful that speed will add to the predictiveness of other tests, such as those of reasoning and verbal comprehension.  Now the PMA is mainly of historical importance.

## The Differential Aptitude Tests

The Differential Aptitude Tests (DAT) were developed by The Psychological Corporation, principally for use in the vocational and educational guidance of high school students (Bennett, Seashore, & Wesman, 1952).  Although the tests were intended for use with students in grades 8 through 12, they have a sufficient range of item difficulty so that they can be used with most adult groups.  The tests were not developed directly out of factor-analytic work, but were composed in such a way as to incorporate some of the major findings from factor analysis.

The subtests of the DAT are as follows (see Figure 9-6 for sample items):

1. *Verbal Reasoning.*    The items consist of verbal analogies, in which the reasoning component rather than the difficulty of words is emphasized. The test is more concerned with the reasoning factors than with verbal comprehension.
2. *Numerical Ability.*    The test covers a wide range of numerical computations. It should be a good measure of the numerical computation factor, as it was previously described.
3. *Abstract Reasoning.*    This test differs from the verbal reasoning test in that all the problems deal with abstract patterns.
4. *Spatial Relations.*    The test items concern the individual's ability to imagine how objects would look if they were rotated in space and to visualize a three-dimensional object from a two-dimensional pattern.

5. *Mechanical Reasoning.*     The test items consist of pictures which portray mechanical problems. The subject is asked questions about each picture.
6. *Clerical Speed and Accuracy.*     The test is modeled closely after the perceptual speed factor. The subject is required to find identical sets of numbers of figures.
7. *Language Usage.*     This test is more concerned with acquired knowledge, or achievement, than with a specific aptitude. The two parts of the test concern spelling ability and grammatical usage in sentences.

Although the DAT were not derived directly from factor analysis, the tests represent a collection of reasonably independent measures which range broadly over those factors most directly related to school achievement.   The tests were constructed primarily for school programs, and it is doubtful that they would meet with the same level of success in other testing situations.   The correlations between the tests vary considerably, ranging from .06 to as high as .67. The intercorrelations run about .50 on the average.   Although it is desirable to have lower correlations, they are not so high as to prevent the battery from functioning as a measure of differential aptitudes.

The reliabilities of the tests are generally high, ranging from .85 to .93 for all except the mechanical comprehension test.   The reliability for men on the mechanical comprehension test is sufficiently high, with a mean coefficient of .85, but the reliability for women is only .71.

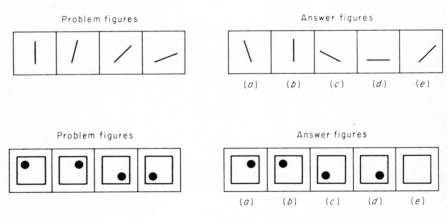

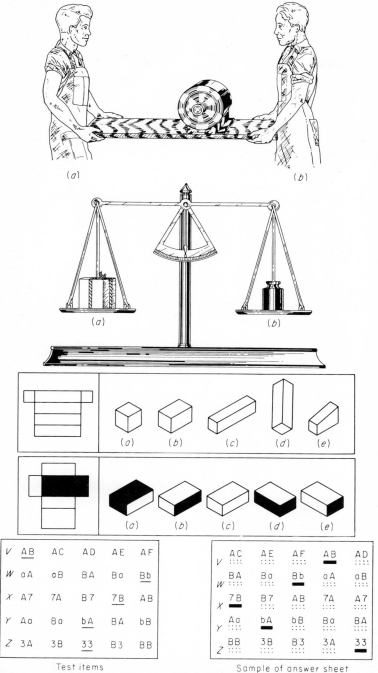

**FIGURE 9-6**    Sample items from the Differential Aptitude Tests (*Reproduced by per-*
*mission.    Copyright 1947,* © *1961 by The Psychological Corporation, New York, N.Y.    All*
*rights reserved.*)

A particular point in favor of the DAT is the large amount of research that went into the standardization and validation of the instrument. The norms are based on the testing of 47,000 students in grades 8 to 12 in schools scattered widely over the United States. Because sizable sex differences were found on some of the tests, separate norms are given for boys and girls.

Thousands of correlations between DAT scores and various criteria have been computed. Some correlations between test scores and school grades are shown in Table 9-5. A follow-up study was undertaken of students two years after completing high school. The results are shown in Table 9-6. In Table 9-6, scores for the total group are broken down in terms of subsequent occupation or college specialty. Some of the groups are represented by only several dozen individuals, and consequently the results should be considered tentative. More research of this kind will provide the DAT and other similar test batteries with a firmer basis for use in vocational counseling. The DAT is a model of careful test design, practicality, thoroughness of research, and frankness of reporting. Other test batteries for the measurement of differential abilities are described in Appendix C.

## uses of multifactor test batteries

In spite of the overwhelming evidence indicating that there are numerous factors of ability, multifactor test batteries still are not used widely. Instead, in most situations only a measure of general ability is employed, or only two tests are employed (these typically being a measure of verbal comprehension, such as verbal analogies, and a measure of general reasoning, usually with items concerning arithmetical reasoning). The present limited use of multifactor batteries is due partly to the fact that they are more expensive, more time-consuming to administer, and more difficult to interpret than tests of general ability (intelligence tests). Also, multifactor batteries are not used more frequently because of a "cultural lag" in many applied settings regarding the nature of human abilities and the potential uses for such batteries of tests. In addition, much more research needs to be done in the development of truly effective batteries for measuring the more important factors. In the following sections, the major factors that are important in the settings in which multifactor batteries might be useful will be discussed.

### Education

After looking at the factors presented in previous sections and considering that these are only some of the many factors that have been found, the reader is likely to have the discomforting feeling that the schoolchild is fragmented into many different pieces which are hard to put together in a living image. Fortunately, the problem is not quite that complex. Some of the factors which

**TABLE 9-5**    Median correlations of differential aptitude test scores with school grades*

| TEST | ENGLISH | MATHEMATICS | SCIENCE | SOCIAL STUDIES, HISTORY | LANGUAGES | TYPING | SHORTHAND |
|---|---|---|---|---|---|---|---|
| Verbal Reasoning (VR) | 50 | 39 | 54 | 50 | 30 | 19 | 44 |
| Numerical Ability (NA) | 48 | 50 | 51 | 48 | 42 | 32 | 27 |
| Abstract Reasoning (AR) | 36 | 35 | 44 | 35 | 25 | 27 | 24 |
| Spatial Relations (SR) | 27 | 32 | 36 | 26 | 15 | 16 | 16 |
| Mechanical Reasoning (MR) | 24 | 22 | 38 | 24 | 17 | 14 | 14 |
| Clerical Speed and Accuracy (CSA) | 24 | 19 | 26 | 26 | 23 | 26 | 14 |
| Language Usage: | | | | | | | |
| Spelling (Spell.) | 44 | 29 | 36 | 36 | 31 | 26 | 55 |
| Sentences (Sent.) | 52 | 36 | 48 | 46 | 40 | 30 | 49 |

* Decimal points omitted.
SOURCE: *Adapted from Bennett et al., 1952; reproduced by permission of The Psychological Corporation.*

**TABLE 9-6**     Percentile equivalents of average scores on the DAT for men in various educational and occupational groups

| GROUP | | PERCENTILES | | | | | | | |
|---|---|---|---|---|---|---|---|---|---|
| | No. | VR | NA | AR | SR | MR | CSA | Spell. | Sent. |
| Degree-seeking students: | | | | | | | | | |
| Premedical | 24 | 88 | 86 | 81 | 72 | 77 | 77 | 90 | 90 |
| Science (biology, chemistry, and mathematics) | 25 | 81 | 85 | 60 | 67 | 68 | 74 | 81 | 72 |
| Engineering (includes architectural) | 70 | 80 | 86 | 80 | 81 | 82 | 67 | 68 | 74 |
| Liberal arts (includes prelaw) | 68 | 79 | 75 | 78 | 61 | 64 | 75 | 78 | 81 |
| Business administration | 64 | 72 | 73 | 61 | 63 | 60 | 71 | 67 | 68 |
| Education (includes physical education) | 25 | 68 | 66 | 58 | 57 | 48 | 68 | 67 | 66 |
| Various: predental, agricultural, etc. | 30 | 64 | 67 | 74 | 60 | 73 | 59 | 55 | 64 |
| Non-degree-seeking students in two-year schools: | | | | | | | | | |
| Business, technical, fine arts, etc. | 43 | 63 | 62 | 71 | 72 | 68 | 60 | 54 | 61 |
| Employed: | | | | | | | | | |
| Salesmen | 23 | 56 | 53 | 53 | 52 | 57 | 44 | 50 | 49 |
| Clerks: general office work | 55 | 45 | 42 | 52 | 44 | 41 | 41 | 52 | 53 |
| Mechanical, electrical, and building trades | 66 | 34 | 41 | 46 | 49 | 56 | 44 | 28 | 29 |
| Various skilled: butcher, baker, etc. | 26 | 47 | 37 | 43 | 41 | 49 | 51 | 52 | 45 |
| Various unskilled: truck driver, laborer, etc. | 85 | 35 | 30 | 36 | 42 | 49 | 37 | 35 | 36 |
| Military service | 129 | 46 | 42 | 46 | 51 | 50 | 49 | 46 | 41 |
| Unclassified: | | | | | | | | | |
| No consistent work or school record | 58 | 53 | 48 | 51 | 54 | 54 | 46 | 47 | 52 |

SOURCE: *Adapted from Bennett et al., 1952; reproduced by permission of The Psychological Corporation.*

have been cited, and most of the many which have not been cited, are of relatively little importance for the teacher in the classroom. Although a great deal more research needs to be done before we can say with confidence how factors of ability grow, change, and interact with success in daily life, there are some guideposts that can be used.

Verbal comprehension is by far the most important factor to consider in relation to schoolwork. Schoolwork consists mainly of words—printed and spoken. The child reads his assignments, learns the meaning of new words, gives verbal replies to questions by the teacher, talks to his friends in relation to group projects, and writes paragraph descriptions of recent events. The school setting is a highly verbal world, and unless the child has an understanding of words and how words go together in sentences, paragraphs, and books, he is crippled. It may be that, depending on his vocation, he will not be so dependent on verbal comprehension in later life, but in the school setting it is all-important. The first four or five grades of elementary school are almost synonymous with the development of verbal comprehension. Because it is of such central importance, a good test of vocabulary or reading comprehension is the best indicator of scholastic aptitude as shown in the primary grades. If a child is very high in verbal comprehension and only average in some of the other important factors (which is a rare occurrence), he still will probably do well in schoolwork. His lack of ability in other areas, such as in the areas of reasoning factors, may hinder him in higher education and in vocational pursuits, but because of the centrality of verbal comprehension for schoolwork, he will probably manage to make good grades, at least at the elementary school level.

Verbal fluency provides the student with a special advantage. He can talk fluently, and he makes a good impression on others. As was mentioned previously, although, statistically speaking, verbal comprehension and verbal fluency tend to go together, there are some real exceptions. Consequently, the teacher should be on guard not to mistake sheer fluency for the deeper understanding of words and written material. Verbal fluency allows an individual to "sell himself," and because it is not always matched by a high level on other important factors of ability, an individual who is high on verbal fluency often oversells himself, to the subsequent disappointment of teachers in school situations and employers and coworkers later in life.

The numerical computation factor is important mainly for some topics in the early elementary grades. Children must learn to add and subtract, divide, obtain square roots, and develop other numerical skills. Nothing is more frustrating to a teacher than to have a child who consistently flounders in numerical skills. Although there is some correlation between numerical computation and other important factors, such as verbal comprehension and the reasoning factors, such correlations tend to be relatively low. Consequently, a child can have difficulty in numerical skills and still be superior with respect to more important factors of ability. When the deficiency in numerical skills is very extreme, as in the case of an eighth-grade child who still cannot add and subtract, it probably indicates an overall deficiency in intellectual abilities. Except for these extremes, facility in numerical computation is a nice thing to possess, but is not intimately related to eventual achievement in most careers. Even some of the better mathematicians (whose abilities depend more on the reasoning factors) are poor at numerical computations.

The reasoning factors are, of course, all-important for high-level vocational and professional activities later in life. They also play some part in success in school situations, more so in high school and college than in the elementary grades. The reasoning factors are directly involved in learning mathematics (not numerical skills) in the form of simple algebraic problems in the higher levels of elementary school and in learning mathematical topics presented in high school and in college. In school situations, the reasoning factors come into play mainly when the student is required to do something on his own, such as write an essay on world government. In such instances, the child who can invent solutions to problems, see logical consequences, and see parallels between historical trends and what is going on now has a distinct advantage.

Memory factors come into play mainly when there are many simple facts, dates, and names to be mastered. The memory abilities are not intimately related to the "higher" abilities—verbal comprehension and the reasoning factors. A child can be quite intelligent in other ways and have great difficulty in memorizing simple facts and details. Memory is apparently strongly influenced by the desire to memorize and the patience to work at it. As is true of nearly all the ability factors, when the deficiency is quite extreme, e.g., in the case of a twelve-year-old child who is unable to memorize the multiplication tables, it suggests an overall deficiency. Otherwise, memory factors are not highly prognostic of eventual high-level success in college and beyond. Memory plays a very important part in the first several grades at the primary level. Much of the child's time is consumed with memorizing the alphabet, sounds relating to alphabetical letters, the sequence of numbers, names, and simple facts. Although verbal comprehension also plays an important part in the first several grades, the important part played by memory factors often obscures the true ability of some children and causes the teacher to overestimate the ability of others. Some children who perform poorly when details must be memorized manifest a superior ability in later schoolwork.

Nearly all children (excepting some true mental deficients) can be taught to memorize the essential details in schoolwork. First, it would be better if teachers discouraged memorizing for its own sake, e.g., memorizing long lists of names, places, and dates. This does not constitute true intellectual accomplishment, and the child will soon forget most of what he has memorized. Second, where memorization is essential for subsequent understanding, e.g., memorization of the multiplication tables, the ability of all students to memorize material can be greatly increased by the gifted teacher who turns memorizing into pleasant games rather than dull activities.

The spatial and perceptual factors play only a modest part in successful performance in elementary and secondary school. Spatial factors are somewhat important for secondary mathematics, for special mathematics courses in high school (e.g., geometry and trigonometry), and, to some extent, for physics. Perceptual factors are largely auxiliary skills that help students to only a small extent, e.g., in proofreading an English theme for spelling errors. Spatial and perceptual factors come into play when students are out of school engaging in professional and vocational pursuits. Airplane pilots must have spatial orientation; visualization is essential to the draftsman; and perceptual speed is important for file clerks. Tests of spatial and perceptual abilities are quite useful in batteries employed in high school for vocational counseling.

The need to test for many different factors of ability, rather than for general ability only, varies directly with the school level. In the primary grades only several of the factors we have discussed are important, mainly verbal comprehension. Later in elementary school some of the other factors play an important part: deduction, seeing relations, word fluency, and others. In high school some specialized topics, such as typing and mechanical drawing, bring into play some of the more specialized perceptual and spatial factors which were of relatively little importance earlier. As the student goes into college and eventually enters a vocation or profession, an even wider array of factors must be taken into account.

The schoolday world of the child is comparatively simple. He must possess verbal comprehension, some reasoning ability, and at least a modicum of skill in verbal fluency and the memory factors. If he has these, he will succeed. In contrast, vocational and professional skills are quite complex and in many instances may depend on esoteric factors which we seldom consider and which are presently very difficult to measure. Because of the changing intellectual requirements, it can be said that abilities are actually more general in children than in adults. The intellectual demands made on children are more general in that they relate to only several of the factors which we have discussed, and, in a sense, intellectual functions are more general in children. Apparently the many specialized factors which are found in factor-analytic studies, e.g., spatial visualization, are due to the special interests that the individual acquires and the experiences he has as he matures. Because children in the elementary grades have not been exposed to so many varied activities, differences in related skills are not important factors. The greater generality of intellectual functions in children and the generality of requirements at the elementary levels make it feasible to test for general ability without losing a great deal of information. Because only a few of the factors are very important in the elementary grades, and because these tend to correlate with one another, it makes some sense to add them all together in one test of general ability.

What has been said and shown about the factors of intellect has two important implications for teachers. First, as human abilities grow more complex during the high school years, it is important to give measures of some of the most significant factors rather than to test for general ability only. Such measures will prove useful in advising students about future schooling and vocations. Second, the factor-analytic results provide a lesson that abilities, even in the primary grades, are not perfectly general. Students are not uniformly good or poor at all the kinds of tasks that are presented, and every now and then we see a child who is quite uneven in his abilities, e.g., very high in the memory factors but very poor in verbal comprehension. In addition to making overall measures and appraisals of students' abilities, teachers should be on guard to look at the differential abilities of each student. Some students are simply better at certain kinds of intellectual tasks than at others, and there is nothing "wrong" when this occurs. Because a student is very high in several intellectual dimensions, e.g., the verbal dimensions, teachers often wrongly conclude that he should be very high in others, such as general reasoning. Some unevenness in levels of ability is to be expected of all students. Consequently, rather than ask the oversimplified question of how bright Ted Bronson is, it would be more meaningful to ask how high he is in verbal comprehension, what his level of verbal fluency is, how he does on rote memorization, and how well he performs in numerical computation. To have to consider these somewhat different dimensions of intellectual activity, rather than talk about one overall dimension of intelligence, complicates our work considerably, but it brings us closer to a faithful map of human ability.

## Vocations

Multifactor test batteries come into their own in advising people about, and selecting them for, particular vocations. Whereas only several factors are highly important for most schoolwork, and a measure of general ability goes a long way toward tapping those factors, different vocations frequently require quite different factors of ability. Consequently, multifactor batteries are used widely in vocational counseling in high school, college, governmental counseling services, and other places. Also, multifactor batteries are used widely for selecting persons for particular jobs in industry and governmental agencies, e.g., television repairmen and secretaries for governmental offices; for placing men in different training programs in the armed forces, e.g., programs in mechanics, radar maintenance, and control-tower operation; and for selecting people for certain types of advanced training in universities, e.g., dentistry. The differential aptitude batteries discussed in Appendix C are frequently employed with respect to the foregoing kinds of selection. Also, because different vocations frequently require different factors of ability, numerous special batteries have been constructed for particular uses. This is the case, for example, with the selection of students in dentistry, where some of the motor abilities, particularly finger dexterity, are important. This is also the case with respect to the placement of men in different forms of technical training in the Air Force, where spatial, perceptual, and motor abilities differ in their importance for different specialties.

### Basic research

It is reasonable to predict that eventually multifactor batteries will be used frequently in controlled experiments in psychology, but at the present time they are being used very little for that purpose. Studies of the learning of motor skills provide an interesting example, e.g., a task requiring an unusual type of two-hand coordination. By correlating measures of performance after different amounts of practice with scores on a multifactor battery administered prior to training, it has been possible to determine the importance of different factors at different levels of training. Research of this kind was discussed earlier in this chapter.

Multifactor batteries of ability tests would provide very helpful information in many controlled experiments in psychology, such as in experiments on perception, learning, immediate memory, and human physiological reactions to stress. It is unfortunately the case at the present time that most experimentalists ignore individual differences in human ability. As one consequence, the experimentalist frequently has to treat the wide individual differences that actually occur in experiments as "error." A proper measurement of the abilities involved would permit the use of much more powerful experimental designs. A second consequence is that the experimentalist frequently does not understand what is being measured in his experiments. He may, for example, be employing four different measures of memory which tap somewhat different factors of ability.

A marriage is needed between experimental psychology and differential psychology (study of individual differences). Specialists in differential psychology have been as guilty of shunning wedlock as the experimentalists have. Without a close relationship with experimental psychology, differential psychology is a dreary descriptive enterprise, in which much technical elegance is lavished on finding more and more factors but in which the factors are not really understood. A more complete science of psychology requires a closer affiliation of these two traditions.

### Summary

There has been a historic controversy about human abilities, that concerning whether human abilities are perfectly general, as is implied by the use of measures of general intelligence, or whether instead there are separable factors of intellect. There is something to say for both points of view. Most tests of ability correlate positively, even if some of the correlations are negligible. This is evidence for the generality of ability. However, modern methods of factor analysis have clearly shown that the patterns of correlations between tests lead inescapably to the conclusion that there are numerous separable, but not entirely independent, factors of human ability.

The problem now is not one of finding new factors of human ability but rather one of separating the wheat from the chaff among the many factors that have already been found. There are standards for deciding the importance of factors. One important standard is that the factor should relate to a broad range of item content, as the factor of verbal comprehension does. A second standard is that some, but not necessarily all, factors should demonstrate the ability to predict successful performance in applied situations. A third standard is that the factor should relate to mathematical models concerning human abilities, such as the hierarchical model. A fourth standard, perhaps the most important one, is that factors should demonstrate their importance in controlled experiments in psychology, e.g., in experiments on learning, motivation, perception, and physiological processes. Despite the fact that many, many factors have reared their heads in statistical analyses of correlations between tests, only a handful of those factors have proved their importance with respect to the aforementioned standards.

Although existing multifactor batteries fall short of perfection, they are definitely improvements in many situations over the use of only a measure of general intelligence. Such multifactor batteries are useful in school situations, in vocational settings, and in basic research in psychology.

### Suggested additional readings

Anastasi, A. *Psychological testing.* (3rd ed.) New York: Macmillan, 1968. Chs. 13–15.

Cronbach, L. J. *Essentials of psychological testing.* (Rev. ed.) New York: Harper & Row, 1960. Chs. 7, 9.

Guilford, J. P. Factorial angles to psychology. *Psychological Review*, 1961, 68, 1–20.

Guilford, J. P. *The nature of human intelligence.* New York: McGraw-Hill, 1967.

Nunnally, J. C. *Psychometric theory.* New York: McGraw-Hill, 1967. Ch. 12.

Spearman, C. *The abilities of man.* New York: Macmillan, 1927.

# CHAPTER 10

## General
## intelligence

Parents, mostly mothers, are making the supreme sacrifice in behalf of togetherness with their sons by attending the monthly cub scout pack meeting. While there is a lull in the ceremonies in preparation for awarding badges, insignia, and many special citations, the mothers are talking, as they often are, about their children. Mrs. Crankston wonders whether the school is doing enough for "gifted children." Her Charlie has been tested by a psychologist and, so she says, "has a high IQ, but they are not giving him any special instruction at Belmont." At the mention of "IQ" the other mothers assume a look of awe, as though something sacred had been broached.

No other product of psychology has had the same impact on the public as intelligence tests. Their results are too often reported as though they were infallible guides to all that is wise and good. Such tests do serve many purposes well, but only if they are expertly administered and only if they are interpreted in the light of the limitations of the tests, the personality of the child, and the special abilities which the child possesses. The purpose of this chapter is to explain the composition, use, and proper interpretation of intelligence tests.

The term "intelligence tests" has been used with some misgiving because it implies more than can be expected from any test. Consequently, the first issue to be discussed will be that of what the so-called intelligence tests actually contain.

## the content of intelligence tests

In the previous chapter it was shown that there are a number of semi-independent kinds, or factors, of intelligence, and it was said that it is somewhat misleading to lump all these together in one overall measure. That is what the intelligence tests do—they sample from the content of a number of factors of intellect. In other words, they seek to measure how intelligent a person is in general (or on the average), without specifying the particular ways in which he is more or less capable. Because they sample content from a number of factors, it is more appropriate to refer to them as "measures of general ability" than to use the more grandiose name "intelligence tests."

For several reasons, tests of general ability have been very useful in the past, and will probably continue to be for some time to come, in spite of the fact that they measure a conglomerate of separable mental functions. Sheer expediency is one reason why it has been necessary to rely heavily on measures of general ability. It is very difficult to construct the extensive batteries which are needed to measure even a few of the more important factors described in the previous chapter. Such batteries are expensive for schools to use and time-consuming to administer. Even after the scores on multifactor batteries have been obtained, they are usually difficult for most persons to interpret.

Another reason why it is defensible to use measures of general ability is that they are not as conglomerate as might be thought. Rather than spreading their content evenly over many different factors, they tend to concentrate on only several of the more important ones. In particular, they tend to concentrate on the factors of verbal comprehension, general reasoning, seeing relationships, and numerical facility. To a lesser extent, they sample items from memory, perceptual, and spatial factors. The factors which predominate in most tests of general ability are the ones that intuitively "look" important, and as studies have shown, they are the ones that are most important in schoolwork. These factors also tend to correlate well with one another. For these reasons, tests of general ability measure primarily some of the more "important" factors rather than an entirely illogical hodgepodge of mental functions.

The factor content of most tests of general ability was not specifically planned. Rather, each test constructor selected items that looked as if they measured intelligence. In later factor-analytic studies, it was found that most tests tend to measure the same factors and, consequently, that most of them correlate highly with one another. Some examples of the types of items that tend to predominate in measures of general ability are as follows:

### Vocabulary

*Indignant* means most nearly the same as

1. poor
2. lazy

3. angry
4. spiteful

## Verbal Relations

*Ship* is to *sail* as *automobile* is to _____.

## Verbal Meaning

What is the meaning of the saying "penny-wise and pound-foolish"?

## Figural Relations

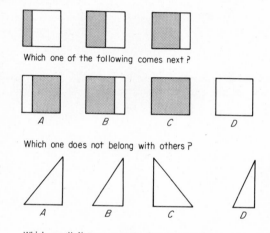

Which one of the following comes next ?

Which one does not belong with others ?

Which small figure correctly fills the missing part ?

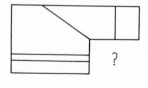

## Arithmetic Reasoning

A boy has 12 apples. He gives half of these to his mother and half of the rest to a friend. How many apples does he have left for himself?

*a.* 8   *b.* 2   *c.* 4   *d.* 3

### General Reasoning

A boy goes to a stream with one 2-quart bucket and one 3-quart bucket. How can he arrange it so that he will take back exactly 4 quarts of water?

### General Information

What time is it when the minute hand is pointing straight up and the hour hand is pointing straight down?
What is the smallest state in the United States?

### Practical Judgment

Suppose that you are walking by yourself and you see a house on fire. No one else sees the fire. What should you do?

### Absurdities

Billy's mother said, "You are going to be late for school." To make sure that he got there on time, he set the hands on the kitchen clock back one hour. What is foolish about that?

### Object Assembly

Put the pieces together to make a square.

## achievement and aptitude

Teacher-made tests and standardized achievement tests are intended to measure how much a student has learned in school. Tests of general ability are intended to measure how much the student *can* learn in the *future* if ideal conditions prevail. Another way of saying this is to say that tests of general ability are intended to measure the *capacity* to learn rather than, as with achievement tests, how much has been learned up to a particular point in time.

The distinction between aptitude and achievement is commonplace in daily life. We say such things as: "If he wanted to, he could be an excellent student." "Even though he has only limited ability, he makes good grades by studying night and day." "His real ability is hidden because of the poor schools which he previously attended."

It would indeed be helpful if we had pure measures of aptitude. They would be particularly helpful in spotting children who would do much better in school if they were given better training or if their personal and home environments could be improved. Unfortunately, this goal is only partially accomplished by the currently available measures of general ability. At the present time we do not know how to measure aptitude other than by measuring what the child can accomplish at a particular point in time. There is no way to "get inside" the child to obtain a pure measure of how much he could accomplish in ideal situations. Rather, what the tests of general ability tend to do is measure relatively *abstract* ability, ability that is not as dependent on specific types of school instruction as that measured by achievement tests.

A child probably would not be able to answer questions about the mineral resources of Africa or about the United States Constitution unless he had had good instruction in those topics in school and unless he had made a concentrated effort to study the materials. Such questions are closely bound to the quality of instruction and the energetic study of the student. In contrast, some of the types of items used on tests of general ability are not highly related to the richness of the student's school and home environment. For example, the figural relations items shown previously do not obviously relate to anything that is learned in the home or in school.

The value of most tests of general ability is that they contain items not as directly related to school and home environment as those found on most achievement tests. The effort in measures of general ability is to use questions that any intelligent person could answer from his daily experience rather than ones that require specific types of instruction. This is true even of items measuring vocabulary and general information. Efforts are usually made to employ largely words and facts that could be learned by any intelligent person.

Even with the best of efforts, it presently is not possible to measure aptitude completely apart from achievement. The same factors that make for achievement in school also, to a large extent, make for success on tests of general ability.  The two types of tests usually correlate highly, usually around .70, with the exact size of the relationship depending on the type of school and the year in school.  The difference is more a matter of degree than of kind.  Achievement tests are relatively *more* concerned with present accomplishment; aptitude tests are relatively *more* concerned with abstract ability.

When students' scores are compared on achievement tests and tests of general ability, the differences usually are not large, and many of the apparent differences are due only to measurement error.  However, when such differences are quite large, they provide important diagnostic information about students.  It is in these instances that the major usefulness of tests of general ability is shown.

## individual versus group tests

Tests can be given to each individual separately, or a group of individuals can be tested at one time.  Although this is a consideration for tests of all kinds, it is a particularly important issue in the use of general intelligence tests.  The multifactor batteries are almost always group tests.  There is considerable competition between individual and group tests of general intelligence.  Numerous articles have appeared in the psychological literature arguing about whether group or individual tests should be used with particular age groups.

### Individual tests

The first practical general intelligence test, the Binet-Simon scale, was administered individually.  This was necessary because the subjects were young children.  The individual test requires a highly experienced examiner.  The examiner is in essence a part of the standardized testing procedure, and he must standardize his own treatment of the child to conform to established methods.

Many of the items on individual tests cannot be scored unambiguously as right or wrong.  Instead there may be a number of acceptable responses, and different scores are often required to indicate the degree of correctness.  The better-established individual tests go to considerable lengths to specify just what will be considered a correct response and how much credit should be given for a response.  The examiner must follow the established scoring procedures meticulously and not permit his subjective judgment of a child to influence the test results.  Any idiosyncrasies in scoring will make the test less reliable.

### Group tests

The first practical group tests of general intelligence were developed for the armed forces during World War I.  The number of men to be tested required a quick and economical measurement device, and the individual test was unsuited for that purpose.

Most group tests are sufficiently self-explanatory so that the test examiner need have little or no specialized knowledge of testing procedures. The test forms are simply passed out to the subjects; either they are allowed to work at their chosen rate or the examiner directs them when to start and stop.

## Comparison of individual and group tests

Although the following rules are not precisely correct for all group and individual tests, they are sufficiently general to offer a reasonable basis for choosing between the two kinds of tests in most situations:

1. *Individual tests are required with young children.*    Starting at the earliest age, there are no group tests that can be used with infants. Each infant must be examined separately, and any effort at standardization of procedures is difficult. With preschool children, it is usually necessary to use individual tests. Young children either cannot read at all or lack the reading ability to take the self-explanatory group forms. As an additional factor, young children are highly distractible, and it is all that the expert examiner can do to keep one child working at the test materials. Young children are often not motivated to do well on tests, and it is only through the examiner's careful, but standardized, encouragement that a meaningful measure can be obtained.

2. *Group tests are more frequently used for testing "normal" adults.*    The well-standardized group tests prove to be as good predictors as the individual tests when working with most teenage and adult groups. Although the evidence is clear that individual tests are better predictors for young children and that group tests do as well with adolescents or older persons, it is not certain which kind of test is generally more valid with the in-between age group.

Adolescents and older persons are usually motivated and attentive enough to manifest a meaningful score on a group test. Also, they are probably less embarrassed by the group testing situation than they would be in the face-to-face individual testing situation.

Because group tests tend to be as valid as individual tests when administered to adults, they are much to be preferred in practical work. Group tests are much less expensive and time-consuming. It takes no more time to administer and score 20 group tests than it does to administer and score one individual test.

3. *Individual tests are often useful in clinical settings.*    The school psychologist can often learn considerably more from the individual test than the subject's score would indicate. The child who appears dull in the classroom may be only hard of hearing. Another child may do poorly in schoolwork because he wants to do poorly, giving wrong answers when he knows what is correct. The older adult may appear to be demented because he is discouraged and withdrawn. These things probably would not be found in group testing situations, but an experienced clinician can often use the individual testing situation to diagnose why an individual is performing poorly.

4. *Group tests are usually easier to construct than individual tests.*    The person who plans to construct a test should not undertake an individual test unless measurement specialists are available and it is planned to expend a considerable amount of time and money on test construction. The difficulties in constructing test materials,

in standardizing the test, and particularly in setting instructions for administration and scoring make the development of an individual test a time-consuming, expensive job.  Training test examiners for the individual test creates additional expense.

## verbal versus performance tests

There has been some confusion about the difference between "verbal" tests and "performance" tests, and the distinction is itself somewhat misleading. The following outline of verbal components in tests is offered as a basis for discussing test content:

### Verbal Requirements

1. Understand spoken language
2. Understand written language
3. Speak language
4. Write language
5. Verbal comprehension factor

There are many different combinations of these requirements in particular tests.  A test may require the first four items, but deal with language at so simple a level that very little ability in verbal comprehension is required to obtain a high score.  It is possible to make up a test in which almost none of the five aspects is required.  This can be done by giving the test instructions in pantomime and using test materials that require neither written nor spoken responses.  It is also possible to compose a test in which none of the first four aspects is present and in which the fifth aspect, verbal comprehension, is a cardinal requirement.  If the test requires the child to manipulate abstract symbols or to deal with pictures, this will tap, in part, the verbal comprehension factor.  Each test should be examined in terms of its combination of verbal requirements rather than simply classified as "verbal" or "nonverbal."

It is also possible to distinguish between tests on the basis of the way in which responses are made:

1. *Symbolic response.*    The subject indicates the correct answer either through the use of language or by marking one of a number of choices.  The symbolic response might be made with respect to objects rather than printed materials, although this is usually not done.
2. *Manipulative response (performance).*    The subject is required to handle objects in such a way as to complete a specified product.  The product may be anything from a completely finished piece of machinery to the arrangement of a set of blocks.

Some items are not clearly differentiated in terms of the two kinds of responses.  For example, in maze tracing, the child is required to coordinate the pencil and move to the goal—the response is as symbolic as it is manipulative.

It has been the custom to call instruments "performance" tests if they de-emphasize language requirements, employ three-dimensional materials, and require manipulative responses. Because of these components, the performance tests usually measure motor coordination, speed, perceptual factors, and spatial factors. Instruments are usually referred to as "verbal" tests if they are printed forms, emphasize verbal comprehension, and require symbolic responses. Because of the ease with which certain kinds of test materials can be placed on printed forms, the verbal tests tend to measure verbal comprehension, numerical computation, and the reasoning factors. There is no clear-cut separation between the factors found in verbal and performance tests, but there is a tendency for different factors to arise in the two kinds of materials.

In addition to the two extreme types of measures—one extreme type heavily involved in verbal requirements and the other extreme type almost exclusively manipulative—there is a third important type of test, which is variously referred to as "nonlanguage," "culture-free," and "culture-fair." In this third type of test, the student is required neither to use and understand language nor to manipulate three-dimensional objects. Rather, the test items consist of symbolic responses (multiple choice) to relationships between figures and designs. Typical of such items are the examples given earlier of items involving figural relations. These tests have a very important place. They avoid complete dependence on verbal ability, and they apparently measure more important intellectual functions than performance tests.

The following sections will describe some typical group and individual tests of general ability. Representative tests will be described for different age groups. As is the rule throughout this book, no effort will be made to present an exhaustive (and, consequently, unreadable) list of all the good measures available. Mention is made of other good tests of general ability in Appendix C. After representative tests are described, some of the major research findings about general ability will be discussed, and some recommendations will be made for the use of tests of general ability in elementary and secondary schools.

## the Binet test and its followers

As will be recalled from the previous chapter, Alfred Binet pioneered in the theory and practice of measuring general ability. His immediate practical problem was to construct tests to be used with "problem children" in French elementary schools. Among those children who were failing in school, some method was needed for distinguishing those who lacked the capacity to learn from those who might profit by special instruction. Binet's point of view was that, for practical purposes, it would not be feasible to measure intelligence in terms of the many constituent factors involved but, rather, that it would be necessary to measure general ability by its end products. Consequently, in his tests Binet emphasized the ability to make correct judgments, the ability to solve problems, and the ability to understand words and written material.

Working with Simon, in 1905 Binet (Binet & Simon, 1905) produced the first crude measure of general ability. The test consisted of 30 items, graded in difficulty. The first 15 items in the list were as follows:

1. Follow a lighted match with head and eyes.
2. Grasp a cube placed on the palm.
3. Grasp a cube held in the line of vision.
4. Make a choice between pieces of wood and chocolate.
5. Unwrap paper from chocolate.
6. Execute simple orders.
7. Touch head, nose, ear, cap, key, and string.
8. Point to objects which the examiner names in a picture.
9. Name objects pointed out in a picture.
10. Judge which of two lines is the longer.
11. Repeat immediately three digits read by the examiner.
12. Judge which of two weights is heavier.
13. Solve problems that embody novel, ambiguous, or contradictory solutions.
14. Define "house," "horse," "fork," and "mamma."
15. Repeat sentence of 15 words after a single hearing.

The list of problems was tried out on about fifty children, and provisional norms were established. It was found that the first five items could be passed by idiots and normal two-year-olds. Most three-year-olds could go no further than about the ninth item. Most five-year-olds could go no further than about the fourteenth item.

The original test was obviously only a rough beginning to the measurement of general ability, but it constituted a very important first step. Binet's conceptions of how general ability should be measured and the types of items which should be used have dominated most tests of general ability to this day.

Binet later made revisions of his test, employed more items, gathered responses from larger groups of children, and developed more dependable norms. However, the center of activity in the development and use of measures of intelligence soon shifted to America. During the first decade of this century, the Binet-Simon tests became very popular in this country. Such instruments were needed in the care of the feebleminded, in educational research, and in understanding juvenile delinquency. Several translations into English were made of the scales, and efforts were made to broaden and further standardize the tests.

### The Terman and Merrill revisions

The most extensive revisions of the Binet-Simon scales were made first by Terman in 1916 and then by Terman and Merrill in 1937 and 1960 (Terman & Merrill, 1960). Because their work was done at Stanford University, their revisions were named the Stanford-Binet tests. Their work has so extensively revised and extended Binet's tests that it is only out of respect to him that the current form of the test still bears his name. The major ways in which Terman and Merrill improved the tests were (1) they tried out a large number of items; (2) they used statistical analysis to obtain the most effective items; (3) they wrote detailed, explicit instructions for administration and scoring; and (4) they gathered norms from a large number of representative children and adults. Since the scales were revised in 1916, the Stanford-Binet series of tests has been used very widely in this country and has been translated into many other languages.

## Construction of the Stanford-Binet tests

The Stanford-Binet contains six subtests and one alternative (in case something goes wrong in the testing) to be administered at half-year intervals from two to five years of age, at yearly intervals from five to fourteen, and at four levels of adult performance. (At the "average adult" level there are eight rather than six subtests.) The items at each level were carefully selected according to three principles. First, all items were selected because they "looked" as if they measured intelligence (see the examples cited earlier). Second, it was expected that all items retained for the scale would correlate highly with chronological age. Although we may argue about what constitutes "intelligence," all will agree that it grows with the child. Of course, age differentiation is not the *only* desirable standard for selecting such items. The length of the foot also increases with age, but it goes without saying that no one would consider that a measure of intelligence. With respect to the standard of age differentiation, a suitable item for the seven-year subtest would be one that few of the six-year-olds answer correctly, over half of the seven-year-olds answer correctly, and most of the eight-year-olds answer correctly. Needless to say, it is very difficult to find items that meet this standard.

The third standard which was applied to the items was that of homogeneity. For this standard, each item was correlated with the total test, which gives an index of how well the individual items measure the same thing as compared with the whole test. This is a sensible standard in constructing a measure of general ability because, even though the total test may not be a perfect measure, it is logically a better measure than any item taken separately. When these procedures are followed, the final collection of items will (1) consist of problems that intuitively relate to general ability, (2) differentiate well between adjacent age groups, and (3) be relatively homogeneous in content.

## The 1960 revision

The most recent revision of the Stanford-Binet (Terman & Merrill, 1960) involved largely recombining items and making minor changes in items used

in previous forms.  The 1937 revision consisted of two alternative forms, Forms
L and M, respectively.  Having an alternative form available made it possible
to retest children after short periods of time without having the results affected
by memory.  However, little use was made of Form M.  Consequently, in the
1960 revision the best items were selected from both the older Forms L and
M, and the present form is referred to as L-M.  Except for the combining of
items from the two older forms, the only other major change was the obtaining
of up-to-date norms.  Because of the similarity between the present test and
those published in 1937, many of the findings with respect to the earlier tests
probably still hold true.

## Content of the Stanford-Binet

The present test bears many of the earmarks of the original Binet test.  A
knowledge of words and the comprehension of written material play a predominant part in the scale, particularly at the upper age levels.  Although a number
of performance items appear at earlier age levels, these concern primarily the
child's recognition and use of common objects.  A few items concerning spatial
and perceptual abilities are found at different age levels.  Many of the items
relate to one or more of the reasoning factors discussed in the previous chapter.
Three types of memory items appear at one or more age levels, including serial
memory of digits, paragraph memory, and memory of geometric designs.  To
illustrate the nature of the scale, the items at four different age levels are described as follows:

### Two-year Level

1. *Three-hole form board.*     The child is shown a form board containing a cutout
square, circle, and triangle.  The pieces are removed, and the child is asked to put
them in their places.  The child receives credit if all three objects are put in place.
2. *Delayed response.*     The child is shown three small boxes and a toy cat.  The
examiner says, "Look, I am going to hide the kitty and see whether you can find it."
While the child is watching, the toy cat is placed under the middle box.  Then a
screen is placed in front of the boxes for about 10 seconds.  When the screen is
withdrawn, the child is asked to choose the box containing the cat.  The examiner
repeats the procedure, putting the cat under the box on the right and then under the
box on the left.  The child is given credit if two out of three first selections are correct.
3. *Identifying parts of the body.*     The child is shown a large paper doll and is
asked to point to parts of the body.  ("Show me the dolly's hair," etc.)  Credit is
received for correctly pointing out three of the parts.
4. *Block building.*     A box of blocks is placed before the child.  The examiner
builds a tower of four blocks and asks the child to do the same.  Credit is received
if the child makes a tower of at least four blocks.
5. *Picture vocabulary.*     The child is presented with 18 cards showing pictures of
common objects and is asked to tell what each object is.  Credit is given if the child
names at least two of the objects.
6. *Word combinations.*     The examiner notes the spontaneous speech of the child

during the test. Credit is given if the child uses at least a two-word combination such as "see kitty."

## Six-year Level

1. *Vocabulary.*     The child is asked the meaning of words from a graded list of 45 terms.  Credit is given for five correct definitions.  (The same list of words is used throughout all higher age levels.)
2. *Differences.*     The child is asked to tell the difference between three pairs of words, e.g., "bird" and "dog."  Credit is given for making at least two correct responses out of three.
3. *Mutilated pictures.*     The child is shown five pictures in which an object has a missing part, e.g., a wagon with only three wheels, and is asked to say what is missing in each.  Credit is given for getting as many as four of the problems correct.
4. *Number concepts.*     Twelve blocks are put in front of the child.  He is asked to give different numbers of blocks to the examiner.  Credit is given for selecting three correct numbers of blocks out of four trials.
5. *Opposite analogies.*     The child is asked to complete sentences such as the following: "A table is made of wood; a window, of _____."  Credit is given for at least three out of four correct responses.
6. *Maze tracing.*     The child is shown three designs, each of which shows two ways for a person to get home.  One route is longer than the other.  The child is asked to trace the shorter route.  Credit is given for two correct responses out of three.

## Ten-year Level

1. *Vocabulary.*     The child is asked to define words from the standard list.  Credit is given for 11 or more correct definitions.
2. *Block counting.*     The child is shown pictures of piles of blocks.  Some of the blocks are directly visible, and others are stacked behind and beneath.  He is asked how many blocks are in each pile.  Credit is given for correct responses to at least 8 of the 11 pictures.
3. *Abstract words.*     "What do we mean by _____?" e.g., "curiosity."  Credit is given for correctly interpreting at least two of the four words presented.
4. *Finding reasons.*     The child is asked to explain why two social rules are necessary, e.g., why children should not be too noisy in school.  Credit is given for supplying two reasons.
5. *Word naming.*     The child is asked to name as many words as he can in two minutes.  Credit is given for 28 words or more.
6. *Repeating six digits.*     Six digits such as 4, 8, 2, 1, 6, 3 are read at one-second intervals.  The child is asked to repeat the digits in the correct order.  Credit is given if one or more complete series out of three are recalled correctly.

## Average Adult Level (Age Fifteen and Older)

1. *Vocabulary.*     The subject is asked for definitions of words in the standard list.  Credit is given if 20 or more are defined.
2. *Ingenuity.*     Three problems are given, such as the following: "A boy is sent to the river to get exactly 3 pints of water, and he has only a 7-pint container and a 4-

pint container. How can he measure the water?" Credit is given if two problems are solved.

3. *Differences between abstract words.*    The subject is asked to distinguish between three pairs of associated words, e.g., "poverty" and "misery." Credit is given if two or more of the distinctions are correct.

4. *Arithmetical reasoning.*    The subject is asked to solve three problems, e.g., "If two pencils cost 5 cents, how many pencils can you buy for 50 cents?" Credit is given for two or more correct solutions.

5. *Proverbs.*    The subject is asked to explain the meaning of three proverbs, e.g., "A burnt child dreads the fire." Credit is given for two or more correct interpretations.

6. *Orientation.*    Questions are asked which require the understanding of compass directions, e.g., "Which direction would you have to face so that your right hand would be toward the North?" Credit is given for correctly answering at least four of the five questions.

7. *Essential differences.*    The subject is asked, for example, "What is the principal difference between work and play?" Credit is given for correctly answering at least two of the three questions.

8. *Abstract words.*    The subject is asked to define five abstract words, such as "generosity." Credit is given for at least four correct responses.

## Administration of the Stanford-Binet

The test materials include a box of performance items (beads, toys, pictures, etc.), test blanks on which the child's responses are recorded, and a manual of instructions. Some of the test materials are shown in Figure 10-1. As was mentioned previously, the administration of an individual test of this kind requires a highly trained examiner, and no faith should be placed in the scores obtained by an amateur tester. The test can usually be given in a period of 50 to 75 minutes.

No one is administered all the items. Instead, the individual is started slightly lower in the age scale than he is expected to reach. For example, a typical procedure would be to start a seven-year-old off on the five-year-level questions. The child is then taken up through all the age levels as far as he can go.

In previous forms of the Stanford-Binet, IQ was obtained by dividing mental age by chronological age. As was described in Chapter 3, such quotient scores are fraught with statistical and conceptual difficulties. Consequently, IQs on Form L-M are determined by a more sensible procedure. Now IQs are simply transformed standard scores, with a mean of 100 and a standard deviation of 16 for each age level. The manual provides tables for rapidly transforming mental age scores directly into IQ scores.

## Evaluation of the Stanford-Binet

The primary purpose of the Stanford-Binet is to provide information which helps in making decisions about the educational progress of students in elemen-

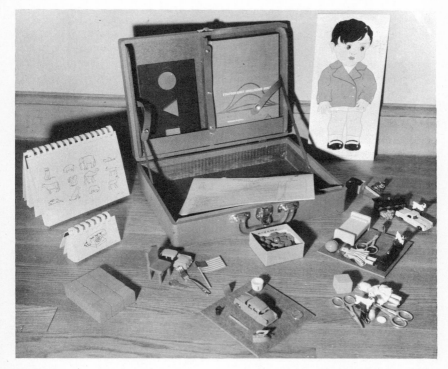

**FIGURE 10-1**     Some of the test materials used with the Stanford-Binet (*Reproduced by permission of Houghton Mifflin Company.*)

tary and secondary school. The evidence is that it serves that purpose very well. Some of the salient features of the test are as follows:

1. *Construction.*    The test was very carefully constructed and standardized. A particularly good feature of the test is the care that went into providing detailed instructions for scoring each item.

2. *Reliability.*    Very careful research was undertaken to determine the reliability of the Stanford-Binet IQ at different age levels. An equivalent-form reliability estimate was made separately for each age. Correlations were found between the scores obtained on Form L and Form M administered to the same subjects within one week's time. In general, the findings show that the Stanford-Binet is a highly reliable scale, with most of the reliability coefficients equal to, or greater than, .90. Scores tend to be more reliable for persons in their teens than they do for young children. The studies also show that low scores are somewhat more reliable than high scores in each age range. In other words, a bit more faith can be placed in the precision of a very low score than in that of a very high score.

3. *Predictive efficiency.*    The test has shown itself to be a good predictor of dif-

ferent criteria, particularly of school grades.    In general, the findings have been that Stanford-Binet IQs correlate in the neighborhood of .70 with elementary school grades, .60 with high school grades, and .50 with college grades.    (The decline in validity is probably due to the progressively decreasing dispersion of intellectual ability.)    The following correlations (Bond, 1940) were found between Form L IQ and high school achievement test scores.    The number of students ranged from 78 to 200.

| | | | |
|---|---|---|---|
| Reading comprehension | .73 | Spelling | .46 |
| Reading speed | .43 | History | .59 |
| English usage | .59 | Geometry | .48 |
| Literature acquaintance | .60 | Biology | .54 |

4. *Testing of adults.*    On both subjective and empirical grounds there is reason to believe that the Stanford-Binet is a better test for children than for adults (age fifteen and over).    One reason for this is that the concept of general intelligence is more meaningful with children than with adults.    This point will be discussed later in the chapter.    The Stanford-Binet does not have a high enough "ceiling" to measure the ability of superior adults.    That is, the range of difficulty at the adult level is not sufficient to tap the ability of highly gifted individuals.    Because no persons over eighteen years were included in the standardization sample, the norms for adults are suspect.

5. *Clinical utility.*    Presumably, a test like the Stanford-Binet should be judged, in the long run, by the success with which it predicts different criteria.    Many of the uses, however, to which this and other general intelligence tests are put are so subtle as to make direct empirical validation difficult.    For example, the test might be used to decide what type of psychotherapy should be used with a disturbed child.    Because of the difficulty in measuring therapeutic success and the difficulty in deciding the importance of intelligence for the outcome, it is hard to determine how well the test works in such a situation.    In many situations only the clinical impression of how well the test performs a particular job can at present be used as an indication of "validity."    Judging from the wide acceptance of the test in clinical settings, it is apparent that the Stanford-Binet is considered to be as valuable as, or more valuable than, any other test for use with children.

## the Wechsler scales

The Wechsler scales are competitive with the Stanford-Binet as individually administered tests of general ability.    There are separate Wechsler scales for adults and children, described below, which is not true of the Stanford-Binet.

### WAIS

Wechsler began his work on the measurement of general ability with the development of an adult test.    The test is frequently used with students aged fifteen and older.    The presently used form is called the Wechsler Adult Intelligence Scale (Wechsler, 1955).    The adult scale was intended to differ from the Stanford-Binet in the following respects:

1. The test items were to be more appropriate for adults, and representative norms for adults were to be obtained.

2. Age levels were to be discarded in favor of a number of subtests which all subjects would take.

3. Separate sets of verbal and performance tests were to be constructed, allowing for both a verbal and a performance IQ.

The WAIS consists of 11 subtests, which are described as follows:

## Verbal Scale

1. *General Information.* The subject is asked 25 questions concerning a wide variety of facts. The questions are not intended to tap academic training or specialized branches of knowledge. They are meant to cover the kinds of information that any alert individual can learn from his cultural contacts.

2. *General Comprehension.* The test contains 10 items concerning why certain social rules are necessary and how everyday problems are solved.

3. *Arithmetical Reasoning.* Ten problems of the kind that would be typically encountered in elementary school arithmetic are given. Both speed and correctness of response are scored.

4. *Similarities.* The subject is asked to tell what is similar about 12 pairs of terms. This subtest is very similar to material found on the Stanford-Binet.

5. *Digit Span.* This is the familiar memory for digits, which also appears at different levels of the Stanford-Binet. From three to nine digits are read to the subject, and he is asked to repeat them in the exact order presented. In the second part of the test, the subject is asked to repeat the digit series backward.

6. *Vocabulary.* Forty words of increasing difficulty are presented. The subject is asked what each one means.

## PERFORMANCE SCALE:

7. *Digit Symbol.* This is an adaptation of the familiar coding test. The subject is given a sheet of paper on which nine symbols are paired with nine numbers. Further down on the page a jumbled list of the numbers is given, and the subject is asked to write in the matching symbols.

8. *Picture Completion.* The subject is shown 15 incomplete pictures and is asked to describe the missing part in each. This is also very much like material found on the Stanford-Binet.

9. *Block Design.* The subject is shown a set of small blocks, the surfaces of which are painted white, red, and red and white. The subject is presented with a picture of a design and is asked to reproduce it with the blocks. Seven designs are given in turn. Both speed and accuracy are scored.

10. *Picture Arrangement.* The subject is handed a set of pictures and is asked to arrange them in an order that tells a story. Six sets of pictures are given. Both speed and accuracy are scored.

11. *Object Assembly.* The subject is asked to put together three jigsaw puzzles. Each puzzle pictures some part of the human body. Both speed and accuracy are scored.

## WISC

A separate scale is available for children, which is called the Wechsler Intelligence Scale for Children (Wechsler, 1949). The WISC is used for students aged five to fifteen, and the WAIS is used for all older age groups. The WISC is very similar to the WAIS, the major difference being that the WISC contains material more appropriate for, and more interesting to, younger people. The subtests of the WISC are as follows:

*Verbal scale*
1. General Information
2. General Comprehension
3. Arithmetic
4. Similarities
5. Vocabulary
6. Digit Span (alternative)
*Performance scale*
1. Picture Completion
2. Picture Arrangement
3. Block Design
4. Object Assembly
5. Coding
6. Mazes (can be used as an alternative for Coding)

On the verbal scale, Digit Span is given as an alternative if, for some reason, one of the other tests is not usable. On the performance scale (see Figure 10-2), the examiner has the choice of using either Coding or Mazes. The

**FIGURE 10-2**   Child being administered performance materials from the WISC (*Reproduced by permission. Copyright 1949 by The Psychological Corporation, New York, N.Y. All rights reserved.*)

Coding test on the WISC is similar to the Digit Symbol test on the WAIS. The Mazes test is the only one that does not appear on the adult form. It consists of eight paper-and-pencil mazes of increasing difficulty, performance being scored in terms of both speed and number of errors.

IQs on the WISC are determined in the same general manner as on the adult test. As in the adult form, IQs can be obtained separately for total scale, verbal scale, and performance scale. All IQs are simply transformed standard scores with a mean of 100 and a standard deviation of 15.

The manual (Wechsler, 1949) states the percentages of children falling at different IQ levels, with a verbal description of what particular scores mean (see Table 10-1).

### WPPSI

For a number of years those who used the Wechsler scales felt the need for a separate intelligence scale that would more adequately appraise the abilities of the preschool child. Although the WISC can be used with children as young as five years, it was felt that the period from four to six years constitutes a well-defined landmark in the young child's mental development and that therefore a scale specifically designed for use with this age group was desirable. In response to this need, the Wechsler Preschool and Primary Scale of Intelligence (WPPSI) was published in 1963 for use with children aged 4 to 6½ years.

While similar to the WISC in form and content, the WPPSI is a separate and distinct scale which takes into account the special problems of testing the child in this age group. The majority of the 11 subtests on the WPPSI are simply modifications of WISC subtests; however, three subtests are unique to the WPPSI. These three new subtests (Sentences, Animal House, and Geometric Design) replace Digit Span, Picture Arrangement, Object Assembly, and Coding on the WISC, which could not be adapted to the WPPSI.

Like the WISC, each of the subtests on the WPPSI may be treated separately as measuring different abilities, or they may be combined into a com-

**TABLE 10-1**     Classification of IQs on the WISC*

| DESCRIPTION | IQ RANGES | PERCENT OF CHILDREN |
|---|---|---|
| Very superior | 130 and above | 2.2 |
| Superior | 120–129 | 6.7 |
| Bright | 110–119 | 16.1 |
| Average | 90–109 | 50.0 |
| Dull normal | 80–89 | 16.1 |
| Borderline | 70–79 | 6.7 |
| Mental defective | 69 and below | 2.2 |

posite score as a measure of overall intellectual ability.  Both the method of computing the IQ and the evaluation scores of different levels (Wechsler, 1967) are the same as for the WISC.

## Evaluation of the Wechsler scales

Most of the good things that can be said about the Stanford-Binet apply equally well to the Wechsler scales.  In fact, the two types of tests correlate so highly at most age levels that it is illogical to argue which is "better" in general.  Although there are some advantages of one type of test over the other for particular purposes, the choice of whether to use one rather than the other type of scale often boils down to the personal preferences of the test user.  Some of the salient features of the Wechsler scales are as follows:

1. *Administration.*    Although, like the Stanford-Binet, the Wechsler scales are individually administered, they are somewhat easier to administer than the Stanford-Binet.  The full WAIS or WISC can usually be administered in no more than one hour.

2. *Standardization.*    The manual provides relatively detailed instructions for scoring each test.  The norms were based on representative samples of children and adults.  The care that went into the construction of norms is illustrated by the normative samples used for the WISC.  One hundred boys and one hundred girls were tested at each age level, giving a total of 2,200 children in the standardization sample.  A strenuous effort was made to choose a representative cross section of white children in the United States.  The sample was drawn from 85 communities in 11 states.  The distribution of subjects closely resembled the country at large in terms of urban-rural proportion, geographical area, and parental occupation.  The WISC standardization sample is as representative as that used in almost any current measure of general ability.

3. *Reliability.*    The Wechsler scales are highly reliable; that is, the pure chance factors influencing test results are quite small.  Because no alternative forms are available, split-half reliability estimates were used at various age levels.  The results at various ages indicate an overall reliability for the total scale of about .95, which, to say the least, is quite good.

4. *Performance scale.*    The performance items on the Wechsler tests constitute an advantage over the Stanford-Binet for certain purposes.  For most students, the more "verbal" types of items, such as appear throughout the Stanford-Binet and on the verbal scales of the Wechsler tests, are more predictive of achievement in school.  However, for certain types of "unusual" children, the performance items on the Wechsler scale are quite helpful.  They are helpful for children with various types of language problems, with the deaf, and with children who have been reared in other countries.  They are also useful with children who have led "impoverished" lives of a kind that would markedly hinder their performance on more verbal tests.  Although the verbal and performance scales correlate highly, when a child shows very different scores on the two types of scales, it is of real diagnostic importance.

5. *Testing adults.*    Most will agree that the WAIS is better than the Stanford-Binet for testing most adults, particularly those adults who are well above average in general ability.  The WAIS has items which are more appropriate for adults and more interesting to them, and the test has a higher "ceiling" than the Stanford-Binet.

Because the WISC does not extend below the five-year level, the Stanford-Binet dominates the testing of preschool children. Between the ages of five and fifteen, it is hard to choose between the two tests.

6. *Predictive efficiency.*    Although not as much research has been done with the Wechsler scales to predict school achievement and vocational success, the available evidence indicates that the scales will do approximately as well as the Stanford-Binet. Respectable correlations have been found with both grades in school and indices of vocational accomplishment.

7. *Clinical utility.*    As is true of the Stanford-Binet, many of the uses of the Wechsler by educational and pychological specialists are so subtle as to make direct appraisal quite difficult, and it is necessary to rely on impressions of how well the tests work. Evidently, the Wechsler scales are thought to be very useful in school settings and clinical settings.

## group tests of general ability

Like the individual tests of general intelligence, the group tests are usually composed of verbal comprehension, numerical computation, and various mixtures of the reasoning factors. Although the tests differ from one another in appearance and sometimes in their factor composition, they tend to correlate highly with one another. At the teenage and adult levels the group tests correlate highly with the individual tests, such as the WAIS. We see the interesting result that people who started off to compose intelligence tests in seemingly different directions ended up with rather similar measures. Where the group tests differ from one another is in their practical advantages. Some are longer and thus more reliable than others. Some have obtained norms in a careful and representative manner; others have only scant or misleading information on norms. Some have either higher or lower ceilings, making them more useful with one or the other extreme of ability. Considerable research has been done with some of the tests, and only "face validity" can be claimed for others.

The Binet and Wechsler scales dominate the field of individual tests of general intelligence. Among group measures neither one nor several tests have dominated the field. Therefore, the tests which will be discussed here are only examples of the measures available.

### Group tests for young children

The youngest age levels at which it has proved feasible to use group tests are the five- and six-year levels. Only small groups of approximately a dozen children can be tested in this way, and even then the examiner must exercise considerable skill to obtain the necessary cooperation and attention. Tests at this age level cannot employ written language, and the child cannot be expected to write his own responses. Test instructions must be given orally and supported by illustrations and gestures.

One of the most widely used tests for young children is the Pintner-Cunningham Primary Test (Pintner, Cunningham, & Durost, 1946), which has been in use for over twenty years. The test is available in three equivalent forms, A, B, and C. Each form is composed of seven subtests which are added together to obtain one score. (Illustrative items are shown in Figure 10-3.)

Equivalent-form reliabilities are found to be generally high for groups of kindergarten and first-grade children, ranging from .83 to .89. Correlations between the Pintner-Cunningham and the Stanford-Binet are usually about .80. In a group of 260 first-grade children, the Pintner-Cunningham correlated .63 with scores on a reading test.

Test 1. Mark the things that mother uses when she sews her apron

Test 2. Mark the prettiest girl

Test 3. Mark the two things that belong together

Test 7. Look at how each picture is drawn; make another one like it in the dots

**FIGURE  10-3**     Illustrative items from Form A of the Pintner-Cunningham Primary Test (*Reproduced by permission of Harcourt, Brace, & World, Inc.*)

## Group tests for the elementary school level

As children progress through the elementary school levels, more and more written material can be employed in tests. In the first several grades it is still necessary to rely heavily on oral instructions and pictorial test materials. One of the best available batteries for the elementary grades is the Lorge-Thorndike Intelligence Tests (Lorge & Thorndike, 1957), which include tests at five levels ranging from those appropriate for use with kindergarten children up to those for use with twelfth-grade students. At all levels the tests emphasize verbal comprehension, numerical skills, and reasoning abilities. (Illustrative items are shown in Figure 10-4.) The test can be given in about thirty minutes. A particularly good feature of the tests is that up through grade 3 they are "non-verbal," all the items concerning pictures and designs. This is good because it provides a relatively pure measure of "abstract" ability, which is not highly dependent on the fortuitous circumstances that influence the early acquirement of reading skills. Alternative forms are available at each age level. The manual of instructions presents simplified procedures that would permit any conscientious teacher to administer the tests in the classroom.

Even though the tests take only a short time to administer, they are highly reliable. Alternative-form and split-half correlations are respectably high. The tests correlate well with the Stanford-Binet, with some other group tests of general ability, and with some achievement tests.

## general intelligence tests for infants and preschool children

A separate section has been reserved here for the discussion of tests for infants and preschool children because of the special problems that are involved. One

Teacher says, "Circle the one showing the boy diving."

"Circle the one showing a girl eating."

"Circle the empty box."

**FIGURE 10-4** Sample items from the Lorge-Thorndike Intelligence Tests, kindergarten and first-grade level (*Reproduced by permission of Houghton Mifflin Company.*)

of the pioneers in the testing of infants was Arnold Gesell. For over twenty years he and his colleagues performed longitudinal studies of child development. A group of 107 infants was systematically observed at four, six, and eight weeks and at every four-week interval to fifty-six weeks. The children were studied again at eighteen months and at the ages of two, three, four, five, and six years. On the basis of these observations the Gesell Developmental Schedules were prepared (Gesell & Amatruda, 1949). They are intended to measure the following attributes:

1. *Motor behavior.*    How well the child can hold his balance, coordinate, stand, walk, and manipulate objects.
2. *Adaptive behavior.*    How well the child can solve the problems of his small world: obtain objects, remove obstacles, solve puzzles, and react to stimuli.
3. *Language behavior.*    How well the child can communicate, using the word in its broadest sense to include the use of gestures and primitive words as well as the later development of real language.
4. *Personal-social behavior.*    How well the child learns habits of personal care such as toilet training, dressing, and feeding himself. At a later age consideration is given to how the child manages himself in social situations and in play activity.

During the first year of life, when the Gesell scales would supposedly have their unique value, most of the observations have to be made about motor behavior. The four-week-old infant cannot, of course, talk or follow oral instructions of any kind. The most that can be done at the infant stage is to watch the child's spontaneous movements and note how he reacts to various stimuli. At 1.4 months the average child can coordinate his eyes on an object held before him. At 3 months he will make reaching movements for an object. At 5.5 months he will react differently to strangers from the way he reacts to his parents. (See Figure 10-5 for illustrative test materials.) Other tests for infants are the Cattell Infant Intelligence Scale (P. Cattell, 1947), the Bayley Infant Scales of Development (Bayley, 1968), and the Northwestern Infant Intelligence Tests (Gilliland, 1949).

### Analysis of infant tests

Tests for infants are difficult to standardize, administer, and score. They are, of course, all individual measures. Infant tests are less reliable than tests for older children. The reliability is considerably lower during the first six months than afterward. Several studies of different tests have found reliabilities around .65 for testing during the first six months. After six months the reliabilities move up to respectable figures in the range from .80 to .90. Except for the first weeks and months, the infant tests do measure something consistently. The question is: What do they measure? A real difficulty in validating infant scales is that there are almost no criteria available for preschool children. A customary procedure has been to correlate infant tests with scores

**FIGURE 10-5**    Test materials used with the Gesell Developmental Schedules (*Reproduced by permission of The Psychological Corporation.*)

made several years later on more established intelligence tests like the Stanford-Binet.  Studies have shown that infant tests given at the age of one year or less correlate about zero with intelligence tests given five, ten, and fifteen years later to the same persons.  It is obvious that infant tests do not measure intelligence as it is customarily measured in older children.  The key to this dilemma seems to be that the infant scales measure primarily motor and sensory abilities, and the research on reliability shows that there is some consistency in the development of these attributes.  It is quite likely that the infant tests would predict motor and sensory skills later in life, but interestingly enough, almost nothing has been done to test this hypothesis.

### Preschool tests

Between the ages of two and five the developing intellectual processes become accessible to psychological tests.  After the child develops speech, can manipulate objects, and becomes acquainted with the world about him, he can be tested with some of the materials that are customarily used in intelligence tests.  However, many of the difficulties in test standardization and administration still remain.  The test materials must be largely pictorial or consist of performance problems.

The difficulty in testing infants is that they usually do little, one way or the other, to indicate their intellectual abilities. Children between the ages of two and five do too much. They are so active and distractible that it is difficult to carry on any formal testing procedures. Many children in this age group are shy with strangers and will give little if any cooperation to the examiner. They often are not highly motivated to impress the examiner or themselves with how well they can perform. Consequently, the test must be posed as an interesting game to the child, and much depends on the examiner's skill.

One of the most prominent tests for young children is the Minnesota Preschool Scale (Goodenough & Van Wagenen, 1940). There are two equivalent forms, each with 26 items. Some of the items are as follows (see Figure 10-6 for an illustration of some of the testing materials):

1. Pointing to parts of the body on a doll
2. Telling what a picture is about
3. Naming colors
4. Digit span
5. Naming objects from memory
6. Vocabulary
7. Copying simple geometric designs
8. Block building
9. Doing a jigsaw puzzle
10. Indicating missing part in pictures

Many of the items are similar to those at the lower age levels of the Stanford-Binet. The instrument is largely a power test with no emphasis on speed, and the items are little concerned with motor skills. Tests at this age level which depend on speed and motor skills are probably poorer measures.

The Minnesota scale was standardized on a group of 900 children ranging in age from 1½ to 6 years. Equivalent-form reliabilities of the total scale vary from .80 to .94. There are some reasons to believe that the Minnesota scale is not an entirely adequate measure below the age of three. Although scores for children above three tend to correlate highly with Stanford-Binet scores obtained later, the correlation for children below the age of three is only .21. Also, clinical experience indicates that some of the test materials are not sufficiently interesting to hold the attention of children below the age of three. Two other preschool tests are the Intelligence Test for Young Children (Valentine, 1945) and the Merrill Palmer Scale (Stutsman, 1931).

## the nature of general intelligence

It has been shown that in spite of the separable factors that underlie tests of human ability, ability functions have a common ground that can be reliably and usefully measured. The "verbal" intelligence tests, both individual and

**FIGURE 10-6**    Test materials used in the Minnesota Preschool Scale (*Reproduced by permission of Educational Test Bureau, Minneapolis.*)

group, generally correlate highly enough with one another for us to speak of their common characteristics. If a marked difference in test scores is found between two kinds of people with one of the tests, the difference would most likely be reflected in the others. The wide use of intelligence tests during the last half century has shown a number of things about the underlying process:

(1) Intelligence cannot at present be measured in children below the age of two years and not very well below the age of five or six years. Earlier in the chapter the difficulties of constructing tests for infants and preschool children were discussed. Perhaps the next decade will show an improvement in the early measurement of general ability.

(2) The concept of general intelligence is more meaningful with children than with adults. Although the evidence on this point is somewhat conflicting, it seems that abilities are more "general" in children. Some of the factors which are found in adult populations are not found with children. The factorial diversity of abilities in adults is probably due to different life experiences and different kinds of school and vocational training. It makes more sense to use tests of general intelligence with children than with adults.

(3) Intelligence as measured by current "verbal" tests is due partly to heredity and partly to environment. The most telling arguments for this posi-

tion come from the studies of resemblance between family members in intelligence. Conrad and Jones (1940) administered intelligence tests to over two hundred families in rural New England. They found that for children above the age of five years, intelligence of parents and children correlates .49. Numerous other studies have found correlations very close to .50. Conrad and Jones also found a correlation of .49 between siblings (between brothers, between sisters, or between brothers and sisters). Roberts (1941) pointed out that a correlation of .50 between siblings is what would be expected from multifactor inheritance. It is possible that the correlations which have been found between family members could be due to environment rather than heredity. Family members tend to share the same environment, talk about the same topics, and have similar kinds of schooling. Environment may explain part of the resemblance, but studies of twins make it apparent that this is not a complete explanation. Correlations between the intelligence test scores of fraternal twins (dizygotic) are usually higher than correlations between those of siblings, ordinarily ranging from .50 to .70. Correlations between scores of identical twins (monozygotic) are usually around .90—almost as high as the reliability of the tests! Fraternal twins can have very different genetic structures, but the genetic structures of identical twins are exactly alike. This leaves little doubt that at least a portion, and apparently a sizable portion, of intelligence is due to inheritance.

(4) After the age of about six years, the individual's intelligence tends to remain stable with respect to his age group. That is, the superior people at one age level tend to be the superior people at other age levels (see Figure 10-7 for evidence on this point). The relationship is far from perfect, and isolated individuals may show drastic changes over a period of years.

(5) There are definite group differences in intelligence test scores. Lower scores on the average are made by people of low socioeconomic status, people living in rural areas, people living in the Southern or Southwestern part of the United States, immigrants from southern Europe, and Indians and Negroes. The interpretation of differences of this kind places a large strain on the logical foundation of intelligence tests. As was discussed previously in this chapter, the traditional measures of intelligence are constructed in such a way as to favor certain groups. The question is whether or not the subgroups which tend to make lower scores would make high scores if afforded the advantages of the wider culture. There is some evidence to show that they would. It was found (Klineberg, 1935) that the longer Southern Negro children who migrate to New York have been in the city environment, the higher scores they make. Another point that should be considered is that even though some subgroups score lower on the average than others, at least some high-scoring individuals can be found in each. The whole question of ethnic and socioeconomic differences is highly charged with emotion in both professional and lay circles and is a point about which much more information needs to be obtained.

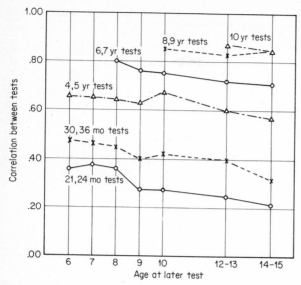

**FIGURE 10-7** Effect of age at initial testing and test-retest interval on prediction of later Stanford-Binet IQ from earlier test (*Adapted from Honzik, McFarlane, & Allen, 1948.*)

(6) Many different kinds of attainment involve intelligence as measured by traditional "verbal" instruments. In particular, intelligence is one of the major factors in successful schoolwork. Numerous correlations of .50 and above between particular tests and school grades were cited in this chapter. Intelligence test scores differentiate occupational groups (see Table 10-2). However, it should be noted that there is considerable overlap among most groups. Comparing the extremes in Table 10-2, the top 10 percent of lumberjacks score higher than the lower 10 percent of accountants. Scores on intelligence tests are predictive of success on many but not all jobs (see Table 10-3). The fact that the correlations between test scores and job success are near zero in some cases does not necessarily mean that intelligence is not important for the job. The dispersion of intellectual ability is usually narrowed considerably in most jobs by the individual's gravitating toward a job at which he can work comfortably and by the selection procedures that are used in industrial settings. Also, it is important to note that the variability of intelligence test scores is higher for lower-level than for higher-level jobs. This indicates that, as would be expected, intelligence is a more important determiner of success in high-level occupations. The individual's ability to succeed is determined by his intelligence and by a host of other things as well: abilities not measured by intelligence tests, interests, personality traits, and just plain luck.

**TABLE 10-2**    AGCT standard scores of occupational groups in World War II

| OCCUPATIONAL GROUPS | PERCENTILE | | | | |
|---|---|---|---|---|---|
| | 10 | 25 | 50 | 75 | 90 |
| Accountant | 114 | 121 | 129 | 136 | 143 |
| Teacher | 110 | 117 | 124 | 132 | 140 |
| Lawyer | 112 | 118 | 124 | 132 | 141 |
| Bookkeeper, general | 108 | 114 | 122 | 129 | 138 |
| Chief clerk | 107 | 114 | 122 | 131 | 141 |
| Draftsman | 99 | 109 | 120 | 127 | 137 |
| Postal clerk | 100 | 109 | 119 | 126 | 136 |
| Clerk, general | 97 | 108 | 117 | 125 | 133 |
| Radio repairman | 97 | 108 | 117 | 125 | 136 |
| Salesman | 94 | 107 | 115 | 125 | 133 |
| Store manager | 91 | 104 | 115 | 124 | 133 |
| Toolmaker | 92 | 101 | 112 | 123 | 129 |
| Stock clerk | 85 | 99 | 110 | 120 | 127 |
| Machinist | 86 | 99 | 110 | 120 | 127 |
| Policeman | 86 | 96 | 109 | 118 | 128 |
| Electrician | 83 | 96 | 109 | 118 | 124 |
| Meatcutter | 80 | 94 | 108 | 117 | 126 |
| Sheet metalworker | 82 | 95 | 107 | 117 | 126 |
| Machine operator | 77 | 89 | 103 | 114 | 123 |
| Automobile mechanic | 75 | 89 | 102 | 114 | 122 |
| Carpenter, general | 73 | 86 | 101 | 113 | 123 |
| Baker | 69 | 83 | 99 | 113 | 123 |
| Truck driver, heavy | 71 | 83 | 98 | 111 | 120 |
| Cook | 67 | 79 | 96 | 111 | 120 |
| Laborer | 65 | 76 | 93 | 108 | 119 |
| Barber | 66 | 79 | 93 | 109 | 120 |
| Miner | 67 | 75 | 87 | 103 | 119 |
| Farm worker | 61 | 70 | 86 | 103 | 115 |
| Lumberjack | 60 | 70 | 85 | 100 | 116 |

SOURCE: *Adapted from Stewart, 1947.*

## using tests of general ability

In school settings, tests of general ability are potentially useful in helping to make decisions about (1) grade placement, (2) ability grouping within grades, (3) special instruction, (4) counseling, (5) vocational guidance, and (6) planning for higher education. Tests of general ability are also useful in making decisions about people in many vocational settings, including industry, the civil service, and the armed forces. In addition, tests of general ability play very important parts in basic research in psychology and education.

### Uses in vocational settings

Besides having applied uses in school settings, tests of general ability also have many applied uses in vocational settings, including industry, civil services,

**TABLE 10-3**    Median validity coefficients of intelligence tests for various occupational groups in the prediction of job proficiency

| OCCUPATIONAL GROUP | MEDIAN VALIDITY COEFFICIENT | NUMBER OF VALIDITY COEFFICIENTS |
|---|---|---|
| Clerical workers | .35 | 85 |
| Supervisors | .40 | 9 |
| Salesmen | .33 | 4 |
| Salesclerks | −.09 | 18 |
| Protective service | .25 | 6 |
| Skilled workers | .55 | 6 |
| Semiskilled workers | .20 | 45 |
| Unskilled workers | .08 | 13 |

SOURCE: *Adapted from Ghiselli & Brown, 1948, p. 577; reproduced by permission of the American Psychological Association.*

and the armed forces. For example, tests of general ability have a moderate amount of validity for the selection of management personnel in industry and for the selection of officer candidates in the armed forces. As was mentioned previously, such tests are generally more valid for selecting people for high-level jobs than for low-level jobs. In vocational settings, a frequent practice is to employ measures of general ability to admit individuals to an institution or program within an institution; then later a test of differential aptitudes is employed to assign individuals to specific positions. For example, a test of general ability has been employed to admit candidates into officer training in the Air Force. Later a test of differential aptitudes was employed to assign men to training as pilot, navigator, bombardier, or other specialty.

### Uses in basic research

In addition to applied uses of tests of general ability, there are many, many uses of such tests in basic research in psychology. Tests of general ability are very useful both in basic research on individual differences and in controlled experiments. In studies of individual differences, only problems concerning time and expense should prevent the inclusion of a group measure of general ability in every correlational study of individual differences. Tests of general ability correlate with so many different measures that, unless a measure can be shown to add something to what can be explained by measures of general ability, scientific parsimony demands that no importance be attached to the measure. For example, it has been hypothesized that certain perceptual abilities correlate with learning to read. If it is found that perceptual abilities add nothing to the prediction of learning to read above that which can be predicted from tests of general ability alone, the finding of a positive correlation between perceptual abilities and learning to read is of little scientific interest.

Although they are not employed as much as they should be in this regard, tests of general ability are also important explainers of the results of controlled experiments, particularly any type of experiment concerned with human learning. In a study of paired-associate learning (e.g., pairing nonsense syllables such as *keb* with real words such as "conglomerate"), memory factors and verbal factors enter the picture. In a study concerning the effects of different dosages of a drug on tasks concerning concept formation, factors of reasoning are important. Because factors such as those in the foregoing examples are important components of tests of general ability, it follows that such tests could explain some of the variability of scores within treatment conditions. There is no other variable in psychology that has the same wide explanatory power in studies of individual differences and in controlled experiments as that of general intelligence. Some of the important principles for using tests of general ability in these ways are described below.

### Choice of tests

In this chapter numerous different types of tests have been described. Which ones should be used for helping to make particular kinds of decisions? There are some rules that partially answer the question.

Most schools employ standardized tests of achievement. As has been mentioned in a number of places in this book, tests of general ability tend to correlate highly with achievement tests. Consequently, tests of general ability should be used only if they *add* something to what can be obtained from achievement tests alone. Tests of general ability (at least the good ones) definitely add something when used with children from five to about ten. During those years, the child is still getting used to school, and he has not had enough "book learning" for achievement tests to predict accurately what he may accomplish later. Because most tests of general ability, particularly at the earlier age levels, are relatively more concerned with "abstract" ability, they are more prognostic of later achievement than achievement tests given in the primary grades.

Because the abstractness of many measures of general ability is an asset in dealing with children from five to ten, the more abstract the test, the better. At those age levels, the Stanford-Binet and the WISC are semi-independent of school learning, which is why they are highly recommended. The fact that the Lorge-Thorndike group test (described earlier in this chapter) is "nonverbal" up to the third-grade level is considered an advantage. It can be expected that, in order to add something to what can be obtained from routinely administered achievement tests, tests of general ability will become even more abstract. One step in this direction is to employ more items concerning figural relations such as those illustrated early in this chapter.

The choices concerning whether to use group or individual tests in general and when to use one rather than the other are relatively easy to make. The individual tests are simply far too expensive to be routinely given to all children. Consequently, most schools will have to rely on one of the group tests of general ability for routine testing of students. The individual tests are necessary, and worth the expense, when the child constitutes a problem in some sense.

For several reasons, tests of general ability are more valuable in the elementary grades than in high school. One reason is that, as was argued previously, the abilities of children are more general; therefore, one general measure will tell much about the child. Beginning with the teens, it is advisable to use one of the multifactor batteries when possible. Another reason is that much of the need for a test of general ability no longer exists by the time the student is well along in high school. The major value of such tests is in getting students off to a good start in school, and by the time the student is in high school, much of the "good" or "evil" has already been done. A third reason is that tests of general ability for teenagers and average adults (in contrast to some of those for young children) are so saturated with "book learning" that they closely resemble tests of achievement and tend to add only a small amount of additional information. At the early age levels, the school needs *both* measures of general ability and measures of achievement. In the later years of high school, the need is for *either* a measure of general ability or a measure of achievement. Although even at the upper age levels most tests of general ability still add something to routinely employed measures of achievement, it is a real question whether most schools can pay the price for the relatively small amount of additional information obtained.

## Counseling and guidance

Tests of general ability would be worthwhile if for no other reason than the important part they play with problem children. In a typical problem the first-grade child is overactive, runs around the room rather than working on exercises, will not follow instructions, and is apparently incapable of doing first-grade work. The teacher suffers it for a month and then tells the principal that something has to be done. The principal gets in touch with a school psychologist, who administers the Stanford-Binet as one part of the clinical workup. What the test shows has an important bearing on the child. If his score is very high, he may be restless out of boredom and need more challenging fare. If he is near average, he may have emotional problems centered in the home, or he may be poorly disciplined. If his score is very low, he may be totally unable to master the first grade and be causing trouble because he is frustrated and angry. Regardless of what the tests show, they supply one important type of information to help in making decisions about problem children.

Individually administered tests are particularly helpful in dealing with prob-

lem children.  Many children who are too disturbed to perform well in class
or on achievement tests often show high ability when carefully drawn out by
the expert examiner.  Also, the individual testing situation provides the examiner with many opportunities to observe the emotional behavior of the
child, his habits, and his methods of approach to problem-solving situations.

### Curriculum management

Some school systems use tests of general ability to decide when children may
be admitted to the first grade.  If children score high enough, they can be
admitted when they are only 5½ or even younger.  Although the practice is
controversial, the merit probably outweighs the potential dangers involved.
Children of the same chronological age are not of the same mental age.  Basing grade placement on chronological age is, if anything, less logical than basing
it on mental age obtained from a good test.

An even more controversial practice is that of placing children in ability
groups within particular grades.  There are both very good and very bad things
to be said about this practice.  On the bad side, it potentially can (1) make
the slow learners feel inferior, (2) place an unhealthy emphasis on intelligence,
and (3) deprive all students of the opportunity to learn about other children
in general rather than about their "own kind."  On the good side, ability
grouping potentially can (1) let every student learn at his own pace without
either dragging along or being dragged along by the others, (2) let slow learners
work with students of their own level of ability, and (3) simplify the teacher's
work by giving him students who can do, and are interested in, much the same
materials.  No attempt will be made here to reach a final decision as to whether
the potentially good features of ability grouping outweigh the potentially bad
ones, but should ability groups be used, tests of general ability are very helpful.
Up to about the fourth or fifth grade, tests of general ability offer the best
measures currently available for grouping children in terms of ability.  After
that point, standardized achievement tests do as well or better.

### Classroom instruction

To the child, "school" means the day-to-day interactions with his teacher
and with fellow students.  How can, and should, tests of general ability interact with that all-important (for the child) environment?  Some argue that
teachers and students would be better off if IQ tests had not been invented,
and there is some truth in this.  On the negative side, teachers often display
a naïve faith in the tests.  They forget that they are man-made and are only as
good as men know how to make them at the present time.

Teachers must be careful not to let the IQ become an index of value or
moral goodness.  Good character, sportsmanship, pleasantness of personality,

and most other desirable personal attributes are *not* related to measures of general ability. If the teacher wants to single out a student who is in need of special attention and consideration, it should be the child with a low IQ. School will always be an uphill fight for him, and he will have to settle for less in life than his brighter schoolmates can expect. If the teacher has any energy left after trying to love them all, that last ounce of affection and concern should go to the child who needs it most.

Tests of general ability give the teacher an approximate idea of what to expect from each child. If a child has a very high score, he can be expected to perform well above the average. If he has a very low score, he may need special instruction. However, teachers must remember that *general* measures are just that—they do not indicate the particular ways in which the child is more and less bright. If the child makes a very high score, he can probably perform well in most school topics. If he makes a very low score, he will probably have trouble in most school topics. However, most children are not at the extremes, and for them tests of general ability leave many unanswered questions. Although all abilities tend to go together, there are definite exceptions. Consequently, one child may show an average IQ but be high in mathematical ability and low in other respects, and many other patterns of ability are possible. Teachers should look for the child's particular abilities rather than rely solely on one index of general ability.

Tests of general ability do not necessarily measure creative potential. Although students who make low scores seldom become creative adults, there is far from a one-to-one correspondence between IQ and creativity for above-average students. Some students with very high IQs do not grow to be creative adults, and some students with only moderately high IQs produce truly creative works. Tests of general ability are useful primarily for predicting how well children will do in school.

In using tests of general ability to predict success in school, teachers must remember that such tests are useful primarily for predicting and making decisions about the *next step*. A test of general ability given to a five-year-old is highly predictive of how well he will perform in the first several grades. A test of general ability given at the beginning of junior high is quite predictive of progress during the ensuing several years. However, tests of general ability are *not* highly predictive of performance many years after they are administered. For example, the correlation between measures of general ability given to five-year-olds and successful performance in college is nil.

Although children's mental abilities change quite slowly, they do change. Mental abilities of children are not highly "crystallized." The child who appears only average at age six may appear superior at age eighteen. The child who appears above average at seven may appear below average as an adult. Children grow at different rates, both physically and mentally, and it is no more sensible to expect a test of general ability given at age six to be an infallible judge of adult ability than it would be to expect a measure of height at that age to be an infallible predictor of how tall the adult will be. As is true of all tests, more faith should be placed in the extremes. The child who obtains a score typical of mental defectives is probably always going to have trouble. The child whose score is typical of only the top 1 percent of the population is probably going to do quite well in school. In between it is somewhat hazardous to make long-range forecasts with tests of general ability. Rather, the results of such tests should be considered primarily to be good indications of how well children will perform during the ensuing several years.

## Summary

The purpose of intelligence tests is to measure *abstract* ability, which is distinct from actual accomplishment in school as evidenced in achievement tests and teacher-made examinations. The potential usefulness of measures of abstract ability is that they could forecast how well some children might do if their home and school environments were improved. Also, they point to children who are, in a sense, performing better in school than they "should," children who are highly motivated to achieve or who overly impress teachers with their accomplishments. These two types of children are often spoken of as "underachievers" and "overachievers," respectively. It is very important to know about both types (regardless of what is done about them), and, potentially, intelligence tests can help spot these children.

Unfortunately it is not possible to measure abstract ability entirely apart from actual achievement in school. Many of the items on intelligence tests and achievement tests are very similar, and the two types of tests correlate highly. However, in those few cases where large differences are found between scores on the two types of tests, this can provide very important diagnostic information.

The content of most tests of intelligence was determined largely by the intuitions of the test constructors, plus statistical analyses of test data. In spite of their intuitive beginnings, all the tests tend to share some common properties. They all capitalize on several factors of intellect, particularly verbal comprehension. The dominant factors in the tests tend to be the ones that are most involved in successful performance in elementary and secondary school. Because of the similarity of their content, all the tests tend to correlate rather highly with one another, and choices among them for particular uses often must be made on practical grounds.

In schools, intelligence tests have many uses, if they are employed wisely. Teachers must realize that intelligence tests are not intended to measure what students have actually accomplished and that they are not perfect predictors of future accomplishment. The value of intelligence tests is in the clues they provide about underachievers and overachievers. It is particularly important for teachers to realize that the IQ is not the only important aspect of intellectual potential and personal worth. The IQ does not (1) indicate special abilities, (2) provide a sure index of creativity, or (3) strongly relate to personality and character.

In addition to their uses in educational and vocational settings, tests of general ability have many uses in basic research in psychology and education. Both in studies of individual differences and in controlled experiments with people, it is a truism that scores on most tasks correlate modestly or higher with measures of general intelligence.

There are many good measures of general ability for the different requirements in applied settings and in basic research. Among individually administered tests, the Stanford-Binet test and the Wechsler tests lead the field. There are many different group tests of general intelligence, ranging from ones that are suitable for use with preschool children to ones that are suitable for use with superior adults. It is safe to say that up until now, these instruments have had more impact on the general public than any other products of psychology.

## Suggested additional readings

Anastasi, A. *Psychological testing.* (3rd ed.) New York: Macmillan, 1968. Chs. 8–12.

Cronbach, L. J. *Essentials of psychological testing.* (2nd ed.) New York: Harper & Row, 1960. Chs. 7, 8.

Thorndike, R. L., & Hagen, E. *Measurement and evaluation in psychology and education.* (2nd ed.) New York: Wiley, 1961.

# CHAPTER 11

# Special abilities

There are many human attributes to measure other than the kinds of abilities which were discussed in the previous two chapters. There we talked about the components of intelligence or intellectual ability. These are usually thought of as the "higher processes," the most prized of abilities. However, individual differences are as easily found, and sometimes as important to study, in sensory, motor, mechanical, and artistic abilities.

In order to understand fully an individual's potentialities and liabilities, much must be learned about him in addition to his intellectual capabilities. Two persons could make the same score on a general intelligence test and yet be very different in other important ways. Similarly, for all the factors which were described in Chapter 9, two persons could have exactly the same profile of scores and differ importantly in terms of other abilities. One person might be underweight and frail, and the other an excellent physical specimen. This would make quite a difference if they were both being considered for jobs as Arctic explorers, test pilots, or steeplejacks. One person might have a flair for mechanical work, whereas the other could have little such ability. This would be important to know if they were both considering careers as mechanical engineers. There are many, many other ways in which the two persons could differ importantly—in auditory acuity, depth perception, finger coordination, musical ability, sense of balance, athletic ability, resistance to disease, and so on.

In addition to discussing special abilities relating to the practical aspects of intelligence, we shall consider measures of creativity in the final section of this chapter. Eventually, various dimensions of creativity will be treated as parts of a general structure of intellect, as it was discussed in Chapter 9. However, the measurement of creativity is so new, and many of the measures are so different in kind from those employed in present multifactor test batteries, that creativity will be treated here as a set of special abilities.

## sensory tests

The first tests in psychology, those of Galton and his immediate followers, were largely measures of sensory ability: the fineness of sensory thresholds, reaction time, and sensory acuity. The early investigators became discouraged with these measures because they failed to predict school grades, teachers' ratings of intelligence, and other criteria of intellectual accomplishment. However, sensory tests have come back in the last several decades as important measures in their own right. Attention will be given here to some components of vision and audition, omitting the interesting individual differences to be found in relation to the other three "senses": touch, smell, and taste. Indeed, the range of individual differences extends to numerous other senses that are seldom listed. There are internal senses like thirst, sensitivity to movement of the limbs, and awareness of specific organic tensions.

## vision

The popular practice of talking about "good" and "poor" eyesight does considerable injustice to the complexity of visual functions. There are a number of separable and only partially related kinds of good vision. A primary distinction must be made between near acuity and far acuity. Near acuity concerns how well the individual can discern visual forms within 1 or 2 feet of his eyes. Far acuity concerns how well he can discern visual forms placed 20 or more feet away. A third component of good vision is depth perception, the ability to judge the proximity of objects to one another. Another component is the ability to distinguish colors. Although it is commonplace to think of "color blindness" as a unitary characteristic, there are different kinds of color blindness. Also, the ability to distinguish colors is partly a matter of degree rather than an all-or-none attribute.

### Wall charts

The most familiar measure of visual ability is the ordinary wall chart, which nearly everyone has encountered during a routine physical examination. The Snellen Chart is used extensively for this purpose. It consists of rows of letters, each lower row containing smaller letters than the one above it. The chart is placed 20 feet from the subject. If he can read the row of letters that the average man can, he is said to have 20/20 vision. If he can read the row of letters that the average person can read at only 15 feet from the chart, he is said to have 20/15 vision. Similarly, if he needs to stand 20 feet from the chart to read the row that the average person can read from 40 feet, he is said to have 20/40 vision.

Although the Snellen Chart is an adequate device for detecting gross deficiencies in visual acuity, it has a number of disadvantages. Like all the wall charts, it tests only far acuity. A schoolchild could have excellent far acuity and still have crippling visual defects of other kinds. Some letters are easier to distinguish than others, and this is not taken into account when using the Snellen Chart. Also, the rows of letters are easy to remember, and the test can often be "faked" by the person who has some prior knowledge of the chart. The amount of light on wall charts should be carefully controlled, but in much practical work this is given little consideration. When controlled conditions are obtained, the reliabilities of the Snellen and other wall charts are satisfactorily high. One study (Studies in Visual Acuity, 1948) reports a reliability coefficient of .88 for the Snellen Chart.

### Color vision

One of the oldest tests for color vision is the Holmgren Woolens. The subject is given different colors of yarn and is asked to sort the ones that are alike. It is a crude test which serves only to distinguish persons who are very deficient in color vision. A more systematic measure can be obtained with the Ishihara color plates.[1] The plates are composed of small patches of color. The person who has good color vision can see a number on the plate. The person with deficient color vision either does not see the number or sees a different number. More recent color-vision tests are the Farnsworth Dichotomous Test for Color Blindness (D. Farnsworth, 1947), the Farnsworth-Munsell 100 Hue Test (D. Farnsworth, 1949), and the Illuminant-Stable Color Vision Test (Freeman & Zaccaria, 1948). In order to keep color-vision tests adequately standardized, they must be used in the same illumination and protected from fading or soilage.

### Multiple-component tests of vision

In recent years devices have been constructed which test a number of different aspects of vision. The three best-known instruments are the Ortho-Rater (Bausch and Lomb), the Sight-Screener (American Optical Company), and the Telebinocular (Keystone View Company). Each of these instruments tests

[1] Obtainable from C. H. Stoelting Company.

near vision, far vision, depth perception, color discrimination, and control of the eye muscles. In general, the multiple-component instruments are a considerable advance over the older, single-component tests.

## audition

The sense of hearing is also composed of a number of different functions. Only auditory acuity will be treated here, the ability to detect faint sounds. Auditory acuity is itself complex: the person who can hear well at one tone level may be nearly deaf at higher or lower frequencies. Because of their relevance to musical aptitude, some of the other auditory functions will be considered in a later section.

The older tests of auditory acuity employed sound sources like whispered speech or the ticking of a clock. In the whispered-speech test, the examiner stands some distance from the subject and whispers a number of words. The subject tries to repeat each word in turn. The examiner walks farther and farther from the subject to determine the distance at which the whispered words can be heard. Although tests of this kind are adequate for detecting gross losses of hearing, they have a number of defects. It is difficult to standardize both the loudness and the clarity of whispered speech. One examiner will inevitably whisper a bit louder and/or more clearly than another in spite of the best efforts at standardization. Such tests measure auditory acuity within a narrow range of the tone, or frequency, continuum. The person who can hear whispered speech well might not be able to hear sound at a different frequency, such as the sound of a ticking clock. The differences in the acoustical properties of testing rooms and the problem of ruling out extraneous noises add to the difficulty of standardizing this type of test.

A number of instruments have been developed for measuring auditory acuity at different points on the frequency continuum. These are called *pure-tone audiometers* (H. Davis, 1947; Watson & Tolan, 1949). Earphones are used to test one ear at a time. The standard procedure is to gradually raise the sound intensity until the subject indicates that he can hear the tone clearly; then the intensity is lowered to a point where it can no longer be heard. (The reader will remember this as one of the psychophysical methods for determining *thresholds*.) The procedure is repeated at different frequency levels. The resulting data can be plotted as a profile of auditory acuity (see Figure 11-1).

Pure-tone audiometers are now available for group testing. Earphones are given to all the subjects, who use standard answer sheets to indicate whether or not they hear the tone at different intensities. It is not possible to determine the individual's auditory acuity as finely in the group testing situation. The individual who shows a marked loss in any frequency range on the group test should, if possible, be given the individual test to determine more accurately the nature of his hearing deficiency.

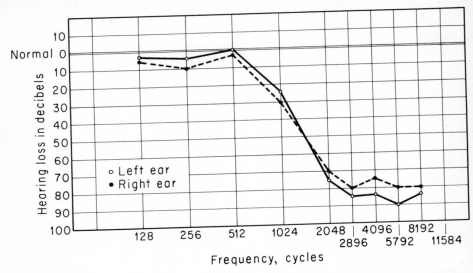

**FIGURE 11-1**    Audiogram of a child with severe high-tone deafness (*Adapted from Watson & Tolan, 1949.*)

## practical uses for sensory tests

The individual with a visual or hearing defect is at a definite disadvantage in many performance situations. Particularly, the young schoolchild is handicapped. It is sometimes found that poor vision or hearing is responsible for apparent dullness. The child who cannot see the blackboard or hear the teacher will learn very little, regardless of his latent capacity for learning. Reading difficulties can often be traced to visual defects.

In order to speak correctly, the child must imitate the speech of others. He cannot imitate what he cannot hear. To do well on most psychological tests, the child must be able to hear the instructions and to read the test content. As is common practice in many school programs, children should be systematically tested at different age levels for auditory and visual ability.

Even the sophisticated adult is often unaware that he has a visual or auditory defect. It often happens that individuals who wear glasses for the first time are surprised that the world "looks that way." Persons with poor far acuity often take it for granted that everyone sees objects more than 50 feet away as "big blurs." Consequently, the individual cannot be relied upon to detect his own sensory difficulty and seek help. He is likely to blame his inability to perform well on "dumbness" rather than on a visual or hearing loss.

Sensory ability is necessary for many different occupations. The classic example is the baseball umpire's dependence on "good eyesight." Color discrimination is paramount to the interior decorator, the tailor, and the artist. A moderate level of auditory acuity is necessary for most jobs, particularly those which involve talking with others or following spoken instructions. However, there are few jobs in which high-level sensory ability is the primary attribute required. Even jobs that would seem to depend heavily on sensory acuity usually require only average ability, for example, the job of a sonar operator, who uses a sound-echoing device to detect submerged objects. It has been found that up to a certain point, auditory acuity is a "must" for this job, but above the level of average hearing it is not a predictor of good and poor performance.

## motor dexterity

It has long been recognized that the person who works well with his "head" does not necessarily work well with his hands. Accomplishments like shaping a fine piece of pottery, hitting a home run, and operating complex machinery have little to do with intelligence or with formal school training.

Among the oldest motor tests are the pegboards, designed to measure arm, hand, and finger dexterity. A typical example is the Stromberg Dexterity Test (Stromberg, 1951; see Figure 11-2). The first part of the test requires the subject to place 60 cylindrical blocks into holes as fast as he can. In the second part, the blocks are removed, turned over, and put back in the holes. Another widely used test is the Crawford Small Parts Dexterity Test (Crawford & Crawford, 1949; see Figure 11-3). In the first part of the test, the subject uses tweezers to place pins in holes and then places a small collar over each pin. In the second part, he puts small screws in place with a screwdriver.

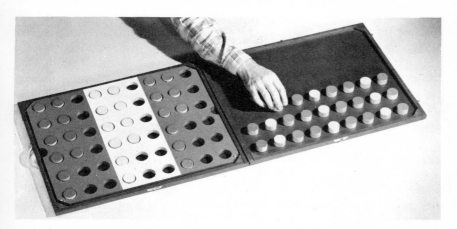

**FIGURE 11-2**    Stromberg Dexterity Test (*Reproduced by permission of The Psychological Corporation.*)

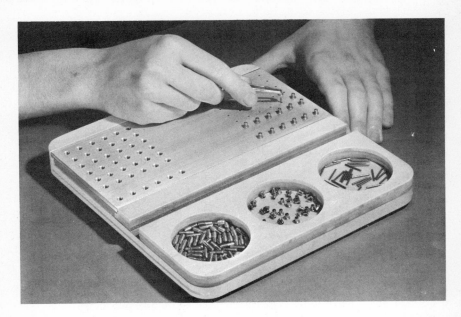

**FIGURE 11-3** Crawford Small Parts Dexterity Test *(Reproduced by permission of The Psychological Corporation.)*

Some tests are designed specifically to test how well the individual can work with tools and small mechanical parts. A typical test of this kind is the Bennett Hand-tool Dexterity Test (Bennett, 1947; see Figure 11-4). The test requires the subject to remove and replace nuts and bolts as quickly as possible.

More complex tests involving hand, arm, and leg coordination have been designed for particular jobs. One of the best known of these is the Complex Coordination Test (Melton, 1947), which the Air Force uses in selecting pilots (see Figure 11-5). The test consists of a partial replica of an airplane cockpit, complete with stick and rudder, and lights on a control panel simulate the maneuvers of an airplane. The subject must use the stick and rudder to match the stimulus lights, the counterpart in the test of coordinating the stick and rudder as required by the situation in the airplane.

### Analysis of motor tests

Most tests of motor dexterity are highly dependent on speed. Consequently, they prove to be better predictors of jobs in which speed rather than quality is important. There are many jobs in which speed is only a minor consideration. The person who can saw a board quickly does not necessarily have the craftsmanship of the skilled cabinetmaker.

An important characteristic of motor tests is that they tend to correlate very little with one another.  Slightly different manipulations of the same material often have little in common.  For example, the two parts of the Crawford Small Parts Dexterity Test correlate on the average less than .50 (Crawford & Crawford, 1949).  A correlation of only .57 was found between the two parts of the Stromberg Dexterity Test (Stromberg, 1951).  Correlations between different motor tests prove to be even smaller.  Factor-analytic studies of motor dexterity tests have generally found few broad common factors.  Tests in this area tend to be characterized by specificity.

Because of the small overlap between motor dexterity tests, there are no general measures of motor ability such as the general intelligence tests supply for intellectual functions.  Motor tests are thus of relatively little use in vocational counseling.  They are most legitimately used in industrial selection where the job is simple, requires a definite set of motor skills, and is highly dependent on speed.  Among jobs of this kind are those in production-line work, sewing-machine operation, and packaging.

Motor dexterity tests show at best only moderate predictive validity for most situations in which they are used (see Tables 11-1 to 11-4).  However, if they

**FIGURE 11-4**    Bennett Hand-tool Dexterity Test (*Reproduced by permission of The Psychological Corporation.*)

**FIGURE 11-5**     Complex Coordination Test (*Reproduced by permission of the U.S. Air Force.*)

are used in conjunction with other ability tests, they often add a small, but important, increment to the overall validity of the battery. Motor tests tend to be more valid when they are made to resemble the actual machine or instrument which is featured on the job. Tests designed in this way are called *job miniatures*. If the job is that of lathe operator in a machine shop, the best motor test would employ a miniature lathe with the same kinds of dials, handles, and controls that appear on the real lathe. During World War II, the Army Air Force used a variety of motor tests for the selection of pilot trainees. The Complex Coordination Test, which resembles most closely what the pilot actually does, generally proved to be one of the most valid instruments.

## mechanical aptitude

Mechanical ability is popularly thought of as concerning the making and fixing of things, as distinct from clerical, sales, administrative, and professional abilities. In general, we speak of mechanical ability in relation to *trades* and various levels of skilled work. There is no fine dividing line between mechanical occupations and those which are not mechanical. Some occupations that most of us would classify as mechanical are those of a plumber, carpenter, automobile mechanic, and boatbuilder.

There is no one type of test function which underlies mechanical work to the same extent that the general intelligence tests relate to schoolwork. In order satisfactorily to predict a particular mechanical job, a range of different kinds of tests must be used in a battery. Different combinations of tests are usually needed for different jobs. Some of the kinds of tests that have proved useful in the prediction of success at mechanical work and in vocational guidance are described in the following sections.

### Intellectual ability

The fact that an individual is involved in making and fixing things does not mean that intelligence is an unimportant attribute. When it is possible to do so, either a battery of the major intellectual factors or at least a general intelligence test should be tried as a predictor. The spatial and perceptual factors

**TABLE 11-1**    Correlations of ability test scores with measures of job performance

| TEST | TYPE OF JOB | | | | |
| --- | --- | --- | --- | --- | --- |
| | Clerical | Protective service | Skilled trade | Semi-skilled | Unskilled |
| General intelligence | .36 | .28 | .45 | .20 | .16 |
| Arithmetic | .42 | −.12 | . . . | .15 | |
| Number comparison | .28 | .25 | . . . | .15 | .15 |
| Spatial relations | .06 | . . . | .45 | .30 | .27 |
| Mechanical principles | . . . | . . . | .45 | .25 | |
| Finger dexterity | .22 | .20 | .21 | .30 | .05 |

SOURCE: *Adapted from Ghiselli & Brown, 1955.*

**TABLE 11-2**  Average validity coefficients of various aptitude tests for industrial occupations

| TYPE OF TEST | MECHANICAL REPAIRMEN | | ELECTRICAL WORKERS | | STRUCTURAL WORKERS | | PROCESSING WORKERS | | COMPLEX MACHINE OPERATORS | | MACHINING WORKERS | | AVERAGE, ALL TRADES AND CRAFTS | |
|---|---|---|---|---|---|---|---|---|---|---|---|---|---|---|
| | Train-ing | Prof-ciency | Train-ing | Prof-ciency | Train-ing | Prof-ciency | Train-ing | Prof-ciency | Train-ing | Prof-ciency | Train-ing | Prof-ciency | Train-ing | Prof-ciency |
| Intellectual: | | | | | | | | | | | | | | |
| Intelligence | .38 | .04 | .43 | .47 | .29 | .09 | .35 | .24 | .34 | .28 | .30 | .08 | .35 | .20 |
| Immediate memory | .30 | ... | .31 | ... | .13 | .13 | .31 | .15 | ... | .30 | .12 | -.02 | .23 | .17 |
| Substitution | ... | ... | ... | ... | .31 | ... | ... | ... | ... | .26 | .27 | .21 | .29 | .24 |
| Arithmetic | .40 | .19 | .45 | .07 | .30 | .15 | .35 | ... | ... | .29 | .33 | .20 | .37 | .18 |
| Number comparison | ... | ... | ... | ... | -.04 | .08 | .24 | .20 | .20 | .14 | .02 | ... | .07 | .11 |
| Name comparison | ... | ... | ... | ... | -.01 | .08 | .14 | ... | ... | .22 | -.02 | ... | .08 | .17 |
| Cancellation | ... | ... | ... | ... | ... | ... | ... | ... | ... | ... | .28 | | | |
| Spatial and perceptual: | | | | | | | | | | | | | | |
| Tracing | .21 | ... | .24 | .15 | ... | .30 | .17 | .24 | .22 | .19 | .21 | .06 | .21 | .19 |
| Location | .24 | ... | .24 | .23 | .23 | .23 | .24 | .21 | .28 | .25 | .24 | .04 | .25 | .22 |
| Pursuit | .17 | ... | .12 | .32 | ... | ... | ... | .17 | ... | .33 | ... | .01 | .15 | .21 |
| Spatial relations | .34 | .19 | .33 | .33 | .28 | .31 | .35 | .16 | .36 | .30 | .33 | .11 | .33 | .23 |
| Speed of perception | .40 | ... | .43 | ... | .29 | .35 | .34 | .19 | ... | ... | .35 | ... | .36 | .27 |
| Mechanical principles | .37 | .29 | .40 | ... | .31 | ... | .40 | ... | ... | .40 | .33 | .57 | .36 | .42 |
| Motor: | | | | | | | | | | | | | | |
| Tapping | -.01 | ... | ... | .19 | .20 | .18 | -.01 | ... | ... | .19 | .05 | .08 | .06 | .16 |
| Dotting | .20 | ... | ... | ... | .13 | .20 | .02 | ... | ... | .11 | .14 | .06 | .12 | .12 |
| Finger dexterity | .19 | .16 | .15 | .18 | .24 | .30 | .22 | .30 | .11 | .14 | .24 | .08 | .19 | .19 |
| Hand dexterity | .17 | .12 | ... | ... | ... | ... | ... | ... | ... | ... | ... | .29 | ... | ... |
| Arm dexterity | .08 | ... | ... | ... | ... | ... | ... | .32 | ... | ... | -.03 | .11 | .03 | .22 |

SOURCE: *Ghiselli & Brown, 1955, p. 234.*

**TABLE 11-3** Average validity coefficients of various aptitude tests for industrial occupations

| TYPE OF TEST | MACHINE TENDERS | | ASSEMBLERS | | INSPECTORS | | PACKERS AND WRAPPERS | | GROSS MANUAL | | OBSERVATIONAL | | AVERAGE, ALL MANIPULATIVE AND OBSERVATIONAL | |
|---|---|---|---|---|---|---|---|---|---|---|---|---|---|---|
| | Train-ing | Profi-ciency | Train-ing | Profi-ciency | Train-ing | Profi-ciency | Train-ing | Profi-ciency | Train-ing | Profi-ciency | Train-ing | Profi-ciency | Train-ing | Profi-ciency |
| **Intellectual:** | | | | | | | | | | | | | | |
| Intelligence | … | .16 | .02 | .22 | .19 | .35 | .22 | .13 | −.03 | .26 | … | … | .10 | .22 |
| Immediate memory | … | .17 | … | .06 | … | .14 | … | .24 | … | … | … | … | … | .13 |
| Substitution | … | .19 | … | .12 | … | −.01 | … | .16 | … | … | … | … | … | .12 |
| Arithmetic | … | .15 | .39 | .09 | … | .18 | .43 | .14 | … | … | … | … | .41 | .14 |
| Number comparison | … | .20 | … | .15 | … | −.02 | … | .13 | … | … | … | … | … | .12 |
| Name comparison | … | .17 | … | .10 | … | .17 | … | .20 | … | … | … | … | … | .16 |
| Cancellation | … | .25 | … | .36 | … | … | … | .24 | … | … | … | … | … | .28 |
| **Spatial and perceptual:** | | | | | | | | | | | | | | |
| Tracing | … | .16 | .16 | .18 | … | .20 | … | .12 | … | … | … | … | … | .17 |
| Location | … | .11 | .29 | .19 | .19 | .18 | … | .16 | … | … | … | … | .24 | .16 |
| Pursuit | … | .15 | .28 | .15 | .09 | .09 | … | .16 | … | … | … | … | .19 | .14 |
| Spatial relations | … | .11 | .24 | .15 | .27 | .24 | … | .13 | … | … | … | … | .24 | .16 |
| Speed of perception | … | … | .26 | .27 | .22 | … | .22 | … | … | … | … | … | .24 | … |
| Mechanical principles | … | … | … | .56 | … | .42 | … | … | … | … | … | … | … | .49 |
| **Motor:** | | | | | | | | | | | | | | |
| Tapping | … | .12 | .16 | .14 | .10 | .06 | … | .14 | … | … | … | … | .13 | .12 |
| Dotting | … | .15 | .22 | .15 | … | .06 | … | .13 | … | … | … | … | … | .12 |
| Finger dexterity | … | .15 | .44 | .25 | .00 | .14 | … | .08 | … | .15 | … | … | .22 | .15 |
| Hand dexterity | … | .23 | .50 | .14 | … | −.02 | … | .15 | … | … | … | … | … | .13 |
| Arm dexterity | … | .15 | .54 | .24 | … | .00 | … | .24 | … | .43 | … | … | … | .21 |

SOURCE: *Ghiselli & Brown, 1955, p. 234.*

**TABLE 11-4**    Average validity coefficients of various aptitude tests for protective occupations, service occupations, and vehicle operators

| TYPE OF TEST | PROTECTIVE OCCUPATIONS | | SERVICE OCCUPATIONS | | VEHICLE OPERATORS | |
|---|---|---|---|---|---|---|
| | *Training* | *Proficiency* | *Training* | *Proficiency* | *Training* | *Proficiency* |
| Intellectual: | | | | | | |
| *Intelligence* | .46 | .26 | .50 | .07 | .18 | .14 |
| *Immediate memory* | .28 | .26 | | | | |
| *Arithmetic* | .30 | .08 | .59 | −.11 | .14 | .04 |
| *Number comparison* | ... | .25 | ... | .14 | | |
| *Name comparison* | ... | .36 | ... | −.17 | | |
| *Cancellation* | ... | ... | ... | −.27 | | |
| Spatial and perceptual: | | | | | | |
| *Location* | ... | ... | ... | ... | ... | .18 |
| *Spatial relations* | .33 | .04 | .42 | ... | .21 | |
| *Speed of perception* | .30 | ... | ... | ... | .08 | |
| *Mechanical principles* | .41 | .20 | ... | ... | .36 | .21 |
| Motor: | | | | | | |
| *Tapping* | ... | ... | ... | ... | ... | .32 |
| *Dotting* | ... | ... | ... | ... | ... | .28 |
| *Finger dexterity* | .19 | | | | | |
| *Hand dexterity* | ... | ... | ... | −.09 | | |
| *Arm dexterity* | ... | ... | ... | −.01 | | |
| *Simple reaction time* | ... | ... | ... | ... | ... | .27 |
| *Complex reaction* | ... | ... | ... | ... | ... | .35 |

SOURCE: *Ghiselli & Brown, 1955, p, 229.*

are very useful in predicting success in many mechanical jobs. Some tests embodying these functions will be considered in the subsequent discussion. However, it is important to consider the verbal, numerical, and reasoning factors as well in the prediction of success in mechanical work. Because general intelligence tests are composed mainly of these factors, a good general intelligence test is often one of the best predictors of job success (see Tables 11-1 to 11-5).

General intelligence tests tend to be more predictive of how well the individual will do in job training than of how well he will perform subsequently on the job. This is probably due to the fact that the training phase requires more abstract ability. In many cases the training program involves classroom-like procedures, the reading of materials, and the learning of machine operations. Success at activities of this sort is what intelligence tests predict best.

Predictor tests in general tend to correlate more highly with performance in training than with later job performance because, as a rule, performance is more reliably measured in training than on the job. Progress in training is usually graded more carefully. There is a greater opportunity to observe the

**TABLE 11-5**       Minimum mental ages for several jobs

| MENTAL AGE, YEARS | BOYS | GIRLS |
|---|---|---|
| 5 | Dishwasher | Sewer (simple patterns) |
| 6 | Mixer of cement | Vegetable parer<br>Mangle operator |
| 7 | Freight handler<br>Painter (rough work) | Crocheter (open mesh)<br>Cross stitcher |
| 8 | Shoe repairer (simple tasks)<br>Haircutting and shaving<br>Gardener | Hand-iron operator<br>Scarf-loom operator<br>Dressmaker (not including pattern work) |
| 9 | Foot-power printing-press operator | Fancy-basket maker |
| 10 | Mattress and pillow maker<br>Sign painter<br>Painter (shellacking and varnishing) | Cook (simpler dishes)<br>Sweater-machine operator<br>Launderer |
| 11 | Storekeeper<br>Greenhouse attendant | Librarian's assistant<br>Power sealer in cannery |

SOURCE: *Beckman, 1930.*

worker, and in many cases achievement tests are used to assess progress in training.

The general intelligence tests tend to be more predictive of success in high-skill than in low-skill jobs. That is, validities are usually higher for jobs such as that of electrical technician or complex machine operator than for jobs such as that of truck driver or furniture mover. The difference in validity is probably due to the increased importance of abstract ability in more highly skilled work. In selecting people for unskilled work, the problem is to set up minimum standards of intelligence rather than to seek persons of high intelligence (see Table 11-5).

## Spatial and perceptual tests

A wide variety of mechanical work requires the spatial and perceptual factors which were described in Chapter 9. The automobile mechanic needs *spatial orientation* in his work. In a typical job situation he is lying under the automobile and must remove a nut from the engine above him. The nut is slanted at a 45-degree angle, and he must remove it with a wrench that has two joints. He must orient himself spatially to the complex of angles and movements in order to do such work. In draftsmanship, it is necessary to portray three-dimensional objects on two-dimensional pieces of paper. In some drawings the objects must be shown in tilted positions or partially disassembled. Spatial ability, both *spatial orientation* and *visualization*, is required to work as a draftsman and at many other jobs.

One of the best-known spatial tests for mechanical aptitude is the Minnesota Paper Form Board Test (Likert & Quasha, 1948). It is a useful predictor of grades in shop courses, supervisors' ratings of workmanship, objective production records, and many other measures of mechanical performance (see Figure 11-6).

Perceptual ability is required in a variety of jobs. The *perceptual speed* factor has been used most often as a predictor, but it is likely that the other perceptual factors will eventually find their place in vocational guidance and job selection. The individual who sits by a fast-moving conveyor belt and looks for flaws in manufactured products uses perceptual ability. Any job in which it is necessary to detect aspects of a visual scene requires perceptual ability to some extent.

Examples of perceptual tests can be found in some of the multifactor batteries which were discussed in Chapter 9. Some tests designed specifically for industrial selection will be described in the section on clerical aptitude. (See Tables 11-1 to 11-4 for typical validities.)

### Motor dexterity

The kinds of motor tests which were discussed earlier in this chapter are often featured in mechanical aptitude batteries. Motor tests were discussed in a separate section because they are involved in a number of aptitudes other than

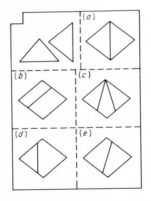 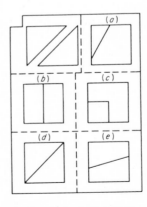

**FIGURE 11-6** Sample items from the Revised Minnesota Paper Form Board Test. For each item, the subject must choose the figure which would result if the pieces in the first section were assembled. (Reproduced by permission. Copyright 1941, renewed 1969 by The Psychological Corporation, New York, N.Y. All rights reserved.)

mechanical aptitude, for example, athletic aptitudes.  (See Tables 11-1 to 11-4 for typical validities.)

## Mechanical comprehension

Among the most successful tests of mechanical aptitude are those designed to measure the mastery of mechanical principles, or the ability to reason with mechanical problems.  In a typical problem, a truck driver is rushing medical supplies to a fire-damaged town.  He discovers that his truck is about an inch too tall to clear a bridge leading to the town.  What should he do?  The answer is to let some air out of the tires.  As another example, a motorist must remove a boulder which blocks the road.  He finds a long, stout pole to do the job.  He must then decide whether to use the pole as a pry or a lever.  He can construct a lever by balancing the pole on a rock placed between the boulder and himself (the lever exerts more force than a pry).  After deciding to use the lever action with the rock as a balancer (a *fulcrum*), he must then decide where to place the balancer (rock) and how to exert his strength best against the pole.  As a third example, a hoist is being built to lift tree trunks into the bed of a truck.  A system of gears and chains is set up to transfer the power from an electric motor to the hoist.  It must be decided how large the different gears should be to give the desired power to the hoist.

The three problems above are typical of those found in mechanical comprehension tests.  Tests of this kind tend to range over several ability factors.  Because of the paucity of factor-analytic studies of mechanical comprehension tests, it is not always possible to say just what a particular test measures.  Some of them emphasize the spatial factors, which are prominently involved in many tests of mechanical aptitude.  Other functions which appear in some mechanical comprehension tests are *numerical facility*, various aspects of the reasoning factors, and familiarity with tools and machinery.  Examples of mechanical comprehension tests are the Bennett Mechanical Comprehension Test (Bennett, 1948, 1951; see Figure 11-7), the Mechanical Reasoning Test of the DAT (discussed in Chapter 9), and the SRA Mechanical Aptitude Test (Richardson, Bellows, Henry, and Company, Inc., 1950).

## Mechanical information

One of the most useful measures for the selection of skilled and semiskilled workers is a test of information, or knowledge, about tools and machinery.  For example, a set of questions like the following would be useful in the selection of automobile mechanics:

1. What is a torque converter?
2. What is a ratchet?
3. Where is the "needle valve" in an automobile?

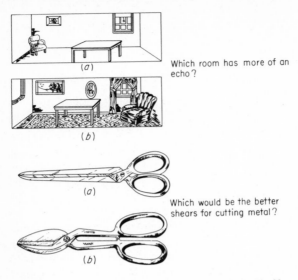

Which room has more of an echo?

Which would be the better shears for cutting metal?

**FIGURE 11-7**    Sample items from the Bennett Mechanical Comprehension Test, Form AA (*Reproduced by permission.    Copyright 1940, renewed 1967 by The Psychological Corporation, New York, N.Y. All rights reserved.*)

4. What source of power is used to run the alternator in most automobiles?
5. How do you recognize "preignition"?

Information tests can be constructed to measure either general knowledge of mechanical work or knowledge of one particular job.    It is usually the case that a test constructed specifically for one job, such as television repairman, will be more predictive than a test of knowledge in general about mechanical work. However, the test which is constructed specifically for one job is likely to be useful only for selecting personnel for that job or for closely related jobs.    Also, because of the specific knowledge which the instrument measures, it is of little use in vocational guidance, where it is usually necessary to measure broad functions rather than highly specialized information.    A more general measure of mechanical knowledge is often useful in vocational guidance.

## Analysis of mechanical aptitude tests

A sufficient personnel-selection program usually requires a careful study of the particular industrial setting.    The diversity of psychological functions required by different jobs makes it necessary to try out a range of tests to find the ones that will work well in practice.    Also, it is often necessary to invent and construct tests for particular jobs.

Few of the mechanical aptitude tests have been studied as extensively as the tests of intellectual ability.    Consequently, it is usually necessary to perform considerable research in the job setting to determine the utility of particular tests. In few cases have norms for the tests been obtained on a sufficiently representative sample to allow their use as dependable guides. It is generally more meaningful to obtain local norms for particular personnel selection or school programs.

Mechanical aptitude tests have modest validity for many different jobs, the amount varying considerably with the job. The seemingly small validities for some jobs should be regarded from a number of standpoints. Primarily there is the possibility that formal abilities such as those measured in psychological tests have little to do with job success. Another possibility is that the criterion of job success is unreliable and consequently cannot be predicted. If the criterion is determined only from the sketchy impressions of foremen and managers, it is seldom very reliable. It is meaningful in this instance to make the correction for attenuation as discussed in Chapter 5, correcting for the unreliability of the criterion. Because of the unreliability inherent in most criteria, mechanical aptitude tests are often more valid than is apparent from the correlation coefficients. The third point to consider is that the modest to low individual validities should not obscure the fact that a combination of several tests in a battery will often produce reasonably good predictive efficiency.

## clerical and stenographic aptitudes

### Clerical aptitude

Clerical aptitude, as it will be discussed here, concerns the office clerk, the individual who deals with files, ledgers, accounts, and correspondence. The term "clerk" is much more general than this usage suggests, referring variously to grocery clerk, department store clerk, and even court clerk. *Perceptual speed* tests have a special importance in the prediction of clerical performance. Perceptual speed is involved in chores like proofreading letters, searching for particular accounts in a long list, and alphabetizing names.

A typical test which emphasizes perceptual speed is the Minnesota Clerical Test (Andrew & Paterson, 1946). The test is divided into two separately timed parts, Number Comparison and Name Comparison (see Figure 11-8). Retest reliabilities range from .85 to .91. Extensive validation research shows that correlations range up to .60 between the Minnesota Clerical Test and business school and job performance criteria. Other perceptual speed tests for clerical aptitude are the Clerical Speed and Accuracy Test of the DAT, the Clerical Perception Test of the GATB, and parts of the General Clerical Test (Psychological Corporation, 1950).

Perceptual speed is a necessary component of many clerical jobs, but other functions should be tested as well. *Verbal comprehension* is a desirable attribute, especially a knowledge of spelling and grammar. Clerical work often involves routine arithmetical operations, and therefore a test of numerical

66273894 _____ 66273984
527384578 _____ 527384578
New York World _____ New York World
Cargill Grain Co. _____ Cargil Grain Co.

If the two names or numbers of a pair are exactly alike, make a check mark on the line between them.

**FIGURE 11-8**     Sample items from the Minnesota Clerical Test (*Reproduced by permission. Copyright 1933, renewed 1961 by The Psychological Corporation, New York, N.Y. All rights reserved.*)

facility is likely to be a useful selection instrument. If the clerical job requires the use of accounting machines or other equipment, some of the motor dexterity tests may be of use. The DAT tests not only perceptual speed but also a variety of verbal and arithmetical abilities; hence, it would probably serve well in the selection of office clerks. The General Clerical Test (Psychological Corporation, 1950) is a short battery designed to cover the major functions required in clerical work. Scores on nine subtests are combined to form clerical, numerical, and verbal scores.

### Stenographic ability

The selection of stenographers is best made on the basis of specific job requirements. Typing and shorthand ability are the major requirements in most stenographic jobs. Therefore, proficiency tests in these skills offer a sound basis for the selection of stenographers (for typical tests, see Bisbee, 1933; Blackstone & McLaughlin, 1932; H. Seashore & Bennett, 1946; L. L. Thurstone, 1922). Here, as in many other testing problems, the needs of a selection program are not always the same as those of the vocational guidance situation. In vocational guidance, before the individual has had an opportunity to test himself in specialized training or on the job, some prediction must be made as to how well he will perform. Although an insufficient amount of research has been done on the aptitude for stenographic work to allow us to speak with certainty, the most promising attributes seem to be the motor skills involved in typing, verbal comprehension and language usage, and interest in stenographic work.

### artistic aptitudes

The nature of art and artistic ability has been a matter of interest to psychologists for well over a hundred years, since before the time of Fechner. In spite of this prolonged interest, the measurement of artistic ability lags behind the testing of other ability functions. This is due in part to practical considerations. There has always been a more urgent need for intellectual and vocational tests than for tests of artistic ability. Research on classifying men in the Armed Forces, testing children in school, and selecting men in industry has won financial support because of the immediate gains to be expected. Although the study of artistic ability offers some practical advantages, it has never promised a sufficient commercial market to attract large amounts of research.

Another reason why tests of artistic ability lag behind is that the functions to be measured are intrinsically complex. In this area, it is very difficult to distinguish aptitude from achievement. The accomplished musician or painter can be judged by what he currently does, but it is difficult to find the underlying aptitudes that give one child an advantage over another in terms of eventual artistic accomplishment.

Good art is largely a matter of time and place. Chinese music sounds cacophonous to us, and no doubt much of our music seems strange to the Chinese. Some primitive music centers almost entirely on the drum and other percussion instruments. The complex rhythmic patterns used are too elusive for the "civilized" ear. We lack the aesthetic appreciation that the primitive has for his music, just as he would be baffled by a symphony orchestra. The delicate sensitivities of a Japanese poem may be lost on an Occidental audience. We might cite many other examples to show that art is a matter of values. Different people have different values, and values change over the ages.

Different abilities are involved in the production of art and in the appreciation of art. The music critic may not be a musician at all; the art historian may never have painted. Different abilities are required in the production of different kinds of artwork.

The measurement of artistic aptitude evolves into several components. For producing works of art, there are probably some underlying abilities that cut across different times and different cultures. Most painting requires the ability to make line drawings, to combine colors, and to achieve properties of "balance." In musical ability there are the basic sensory skills of tonal memory, sense of pitch, and recognition of rhythms, which to some extent cut across different kinds of musical production.

Another attribute which can be tested is the appreciation of art forms. Appreciation is dependent on the values in a particular culture and on the individual's knowledge and acceptance of those values. Finally, tests can be made of how well the individual can produce particular art forms; such achievement is dependent on both his initial aptitude and the training that he has had.

## musical aptitude

### Seashore measures

One of the oldest and most widely used musical tests is the Seashore Measures of Musical Talents (C. E. Seashore, Lewis, & Saetveit, 1939). The test stimuli are reproduced on phonograph records, which can be used for the testing of moderate-sized groups of subjects. The battery includes the following subtests:

1. *Pitch Discrimination.*    The subject is asked whether the second of two tones is higher or lower than the first. The items are made progressively more difficult by decreasing the difference in pitch between the pairs of tones.
2. *Loudness Discrimination.*    The subject judges which of two tones is louder.
3. *Time Discrimination.*    One tone is presented for a longer period of time than another. The subject judges which of the two tones is longer.
4. *Rhythm Judgment.*    The subject judges whether two rhythmic patterns are the same or different.
5. *Timbre Judgment.*    The subject judges whether or not two tones are of the same musical quality.
6. *Tonal Memory.*    Two series of notes are played. In the second series one of the notes is altered. The subject judges which of the notes is different.

Scores on the subtests correlate near zero on the average with intelligence tests (P. R. Farnsworth, 1931). The subtest scores are partly independent, with median intercorrelations ranging from .48 to .25 for different samples (P. R. Farnsworth, 1931). Split-half reliability estimates for the subtests range from .62 to .88. Rhythm and timbre are the least reliable. If, as is often done, the six subtests are added to form one general measure, high reliability can be expected for the test. Except for large differences in scores, the subtests are not sufficiently reliable for considering differential aptitudes within the test.

Scores on the Seashore test are affected very little by age. Similar norms are found for grammar school, high school, and adult populations. Although the research results are somewhat contradictory (P. R. Farnsworth, 1931; C. E. Seashore, 1938; Stanton, 1935), it seems that scores are affected only slightly by musical training. These two findings taken together suggest that the Seashore subtests measure some basic aptitudinal functions which are partly inherited. The larger question is whether the aptitudinal functions involved in the tests are of any importance in predicting musical accomplishment.

An insufficient amount of research has been done with the Seashore test to allow us to speak with firmness about its predictive utility. Modest to small correlations have been found with grades in music classes and with teachers' ratings of musical ability (Drake, 1933; Highsmith, 1929; Larson, 1930; Mursell, 1937). The test differentiates moderately well between students who complete specialized musical training and those who drop out. It is reasonable to think that at the level of specialized musical training, most of the persons who do poorly on the Seashore type of measures will have already been eliminated.

A number of persons have argued that the Seashore measures do not involve skills that are very similar to those used in the actual production of music. The Seashore subtests measure certain types of sensory discrimination which might be necessary for musical ability but not sufficient.  The Seashore test would be most valuable in helping parents decide whether their children would be likely to profit from extensive musical training.  It could save parents considerable expense and would spare the neighbors from having to hear little Susan grind away for years at an instrument she will never master.  At present the Seashore test is difficult to administer below the age of ten, and the predictive validity of the test at younger ages is not known.

### Wing test

The Wing Standardized Tests of Musical Intelligence (Wing, 1948) were designed to involve as closely as possible the skills required for musical production and appreciation.  Like the Seashore test, the Wing test uses phonograph recordings.  The following seven functions are tested:

1. *Chord analysis.*    Judging the number of notes in a chord.
2. *Pitch change.*    Judging the direction of change of notes in a repeated chord.
3. *Memory.*    Judging which note is changed in a repeated melodic phrase.
4. *Rhythmic accent.*    Judging which performance of a musical phrase has the better rhythmic pattern.
5. *Harmony.*    Judging which of two harmonies is better for a particular melody.
6. *Intensity.*    Judging which of two pieces has the more appropriate pattern of dynamics, or emphasis.
7. *Phrasing.*    Judging which of two versions has the more appropriate phrasing.

The first three subtests measure complex sensory abilities.  The other four concern the aesthetic value of different compositions.  The subtest scores are added to form one general measure of musical aptitude.

The Wing test has received a favorable response from teachers of music, who feel that the test covers many of the skills that are important in musical training.  Little is known about how well the test can predict available criteria. Wing (1948) reports correlations of .60 and above between the test and teachers' ratings of musical ability.  It is possible that the Wing test will prove to be a better differentiator of musical talent at higher levels of ability than the Seashore.  The Wing test might then be useful in the guidance and selection of students who want to go on from some initial musical training to more advanced training.

### Analysis of musical aptitude tests

Not enough research has been done to say how well the current tests work. A particular problem is the dearth of adequate criteria of musical accomplishment.  School grades in the history, techniques, and general knowledge of music are the most reliable indices, but these are not the same as artistry in musical production.  Judgment of the actual mastery of musical instruments must necessarily be based on the impressions of teachers and other persons, and impressions of this kind usually have only modest reliability. Even if there are some difficulties in validating the instruments, much more research should be done to determine how well they work.

The tests which were discussed in the previous sections are all, strictly speaking, tests of judgment. That is, the subject is not required actually to play an instrument but only to listen and judge what he hears. However, some of the complex judgments involved seem to underlie the skills that are needed in musical production. It is likely that other types of tests could be used in conjunction with the conventional measures to obtain a better estimate of musical ability. Motor skills are involved in playing most musical instruments, the piano being an outstanding example. Motor tests might be profitably used in the prediction of musical accomplishment. Although intelligence tests correlate very little with the available musical tests, this does not mean that they would be of no use in predicting musical accomplishment. It would be expected that intelligence and, more generally, the factors which underlie differential aptitude tests would be useful in the prediction of course grades in musical curricula and in special music schools.

It is likely that an individual's interest in musical work will be as predictive of later success as tests of the ability type. Two such interest tests are the Farnsworth Scales (P. R. Farnsworth, 1949) and the Seashore-Hevner Tests for Attitude toward Music (R. H. Seashore & Hevner, 1933). The small amount of research that has been done indicates some promise for tests of musical interest.

## graphic art

### McAdory test

The field of graphic-art testing has been dominated by a particular type of item, in which a "masterpiece" is compared with one or more altered versions of the same work. One of the oldest tests of this kind is the McAdory Art Test (McAdory, 1929), which came out in 1929. It is now of only historical interest. The test contains pictures of 72 works of art covering a wide variety of then contemporary art forms, ranging from pictures of furniture and automobiles to works of art in museums. Four versions of each work are given; these differ in shape, arrangement, shading, and use of color. The subject is required to rank-order the four versions in terms of his preferences.

Items for the McAdory test were selected on the basis of the judgments of experts, including teachers, critics, and artists. Items were retained only if at least 64 percent of the judges agreed on the ranking of the four versions of each picture. A primary weakness of the test is its dependence on art values current at the time it was constructed. For example, taste in automobile design has obviously changed since 1929, as have preferences for furniture styles and even paintings.

Meier test

The Meier Art Judgment Test (Meier, 1942) is by far the most widely used test of art appreciation. It also uses the altered-version type of item. The test differs from the McAdory in that only one alternative version is given for each original work of art, and the items concern relatively timeless art master-pieces. The items are all in black and white. The altered version of each masterpiece is meant to destroy the aesthetic organization. In a typical altered version, one figure is moved to the side in such a way as to change the balance of the painting (see Figure 11-9).

The initial selection of items was made on the basis of expert judgments. Items on which there was high agreement among 25 experts were retained. The items were further pared down in terms of internal-consistency statistics.

**FIGURE 11-9**    Illustrative items from Meier Art Judgment Test *(Reproduced by permission of Norman C. Meier.)*

Only those items showing a high correlation with the total score were placed in the final form.

Split-half reliabilities for the Meier test range from .70 to .84 in relatively homogeneous groups of subjects. Scores correlate only negligibly with traditional measures of intelligence. Only a small amount of research has been done to determine how well the test predicts available criteria. It has been shown that the test differentiates art students from non-art students and different art students in terms of the amount of training that they have had. A correlation of .46 was found with the grades of 50 art students (Kinter, 1933). Correlations ranging from .40 to .69 were found with ratings of creative artistic talent (Carroll, 1933; Morrow, 1938).

### Graves test

The Graves Design Judgment Test (Graves, 1948, 1951) consists entirely of abstract designs, which makes it as independent as possible of traditional and contemporary art values (see Figure 11-10). Each test item consists of either

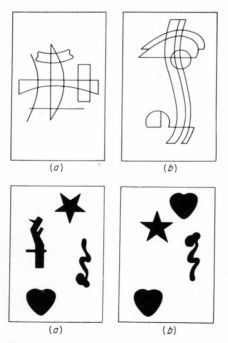

(a)               (b)

(a)               (b)

**FIGURE 11-10**     Illustrative items from Graves Design Judgment Test (Reproduced by permission. Copyright 1946 by The Psychological Corporation, New York, N.Y. All rights reserved.)

two or three versions of the same basic design.   The altered version or versions were constructed to violate accepted aesthetic principles.   The judgments of art teachers and art students were used to select the best 90 items from an original list of 150.   Split-half reliability estimates range from .81 to .93.   Although the Graves test gives promise of being a useful measure, only a small amount of empirical work has been done with it.

## Worksample tests

A number of tests have been designed to measure how well individuals can actually produce graphic art.

Typical of these is the Horn Art Aptitude Inventory (Horn, 1944; Horn & Smith, 1945), which includes the following subtests (see Figure 11-11):

1. *Scribble Exercise.*    Making outline drawings of 20 simple objects
2. *Doodle Exercise.*    Making abstract compositions out of simple geometric forms
3. *Imagery.*    Working from a given set of lines to a completed composition

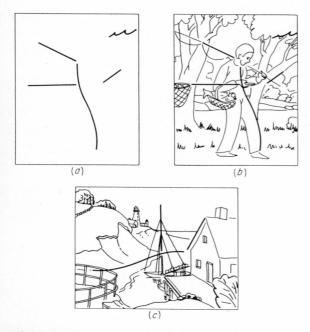

FIGURE 11-11    Sample item from the imagery test of the Horn Art Aptitude Inventory.  The subject is shown only the lines in rectangle (a), from which he is to make a drawing.   Examples of completed drawings are shown in (b) and (c).    (From Horn & Smith, 1945, p. 351; reproduced by permission of the American Psychological Association.)

Other tests which are concerned largely with the production of art are the Knauber Art Ability Test (Knauber, 1935b) and the Lewerenz Tests in Fundamental Abilities of Visual Art (Lewerenz, 1927).

The worksample tests must rely on the judgments of graders. Product scales are used, in which a particular drawing is compared with a standard set. Sample drawings are available for each score level. The grader gives a score in accordance with the apparent nearness in quality of the subject's drawings to the product-scale examples. In spite of the apparent subjectivity of the scoring system, moderately high reliabilities are reported for tests of the worksample type (Horn, 1944; Horn & Smith, 1945; Knauber, 1935a, 1935b). Current evidence indicates that the worksample tests predict course grades as well as the appreciation tests and do a better job of predicting teachers' ratings of creative ability (Barrett, 1949; Horn & Smith, 1945).

### Analysis of graphic-art tests

The difficulties of defining and measuring graphic-art aptitude are even greater than those of defining and measuring musical aptitude. Since the graphic arts are more dependent on fashion, criteria of accomplishment are weaker; hence the underlying aptitudes are more difficult to determine. Unlike the sensory discrimination functions in musical aptitude, the current measures of graphic-art aptitude appear to depend heavily on training. Consequently, they are of less use in the early guidance of prospective art students, where all tests of art aptitude would seem to have their most promising use.

Current tests are biased toward certain cultural groups. For example, it was found (Steggerda, 1936) that much lower scores on the McAdory test are made by Navajo Indian children than by children in New York City, in spite of the fact that the Navajo culture has a highly developed art form of its own. The available tests appear in most cases to be clever and well designed, but the paucity of research which characterizes the testing of artistic abilities leaves many questions about how well the tests work in practice. Perhaps future factor-analytic studies of graphic-art tests will lead to a better knowledge of the underlying functions and how they can best be measured.

## creativity

So far we have not discussed the abilities which are involved in truly creative work, as evidenced in the work of leading scientists, scholars, and artists. What types of children grow into creative adults? What types of instruments can be used to measure creativity? What can the teacher do to promote the creative potentials of all children? In spite of the obvious importance of these questions, firm answers are not yet available. Considerable theorizing and research have been done on creativity, and some of the results are quite promising, but much more needs to be done before we can speak with certainty about the circumstances that surround and promote human creativity. This section will discuss some of the factors which are currently thought to determine creativity.

## What is creativity?

In spite of the widespread use of the term, people seldom stop to state what they mean by "creativity." Implicit in most discussions is the notion of *creative products*; that is, before we can talk meaningfully about the creativity of individuals, we must talk about the creativity of some of their productions. We first look at what the person has done (whatever it may be) and then judge the creativity of the accomplishment. Until some products are available to be judged, it is rather meaningless to argue about the creative abilities of particular individuals.

If creative products are essential to judge creative ability, what types of products meet the standards? More than sheer "goodness" is usually required before a person's work can be labeled "creative." For example, most of us would not use the word "creative" to describe (1) a well-performed surgical operation, (2) the solution of a difficult mathematical problem, or (3) the construction of an excellent piece of furniture. In describing these accomplishments, we would more likely use terms such as "highly skilled" or "knowledgeable."

In essence, the word "creative" concerns the *invention* of something, the production of something that is new, rather than the accumulation of skills or the exercise of book-learned knowledge. Creativity concerns what people *add* to the store of knowledge which was on hand before they came upon the scene. Of course, the "inventions" of children more often than not are rediscoveries of existing pieces of knowledge, but if this knowledge is not available to them from books, class discussion, and other sources, such rediscoveries constitute genuine creative acts. Also, children are sometimes creative in the sense of actually adding to the existing store of knowledge.

Conceivably, creativity could be manifested in anything one did; however, here we shall be concerned primarily with creativity as manifested in (1) scientific research, including the social and biological as well as the physical sciences; (2) scholarly work, such as in philosophy and history; and (3) artistic productions. It is not known whether the traits that make for creative ability in one of these three areas would lead to success in the others, and it may be that different types of home and school environments are necessary to nurture creative people for the three areas. Current research evidence suggests that there is enough common ground among different types of creativity so that we can talk about traits that make for creativity in general and environments that help promote creativity in general.

## traits relating to creativity

What are some of the characteristics of the creative person? Because, as was said previously, it is necessary to witness creative products in order to judge creativity, it is difficult to judge the creative ability of students, particularly that of students in the elementary grades. Few obviously creative works come from children. We may regard some of their products as clever or unusual, but seldom do they make a real imprint on the world. Consequently, determining whether or not a student is actually creative often involves a considerable amount of guesswork. In children, creativity is best judged by the tendency to be original in many ways and on many occasions rather than on the basis of a few obviously creative productions of a kind that we associate with adult creativity. For example, the child who has creative potential as a scientist is not likely to manifest his creativity by actually producing an important new law of physics, but rather by showing unusual insight into the implications of simple physical principles and by having many clever (for his age) ideas about how such principles relate to daily life. Similarly, the child who has creative potential as a writer is not likely to manifest his gift by writing a best-selling novel, but rather by showing an unusual sensitivity to the meaning and use of words in themes and poems.

Because of the complexity of the issues involved, solid research on creativity is difficult to perform. Consequently, only a small store of information is available about the psychological traits that relate to creativity and the most effective methods for predicting eventual creativity in life. Also, some studies of creativity provide contradictory findings. For these reasons, what is said in this chapter about the nature of creativity and the measurement of creative potential depends heavily on the author's personal interpretation of existing research reports. (Unfortunately, no up-to-date, comprehensive reference book on creativity is available.)

In discussing the characteristics that often go along with creativity, it will be necessary to talk about a "type" of person. Of course, types are only handy fictions that facilitate discussion. It is important to keep in mind that many creative persons will be exceptions to the rule. Some will have none of the characteristics which will be discussed, and the majority will "go in opposite directions" on at least one of them. The following characteristics are currently *thought* to typify creative people *as a group*.

### General ability

How well do creative people score on tests of general ability, such as those discussed in Chapter 10? Some suggest, or apparently assume, that people who score only average, or even below average, may possess outstanding creative ability. All the evidence indicates that this is definitely a misconception. Although *all* people who perform well on tests of general ability are not creative, it is incorrect to leap from this observation to the conclusion that some people who do poorly on tests of general ability are quite creative.  By any standard one chooses to apply, those persons who are judged to be creative, as a group, score moderately high on tests of general ability.  Most creative people are in the top 10 or 15 percent on intelligence tests.  Almost never does one find a person who is average, or below average, on tests of general ability whose products strongly indicate creative potential.

The real question is why only *some* of the people with high IQs are creative.  Rather than make a distinction between the intelligent and the creative, it is more appropriate to make a distinction between the intelligent but not creative and the intelligent and creative.  Apparently, to be creative it is necessary to have a moderately high level of ability as represented by conventional tests of general ability, but beyond that point such tests are not indicative of creative potential.

One of the difficulties in untangling the difference between intelligence and creativity is that the so-called intelligence tests have usurped a name that has broad connotations.  Tests of general ability require mainly an *understanding* of questions and problems; they do not necessarily relate highly to *invention* and *discovery*.

### Success in school

Another misconception is that many creative persons do only average school-work or even quite poor schoolwork.  The research evidence strongly suggests that this is not true.  The studies show that those persons who are judged to be creative, as a group, perform rather well in school.  They may not make all A's, but it would be quite rare to find a creative person who did not generally do at least B work.  Although creative people are often bored by the routines of schoolwork and are distracted by their own special interests, they usually have sufficient energy and general ability to carry them to at least moderate success in the classroom.

### Introspectiveness

Creative children typically like to think, and they enjoy having some time to be alone with their thoughts.  They are not always the happy extroverts which, for some reason, we tend to cultivate.  They may appear absentminded and distracted, and, of all sins, they do not always listen when the teacher talks.  Because of their introspectiveness, creative children are seldom voted "most liked" by their peers, and they may not enjoy the same social life in and out of school as their less creative classmates.

### Adjustment

By ordinary standards (which perhaps we should revise) the creative child is often not as well adjusted as his noncreative peers.  The creative child tends to be different in many ways. His searching mind goes far beyond that of his peers, and quite often beyond that of his teachers. In a sense, he knows too much—too much to take the "childishness" of his peers seriously and too much to take seriously all that the teacher says and does. The creative child is in much the same position that the college graduate would be in if he were required to sit in a fourth-grade class and take it all seriously. He would be rather maladjusted in his surroundings.

Perhaps creative children as a group would not appear somewhat maladjusted if we were better able to recognize creativity and better able to nourish it when we found it. However, at the present time, by present standards, children who are thought to be creative tend to be, variously, shy, nervous, recalcitrant, and socially awkward.

In addition to a tendency to be somewhat maladjusted, creative children tend to possess some other personality characteristics. One of these is that they are not strongly influenced by the values and standards of others. They typically consider their own values to be best and will stick to them regardless of what others think. They often maintain a cynical view of what the teacher and the other students value, which serves to isolate them from the group.

Another characteristic of many creative children is that they are very flexible in their ideas. They can change their minds quite readily, without feeling a strong need to have a "pat answer." They are always exploring new ways of looking at issues and are not very disturbed if one point of view proves to be faulty. In contrast, most intelligent but not creative children look for, and want, pat answers and are disturbed by finding that a seemingly well-established point of view must be abandoned. To the creative child, thinking is like a game of chess, in which the game itself is enjoyable and long periods of contemplation before each move are savored. To the noncreative child, thinking is, at best, a means to an end. He is happiest when the issue is settled and done and is glad that he has to think no more. The noncreative child wants to learn "how to do it," "what the facts are," and "how the problems are to be solved." The creative child has a less passive (and, in a sense, less disciplined) intellect. He dwells on what he considers to be intrinsically interesting, goes off on fascinating tangents, and soars above the mental level of the issue at hand. These are more reasons why he is different, and being so different he is likely to be labeled as odd, unfriendly, and troublesome.

Creative children usually have a great deal of faith in their own ideas. Because they actually do more thinking, and do it better than the people around them, they soon learn to trust their own ideas. In the classroom this often makes them appear unreasonably stubborn.

There is a type of teacher (rare, we hope) who is concerned primarily with convincing students of his vast store of knowledge. Such an inflexible fellow is disturbed by the creative child who thinks that his own ideas are better than those of the teacher. This is why the creative child is seldom made teacher's pet. When asked to rate the likability of their students, teachers typically show a preference for intelligent but not creative children over intelligent and creative children.

## Home environments

Creative children tend to come from unusual home environments, and they typically are unusual in the sense that, by common standards, they are often bad. Studies of highly creative adults indicate that, as a group, few of them came from happy, well-structured home environments. Many creative children come from broken homes or from homes where either there is constant strife between the parents or the relationship is cold.

Some of the other ways in which the homelives of creative children tend to be unusual are (1) the mother spends much time away from home in vocational or avocational pusuits; (2) the child is rejected by one or both parents; (3) the father is poorly adjusted as a man and as a family member; (4) the family moves frequently, with the result that the child changes schools often; and (5) the child lives with foster parents or with only one parent.

Of course no creative child has a home environment characterized by all the bad features mentioned above, and because we are talking about group trends, many creative children do come from stable, happy homes. However, there is a tendency for there to be something unsavory about the home environment.

There is apparently some truth in the saying that "genius is born of misery." This is not necessarily so, one would hope, but too many creative people have unhappy beginnings to deny that the saying has some validity. Perhaps many creative children withdraw somewhat to escape the unpleasant features of their environments. They find pleasure in thought and fantasy that they do not find in their outside worlds. Thinking then becomes a habit which they carry with them all their lives. Conversely, it may be that many children who are intelligent but not creative are absorbed by the pleasant features of their external worlds; therefore, they have no need for, and derive little enjoyment from, retreating into their own thoughts. If these things are so (and, admittedly, there is much conjecturing here), some way must be found for using methods of training to bring out the creative potential in all children rather than depending on "misery" to bring out the best in some of them.

## measuring creativity

The measurement of creativity is still in its infancy. Consequently, the measures discussed in this section are only illustrative of the efforts which are currently being made.

## General ability

It must be remembered that even though all students who make relatively high scores on intelligence tests are not creative, the converse does not hold:

almost none of the students who make low scores on tests of general ability will prove to be creative.  Up to a point, then, tests of general ability are among the best predictors of creative ability.  The question does not concern whether students need relatively high IQs in order to be creative, but rather what they need *in addition* to high IQs.

## Personality characteristics

Personality characteristics are among the most important determiners of creative ability.  Some of the traits which apparently relate to creativity are (1) introversiveness, (2) flexibility of opinions, (3) intellectual self-confidence, (4) self-willed independence, and (5) immense energy for intellectual tasks.  Some of the methods which are used to measure these personality characteristics are (1) observations and ratings, (2) self-reports in personality inventories, and (3) projective tests.  More will be said about all these methods of attempting to measure personality characteristics in Chapters 12 and 13.  Suffice it to say that none of these is as effective as we would like.  Presently we have few truly satisfactory methods for measuring any personality characteristics, including those relating to creativity.  Until such time as we do have excellent methods for measuring those personality characteristics which relate to creativity, the approximate methods mentioned above will have to be used.

## Unusual uses

Supposedly one aspect of creativity is the ability to see new and unusual uses for old objects and methods.  This is illustrated by the pilot who, in a pioneering oceanic flight, thought of filling the wings of his plane with Ping-Pong balls to keep the craft afloat in case of engine failure over open water.  Most of us noncreative folk could look at a Ping-Pong ball for hours and not think of such a clever way to use it.  Of course, one such clever idea does not make a person creative.  The creative person is forever seeing clever, unusual uses for common objects and methods.

Test items can be composed to measure students' abilities to see unusual uses for objects and methods.  For example, students can be asked, "What are some uses that can be made of empty tin cans?"  Both the number and quality of answers are important.  The noncreative student will think of "carry water," "plant flowers," and "hold marbles" and then be at a loss to provide more answers.  The really creative child will produce a flood of answers, suggesting not only many ordinary uses such as those mentioned above but also such clever ones as "cut out the tops and bottoms and weld them together to make a stove chimney," "put them in the ground to make golf cups," and "cut holes in the bottoms and use them to spread grass seed."  Similar items can be composed relating to screwdrivers, paper clips, bottle caps, and many other objects.

## Consequences

One facet of creativity is the ability to see the many consequences that would follow from a particular action or event. For example, what would some of the effects be if the average temperature of the earth were raised by 10 degrees? Some obvious consequences would be that less heating would be needed in homes, there would be less need for winter clothing, and people could swim most of the year. Some more remote (and perhaps creative) responses would be that the polar ice cap would melt and flood many coastal cities, Eskimos would have to change their way of life drastically, and many new regions could be opened up to farming. Many other such items can be composed to measure the ability to visualize consequences.

## Original responses to specific events

One of the characteristics of many creative persons is that they are often able to produce quite clever slogans, captions for cartoons, and endings to stories. In these instances creative persons manifest the inventive side of verbal ability, which goes beyond the passive aspect that is traditionally measured in tests of vocabulary and reading comprehension. An illustrative item would be as follows. The student is asked to invent a clever title for a picture of a sleepy child standing near a worn-out tire. Noncreative students would suggest titles like "Off to Bed," "Who Is Going to Blow out the Candle?" and "School in the Morning." The creative student is likely to think of something quite clever, such as "Time to Retire" (item from Guilford, as presented in C. W. Taylor, 1961).

In another type of item, students are asked to supply clever endings to a sentence or a short narrative. Following is an example:

John walked through the snow and up the porch steps. After fumbling for his key and not finding it, he pushed against the door and found it was unlocked. Inside no one greeted him, and when he called, "I'm home," no one answered. With his eyes fixed on the light coming from an upstairs bedroom, he slowly climbed the stairs. As he reached the top stair, he stopped suddenly and said, "Oh, my goodness, _____ _____."

Noncreative students would complete the story with endings like "I forgot to let the dog in the house," "I meant to mail that letter," or "There's a ghost." More creative students would provide endings like "I took a bus home and left the family sitting in the car in front of my office" or "I don't live in a two-story house." Many other such items can be constructed to test the creative ability to supply unusually clever verbal responses.

Fluency

Apparently one aspect of creativity is the sheer fluency with which words, ideas, and solutions to problems are produced. One aspect of fluency was considered in Chapter 9: verbal fluency, which concerns the rapid production of words. An illustrative item would require students to produce as many words beginning with "s" as possible in two minutes' time. Although word fluency is only moderately well correlated with measures of general ability, it apparently does go along to some extent with measures of creativity.

Another type of fluency, one that apparently is related to creativity, is the ability to rapidly produce words in specific categories or words that bear specified relationships to one another. An item designed to test the former ability would require the student to quickly produce the names of objects that roll on wheels or the names of creatures that live in water. An item testing the latter would require him to produce words that mean much the same as a given word, e.g., synonyms for "intelligent," such as "smart," "bright," and "clever."

Another aspect of fluency is ideational fluency. Creative persons not only have better ideas but also have many more of them. Ideational fluency can be measured by counting the number of ideas and solutions which students produce. This can be done with respect to some of the traits mentioned above: unusual uses, consequences, and original responses. Besides scoring for cleverness, simple counts can be made of the number of responses produced.

In addition to scoring other types of creativity measures for the fluency of ideas, items can be constructed specifically for that purpose. An example is as follows:

> Imagine that you own a company which produces bicycles and that you want to make many improvements in your product. What changes would you make in the bicycles? What would you do to make them better? During the next five minutes write down as many improvements as you can. Try to give good ideas, and give as many of them as you can.

The number of different improvements listed would be one index of ideational fluency.

Apparently, the various types of fluency are very important for some types of creativity. Creative people typically have floods of ideas, most of which are impractical but a few of which are highly ingenious. Sometimes creative people are unable to evaluate the "good" and "bad" among their own ideas. This is why some creative people work better with a partner or as a member of a team. They are the "idea men" who must be supplemented by others who can carefully evaluate, experiment with, and test their productions.

It is a mistake to judge the creative abilities of either adults or children by the number of unworkable ideas they produce; rather, they should be judged by the number of ideas that do work.  Because of the typical fluency of creative people, they are bound to produce many "whacky" ideas along with their good ones.

Perhaps one of the reasons why more people are not creative is that they are not willing to let themselves be fluent, not willing to let themselves go mentally and produce a flood of ideas.  Because many such ideas are bound to appear silly to ourselves and others, we often stifle our thought processes rather than endure self-ridicule or the ridicule of others.  To be creative, a flood of ideas must be produced, and the bad ones must be accepted as a natural part of the process.

## Ingenious solutions to problems

Creativity concerns not only having many new and unusual ideas but also thinking of very clever ways to solve ordinary problems that occur in daily life.  One such ingenious solution to a problem was arrived at long ago during the construction of a church in New Orleans.  The water level in the ground was so high and the ground so soft that any ordinary foundation for the church would have soon collapsed.  The solution: Hundreds of bales of cotton were buried in the mud, and the foundation was laid over these.  The church, to this day, literally floats on bales of cotton.

Although it takes a skillful person, and takes him much time, test items can be composed to measure the ability to produce or recognize ingenious solutions to problems.

By its nature most people would think that creativity could not be measured with multiple-choice items.  Creativity concerns the invention of something.  In contrast, multiple-choice items usually concern the recognition of correct answers.  However, if the alternative responses contain only a key word or some letters in key words in the solution, multiple-choice items can actually measure inventiveness.  An example is as follows:

A farmer living in a remote region finds that a 2-foot length of pipe has burst in the series of pipes that carries water from the pump to the house and barn.  It is urgent that he get the water flowing again.  He uses a wrench to remove the burst section of pipe.  He looks in his tool shed and finds only one piece of pipe of the right length and diameter.  On inspecting the piece of pipe, he finds that both ends are threaded clockwise, which means that the turning motion that would be required to screw the pipe in at one end would be the opposite of the direction of turning that would be required to screw the pipe in at the other end.  If he turns the pipe clockwise with his wrench, the pipe will screw in at one end but not the other, and vice versa if he turns the pipe counterclockwise.  He has no other pipe and no special tools for rethreading pipe, nor does he have welding equipment or any material sufficiently strong to bind one end of the pipe. A key word involved in a temporary solution to the problem is

1. frozen
2. halfway
3. bury
4. slide
5. burn

The alternative answers give the student few clues, and consequently he must think of good solutions and see whether any of the terms apply. In the example above, only one word, "halfway," involves a good solution. The solution is to screw the pipe in tightly at one end and then, pressing the unattached ends together, unscrew it halfway, which will leave both ends halfway screwed into their respective attachments. The arrangement might leak slightly, but it would be a clever temporary solution, better than any that could be arrived at using any of the other terms.

To provide even fewer cues to students, only the first letter of one or more key terms can be placed in the alternatives. An example is as follows:

In a factory a hole has developed in a large steel container which is used to carry hot water from one vat to another. The container is part of an elaborate system of wheels and cables which is used to do the job. It may take several weeks to get a new container installed. The foreman tries to cover the hole with a steel disk, but because of vibration from the machinery, the disk keeps slipping away from the hole. Since the water is so hot, glue will not work, and no equipment is available to weld or bolt the disk over the hole. The disk can be held over the hole with a

1. t _____
2. p _____
3. h _____
4. s _____
5. m _____

The best solution involves the letter "m." A magnet placed on the bottom of the container under the hole would hold the steel disk firmly in place.

## Creative productions

One of the most straightforward, and in many ways the best, method of testing for creative potential is to give the student an issue or problem and ask him to produce creative responses. This is essentially what is involved in parts of the Horn Aptitude Inventory, which was discussed previously. The student is given a piece of paper on which several lines have been drawn, and, starting with these, he is asked to "create" something.  Similar tests of creativity in the arts can be made using designs, parts of figures, and splotches of color.  Starting from these bare beginnings, the student must create something on his own.

Productions can also be used to test literary creativity.  Students can be given the first two lines of a poem and asked to go on from that point to a finished product, or they can be given the first paragraph of a story and asked to complete it.

Productions can also be used to measure scientific and scholarly creativity.  For example, a problem that could be used with high school students in science courses is as follows:

Design and describe a vehicle for transporting people and supplies on the moon.  Consider (1) the type of power supply needed, (2) the fuel that would be used, (3) the type of "wheels" that would be used, (4) special gadgets that would be needed for operating on the moon's surface, and (5) any other properties that you consider relevant.

A problem that could be used with students in the elementary grades is as follows:

Suppose that we were going to build a new school and you were asked to design it.  You would like the school to be very modern and to contain many new ideas.  What are some of the things that you would put in your school?

Relatively noncreative students will give such answers as "pretty flowers," "a better ball diamond," and "more chairs in the lunchroom."  More creative students will give answers such as "blinds run by motors that keep just the right amount of light coming in," "sliding walls that let you make rooms bigger or smaller," "little television sets on each desk that the teacher can show exercises on and that will tell you whether you have the right answers," and "tape recorders so that you can talk into them and then see whether you are pronouncing words right."

If it were not for one salient difficulty, the production methods would be used quite widely in measuring creative ability.  The difficulty lies in how the responses are to be scored.  One part of the problem is that of finding scorers who can recognize creative answers when they see them.  How can we score the productions of persons who are more creative than we are?  Actually this is not so much of a problem with students in the elementary grades.  What would be creative responses for most of them are not beyond the mental comprehension of most teachers.  It does get to be a problem with high school and college students, where some of the complex ideas creative students have are beyond the understanding of many teachers.  Fortunately, it is not always necessary to be highly creative to recognize creative products.  Even though we might not be clever enough to make the drawing, compose the poem, or design the school, we can usually recognize clever productions when we see them.

In most commercially distributed tests relating to productions, product scales are used for scoring.  Expert judges score many different productions.  From these, standard examples are chosen to represent different levels of performance.  Productions of students are then scored by comparing them with the standard samples.  This still involves an element of subjectivity, but carefully constructed product scales often have high reliability.

Another problem that is encountered in the scoring of production is the sheer labor involved.  Scoring each one is like scoring a difficult essay question.  If it were not for the vast amount of time needed to score responses, production items would probably be used quite widely to measure creative ability.

### Perceptual tests

In addition to the types of measures mentioned previously, it is currently thought that some types of perceptual measures actually relate to creativity.  We often talk about creative thinking as though there were some connection with perception.  For example, in discussing creative processes, we talk about the ability to "see through" arguments, the ability to "focus" on important issues, and the ability not to be "distracted" by irrelevant cues.  Not enough research has been done for us to be sure that creativity actually relates to perceptual processes, but some of the evidence is sufficiently interesting to encourage more research.

One type of perceptual problem that is thought to be related to creativity is illustrated in Figure 11-12.  In each of the two items, the figure on the left is embedded in one or more of the complex figures on the right.  In order to mark the correct figure, it is necessary to "see through" the maze of distracting lines and competing figures within the complex pattern.  There is some evidence to suggest a relationship between this type of perceptual ability and the ability to see through irrelevancies in scientific problems.  This and other types of perceptual abilities may relate to some extent to creativity.

### Summary

The so-called special abilities are special only in the sense that they are somewhat different from the abilities measured by most multifactor batteries of tests.  Sensory abilities, such as vision and audition, are rather straightforwardly measured, and measures of such abilities are important to consider in school settings and numerous vocational activities.

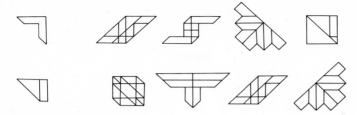

**FIGURE 11-12**    Two items concerning the ability to detect embedded figures    (*Reproduced by permission of the publishers, Science Research Associates, Inc.*)

Mechanical aptitudes depend on a variety of things, including (1) motor skills in some vocations, (2) general intelligence in most occupations, (3) information concerning particular jobs, and (4) varying with the job, mechanical comprehension, perceptual factors, and spatial factors. Because of the wide differences in skills required for different mechanical occupations, it is difficult to develop and use general batteries of tests in vocational guidance. There are some factors that come into play in many different mechanical occupations, such as mechanical comprehension and the spatial factors, but other aspects of mechanical aptitude tend to be highly specific with respect to the particular job, as is the case with the motor skills that relate to success on different jobs. For these reasons, one frequently finds tailor-made batteries of tests to select people for particular jobs, e.g., persons who assemble television sets.

The measurement of artistic aptitudes has lagged behind the measurement of most other types of aptitudes. This is due to the intrinsic difficulty of measuring artistic aptitudes and to the fact that relatively more practical importance is attached to the development of other types of measures. Measures of musical aptitudes are based mainly on sensory judgments that logically underlie the development of actual musical skills. Most measures of aptitudes in the graphic arts concern art appreciation, and they apparently serve that purpose well. Some more recent tests have attempted to measure aspects of actual skill in artistic production.

Some students possess creative talents, beyond the ability to master subjects taught in the classroom, which, if properly nourished, will allow them to make important contributions to society. Unfortunately, at the present time we are only beginning to develop methods for measuring creative ability. Studies of creative students and adults suggest a number of characteristics relating to creativity. Creative people tend to score relatively well on intelligence tests, and they tend to make at least moderately good grades in school. Creative people tend to be different—they tend to come from unusual home and social environments, and they differ from other people in the ways in which they approach intellectual problems. Some of the mental characteristics which are currently thought to distinguish creative students are (1) a strong drive for intellectual accomplishment, (2) the ability to see unusual aspects of problems and unusual solutions, (3) the generation of floods of ideas, and (4) the ability to visualize the consequences of particular courses of action. It is feasible to measure these and other aspects of creativity with psychological tests, but much more research will have to be done before the necessary hardware is available. Such tests will probably be more time-consuming and difficult to administer and score than most current measures of human ability. Also, psychologists will have to muster their own creativity in order to construct the instruments that are required.

# PART 6:

Examples of Methods
for Measuring
Personality and Sentiments

# CHAPTER 12

## Measurement of personality traits: inventories and observational methods

Before we can meaningfully discuss the measurement of personality traits, we must define "personality." Since, however, different persons attach somewhat different meanings to the word, the best we can do is to indicate some types of human traits that most people agree relate to personality. To some nonpsychologists, the word "personality" connotes social effectiveness and charm, which, of course, psychologists would consider to occupy only one corner of the total domain of personality characteristics.

Some psychologists have given overly comprehensive and elegantly vague definitions of personality such as "the total functioning individual interacting with his environment." Such definitions would include all traits of human ability, which we have chosen to discuss separately from personality.

The overall study of personality concerns two broad issues: (1) what people are like at any point in time and (2) how they got that way. Personality measurement is concerned mainly with the first issue, the purpose of measurement being to describe individuals in terms of traits relating to dominance, extroversion, and other characteristics. The second issue relates to heredity and past experience. To explain how an individual developed a particular set of traits, one must resort either to genetic mechanisms or to learning theory. Of course, at the present time we know very little about possible genetic mechanisms relating to human traits; although we think that we know considerably more about the types of social learning that influence particular traits, there is still much speculation in this area.

Specialists in the study of personality can, and sometimes do, argue that a discussion of personality measurement is not a total discussion of personality. There is much merit in this argument. Although this chapter will be concerned solely with personality measurement, it is freely recognized that this is only one of the two issues discussed above. Also, we might have better measures of personality if all the persons who specialize in personality measurement had closer contacts with studies and theories concerning personality development.

As is true of the measurement of human abilities, the measurement of personality traits is concerned mainly with individual differences. We shall speak of personality measurement as concerning the following four broad classes of traits:

1. *Social traits.*    The characteristic behavior of individuals with respect to other people. Typical social traits are honesty, gregariousness, shyness, dominance, and humor. Social traits are often said to constitute the surface layer of personality, the way that an individual appears in society.

2. *Motives.*    Individual differences in "needs" or "drives," particularly the "non-biological" drives such as the needs for affiliation, aggression, and achievement. Motives are often spoken of as constituting personality "dynamics."

3. *Personal conceptions.*    Individual differences in what people think of themselves and how they view the world, such as differences in self-esteem, interests, attitudes, and values.

4. *Adjustment versus maladjustment.*    The relative freedom from emotional distress and/or socially disruptive behavior. Maladjustment relates to the so-called neuroses and psychoses, and adjustment relates to the opposite of these.

One could make further subdivisions of the above categories of personality traits—for example, by dividing social traits into character and temperament—but the four categories should suffice for the discussion in this chapter. Of course, these four kinds of traits are not independent. A person's motives certainly influence his social behavior, but there is no one-to-one correspondence. For example, even though it may be meaningful to speak of a person as having hostile motives, he may not act very hostile, except in subtle ways that only the expert would recognize. Social traits can be observed directly, and it is for this reason that many of the standardized measures of personality concern social traits. Motives, or dynamics, cannot be observed directly, but must be inferred from overt responses, e.g., as is done with projective techniques such as the Rorschach.

Personal conceptions relate to social traits and to motives, but logically they are not the same. A person may be strongly prejudiced against a particular racial group (a type of personal conception), but because of the feelings of other people in his environment, he might not speak in hostile terms about members of that group or act in a hostile manner toward them (which would represent social traits). Similarly, a person might have homosexual urges (a motive), but repress this to the point where it is not evidenced in personal conceptions. In this chapter we shall discuss only those aspects of personal conceptions which pertain to self-conceptions—conceptions the individual has of himself. Although interests, attitudes, and values are also rightly considered personality traits, somewhat different principles hold for their measurement from those which apply to the measurement of other types of personality traits. Consequently, Chapter 14 will be reserved for a discussion of the measurement of interests, attitudes, and values.

Adjustment and maladjustment are related to the other three categories of traits. Whenever an individual is very extreme in social traits, motives, or personal conception, he is usually maladjusted also. There are, however, some traits relating to adjustment that are not easily thought of as being motives, personal conceptions, or social traits, e.g., hallucinations, imaginary illness, and bizarre associations. Definitions of adjustment and maladjustment necessarily concern values—what the individual values and what is valued by the society as a whole. If the individual is distressed by his own feelings and behavior and/or if his behavior is highly distressful to others, we say that he is maladjusted.

## Personality traits

The title of this chapter speaks of the measurement of personality *traits*, the word "trait" being a synonym for "attribute" or "characteristic," as those terms have been used in previous chapters. A trait is simply a measurable dimension of behavior, either one that is measurable only dichotomously or one that is measurable in finer gradations. Traits vary in generality from specific habits, such as smoking rather than not smoking, to very general dimensions of behavior, such as extroversion rather than introversion. To have parsimonious descriptions of personality, it is necessary to find general traits, ones more general than specific habits.

## Idiographic and nomothetic theories

For some years now a controversy has existed over whether or not general traits of personality exist. The controversy has been between those who espouse a *nomothetic* and those who espouse an *idiographic* point of view, the former referring to "general laws" applicable to all people and the latter referring to a personalized approach. Essentially, the idiographic point of view is that each person is a law unto himself. In terms of factor-analytic approaches, this means that either there are no general factors among personality characteristics or those which do exist fail to capture the "essence" of the individual. The idiographic approach is the one used by novelists who explore in detail the inner workings and behavioral characteristics of one person. This is in contrast to the nomothetic approach, which strives to represent the important personality characteristics of all people in terms of profiles of measurable traits.

The idiographists have an important point: To find general traits (factors) of personality, it is necessary to find correlations between specific traits (habits); but everyday experience suggests that such correlations are frequently either very low or absent altogether. For example, it makes sense to deal with a general trait of dominance only if there are positive correlations between tendencies to be dominant in specific situations; however, some persons are dominant with their wives but not dominant at work, dominant with men but not with women, dominant in intellectual matters but not in practical matters, and so on.

In order to be successful, the nomotheticist must hypothesize a general trait of personality and find it evidenced in the correlations between more specific traits, or if he has no hypotheses, he must find such clusters of correlated traits in his factor-analytic explorations. If the nomotheticist does not find important factors by means of these approaches (important in terms of criteria discussed in Chapter 9), he has failed. Enough failures of this kind would eventually lead to the admission that the idiographists are correct—that personality traits are "scattered" among people in such a way that the only approach to understanding the individual is to trace back through all the "life threads" that made him what he is. Then it would have to be admitted that there are no general traits of dominance, extroversion, or other characteristics; instead, each individual would need to be considered a unique configuration of specific traits (habits).

The idiographists may be entirely correct, but if they are, it is a sad day for psychology. Idiography is an antiscience point of view: it discourages the search for general laws and instead encourages the description of particular phenomena (people). The idiographist is like the astronomer who despairs of finding any general laws relating to heavenly bodies and instead devotes the rest of his life to describing the particular features of the planet Neptune.

Essentially the idiographic point of view is that, because of highly individualized learning experiences and constitutional factors, each individual is an idiosyncratic mosaic of behavioral tendencies, which cannot be accurately summarized by any general factors of personality. To illustrate such crazy-quilt combinations of behavioral tendencies, however, the idiographists usually choose the average person. Thus, with respect to the trait of dominance, the average person is somewhat dominant in some situations and somewhat submissive in others, which is what would be expected from a psychometric point of view and exactly what one finds in terms of test scores. The average person tends to mark about half of the items in the direction keyed "dominant" and the other half in the direction keyed "submissive." What the idiographic point of view neglects to encompass is the fact that some individuals actually are dominant in almost all situations and others actually are submissive in almost all situations. At least this is what one finds in examining the item scores of individuals who score on the extremes of the trait being investigated. What the evidence then shows is that it does make sense to speak of some people as being dominant in a general sense, of others as being submissive in a general sense, and of most of the people in between the extremes as being neither very dominant nor very submissive. Why should such straightforward findings be used to support the gloomy conclusion that there are no general traits of personality? Also, it must be remembered that the extremes are the important points on the continuum, both for issues relating to basic research and for applied concerns.

Efforts to measure personality traits are based on the hypothesis that the idiographists are not entirely correct, that there are some general traits of human personality. To accept the nomothetic point of view in advance is to postulate that only chaos prevails in the description of human personalities. The remainder of this chapter and the following chapter will be concerned with efforts to measure general traits of personality.

## Approaches to the measurement of personality

In contrast to the measurement of human abilities, the measurement of personality traits involves a number of different basic approaches. Most measures of human ability, particularly those of the "intellectual" functions, are printed tests. In each such test, the subject understands that he is required to solve some type of problem, broadly speaking. In most tests of human ability, it is obvious how responses should be scored. With measures of personality, these matters are not nearly so clear. Personality traits are not highly concerned with "how well" a person can perform; rather, they are concerned mainly with the typical amount of gregariousness or hostility. How such typical behavior is to be measured, if it can be, is a matter of dispute, and consequently various schools of thought have come forward. Also, the logic of measurement depends on the kind of personality trait which is being studied. Thus the logic of measurement required for the measurement of social traits might be different from that required for the measurement of motives.

The major approaches to the measurement of personality traits are with (1) self-inventories, (2) observational methods, (3) projective techniques, (4) physiological variables, and (5) perceptual variables. The remainder of this chapter will be concerned with self-inventories and observational methods; the other approaches to the measurement of personality will be discussed in Chapter 13.

## Current status of personality measurement

Before going into particular approaches to the measurement of personality characteristics, we should state in advance that such measurement is still in an embryonic stage.

In speculating about why efforts to measure personality attributes to date have not been highly successful, one must realize that this is not due to the fact that the problem has been neglected. Galton was interested in the measurement of personality traits and made some attempts to develop valid instruments, and the same was true of Binet, Spearman, Thurstone, and the other "greats" in psychometric theory. On the scene now are numerous distinguished psychologists who have devoted themselves in large measure to the study of personality traits. At the present time, it is safe to say that much more effort is being expended to develop measures of personality traits than to develop measures of human ability. In spite of all this effort and in spite of the talent that has been associated with some of it, the search has met with only modest success. As will be discussed later in this chapter and in the following chapter, however, some approaches to measuring personality have been overly maligned, others can be markedly improved, and promising new approaches are coming into view.

The rapid success of early efforts to measure human abilities may have beguiled psychologists into thinking it would be easy to measure personality traits. Also, the fact that printed tests of human abilities proved successful probably encouraged the idea that printed tests of personality would be equally successful.

The present state of personality measurement is in strong contrast to the need for such measures. Psychological theories are populated with personality traits such as anxiety, self-esteem, ego strength, dogmatism, empathy, and rigidity—few of which can be measured very well at the present time. In addition, there are many needs for measures of personality traits in applied settings —in psychological clinics, schools, psychiatric practice, industry, the armed forces, and others. In spite of these obvious needs, there are very few instances in which supposed measures of personality traits have proved to be consistently valid. This point is emphasized by the fact that whereas vocabulary tests are consistently valid for selecting college freshmen for many different colleges, no personality test (as far as the author knows) has shown itself to be consistently valid for the same purpose.

## self-inventory measures

By far the most frequently employed approach to personality measurement is with printed tests in which the individual is required to describe himself. Self-inventories obviously concern personal conceptions, and they are also frequently used to measure social traits, motives, and adjustment. The overriding problem is that whereas personal conceptions do overlap to some extent with the other three aspects of personality, the overlap is less than 100 percent. The issues relating to the use of self-inventories to measure personality traits other than personal conceptions will be discussed in detail later in this chapter. Examples of typical items on self-inventories are as follows:

Social traits:
1. I usually lead the discussion in group situations.
2. I seldom hurt other people's feelings.
3. I am very frank in giving people my opinions.
4. I am frequently late for appointments.

Motives:
1. My sexual needs are greater than those of the average person.
2. I enjoy being guided by strong people in my life.
3. I like the feeling of power when I am in a position of responsibility.
4. I frequently daydream of becoming an important person.

Personal conceptions:
1. I consider myself to be a valuable member of society.  (An item concerning self-esteem.)
2. I would rather fix a broken clock than read a novel.  (An item concerning interests.)
3. I do not think that we should allow Orientals to become citizens of our country. (An item concerning attitudes.)
4. I believe that it is more important to work for the betterment of mankind than to strive for personal success.  (An item concerning values.)

Adjustment:
1. I have no major personal problems.
2. I frequently become anxious for no apparent reason.
3. I enjoy life more than the average person does.
4. I have no true friends.

Although self-inventories have been used for a long time (Galton used one to measure individual differences in imagery), the first systematic effort to develop them is credited to Woodworth (1918).  During World War I, the Army neeeded some means for weeding out emotionally unfit men before they were sent overseas.  Previously such screening had been done by psychiatric interviewers, but there were not nearly enough interviewers to do the job.  Essentially, Woodworth's solution was to have each man "interview himself."  Questions were obtained from a search of the psychiatric literature and from among those frequently used by psychiatrists in interviews.  Some of them were as follows:

1. Do you often have the feeling of suffocating?
2. Have you ever had convulsions?
3. Can you stand the sight of blood?
4. Did you have a happy childhood?
5. Have you ever had a vision?
6. Did you ever have a strong desire to commit suicide?

A list of 116 such questions constituted a printed form called the Personal Data Sheet.  A neurotic-tendency score for each person was obtained by counting the number of problems he marked.  A small amount of standardization research was performed with the instrument.  Items were eliminated if the "neurotic" response was given by more than 25 percent of normal soldiers.

Comparisons were made of responses given by unselected soldiers and by a small group of declared neurotic soldiers.

The Personal Data Sheet was considered not a test, in the stricter meaning of the term, but an aid to interviewing. Persons who gave numerous "neurotic" responses were called in for detailed psychiatric interviews. Although little direct evidence of validity was obtained, persons who worked with the Personal Data Sheet during World War I were generally pleased with it. After World War I, interest developed in the construction of tests of all kinds, personality self-inventories included. Many of the inventories were modeled after the Personal Data Sheet, to the extent of using some of the same items. Now there are literally hundreds of self-inventories employed for one purpose or another.

In the following section, a very widely used self-inventory will be described and illustrated. (Other self-inventories are described in Appendix C.) After that, some general principles will be discussed regarding the development and use of self-inventories.

### Minnesota Multiphasic Personality Inventory (MMPI)

The MMPI represents the apex of research and detailed test construction in the area of adjustment inventories (Hathaway & McKinley, 1967; Hathaway & Meehl, 1951). Research on this instrument has gone on for many years now, and hundreds of journal articles have been devoted to its construction, refinement, and use. The MMPI is intended to measure the relative presence or absence of eight forms of mental illness; in addition, there is a ninth scale to measure masculinity-femininity. Two related items are shown for each type of mental illness. A plus sign means that persons who have the illness are likely to agree with the item; a minus sign means that they are likely to disagree.

**Hypochondriasis (Hs)**

Overconcern with bodily functions and imagined illness.
Related items:

I do not tire quickly. (−)
The top of my head sometimes feels tender. (+)

**Depression (D)**

This term is used in the conventional sense to imply strong feelings of "blueness," despondency, and worthlessness.
Related items:

I am easily awakened by noise. (+)
Everything is turning out just as the prophets of the Bible said it would. (+)

## Hysteria (Hy)

The development of physical disorders such as blindness, paralysis, and vomiting as an escape from emotional problems.
Related items:

I am likely not to speak to people until they speak to me. (+)
I get mad easily and then get over it soon. (+)

## Psychopathic deviate (Pd)

An individual who lacks "conscience," who has little regard for the feelings of others, and who gets into trouble frequently.
Related items:

My family does not like the work I have chosen. (+)
What others think of me does not bother me. (+)

## Paranoia (Pa)

Extreme suspiciousness to the point of imagining elaborate plots.
Related items:

I am sure I am being talked about. (+)
Someone has control over my mind. (+)

## Psychasthenia (Pt)

Strong fears and compulsions.
Related items:

I become impatient with people easily. (+)
I wish I could be as happy as others seem to be. (+)

## Schizophrenia (Sc)

Bizarre thoughts and actions, out of communication with the world.
Related items:

I have never been in love with anyone. (+)
I loved my mother. (−)

## Hypomania (Ma)

Overactivity; inability to concentrate on one thing for more than a moment.
Related items:

I don't blame anyone for trying to grab everything he can get in this world. (+)
When I get bored I like to stir up some excitement. (+)

### Masculinity-femininity (Mf)

The relative balance of male versus female interests.
Related items:

I like movie love scenes. (F)
I used to keep a diary. (F)

There are several noteworthy features of the MMPI which set it above most inventories that are used to detect maladjustment. Face validity was not a concern in the construction of the instrument. The scales used to measure the various kinds of mental illness were developed on an empirical basis. A large group of items was administered initially to several hundred normal persons and to groups of mental-hospital patients whose symptoms matched one of the kinds of mental illness. Item analyses were undertaken to find the scoring key for each illness scale which would best differentiate the patients of one type from normals and from other types of patients.

In addition to the mental-illness scales available on the MMPI, four so-called validity scores are used. These supposedly provide some information about the test-taking attitude of the subject and the relative honesty with which he made his responses. The "validity scores" are as follows:

1. *The question score* (?).    This consists of the number of items marked in the "cannot say" category. The interpretation is that if a person has a high question score, the scale scores for the different kinds of illness appear lower than they should be. If a person has as many as 130 "cannot say" responses, his test record is assumed to be invalid.

2. *The lie score* (L).    This scale consists of 15 items concerning socially desirable actions which few people could truthfully endorse, e.g., "I never get angry at anybody." It is assumed that a person who endorses numerous items of this kind is falsifying the inventory.

3. *The validity score* (F).    This consists of 64 items which are endorsed infrequently by normal subjects. They concern a hodgepodge of symptoms which are not likely to occur in any one mental illness. The interpretation is that a person who endorses a number of these items is careless or does not understand the test instructions.

4. *The correction score* (K).    This consists of 30 items which were found to differentiate clinical patients whose scale scores appeared normal from persons who were actually normal. The responses to these items can be used to correct the illness scores for particular persons.

It should not be assumed that "validity scores" like those on the MMPI are a panacea in the use of personality inventories. There is not enough evidence yet to support the contention that the validity scores actually measure what they are purported to measure. The question, lie, and validity scores may indicate that a respondent gives misleading responses, but nothing can be done except to throw away the test record. The correction score (K) offers a more positive approach, but not enough research has been done to enable us to say how well it works.

The results of the MMPI can be plotted as a profile showing scores on the illness scales and those on the four validity scales (see Figure 12-1 for illustrative profiles). It is seldom found that a person scores high (the maladjusted direction) on only one of the scales. Typically, the maladjustment spreads across several of the scales. Some of the scales correlate substantially with the others, which is to be expected because mental illness seldom occurs as one specific pattern of traits. It is usually the case that the patient has a mixture of different kinds of mental illness.

Complex pattern scoring methods have been devised to interpret the MMPI profile (Hathaway & Meehl, 1951). Even with these it is necessary to have an experienced clinical psychologist to interpret the results. As is true of many clinical methods, a complex lore has developed about the meaning of different kinds of MMPI profiles, much of which has only slight grounding in empirical fact.

Much stands or falls on the eventual validity of the MMPI. Never before has so much careful research gone into the empirical derivation of a self-description inventory to measure different kinds of maladjustment, and perhaps such efforts will never be made again. The success of this venture will have a strong effect on the future course of personality measurement.

### Types of inventories

In a discussion of inventories, it is important to make a distinction between self-inventories and other types of inventories, even though the distinction is

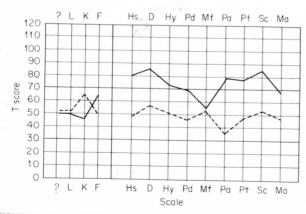

**FIGURE 12-1**      MMPI profiles for a normal adult (- - -) and for a "typical psychotic" (——) (Adapted from Gough, 1953, pp. 554, 563; reproduced by permission of The Ronald Press Company)

sometimes not clear.  A self-inventory is one in which the individual describes his own traits, as is the case in the MMPI.  Essentially, self-inventories ask the individual: "What are you like as a person?  Show us by responding frankly to the following items."  Such self-inventories should be distinguished from inventories that do not require the subject to describe himself.  It has been the custom to refer to any objective (as regards scoring) printed test as an *inventory*.  (It is unfortunate to group tests in terms of whether they are printed forms or appear in some other guise because there are better ways to classify them.)  As an example of an inventory which does not directly concern self-description, efforts have been made to develop measures of personality attributes from aesthetic preferences among different types of geometric forms, e.g., choosing between regular and irregular forms.  It is important to distinguish self-inventories from other types of printed tests of personality because self-inventories have their own logic and their own particular problems, ones that are not necessarily associated with other printed tests of personality.  This section concerns self-inventories; other printed tests for measuring personality traits will be mentioned at various points in the remainder of this chapter and in the following chapter.

### Types of self-inventory items

There are numerous types of items that can be employed in self-inventories. Most typically, the subject is presented with a list of statements and is asked to mark "yes" or "no," "true" or "false," or "agree" or "disagree."  Various types of rating scales can also be employed with such statements, such as seven-step scales of agreement-disagreement, percentage scales comparing the individual with people in general, and others.  Instead of employing such absolute rating methods, the experimenter can use various types of comparative rating methods.  These include forced-choice scales, ranking of statements, and others.  Issues regarding the psychometric properties of these different ways of obtaining responses were discussed in Chapter 7.  Special issues in the development and use of rating methods in the study of personality and in the study of attitudes will be discussed in Chapter 14.  Such technical considerations regarding how responses are elicited, however, are secondary to other issues in the measurement of personality traits.  If it were not for the other problems discussed in this chapter, any or all of the rating methods could probably be successfully employed in the measurement of personality.

### factors in self-inventory items

There is an interesting parallel between the growth of knowledge about factors in self-inventories and the growth of knowledge about factors in tests of human abilities. At first only several factors were proposed, e.g., adjustment and introversion-extroversion. Then others were proposed, such as dominance and sociability, and the list grew and grew. In the attempt to make sense out of the increasingly long list of proposed factors, factor-analytic studies were undertaken. (Guilford, 1959, provides a comprehensive discussion of the history of this work, the many factors which have been proposed, and one man's view of the evidence.) Just as it was necessary to make yearly revisions of the number of factors of human ability that existed, it was necessary to make yearly revisions of the number of factors of personality that existed. At the present time, it is difficult to say how many factors have been found in self-inventories because (1) the statistical evidence for some of the factors is so weak, (2) different investigators include different types of traits under the heading of "personality," and (3) it is difficult to compare factors reported by different investigators. The most conservative estimate, however, is that over twenty factors have been reported in self-inventories. R. B. Cattell (1957) reports over forty-five factors of personality, and Guilford (1959) apparently thinks in terms of similar numbers. (Some of these factors were defined mainly by measurement methods other than self-inventories.)

The following 10 factors from the Guilford-Zimmerman Temperament Survey (Guilford & Zimmerman, 1949) are typical of those which have been found in self-inventories:

1. *General activity.* High energy, quickness of action, liking for speed, efficiency
2. *Restraint.* Deliberateness, serious-mindedness, persistence
3. *Ascendance.* Leadership, initiative, persuasiveness
4. *Sociability.* Having many friends and liking social activities
5. *Emotional stability.* Composure, cheerfulness, evenness of moods
6. *Objectivity.* Freedom from suspiciousness, from hypersensitivity, and from getting into trouble
7. *Friendliness.* Respect for others, acceptance of domination, toleration of hostility
8. *Thoughtfulness.* Reflectiveness, meditativeness, observation of self and others
9. *Personal relations.* Tolerance of people, faith in social institutions, freedom from faultfinding and from self-pity
10. *Masculinity.* Interest in masculine activities, hard-boiled attitude, not easily disgusted, versus (for femininity) romantic and emotionally expressive

## Evidence for the factors

In spite of the many reported factors in self-inventories, there is serious doubt that more than several *important* factors are presently known (important in terms of the criteria discussed in Chapter 9). Statistical evidence for most of the reported factors is rather weak. Because constructing tests before resorting to factor analysis has proved difficult, in many cases it has been necessary to perform factor analyses of items. Because of the low correlations typically found between such items and the small variance of such correlations in a matrix, the results have generally been unclear. Typically only a relatively small number of items load on each factor, and loadings are frequently tiny. As a result, some of the factors have very low reliabilities, and many of them are difficult to interpret.

These factor-analytic practices have resulted in a large number of groups of items, each supposedly relating to a different factor. Since the number of items relating to each factor is usually less than 20, reliabilities of factors are usually low. Usually there are substantial correlations between those groups of items, so high in some cases that nearly all the reliable variance in one group of items can be explained (by multiple regression) from other groups of items.

It is probably a mistake to interpret this statistical mess as meaningfully portraying the important factors in self-inventories; it would be better to employ one of three complementary approaches. One approach is to hypothesize whole tests relating to personality constructs (e.g., anxiety), to develop homogeneous tests by methods discussed in previous chapters, and then to submit those tests to factor analysis. As a second approach, if one does not attempt to analyze whole tests but works with individual items instead, it is better to retain only the several strong factors that are obtained. A third approach is to intercorrelate the groups of items that have been found as factors in previous studies and to submit those correlations to factor analysis.

When any of the foregoing three approaches is tried, one comes to the conclusion that presently there is evidence for only several broad statistically strong factors in self-inventories. Careful analyses of these kinds led Peterson (1965) to the following conclusions:

Factor analysis of verbal personality measures have typically generated highly complex multidimensional structural systems. Available evidence now suggests that the most dependable dimensions drawn from conventional factor analyses of ratings and questionnaires are simple, familiar dimensions of broad scope. It also appears that most of the initially obscure, apparently more precise, more narrowly defined factors many investigators claim to have revealed are either trivial, artifactual, capricious, or all three. Verbal descriptions of personality were reduced to two factors, and the two factors were reduced to two ratings, one concerning perceived adjustment and the other related to introversion-extroversion.

As Peterson says, at the present time two factors explain much of the common variance among self-inventories: adjustment and introversion-extroversion, the former being much more prominent than the latter. This is essentially the same position Eysenck (1960) has held for years, except that he interprets the opposite pole of adjustment and calls it "neuroticism," and he also deals with a third major factor, "psychoticism." This author's inclination is to interpret the dominant factor as *the tendency to say good rather than bad things about oneself,* or, as Edwards (1957a) refers to it, *social desirability.* The most obvious thing about the dominant factor is that people who are high on it mark "yes" on socially desirable traits and "no" on socially undesirable traits, and vice versa for persons who are low on the factor. The assumption that the former type of person is "adjusted" and the latter type of person is "neurotic" has not yet been proved correct.

The broadness of the factor of introversion-extroversion is a matter of dispute (Carrigan, 1960), but there is enough evidence for such a factor to encourage continued investigation. Eysenck's factor of "psychoticism" is probably statistically strong only in comparing psychotics with supposedly normal people. In studies of college students, for example, most of the variance attributable to that factor would probably be explained by social desirability and introversion-extroversion.

Before leaving this section, it should be made clear that the three factors discussed previously are not the only factors in self-inventories. Numerous others have been found, but so far none of them have met all the standards of (1) replicability from one laboratory to the next, (2) broadness of item content, (3) statistical strength in the form of high factor loadings, (4) high reliability, (5) relative independence of the three major factors discussed above, and (6) predictive validity and construct validity. As more research is done, surely more important factors from self-inventories will prove measurable.

## social desirability in self-inventories

As was mentioned in the previous section, one of the present problems in employing self-inventories to measure personality traits is that such self-inventories are dominated by a general factor of social desirability. Although this fact was suspected for a long time, it remained for Edwards (1957a) and his colleagues to explore the matter thoroughly. In the first major study (Edwards, 1953), 152 subjects rated the social desirability of 140 self-inventory items. Each item was rated on a nine-point scale. The mean rating of each item represented the social desirability of the item as viewed by the subjects as a group. Next, Edwards placed the 140 items in a self-inventory and obtained yes-no responses from a group of subjects. He found a correlation (over items) of .87 between the mean desirability ratings and the proportion of people endorsing each item. This is strong evidence that the average person tends to describe himself in a socially desirable manner on self-inventories.

The above evidence regarding social desirability, however, said nothing directly about *individual differences* in the tendency to say good things about oneself; rather, it pointed to a bias in that regard for the average person. More recent evidence has made it quite clear that individual differences in that tendency do explain much of the variance on self-inventories.

A direct type of evidence for the importance of individual differences in social desirability comes from the following type of study. Edwards (1957a) developed a self-inventory to measure the extent to which each individual rates himself as socially desirable rather than socially undesirable. Items were obtained from different scales of the MMPI on the basis of ratings of social desirability, by the method discussed previously. Each item so selected was rated as either definitely desirable or definitely undesirable. The items were selected in such a way that approximately half of them were keyed "no" for the desirable response and the others were keyed "yes" for the desirable response. When the items are used in a self-inventory, scores should reflect individual differences in rated self-desirability (the tendency to say good things about oneself). Other psychologists have developed scales by similar methods for measuring individual differences in rated self-desirability. (These scales, and the evidence gained from employing them, are discussed by Holtzman, 1965.) It has been found that these scales correlate substantially with many different self-inventories, the directions of the correlations depending on whether the inventories are keyed for "good" or "bad" traits, e.g., adjustment versus maladjustment. In some cases the correlations are almost as high as the reliabilities of the self-inventories.

There is no longer room for argument about the statistical importance of scales constructed to measure self-desirability. They explain so much of the variance of individual differences in responses to self-inventories that statistical arguments concern whether or not there is enough independent variance in such inventories to justify further investigation of them. The major arguments now concern the psychological nature of self-desirability scores. Some speak of such scores as concerning only *response styles*, individual differences in test-taking habits which are unrelated to the purpose of the instruments. Others have gone so far as to suggest that the variance in self-desirability ratings represents individual differences only in conscious faking, which in turn implies that self-inventories in general tend to measure only individual differences in the tendency to "fake well." At the other extreme, some argue that the correlations between self-desirability scores and scores on self-inventories do not invalidate the latter, but rather serve to show that adjustment and self-desirability (or self-esteem) are much the same thing. It could further be argued that to picture oneself as socially desirable, one must know what is desirable in particular situations, and that if an individual is unable to fake well, this indicates that he has been subjected to highly unusual environmental influences. In other words, only a poorly adjusted person would be so unfamiliar with social expectations that he would not know how to fake well on a self-inventory.

Admittedly, the dominant factor in self-inventories (social desirability) is quite complex. The major components of social desirability are probably (1) the individual's actual adjustment, (2) the knowledge he has about his own traits, and (3) his frankness in stating what he knows. An individual could be maladjusted (by popular standards) and not know it, and thus he might rate himself as being high in social desirability. In contrast, a person could be maladjusted and know it, but consciously distort his responses so as to appear socially desirable. Another possibility would be an individual who is highly adjusted, knows it, and frankly describes himself as being high in social desirability. Since each of these three component characteristics can be thought of as relatively continuous, the expressed self-desirability of each person can be thought of as some combination of the three.

The major indictment of self-report measures of personality—that they can be faked—is an issue that has been misunderstood both by laymen and apparently even by some specialists in psychological measurement. There are three separate, and largely unrelated, questions regarding faking (lack of frankness) in self-report measures: (1) Can most such measures be faked? (2) Do people actually fake scores, either in applied settings or in basic research on personality characteristics? (3) If people do fake scores, does this have any effect at all on the validity of self-report measures? Most of the evidence requires us to answer "yes" to question 1. The strongest evidence comes from investigations in which either the same subjects or different subjects are administered a self-report measure under different instructions regarding faking. As an example, a group of subjects is given a measure of personal adjustment on two occasions under two different instructions. On the first occasion, the inventory is administered under the usual instructions to be frank. On the second occasion, the subjects are essentially told to play a game in such a way as to appear as well adjusted as possible. In such investigations, it is usually found that the mean score shifts somewhat toward the well-adjusted end of the scale. Findings such as these have sometimes been used as evidence that the answers to questions 2 and 3 are "yes," which is strange reasoning indeed.

Regarding question 2, even if it is true that people can fake most measures of self-report, this is no evidence at all that they actually do fake such instruments either in applied settings or in basic research in psychology. When asked the time of day, a person could always add an hour to what his watch shows, but who actually does that? There is a great deal of positive evidence to show that many measures of self-report are reasonably valid. For example, if one takes a close look at people scoring in the highest decile on a measure of anxiety, he will find a great deal of circumstantial evidence to indicate that those people as a group are highly anxious. Although no one would claim that the MMPI is a perfect measure of various facets of maladjustment, people who obtain high scores on the various scales tend to be rather sick individuals. For the sake of argument, however, let us assume that the answer to question 2 is "yes" and then see what implications, if any, this has for question 3, which is really the important question to ask.

If the average person can and does fake scores on self-report measures in such a way as to put himself in a better light, all this indicates for sure is that the mean of the obtained distribution of scores is somewhat different from that of a hypothetically valid measure of the same trait. But as is well known, the mean of a distribution of scores is of relatively little consequence either in applied settings or in basic research. Such scores are almost always interpreted in a relative sense, as when scores are converted to percentiles or some type of standard scores.

The real issue regarding question 3 is how well scores obtained from self-report measures would correlate with scores obtained in a situation where people were absolutely frank. There are two reasons why that correlation might be relatively low. First, faking may introduce a source of unreliability into scores obtained from the usual administration of self-report measures. The evidence is against this possibility. It is usually not difficult to develop a highly reliable self-report measure of personality, such as a measure of anxiety. One frequently sees rather low reliabilities, but this is almost always due to the fact that not enough items are included to obtain a reliable scale. For any set number of items, self-report measures of personality tend to be as reliable as measures of human ability, such as measures of vocabulary and arithmetic skills.

The second reason why the correlation might be low is that faking results in a change in the factorial composition of a measure over that which would be obtained in a condition where no faking was present. A measure for that purpose is obtained by dividing the squared correlation between two measures by the product of their respective reliabilities. This indicates the percentage of shared common variance and, consequently, the extent to which two measures have the same factorial composition, when measurement error is excluded. As far as the author is aware, there is almost no evidence at all that the shared common variance is less than 100 percent between measures obtained in practice and measures obtained under special experimental conditions concerning faking. Circumstantial evidence here would be obtained by computing the shared common variance for scores found under the usual instructions to fake well. The author has never seen any evidence of that kind and hypothesizes that, when it is obtained, the shared common variance will be surprisingly high. If that hypothesis is correct, the distribution of scores seen in practice will be one in which the mean is moved somewhat from its true position and the distribution shape might be slightly altered but in which people tend to retain the same rank-order positions they would on the measure when no faking is present.

The foregoing three questions can be illustrated with the variable of chronological age of women as found in census reports. Anyone can fake his age, so the answer to question 1 is "yes." The folklore has it that women as a group tend to understate their ages somewhat, so we shall accept the answer to question 2 as "yes." Regarding question 3, however, the answer might be "no." The shared common variance might be very high between actual ages and ages stated on the reports. There would probably be a monotonic function relating amount of faking to age. The younger women would tend to give their correct ages, women in their late thirties might tend to take off a year or two on the average, and older women might shave the years by quite a bit. Then, if one is interested only in *individual differences* in ages between the women, the obtained measure is approximately as valid as the true measure. The same may very well be true of most self-report measures of personality. We may have overly damned self-report measures of personality on this score.

## other issues concerning self-inventories

There are other problems in the use of self-inventories to measure personality traits that should be mentioned, in addition to those we have discussed so far. Such inventories are beset with *semantic problems*, which occur both in communicating the meaning of items to subjects and in communicating the results of studies to researchers. The former type of problem can be illustrated with the following item: "Do you usually lead the discussion in group situations?" First, the individual must decide what is meant by "group situations." Does this pertain to family settings as well as to groups outside the home? Does it pertain only to formal groups, such as clubs and business groups, or does it also apply to informal group situations? Second, the subject must decide what is meant by "lead." Does this mean to speak the most, to make the best points, or to have the last say? Third, the subject must decide what is meant by "usually." Does that mean nearly all the time, most of the time, or at least half the time?

Anyone who works with self-inventories should, on at least one occasion, ask several subjects how they interpret each item on a typical inventory. When one does this, he is rather appalled by the different interpretations of different subjects and by the extent to which all subjects are somewhat confused by some of the items. For these reasons, it is frequently found that subjects give different responses to sizable percentages of the items when responding to the same self-inventory on two or more occasions. This, of course, relates only to the general confusion about the meanings of items. In contrast, if an individual makes a definite but erroneous interpretation of an item, he will consistently respond erroneously to the item.

A second semantic problem occurs in communicating the results of studies with self-inventories to other researchers. Factor names and descriptions tend to be less clear than is the case with factors of human ability. This is due partly to the fact that researchers employ terms in common parlance to describe factors, and people do not entirely agree about the meanings of such terms. For example, the factor that Guilford calls "thoughtfulness" might be misinterpreted by many as relating to considerateness, whereas it actually relates to contemplativeness. Admitting that it is difficult to find precise terms for communicating about personality traits, some investigators have gone out of their way to employ vague terms, e.g., "rhathymia" and "adventurous cyclothymia."

Another major problem with self-inventories is that scores are somewhat affected by situational factors. (Evidence for this is summarized by Guilford, 1959.) For example, if a self-inventory is used in personnel selection, individuals are likely to give somewhat different answers when applying for a job from those which they will give sometime later when they are performing satisfactorily on the job. Numerous studies have shown that responses are somewhat different when the same subjects are required to take the same inventory under different instructions, e.g., under instructions to appear adjusted, to appear maladjusted, and to be frank. Although there is not enough evidence to know for sure, it might be that self-inventories used in basic research are affected to some extent by the subject's conceptions of the intents and purposes of the research. For example, if the subject thinks the research concerns emotions, he might make somewhat different responses on an inventory from those he would make if he thought the research concerned learning.

It should be pointed out that the foregoing and other problems with items on self-inventories do not make it impossible to develop highly valid measures of personality traits. As should be remembered from the discussion in Chapter 8, the individual item on almost any test has only a very modest amount of validity. However, the total score obtained over all items in a test can be highly valid even if the average item has only modest validity.

### Directions for research

Since individual differences in social desirability are so strongly represented in most self-inventories, plans for improving such inventories must consider what is to be done about that variable. As was mentioned previously, it is an interesting variable which merits investigation in its own right, but it is serving to cloud the measurement of other personality traits. Numerous suggestions have been made for ways to delete the social-desirability factor in self-report inventories, but none of these has proved very satisfactory. One possible way to deal with social desirability is to employ items that are neutral with respect to social desirability. Logically this is very difficult because, to varying degrees, personality traits are intrinsically related to social desirability. Thus dominance is considered more desirable than submissiveness, sociability is considered more desirable than nonsociability, being energetic is considered more desirable than being lazy, and so on for other personality traits. For these reasons, it is very difficult to find neutral items that actually measure personality traits; however, by employing items that are not extreme with respect to social desirability, one should be able to obtain some reduction of the importance of that factor.

Rather than attempt to employ items that are neutral with respect to social desirability, another approach is to employ forced-choice items that are matched for social desirability. Two examples are:

Do you worry more about

_____ social problems

or

_____ health problems?

Do most of your friends consider you more

_____frank

or

_____ tenderhearted?

Although the use of forced-choice self-inventories has stirred much interest and considerable work has been done to develop such inventories, the forced-choice item by no means constitutes a panacea for the problems that beset self-inventories. One major problem is that it is very difficult to equate alternatives for social desirability. Even when the alternatives have almost identical ratings of social desirability when rated separately, they are not rated equal in social desirability when paired. This is probably due to the fact that comparative ratings are more precise in this instance, for reasons that were discussed in Chapter 7. For example, even if frankness and tenderheartedness receive the same mean rating of 6.0 on a seven-step social-desirability scale, 60 percent of the people may say that frankness is more desirable than tenderheartedness when they are actually paired. Apparently, in forced-choice inventories, people are able to detect fine differences in social desirability, which partly destroys the purpose of using such instruments.

Another problem with forced-choice inventories concerns public relations, particularly in applied settings. People tend to feel "trapped" by forced-choice inventories, and in many cases rightly so. As extreme examples, almost anyone would feel uncomfortable in responding to the following two items:

Are you more

_____ honest

or

_____ intelligent?

Are you more

_____ cowardly

or

_____ cruel?

Self-report has been used in the effort to measure all four of the kinds of personality traits mentioned previously—social traits, motives, personal conceptions, and adjustment. If one will think carefully and look at the available evidence, he will see that self-report measures have had their major problems in the area of social traits. Measures of social traits tend to be dominated by a huge factor of expressed self-esteem, or social desirability, as Edwards (1957a) calls it. Beyond that factor, the idiographists have had a field day in showing that it is hard to demonstrate other broad, statistically strong factors in self-report measures of social traits. As was mentioned previously, the idiographists have overstated their case, and also there are some possibilities of reducing the factor of expressed self-esteem to the point where other broad, statistically strong factors can arise from self-report measures of social traits. But even so, it is in the area of social traits that self-report measures have encountered the most trouble.

Very encouraging signs have appeared regarding the development of self-report measures of personality characteristics relating to personal conceptions, such as with respect to measures of attitudes and values. An example is the Locus of Control Scale (McConnell, 1966), which concerns the extent to which the individual conceives of the good things in life as being due to luck and machinations by other people rather than to his own talents and efforts. There are very interesting developmental trends with respect to scores on the scale, and the scores relate to various aspects of problem solving.

Idiography does not hold in the area of personal conceptions to the extent that it does in self-report measures of social traits. This is evidenced in the relatively high correlations between items on many measures of personal conceptions and the consequent high reliability of scales. What has been lacking in the study of personal conceptions through self-report is a consistent attack on personal conceptions as a whole. Individual scales of values and attitudes have been developed, but have not been followed up with factor-analytic investigations. If different facets of personal conceptions were hypothesized and investigated by factor analysis, self-report might lead to some very interesting dimensions of personality.

The condemnation of self-report measures of personality by many psychologists may be due in part to epistemological biases regarding the acceptability of different kinds of data from human subjects. Although very few psychologists will confess it, we have tended to reject verbal reports as somehow unacceptable as scientific data. This attitude has probably been brought about because of (1) an overly zealous rejection of turn-of-the-century introspectionism, (2) an equally overzealous interpretation of behaviorism, and (3) such a large amount of research with animals that cannot talk. It may prove to be the case that, because he can talk, man will eventually be the only animal for which a complete psychology is obtainable. Having been shunned by many people for over twenty years, verbal reports are very much coming back into experimental psychology, such as in the investigations of verbal reports of problem-solving strategies in studies of computer simulation.

## observational methods

Related to self-inventories are observational methods for the measurement of personality traits, the difference being that in the latter method the individual is asked to describe someone else rather than himself. In most observational methods, the interest is in the personality traits of the person being observed, and the intention is for the observer to be an impartial, accurate judge of the traits of the other person. In some observational methods, however, it is really the personality traits of the observer that are at issue, and the observer's observations are used to infer something about his personality. This is the case in studies of "person perception," to be discussed later.

In most observational methods, the validity of the measurements is completely at the mercy of the observers. They make judgments about the personality traits of other people, and such judgments can be accurate only if the experimenter asks the right questions of the observers and only if the observers know the correct answers. It is proper to say that such observational methods are "subjective," in that judgments necessarily flow from the silent intuitive processes of the observers. Such subjective judgments surely constitute the oldest approach to the understanding of personality traits. Men have always observed other men and tried to describe their characteristics with words relating to personality. What has been done in psychometric research on observational methods is to objectify the recording of impressions (e.g., with rating scales) and to objectify the analysis of results.

In contrast to most observational methods, which are based on subjective judgments of personality traits, some observational methods are quite objective, in that all the observer does is record what the subject actually does, e.g., how many questions a child asks in an interview situation. In other instances, observational methods are "almost" objective, in that the observer is required to make ratings that entail only a low level of inference, e.g., that a child is shy in an interview situation.

What is typically found is that the more objective the behavior to be observed, the more molecular the trait involved. It is easy to be objective about traits at the level of simple "habits," e.g., number of questions asked, amount of time spent in different activities, and number of words of different kinds uttered by the person being observed. When observations are being made of more general personality traits, however, judgments are usually highly subjective, e.g., judging personality traits like anxiety, dominance, and achievement motivation. Thus efforts to make observational methods more objective usually result in narrowing the traits under investigation to the level of highly specific modes of response (or habits). Then there is a question of how to combine such highly specific responses into measures of more general personality traits. To do so requires a great deal of construct validation, very little of which has been done at the present time. If one goes to the other extreme and deals directly with general traits of personality, much credence must be placed in the accuracy of subjective judgments by observers.

Most observational methods employ rating scales to record impressions, e.g., a seven-step scale bounded by the adjectives "anxious" and "calm" to be used in rating psychiatric patients in an interview. Some psychometric properties of rating methods will be discussed in Chapter 14; here we shall consider the types of situations in which such rating scales are employed. There is a large literature on observational methods, so large that it is not possible here to summarize all the evidence with respect to the many approaches that have been explored. We shall mention only some of the outstanding properties of the major observational methods. (Guilford, 1959, provides a detailed summary of methods and results.)

### Observation in daily life

Observation in daily life is probably employed more frequently than any other observational method for the measurement of personality traits. For example, a teacher rates the personality traits of his students, parents rate the personality traits of their children, and students rate one another's personality traits. (A typical rating form used in educational settings is presented in Figure 12-2.) Such observations are analogous to having one individual fill out a self-inventory for someone else, and consequently both methods tend to run into the same types of problems. Ratings of persons in daily life tend to be dominated by a general factor, not unlike the factor of social desirability found in self-inventories (Peterson, 1965). Such ratings tend to concern rather obviously good- and bad-sounding traits, e.g., anxious rather than calm, and friendly rather than hostile. Much of the common variance among scales in a typical study can be accounted for by a general factor. This is particularly so in ratings of social traits and motives of normal people. Apparently there is less tendency for a general factor to prevail in studies of symptoms of malad-

| | Much below average | Below average | Average | Above average | Much above average |
|---|---|---|---|---|---|
| Courtesy | | | | | |
| Intelligence | | | | | |
| Moral character | | | | | |
| Personal appearance | | | | | |
| Health | | | | | |
| Ambitiousness | | | | | |
| Friendliness | | | | | |
| Creative ability | | | | | |
| General knowledge | | | | | |
| Writing skill | | | | | |
| Emotional stability | | | | | |
| Diligence | | | | | |

**FIGURE 12-2**     A typical set of rating scales

justment in groups of neurotics and psychotics. This is demonstrated, for example, in the study by Grinker, Miller, Sabshin, Nunn, and Nunnally (1961), which produced 15 factors relating to the symptoms of depressed patients.

The general factor that usually appears in self-inventories concerns self-desirability (or rated self-esteem). The general factor that appears in most ratings of normal people concerns *leniency*, the tendency to say good things or bad things about people in general. This might be thought of as other-desirability rather than self-desirability. Individual differences in the former tendency have been documented on numerous occasions, where it has been found that raters differ in their average ratings of other people.

The factor of other-desirability, besides making it difficult to document additional factors in ratings, also introduces a source of bias into ratings. The ratings made of a person depend to some extent on the rater's level of other-desirability, which is a source of unreliability. Obviously this bias would lead to some faulty decisions about people in applied situations, e.g., in ratings of workers by foremen and in the ratings of psychiatric patients by nurses.

Just as self-desirability in self-inventories is influenced by the frankness of the subject, the rated social desirability of other persons is influenced by personal prejudices. For example, parents are prone to give more favorable ratings to their children than to other peoples' children, and teachers are influenced in the rating of students by their personal likes and dislikes.

Just as self-inventories are limited to what the individual knows about himself, ratings in daily life are limited to what the observer knows about the person being rated. Actually, this is more of a problem with observational methods than with self-inventories because with the latter, it can at least be assumed that the individual "lives with himself" and has myriad opportunities to observe himself in action, whether or not he actually does so. Frequently ratings are made by people who barely know the person being rated or have had opportunities to observe him only in highly restricted settings.

Even if the observer has had considerable opportunity to observe an individual in one type of situation, he may have had practically no opportunity to observe him in situations relevant to the traits being rated. This frequently occurs in university settings, where professors are asked to rate personality characteristics of students in applications for graduate work or for a particular position. The professor may have only the vaguest idea about some of a student's social traits.

In spite of the problems involved, observations in daily life tend to be superior to the other types of observational methods. Although such ratings frequently suffer because the observer has not had sufficient opportunities to observe the individual in circumstances relevant to the traits being rated, the situation in this regard tends to be much worse in the case of the other observational methods. Typically the latter methods permit the observer to witness only a tiny sample of the individual's behavior, and frequently that is done in highly artificial situations.   If nothing else, observations in daily life provide a much more economical way of obtaining approximate information about personality characteristics than is provided by other observational methods.

## Interviews

The interview is simply one type of observational situation.   It is seldom used for observing personality traits in general; rather, it is usually restricted to "sizing up" an individual with respect to particular decisions about him, as in a job interview or a psychiatric interview.   Usually the interviewer either has never previously met the person being interviewed or has known him only casually.   Because of the small amount of time available to observe the individual (usually less than one hour), interviews make sense only if it can be assumed that (1) the interviewer is particularly talented at observing some important traits and (2) the purpose of the interview is limited to obtaining information about only a small number of traits.   Because the results of interviews naturally depend on the questions asked by the interviewers, efforts have been made to "structure" such interviews with standard lists of questions and other ways of establishing uniformity.

Even with the best efforts, ratings based on interviews tend to have only a low level of reliability and validity (Guilford, 1959; Ulrich & Trumbo, 1965).   Since interviews are usually employed in making personnel decisions, validity is determined by correlating ratings with specific criteria.   When that is done, it is usually found that ratings add little to the predictive validity that is obtainable from objective tests of ability, personality, and interest.   In spite of this fact, interviews will probably continue to be used for some time because in some instances there is nothing else that can be used, as is the case with psychiatric interviews.   It is surprising, however, that some people who castigate standardized tests place inordinate faith in what can be obtained from a 30-minute interview.   It is clear that the interview does not provide a valid general tool for the measurement of personality traits.

Although the interview does not constitute a valid general tool for the measurement of personality characteristics, it is obviously very useful in obtaining particular information about persons in applied settings.   For example, in an interview with a job applicant, it might be learned that the applicant owns a truck that would be useful on the particular job.   In an interview with a newly admitted psychiatric patient, it might be learned that the patient has a paranoid delusion concerning one of the hospital staff members, which would be important to know both for the sake of treatment and in the interests of security precautions.   The interview is very valuable for obtaining such bits of information about people, but for sizing them up with respect to general traits of personality (such as honesty, intelligence, and gregariousness), other methods of measurement tend to be more valid.

### Observations in contrived situations

One approach to observation is to have the individual participate in a contrived situation, which is frequently spoken of as a *situational test*. One of the pioneering efforts of this kind was the screening program developed by the Office of Strategic Services during World War II. The purpose was to select men for military intelligence work, espionage, and other dangerous assignments. In addition to taking standardized tests of personality and ability, each candidate was given a series of situational tests, with each situation involving a type of problem that might be encountered in actual duty. The candidate's performance was rated in terms of ability to think quickly and effectively and in terms of emotional stability and leadership. In one such situation, the candidate was told to imagine that he was caught in a government office going through files marked "secret," that he did not work in the building, and that he carried no identification papers. He was given 12 minutes to construct an alibi for his presence under such suspicious circumstances. Then he was subjected to a harrowing interrogation, in which attempts were made to break his alibi and to make his statements appear foolish. The candidate was rated on how convincing his story was and his ability to support it under interrogation.

A large-scale use of situational tests was made in a study to develop selection instruments for clinical psychology trainees (Kelly & Fiske, 1951). In one such test, each candidate was required to express in pantomime the meaning of different emotions. In that study, situational tests added nothing to the prediction of success in clinical practice over what was provided by standardized tests of ability and personality (and the same was true for interviews).

By their nature, observations in contrived situations are not suited to the measurement of personality traits in general; rather, they are restricted to a very limited number of traits relating to the particular contrived situations. Also, since in many cases they are extremely laborious and time-consuming, they should not be employed unless they add something to results obtained with simpler methods of measurement, and most of the evidence on that score is negative. Perhaps in some situations such observations are no more valid than they are because the situations are so obviously contrived. Some situations amount to "playacting," and it is reasonable to believe that such playacting is not entirely representative of behavior in real life. For example, the individual who shows leadership qualities in daily life might regard situational tests as silly and thus might appear to perform rather poorly.

Observations in contrived situations will probably continue to be used only with respect to applied problems of personnel selection. There is evidence (Guilford, 1959) that some of the approaches work reasonably well for that purpose, particularly when the situations are made "natural" for the persons to be observed. An example is the "leaderless group discussion," in which half a dozen persons are observed while they discuss some issue. Ratings of leadership qualities in such situations correlate reasonably well with actual performance in supervisory positions.

### Behavioral tests

In some observational situations, directly observable aspects of the subject's behavior are used as measures of personality characteristics. Because the observations concern observable behavior, the situations in which such observations are made are usually referred to as *behavioral tests*. Like situational tests, behavioral tests consist of contrived situations. One of the earliest and still the best-known use of behavioral tests was that of Hartshorne, May, and Shuttleworth (1930) in the Character Educational Inquiry. They wanted to measure traits in schoolchildren such as honesty, truthfulness, cooperativeness, and self-control. Rather than use conventional tests or ratings to measure those characteristics, they chose to observe the actual behavior of children with respect to the traits. The observations were made in the normal routine of school activities—in athletics, recreation, and classroom work.

Observations were made so as to provide objective scores. For example, one of the measures of honesty was made by allowing students to grade their own papers. Since a duplicate copy of each paper had been prepared before it was given to the student, it was a simple matter to check the student's honesty in that situation. Another behavioral test in that study concerned the trait of "charity," in which children were first given an attractive kit of school supplies and then were allowed to donate some of the items to "less fortunate children." The donations appeared to be anonymous, but the experimenters had marked the items so as to be able to count the number of items donated by each child.

Another type of behavioral test is the Minimal Social Behavior Scale (Farina, Arenberg, & Guskin, 1957), in which mental patients are submitted to a structured interview. In one "item," the interviewer offers the patient a pencil, and the item is scored "correct" if the patient accepts the pencil or acknowledges the offer in some other way. In another item, the interviewer places a cigarette in his mouth and fumbles for a match, during which time a book of matches is in plain view of the patient but is not visible to the interviewer. The item is scored "correct" if the patient mentions the matches or offers a match from his own pocket.

When behavioral tests can be employed, they have a number of attractive advantages. The use of actual behavioral products frees the measurement methods from the subjectivity of rating scales. If observations can be made in natural settings where the subject is unaware that he is being tested in any sense, the results are probably more valid. There have, however, been so few systematic uses of behavioral tests that it is difficult to judge how useful they will be in the measurement of personality traits. They will probably continue to be used more with children than with adults because it is easier to place children in the test situations without having them suspect an ulterior purpose. Also, the relevant behaviors of children are more easily observed than complex adult interactions.

For a number of reasons, it is doubtful that behavioral tests will occupy more than a modest place in the measurement of personality traits. Like all observations in contrived situations, they are expensive and time-consuming to apply. More important, it is very difficult to think of behavioral products that might relate to most personality traits. For example, what behavioral products in adults might relate to dominance or sociability? Behavioral tests will probably continue to be used only for rather special purposes, such as in the basic research of Hartshorne, May, and Shuttleworth on character traits in children or for diagnosing rather specific traits in clinical populations.

### Person perception

As was mentioned previously, in some instances observational methods are employed in the effort to learn something about the personality of the observer rather than about the persons being observed. Such methods are said to concern person perception. For example, previously it was said that observers differ in other-desirability, as manifested in mean differences between observers in their ratings of the social desirability of persons in general. It might be thought that such differences in other-desirability would relate to the personalities of observers—that observers who generally rate all people as "positive" are accepting and friendly and that observers who tend to rate all people as "negative" are sullen grouches. If differences in mean favorableness ratings relate to personality characteristics of observers, convincing evidence is yet to be obtained. More likely, most of the variance among observers in that regard is due to "sets" regarding the use of rating scales. In most cases observers would probably change their mean ratings of other people if they learned that their ratings were well above or below the mean ratings given by other observers.

Another aspect of person perception concerns the ability to guess how another person will rate himself, which has been referred to as *empathy*. One way of attempting to measure this supposed trait is to have an individual respond to the items on a self-inventory and then have a friend attempt to guess how the person responded to each item. The percentage of correct guesses is taken as an empathy score. This approach has been used to investigate the amount of empathy of psychotherapists, in which case the therapist is required to guess the responses of his client. Unfortunately, accuracy scores tend to be rather specific to the "target" person. A person might have a rather high empathy score in guessing the responses of one person but a rather low empathy score in guessing the responses of another person. What consistency there is in such judgments has not found much construct validity for the measurement of a trait of empathy (Guilford, 1959).

A third aspect of person perception concerns *assumed similarity*, the degree to which a person rates other persons as much the same as one another or different from one another. One approach is to ask an individual to rate a person whom he likes very much and a person whom he dislikes on a list of rating scales, each rating scale being bounded by bipolar adjectives such as kind-cruel, friendly-unfriendly, wise-foolish, and strong-weak. An assumed-similarity score is obtained from a statistical comparison of the ratings given to the two persons. One of the major problems with studies of assumed similarity is that they are beset with numerous artifacts that are very difficult to control (these are discussed by Cronbach & Meehl, 1955). For example, the assumed-similarity score obtained from comparing "most liked person" with "least liked person" depends on the persons that the rater has in mind, and thus it may be more an indication of the wideness of the person's acquaintance with other people than an indication of the tendency to view others as much the same rather than as different from one another. There is little convincing evidence that measures of assumed similarity are important measures of personality traits.

### Evaluation of observational methods

As can be seen from the foregoing discussion, observational methods as a group have severe limitations as approaches to the measurement of personality traits. Individual methods tend to suffer from one or all of the problems of being (1) based on insufficient experience with the person being observed, (2) dependent on the subjective judgment of observers, (3) dominated by a general factor of other-desirability in ratings, (4) logically restricted to the measurement of only a limited range of traits, (5) of only modest to low interobserver reliability, and (6) in those instances where a particular criterion is to be predicted of little predictive validity. As a general tool, the best approach of this lot is the method of obtaining ratings in daily life. If there is a truism concerning the use of observational methods, it is that the validity depends much more on the amount of experience the observer has had with the ratee in situations relative to the traits being rated than it does on the qualifications of the rater in other regards. For example, in military settings it is consistently found that trainees in officer candidate schools do a better job of rating one another than the officers do in rating the trainees, probably because the trainees know one another much better than their officers know them. As another example, in a study by Grinker et al. (1961), an *inverse* relationship was found between the years of experience of psychiatrists and the reliability of rating depressive patients in hospitals. They hypothesized that this was due to the fact that the younger psychiatrists had much more direct experience with the patients, seeing them on numerous occasions on the ward, whereas the senior psychiatrists saw the patients only in interviews and briefly on other occasions.

Even when observers have approximately the same amount of information about persons being rated, there are individual differences in the ability of observers to make accurate ratings (Guilford, 1959), and the accuracy of the rater interacts with the type of person being rated. This is analogous to the case of intelligence testers who differ in their overall accuracy of administering tests and who do a better job with some types of persons than with others. This must happen to some extent with intelligence tests, but it surely happens to a much greater extent in ratings. To the extent that there are differences in accuracy of raters and these differences interact with the persons being rated, ratings simply are not standardized measures of personality traits. With respect to basic research on personality traits, all observational methods are mainly stopgap approaches that will probably be replaced one day by better methods for the measurement of personality traits.

Surely observational methods will continue to be employed in applied settings in education, industry, military organizations, hospitals, and other institutions. It is very difficult to imagine how some types of important information could be obtained by any other means.


## Summary

In spite of the vast importance of personality traits in basic research and in applied psychology, the measurement of these traits is still in its infancy, not because the problem has been neglected, but rather because of the intrinsic difficulties of developing valid measures of personality traits. There are those (the idiographists) who claim that it is futile to search for general yardsticks concerning personality, that instead it is necessary to study each individual as an idiosyncratic pattern of behavioral tendencies. The idiographic point of view is an unhealthy scientific standpoint, and the available facts do not require one to subscribe to that gloomy outlook.

A fourfold taxonomy is useful for discussing different types of personality traits. Social traits, such as gregariousness and aggressiveness, relate to how an individual behaves overtly in his social environment. Motives concern the inner urges—drives, needs, and emotions. Although they frequently go by the same names, motives differ from social traits in that they are frequently obscure in overt behavior. Personal conceptions concern the way a person views the world and his place in it—self-concept, interests, attitudes, and values. Adjustment, as contrasted with maladjustment, appears mainly in the form of various mixtures of the extremes of the foregoing three types of personality characteristics.

Two approaches to the measurement of the aforementioned types of personality traits are with respect to (1) self-inventories and (2) observational methods. With self-inventories, essentially subjects are asked to describe their own personalities by answering questions on printed forms or by marking rating scales. The major potential virtue of self-inventories is that, since the individual experiences his own insides and has had many opportunities to watch his own behavior, self-report should offer a gold mine of information about personality characteristics. There are numerous problems, however, in mining that gold with existing self-inventories.

Responses to self-inventories are based on a mixture of (1) what a person actually knows about himself, (2) what he is willing to relate, and (3) what his personality traits actually are. Regarding the first point, if an individual actually does not understand himself, valid measurement of personality traits with self-inventories is not possible. Potentially this is a bigger problem with some types of personality traits than with others; e.g., it would be a larger issue when asking an individual to describe how other people feel about him than when asking him how he feels about other people.

Regarding the second point above, self-inventories have been roundly criticized because it is assumed that (1) such inventories can be faked easily, (2) people generally do fake them in such a way as to appear healthy-minded, and (3) such faking prevents the instruments from being valid measures of individual differences in personality traits. The evidence regarding the first point is strong; the evidence regarding the second point is weak; and the evidence regarding the third point is almost nonexistent.

In spite of the problems inherent in their use, self-inventories offer the most practicable and valid approach currently available for the measurement of personality traits in general. The other approaches either are known to be limited in applicability or involve even more problems than self-inventories.

Instead of employing self-inventories, observational methods can be used for the measurement of personality traits. Rather than being asked to describe himself, the individual is asked to describe someone else. With observational methods, it is important to consider the extent to which opportunities for observations are structured, or controlled, by the researcher. At one extreme, observations in daily life are not structured at all. At the other extreme, in *behavioral tests* and *situational tests* observations are obtained regarding behavior in controlled social situations.

It has been found that the validity of observational methods depends more on the opportunities to observe an individual in situations relative to the personality characteristics being judged than it does on the training or qualifications of the judge. For this and other reasons, only observations based on informal acquaintance in daily life have much chance of providing important general tools for the measurement of personality characteristics.

## Suggested additional readings

Cattell, R. B. *Personality and motivation structure and measurement.* New York: Harcourt, Brace & World, 1957.

Eysenck, H. J. *The structure of human personality.* London: Methuen, 1960.

Guilford, J. P. *Personality.* New York: McGraw-Hill, 1959.

# CHAPTER 13

## Measurement of personality traits: methods based on projection, physiological processes, and perception

The methods for measuring personality characteristics discussed in Chapter 12 (self-inventories and observational methods) depend upon the accuracy of the reporting of human subjects. With self-inventories, the individual must know himself well and honestly report what he knows. With observational methods, the observer must know the "target" person well and report what he knows without bias. In contrast to self-inventories and observational methods, there are methods of personality measurement which do not depend heavily on the knowledge and honesty of human subjects. The latter type of methods will be discussed in this chapter.

### projective techniques

The projective techniques offer an approach to the measurement of personality which is interestingly different from that of the self-description inventories. Whereas the self-description inventories require the subject to describe himself, the projective techniques require him to describe or to interpret objects other than himself. The projective techniques are based on the hypothesis that an individual's responses to an "unstructured" stimulus are influenced by his needs, motives, fears, expectations, and concerns.

If there is an agreed-upon public meaning for a stimulus, it is referred to as a *structured* stimulus. If there is no agreed-upon public meaning for a stimulus, and in consequence there is considerable latitude for individual interpretation, it is referred to as an *unstructured* stimulus. A structured stimulus is compared with an unstructured stimulus in Figure 13-1. First, what is pictured in Figure 13-1*a*? Nearly everyone will say that it is a house. A few people might call it a school or even a jail, but people will generally agree that it is a building of some kind. The shape of a house is a highly structured stimulus. Now what is pictured in Figure 13-1*b*? There is no accepted common meaning for that stimulus pattern. It might be interpreted as a thunderstorm, a dog, or an artist's palette.

There is much evidence from everyday life to show that interpretations of relatively unstructured stimuli are related to moods, needs, and expectations. An experience common to most of us is the misreading of printed material in a way that indicates our concerns of the moment. For example, the student who is worried about an examination he has to take the next day is likely to see in a hasty glance at the evening paper that "The police will give the examination tomorrow," whereas a careful reading will show that "The police will give the explanation tomorrow."

As another example, the individual who has strong hostile motives himself very frequently attributes hostile motives to other people. Potentially, projective techniques provide a very useful method for the measurement of motives such as aggression, sex, affiliation, achievement, and others (as distinct from the social traits relating to the way such motives appear on the surface).

If the individual interprets Figure 13-1*b* as a thunderstorm rather than a dog, this may indicate something about him personally. However, it is one thing to say that a response is significant and quite another thing to say just what it indicates about the person.

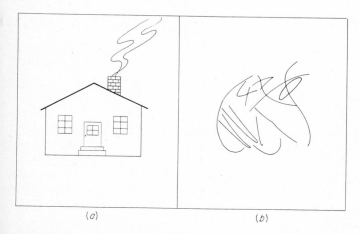

(*a*)                    (*b*)

**FIGURE 13-1**    Comparison of (*a*) a relatively structured stimulus with (*b*) a relatively unstructured stimulus

The instruments which will be described in this discussion of projective techniques are based primarily on the interpretation of personality characteristics from responses to relatively unstructured stimuli. The ultimate in unstructured stimuli is found in one of the pictures in the Thematic Apperception Test (TAT). The subject is asked to make up a story about a completely blank card. Other stimuli are structured to some extent to obtain information about particular needs and concerns. For example, in an instrument used to study attitudes, a picture which shows a white person and a Negro talking can be used. The stimulus is structured to that extent and in that manner in order to learn about attitudes toward Negroes.

The term "projective tests," which is used to refer to the kinds of instruments to be discussed here, is something of a misnomer. The more strict meaning of the term "projection" is the tendency of an individual to see his own unwanted traits, ideas, and concerns in other people. Here we shall be concerned not only with projection in the stricter sense but also with the many ways in which the interpretation of unstructured stimuli can be used to detect personality characteristics.

### Rorschach technique

By far the most widely used projective technique is the Rorschach. It was developed during and after World War I by Hermann Rorschach, a Swiss psychiatrist. He experimented with different inkblots to find a set which would provide the most insight into the nature of mental disorder. The 10 inkblots which he settled on are still in use. An inkblot like those used in the test is shown in Figure 13-2. Five of the inkblot cards are made in shades of black and gray only. Two of the remaining cards contain bright patches of red in addition to shades of gray. The three remaining cards employ various colors.

### Administration

The Rorschach, like the other projective devices, should be administered only by a highly trained examiner. The results will depend very much on the examiner's skill. Although there are several schools of thought as to how the Rorschach should be administered and interpreted, a similar approach is used by most examiners. The most widely used approaches are those advocated by Beck (1944) and by Klopfer and Kelley (1942).

The ususal procedure followed in administering the Rorschach is to talk with the respondent a minute or so to gain rapport, seat him with his back to the examiner, and then introduce the task with approximately the following instructions: "People see all sorts of things in these inkblot pictures; now tell me what you see, what it might be for you, what it makes you think of" (Klopfer & Kelley, 1942, p. 32). The respondent is allowed to give as many interpretations as he likes. If he gives only one response and apparently tries to give no

**FIGURE 13-2**    An inkblot of the type used in the Rorschach
test

more, the examiner suggests that he look for other things, saying something
like, "People usually see more than one thing."   In a typical series of responses
to one card, the subject would report, "It all looks like a bat" and "This part
looks like a vase."   After looking at the card for a few more seconds, he might
give as his final response, "This little bit looks like a nose."

After the respondent runs out of interpretations for the first card, he is
handed the next one, and so on for all 10 cards.   The examiner is kept busy
ordering the materials, measuring the time taken to give each response, and
writing down verbatim what the respondent says.   After the series of inkblots
is administered, the examiner conducts what is called the "inquiry."   This
consists of asking the subject questions about each of his responses to learn
what part of the blot is involved in the interpretation and why the particular
part gives rise to the response.

## Scoring

There are a number of different kinds of scores given to each response.   The
major scoring categories relate to *content, location,* and *determinants.*   The interpretation of a response depends on the scores received from all three cate-

gories. Consequently, only very general implications can be given to scores in one category alone.

Some of the major categories of content are listed and illustrated below, along with typical responses:

*Human.*    "A man doing a dance."
*Human detail.*    "A nose."
*Animal.*    "A bat."
*Anatomy.*    "Bones."
*Clothing.*    "A nun's habit."
*Nature.*    "Northern lights."
*Sex.*    "A woman's breast."
*Landscape.*    "A Lake."
*Food.*    "A steak with mushrooms."

If a person gives almost all animal responses, this is taken as an indication of low "functioning intelligence." A predominance of anatomy responses is usually interpreted as an indication of depressive tendency or of overconcern with health. If an individual gives many more responses in one content category than in others, e.g., many food responses, this is taken as evidence of a particular personality need.

Location refers to the part of the inkblot which instigates a particular response. This information is usually obtained in the inquiry. The response is scored W if the whole blot is used in the response. Typical W responses are "a bat," "a sky full of dark clouds," and "a garden of flowers." The response is scored D if the location is a commonly perceived subdivision of the total blot. Typical D responses are to call a large part of an inkblot "a bird's head" and another part of the same blot "a statue." The response is scored Dd if the location is a small and usually unnoticed part of the inkblot. A typical Dd response is to interpret a small patch of gray off from the main figure as "a face."

The location of responses is thought to indicate the subject's mental approach to life, whether he deals in sweeping generalizations, considers details systematically, or gets lost in the compulsive consideration of unimportant side issues. The number and kind of W responses supposedly reflect potential intelligence. The intelligent, creative person is thought to give numerous, well-organized W responses. The person who emphasizes D responses is thought to have a commonsense, matter-of-fact approach to life problems. An emphasis on Dd responses is taken as an indication of compulsive tendency or mental disorganization. The Rorschach responses of the average adult contain approximately 6 W responses, 20 D, and 4 Dd.

The scoring of determinants is both more complex and more subjective than the scoring of content and location. If the response is determined by the shape or outline of either the whole or part of the inkblot, it is scored as a form response (F). Form responses are further scored either "plus," if they are adequate responses of the kind that normal and superior people would give, or "minus," if they are not adequate interpretations. A response is scored M if the interpretation involves movement, e.g., "two women dancing." If the response is apparently determined by the color of the part which is interpreted, it is scored C. If the response is "seawater" and in the inquiry the subject gives as his reason, "because it's green," it would be scored as a color response. A response is scored Y if it is determined by the shades of gray within a blot. A typical Y response is "dark clouds." It is usually the case that a response must be scored on more than one determinant. For example, an FC score means that the response is determined mainly by form and that color enters as a secondary determinant. A CF response means that color is the primary determinant and form the secondary determinant.

Form responses are thought to indicate a factual, rational approach to life. Color responses are thought to indicate emotional reactions. If a person gives considerably more form than color responses, this is taken as a sign of emotional impoverishment and repression of feelings. If color predominates over form, this is said to indicate impulsiveness, lack of emotional control, and dominance of emotion over reason.

Movement responses are considered to be indicators of the richness of imagination and "inner life." When movement responses predominate over color responses, the interpretation is that the individual is introversive. If color responses are more numerous than movement responses, the subject is said to be extratensive, more concerned with the "outer" rather than the "inner" life. Shading responses are taken to indicate uncertainty, worry, depression, and anxiety.

After each response has been scored in terms of content, location, and determinants, scores are added up over all responses, forming the "response summary." The total number of responses given and the time taken to respond are also considered in the summary.

### Interpretation

Rorschach responses are interpreted in terms of psychoanalytic and other "depth" psychologies. The response summary alone is only a part of the material used in the interpretation. The trained examiner takes note of many complex relationships between content, location, and determinants. Thus in terms of the other responses in the record, the interpretation of the movement response "children playing ball" might be quite different from that of "men playing ball." A response that would be interpreted one way for a man is often interpreted differently for a woman. If a person who has never finished high school gives numerous anatomical responses, this might be taken as an indication of morbid thoughts. If a college student gives many anatomical responses, this might be interpreted as interest in, and familiarity with, biology.

The interpretation of Rorschach responses is an extremely complex task. Although there are reasonably clear-cut rules for scoring individual responses, there are only general standards and examples to direct the final interpretation. The interpretation depends heavily on the subjective impression of the examiner. It takes about two years of practice, usually working in close collaboration with experienced examiners, to become proficient at interpreting Rorschach responses.

### the Thematic Apperception Test (TAT)

The TAT, developed by Murray (1943) and his associates, consists of pictures of people in various settings. One of the pictures is shown in Figure 13-3. Some of the pictures are more suited to young than to older people, and some are more suited to men than to women. The pictures are structured in such

**FIGURE 13-3**    One of the pictures used in the Thematic Apperception Test (*Reproduced by permission of Harvard University Press.*)

a way as to elicit responses concerning various social roles and responses relating to different emotions. The pictures are unstructured in the sense that a wide variety of interpretations can be given about the feelings and actions of the persons shown.

## Administration

The examiner has a choice as to how many of the pictures and what kinds will be used with a subject. If the standard set of 20 pictures is used, usually more than one testing session is required to complete the series. In many cases the examiner uses only the half dozen or so pictures which he thinks will elicit the most pertinent information from a particular subject. The subject is told to make up a story about each picture in turn. The instructions are approximately as follows: "I am going to show you some pictures. I want you to tell me a story about what is going on in each picture. What led up to it, and what will the outcome be?" Either the responses are written down verbatim or an auditory recording is made.

## Scoring and interpretation

Murray originally scored TAT responses in terms of *needs* and *presses*. A need is something that the individual is trying to obtain. Some of the needs listed by Murray are achievement, aggression, nurturance, passivity, and sex. Presses are the outside influences which help or hinder the attainment of needs, such as aggression, dominance, and rejection by other persons. Each story can be inspected for the needs and presses which are portrayed.

Murray's system of scoring also considered the *hero* in each story and the *outcome*. The hero is the person in the story with whom the subject apparently identifies. For example, responses to the picture shown in Figure 13-3 could concern stories about either the older woman or the younger woman. Sometimes the hero is a person outside the picture. For example, a story about the picture shown in Figure 13-3 could concern a relative of one of the persons depicted.

Although needs, presses, hero, and outcomes are considered by most of the people who work with the TAT, apparently few examiners make detailed scorings of them. In fact, no formal scoring system of any kind is used by the majority of TAT examiners. The examiner interprets the responses in terms of his knowledge of personality and his experience with the instrument. Some interpretations are of a commonsense kind with which most examiners would agree. If a male subject imputes unfriendly motives and actions to all the female characters, this strongly suggests he is having troubled relations with women in real-life situations. If all the stories end in disappointment, embarrassment, and failure, it is likely that the subject feels defeated and depressed.

If the stories are lacking in passion and violence, even where strong emotion is the evident theme of the picture, this might indicate that the subject is suppressing his own emotions. If any one type of social interaction, such as adultery, is seen in numerous pictures and in pictures where there is little to suggest it, this indicates that the subject is overly concerned about a particular issue. Responses to the TAT pictures provide many hints about the subject's motives, his conception of himself, and the way he views his human environment.

## Special uses for TAT pictures

The original set of pictures developed by Murray and his coworkers is only one of many such sets of pictures that are presently in use. Pictures can be made for many different kinds of special studies. For example, a special set of pictures could be used to study the attitudes that management and labor hold toward each other. Persons dressed like foremen, workmen, union executives, and vice-presidents could be shown in settings pertinent to the problems under study. The pictures could be structured to the extent that attitudes about certain kinds of social interactions would be elicited. Special sets of pictures have been composed for Negroes, Indians, and other racial and ethnic groups. Pictures of the TAT kind have been used to study anti-Semitism, family relations, attitudes toward military life, and problems in many other areas.

### other projective techniques

In addition to the Rorschach and the TAT, there are numerous procedures for evaluating personality which are best thought of as projective techniques. Almost anything that can be described, completed, or interpreted serves to some extent as a projective test. We tend to read our concerns and expectations into everything we do.

## Word association

An old technique for learning about personality is to have an individual associate words. Various lists of words (see Kent & Rosanoff, 1910; Rapaport, 1968) have been employed to elicit particular kinds of reactions. The usual practice is to place certain emotionally tinged words among relatively neutral ones. The following list of words would be useful in studying the home and school adjustment of adolescents:

1. Hair  _____
2. Mother _____
3. Home  _____
4. Desk  _____

5. Book  _____
6. Father _____
7. School _____
8. Love  _____

|   |   |   |   |
|---|---|---|---|
| 9. Tree | _____ | 15. Sister | _____ |
| 10. Hate | _____ | 16. Cake | _____ |
| 11. Paper | _____ | 17. Body | _____ |
| 12. Shoe | _____ | 18. Me | _____ |
| 13. Fight | _____ | 19. Brother | _____ |
| 14. String | _____ | 20. Friend | _____ |

The words are read to the subject one at a time, and he is asked to give the first word that comes into his mind as he hears each one. The examiner records the responses and notes the time taken to respond. The results are interpreted in several ways. The words which are associated often indicate the subject's attitudes toward persons and activities. For example, where the association to "father" is "spanking" and the association to "hate" is "father," there is the strong suggestion of a negative reaction to the father. Equally revealing are the emotional reactions to the initial terms. If the subject takes a relatively long time to respond or gives sign of being embarrassed, a strong emotional reaction is suggested. Thus, even though the subject eventually supplies an innocuous association for "father," such as "hat," the long time taken to respond would suggest "blocking" and underlying conflict. A third type of information used in the interpretation is the tendency to give unusual associations. For example, most persons will associate "table" with "chair" or respond with some other related item of furniture. It is unusual to hear the response "tiger" to "chair," and when numerous such associations are made, there might be a relation to mental illness.

### Sentence completion

The sentence-completion technique is similar to word association (see Rotter & Rafferty, 1950). Examples are as follows:

1. I dislike most to _____
2. I wish that I had never _____
3. Most people are _____
4. I become embarrassed _____
5. The people I like most _____

The usual procedure is to have subjects write their responses, which permits the testing of a number of persons at one time. The sentences can be structured to provide information on different areas of adjustment. No effort is made to "time" the responses. Consequently, the subject has time to make up whatever responses he chooses. The responses are analyzed similarly to the way those on the TAT are interpreted. That is, the moods, motives, solutions, and expectations portrayed in the responses are interpreted with respect to the subject's personality. Semiobjective methods of scoring have been developed for some sentence-completion tests which go a long way toward standardizing interpretations.

### Play techniques

A method which is especially useful with children is to employ play materials as a projective device (see Bell, 1948, Ch. 22). Children betray their feelings quite readily in play activities of all kinds, and almost any set of play materials serves as a "test." Dolls and puppets are used most often for this purpose. The situation can be structured by, for example, naming the dolls "mother," "father," "little brother," "me," and so on. The environment for the dolls can also be structured to some extent by having present toy implements, such as a baby bottle, a toilet, a bed, doll clothing, and others. The child is encouraged to play with the material in whatever way he chooses. A revealing set of actions would be for the child to place the doll for "mother" and "little brother" with their faces to the wall while "father" gives the bottle to "me." Play activity of this kind is usually very rich in suggestions about children's feelings and concerns.

### Drawings, paintings, and sculpture

Artistic productions can be used as projective devices. These may be almost completely unstructured, like finger painting (see Anderson & Anderson, 1951, Ch. 14), or they may be structured to the point of asking for the drawing of a man (see Machover, 1949). The advantage of the relatively unstructured task is that it is often not perceived as a test. A widely used procedure is to furnish clay to children and to let them make whatever they like. The product can be analyzed for the symbolism apparent or simply in terms of the actions imputed to the clay figures. If the child makes a clay image of himself, it is important to note whether the bodily parts are in proper proportion. An outsized nose or excessively small arms might offer suggestions about the child's concept of himself. Children often manifest strong emotions in artistic productions that they would not talk about openly. For example, a disturbed child might make a clay figure of his mother and then run over it with a toy car, tear off the arms, and finally throw it in the wastebasket.

Finger painting is used with both adults and children. The subject is presented with a variety of paints and is encouraged to use his fingers to make whatever he likes. The way in which the subject approaches the task is thought to be as important as what he paints. Some persons are very reticent about putting their fingers in the paint or making a mess with the materials. Others take a childlike glee in smearing the paints and making the biggest mess possible. The colors which the individual chooses are thought to be important. The proportioning, balance, and integration of the finished painting are also used in the interpretation. For example, making only swirling smears with one color might be considered a sign of schizophrenia.

## evaluation of projective techniques

### Objectivity

It is sometimes said that projective techniques are subjective methods, whereas self-inventories are objective methods. Actually, both of them are subjective but in different ways. The objectivity in self-inventories is in the scoring, but the validity of the results depends on the subjective processes of the subject. In contrast, the projective techniques do not depend on the subjective processes of the subject in describing his personality, but most of these techniques depend very much on the subjective processes of the test examiner in interpreting the responses. Rather than speak of objectivity, it would be better to say that self-inventories are much more highly *standardized* than projective techniques, a matter that will be discussed in more detail later.

The growth of projective techniques has paralleled the growth of self-inventories, but they have been nourished by somewhat different traditions. Projective techniques have been developed mainly in conjunction with psychiatry and clinical psychology, but to a large extent self-inventories have been developed in conjunction with basic research on personality traits and with personnel-selection programs in military and vocational settings. Because of the affiliation of projective techniques with clinical activities, they are frequently spoken of as "diagnostic instruments." In clinical settings, projective techniques are used mainly to specify what is particularly "sick" about an individual who, at the outset, is known to have serious problems.

Whereas self-inventories tend to be concerned more with social traits and personal conceptions than with motives or specific forms of maladjustment, the reverse is true in most uses of projective techniques. Since motives must be inferred rather than observed directly, some people claim that projective techniques offer rich material for making such inferences. If so, projective techniques will be an improvement over self-inventories in the measurement of motives because the social-desirability factor in self-inventories tends to obscure the valid measurement of motives.

### Validity

Apparently most projective techniques do a rather poor job of measuring personality traits. (Evidence regarding statements in this and following sections is found in the summaries of literature on projective techniques by Guilford, 1959, and Masling, 1960.) Most of the traits measured by projective techniques require construct validity, but there is very little positive evidence in that regard available. For example, there is no convincing evidence that any projective technique validly measures the trait of anxiety or the trait of dominance.

In applied settings, the evidence is clear that projective techniques have, at most, only a low level of validity in predicting particular criteria. They tend to correlate very little with criteria of vocational success. Also, they do a poor job of differentiating normal people from people who are diagnosed as neurotic, and they do a poor job of differentiating different types of mentally ill persons. There are scattered findings that particular techniques are valid for particular purposes, but the total evidence points to the fact that, as a group, projective techniques do not provide very valid measures of personality traits. The following sections will consider some of the reasons for this state of affairs.

### Reliability

Although there are some exceptions to the rule, projective techniques tend to have unacceptably low reliabilities. There are arguments about how the reliability of projective techniques should be measured; but however it is measured, the typical finding is a reliability around .60, and very few reliabilities as high as .80 are found.

Logically, the most appropriate measure of reliability with projective techniques is the correlation of alternative forms administered and scored by different examiners, but very few studies of this kind have been done. With projective techniques, it is particularly important to develop alternative forms because it is usually difficult to define the domain of content. For example, what is the domain of content for the Rorschach test? Is it all possible inkblots, all inkblots of particular kinds, or what? If an alternative form can be constructed and the two forms correlate highly, one can have confidence that a definable domain of content is involved. Some of the projective techniques (e.g., the original Rorschach inkblots), have no alternative form, and consequently the alternative-form reliability is unknown. Alternative forms would also be useful for practical purposes, such as in testing the amount of improvement during psychotherapy.

In addition to the need for alternative forms in studying the reliability of projective techniques, it is necessary to investigate the measurement error due to the examiner. The interpretation of most projective techniques is highly subjective, and in such instances one is likely to find considerable measurement error due to differences in interpretations by different examiners.

In many cases the reliabilities of projective techniques are not too low to permit their use in research, but in most cases they are far too low to permit their use in those applied settings where important issues about people are at stake. When important decisions about people are based on psychological measures, even a reliability of .90 is not high enough. Since the typical reliability of trait measures from projective techniques is around .60, the standard error of measurement is 0.63 times as large as the standard deviation of the trait. Such a large dose of measurement error cannot be tolerated in situations where measures have important impacts on people's lives.

### Standardization

As has been mentioned in a number of places elsewhere in this book, the essence of measurement in science is the standardization of the measurement procedures. If measures are standardized, the results are repeatable by the same individual employing different forms of the same instrument and by different individuals. Because the results depend very much on the tester, most projective techniques are rather unstandardized. The tester influences the kinds of responses that the subject gives, and interpretations of responses vary considerably with the tester. For example, studies with the Rorschach have found that different examiners tend to obtain different numbers of responses from subjects. Some examiners typically obtain only 20 responses, and others typically obtain 40 or more. Many of the Rorschach scores correlate with the total number of responses given and thus depend to some extent on the person administering the test. Male examiners tend to obtain different types of responses from those elicited by female examiners, and different examiners tend to elicit different types of responses in particular categories (Masling, 1960).

The examiner, in addition to his influence on the responses given to projective techniques, has an even more marked influence on the interpretation of results. With most projective techniques, the end result is not a set of trait scores but a description of some aspects of the subject. On the Rorschach, for example, a semiobjective method is used for scoring individual responses, but going from those scores to the interpretation involves a highly intuitive process. Thus, after studying a subject's responses, the examiner might conclude, among other things, that he "is rigid, overintellectualizes, and has much free anxiety." There are, however, only rough guides for making such interpretations, which is the major reason why some projective techniques are so unstandardized.

There is some evidence that projective techniques are projective both for the examiner and for the subject (Masling, 1960). For example, one study found that examiners who were rated by their colleagues as hostile tended to interpret the responses of psychiatric patients to a projective technique as being hostile. Aside from particular differences between examiners in the interpretation of responses, there are surely important differences between them in overall validity. One gets the impression that some examiners are very accurate in their interpretations and that others tend to miss the mark entirely. This is much like a situation in which some meteorologists were very accurate in measuring humidity and others were very poor in that regard, with the result that the accuracy of weather forecasting would differ greatly from locality to locality and the data obtained from such observations would not aid the science of meteorology.

Since the validity of most projective techniques depends on the interaction of examiner, subject, technique, situation, and trait being measured, these techniques are unstandardized and thus should not be called "tests." (Some exceptions will be discussed later.) Since it is obviously impossible to determine the validity of these myriad possible interactions of examiners and other factors, it is not possible to know the validity with which projective techniques are employed in particular instances. It is better to think of most projective techniques as "aids to interviewing." Although it is not clear that they actually aid interviewing, they certainly cannot be classified as standardized measures of personality traits.

### Directions for research

In spite of the weaknesses of most projective techniques, the concept of projective testing is still promising in that there is so much everyday experience to support the notion that people tend to interpret unstructured stimuli in ways that relate to their personalities. The problem is that most projective techniques are psychometrically unsound vehicles for measuring anything. Projective testing might be advanced considerably by efforts to develop homogeneous scales for particular traits, e.g., the gathering of responses to inkblots that are thought to measure anxiety, standardization of procedures of administration and scoring, factor analysis of correlations between scales, and construct validation of the obtained factors. This would not necessarily be more difficult than the other approaches to the measurement of personality traits, but it is surprising how little work has been done in this regard.

The good things that can be done with projective techniques are exemplified by the work of Holtzman, Thorpe, Swartz, and Herron (1961) on inkblot tests. After careful psychometric work, they constructed alternative forms of an inkblot test, each test consisting of 45 blots. Homogeneous scales were developed for scoring particular types of responses, e.g., the tendency to see "good forms" and the tendency to respond to colors. Each subject makes only one response to each blot, and consequently there is no possibility of variation in that regard influencing results. Instructions and scoring are well standardized, and alternative-form reliabilities of most trait measures are acceptable. Norms were obtained from diverse groups across the country, and comparisons were made of average scores given by normal, neurotic, and psychotic populations. Correlations were made between scales on the inkblot test and those on self-inventories (which, interestingly enough, were all nil). Similar efforts have been made to develop standardized versions of sentence-completion tests (discussed in Guilford, 1959).

In the development of standardized projective techniques, more attention should be given to the place of *structure* in such instruments. Projective techniques are founded on responses to unstructured stimuli, and that is good because it allows one to investigate interpretative responses. However, one can overemphasize the lack of structure in projective techniques. Some projective testers apparently assume that *everything* in the situation should be unstructured. Consequently, they do almost nothing to direct subjects' responses in one way or another, and they employ complex materials (e.g., TAT pictures of people in social situations) which permit subjects to go off in many different directions. A better approach is to have projective techniques entirely structured except for responses relating to a particular dimension, e.g., hostility. Materials should be such that all subjects are forced to say something that relates to a single dimension. To do that requires simpler materials than are sometimes employed—materials that direct the subject toward responses that are related to the trait of interest—and/or instructions by the examiner that elicit relevant responses. For example, the subject can be shown a simple picture of two boys fighting. It is obvious that they are fighting, and there are no other persons or objects in the picture to elicit nonrelevant responses. To ensure that the subject gives responses that relate to hostility, the examiner could ask, "Why do you think they are fighting?"

The success that has been achieved in the standardization of sentence-completion tests is probably due to the fact that such tests structure responses up to the point where lack of structure is called for. For example, even though the following sentences do not structure the subject's responses entirely, they do ensure that his responses will relate to guilt feelings:

1. I wish that I had never _____
2. I feel guilty when _____
3. When I hurt others _____

Because many projective techniques are so entirely unstructured, they do not obtain comparable information from subjects. One subject might give 10 responses that relate to anxiety, and another subject might not give any, but this may have nothing to do with the amount of that trait in the two subjects. If both subjects were required to give 20 responses structured so that they would provide information about anxiety, the latter person might prove to be more anxious. Also, because many of the techniques are so unstructured, the results must be influenced by incidental sets that subjects form. Most subjects, particularly adults, know that they are taking a personality test, and since the situation is so unstructured, they formulate hypotheses about how to respond. For example, on seeing an inkblot, an adult may think that it is a test of "childish imagination," since, after all, it is an inkblot and to call it anything else would be make-believe. Consequently, the subject gives as few responses as possible, and the responses that he does give concern physical resemblances between parts of the blot and objects in daily life. College students, being on their mettle in this regard, might react to the inkblot as constituting an intellectual task and consequently give many clever interpretations interspersed with classical references. One of the problems with such sets is that they frequently produce "pseudoreliability." Although the set may have been formulated quite capriciously when the subject first saw the testing materials and although it may have nothing to do with the traits under study, the subject may hold his set throughout the testing session, which will make the internal consistency high. Also, subjects may hold the same set when responding to an alternative form on another occasion. In both instances this leads to pseudoreliability, the true reliability being obtainable only in the science-fiction circumstance where memory of each response is erased after it is made.

## physiological measures of personality traits

This discussion will be short because not much space is required to summarize what is presently known about the possibilities of employing physiological variables as measures of personality traits. In spite of the fact that personality traits must have some type of physical representation inside the individual, to date there has been very little success in deriving measures of such traits from physiological processes. No physiological variable (or group of such variables) is known to correlate substantially with self-inventories, ratings, projective techniques, or other indicants of personality traits, and no physiological variables are known to distinguish sharply between mentally ill people and normal people or between different types of mentally ill persons. (Evidence for these and other assertions about relations between physiological variables and personality traits is summarized by Guilford, 1959, and by Stern & McDonald, 1965.)

### Physique

For centuries it has been thought that different types of body builds are related to different patterns of temperament, e.g., that the fat person is jolly, the thin person is contemplative and morose, and the muscular person is extroversive and dominant. Factor analyses of bodily measurements have produced half a dozen factors (discussed in Guilford, 1959), such as trunk length, trunk depth, and muscular thickness. There is little evidence that these factors relate to personality characteristics, and consequently the age-old assumption of relations between physique and personality is much in doubt.

### Blood chemistry

It is reasonable to hypothesize that some personality traits relate to some of the myriad chemical components of the bloodstream. The numerous attempts to find such relations have, however, not yet met with success. Most of the efforts along these lines have been directed toward finding chemical differences between mentally ill persons and normal persons. Although there have been numerous suggestive findings (Stern & McDonald, 1965), the evidence so far for the importance of any one chemical substance is rather weak. Very little is known about relations between blood chemistry and personality traits in normal people.

## Autonomic functioning

One of the richest potential sources of personality correlates is in the functioning of the autonomic nervous system. This system participates in the activation and deactivation of the organism. It might, for example, be thought that anxious persons would show a pattern of autonomic responses typical of activation and that certain types of lethargic neurotic and psychotic persons would show a pattern of autonomic responses typical of deactivation. There are some small correlations between measures of autonomic functioning and self-inventories; otherwise, few relations have been found between autonomic functioning and personality.

## Regulatory processes

One might expect to find personality correlates in various regulatory processes, such as heart rate, blood pressure, breathing rate, typical amounts of sleep, fluid intake, and others. For example, one hears of the "hypertension syndrome," supposedly typical of the individual whose psychological tension is manifested in heart rate, blood pressure, and other physiological variables. There is, however, very little evidence for these and other correlations between personality traits and regulatory processes. In an extensive review of the literature on studies relating blood pressure to personality traits (McGinn, Harburg, Julius, & McLeod, 1964), for example, few consistent correlations, if any, could be reported.

## Brain functioning

Since personality traits must be represented in some form in the brain, it is logical to hope that someday various aspects of brain functioning may be used as measures of personality traits. The problem, of course, is that it is so very hard to get at the brains of living people, and consequently, until better techniques are available, there is little that can be done to find measures of personality traits in terms of brain functioning. The most that has been done so far is to compare brain waves of normal people with those of groups of abnormal persons. Some suggestive small differences in that regard have been reported (Stern & McDonald, 1965), but few correlations, if any, have been found between brain waves and personality characteristics in normal people.

## Reactions to stress

The studies of physiological variables discussed above concern measurements taken in normal states, for example, while the subject lies on a comfortable couch. Of equal interest are physiological reactions to stress. It has been hypothesized, for example, that anxious persons recover more slowly in their physiological reactions to stress than nonanxious persons. Typical stressful situations that have been employed in these studies involve electric shock, sudden loud noises, and highly speeded, difficult tests of ability. What has been found in such studies is that different persons respond in terms of *different physiological* indicators. For example, whereas one person typically responds to different stressful situations with increased blood pressure but not with increased rate of breathing, the reverse is true for another person. This tells us something interesting about physiological responses to stress, but it provides little encouragement for the measurement of personality traits in terms of physiological variables.

## Problems in measuring personality traits with physiological variables

One of the major problems in searching for physiological correlates of personality traits is that people's somatic complaints frequently are not matched by actual somatic responses (Stern & McDonald, 1965). The person who complains of rapid heartbeat frequently does not have a rapid heart rate. The person who complains of difficulty in breathing may show no abnormality in actual breathing. Consequently, it is necessary to make a careful distinction between the labels that people employ for conscious states (e.g., "tension") and physical states that go by the same names. Apparently this semantic confusion has led us to expect that it would be rather easy to find physiological correlates of some personality traits (e.g., anxiety), but that certainly has not been the case.

A second problem in the use of physiological variables as measures of personality traits is that many of the measures have very low reliabilities. In a study by Wenger (1948) of 19 physiological variables which were repeated after one day, only one variable had a reliability as high as .80, numerous were below .50, and one was only .11 (sublingual temperature). Repeated measures after three months tended to show even lower reliabilities. The reliabilities of individual variables were not so low, however, that it would not be possible to obtain highly reliable combinations of them.

A third problem in the use of physiological variables as measures of personality is that, at the present time, we are sorely lacking in techniques for measuring many physiological variables. Physiological psychology has burgeoned in recent years partly because of the development of ingenious measurement techniques, e.g., the techniques for measuring electrical activity in single cells of the brain. Many of these techniques, however, either kill or maim the organism. Until comparable measurements can be taken without hurting people, they cannot, of course, be used in the search for measures of personality traits. Some of the physiological variables that might relate to personality traits (e.g., chemical changes at the synapses of neurons in the brain) are so microscopic in locus and so "delicate" that it may be some time before adequate measurement techniques are developed.

The fourth, and major, problem in employing physiological indices as measures of personality traits concerns the basic logic of such investigations. It is hard to disagree with the statement that if general traits of personality exist, they are entirely represented within the physical structure of the person. It is quite another thing, however, to assume that personality traits are manifested in the same ways in different people or that they are manifested in ways that will lend themselves to measurement. Present evidence suggests that many physiological variables do not obey general laws (e.g., reaction to stress, mentioned previously); rather, they tend to behave idiographically. It is as though people developed largely different "styles" of responding to the same types of conscious states. For this reason, the "visceral" variables (those outside the central nervous system) may not be usable as measures of personality traits. If that is true, it means that one must search for measures of personality traits in the central nervous system, particularly in the brain. At the present time, however, the workings of the brain are so poorly understood and techniques for learning more about those functions are so limited that it is hard to know how to proceed. Also, personality may not be fully represented in gross structural or chemical differences between people, but rather may be represented in terms of what is "stored" as habits and memories in the brain. It is quite baffling to consider how one would ever recover those through measurements of brain processes in living humans. Even if that ever comes about, it may prove to be much more economical to measure personality traits in terms of overt behavior, as is done with printed tests of personality. It is obviously worthwhile to continue exploring the possibilities of measuring some personality traits with physiological variables, but at the same time it is also obviously worthwhile to continue trying to develop measures of personality traits in terms of overt behavior (including verbal responses).

## personality traits in perception and judgment

One of the most promising areas in terms of finding valid measures of personality traits is that of individual differences in laboratory investigations of perception and judgment. Of course, such studies have a long tradition in experimental psychology, but it has been only during the last 20 years that individual differences in those situations have been related to personality. Whereas such studies ostensibly concern *abilities*, it may be that individual differences actually relate to personality traits.

Although the evidence so far for measuring personality traits in terms of perception and judgment is only suggestive, the approach has a number of attractive features. In contrast to observational methods and projective techniques, measures of judgment and perception are not dependent on the subjective processes of observers and test examiners, and in contrast to self-inventories, they are not fraught with technical difficulties.

## Visual acuity

Surprisingly enough, there is suggestive evidence that some aspects of visual acuity are related to personality traits. The most significant findings to date concern correlations between dark vision and self-inventory measures of neuroticism. In one study, Eysenck (1947) found a correlation of .60 between the two variables! It is hard to believe that correlations of that magnitude will generally be found between aspects of visual acuity and personality traits, but the evidence so far does suggest that whereas visual acuity has been considered a passive perceptual function, it may, in part, be dynamically related to personality.

## Field dependence

One of the most encouraging lines of evidence for the measurement of personality variables with tasks concerning perception and judgment comes from studies of field dependence (these studies are summarized by Holtzman, 1965). The rod-and-frame test was first used as a measure of field dependence. In the test, the subject sits in a darkened room and looks at a luminous square wooden frame. The frame can be rotated to the left or to the right by the experimenter. In the center of the frame is a luminous rod, which the subject can rotate with remote controls. With the frame tilted to the left or right at various angles, the subject tries to adjust the rod so that it is in a vertical position. This is difficult to do without being influenced by the frame. The frame is spoken of as the *field*, and to the extent that the subject places the rod in a vertical position with respect to the frame rather than the room, he is said to be *field-dependent*.

Field-dependency scores on the rod-and-frame test correlate with other perceptual measures that also appear to concern field dependence. One of these is the embedded-figures test. On each item of the test, the subject tries to locate a simple geometric form embedded in a complex form. The total figure constitutes the perceptual field, from which the subject must differentiate the embedded figure. Numerous studies have found substantial correlations between the rod-and-frame test and the embedded-figures test, and both tests tend to correlate with other perceptual measures that apparently concern field dependence (Holtzman, 1965). Suggestive correlations have been found between these measures and conventional measures of personality. The evidence is that the individual who appears "dependent" in tests of field dependence also tends to be dependent in his social behavior.

### Categorizing behavior

Efforts have been made to develop personality measures from the ways in which people employ categories in tasks concerning judgment (this research is summarized in Holtzman, 1965). The task which has been used most frequently for that purpose is the object-sorting test. Typically the subject is presented with a miscellaneous collection of 50 or more objects (a spool, a small rubber ball, a paper clip, etc.) and is told to sort them into groups of objects in any way that he likes. The measure which has been studied most often is simply the number of groups or categories formed, which is thought to relate to *conceptual differentiation*. The person who employs many categories is thought to make fine conceptual differentiations, and the person who employs only a small number of categories is thought to make coarse conceptual differentiations.

Another task relating to categorizing behavior is the Category Width Scale (Pettigrew, 1958). The items concern judgments about the largest and smallest members of particular classes of objects, e.g., the lengths of the largest whale and the smallest whale. It has been hypothesized that the person who manifests "broad categories" on the Category Width Scale will also employ only a small number of categories. The evidence (Gardner & Schoen, 1962) is that these and other tests concerning conceptual differentiation tend to have positive correlations with one another, although the correlations tend to be modest. Also, suggestive correlations have been found between measures of conceptual differentiation and conventional measures of personality.

### Eye movements

There is suggestive evidence that eye movements relate to personality variables. Gardner and his colleagues have investigated *scanning behavior* as measured by the amount of the subject's eye movement when he is judging the size of one geometric form in the context of distracting forms (summarized in Messick & Ross, 1962). Some subjects typically focus only on the relevant form, and the eyes of other subjects wander constantly about both the relevant form and irrelevant forms. There is suggestive evidence that extensive scanners tend to be obsessive or compulsive people, in contrast to restricted scanners, who tend to be the opposite.

In addition to studies directly concerned with personality correlates of eye movements, laboratory investigations of eye movements suggest that they might be fruitfully studied as measures of some personality traits. It has been found that eye movements of subjects tend to "approach" objects that are pleasant and to "avoid" objects that are neutral or negative (Nunnally, Stevens, & Hall, 1965). In a typical study, children's eye movements are photographed while they look at a display showing nonsense syllables that previously have been associated with reward, punishment, or neither. Children look most at reward syllables, next most at neutral syllables, and least at punishment syllables. Since so much of personality concerns individual differences in what people "approach" and "avoid," it is logical to think that eye movements in looking at visual displays of different kinds could provide information relating to personality traits.

### Pupillary response

There is suggestive evidence that pupillary response might be used for the measurement of personality traits (Hess, 1965). Pupillary dilation occurs when an individual looks at anything that arouses him. Particularly, it has been found that pupillary dilation occurs when the individual encounters any pleasant object, e.g., a picture of food for a hungry subject or a picture of a cool-looking drink for a thirsty subject. This response is involuntary, and since there is no feedback from the pupil, the subject is not directly aware of pupillary changes.

Since pupillary response is affected by the pleasantness of objects, individual differences in response might be related to the degree that different objects are pleasant to different persons. (The relationship here is apparently most clearcut in comparing objects ranging from neutral to intensely pleasant. It may be that unpleasant objects also induce dilation.) It has been found, for example, that men dilate more to a picture of a seminude female than to a picture of a seminude male, and vice versa for pupillary response in female subjects. Homosexual males dilate more to a picture of a seminude male than to a picture of a seminude female. Women dilate to a picture of a baby, but men dilate little to the same picture. There is other evidence (Hess, 1965) that individual differences in pupillary response to different kinds of stimuli relate to motives and other aspects of personality. There is then the possibility of developing personality tests in which the "scores" consist of amount of dilation to different types of visual and auditory stimuli.

### Looking time

A perceptual variable that might be useful for the measurement of personality traits is the amount of time that individuals choose to look at different visual displays. A procedure that is employed for that purpose is as follows (Nunnally, Duchnowski, & Parker, 1965). The subject is presented with a metal box, on the front face of which are six windows. By pressing the proper button, he can turn on a light behind any window, which permits him to view a particular picture. The subject is allowed to press buttons at will to look at what he likes. The amount of time he spends looking at each picture is automatically recorded. Studies have found that children look at nonsense syllables and geometric forms that have been associated with rewards more than at neutral stimuli and that they look at neutral stimuli more than at ones that have been associated with punishment. Also, it has been found that the amount of time the subject spends viewing real-life objects is related to the pleasantness of the object. For example, children spend more time looking at a picture of a quarter than at a picture of a dime, and more time looking at a picture of a dime than at a picture of a penny.

Although the author knows of no studies to date on the topic, looking time might be useful as a measure of motives in children. (Adults probably would not perform "naturally" in the situation, and consequently it is doubtful that the results would have any orderly relations with personality characteristics.) Looking time could be measured not only for material objects but also for pictures of different kinds of persons in different types of situations. For this purpose, one could employ scenes concerning aggression, health, and affection, for example. The amount of time children spend looking at such stimuli might be related to their motives, needs, and problems.

### Directions for research

So far the surface has only been scratched in the search for personality measures in situations involving perception and judgment. It would be best to summarize all the research to date in that regard as being only suggestive. The methods which have been presented in this discussion of personality traits in perception and judgment are illustrative only of what might be done, not of what has actually been accomplished.

A principle that should be kept in mind is that it is not likely that strong correlations will be found between personality traits and *accuracy* of perception and judgment. Accuracy would be involved, for example, in estimating the size of illusory geometric forms or in the recognition threshold for emotionally toned words. In all psychophysical studies, individual differences in accuracy tend to be slight, and usually what reliable variance there is in that regard can be accounted for by factors other than personality traits. Selective attention and the *style* with which an individual perceives and makes judgments provide richer ground for finding measures of personality traits. For example, scanning behavior, as discussed previously, concerns individual differences in style of inspecting visual displays rather than in accuracy of size estimation (although the two are not entirely unrelated). The previously discussed studies of eye movements with respect to displays of pleasant and unpleasant objects concerned selective attention to different objects, and accuracy of perception was not at issue. Also, accuracy is not involved in studies of pupillary response and looking time; rather, such studies are concerned with intensity of attention and selective attention, respectively.

## other methods for the measurement of personality

In addition to the major approaches to the measurement of personality, there are numerous other approaches which do not fit any of the major classifications. A number of these will be illustrated here. More detailed accounts of the "other" approaches are given in the Suggested Additional Readings at the end of this chapter.

### Response styles

Response styles are hypothesized to constitute reliable individual differences in test-taking habits. One of these is *acquiescence*, supposedly a tendency to say "yes" or to agree rather than the opposite when an issue is ambiguous or very difficult. Another response style is *cautiousness*, which supposedly concerns the tendency to leave items on ability tests blank when the correct answer is in doubt. A third response style is *extremeness*, which supposedly relates to the tendency to mark the extremes of rating scales rather than points toward the middle.

Unless one wants to call the social-desirability factor in self-inventories a response style (the author prefers not to), there is very little evidence that measures of response style relate to personality, not because there is a lack of studies in that regard, but because the many studies that have been done have generally failed to produce positive evidence. This work is critically evaluated by Rorer (1965) in an article which is aptly entitled "The Great Response-style Myth."

The major problem in employing measures of response style as measures of personality is that response styles apparently are highly specific to the measuring instrument. For example, numerous measures of acquiescence have been proposed, all of which make sense in terms of appearances, but the correlations between the different measures are very low. As another example, in the effort to measure the extremeness tendency, it is found that correlations of extremeness scores in different rating tasks are very low. Reliabilities are often high in terms of internal consistency, repeated measures, and alternative forms; consequently each type of test tends to measure something consistently, but different measures of the same response style are inconsistent with one another.

## Products of ability tests

Tests that superficially concern abilities can also be used in the attempt to measure personality traits. Such tests are frequently spoken of as "objective" tests of personality. An example is as follows. One page of a test is filled with randomly ordered letters. Subjects are told to circle each "a" and to mark an X through each "b," and they are required to work quickly. On the next page of the test, subjects are told to reverse their method of operation—to mark an X through each "a" and circle each "b." The extent to which the first task interferes with the second task is determined by subtracting the score on the first task from that on the second task. The amount of interference in that regard has been hypothesized as relating to personality.

Another ability test that has been used as a personality test is the *color-word test.* The subject is given a stack of cards, on each of which is the name of a color. In each case the color name is printed in a different color; e.g., "blue" is printed in red. The subject is required to say the words as rapidly as he can. Next he is asked to go back through the cards and state the color in which each word is printed. Supposedly the colors and names of colors will interfere with each other, and individual differences in the amount of this interference might be related to personality traits.

Products of ability tests have been used in the hope of measuring a trait of *rigidity.* A typical test is as follows. The subject is given a list of reasoning problems, all of the same basic type. The first 10 problems are rather easily solved by the application of a simple principle. The remaining items can be solved by the same principle, but they are much more easily solved by a second principle. To the extent that a subject fails to switch from employing the first principle to employing the second principle, he is said to be rigid.

The possibility of obtaining measures of personality from the products of ability tests is quite attractive because such tests are not beset with some of the unfortunate features of other approaches to the measurement of personality; e.g., logically they are not influenced by the social-desirability factor. The results to date with such measures, however, have not been very successful (evidence is summarized by Holtzman, 1965). Different tests intended to measure the same trait frequently do not correlate well with one another, and consequently the factor structures among such tests tend to be "weak." Also, personality measures obtained from ability tests correlate very little with other measures of personality, such as with ratings and self-inventories.

## Biographical inventories

Unlike self-inventories, biographical inventories ask the subject factual questions about his personal history, e.g., about ages of parents and siblings, types of schools attended, hobbies, health problems, and membership in organizations. Inventories of this type have been rather successful in selecting personnel for particular vocations, but very little has been done to form general measures of personality traits from them. For two reasons, however, the possibility is attractive. First, to the extent that the questions concern factual matters, test scores are not likely to be strongly influenced by social desirability. Second, information about personal history logically should be rich in information about personality. If it were possible to learn enough about what has happened to a person and how he has behaved in the past, it should be possible to make good predictions of his behavior in the future.

A major problem in employing biographical inventories is that people frequently do not know the answers to many important questions about themselves, e.g., behavior in early childhood or body weight at different ages. Another problem is that it is difficult to find a standard list of questions that will get at the important background characteristics of people in general. To a large extent these may be particular to the person. The construction of biographical inventories has been dominated by "shotgun empiricism," with little theory being used to guide the work. More careful thought about the background characteristics that theoretically should relate to personality traits might lead to biographical inventories that validly measure some aspects of personality.

### Verbal behavior

Another possible approach to personality measurement is with respect to the words that individuals typically employ. It may prove to be the case that "words are the mark of a man," more so than clothes are. For example, by listening to the words that a person employs, we frequently judge him to be either an intellectual, a beatnik, a psychotic person, or a person in a particular profession. It may be that more subtle differences in word usage relate to personality characteristics.

One approach to investigating individual differences in word usage is with binary-choice measures of association (Nunnally & Hodges, 1965). Typical items are as follows:

1. Snake: _____ dangerous _____ long
2. Orange: _____ sweet _____ round
3. Coal: _____ burn _____ dirty

In each item the subject picks the response word that he thinks is the best associate for the stimulus word. The responses of each subject are scored in terms of the tendency to give associations in different categories, some of these categories being (1) positive evaluations, e.g., orange——sweet and priest——kind; (2) negative evaluations, e.g., snake——dangerous and knife——hurt; and (3) antonyms, e.g., night——day and fast——slow. Factor analyses of associations have produced six factors (Nunnally & Hodges, 1965). Some interesting differences have been found on the factors for different types of people (e.g., psychotic and normal persons), and some small correlations have been found with self-inventories. As is true of so many of the approaches to measuring personality discussed in this chapter, a great deal more research will have to be done on individual differences in verbal behavior to determine whether or not this approach can contribute to the measurement of personality traits.


## Summary

In addition to the measurement of personality characteristics with self-inventories and observational methods, other major approaches are with respect to (1) projective techniques, (2) physiological processes, and (3) results of controlled experiments on perception and judgment. Self-inventories and observational methods differ from the three latter methods in that they depend heavily on the accuracy with which an individual reports his own personality characteristics or the characteristics of other persons.

Projective techniques hinge on the assumption that interpretations of unstructured stimuli are influenced by motives, drives, emotions, and the other internal urges. Thus, if a person is chronically anxious, he might interpret an ambiguous picture as containing threatening objects and actions. There is much common sense in the argument that interpretations of unstructured stimuli are rich in material relating to personality, but as a group the currently available projective techniques are unsound psychometric vehicles for measuring anything. This is due to the fact that, in a very general sense, they are unstandardized. In few instances were they based on sound principles of test construction, such as those discussed in Chapter 8 regarding the development of reliable, homogeneous scales. Because the results of many projective techniques depend heavily on the subjective processes of the test examiner, it is nearly impossible to perform overall studies of validity or to know how validly instruments are used in particular situations. Because of these and other ways in which projective techniques are unstandardized, reliability tends to be low. As a group, there is very little evidence of either predictive validity or construct validity for projective tests.

In spite of the aforementioned considerations, the concept of projective testing is still appealing. What is needed now is the careful psychometric work required to develop all valid measures of psychological traits. The good things that can be done in that regard are illustrated by some of the more recent efforts to develop standardized measures relating to sentence-completion tests and inkblot tests.

Another approach to the measurement of personality traits is through physiological processes, such processes as blood pressure, activity of the autonomic nervous system, chemical composition of the blood, body build, and brain waves. However, the evidence to date on this score is rather discouraging. So far, no physiological measure has been found to be highly correlated with other indicators of personality traits, but there is still hope for the future.

A promising route to the measurement of personality traits is through the by-products of controlled experiments on perception and judgment, for example, in terms of individual differences in the styles with which subjects scan visual displays or individual differences in pupillary response to emotion-provoking stimuli. However, the results to date from such methods are only suggestive.

In addition to the foregoing approaches to the measurement of personality traits, there are numerous other approaches that might prove fruitful, such as the measurement of response styles, incidental products of ability tests, biographical information, and verbal behavior.

A thorough analysis of all major methods for the measurement of personality leads to the conclusion that only self-inventories provide a practicable and even semivalid approach. Surely other methods will prove workable in the future, but until that time, the measurement of personality characteristics will depend heavily on what the individual knows about himself and is willing to relate.

## Suggested additional readings

Cattell, R. B. *Personality and motivation structure and measurement.* New York: Harcourt, Brace & World, 1957.

Eysenck, H. J. *The structure of human personality.* London: Methuen, 1960.

Guilford, J. P. *Personality.* New York: McGraw-Hill, 1959.

# CHAPTER 14

# Measurement
# of sentiments

Although the boundaries are not crystal clear, it is useful to distinguish sentiments from abilities and from other personality traits. In Chapter 7, it was said that "sentiment" is a generic term for all forms of likes and dislikes, and a distinction was made between psychophysical methods concerning judgments and those concerning sentiments. In this chapter we shall discuss some methods for measuring various types of sentiments; major consideration will be given to rating methods since they are most frequently employed for measuring sentiments. Two widely used rating methods, the semantic differential and the Q sort, will be discussed in some detail.

The distinctions between different types of sentiments are less clear than those between sentiments, abilities, and personality traits. Sentiments are usually divided into three overlapping groups: interests, values, and attitudes.

## measurement of interests

Interests are preferences for particular activities. Examples of statements relating to interests are as follows:

1. I would rather repair a clock than write a letter.
2. I like to supervise the work of others.
3. I would enjoy keeping a stamp collection.
4. I prefer outdoor work to work in an office.

Although investigations have been made of interests in many different types of activities, such as hobbies and reading habits, they are most frequently made of interests relating to vocational pursuits. Measures of vocational interests are used so widely for career planning in schools, industry, government agencies, and the armed forces that it is rare to find a person who has not "taken" at least one of the available inventories.

Interest inventories depend on the individual's honest and accurate reporting of what he likes to do. At the outset some justification needs to be given for using interest inventories because the most obvious approach would be simply to ask the individual what occupations he prefers. If the individual is already convinced that he wants to be a physician, a sea captain, or a fireman, having him record his preferences on a printed form would appear to be a waste of time. The purpose in administering tests is to gain some *new* information about people.

There is a considerable amount of evidence to show that stated preferences for occupations are unrealistic. This is particularly so in the case of adolescents and young adults, with whom interest inventories are most needed. Young people are usually quite unaware of the specific activities which are entailed in different occupations. Their stated preferences for occupations are often prompted by glamorized stereotypes. The physician is remembered as the heroic figure who performs the miraculous operation while the gallery looks down in silent awe. The sea captain is seen holding steadfast to the helm against the stormy onslaught of the sea. The mental picture of the fireman has him descending the ladder with the rescued maiden on his shoulder. All these images are, of course, very unrealistic. Few physicians do surgery at all. They must spend many hours in unheroic activities such as reading medical texts, writing reports, and calming the fears of anxious patients. The sea captain has scant opportunity to steer the ship because of the modern electronic gadgetry which automatically navigates. The captain is usually a sea-going businessman, ambassador to passengers and clients, who must be concerned with such matters as bookkeeping, personnel management, and correspondence. No one considers what the fireman does during the larger portion of his time—tending equipment, collecting funds for charities, and helping rescue cats from inaccessible perches.

The purpose of the interest inventory is to ask the individual about his preferences for a wide range of relatively specific activities such as mending a clock, preparing written reports, and talking to groups of people. From these a diagnosis is made of the occupations which most closely match his interests. A fundamental assumption in the use of interest inventories is that people in different occupations have at least partially different interests. Otherwise there would be no way in which interest tests could be used successfully to advise people to consider one occupation rather than another.

## The Strong Vocational Interest Blank

One of the earliest and still most widely used measures of interests is the Vocational Interest Blank (VIB), developed by E. K. Strong (1951c). Separate forms are available for men and women. The VIB employs 400 questions, mostly about relatively specific activities. On most of the items the subject indicates his preferences by marking one of the three categories "like," "indifferent," and "dislike." Some illustrative items from the men's form are as follows:

| | | | |
|---|---|---|---|
| Buying merchandise for a store | L | I | D |
| Adjusting a carburetor | L | I | D |
| Interviewing men for a job | L | I | D |

Responses to the VIB can be scored in terms of 47 occupations on the men's forms and 28 occupations on the women's forms. A separate scoring key is available for each occupation. The scoring keys were developed from the responses to the VIB made by successful persons in each of the occupational groups. Each scoring key is composed in such a way as to differentiate the people in a particular profession from professional people in general. This procedure for developing scoring keys is referred to as *criterion keying.* Each scoring key consists of a set of weights to be applied to the item responses. The weights range from +4 to −4. A positive weight means that people in the profession—say, in accounting—mark "like" on the item more frequently than professional people in general. A negative weight means that accountants mark the "like" category less frequently than people in general. The larger the difference between the profession and people in general, the larger the weight. If an item does not differentiate a profession from people in general, it receives a zero weight. A considerable amount of research was required to obtain the occupational keys, and scoring keys for new occupations are gradually being developed.

An individual's responses are scored on either some or all of the professions. The scores can be converted to standard scores, to percentiles, or to a grading system ranging from A to C. The resulting profile of scores is used to interpret the individual's interests. People usually express high interest in a number of related professions, such as mathematician, engineer, and chemist. Interest inventories in addition to the VIB are described in Appendix C.

## Uses of interest inventories

The fact that a person is interested in certain activities, such as those relating to engineering, does not necessarily mean that he has the capacity for accomplishment in that field. The relationship between interests and ability is particularly tenuous in children and young adolescents. The child who professes an interest in athletic activities, for example, may have little athletic ability, and the same is true in the case of artistic and scientific pursuits. However, there is an increasing congruence between interests and ability as the individual matures. It is very difficult for a person to maintain an interest in activities in which he constantly performs poorly. As the child matures, his interests gradually shift to the things that he can do at least relatively well.

Without some stability over time, scores on interest inventories would be of little use in advising people about vocational choices. Interests are notoriously unstable in children and adolescents. They begin to stabilize in the late teens and remain remarkably stable throughout adulthood. Strong (1951b) found retest correlations in the .70s and .80s over intervals as long as 22 years. This is both a credit to the VIB and strong evidence that interests are relatively enduring characteristics of human adults.

Interest inventories are second only to intelligence tests as aids to vocational guidance. Interests are very important to consider in choosing occupations. If an individual really likes a particular type of work, often he can succeed in spite of only a moderate amount of aptitude. No matter how much initial aptitude a person has, he can fail in a line of work through inattention and lack of effort.

In vocational guidance, interest inventories are used for two related purposes: to predict satisfaction in the work and to predict successful performance. The criterion keying on the Strong inventory provides some supporting evidence that interest tests can predict future satisfaction on the job. Another type of evidence is that follow-up studies of individuals who completed the VIB in college show a strong tendency for people to enter occupations related to their expressed interests. Both these pieces of evidence also tend to support the hypothesis that interests are predictive, at least to some extent, of job performance. Strong (1951a, 1951c) has gathered more direct evidence to show that interest scores are predictive of performance in some occupations. For example, there is a relationship between the amount of interest shown on the key for insurance agents and the amount of insurance which agents sell.

Even though interests are very important to consider in choosing occupations, it does not necessarily follow that the available instruments are maximally effective measures of interests. As is true in most areas of testing, a great deal more research with interest inventories is needed.

It is unfortunate that interest tests cannot be used as successfully in the selection of people for particular jobs as they can in vocational guidance. It has been shown repeatedly that people can fake interest tests to a marked extent. If a person is told to mark the Strong inventory as a successful engineer would, for example, he will obtain a profile similar to that which a person in the profession would obtain.

People usually give honest responses in a vocational guidance situation. They are there for information and advice, and there is little to gain by faking an interest inventory one way or the other. If, as is usually the case, the vocational guidance facility is not connected with personnel-selection programs, there is no way in which test scores can lower the individual's chances of getting a particular job. When an individual applies for a particular job, he is seldom as desirous of learning about himself as he is of obtaining the position. If he is applying for a job as an electrician, he knows that it behooves him to answer "yes" to an interest item such as, "Do you like to repair electric motors?" The small amount of success that interest inventories have in personnel-selection programs should not detract from their importance in vocational guidance.

## measurement of values

Values concern preferences for "life goals" and "ways of life," in contrast to interests, which concern preferences for particular activities. Examples of statements relating to values are as follows:

1. I consider it more important to have people respect me than to like me.
2. A man's duty to his family comes before his duty to society.
3. I do not think it is right for some people to have much more money than others.
4. Service to others is more important to me than personal ambition.

In contrast to measures of interests, measures of values are seldom used in applied activities; instead, they are usually employed in basic research in sociology and social psychology. Also, in many cases the statements used in studies of values are similar to those employed in self-inventory measures of personality. Not nearly so much research has been done on values as has been done on interests and attitudes.

Because very little has been done to systematically explore the domain of human values, there are no satisfactory general-purpose batteries of inventories available. The nearest approximation is the Study of Values, which attempts to measure values in six categories: theoretical, economic, aesthetic, social, political, and religious. However, that instrument was not developed as carefully as it should have been (see the critique by Gage, in Buros, 1959, pp. 119–202). Most scales of values have been developed for particular research projects and concern only one type of value, e.g., a scale to measure religious values.

As was mentioned in Chapter 12, values (along with interests and attitudes) are important aspects of personal conceptions, one of the four divisions of personality traits. Because values are important in personality theory and certainly important in daily life, it would be worthwhile to explore more systematically the domain of values. This would require the application of all the principles discussed in this book regarding the development of valid measures, including the development of homogeneous scales to measure each type of value and the development of a taxonomy by factor analysis.

## measurement of attitudes

Attitudes concern feelings about particular social objects—physical objects, types of people, particular persons, social institutions, government policies, and others. Some statements relating to attitudes are as follows:

1. The United Nations is a constructive force in the world today.
2. Trade unions have too much effect on our economy.
3. All public schools should be fully integrated.
4. Fraternities and sororities do more harm than good.

Attitudes are distinguished from interests and values by the fact that they always concern a particular "target" or object. In contrast, interests and values concern numerous activities—specific activities in measures of interests and very broad categories of activities in measures of values.

For several reasons, more attention will be given in the remainder of this chapter to the measurement of attitudes and values than to the measurement of interests. There is not much need to discuss in detail the logic and methodology of the measurement of interests because they are rather simple. In the measurement of interests, the purpose is to predict occupational choice and satisfaction in occupational endeavors. In other words, interest inventories are predictor instruments, and the logic of constructing and validating predictor instruments has been discussed in previous chapters. Except in the case of some indirect approaches to the measurement of interests (summarized in Guilford, 1959), interest inventories contain simple statements about preferences for activities relating to occupations. More attention will be given in the remainder of this chapter to the measurement of attitudes than to the measurement of values because (1) there is presently a great deal more research activity concerning attitudes than there is concerning values and (2) the logic and methodology for the investigation of the two are essentially the same.

### Approaches to the measurement of attitudes

The most direct approach to the measurement of attitudes is to ask people, in one manner or another, what their attitudes are. For example, subjects are presented with a list containing favorable and unfavorable statements toward the United Nations and are asked to agree or disagree with each. Such self-report inventories are called *attitude scales*, and much of the literature on the measurement of attitudes concerns different methods for developing such scales. In addition to self-report methods, numerous other methods have been explored as measures of attitudes (these are discussed in Campbell, 1950, and in Cook & Selltiz, 1964). One approach is with physiological measures. For example, physiological processes, such as the galvanic skin response or pupillary response, can be measured while an individual reads statements relating to a particular national group or while he looks at a picture of Negroes and whites in a social setting. Projective techniques have been employed for the measurement of attitudes, e.g., TAT-type pictures showing Negroes and whites in various social situations. Real or near-real behavior with respect to attitudinal objects has in some cases been explored as a measure of attitudes. For example, individuals have been asked to indicate the degree to which they would be willing to participate in activities relating to desegregation.

Although some of the indirect approaches to the measurement of attitudes seem promising, a great deal more research must be done before such measures will actually be usable. At the present time, most measures of attitudes are based on self-report, and from what evidence there is concerning the validity of different approaches to the measurement of attitudes, it is an easy conclusion that self-report offers the most valid approach currently available.

### Self-report measures of attitudes

Potentially, self-report measures of attitudes are susceptible to the same weaknesses that accompany self-description inventories. In particular, self-report measures of attitudes are limited to what the individual knows about his attitudes and is willing to relate. Both these limitations, however, are probably not so severe in self-report measures of attitudes as they are in self-description inventories. On self-description inventories, some of the items require the subject to make fairly complex judgments about his social behavior; e.g., he may be asked, "Do you usually lead the discussion in group situations?" In contrast, most self-report measures of attitudes concern items relating to direct feelings about a particular object, e.g., "I would not mind having a Japanese immigrant as a neighbor." In comparison to what is the case on self-description inventories, the items on self-report measures of attitudes are usually more understandable, and subjects feel more confident about their responses. (These assertions are based on informal experience with the two types of instruments, but not on any formal evidence.)

Self-report measures of attitudes probably have an advantage over self-description inventories in terms of the extent to which they are influenced by social desirability. Whereas all people tend to have the same concepts of social desirability of personality traits, people differ markedly in their concepts of social desirability of attitudes, as in the case of regional differences in attitudes toward racial segregation. Frankness of responding on self-report measures of attitudes, then, is frequently lessened by pressures from social groups, e.g., the prevalent attitudes in a college fraternity toward intercollegiate athletics or the prevalent attitudes in a factory toward a particular trade union. To the extent that anonymity of responses can be assured, however, self-report measures of attitudes logically should not be strongly influenced by lack of frankness on the part of subjects.

The validity of a self-report measure depends upon the way results are interpreted. At one extreme, there is nothing wrong with the investigator's having a direct interest in reported attitudes, regardless of whether they relate to attitudes measured in any other way. It has been noted on numerous occasions that a verbalized attitude usually does not correlate highly with behavior pertaining to the attitude. (Some evidence on this point is summarized by Guilford, 1959.) This does not necessarily mean, however, that verbalized attitudes are invalid. In some cases they may be highly valid measures of *reported* attitudes, but not valid measures of attitudes measurable in other ways.

Actually, in many instances what people say is more predictive of the course of their social action than what they may feel in any deeper sense. For example, if most of the people in a particular community *say* that they favor school integration, this might bring about rapid integration even if, "down deep," some of the people feel somewhat negatively toward the idea. In some instances it is reasonable to believe that verbalized attitudes represent the "cutting edge" of changes in feelings. Thus a person may start saying that he is in favor of integration before his feeling catches up with his verbalized attitude. Also, verbalized attitudes have powerful effects on courses of social action, as is evidenced by the extent to which government officials are influenced by the results of opinion polls. So, then, one has a right to be directly interested in verbalized attitudes without claiming that they have a high degree of correspondence with other attitude-related forms of behavior.

If one is interested mainly in verbalized attitudes for their own sake, *content validity* (Chapter 6) is the major issue. For that purpose, it must be ensured that a broad sample of item content is obtained, e.g., of statements relating to the United Nations or toward intercollegiate athletics. The broadness of the content must be judged by those who are involved in investigating the particular type of attitude. Next, the investigator must perform item analyses to determine the number and kinds of homogeneous scales that are implicit in the item pool. If a scale developed by this method is highly reliable and correlates highly with scales developed by other investigators using the same or different methods of scale construction, it can be said that the scale has a high degree of content validity for the measurement of verbalized attitudes.

Instead of being interested only in verbalized attitudes, one may be interested in explicating a particular type of attitude as a construct. Previously, an attitude was defined as a *feeling* toward a social object, but, of course, verbalized feelings provide only one indicant of such feelings. To explicate a particular attitude as a construct requires a multi-indicator approach (as discussed by Cook & Selltiz, 1964). For example, in the course of explicating a construct concerning attitudes toward Negroes, one might decide to investigate behavioral tests, projective techniques, and verbal report. If these correlate substantially, some combination of them could be said to have a measure of construct validity. Also, the construct validity of the combination of measures could be further evidenced in changes occurring in controlled experiments, e.g., in studies of attitude change involving persuasive communications or in structured group situations. To the extent that verbal report alone correlated highly with other measures related to the construct and faithfully mirrored changes in controlled experiments, it could be said to have a high degree of construct validity. Then it could be used alone, with some assurance that is was measuring more than verbal report. To the extent that a measure of verbal report had low correlations with other hypothesized indicants of the construct and only weakly differentiated differently treated groups in controlled experiments, it would not suffice as a sufficient measure of the construct.

Of course, it is far easier to talk about these complex approaches to explicating attitudes as constructs than it is to do anything about them. (For some attempts, see Campbell, 1950, and Cook & Selltiz, 1964.) At the present time, most investigations of attitudes in sociology and social psychology are undertaken with self-report measures, and although there is ample evidence that many of these validly measure verbalized attitudes, in most cases there is little or no evidence regarding the extent to which the instruments measure more than verbalized attitudes.

Many of the psychophysical methods discussed in Chapter 7 can be used to measure verbalized attitudes. Various kinds of comparative responses (as distinct from absolute responses) can be investigated for that purpose. For example, the order of preference for different national groups could be obtained by the method of rank order or the method of pair comparisons. Since, however, the comparative-response methods provide no indication of overall level of response to the stimuli as a group, they are not frequently used in studies of attitudes. For example, no matter how much an individual liked or disliked foreigners as a group, this could not be told from his rank ordering of the names of national groups. Comparative methods are more useful for scaling *stimuli* with respect to sentiments than for scaling *individuals* with respect to sentiments. Thus the method of rank order would serve very well to develop a scale of preference for national groups, but it could not be directly employed to measure the attitude of one person toward, say, the Japanese. Since, as previously defined, an attitude concerns feelings about a particular social object rather than comparative differences in feelings about social objects, the comparative methods are not highly appropriate to employ; rather, it is necessary to employ an absolute-response method. The numerous possible particular approaches to obtaining such absolute responses are said to constitute *rating scales*. Because of the importance of rating scales in the scaling of attitudes and values, the next section will discuss rating scales in some detail.

## properties of rating scales

Although it is common practice to speak of *the* rating scale, in actuality there are numerous types of rating scales. Also, different principles apply to the use of rating scales in different situations. These matters will be discussed in the following sections.

### Graphic and numerical scales

We usually think of rating scales as being presented graphically, e.g., as follows:

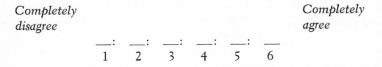

In some instances, however, the numbers are defined and written in spaces opposite the objects to be rated, instead of having the appropriate numbers marked on a graphic scale. It is customary to refer to these as *numerical scales* rather than as graphic scales. The issue, however, usually concerns whether there will be numbers employed with a graphic scale or without a graphic scale. Numbers are used as anchors in most rating scales. The numbers must first be defined, e.g.:

1. Completely disagree
2. Mostly disagree
3. Slightly disagree
4. Slightly agree
5. Mostly agree
6. Completely agree

Employing the above scheme with a so-called numerical scale, the subject would be given a list of statements (say, concerning attitudes toward the United Nations). Opposite each statement would be a blank space, in which the subject would write the number corresponding to his agreement or disagreement. In this instance a graphic scale would be employed as follows. First, as with the numerical scale, the numbers corresponding to scale steps would be defined. Then, rather than write the number in a blank space, the subject would mark a graphic scale, as illustrated above, to indicate his agreement or disagreement with each statement.

For several reasons the use of the graphic scale with numbers is preferable to the use of numbers without the graphic scale. First, because people frequently think of quantities as represented by degrees of physical extension (e.g., by the yardstick and the thermometer), the presence of a graphic scale probably helps to convey the idea of a rating continuum.  Second, the graphic scale should lessen clerical errors in making ratings.  If the meanings of numbers are given only at the beginning of an inventory and subjects have to remember the meanings as they record the numbers in the blank spaces, they are likely to forget the meanings, e.g., to confuse ends of the scale or to assume that 4 means "mostly agree" when it was defined as meaning "slightly agree." The presence of the graphic scale should lessen such errors, particularly if the ends of the scale are anchored by the extremes of the attribute being rated, e.g., "completely agree" and "completely disagree," as in the previous example. Third, if subjects write numbers in blank spaces, in some instances it will be difficult to decipher the numbers.  For example, it might prove difficult to tell whether a particular number is 1, 7, or 9.  Fewer errors in this regard are made in reading the points marked on graphic scales.

### Number of scale steps

In most cases the experimenter has a choice of the number of scale steps to be used.  He might decide to employ a two-step (or dichotomous) scale, as follows:

_____    _____
Disagree    Agree

Or he might choose to employ many steps, as in the following example:

Strongly
disagree
                                                                Strongly
                                                                agree

__: __: __: __: __: __: __: __: __: __: __
 1    2    3    4    5    6    7    8    9    10   11

In terms of psychometric theory, the advantage is always with using more rather than fewer steps. This is demonstrated by the numerous studies showing that the reliability of individual rating scales is a monotonically increasing function of the number of steps (Guilford, 1954).  Essentially the same principle is derivable from another body of evidence, that concerning relations between the number of scale steps and the _information_ (or amount of discrimination) found in classical methods of psychophysical scaling (Garner, 1960).  The amount of discrimination provided by psychophysical scales (e.g., obtained from the average ratings by a group of subjects for 20 stimuli) increases with the number of scale steps up to at least 20 steps.

As the number of scale steps is increased from 2 up to 20, reliability increases, very rapidly at first.  It tends to level off at about 7, and after about 11 steps there is little gain in reliability from increasing the number of steps. To some extent, the monotonic relationship between scale reliability and number of scale steps may be at variance with common sense.  It might, for example, be reasoned that if there are numerous scale steps, the subject will have difficulty making up his mind and might mark a different point on a retest. It is true that as the number of scale points increases, the error variance increases, but at the same time the true-score variance increases at an even more rapid rate.

The only exception to the rule that reliability increases with the number of scale steps would occur in instances where a large number of steps confused subjects or irritated them to the point where they became careless. Then it would be possible to find the reliability coming back down with, say, as many as 20 steps. Isolated studies have reported such results (Guilford, 1954), but findings of this sort are rare. By far the bulk of the studies report increasing reliabilities up to 20 steps (although the increase from about 11 to 20 is usually small).

Another issue regarding the number of steps on rating scales concerns whether an even number of steps or an odd number of steps is generally preferable. The argument for an odd number of steps is that it permits the use of a middle step meaning "neutral," "neither," or "neither agree nor disagree." This is thought to make subjects more "comfortable" in making ratings, and it can also be argued that subjects frequently have neutral reactions which should be measured. On the other hand, it can be argued that the use of a neutral step introduces response styles. Some subjects tend to use the neutral step more than others, and individual differences in that regard might not relate highly to the attitude in question. In looking through responses to attitude scales, one frequently sees the responses of a subject who made all his marks in the neutral step. This might represent a truly neutral attitude, but one has the suspicion that in this way, such a subject is saying that he did not want to participate in the study. More to the point, in some studies it has been found that reliable differentiations can be made between persons who mark the neutral step. This can be investigated as follows. First, subjects are given five-step scales, each of which contains a neutral step. Later the scales are readministered to all subjects who marked the neutral step, except that on the second occasion six steps are employed, with no neutral step present. The variance of ratings over subjects can then be shown to be reliable, indicating that there actually are reliable differences between subjects who marked the neutral step on the first administration of the scale. Although the issue is not highly important, in most cases there is a slight advantage in having an even number of steps rather than an odd number, as was illustrated previously in the six-step scale ranging from "completely disagree" to "completely agree."

## Summative scales

The question of the number of steps to use on a rating scale is very important if one is dealing with only one scale, but it is usually less important if scores are summed over a number of scales. The former would be the case, for example, if attitudes toward the United Nations were measured by only one scale, as follows:

*United Nations*

*Unfavorable*  __:  __:  __:  __:  __.  __  *Favorable*

When only one scale is used to measure attitudes, it is wise to have at least 10 steps. In the usual case, however, one obtains an overall measure of attitudes by summing the ratings given to at least half a dozen scales. One could do this in the example above by having scales for the adjective pairs valuable-worthless, efficient-inefficient, effective-ineffective, and others. As another example of summative ratings, agree-disagree ratings could be summed over a number of positive and negative statements about the United Nations.

The reliability of summative ratings is directly related to the correlations between scales (which, as was discussed in previous chapters, is so in all uses of the summative model for constructing measures). The numbers of steps on rating scales tend to place limits on the sizes of correlations between scales. In the case of a two-step (or dichotomous) scale, the correlations are phi coefficients, and the sizes of phi coefficients are limited by the differences in $p$ values of items. Then, if there is a large standard deviation of $p$ values over items, the average correlation of items with one another will tend to be low, and according to the logic of coefficient alpha, the reliability will tend to be low. When there are three rather than two steps on the scale, the restriction on correlations is less, and it tends to become less and less as the number of scale steps is further increased.

In addition to the effect of the average correlation between items, the reliability of summative scales also depends directly on the number of items. If there are only half a dozen items in the scale, the reliability obtained from two-step scales might be markedly increased by an increase in the number of scale steps. If, on the other hand, there are over 20 items in the summative scale, it is seldom the case that the reliability is materially increased by the addition of scale steps to the individual scales. Of course, in nearly all instances it is safer to have at least five or six steps than to hope that two-step scales will be sufficient. Also, there are seldom practical advantages in having only two steps.

Reliabilities of summative attitude scales tend to be higher (holding numbers of items constant) than those of summative scales of abilities and self-inventory measures of personality. This is true even when two-step scales are employed in the measurement of attitudes. Attitude scales tend to be highly reliable because the items tend to correlate rather highly with one another. This makes the internal-consistency reliability (see Appendix D) high, which, for reasons discussed in previous chapters, is usually a good estimate of the alternative-form reliability measured over relatively short periods of time.

Individual scales on summative attitude scales tend to correlate substantially with one another because they obviously relate to the same thing. For example, in a summative scale to measure attitudes toward the United Nations, the separate statements obviously relate to the same thing. It is easy for the experimenter to intuit items that will correlate highly with one another, and it is easy for the subject to see the common core of meaning in the items. For these reasons, one often finds reliabilities in the nineties for summative scales containing 20 statements rated on a two-step scale of agreement-disagreement. Also, one frequently finds, for example, that a summative scale consisting of 6 eight-step ratings has a reliability above .80. Reliability, then, is usually not a serious problem in the construction of summative attitude scales. At least this is so for the reliability over moderate periods of time (e.g., up to six months), but depending on the attitude being measured, systematic changes might be expected to occur in attitudes over longer periods of time, as, for example, in attitudes toward the Russians or toward contraceptives.

### Physical appearance of scales

One of the *least* important considerations regarding rating scales is physical appearance. One choice, for example, is between placing the scale horizontally or vertically on the page. Some have argued that the vertical scale is more familiar to the average person since it resembles a thermometer, for example. Another choice concerns whether the steps are to be connected or separated, as in the following examples:

| Completely disagree | : | : | : | : | : | Completely agree |

         1    2    3    4    5    6

| Completely disagree | — | — | — | — | — | — | Completely agree |

         1    2    3    4    5    6

The argument for the separation of steps is that it lowers the probability that subjects will mark between steps, which sometimes happens when there are no breaks. The preference for a continuous line is frequently based on the experimenter's superstition that if ratings are made on a continuum, this somehow ensures that the scale numbers can be legitimately interpreted as forming an interval scale. Better arguments for making that assumption were given in Chapter 1.

Another consideration is whether steps will be "open," as shown in previous examples, or "boxed," as illustrated below:

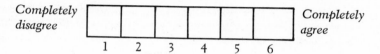

Completely disagree | | | | | | | Completely agree
1 2 3 4 5 6

These and other variations on the physical appearance of rating scales apparently make little difference in the important psychometric properties of ratings. Such differences are usually based more on aesthetic preferences than on psychometric considerations.

### Object rated

There are some important distinctions that should be made between the different types of objects rated on rating scales. In Chapter 12 some of the properties of ratings of personality characteristics were discussed. It was said that such ratings are strongly influenced by (1) the knowledge the observer (or rater) has of the ratee and (2) the rater's tendency to be "lenient" or "severe" in rating other people in general. Numerous other artifacts have been shown to influence ratings (Guilford, 1954). What is important to realize, however, is that in many uses of rating scales, either ratings are not made of people or, if they are made, they do not concern personality characteristics directly. In such cases many of the artifacts that plague ratings of personality characteristics either are logically not present at all or are present to a lesser extent.

In attitude scales, ratings are frequently made of agreement or disagreement with statements, e.g., "The United Nations is our best hope for permanent peace." In rating such statements, neither leniency nor lack of information influences ratings in the same way that they influence ratings of personality characteristics. Leniency in the case of attitude statements would be present only to the extent that the subject appeared to have either favorable or unfavorable attitudes regardless of what social object was being considered. The extent to which that actually occurs is largely unknown, but if it occurred, either it would represent genuine individual differences in the tendency to have favorable rather than unfavorable attitudes or it would represent social desirability. Lack of knowledge affects ratings of statements concerning attitudes differently from the way it affects ratings of people. Lack of information lowers the validity of ratings of people, but it may serve to explain *why* an individual has a particular attitude, although it does not necessarily lead to invalid measurements of what his attitudes actually are.

Instead of making ratings of statements relating to attitudes, in some attitude scales ratings are made of the attitudinal object itself, as would be the case, for example, when the United Nations is rated on a six-point scale bounded by the adjectives "effective" and "ineffective." Other attitudinal objects that could be rated directly are labor unions, Japan, educational television, and intercollegiate athletics. When attitudinal objects are rated directly, leniency (as the term applies in ratings of people) would spring from the same sources that it would in ratings of statements. Individual differences in that regard would represent either differences in favorable attitudes toward social objects of all kinds (which is a rather farfetched notion) or differences in social desirability. Regarding the subject's information about attitudinal objects, the caliber of his information might help explain why he has developed the particular attitude, but it would not influence the validity of measurements of his attitudes at one point in time. A person can, for example, hold genuinely negative or positive attitudes toward the United Nations while having either very little information or much misinformation.

The major point to be made in this section is that the many factors that have been shown to influence ratings of people (Guilford, 1954) do not necessarily have the same kinds and amounts of effects on ratings made for other purposes. The major factor limiting the validity of attitude ratings is probably social desirability, and as was mentioned previously, there are good logical grounds for thinking that social desirability plays a smaller part in attitude scales than it does in self-inventory measures of personality.

### Types of anchors

Before subjects can employ rating scales, steps on the scales must be defined. The definitions of scale steps are referred to as *anchors*, and there are different types of anchors that can be employed. Usually numerical anchors are employed in conjunction with other types. There is no harm in employing numbers on the scale, and they have several distinct advantages. If the meaning of each step on the scale is specified at the beginning of the rating form, as is usually the case, numbers provide an effective means of coordinating those definitions with the rating scales. A second advantage is that numbers on the rating scales constantly remind subjects of the meanings of scale steps. Another advantage of having numbers on the rating scales is that they facilitate the analysis of data, as in placing ratings on cards for computer analyses.

A special type of numerical anchor that is useful in some studies is found on *percentage scales*. On percentage scales, subjects rate themselves or other people on a continuum ranging from zero to 100 percent, either in comparison with people in general or in comparison with some special reference group, e.g., other students in a particular college. The scale is usually divided into 10 steps, corresponding to intervals of 10 percentage points. The subject can rate himself or someone else in terms of attributes such as intelligence and energy, or, less frequently, the percentage scale can be used to measure sentiments. The latter would be the case, for example, if the individual were asked to rate how favorably he feels toward labor unions in comparison with how people in general feel. Then, if he marked the step corresponding to the 70 to 80 percent level, this would mean that he considered himself to have a more favorable attitude than 70 percent of people in general. Where they can be employed, percentage scales are usually highly meaningful to subjects.

A second type of anchor which is widely employed in rating scales is that concerning degrees of agreement and disagreement, as has been amply illustrated previously in this chapter. Where they can be applied, agreement scales are easy to work with. They are easily understood by subjects, and the results obtained from them are rather easily interpreted by researchers. Whereas, superficially, agreement scales might seem to concern judgments rather than sentiments, in attitude scales this is not the case. What an individual does in responding to agreement scales is to indicate his sentiments by agreeing or disagreeing with favorable and unfavorable statements.

Adjectives constitute a third type of anchor for rating scales, as was illustrated previously in the case of scales anchored by valuable-worthless, effective-ineffective, and other pairs of bipolar adjectives. Attitude scales employing bipolar adjectives as anchors are easily constructed and applied to many types of attitudinal objectives. Rating scales employing bipolar adjectives as anchors are said to form a *semantic differential*, a matter that will be discussed in detail later.

A fourth type of anchor for rating scales is in terms of actual behavior, this type of anchor being more useful for the rating of people than for the rating of attitudes and other types of sentiments. A numerical scale for that purpose concerning the tendency of mental patients to have hallucinations is as follows:

1. Shows no signs of having hallucinations.
2. Gestures and talks to himself as if hallucinating on occasions, but does not verbalize hallucinations.
3. Verbalizes hallucinations only occasionally.
4. Actively hallucinates much of the time.

The rater would mark the one statement that best described each patient's tendency to hallucinate. There are three major difficulties with employing behavioral anchors. First, a different set of anchors is needed for each scale, which makes it difficult to construct inventories based on such scales. Second, in some cases it is not at all certain that the different behaviors used as anchors actually represent different levels of the trait in question. For example, in the illustrative four-step scale above for hallucinatory behavior, one might argue that step 2 represents more involvement with hallucinations than step 3. Third, it is frequently difficult to find discrete, easily specified forms of behavior that relate to more general traits. This point was discussed in detail in Chapter 12.

A fifth type of anchor for rating scales concerns comparison stimuli, or *product scales*, as they are called. A classic example is that of a product scale for the legibility of handwriting. A six-step scale is employed, with each of the numbers 1 to 6 being illustrated with samples of handwriting at different levels of legibility.   The samples of handwriting appropriate for the different levels are obtained from prior research, in which experts are asked to make discriminations between samples of handwriting (with one or another of the psychophysical methods).   Once the samples have been chosen for each level of legibility, it is assumed that they (the comparison stimuli) will be helpful in having ratings of handwriting made by people who are not highly expert in that regard.   Usually verbal anchors are used in addition to comparison stimuli; e.g., in the six-step scale for handwriting, 6 equals "excellent" and 1 equals "very poor."   In addition to scales for handwriting, product scales of this kind have been developed for artistic productions, but beyond that, few product scales are reported in the literature.   Although they are attractive approaches to ratings when they can be developed, logically they are restricted to only a few types of ratings.

## models for the scaling of verbalized attitudes

Except in the unusual case where attitudes are measured with only one item, some model must be employed to specify how responses to a collection of items will be translated into an attitude scale.   In Chapter 7 the various models that can be employed for scaling people with respect to all kinds of psychological traits, attitudes included, were discussed.   Here we shall summarize the considerations that lead to an acceptance of one of the models over the others for the scaling of verbalized attitudes in most situations.

### Deterministic models

Deterministic models are ones in which each item is assumed to have a perfect relationship, of one kind or another, with a hypothetical trait.   In the scaling of attitudes, the trait in question is, of course, the set of true scores for subjects on the particular dimension of attitudes being investigated, e.g., verbalized attitudes toward the United Nations.   The only deterministic model that has received wide attention for the scaling of verbalized attitudes is the monotone deterministic model, which is usually referred to as a *Guttman scale*.   In this model, it is hypothesized that each dichotomous item has a perfect biserial (not point-biserial) correlation with the hypothetical trait.

A number of reasons were given in Chapter 7 why the monotone deterministic model is unrealistic for the measurement of most human traits, and these apply with particular force to the scaling of verbalized attitudes.   The model does not take account of the amount of unique variance in each item, and consequently it is very difficult to find items that fit the model.   The scales that do partially fit the model nearly always have only a handful of items; thus only gross discriminations can be made between people.   Also, the model leads only to an ordinal scaling of people with respect to attitudes. In Chapter 1, it was argued that psychology has a legitimate claim to the measurement of human traits on at least interval scales, if not ratio scales. Other reasons were given in Chapter 7 why the Guttman scale is an impractical approach to the measurement of most human traits. Aside from the few instances in which data do fit the models well, the deterministic models are useful mainly as theoretical reference points for the development of practicable models for the actual scaling of attitudes.

## Nonmonotone probability models

A nonmonotone model logically underlies what is called the "Thurstone scale" for the measurement of attitudes. Like the Guttman scale, the Thurstone scale also deals with dichotomous responses to statements concerning attitudes, e.g., agreeing or disagreeing with the statement, "I feel a need for religion, but do not find what I want in any one church." Each item is intended to represent, in a statistical sense, one point on an attitude continuum. Only persons in a narrow zone about that point are expected to agree with the item; persons having either more positive or more negative attitudes are expected to disagree with it. In the ideal case, then, one would expect the item trace line for each item (the curve showing the probability of agreeing with the item as a function of the underlying trait) to be a normal distribution, with the mode corresponding to the true point on the attitude continuum.

The Thurstone scaling method employs judges to establish the scale points for items. In a typical study, 50 judges would rate the attitude implied by each of 100 statements. The judgments could be made on a 11-step continuum ranging from "strong positive attitude" to "strong negative attitude." The mean rating by judges is taken as the scale point for each item. About twenty items are selected for the final scale such that (1) each item has a small standard deviation of ratings over judges and (2) the mean ratings spread evenly from one end of the rating continuum to the other. When the scale is used in subsequent studies to measure the attitudes of people, each subject is instructed to mark only those statements with which he agrees. (Some have advocated restricting subjects to marking the three statements with which they most agree.) The score for the subject is then the scale value of the median item endorsed or the average scale value of the items endorsed.

During the last 40 years, the Thurstone method of attitude scaling has been used very widely in psychology and sociology (this work is summarized by Edwards, 1957b). As was said in Chapter 7, however, there are better methods for the scaling of attitudes. The original assumptions of the model are unrealistic for the scaling of attitude statements. It is simply very difficult to find items that have nonmonotone trace lines. One can find the approximate trace line in this regard by plotting the percentage of people who endorse an item as a function of scores on the total scale. In the effort to obtain non-monotone items, the investigators frequently produce double-barreled statements, as was illustrated in Chapter 7. This is evidenced by the fact that so many of the items on such scales are populated by "and's," "but's," "or's," and other indicators of multiple ideas within statements.

Unless one assumes nonmonotone trace lines for items, it is rather difficult to see how the method of assigning scale scores makes much sense, e.g., taking the median scale point of three items marked as a person's attitude score. In practice, however, few of the items on such scales have nonmonotone trace lines (Edwards, 1957b). Items on the extremes of the scale tend to have monotone trace lines, with the lines sloping downward for negative items and upward for positive items. Items near the middle of the scale tend to have flat trace lines, and thus they do a poor job of discriminating persons in terms of attitudes. The only items that might have distinctly nonmonotone trace lines would be ones that are moderately positive or moderately negative, and such items are typically double-barreled.

The major advantage assumed for Thurstone attitude scales over other types of scales is that they permit a direct interpretation of the attitude of an individual, or the average attitude of a group of people, without recourse to general norms for the attitude in question. In most studies in psychology and sociology, however, that really is not much of an advantage. In most studies, the researcher is interested in correlating individual differences in an attitude with other types of individual differences, or he is interested in the mean differences in attitudes of existing groups of people or of groups of people who are differently treated in controlled experiments. For those purposes, there is little need for a direct interpretation of the attitude of any one person, in an absolute sense.

In cases where direct interpretations of scale values are important, they can be made with only modest precision from Thurstone scales. Even with the best of efforts to select items that judges agree on, the standard deviations of scale values over judges are still considerable. Also, it had been found that different types of judges give markedly different ratings to some of the statements employed in Thurstone scales (discussed in Edwards, 1957b). This is the case, for example, when judgments are made about attitudes toward Negroes by a group of Southern whites and by a group of Negroes. The rank ordering of statements on the scale tends to remain the same, but the absolute scale values shift markedly. Then, if a direct interpretation is made of one person's responses, we must ask the question, "In whose eyes?"

In the next section it will be argued that summative scales do, in general, constitute the best approach to the scaling of verbalized attitudes. Aside from the numerous logical arguments that favor summative scales, it has been repeatedly found that summative scales are somewhat more reliable than Thurstone scales.

## Summative model

As was said in Chapter 7, the summative model is the one that is most generally useful in the scaling of people with respect to psychological traits. It assumes only that individual items are monotonically related to underlying traits and that a summation of item scores is approximately linearly related to the trait. One obtains a total score by adding scores on individual items (reversing the scoring for statements that imply negative attitudes). This same logic is applied both to dichotomous items and to multipoint items.

Because summative scales for the measurement of attitudes were championed by Likert (1932), they are sometimes referred to as "Likert scales." Summative scales have a number of attractive advantages over all other methods: (1) They follow from an appealing model, (2) they are rather easy to construct, (3) they are usually highly reliable, (4) they can be adapted to the measurement of many different kinds of attitudes, and (5) they have produced meaningful results in many studies to date.

## construction of summative scales for verbalized attitudes

The method of constructing summative attitude scales is only a special case of the general method of constructing nonspeeded (power) measures, which was discussed in Chapter 8. Here we shall describe a few of the particular features of constructing summative scales for attitudes. Aspects of scale construction will be illustrated with agree-disagree scales applied to statements concerning attitudes. The methods, however, are general to all summative scales. They apply, for example, to summative scales that one obtains by adding responses to individual rating scales bounded by bipolar adjectives, and they apply to summative scales that one obtains by adding responses to individual rating scales anchored by actual behaviors.

### Item pool

All the statements in the item pool should, of course, concern a particular attitudinal object, e.g., the United Nations or labor unions. Since it is usually easy to obtain a homogeneous scale for the measurement of attitudes, seldom are more than 40 items required in the item pool. Since the purpose of each item on a summative scale is to obtain reliable variance with respect to the attitude in question, most of the items should be either moderately positive or moderately negative. There is no place for truly neutral statements in summative scales. Statements that are very extreme in either direction tend to create less variance than statements that are less extreme. The pool of items should be about evenly divided between positive and negative statements.

### Data for item analysis

The item pool should be administered to a group of subjects that is similar to the groups with which the final instrument will be used, e.g., samples of college students for a scale to be used in research on college students or a broad sample of the general population for a scale that will be used in national surveys. Because it is usually rather easy to develop homogeneous scales of verbalized attitudes, the number of subjects need be no more than five times the number of items, but if larger numbers of subjects are easily obtained, the more subjects the better.

In the development of attitude scales, it is very important that the data for item analysis be obtained under circumstances very similar to those in which the final scale will be employed. For example, the data for an item analysis might be very misleading if they are obtained under conditions of anonymity for subjects and the final scale is intended for use in circumstances where responses of subjects will not be anonymous. Also, it is very important to think out carefully the instructions that will be used with the final instrument and to use those instructions in obtaining data for item analysis.

### Item analysis

Before correlating items with total scale scores, scoring should be reversed for negative statements. (The same result could be obtained by reversing the scoring for positive statements.) For dichotomous items, this would mean scoring 1 for agreement with positive statements and zero for disagreement, and vice versa for negative statements. One reverses scales for negative statements when multipoint items are employed by subtracting each scale position from the number of scale steps plus 1. For example, if a seven-step scale is applied to each statement and 7 means "completely agree," the rating made of each negative statement would be subtracted from 8. This would then treat complete disagreement with a negative statement like complete agreement with a positive statement, and vice versa.

As was mentioned in Chapter 8, one of the difficulties in scoring responses in preparation for item analysis is that with some item pools, the proper directions of scoring for many of the items are difficult to discern. This results in what was called "bipolar item pools." Iterative procedures were mentioned in Chapter 8 for dealing with this situation. In the development of attitude scales (and for the measurement of sentiments in general), however, these procedures are seldom necessary. If, as advised earlier, all the statements are either moderately positive or moderately negative, the proper direction for scoring each item is usually very easy to discern. After the directions of scoring have been established, it is very rare to find any item that has a substantial negative correlation with total scale scores.

After the directions for scoring have been established, one obtains total scores over all items in the item pool by simply summing scores over items. At that point one could compute coefficient alpha (KR-20, for dichotomous items), or since that is usually very high when computed over the total item pool, one could proceed to the correlation of each item with total scores. Correlations would be regular PM coefficients for multipoint scales and point-biserial coefficients for dichotomous scales. Separate rank orderings of the correlations should be made for positive and for negative statements. Then, working from the top of the rank orders downward, one would choose an equal number of positive and negative items for the final scale. Say, for example, that out of a total item pool of 40 items, 10 positive and 10 negative statements are selected. The 20 items would then be combined to form a trial scale, and coefficient alpha (see Appendix D) would be computed for the 20 items. This would require computing the variance of each item and obtaining total scores summed over the 20 items (reversing directions of scoring negative items as before). If coefficient alpha is sufficiently high, the 20 items could be accepted as the final scale. In the construction of summative scales of attitudes, usually 20 statements selected in that way will have a reliability above .80. As was mentioned previously, the size of the reliability relates to the number of scale steps for the rating scale used with each statement.

### Factor analysis of items

In the construction of most types of psychological measures, factor analysis of an item pool should be considered only as a last resort, after efforts to hypothesize homogeneous scales have led to naught. The use of factor analysis is discouraged because the average correlation between items in the typical item pool is small and the standard deviation of such correlations is small. Under these circumstances, the results of factor analyses tend to be very "messy." For two reasons, these conditions tend not to hold in item pools constructed for the measurement of attitudes. First, even if dichotomous items are employed for the measurement of attitudes, the correlations between them tend to be higher than is the case for measures of ability and personality characteristics. Second, the fact that multipoint scales are employed more frequently than dichotomous scales to measure attitudes tends to further increase the size of the average correlation between items. Also, there is frequently enough variance in the sizes of correlations to document "strong" factors.

If one hypothesizes a number of factors relating to a particular attitude, or, lacking hypotheses, if one suspects that an item pool harbors a number of "strong" factors, there is nothing wrong with factor analyzing the item pool initially rather than proceeding directly to the construction of a homogeneous scale, as was outlined previously. The factor structures obtained from multipoint ratings of attitudes are frequently as "strong" as those obtained from factor structures for whole tests of ability and personality characteristics.

An example of a domain of content in which a number of factors might be expected would be in relation to labor unions. A person might feel that labor unions are worthwhile in terms of the national economy but have a stifling influence on cultural values, or he might think that labor unions are "bad" in both these respects but have a constructive influence politically. Factor analysis could be used to test hypotheses about the major factors of attitudes toward labor unions and to construct scales for the measurement of those factors. The use of factor analysis with item pools relating to attitudes is the major exception to the principle that it is usually unwise to start an item analysis with factor analysis.

## semantic-differential scales

A very useful type of scale is one that employs direct ratings of concepts with scales anchored on the extremes by bipolar adjectives, such as the following:

### United Nations

| | | | | | | |
|---|---|---|---|---|---|---|
| Ineffective | __: 1 | __: 2 | __: 3 | __: 4 | __: 5 | __ 6 | Effective |
| Foolish | __: 1 | __: 2 | __: 3 | __: 4 | __: 5 | __ 6 | Wise |
| Weak | __: 1 | __: 2 | __: 3 | __: 4 | __: 5 | __ 6 | Strong |
| Useless | __: 1 | __: 2 | __: 3 | __: 4 | __: 5 | __ 6 | Useful |

A collection of scales such as those above is referred to as a *semantic differential*. Although it will be convenient here to speak of *the* semantic differential, the term is used in a generic sense to refer to any collection of rating scales anchored by bipolar adjectives. Rather than being a particular instrument (or test, as some have called it), the semantic differential is a very flexible approach to obtaining measures of attitudes and other sentiments. The flexibility of the approach is one of its appealing features. The object that is rated is referred to as a *concept*, and anything that can be named can be rated, e.g., Winston Churchill, peach ice cream, labor unions, birth control, my best friend, and automobiles. Not only are bipolar adjectives easily adapted to a multitude of concepts, but it is also easy to apply a list of scales to a number of different concepts in the same rating form. For example, if one is interested in examining attitudes toward a number of different political figures, institutions, and forms of policy, these can all be investigated in the same instrument. Subjects have no trouble in rating 20 concepts on 20 scales in an hour's time or less.   The semantic differential is very flexible in another sense: It makes it easy to construct scales for the measurement of different facets of attitudes, a matter which will be discussed more fully later.

An impressive array of studies have been performed on semantic-differential scales by C. E. Osgood and his colleagues (Osgood, 1962; Osgood, Suci, & Tannenbaum, 1957).   The semantic differential was developed mainly in relation to a mediational theory of learning (Osgood, 1962).   Since in that theory the "meaning" of stimuli occupies a central role, some ways of measuring various facets of meaning are required to give the theory empirical implications. The semantic differential was developed as such a measure.

## Logic of the semantic differential

In spoken and written language, characteristics of ideas and real things are communicated largely by means of adjectives.   Thus a particular person might be described as being polite, urbane, and intelligent, and a particular policy in foreign affairs might be characterized as being outmoded, rigid, and discriminatory.   Consequently, it is reasonable to assume that adjectives can be used to measure various facets of meaning.

Most adjectives have logical opposites, as is evidenced in the pairs sweet-sour, dark-light, and tall-short.   Where an opposing adjective is not obviously available, one can easily be generated with "in-" or "un-," e.g., sufficient-insufficient and satisfactory-unsatisfactory.   All that remains, then, is to (1) generate a wide sample of such pairs of adjectives; (2) use them as anchors on rating scales, as illustrated previously; and (3) search for common factors among the scales.   If strong factors are found and the factors appear in ratings of many different kinds of concepts, they can be used as general measures of different aspects of meaning.

## Factors in semantic-differential scales

Numerous factor analyses have been performed to date on semantic-differential scales (these are summarized by Osgood, 1962).   Different studies have employed different types of concepts, e.g., names of prominent persons, geometric forms, commercial products, persons with different types of physical or mental illness, different animals, and others.   Studies have been performed of ratings made by people in different countries around the world and by different types of persons in this country.   Also, many different adjective pairs have been employed in one or more of the studies.

The numerous factor-analytic studies of semantic-differential scales lead to the conclusion that there are three major factors of meaning involved.   The factors do not always have exactly the same content in different studies, and in some studies more than three prominent factors are found.   The remarkable fact, however, is that three factors with similar content have occurred in so many analyses under such varied conditions. The most frequently found factor is *evaluation*, which is defined by pairs of adjectives like the following:

| | |
|---|---|
| good-bad | honest-dishonest |
| pleasant-unpleasant | positive-negative |
| fair-unfair | sweet-sour |
| wise-foolish | valuable-worthless |
| successful-unsuccessful | clean-dirty |

The evaluative factor is by far the strongest one in semantic-differential scales. In some studies it is so strong that little common variance is left to define other factors. The evaluative factor is prominent because nearly all adjectives imply negative and positive characteristics. Actually, it is difficult to think of bipolar pairs of adjectives that do not hint at evaluation. Even such pairs as wet-dry, long-short, and up-down hint of evaluation. The evaluative factor almost serves as a definition for the term "attitude," and consequently scales on the evaluative factor should serve well as measures of verbalized attitudes.

The second strongest factor that frequently appears in factor analyses of semantic-differential scales is *potency*. Some of the pairs of adjectives that usually load on that factor are as follows:

| | |
|---|---|
| strong-weak | rugged-delicate |
| hard-soft | large-small |
| heavy-light | masculine-feminine |
| thick-thin | severe-lenient |

The third strongest factor that frequently appears is *activity*. Some pairs of adjectives relating to that factor are as follows:

| | |
|---|---|
| active-passive | quick-slow |
| tense-relaxed | hot-cold |
| excitable-calm | sharp-dull |
| impetuous-quiet | busy-lazy |

The factors of potency and activity are not as strong statistically as the factor of evaluation, and whereas one can easily think of many adjective pairs that relate to evaluation, it is difficult to find adjective pairs that clearly measure the other two factors. Typically it is found that even the best scales for measuring potency and activity also correlate with the factor of evaluation. This is particularly so for the potency factor, where one usually finds substantial positive correlations, e.g., between the scales good-bad and strong-weak and between effective-ineffective and rugged-delicate. Correlations also occur between scales to measure activity and scales to measure evaluation, e.g., between the scales valuable-worthless and active-passive and between the scales efficient-inefficient and quick-slow.

Less important than the correlations between scales used to measure the different factors are correlations between estimates of factor scores on the three factors.  Typically half a dozen scales from each of the factors are used to determine factor scores.  For this purpose, ratings are simply summed over the scales in each factor.  When that is done, one typically finds positive correlations between the three factors; i.e., considering the extremes, some concepts tend to be rated as good, strong, and active, and at the other extreme, some concepts tend to be rated as bad, weak, and inactive.  Typically one finds an average correlation between measures of the three factors ranging from about .30 to about .50 in different studies, the size of the average correlation varying with the types of concepts being investigated.

In addition to these three factors that have appeared in numerous analyses, other prominent factors have been found in semantic-differential scales. Nunnally (1961) found a factor of *familiarity* (or *understandability*, as it was called), defined by scales like the following:

| | |
|---|---|
| familiar-unfamiliar | understandable-mysterious |
| usual-unusual | predictable-unpredictable |
| clear-confusing | simple-complex |

Potentially, the factor of familiarity is important for the scaling of stimuli to be used in controlled experiments.  There are numerous instances in which actual familiarity and rated familiarity have proved to be important determiners of rate of verbal learning and rate of perceptual recognition.

Osgood (1962) reports a number of other factors that appear with particular types of scales and concepts.  The factor structure tends to be more "diverse" when ratings are made of concepts relating to human personality, such as a good friend, a mother, and an athlete.  With such concepts, one tends to find about eight factors, and partly because of the limited number of scales that can be employed in a study, only a few scales have substantial loadings on each factor.  In several studies of concepts relating to personality, a factor of rationality has been found, which is defined by scales like logical-intuitive, objective-subjective, and rational-irrational.  In the same studies, a factor of morality was found, with scales like moral-immoral, reputable-disreputable, and wholesome-unwholesome.

### Interactions of scales and concepts

One caution in employing semantic-differential scales is that the meanings of scales sometimes depend on the concept being rated.  For example, whereas "rugged" is positively evaluative when applied to men, it is not positively evaluative when applied to women.  Whereas "sweet" is positively evaluative when applied to many concepts, it certainly is not positively evaluative when applied to the brand names of different beers.  Whereas tough-tender would correlate positively with valuable-worthless in ratings of sports cars, the correlation would obviously be negative in rating the brand names of steaks, lamb chops, hams, and other meats.  Many other examples could be given in which the meanings of scales differ with the concepts being studied and in which the size and directions of correlations between scales differ with the types of concepts.

The interaction of scales with concepts places a limit on the extent to which individual scales can be interpreted in the same way when applied to different concepts, and it also places a limit on the extent to which factors in semantic-differential scales can be employed as general yardsticks (e.g., to measure evaluation) regardless of the concepts in a particular study. There are several lessons to be learned from these points. First, less scale-concept interaction is likely to occur when all the concepts in a particular study are from the same domain of discourse. It would, for example, be better in most studies to have all the concepts be four-legged animals, types of persons, or social institutions, rather than to mix the three types of concepts in one study. There is no harm in having a mixed bag of concepts rated at the same time by the same people, but it usually makes more sense to perform separate analyses, and make separate interpretations, of the data for different types of concepts.

Second, it is wise to perform factor analyses for any type of concept which is to be investigated extensively. For example, if one intended to make extensive use of semantic-differential scales with many different types of geometric designs, it would be wise to investigate the factor structure of such scales with that particular type of concept rather than depend entirely on the factor structures found with other types of concepts. In that instance one would expect the three major factors to have much the same content (e.g., it would be surprising not to find good-bad and pleasant-unpleasant loading substantially on a factor of evaluation), but some of the factor content might be different from that typically found in other studies.

Third, instead of relying blindly on the scales that usually define factors in semantic-differential scales, it is wise to think carefully about possible interactions of scales and concepts in particular studies. For example, although the scale beautiful-ugly usually measures evaluation, anyone would be foolish to employ it for that purpose in ratings of famous statesmen, e.g., Churchill, Napoleon, or Lincoln. In some instances a scale that usually does not load highly on a factor does have a high loading with a particular type of concept. This is the case for the scale effective-ineffective, which has only a moderate-sized loading on the evaluative factor with many types of concepts but has a high loading on that factor when the concepts concern professions, such as psychologist, psychiatrist, engineer, surgeon, and economist. Such concepts tend to "bunch together" on the high end of most scales commonly used to measure the evaluative factor (e.g., good-bad and fair-unfair), but they are drawn apart on the scale effective-ineffective. Though the final test of the wisdom of selecting particular scales to be used with particular concepts is made by factor analyzing the data, careful forethought can lead to a selection of scales that will manifest the desired factor structure.

## What the semantic differential measures

Previously it was said that the initial purpose of the semantic differential was to measure the meaning of concepts. Here we shall go into more detail about the evidence regarding what is measured by semantic-differential scales. "Meaning" is a very global term: in the ultimate it includes all possible reactions that people have to words and things. There are, however, some facets of meaning that can be usefully discussed with respect to the semantic differential. It is useful to distinguish between three overlapping facets of meaning: denotation, connotation, and association. *Denotation* concerns an objective description of an object in terms of its physical characteristics. Thus an orange is denoted as being a round, reddish-yellow fruit with a juicy interior containing seeds, etc. The United Nations is denoted as an international association of governments, the purpose of which is the furthering of world peace, economic advancement, education, etc. Essentially, the denotative aspects of meaning are those which direct a person to a specific object to the exclusion of all other objects.

In addition to denotation there is *connotation*, that is, what implications the object in question has for a particular person. Thus after an individual has completely denoted the orange, he could say, "I like them very much," which would represent a connotation (or sentiment) for him. Similarly, after an individual has completely denoted the United Nations, he could say, "I think that it is a rather ineffective organization," which again would represent a connotation or sentiment.

Overlapping with denotation and connotation is *association*. Associations, as the term will be used here, consist of other objects that are brought to mind when an individual sees or hears about a particular object. Associations are typically obtained by the classical method of free association, in which the subject is presented with one word and is told to write down an associate. Associations to "orange" would be "fruit," "seed," "apple," and "sweet." Associations to "United Nations" would be "world," "New York," "peace," "government," and "Russians."

The semantic differential measures mainly *connotative* aspects of meaning, particularly the evaluative connotations of objects, and it is probably the most valid measure of connotative meaning available. Because of the nature of the instrument, it cannot measure nonconnotative associations; e.g., from the instrument alone there is no way of learning that "apple" is associated with "orange" or that "New York" is associated with "United Nations." The evaluative factor on the semantic differential is almost purely connotative in character rather than denotative or associative (in the sense of object-object associations). This is why it was said previously that the evaluative factor should provide a good measure of attitudes.

Both the semantic differential and the classical method of free association are partly denotative in character, and this is where the three facets of meaning overlap. In the method of free association, denotative associations to "orange" would be "fruit" and "round." Denotative aspects of the concept "orange" would be found in ratings on semantic-differential scales such as sweet-sour and angular-rounded. Both of these approaches, however, only incidentally provide evidence about the denotative meanings of concepts. The semantic differential is dominated by connotative meaning, particularly evaluation. Free association to nouns (concepts or attitudinal objects) is dominated by responses that are also nouns, or "object associates," as the term is used here.

Whereas the factors of potency and activity ostensibly concern denotative aspects of meaning, they do so only in part. First, even though scales on those factors ostensibly concern physical properties of objects (e.g., heavy, large, fast, and active), they are also partly evaluative in nature, and thus they relate partly to connotative rather than denotative aspects of meaning. Second, ratings of potency and activity can be interpreted only with respect to classes of stimuli. To use an example provided by Osgood (1962), a baby would be rated as small, and a railroad spike would be rated as large, but of course the former is actually much larger in physical size than the latter. To explain this, Osgood suggests that objects are rated in comparison with implicit classes of stimuli. Thus a baby is small in the class of all persons, and a railroad spike is large in the class of all naillike objects. Actually, however, this is a good feature of the semantic differential, rather than a bad one. If one really wanted to learn the physical properties of objects (e.g., their strength and speed), measuring those properties directly would be far better than guessing them. The potency and activity factors provide auxiliary information about evaluation beyond that provided by the scales specifically intended to measure evaluation, and they provide suggestions about conceptual classes of objects, e.g., persons and naillike objects.

### Use of semantic-differential scales

In previous sections some general suggestions were made about the employment of semantic-differential scales in research, and some additional points in that regard will be made here. When scores are summed over a number of scales, as is usually the case, the logic of constructing summative measures is the same as that discussed previously for constructing summative scales of verbalized attitudes. That is, by methods of item analysis, one seeks a homogeneous group of scales that meets requirements of reliability. It is usually not difficult to accomplish that goal. One frequently finds, for example, that half a dozen pairs of adjectives rated on eight-step scales have a coefficient alpha as high as .80.

It is well to employ numbers to designate the steps on semantic-differential scales, e.g., the numbers 1 to 8 to designate the steps of an eight-step scale. Also, the meanings of the numbers should be carefully defined and illustrated in the instructions to the inventory. For example, subjects can be told that on the scale good-bad, 5 means "slightly good" rather than "bad," 4 means "slightly bad" rather than "good," and so on for the other steps on the scale.

Rather than employing only the "standard" factors that have been found in studies of diverse concepts, there is nothing wrong with developing particular groups of scales for particular purposes. For example, the following scales would be useful in studying subjective feelings of anxiety in experiments concerning the effects of different types of stressful circumstances:

| | |
|---|---|
| anxious-calm | afraid-unafraid |
| tense-relaxed | nervous-restful |
| disturbed-undisturbed | upset-quiet |

Of course, the advantages of summing scores over a number of scales rather than relying on one scale alone (e.g., anxious-calm) are that (1) it permits finer differentiations between persons and (2) it tends to average out the idiosyncrasy in each scale. Even though such scales may, in general usage, have somewhat different patterns of factor loadings with the "usual" factors, in such special uses as that illustrated above they may correlate highly. Numerous other special groups of scales can be employed in particular studies.

In addition to summing scores over groups of scales, in most studies it is also instructive to compare concepts on individual scales. Thus, as was mentioned previously, the scale effective-ineffective provides useful information about public attitudes toward professional groups, beyond that which is provided by other scales that typically have high loadings on the evaluative factor. As other examples, Nunnally (1961) found that the scale tense-relaxed served better than any other scale to differentiate public attitudes toward neurotic persons and normal persons and that the scale predictable-unpredictable served better than any other scale to differentiate public attitudes toward psychotic persons and normal persons. Such differences between concepts on individual scales provide many hints for subsequent investigations.

An example of the rich information about attitudes obtained from profiles of scores on semantic-differential scales is presented in Figure 14-1, which shows the average ratings given by a broad segment of the general population to the three concepts "old man," "neurotic man," and "me" (self-rating). In terms of overall attitude, note that the concept "me" is rated more favorably than "neurotic man" on all scales, which is evidence of the widely negative attitudes of normal people toward the mentally ill. In terms of the different information about attitudes obtained from different scales, note the wide separation of "neurotic man" from the other two concepts on the scale tense-relaxed and the separation of "me" and "old man" on the scale clean-dirty.

Numerous examples of studies employing the semantic differential are reported by Nunnally (1961), Osgood (1962), and Osgood et al. (1957). A list of 99 scales employed in one or more studies is reported by Nunnally (1959). Sample instructions for inventories containing semantic-differential

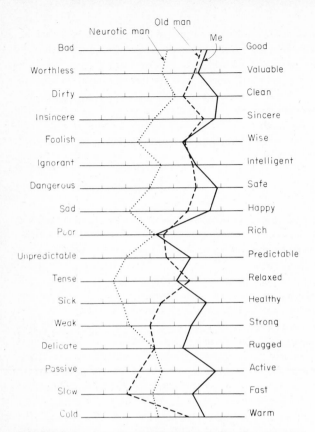

**FIGURE 14-1** Semantic-differential profiles for the concepts "me" (———), "old man" (- - -), and "neurotic man" (. . .). Each point represents the mean rating of 200 subjects.

scales and ratings on a variety of scales for a large number of person concepts are reported by Nunnally (1961). As can be seen from the many studies mentioned in the above sources and from the many particular studies not mentioned in those sources, during the last 10 years the semantic differential has become an important "workhorse" in psychology for the investigation of attitudes and other types of sentiments.

## the Q sort

The Q sort and the semantic differential gained their fame at about the same time, in the early 1950s. Except for that similarity, however, they are very different types of rating tasks. The Q sort grew out of a more general methodology developed by Stephenson (1953) for the study of verbalized attitudes, self-description, preferences, and other issues in social psychology, clinical psychology, and the study of personality. A salient principle in that methodology is that for the advancement of psychology, it is more important to make comparisons between different responses (e.g., statements regarding preferences) within persons than between persons. In other words, basic to Stephenson's methodology is a reliance on *comparative* rating methods and on an analysis of comparative data within persons even when absolute rating methods are employed. The Q sort is a handy comparative rating method that has proved useful for the type of study that Stephenson envisaged. Also, it has been used widely to study numerous issues ranging from psychotherapy to advertising. Wittenborn (1961) surveyed studies employing the Q sort up to 1961. More detailed descriptions of studies employing the Q sort are given by Nunnally (1959) and Stephenson (1953).

### An illustrative study

Before the psychometric properties of the Q sort are discussed, a simple example will illustrate the nature of the rating method. In a study concerning preferences for statues, each of 100 statues appears separately in a photograph. The statues are products of many different cultures around the world and date from many different historical periods. Rather than rate each photograph separately, as would be done with an absolute rating method such as the rating scale, the subject is asked to make comparative preferences by "sorting" the photographs into a specified number of piles. The end piles are designated "prefer most" and "prefer least," respectively. The particular feature of the Q sort is that the subject is required to sort the stimuli in terms of a fixed distribution, usually an approximately normal distribution. A fixed distribution that could be used for the study of 100 statues is as follows:

*Number of Photographs*

| 2 | 4 | 8 | 12 | 14 | 20 | 14 | 12 | 8 | 4 | 2 | |
|---|---|---|----|----|----|----|----|---|---|---|---|
| Prefer | | | | | | | | | | | Prefer |
| 0 | 1 | 2 | 3 | 4 | 5 | 6 | 7 | 8 | 9 | 10 | |
| least | | | | | | | | | | | most |

*Pile Number*

The number for each pile is written on a file card, and the cards are spread out in a line on a large table. To lessen order effects, the investigator shuffles the 100 photographs before giving them to the subject. Before sorting the photographs, the subject is instructed to look at them one at a time and then to spread them out on the table to make comparisons between them. Preparatory to the actual sorting, the subject is frequently asked to place the photographs into three gross classes—ones that he definitely likes, ones that he definitely dislikes, and ones about which he is ambivalent. This is done only to facilitate the subsequent sorting, and judgments made at that time can be changed later.

In the actual sorting of the photographs, the subject is instructed to work from both ends of the continuum toward the middle. The extreme likes and dislikes are usually spotted faster than less extreme preferences. Also, since in correlational studies so much depends on the extreme scores, it is important that the subject pay particular attention to the placements in the two or three extreme piles on each end of the continuum. In a study of preferences, the subject would usually be instructed to work from the "prefer most" end toward the middle. He would be instructed to find the two that he preferred the most and place them in pile 10. From the remaining 98 photographs, he would pick the four that he preferred the most and place them in pile 9. He would continue working in this way down through pile 7. Then he would be instructed to switch to the "prefer least" end of the continuum, pick the two that he least preferred and place them in pile zero, and work upward in that way through pile 3. The subject would then sort the remaining 48 photographs into piles 4, 5, and 6. Finally, he would be instructed to examine the entire ratings to make sure that no photographs were out of place and, if some were, to rearrange the positions of the photographs.

### Nature of the rating task

As was mentioned previously, the Q sort is obviously a comparative rating method rather than an absolute rating method. The task forces all subjects to have the same mean rating, and thus one learns nothing about level of response to the stimuli as a group. A subject could detest all the statues in the example above or like them all very much, but no hint of that would be obtained from the Q sort. All comparative rating tasks (e.g., the method of rank order) force all subjects to have the same mean rating, and thus none of them are intended to provide information about absolute levels of response.

The Q sort also requires subjects to distribute their responses in terms of a fixed distribution, usually an approximately normal distribution. This forces all subjects not only to have the same mean rating but also to have the same standard deviation of ratings and the same curve shape of ratings. The Q sort has been criticized on this score because one could argue that subjects would employ different shapes of distributions if left to their own devices. For a number of reasons, such criticisms are not well justified.

If the intention is to obtain comparative ratings, as it is when the Q sort is employed, it is necessary to sacrifice information about the absolute responses to stimuli. This is exactly what is done in the method of rank order, which is the logical paradigm for all comparative methods. With the Q sort, if subjects are allowed to put as many stimuli as they like in a pile, the method begins to regress to the method of single stimuli (discussed in Chapter 7), a method for studying absolute responses. For example, a photograph would be placed in the top pile not only because it was liked *more* than others but also because it was liked very much in an absolute sense. If one wants to have comparative responses made with respect to all the stimuli in a set, rather than with respect to two at a time, as with the method of pair comparisons or in other subsets, the mean, standard deviation, and curve form must be fixed.

Thus arguments about the use of a fixed distribution in the Q sort boil down to (1) whether a comparative rating method should be used in studies of the kinds in which the Q sort is employed and (2) if so, whether the Q sort should be used in preference to other comparative methods. The first point is well worth considering and will be returned to later, but here let us consider the second point. The major reason for using the Q sort rather than some other comparative rating method is that it greatly conserves the time taken to make ratings. For example, a Q sort of 100 photographs would take no more than 30 minutes on the average, but a complete rank ordering would probably take well over an hour and would prove very tedious to subjects. Because of the time other comparative rating methods take, they would be almost out of the question. For example, if the method of pair comparisons were employed with 100 photographs and each subject judged each pair only once, the subject would have to make 4,950 comparisons. Obviously, most of the comparative rating methods are limited to rather small sets of stimuli. Even with the method of rank order, it is difficult to employ more than 50 stimuli. The Q sort, then, is a useful compromise between two needs: (1) the need to have precise differentiations made between the stimuli, as is done in the method of pair comparisons, and (2) the need to have comparisons made between the members of large sets of stimuli, which is the case in many studies in psychology.

It is best to regard the fixed distribution in the Q sort as an approximation to rank order, a rank ordering in which the number of tied ranks at each point is specified for the subject. The use of an approximately normal distribution rather than some other fixed distribution (e.g., a rectangular distribution) is justified in the general case because (1) so many things in nature are distributed approximately that way and (2) it fits in with the statistical methods applied to the data.

Another reason why criticisms of the fixed Q-sort distribution are largely unjustified is that the exact distribution form has little effect on the kinds of analyses which are made of the data. Correlation coefficients, and the factors obtained from them, are largely insensitive to changes in distribution shapes. Of course, they are not affected at all by artifactual changes in means and standard deviations of raw scores. To the extent that it is meaningful to apply inferential statistics to Q-sort ratings, it is known that the results of such inferential statistics tend to be affected very little by changes in distribution form.

For purposes of analysis, then, even if one allowed subjects to sort stimuli into any distribution form that they chose, differences in distribution forms between subjects would make little difference in the results of statistical analyses.

Actually, those who work extensively with Q sorts recommend that a relatively large number of piles be employed and that the distribution be somewhat flatter than the normal distribution. This allows subjects to make rather fine discriminations between stimuli and tends to increase the reliabilty of ratings, just as an increase in the number of steps on rating scales does.

## Stimulus samples

It is to the credit of Stephenson and his colleagues that research with Q sorts has emphasized the importance of stimulus (or content) sampling. Psychology, and other disciplines as well, is faced with problems concerning two types of sampling—sampling of people and sampling of stimuli. While psychologists are usually careful to sample people adequately, at least to the point of obtaining sufficient numbers of subjects, and while they employ very elegant statistical methods for assessing the error associated with the sampling of people, less is usually done about the sampling of stimuli (or content). To take an oversimplified example, regardless of what type of rating method was employed, one would not learn much about food preferences unless a representative list of food names was sampled. The sample would be inadequate if it left out all meats, included desserts of only certain kinds, or contained numerous foreign dishes that the subjects had never heard of. In more subtle ways, biased samples of content lead to poor measurements, e.g., a vocabulary test for the general population which is loaded with technical terms relating to particular occupations or a scale for verbalized attitudes toward the United Nations that contains statements about only restricted aspects of the organization.

The problem of sampling stimuli occurs in many types of ratings, but for good reasons it has had to be faced more squarely in the use of Q sorts than in the use of other rating methods. One reason for this is that the rating task makes sense only if all stimuli are from a specifiable universe of content. To understand why this is so, imagine that subjects are asked to rate the aesthetic quality of 100 photographs, 50 of which are pictures of statues and 50 of which are pictures of automobiles. In sorting the pictures, not only would the subject have to decide which statues were more aesthetically pleasing and which automobiles were more aesthetically pleasing, but, in essence, he would also have to decide whether statues as a group were more aesthetically pleasing than automobiles as a group. Obviously, the results of such a study would be far more meaningful if separate Q sortings were made of statues and automobiles. Although surely no one would mix such different types of stimuli in a Q sort, the use of Q sorts is constantly plagued by the need to ensure that all stimuli are from some common frame of reference.

The problem with ensuring that all stimuli are from a common frame of reference is that it is hard to define a common frame of reference. In the sampling of people, the problem is one of defining the population which the sample is intended to represent. There are some problems there, e.g., generalizing from studies of college students to people in general or deciding whether American Indians will be included in a national sample for obtaining norms for intelligence tests. The problems in defining populations of people are small, however, in comparison with the problems of defining "populations" of stimuli. These problems are partciularly severe with one type of content that has been used frequently with Q sorts—statements relating to personality traits, such as the following:

1. I have many friends.
2. Most people like me.
3. I am a nervous person.
4. I had an unhappy childhood.
5. I dread the future.
6. I enjoy physical exercise.

It is hard to see how a comparative rating method like the Q sort makes sense with such diverse content as that illustrated in the six statements above. Samples of statements concerning personality used with Q sorts frequently fail to represent a common frame of reference because (1) they mix motives, social traits, personal conceptions, and symptoms of maladjustment; (2) they contain statements relating to the past, present, and future; (3) some statements concern self-description and others concern judgments about what other people think; and (4) some statements concern general traits (e.g., tendency to be anxious), and others concern rather specific habits (e.g., overeating). Even if none of these rather obvious failures to keep all stimuli in a common frame of reference occur, it is frequently difficult to stipulate what domain of content is intended to be covered or to justify the method employed to sample the domain.

## Types of content samples

Two types of content samples are employed with the Q sort: *random* samples and *structured* samples. In both instances, it is important to realize that the so-called sampling is not done in the same way that one samples from populations of persons. Rather, in "sampling" material for a Q sort, one either constructs the materials himself or borrows them from some available source, e.g., a book containing many photographs of statues. The structured sample is one in which the experimenter stipulates the kinds of stimuli that will be included in the content sample in terms of an experimental design. An oversimplified example is as follows. In a study of photographs of statues, the experimenter decides that some of the photographs will be of Oriental statues and that others will be of Occidental statues.  Also, he decides that some of the photographs will show abstract statues and that others will show representational ones.  The structured sample could then be summarized in terms of the following design:

|                    | Oriental | Occidental |
|--------------------|----------|------------|
| Representational   | 25       | 25         |
| Abstract           | 25       | 25         |

The experimenter would employ 25 photographs depicting statues that were both representational and Oriental in origin, 25 that were both abstract and Occidental in origin, and so on for the other two cells of the design.  If there are no other facets of the design, the 25 photographs in each cell should be "random," which the experimenter can best approximate simply by ensuring that they are diversely representative of sculptors and subject matters.

Before any faith can be placed in a structured sample of content, two types of data must be obtained.  First, prior to the use of the sample in $Q$ sorts, judgments should be made by knowledgeable people of the appropriateness of the classifications of stimuli.  In the example above, one could have five artists independently judge the relevance of each photograph for its classification, e.g., by giving each artist the 100 photographs and having him place each photograph in the cell where it belongs.  Only those photographs would be retained that received high agreement among judges.  The second type of assurance for the correctness of cell placements comes from analyzing the responses of subjects who make $Q$ sortings of the stimuli.  If the stimuli in a particular cell actually "hang together," it should be found that the variance of $Q$-sort ratings by each subject for the stimuli in any cell is considerably less than the variance of the $Q$-sort distribution.  If that is not the case, it means that the stimuli that are assigned to a particular cell of the structured sample scatter all up and down the $Q$-sort continuum in the ratings made by each subject.  Then, even if one could argue that there are good logical reasons for the placement of stimuli in a structured sample, it would be obvious that the design did very little to explain the actual ratings made by subjects.

In some cases, it is very difficult to generate a sensible structured sample for the stimuli to be used in a $Q$ sort, as when psychotherapists make $Q$-sort ratings of the day-to-day progress of patients with statements like the following:

1. Spends much time expressing appreciation to me for my understanding.
2. Avoids talking about painful issues.
3. Seems more intent on the future than on what the past was like.
4. Seems discouraged about the possibility of solving major problems.

With such statements, and with many other types of stimuli, the best that can be done is to "randomly sample" the desired number of "things" to be used in a Q sort. What this means is that one tries to obtain a highly diverse collection of materials of the kind to be investigated, e.g., photographs of many different types of statues drawn from a number of different sources, statements about important things to observe in psychotherapy taken from a number of prominent books on the topic, or symptoms of mental illness taken from case histories in the files of a number of different types of psychiatric institutions.

Where it can be employed, the structured sample has obvious advantages over the so-called random sample. The facets of the structure help in communicating the nature of the content to other investigators. One of the problems with many "random" samples of content is that it is very difficult to specify the domain that has been "sampled." Also, the random sample typically attempts to cover too much ground, and consequently it is frequently learned from analyses of Q sorts that insufficient numbers of stimuli of particular kinds were included in the sample. The structured sample serves to limit the content to manageable proportions, and it helps to ensure that sufficient numbers of stimuli of the specified kinds are included. Also, as was mentioned previously, an analysis of the data obtained from investigating a structured sample will provide information about the adequacy of the placement of stimuli in the design. In sum, although the structured sample attempts to cover less ground than the random sample, it does a better job of specifying the ground to be covered, it usually does a better job of covering that ground, and, in addition, the internal checks possible with the structured sample provide evidence regarding the original assignment of stimuli to cells.

When it is not possible to construct a structured sample of content initially, it frequently becomes possible to do so after some investigations have been made with a random sample. The results of statistical analyses may indicate that there are homogeneous groups of items, i.e., a number of items that tend to be given similar placements in Q sorts, regardless of where they are placed as a group by different subjects. Results of these kinds could lead to asserting a structure for the sample. For the final structured sample, then, it would probably be necessary to discard some items that did not relate to the structured design and to add items in some cells to achieve equal numbers. Also, whether one achieves a structured sample initially or only after preliminary research, it frequently happens that additional facets are added to the design as a result of the fact that continued research teaches the investigator how to make important new distinctions between the kinds of stimuli in his domain of interest.

## Analysis of Q-sort data

Many criticisms of research employing the Q sort pertain not so much to the Q sort itself but rather to methods of analysis that have been applied to

Q-sort data. The most popular methods of analysis have concerned correlations, e.g., the correlation of two Q sorts of the same material by the same subject under different conditions or the correlation of Q sorts by different persons. As an example of the former, one person would be required to make "sorts" under two sets of instructions, such as a set pertaining to his aesthetic preferences for 100 statues and a set pertaining to his estimate of what aesthetic preferences the average six-year-old child would have. The PM correlation could then be computed between the sorts made by two persons on a list of statements relating to personality traits. In addition to employing simple correlational methods with Q sorts, many studies have employed more complex methods of correlational analysis, including partial correlation, multiple correlation, and various methods of factor analysis.

Although there is not sufficient space here to go into the many questions concerning various methods of analysis applied to Q-sort data, some of the major issues will be discussed. In this regard, it is important to take separate looks at *inferential statistics* applied to Q-sort data and *descriptive statistics* applied to Q-sort data. Considering the former, it is somewhat difficult to interpret inferential statistics applied in those instances in which the sampling unit is the stimulus rather than the person and in which the sample size is considered to be the number of stimuli (e.g., photographs) rather than the number of persons. This is done when the usual "test for significance" is applied to a correlation between two sorts by the same or different persons. (Such tests of significance are discussed in nearly all texts concerning the use of statistics in psychology, e.g., Walker & Lev, 1958.) Let us say that the correlation is .40 between two sorts by one person and that there are 100 stimuli in the content sample. As has frequently been done, one can find a standard error for the correlation coefficient, inserting 100 as the sample size in the customary formulas.

To compute a standard error for a correlation coefficient in the above way assumes that it is legitimate to define the sample size as the number of stimuli employed in the Q sort. Obviously, since the correlation is computed on the responses from only one subject, there is no basis at all for generalizing to other subjects. Logically, in such cases, inferential statistics concern probability statements about relations between samples of content and a hypothetical "population" (universe or domain) of content. If, by considering the sample size to be the number of stimuli, a correlation of .40 reached acceptable levels of statistical significance, this would provide some statistical confidence that the population correlation was different from zero. The population correlation would be that obtained if the Q sort contained every stimulus in a finite population of stimuli or, in the case of an infinite population of content, that obtained if the hypothetical Q sort were made with an infinite number of stimuli.

As has been mentioned and illustrated at numerous points in this book, the theory of psychological measurement is more intimately related to principles concerning the sampling of content than to principles concerning the sampling of people. That does not mean, however, that it is necessary or wise to employ inferential statistics concerning the sampling of content. One can develop most of the necessary principles in the theory of psychological measurement without considering inferential statistics relating to content sampling.

If one employs inferential statistics with respect to problems of content sampling, as is frequently done with Q-sort data, he must be aware that the assumptions for employing such statistics are much more difficult to justify than in the case of sampling people. First, there must be a definable population (domain or universe), and it is difficult to define domains of content for Q sorts. Second, the sampling unit must be defined. This is obviously the individual person in the usual sampling of people, but it is not so obvious what the sampling unit is with certain types of content, e.g., statements about psychotherapy or statements relating to personality traits. Third, the stimuli must be either randomly sampled overall (the so-called random sample for Q sorts) or randomly sampled within specified categories (as in the structured sample for Q sorts). As was mentioned previously, it is usually uncertain that one is sampling at all when he is obtaining or constructing materials for a Q sort, and it is even less certain that he is sampling randomly.

It is best not to make precise interpretations of the probability values found in applying inferential statistics to problems concerning the sampling of content. One does better to consider them as rough guides to the probable generality of findings over large collections of stimuli of the same general kinds. As an example, assume that the correlation of Q-sort self-descriptions by two persons is .80 and that the correlation with the same stimuli for two other persons is zero. By applying the usual formulas for inferential statistics and using the number of stimuli as the sample size, one finds that the difference in the two correlations is accompanied by an extremely high level of statistical confidence. Then, even if it is usually difficult to justify the assumptions necessary to employ inferential statistics with problems concerning the sampling of content, the level of statistical confidence provides some assurance that the difference in the two correlations is "real" and not entirely due to the fortuitous circumstances that led to the selection of some materials rather than others for the Q sort. In the same way, an informal use of other inferential statistics with problems of content sampling is justified.

In most forms of analysis applied to Q-sort data, however, there is little need to make statistical inferences regarding the generality of results over hypothetical domains of content. Simple correlations, and more complex products of correlational analysis, can be used only as descriptive indices of degrees of relationship.

After descriptive indices have been computed for each person, inferential statistics can be applied to the variabilities of such indices over a priori groups of persons (e.g., men versus women) or differences in differently treated groups in controlled experiments.  An example of the former procedure would be as follows.  The purpose of a study is to compare the aesthetic preferences of college students with those of professional artists.  The mean placement of 25 abstract Oriental statues would be obtained for each person, resulting in a distribution of means for each of the two groups.  The means and variances of those two distributions of means would be obtained, and this information would be used in a test of the significance of the difference in grand means of the two groups.  As another example, patients entering psychotherapy could be asked to make Q-sort descriptions of themselves and how they would like to be ideally.  The two sorts would be correlated for each patient, giving a distribution of such correlations over the number of patients in the study.  All patients would be asked to repeat the two sorts on the completion of psychotherapy. The tendency for the "after" correlations to be higher than the "before" correlations could be assessed by any of the methods of inferential statistics relating to repeated observations.  In many other ways, the results from studies employing Q sorts can be examined in terms of inferential statistics relating to the sampling of persons rather than to the sampling of stimuli.

## Summary remarks about the Q sort

There are advantages and disadvantages to employing the Q sort rather than other rating methods.  The chief advantage is realized in those instances in which one is seeking relatively precise comparative responses among a rather large number of stimuli.  As was mentioned previously, the use of highly precise comparative methods such as pair comparisons is almost out of the question with large numbers of stimuli.  At the other extreme of the continuum of precision, one could make comparative analyses of absolute responses obtained from rating scales.  An example concerning ratings of the handsomeness of men will illustrate the possibilities.  If the stimuli were 100 photographs of men, it would be almost out of the question to employ pair comparisons and difficult to employ rank order.  Comparative ratings could be obtained quickly and easily with the Q sort.

Comparative information about the rated handsomeness of the men could also be obtained as follows.  Instead of having comparisons made between the men with regard to handsomeness, each photograph could be rated on an eight-step scale, anchored on the extremes by "very handsome" and "very ugly." Then one could make comparative analyses between the absolute ratings given by each person.  A first step would be to convert all distributions of ratings by different raters to a common distribution form.  One could do this by standardizing the distribution of 100 ratings for each person.  Then all subjects would have the same mean and standard deviation of ratings, and the standard scores would provide comparative information about the ratings made by each person.  These scores could then be treated in all the ways that scores obtained from Q sorts are treated.

If economy of time, effort, and money were the major consideration, it would pay to make comparative analyses of separate ratings rather than to employ the $Q$ sort. Subjects can make 100 separate ratings in less than half the time they require to perform a $Q$ sort of 100 stimuli. In previous years, the $Q$ sort had a marked advantage in statistical analyses over comparative analyses of separate ratings because in the $Q$ sort, all sets of comparative ratings have a fixed distribution, and consequently there is no need to make conversions to a common distribution, as must be done in order to make comparative analyses of absolute responses. Also, with only a desk calculator, correlations between $Q$ sorts can be computed much faster than correlations between sets of absolute ratings (correlating over stimuli, as is done in the $Q$ sort). Those were very important considerations 15 years ago, but they are no longer significant. Most analyses these days are done on high-speed computers, and the difference between computer time required to make analyses of $Q$ sorts and that necessary for making similar comparative analyses of absolute responses is trivial.

What, then, are the advantages of using $Q$ sorts over performing comparative analyses of absolute ratings? The major potential advantage is that one might obtain more precise comparative information from the $Q$ sort. The $Q$ sort explicitly requires the subject to make comparative responses, but this occurs only incidentally in making separate ratings. The various response styles that accompany absolute ratings (e.g., the tendency to make extreme ratings) could cloud the comparative information in such ratings. Also, the tendency of subjects to shift sets (e.g., to respond more favorably as they proceed from rating to rating) would also tend to cloud the comparative information in the ratings. Then, one would usually expect to find a higher reliability (e.g., retest) for comparative responses obtained from the $Q$ sort than from comparative analyses of absolute ratings.

Aside from questions of reliability, it is also possible that the factor composition of $Q$ sorts is sometimes different from that of comparatively analyzed ratings. In the latter, since the subject does not actually make comparative responses, it is an assumption on the part of the experimenter that a comparative analysis of those responses results in measurement of the same attributes that would be measured by actually obtaining comparative responses.

Even if the $Q$ sort has certain advantages as a method of eliciting comparative responses, a more basic question concerns whether or not it is wise to obtain comparative responses with sets of stimuli of the kinds that are frequently employed with the $Q$ sort. It can be strongly argued that comparative responses make sense only if all the stimuli in a set are from some common frame of reference. As was illustrated previously, it is hard to make a convincing case for this with some of the Q-sort samples that have been employed in studies to date.

The above considerations lead us to four major conclusions about the $Q$ sort and related methods of analysis. First, if one is seeking comparative responses, the $Q$ sort has certain advantages for that purpose. Second, before the $Q$ sort is employed, it is important to ensure that sensible comparative responses can be made among the stimuli employed in a particular study. Third, if one elects to use the Q sort as a rating method, that does not necessarily tie him to the use of particular techniques of statistical analysis rather than others. Fourth, choices among approaches to gathering data (e.g., comparative versus absolute ratings) are mainly matters of taste, hypothesis, and hunch. In the long run we shall learn which approaches are generally more fruitful, but at this early stage in the growth of our science, it is well that all the research eggs are not being placed in the same methodological basket.

## scaling of stimuli

Most of the discussion of rating methods in this chapter has concerned the use of ratings for the scaling of persons with respect to psychological traits. Summative scales based on statements concerning attitudinal objects are used to scale people in terms of their attitudes, e.g., toward the United Nations. Semantic-differential scales are used to measure individual differences in the connotative meanings of concepts. The Q sort is used to measure individual differences in preferences for stimuli of different kinds.

In spite of the important place of rating methods in the scaling of people, it would be appropriate to close this chapter by reminding the reader that rating methods are also very useful for the scaling of stimuli. Numerous methods for scaling stimuli were discussed in Chapter 7, all of which, in essence, are "rating methods." The particular rating methods discussed in this chapter are frequently used for the scaling of stimuli. Summative scales of agree-disagree ratings of statements can be used, for example, to scale typical reactions to different levels of dosage of a particular drug or different levels of reaction to different levels of electric shock. The semantic differential has many uses in the scaling of stimuli, as was illustrated previously in the case of the scaling of nonsense syllables in terms of degree of familiarity and the scaling of geometric designs in terms of pleasantness, complexity, and other aspects of connotative meaning. The Q sort also has many applications to the scaling of stimuli. Words can be sorted in terms of emotionality; statements relating to personality traits can be sorted in terms of social desirability; and patches of gray paper can be sorted in terms of brightness.

When rating scales are used to scale stimuli rather than people, the major assumption is that individual differences are not important in judgments or preferences in relation to the particular set of stimuli. If that is a safe assumption, the experimenter can average over raters to obtain a scale for the stimuli. The assumption is safe with certain classes of stimuli (e.g., patches of gray paper) and not safe with certain other classes (e.g., ratings of food preferences). Whether or not the assumption seems safe a priori, the wisdom of making the assumption can be tested after the data are in hand. The extent to which subjects can be considered replicates of one another can be determined by an inspection of the correlations between subjects or, if necessary, by a factor analysis. Regardless of the details of constructing such scales, it is important to keep in mind that the rating methods discussed in this chapter are important for the scaling of stimuli as well as for the scaling of people.

## Summary

This chapter discussed the measurement of sentiments, "sentiments" being a generic term referring to all types of human preferences, feelings, and likes and dislikes. Individual differences in sentiments are important types of personality traits, aspects of personal conceptions. Major divisions of such traits are interests, values, and attitudes.

Measures of interests are important mainly for career guidance, and in that respect the available instruments are serving well. Measures of interests are based on the sensible premise that if a person enjoys the same types of activities that people in a particular profession do, there is a high probability that he will enjoy working in that profession. Most measures of interests consist of either absolute or relative ratings of preferences for activities. Pioneered by the Strong Vocational Interest Blank, most measures of interests these days are developed by criterion keying, which consists of deriving scales that discriminate people in one vocation (e.g., engineering) from professional people in general.

Measures of values concern principles relating to ways of life. Measures of attitudes concern feelings about particular institutions, practices, and groups of people. In contrast to measures of interests, measures of values and attitudes are employed much more in basic research than in applied settings. Whereas it is useful to distinguish values from attitudes for conceptual purposes, they are both investigated largely with the same methodologies, namely, those based on various rating methods.

Because of the central place of rating methods in the measurement of sentiments, it is important to be aware of some principles concerning their development and use. For example, it is important to know that the reliability of a rating scale tends to increase with the number of scale steps. The logic for constructing summative scales of values and attitudes is essentially the same as that for constructing homogeneous scales presented in Chapter 8.

Although it is common to speak of *the* rating method, as though there were only one approach, there are numerous rating methods. Some of these are (1) scales bounded by bipolar adjectives, (2) agreement scales, (3) percentage scales, (4) scales anchored with behavioral descriptions, and (5) product scales. The type of rating scale that should be used depends upon the type of problem being investigated.

Because of their wide use in research, two rating methods were discussed in detail, the semantic differential and the Q sort. The semantic differential employs absolute ratings of concepts on scales bounded by bipolar adjectives. It is a very useful approach to the measurement of overall attitude. In contrast to the semantic differential, the Q sort is a comparative rating method, in which statements or objects are sorted from "most" to "least" with respect to a stated attribute. The Q sort is nothing more and nothing less than a very handy approach to obtaining comparative responses. Consequently, it is logically very useful in any research problem concerning comparative reactions to a large set of stimuli.

## Suggested additional readings

Edwards, A. L. *Techniques of attitude scale construction.* New York: Appleton-Century-Crofts, 1957.

Guilford, J. P. *Psychometric methods.* (2nd ed.) New York: McGraw-Hill, 1954. Ch. 11.

Guilford, J. P. *Personality.* New York: McGraw-Hill, 1959. Chs. 7, 9.

Osgood, C. E. Studies on the generality of affective meaning systems. *American Psychologist,* 1962, 17, 10–28.

Stephenson, W. *The study of behavior: Q-technique and its methodology.* Chicago: University of Chicago Press, 1953.

# PART 7:

## Examples of Measurement Methods in Basic Research

# CHAPTER 15

# Measurement in general experimental psychology

This and the following chapter will be concerned with principles relating to psychological measurement in controlled experiments. A simple example of such an experiment is one in which three groups of subjects are required to memorize lists of nonsense syllables that vary in the extent to which they resemble real words. The major concern in the experiment is with the average number of syllables correctly recalled by each group.

Traditionally the term "experimental psychology" has meant the study of relatively simple processes such as those involved in perception and learning. Years ago, such simple processes were the only ones that lent themselves to the rigors of experimental control, but these days most studies of psychological processes are, or at least should be, controlled experiments. Psychological measurement in relation to studies of personality, social, and abnormal psychology will be discussed in Chapter 16. Investigations in these areas tend to involve more complex processes than those in experimental psychology, but except for that difference, the two types of investigations are distinguished from each other more as a matter of convenience than because a hard-and-fast distinction must be made.

Literally thousands of measurement methods are used in experimental psychology. An excellent discussion of many of the more frequently used methods is presented by Sidowski (1966). The intention in this chapter is to discuss methods that are illustrative of important problems and/or principles of measurement.

## the nature of experiments

The essence of experimentation in all areas of science is that one or more variables are systematically manipulated and that, to the extent to which this is possible, all other variables are controlled.  A variable which is systematically manipulated is referred to as the *independent variable,* an example of which was given previously in the discussion of an experiment involving the resemblance of nonsense syllables to real words.  The illustrative experiment concerned three levels of the independent variable.  A variable that needs to be controlled in that experiment is the amount of time each group takes to memorize its list of syllables; otherwise, the effects of the independent variable might be obscured by differences between the groups in average amount of rehearsal time.

### Confounding variables

Any uncontrolled variable which influences the results of an experiment is said to *confound* the interpretation of the experiment.  That is, the confounding variable leaves open the possibility that the experimental results are due to the confounding variable rather than to the systematically manipulated independent variable.  In some cases the confounding variable serves only to cloud the results, as was illustrated previously with respect to an uncontrolled amount of rehearsal time in studies of memory.  In other instances the confounding variable produces clear-cut but misleading results.  This would be the case, for example, in the following experiment concerning the effects of different dosages of a particular drug on the activity of rats.  While the drug is taking effect, the rats are confined in a small cage.  Then they are placed in an apparatus that measures the amount of their activity.  Because the larger dosages of the drug require longer times to take effect, the different groups of rats are confined for different amounts of time in their individual small cages.  Then it is possible that different amounts of activity would be found because of the confounding variable of different amounts of confinement time rather than because of the independent variable of drug dosages.  Science is concerned with an endless search for confounding variables and for methods to control them in future research.

A possible confounding variable can be either controlled or systematically manipulated along with one or more independent variables.  In the aforementioned experiment, time could be controlled by keeping all rats in their small cages for the same amount of time, regardless of drug dosages.  However, because this might result in the three dosages' taking effect to different degrees, a better, if more laborious, approach would be to systematically manipulate confinement times in conjunction with drug dosages.  As illustrated in Figure 15-1, this would result in nine groups of rats rather than only the three groups that would be required if confinement time were controlled rather than systematically manipulated. Figure 15-1 illustrates both the use of more than one independent variable in an experiment and the principle that what would be a confounding variable in one experiment can be turned into a systematically manipulated independent variable in another experiment.

One important type of control is obtained by preventing important differences between the subjects assigned to different treatments. This type of control would be violated, for example, if rats of different ages were assigned to the different dosage groups or if the different lists of nonsense syllables were administered to students in different schools. There are two major ways of preventing differences between groups. The first is to randomly assign members of a larger group of subjects to different treatment groups. Then, depending on the number of subjects assigned to each treatment group, it is unlikely that the groups will differ in any important way before the experiment is undertaken. The second major approach is to administer all treatments to all subjects. Then, since the *same* subjects appear in all treatment conditions, there is no possible question of differences between treatment groups.

### Types of experimental designs

When different subjects are assigned to different treatment groups, it is said that a *between-groups* experimental design is being employed. When the same subjects appear in all treatment conditions, it is said that a *within-subjects* experimental design is being employed. If it is feasible to employ within-subjects designs, potentially they have some advantages over between-groups designs. First, more information can be obtained from each subject. For example, if it were feasible to employ a within-subjects design with the experiment depicted in Figure 15-1, the same group of rats could be used in all nine treatment conditions. Similarly, rather than employ three different groups of students for the aforementioned study of memorizing nonsense syllables, the same group of subjects could be administered the three different lists.

The second advantage of within-subjects designs over between-groups designs

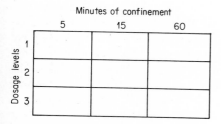

**FIGURE 15-1**    **Experimental design for investigating three levels of drug dosage and three confinement times**

in many circumstances is that they permit the statistical control of individual differences between subjects, which would otherwise be considered "error." For example, some rats are likely to be more active than others under all drug dosages, and some students are likely to be more adept than others at memorizing all types of nonsense syllables. In between-groups designs such individual differences tend to obscure differences between treatment groups. In within-subjects designs, one is concerned with relative performance by each subject in different treatment conditions, which affords the possibility of statistically correcting for consistent individual differences in performances of subjects (by methods that are discussed in numerous graduate-level texts on the statistical analysis of psychological experiments, e.g., Hays, 1963).

Although within-subjects designs offer some potential advantages over between-groups designs, they are not feasible to employ in many circumstances. For example, if the same rats were tested under all nine treatment conditions depicted in Figure 15-1, many of them might be killed by the accumulated effects of the drug before the experiment was completed. Similarly, it would prove difficult to find human subjects who would participate in the numerous treatment conditions that would be required by some within-subjects designs.

### Practice effects

More important for the discussion here than the feasibility of employing within-subjects designs is a major issue that they exemplify regarding psychological measurement. It is frequently the case that the results of applying a measure under one treatment condition are determined partly by the experience subjects have had with the measurement procedure in a previous treatment condition. For example, on repeated exposure to the situation in which activity is measured, rats might become less curious and thus less active, regardless of the effects of drugs. Similarly, regardless of differences between lists of nonsense syllables, students might become more proficient in learning later lists as a function of practice on earlier lists.

The influence of earlier testings on later testings frequently goes by the name *practice effects*, although it should be obvious that more than practice per se is involved. The way both to learn about such practice effects and to partially offset them is to counterbalance the order in which treatments are administered to different groups. For example, one-sixth of the subjects in the study of memorizing nonsense syllables would be administered the lists in the order 1, 2, 3; another one-sixth of the subjects would be administered the lists in the order 3, 2, 1; and so on for the other four possible orders. Then one could determine the extent to which the average response to a particular list was influenced by practice on previous lists. Also, average responses to each list over all six orders would provide a relatively faithful index of difficulty of learning, regardless of any practice effects.

Practice effects are important to consider in studies of individual differences as well as in controlled experiments. An example was mentioned in Chapter 5 regarding practice effects in the retest method of determining reliability.

## Selection and calibration of measures

In some experiments the independent variables concern only qualitative differences in treatments, which would be the case in comparing the effects of two different drugs on activity in rats or in comparing the effects of two different methods of rehearsal on the rate of memorizing nonsense syllables. The aim in most research is to examine the effects of quantitatively different levels of treatment, which means that it is necessary to index, or measure, the degrees of a treatment along some continuum. In most cases the measurement of independent variables poses no major problem, as is the case with such independent variables as level of drug dosage, number of practice trials, brightness of visual displays, percentage of times rewards are given, and others. In such cases the rules and procedures of measurement are quite obvious. Sometimes, however, genuine problems arise with respect to the calibration, or measurement, of treatment variables, as would be the case in the study of the effect of different levels of resemblance of nonsense syllables to real words (the independent variable) on rate of memorization (the dependent variable), discussed above. In that case it is not at all obvious how the independent variable should be measured. What has been done is to develop various supposed measures of the resemblance of nonsense syllables to real words, such as ratings of familiarity and pronounceableness. Since these and other indices correlate highly with one another (Underwood & Schulz, 1960), any one of them can be assumed to have a considerable amount of construct validity for the independent variable of resemblance of nonsense syllables to real words. Consequently, one might choose to select nonsense syllables for the three levels in terms of norms relating to ratings of familiarity.

Usually, but not always, the measurement of dependent variables is a bigger problem than the measurement of independent variables. This is the case, for example, with measures of activity, as illustrated in the aforementioned study of the effects of drugs on activity. There are many different measures of activity, and results obtained with some of them are very different from results obtained with others. Consequently, one must carefully choose the measures of activity that fit the particular hypotheses being investigated, and considerable amounts of construct validation must be undertaken to ensure that measures of activity which are assumed to reflect the same trait actually "behave" in essentially the same way.

Other examples of the problems encountered in measuring the dependent variables in controlled experiments are as follows. For 20 minutes rats are rewarded with food pellets for pressing a lever, and different rats are given different-sized pellets on each trial. Then pellets are withheld from all rats, or, in the jargon of the profession, the rats are run in extinction trials. The question is that of how magnitude of reward on rewarded trials affects rate of extinction of lever pressing on nonrewarded trials. Exactly how to measure performance on extinction trials is not immediately obvious. For example, the most frequently used measure is the number of lever presses during five or so minutes after rewards are withheld, but that does not take account of the possibility that the rats receiving different magnitudes of reward were responding at different rates when rewards were being given.

A more extreme example of an experiment in which measurement of the dependent variables poses problems is an investigation of conditioned emotionality. In a study of college students, the appearance of one geometric form on a screen is consistently paired with painful electric shock, and another form is never paired with shock. Subsequently, the two geometric forms are encountered in another task, and measures are made of the emotional arousal produced by each of the forms. In such an experiment, how to measure emotional arousal is a very difficult question. Competing possibilities would be (1) self-ratings of emotional arousal, (2) changes in pupil size, (3) changes in electrical resistance of the skin, (4) changes in heart rate, and (5) changes in different glandular outputs into the bloodstream, as well as many, many others.

The foregoing examples of problems that arise in measuring dependent variables in some experiments are not intended to suggest that experimental psychology lives in a state of confusion. If there are reasonable alternative approaches to measuring a dependent variable, comparisons should be made of results obtained by the different approaches. If a number of approaches give essentially the same results, it is reasonable to give them a common name (e.g., rate of learning or emotional arousal). If other approaches provide different results, they should not be given the same name. Such findings result in refinements of theories and more precise experimentation. In other words, when there are reasonable alternative approaches to the measurement of a dependent variable, construct validation is required (as discussed in Chapter 6), which is part and parcel of everyday work in all areas of science.

## measurement of animal learning and motivation

The study of learning and motivation in lower animals has come to be called "rat psychology" because up until recent times the white rat was the favored subject. Now psychologists are investigating learning and motivation in a very wide variety of animals, including fish, worms, birds, snakes, monkeys, and many others. Also, it is important to point out that very few psychologists are interested in a particular species of animals for its own sake. Rather, most psychologists are interested in research that has either implications for the whole animal kingdom or particular relevance for the psychology of human beings.

### Discrimination learning

Considerable interest has been shown in the psychological processes whereby animals learn to solve simple problems.  The simplest example of such learning is that of discriminating between two alternative courses of action, one of which leads to a more pleasant outcome than the other.  One measuring instrument used to investigate two-choice discrimination learning is the T maze, a simplified example of which is shown in Figure 15-2.  One arm of the T is painted black, and the other is painted white.  For half of the rats, food is always placed in the cup at the end of the black arm but never in the cup at the end of the white arm, and vice versa for the other half of the rats.  The study concerns the effects of magnitude of reward on rate of learning.  Consequently, the two groups of rats are each subdivided into three groups, which are rewarded for correct choices with one, three, or nine food pellets, respectively.

This simple experiment illustrates two major issues that are important in many experiments on discrimination learning.  First, if the black arm always appeared on the left and the white arm always appeared on the right, one would be unsure whether the measure of correct responding related to black-white

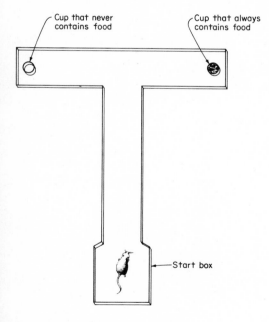

**FIGURE 15-2**      Rat in a T maze

discrimination, left-right discrimination, or some combination of the two. This problem can be largely circumvented by randomly switching the black and white arms from left to right on different trials. Then the measure of correct responding to the black cue by one group or the white cue by the other group will not be confounded by spatial locations of the black and white arms.

A second issue regarding measurement methods illustrated by rat learning in T mazes is that of initial preferences for one mode of responding rather than others. This may appear either in the form of a bias in average performance of subjects as a group or in terms of reliable individual differences in performance. The former possibility is illustrated in the aforementioned study of learning. Rats as a group tend to prefer dark places to bright places. Even if rats are run in a T maze with no food in either goal box, they will tend to go to the dark arm more than the light arm. In a study in which going to the black arm is rewarded, the results will suggest that relatively rapid learning is occurring, and the opposite will be the case if going to the white arm is rewarded. Any overall effect of this type of response bias can be largely eliminted by randomly assigning half of the rats to black-rewarded and the other half to white-rewarded T arms. The average scores obtained over the two groups will be uninfluenced by initial preferences for the black arm of the T maze.

Consistent individual differences in initial preferences for modes of responding are found in the T maze when a spatial discrimination rather than a brightness discrimination is being learned. In that case the arms of the maze would not differ in brightness; e.g., both would be painted dull gray. For half of the rats, food would always appear at the end of the left arm of the maze but never at the end of the right arm, and vice versa for the other half of the rats. Then half of the rats would have to learn to turn right in order to receive food, and the other half would have to learn to turn left. Some error in the findings of such investigations is encountered because of reliable individual differences between rats in the tendency to turn right rather than left, or vice versa, regardless of the food reward. Fortunately, in most investigations the variance of individual differences of such position preferences in rats is not large. The occurrence of any reliable differences in that regard illustrates a problem that is present with all measurement methods that permit individual differences in preferred modes of responding to cloud research results.

In addition to the T maze, many other instruments are used to measure rate of discrimination learning. Complex mazes are used in which, for example, rats must learn to turn right, then left, then left again, then right, and so on for as many as 10 or more choice points. Some complex mazes represent a problem in determining which measure of response to use as the dependent variable. Two of the possible measures in complex mazes are number of errors in running the maze (number of times the rat enters blind alleys) and total time taken to get from the start box to the goal box. Such choices of measures relate to construct validation, as discussed in Chapter 6 and at other places in this book.  One uses (1) a measure that is closely related to a theory, (2) one of several measures from a class of measures that typically produce similar results, or (3) two or more measures to represent different classes of measures that typically produce different results.

Discrimination learning in monkeys and children is frequently investigated with an analog of the T maze, in which on each trial the subject is allowed to lift one of two lids in search of rewards, e.g., a small piece of candy in a study of children.  The lids are distinctively different in some way; e.g., one has a black triangle painted on a white background, and the other has a black circle.  The aforementioned problems that occur in the T maze also occur in this situation, and the same remedies are available.  For example, to correct for position preferences, the two lids are randomly switched in left-right positions from trial to trial.

### Vigor of response

In contrast to measures of discrimination learning, measures of vigor of response concern motivational and emotional effects.  A much-used apparatus for that purpose is illustrated in Figure 15-3, which depicts a runway.  Measurements are made of the length of time the rat takes to run from the start box to the goal box.  Photoelectric devices automatically transmit running times, and recording equipment measures (1) speed of leaving the start box, (2) speed of traversing each segment of the runway, (3) speed of entering the goal box, and (4) total running time.  Supposedly, the faster the rat runs, the more he is motivated to reach the goal box.

A principle of measurement illustrated by the runway is that the results are interpreted differently according to which independent variables are manipulated.  In one experiment, three groups of rats are run under conditions of 1, 8, and 24 hours of food deprivation, respectively.  When some need goes unsatisfied (food in the present example), it is said that a *drive* is being manipulated.  Consequently, the experiment concerns the effects of different levels of hunger drive on vigorousness of response, as measured by running speed.  It is typically found that drive level relates directly to running speed.

Measures of running speed would be interpreted differently in a study of magnitude of reward.  In a typical study, drive is held constant by testing all rats under 24 hours of food deprivation.  Magnitude of reward is manipulated by placing one, three, or nine food pellets in the food cup at the end of the runway.  It is typically found that rats run faster for larger magnitudes of reward than for smaller magnitudes of reward.  Characteristics of rewards are spoken of as "incentives" or "pulls" in motivating behavior.  In contrast, drives are spoken of as "pushes" that cause animals to seek incentive objects and activities.  Consequently, when drive is held constant, measures of vigorousness of response are indicative of different levels of incentive motivation.  Con-

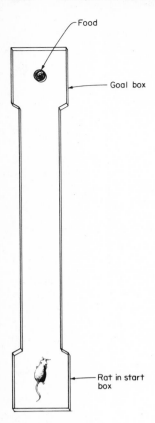
Food

Goal box

Rat in start box

**FIGURE 15-3**     Rat in a
runway

versely, when incentives are held constant, measures of vigorousness of response are indicative of different levels of drive states.

There are numerous other measures of vigorousness of response in addition to speed of responding, and as is usually the case, construct validation is required to determine how different measures are to be interpreted. Even within the confines of so simple a piece of apparatus as the runway, different measures of running time can be obtained. For example, a different interpretation might be placed on speed of leaving the goal box and speed of traversing the runway.

Another measure of vigorousness of response is obtained from the strength with which rats press a lever to obtain food. It is generally found that the same conditions that lead to faster running in the runway also lead to stronger pressing of a lever for rewards.

A third measure of vigorousness of response is rate of lever pressing, as contrasted with strength of pressing. In a simplified illustrative experiment, rats on different hours of food deprivation receive one pellet of food each tenth time a lever is depressed. It is found that hungrier rats press more rapidly than less hungry rats.

A fourth measure concerning vigorousness of response is obtained from an obstruction box. The rat is placed on one side of an electrified grid, which he must cross in order to obtain some type of reward on the other side. The amount of electricity which the animal will tolerate in order to cross the grid serves as a measure of motivation to obtain the goal object. Magnitude of reward is investigated by varying the size of the reward (where magnitude can be measured sensibly in that way). Also, the strengths of different types of motivation are compared by varying the rewarding objects, such as food rewards, thirst quenchers, receptive sex partners, objects that provoke curiosity motivation, and others.

Essentially, most measures of vigorousness of response are intended to index differences in motivational states rather than differences in learning. However, some learning is involved in most measures of vigorousness. For example, no matter what types of drive states or incentive variables are manipulated in the runway, running speed for all groups tends to increase during the early trials. Vigorousness of response in other measurement methods also tends to increase during the early trials, regardless of treatment conditions. These findings suggest that in the early trials, the animal is learning to run the runway or press a lever. Consequently, vigorousness of response during the early trials is a mixture of learning rate and motivation. Then, in order to investigate effects of motivational states on vigorousness of response more purely, it is necessary to make measurements of responses on later trials, after all treatment groups have successfully passed the stage of learning to respond and learning to ignore irrelevant distractions in the test situation.

## Activity

Related to measures of vigorousness of response are measures of activity. Measures of activity have been used primarily with rats and other relatively small four-legged creatures, e.g., rabbits and hedgehogs. One approach to measuring activity is with the tilt-cage, which is a very small (in comparison with the size of the animal) cage that rests on a rocker device. When the animal squirms about, the cage rocks back and forth in small amounts. Each rocking motion is automatically recorded in such a way as to provide a record of the amount of activity over periods of time.

A second approach to the measurement of activity is obtained by the use of photoelectric cells placed on the sides of the animal's home cage. Each time the rat moves in front of one of the photoelectric beams, the movement is automatically recorded. Whereas the animal is rather tightly confined in the tilt-cage, he has somewhat more room to move about in the home cage.

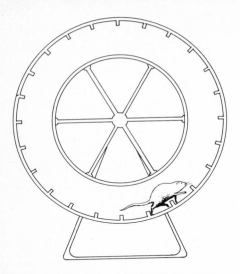

**FIGURE 15-4** Rat in an activity wheel

A third way to measure activity is with the activity wheel, which is illustrated in Figure 15-4. The rat is placed inside the wheel and is allowed to run (if he chooses to do so). The wheel rotates as the rat runs; consequently, the rat remains at approximately the same place in the bottom of the wheel. The faster the rat runs, the faster the wheel rotates. The number of rotations in any period of time serves as a measure of activity.

A fourth approach to the measurement of activity is with the open field, which is illustrated in Figure 15-5. The apparatus is nothing more than a large, empty box, in which the rat or other small animal is placed. A grid of

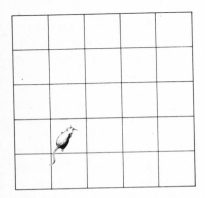

**FIGURE 15-5** Rat in an open field

thin lines is painted on the floor of the box, which serves to partition it into squares (usually about 1 foot on each side). The observer notes the number of times that the rat crosses a line from one square into another, which constitutes the measure of activity.

Although the foregoing are the four measures of activity that are used most frequently in research on lower animals, numerous other measures have been employed. The availability of so many different-appearing measures of activity relates to an important principle of psychological measurement: Measures that bear the same name do not always measure the same thing. The four measures of activity discussed above relate to somewhat different psychological attributes. The tilt-cage tends to measure "fidgetiness" or nervousness, which is not quite the same as the restlessness measured when the animal moves about in the home cage. Also, because the tilt-cage offers the rat almost nothing to explore, behavior in that situation is somewhat differently motivated from that in the home cage, where there are numerous bits of food, debris, and other objects to sniff.

Although there is some overlap in the attributes measured by the tilt-cage and photoelectric cells in the home cage, the activity wheel tends to measure something that is rather different. Movement in the activity wheel tends to be much more rapid and results in a much larger expenditure of energy than is the case with the aforementioned two measures. Consequently, the activity wheel tends to measure "need" for strenuous exercise or "motor release."

The open field tends to measure attributes other than those measured by the tilt-cage, movement in the home cage, and the activity wheel. Movement in the open field tends to be motivated more by curiosity or "exploratory drive" than by nervousness (tilt-cage), sampling stimulation from a highly familiar environment (the home cage), or need for strenuous exercise (the activity wheel). Indeed, the activity elicited by the open field sometimes correlates negatively with that elicited by some of the other measures of activity, depending on the experimental treatments. Because the "willingness" of the rat to explore the open field depends to a large extent on freedom from fear, any experimental treatment that induced fear would tend to make the rat "freeze" in one place in the open field rather than gallop about. In contrast, fear could lead to a sufficient amount of quivering to rock the small tilt-cage back and forth, which would result in a high rate of measured activity.

A more general lesson to be learned from this discussion of activity is that it is necessary to make a careful distinction between construct names (e.g., intelligence, anxiety, exploratory drive) and generic terms that refer to the response systems on which measurements are made (e.g., activity). All the measures of activity obviously do concern some type of motor response, and from the standpoint of being objective about the response systems being investigated, it is meaningful to use the term "activity" in a generic sense in relation to all such measures. In the name of objectivity, however, such generic terms for classes of response systems are frequently confused with psychological constructs. In the development of measures relating to a construct, it is necessary to find a number of measures that "hang together," in the sense that they prove to be largely substitutable. This is not necessarily the case with such generic terms as "activity," which apparently covers a number of different constructs, each of which needs to be investigated in its own right.

There are numerous other examples in experimental psychology of the use of generic terms for response systems in such a way as to imply that a unitary construct is involved. This is the case, for example, with measures of reaction time, of which there are many indeed. What is common to all measures of reaction time is observation of the speed with which responses are made. However, the underlying psychological attributes (constructs) are very different, depending on what subjects are responding to. This is quite evident in contrasting the speed with which a button is pressed with the speed with which subjects give correct answers to simple problems in arithmetic. To reiterate, it is important to make a clear distinction between construct names and generic terms (e.g., activity and reaction time) that refer only to some common property inherent in measures of a variety of constructs. As more and more research is done to develop measures of constructs and to validate them as such, names that refer only to common measurement operations should gradually disappear in favor of construct names.

## human learning and motivation

The fact that this chapter contains separate sections on lower animals and human beings should not lead the reader to assume that the respective psychological processes are qualitatively different in all respects. The two types of subjects are distinguished in this chapter because of the different types of measures that are frequently required to index the same processes. For example, auditory thresholds in human beings can be measured easily by verbal reports, but much more complex methods are required to measure auditory thresholds in lower animals; e.g., a conditioned response is established to the presentation of a tone. As another example, discrimination learning in human beings can be investigated with problems that require button pushing, lid lifting, dial turning, and other such hand movements, but such motor responses would be nearly out of the question with many species of lower animals. Here and throughout this chapter, the measures that will be discussed are ones that illustrate principles of measurement or pose problems of one kind or another.

### Reaction time

As was mentioned previously in this chapter, the term "reaction time" is used in a generic sense in relation to many different types of measures in which response speed is under observation. Historically, studies of reaction time have come to imply the measurement of simple motor responses under instructions to respond as rapidly as possible. Different psychological processes are investigated, depending on the complexity of signal-response relations and other treatment variables. In the simplest type of study of reaction time, a button is pressed at the onset of a tone. This provides a relatively pure measure of the physiological capacity of the human organism for making a simple response to a simple signal. More complex processes are investigated by providing a warning signal preparatory to the onset of the tone. Either in different groups of subjects or on different trials with the same subjects, when a red warning light is flashed one-fifth second, one second, or three seconds before the onset of the tone, it is found that some light-tone intervals facilitate reaction time more than others.

In a more complex study of reaction time, on each trial one of four differently colored lights is lit, and the subject must press one of four buttons. It is generally found that the more light-button combinations there are, the longer it takes the subject to respond correctly. In this type of experimental situation, one is measuring principally decision time rather than raw reaction time.

Although there are no major problems of measurement in the aforementioned types of studies of simple reaction time, the measurement of response speed in some other types of investigations does pose problems. This is the case in the use of speed scores for rats in a straight runway. Even more problems occur in investigating complex processes in human beings, such as in measuring the amount of time that subjects take to identify an object presented in a purposefully vague drawing.

There are two interrelated types of problems encountered in using measures of reaction time in relation to complex psychological processes. First, one frequently finds some highly atypical responses, which present some problems for the statistical analysis of data. For example, every now and then a rat in the runway will stop halfway to the goal box and sit and preen himself interminably, in which case the running time for that rat might be twenty times as long as the average. The same problem is even more likely to occur in the example of identifying ambiguous pictures. Whereas most of the subjects might correctly identify a picture in five seconds, a small percentage will never identify it, at least not until the sun has gone down. Such highly atypical scores present problems for statistical analysis. For example, what reaction-time score does one give to an individual who never completed the task? Even if the subject completes the task, what should be done about a reaction-time score that is twenty times as great as the average? Although there is no completely acceptable way of handling such highly deviant scores, the usual compromise is to set an upper limit to correct responding; if the subject does not make a correct response in that time, the set amount of time is taken as his score on that trial. For example, subjects are given a limit of two minutes to identify each ambiguous picture. If they do not correctly identify the picture in that time, they are given a reaction-time score of two minutes.

A second problem with reaction-time scores in investigating complex processes is that such scores typically are only moderately reliable. Typically, one finds relatively large standard deviations of reaction times over subjects, with only a moderate degree of consistency (correlation) from one trial to the next. Consequently, the variability of scores is largely experimental error, which tends to obscure the results of experimental treatments. The primary method for eliminating the effects of such errors is to average responses over a relatively large number of trials. Then, as is true in all measurement, the measurement error on individual trials (or items) tends to decrease as a function of the number of trials over which scores are summed or averaged.

### Verbal learning

Because man is unique in the animal kingdom in having developed highly complex spoken and written languages, the study of verbal learning in human beings has been very popular in experimental psychology. Rather than being only a special issue in experimental psychology, the study of verbal learning is more like an entire subfield of investigation, partly because there are so many different aspects of verbal learning to investigate, ranging from studies of the memorization of nonsense syllables to studies of how people learn to read. In addition, human verbal learning raises some theoretical issues that are not encountered in most studies of lower animals. For example, people can formulate a nearly infinite number of grammatical sentences, including ones that they have never heard before, such as "Elephants are sad because they have no wings." If one has never heard a particular sentence before, how does he learn to formulate it? Also, how do people recognize that a novel sentence is grammatical even if nonsensical otherwise? These and numerous other human capacities in language usage present problems for the more simplistic theories that are usually marshaled to explain discrimination learning in rats and people. Not only do studies of verbal learning present a challenge to reductionistic theories of learning, but, more importantly, they also pave the way for the development and testing of theories relating to complex forms of behavior.

A type of verbal learning that has been investigated very extensively is that in which subjects are required to memorize the elements in a collection of symbols. Some of the types of symbols used are (1) real words, like "chair" and "house"; (2) nonsense syllables, like *keb* and *zog*; (3) geometric forms; and (4) random sequences of numbers or letters. Symbols are presented either visually or orally. In the former case, either they are presented one at a time or the entire collection is shown in one relatively long presentation. If symbols are presented one at a time, subjects are required to recall them either in the order given or in any order that they choose. These and many other possible sets of experimental procedures illustrate the wide variety of issues that can be investigated even in the confines of studies of rote verbal learning.

Studies of rote verbal learning provide another illustration of a problem that is common to almost all research, that of controlling potential confounding variables. Many studies of rote verbal learning are concerned with effects of various characteristics of the symbols on rate of learning. For example, a variable that has been investigated extensively is that of association strength of words in a list. In the simplest case, one group of subjects is required to memorize words that people tend to associate with one another, such as "chair," "table," "rug," etc. Another group of subjects is required to memorize words that are seldom associated with one another, such as "house," "sheep," "book," etc. In such investigations, it is very difficult to prevent the lists from being different on variables other than association strength. The words in one list might be more familiar than those in the other list, which would lead to differences in rate of learning regardless of association strength. Other potential confounding variables are (1) length of words, (2) frequency of usage in daily life, and (3) whether they are the same or different parts of speech. Indeed, there are so many possible confounding variables in studies of the effects of symbol characteristics on rote verbal learning of real words that one can exhaust the vocabularies of the average subject before finding lists of words that are entirely satisfactory. These difficulties are partially circumvented by employing several lists of each type, e.g., three different lists of words that are minimally associated with one another and three lists of words that are highly associated with one another. By averaging over the three lists of each type, one tends to offset confounding variables, but that is by no means a sure cure; e.g., all three of the lists of one type might contain more familiar words than lists of the other type.

### Classical conditioning

Essentially, classical conditioning concerns the types of experiences whereby one stimulus becomes a partial substitute for another. Pavlov's studies of the conditioning of the salivary response in dogs (discussed in almost any introductory text in psychology) are the classic ones in the field. In an experiment like Pavlov's, the odor of meat powder is blown into a dog's face, which makes him salivate. If a tone is consistently presented before the odor of meat powder is blown into the dog's face, the tone eventually becomes capable of eliciting salivation. Even after the odor of meat powder is no longer presented, the tone persists for numerous trials in its ability to elicit salivation. Then it can be said that the tone has become a partial substitute for the odor of meat powder, at least as regards elicitation of the salivary response.

During the last 30 years or so, considerable attention has been focused on the study of classical conditioning in human beings. Such investigations encounter some methodological problems and some problems of measurement, which are evidenced in the following examples.

One type of study of classical conditioning in human beings concerns the eye-blink response. In a typical study, a tone is sounded shortly before a puff of air is aimed at one eye. The puff of air reliably elicits an eye blink. After many pairings of tone and air puff, the tone alone elicits the eye blink. One problem of measurement found in such investigations is that some subjects try to "help" the experimenter by voluntarily blinking when the tone is sounded, which represents learning only in the sense of learning what the experimenter is attempting to investigate. This artifact of measurement can frequently be detected by an analysis of the characteristics of the eye blink. For example, it is usually the case that a voluntary eye blink is slower than a reflexive blink, and the two differ in other ways that can be detected by delicate recording equipment. Such voluntary responses can be ruled out in the measurements on each subject, and any subject that produces many voluntary responses can be excluded from the investigation. The problem of the subject "getting into the act" is quite widespread in measures used in psychological experiments on human subjects. Other examples will be cited in the remainder of this chapter. When a subject recognizes the purposes of an experiment and actively cooperates in producing an apparent treatment effect when no real effect has been obtained, it is said that he is responding to the *demand characteristics* of the experimental setting.

Another type of study of classical conditioning is that in which a light is conditioned to elicit a change in electrical resistance of the skin. The electrical resistance tends to change when any stimulus is presented that activates the subject. Almost any strong stimulus, presented suddenly, can be used, such as a loud tone. When the light is consistently presented shortly before the onset of the tone, it eventually becomes a conditioned stimulus for eliciting changes in skin resistance (which can be measured in terms of the changes in amount of electric current flowing over several inches on the back of the human hand).

Studies of conditioning the electrical resistance of the skin illustrate a type of measurement artifact that occurs in many measurement problems in psychology, that of *habituation*. The ability of the loud sound to generate changes in skin resistance dwindles throughout an experimental session. Large changes are induced on the first several presentations of the tone, and smaller changes occur on following trials, but after numerous trials almost no change in skin resistance is elicited by the tone. The effectiveness of the conditioned stimulus (the light) in inducing changes in skin resistance would also dwindle throughout an experimental session. Nearly all responses relating to activation or emotion (e.g., heart rate) tend to habituate after being repeatedly elicited in an experimental session. Habituation of this kind gives the impression that the conditioned response is becoming less effective as a function of conditioning trials, which is just the opposite of what is thought to occur. Some ways of reducing the influence of habituation in the measurement of treatment effects are (1) to employ only a relatively small number of conditioning trials or test trials for the conditioned response on any one day, (2) to give the subject frequent rest periods between trials, and (3) to compare the experimental group with various control groups, such as with a group which receives only the light and which has never had the light paired with the loud sound.

### Verbal conditioning

Investigations concerning the development of control over the words that people use have been very popular in recent years. A widely employed procedure is as follows. The experimenter shows the subject a card on each trial. On the card are printed three plural nouns and three singular nouns, and the subject is asked to pronounce one of the words. If he says a plural noun, the experimenter attempts to reward him in some way, usually by saying "good," "OK," or "fine" or by giving some other indication of approval. As subjects proceed through numerous trials with cards showing different sets of nouns, they tend to give more and more plural nouns. Then it is said that they have been "conditioned" to give plural nouns, although the so-called conditioning in this type of study is analogous only to classical conditioning.

The interpretation of results of studies of verbal conditioning involves a measurement problem that is widespread in studies of human beings, that of obtaining valid impressions from subjects regarding their own mental processes. The first several studies of verbal conditioning led many persons to believe that an important type of learning without awareness had been demonstrated. That is, it was suggested that even though subjects were being conditioned to give plural nouns, they had no idea why they were responding in that way. The supposed learning without awareness was based on crude interviews with subjects after experimental sessions were completed. Critics of an interpretation that learning without awareness had been demonstrated developed more refined techniques of interviewing. These new methods for measuring awareness showed quite clearly that those subjects who actually gave a preponderance of plural nouns were highly aware of what they were doing and highly aware that the experimenter was urging them to behave in that way through the use of verbal rewards. What at first was thought to be a type of learning without awareness proved to be a type of learning that cannot occur to a high degree unless there is an acute awareness of correct responses and response-reward contingencies.

The more recent conclusions regarding the psychological processes at work in studies of verbal conditioning were based on refined measures of awareness as evidenced in postexperimental interviews. There are many other instances in experimental psychology in which inadequate measures of human impressions have led to erroneous conclusions.

### Reinforcement of responses

Related to studies of verbal conditioning are the many types of studies of human subjects concerned with the control of behavior through rewards and punishments. Studies of the reinforcement of performance had their beginnings in studies of lower animals, the classic example being that of rewarding rats with food pellets for pressing a lever. The rate of lever pressing was found to depend on numerous treatment parameters, such as the stage of food deprivation, the size of the food pellet, the delay between pressing of the lever and presentation of the food pellet, and the schedules for giving rewards. In recent years, studies of response reinforcement have been extended to human beings, particularly to the treatment of abnormal individuals, for example, the treatment of a child who talks very little or only mumbles. A thorough analysis of the child's behavior indicates that the failure to communicate is due to emotional disturbance rather than to a lack of verbal aptitude. Essentially what the experimenter does is to reward the child every time he talks (e.g., with a small piece of candy) and to withhold rewards when the child tries to obtain them without talking. Although the actual procedures are more complex than can be described in detail here, the essence of the procedures is to establish a highly systematic relationship between the receipt of rewards and the performance of some type of response. Typically, such a child begins to talk more, and as he does, the experimenter switches to rewarding only whole sentences that are clearly enunciated. After large numbers of trials on different days, the child develops better and better habits of communication.

The measurement problem encountered in studies of response reinforcement concerns the independent variable, the reward. Whereas it is assumed that the ostensible reward (such as candy) is the actual reward, sometimes that is only partly true. Frequently it is found that the ostensible reward is less important in motivating correct responses than some incidental form of reward. For example, each time the child says a word, he not only receives a piece of candy but also pleases the experimenter. In some instances, the child may be pleased more by the knowledge that he is performing correctly (being smart) than by the pieces of candy or other supposed agents of reward. An outstanding example of an area in which measurement of the reward dimension would pose severe problems is that of manipulation of the amount of reward, e.g., by giving the child one, three, or nine pieces of candy after each correct response. No difference could be found between the three conditions because something in the situation (e.g., experimenter approval) is more important in reinforcing correct responses than candy. By holding the amount of candy constant on each trial and by manipulating the amount of experimenter approval, it might be found that magnitude of reward is very important in the reinforcement of correct responses.

Similar problems with respect to measurement of the independent variable would occur in studies of delay of reward, schedules of rewards, and other treatment variables. For example, in studies of delay of reward, the experimenter might delay the giving of candy after each correct response, but he might not hide from the child some subtle signs of approval in the interval of delay.

Problems of validly measuring treatment parameters are quite general in studies of the control of human performance with rewards and punishments. This is particularly the case with sophisticated persons, such as college students. Also, in laboratory settings the subject is usually more concerned with appearing intelligent and well adjusted than he is with obtaining the rewards and punishments manipulated by the experimenter. These problems can be largely offset by controlling extraneous sources of rewards and punishments, such as by having the rewards administered by a machine while the experimenter is in another room. Also, it is important to find rewards and punishments that are more effective than any remaining extraneous rewards and punishments.

## sensation and perception

Sensation concerns the raw awareness of some form of stimulation, such as the awareness that a light is turned on or that a sound changes in intensity. Perception concerns interpretation of sensations, or the attribution of meaning. Examples of perception are recognizing a word that is rapidly presented on a screen and judging which of two lines is longer. Actually, the terms "sensation" and "perception" represent differences in degree rather than differences in kinds of processes investigated. When only a very simple response is required to some form of stimulation, it is said that the investigation concerns sensation. When a more complex type of response is required, it is said that the investigation concerns perception.

Some studies of sensation and perception are performed on lower animals. For example, one way to determine the threshold for auditory tones in rats is as follows. The rat is placed in one of two adjoining boxes separated by an inch-high wall. When the rat hears a tone, he must cross the barrier, or an electric shock will be delivered to his feet. If he crosses the barrier before the tone is sounded, he will be shocked on the other side of the barrier. As the intensity of the tone is gradually lowered, the rat's performance deteriorates. When he cannot hear the tone at all, he will behave in an essentially random manner. When the rat is correct on 75 percent of the trials (50 percent better than chance), that tone level is designated as the threshold of sensation.

In addition to studies of simple sensation, it is possible to perform more perceptual types of studies with lower organisms. For example, a rat's ability to recognize differences between briefly presented visual objects can be measured as follows. A small screen appears above a lever. When a black square is projected on the screen, a press of the lever will result in the delivery of a food pellet. When a black triangle appears on the screen, a press of the lever will result in the delivery of an electric shock. A random schedule is estab-lished whereby either the triangle or the square appears on the screen for 20 seconds. The rats learn to press the lever when the square is shown. After they have learned this phase of the experiment, the experimenter gradually shortens the time that each form appears on the screen and lets the screen remain blank during the remaining portion of each 20-second period. Even-tually, the presentation time is down to a fraction of a second. By continuously decreasing the time that geometric forms appear on each trial, the experimenter learns the lowest presentation time at which the rat can meet a specified cri-terion of accuracy, e.g., 90 percent correct responses.

Although, as illustrated above, some types of perceptual experiments can be performed with lower animals, this is usually very difficult. Frequently it in-volves very ingenious, complex procedures and requires a great deal of time and patience on the part of the experimenter. Most studies of perception are much more easily performed on human subjects because one can simply explain to them the nature of the perceptual tasks and they can simply indicate their perceptions verbally or by some mechanical means. For example, the afore-mentioned study of form discrimination in the rat could easily be conducted with human subjects in a few minutes' time. Studies of relatively complex perceptual processes in lower animals are conducted mainly when it would be impractical or unethical to perform such studies on human beings. For exam-ple, one can rear a chimpanzee in darkness in order to study the effects of this on the ability to discriminate between geometric forms, but of course one can-not do that with human infants.

### Perceptual recognition

A considerable amount of research has been performed on the variables that influence the rapid recognition of visual stimuli. Frequently used for the meas-urement of recognition rate is the tachistoscope, or T scope, as it is called. The subject peers into a box, at the other end of which is a screen. The experi-menter projects onto the rear of the screen some type of object, e.g., words, nonsense syllables, geometric forms, or pictures of faces. Timing devices are used to accurately control presentation time to small fractions of a second. One procedure is to start by presenting an object for such a brief time that no one is likely to make a correct response and then gradually to increase the time to levels where the subject is 100 percent accurate.

A phenomenon that is currently of much interest is that of *backward mask-ing*. If, for example, two nonsense syllables are rapidly presented one after the other, the appearance of the second syllable sometimes "blots out" the detec-tion of the first syllable. There are many interesting independent variables that influence the amount of masking, such as the time interval between presenta-tion of the two syllables.

Studies of perceptual recognition encounter a problem of measurement that occurs rather generally in psychology, that of *response bias*. Response biases in studies of perceptual recognition concern tendencies to respond in one way or another regardless of what materials are actually presented and regardless of what is actually perceived.

One type of response bias occurred in a study of the following type. In the T scope, male college students were required to recognize words that differed in emotional tone. Some words had positive emotional tones, words like "love," "friend," and "pleasant." Others were neutral in emotional tone, such as "chair," "brick," and "tree." The third group of words was intended to be negative in emotional tone, these consisting of four-letter "dirty" words. The finding of interest was that the "dirty" words appeared to be more difficult for the students to recognize than either the positive words or the neutral words. Findings of this type started a whole school of perception, which was predicated on preperception, or subception, as some called it. It was hypothesized that percepts must pass some type of censor before they are admitted into conscious awareness. Any object that is likely to cause the person anxiety is resisted by the censoring mechanism, and consequently the threshold of recognition is raised.

Subsequent to the early studies using "dirty" words, it was found that the results were due to a form of response bias rather than to preperceptual mechanisms. The bias consisted simply in the reluctance of students to say the words until the presentation times had become so long that it was quite obvious what was being shown. In contrast, when still not perfectly sure of what appeared on the screen, subjects were not reluctant to say the neutral words and positive words. It was found, for example, that when the experimenter was a young female, the "thresholds" for the "dirty" words were higher than they were when the experimenter was a male graduate student. It was found that "dirty" words were reported as accurately as other types of words when subjects were informed that some "dirty" words would be mixed in with other types of words and when subjects were encouraged to report all types of words as accurately as possible.

Another type of response bias was found in studies of the effects of prior familiarization on perceptual recognition. In a typical experiment, subjects were shown one nonsense syllable 1 time, another syllable 3 times, a third syllable 9 times, and a fourth syllable 27 times. Subsequently, the subjects were required to guess on each trial which of the four syllables appeared on the screen of a T scope. Generally such studies have found that more familiar words are more frequently recognized than less familiar words. Some ingenious research, however, showed that the apparent results were due to a form of response bias. Subjects more frequently guessed that the more familiar words were on the screen even when no syllables were presented. The tendency to guess with the more familiar words had produced the results of previous studies.

One can see what would happen, for instance, if a subject in the previously described experiment reported on every trial only the syllable that had been seen 27 times. He would be 100 percent accurate when that syllable actually appeared, but he would be accurate none of the other times.

Response biases are encountered quite generally in efforts to measure psychological processes. They are particularly annoying because there are few general rules that stipulate how they can be controlled or how statistical corrections can be made. Rather, it is necessary to learn about the particular forms of bias that enter particular types of measures and to learn how to control them either through arrangements of the experiment or by statistical corrections. How this was done through arrangements of the experiment was illustrated in the studies of preperception.

A statistical approach to the handling of response bias is illustrated in studies of signal detection. Earphones present a continuous hum (white noise) to the subjects' ears. When a light appears, either a tone is added to the hum or the hum is left unchanged. A random schedule is established for presenting the tone. An important type of investigation concerns the increasing accuracy of subjects in detecting the tone as the intensity of the tone is varied. The bias in such investigations occurs because of the different criteria that subjects use for reporting the tone. Some subjects indicate that the tone was presented even when they are only guessing, and other subjects will report the presentation of the tone only if they are very sure they heard it. Obviously, if a subject reported the tone on every trial, he would be 100 percent accurate when the tone was actually presented, but he would be incorrect on all trials when the tone was not presented. By taking account of the different amounts of accuracy on the trials when tones are presented and when tones are not presented, statistical estimates can be made of the accuracy of detection that would be obtained if the response bias of accuracy criterion were not present. (This type of research and the statistical methods required for correcting the response bias are discussed in Treisman & Watts, 1966.)

## Perceptual illusions

Perceptual illusions concern phenomena in which the features of a physical object cause people to misjudge the length, area, apparent depth, or some other characteristic of the actual object. The classic example is the Müller-Lyer illusion, which is shown in Figure 15-6. The arrowhead in the middle, 2, is midway between 1 and 3; however, the distance between 1 and 2 appears greater than that between 2 and 3. If 3 is attached to a cord and can be moved to the right or left by a subject, a measure can be obtained of the extent of the illusion. The arrowhead at 3 can be set far to the right, and the subject can be asked to adjust it to a point where the two distances appear equal. The experimenter can then measure the differences between the two lines to deter-

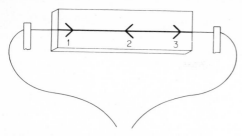

**FIGURE 15-6**    An apparatus for measuring the effect of the Müller-Lyer illusion

mine the effect of the illusion.   The effects of many other illusions can be measured by similar means.

   *Stimulus error*, a problem that occurs in numerous other types of psychological measures, is also encountered in measures of illusions.   The error consists in the subject's responding in terms of how he thinks the physical object is rather than in terms of the way it actually appears.   This type of measurement artifact occurs most frequently when the subject knows something about the illusory qualities of the stimulus.   This would be the case, for example, if the extent of the Müller-Lyer illusion were measured on college students who had completed a course in introductory psychology.   They would be familiar with the nature of some types of illusions.   In order not to be "fooled" by the illusion, some of the students would try to appear clever by distorting their actual perceptions.   The way to circumvent this simple form of stimulus error is to deal with subjects who know practically nothing about illusions.   Also, to prevent the stimulus error from occurring in all types of studies of perception, it is important to emphasize strongly to subjects that the experimenter is interested in how things actually look, sound, or are otherwise perceived, rather than in any knowledge the subjects have about the physical properties of stimuli.

## physiological psychology

Physiological psychology is concerned with internal bodily correlates of overt motor and verbal behavior.   The physiological psychologist is interested in the following types of questions: What goes on in the nervous system while an animal attends acutely to an object?   How does the pupil of the eye respond when a student performs difficult problems in arithmetic?   How is reaction time affected by increased output from the adrenal gland?   How do individual nerve cells in the auditory receiving areas of the brain respond when a tone is sounded?

   Physiological psychology as a whole represents a problem in psychological measurement, that of mechanical difficulties in reliably measuring responses.

Most measures in psychology do not require highly elaborate mechanical paraphernalia such as is the case in physics, chemistry, astronomy, and other physical sciences. Most measures of human ability and personality require only printed forms or a simple mechanical apparatus (e.g., in the measurement of motor skills). Most measures in experimental psychology are relatively simple in terms of mechanics, at least in comparison with many of those in the physical sciences.

Physiological psychology is a definite exception regarding the mechanical complexity of equipment required to measure important variables. How, for example, does one measure the microscopic and highly delicate chemical variations that result in transmission of "signals" from one nerve cell to the next? As another example, how does one measure electrical activity of a single nerve cell deep in the brain? Partial solutions to these mechanical problems have been obtained, but with these and many other measurement problems in physiological psychology, very elaborate apparatus and procedures are required.

For many years physiological psychology lay largely dormant because of the immense technical problems in measuring important variables. Up until about 1945, physiological psychology was largely speculative, but during recent years, technical advances have greatly accelerated research in that area. Now the typical research laboratory in physiological psychology is chock-full of highly elaborate electronic, computerized equipment.

### Studies of brain lesions

One way to investigate functions of the brain is to destroy some portion of it and then measure effects on behavior (which, of course, must be done on lower animals rather than human beings). A destroyed area is referred to as a *lesion*, and techniques for systematically destroying areas of the brain are referred to as methods of *ablation*. In the old days, ablation consisted mainly of actually cutting out particular portions of the brain. These days most lesions are made by tiny electrodes, which electrically destroy specific structures. Other methods are now available for performing relatively precise lesions. The remaining imprecision in making lesions, however, constitutes an important problem for measurement of the independent variables of lesion location and size.

After an experiment concerning brain lesions is completed, it is necessary to sacrifice the animal and inspect the lesion. This is done by examining thin slices of the particular brain structure with a microscope. It is usually found that the lesions were not made correctly in a sizable percentage of the animals. Some of the lesions are too large or too small, or they intrude into brain structures other than the one being investigated. This problem is partially offset by analyzing the data from only those animals in which the proper lesions were made, but this brings up two additional problems: (1) decisions to include an animal in the analysis involve some subjectivity regarding the correctness of the lesion, and (2) in some experiments there is a large loss of data because of the number of animals that must be excluded. The long-range solution is to develop even more refined techniques of making lesions.

## Physiological activation

Considerable interest has been shown in studying the physiological corre-lates of external stimuli that tend to activate, or arouse, the organism. The construct of activation concerns the many observations that, in a very general sense, organismic states vary on a continuum ranging from somnolence to alert-ness to a state of panic. Although different forms of stimulation have their particular physiological effects, it is also meaningful to order stimuli in terms of the extent to which they generate an overall state of activation. Degrees of activation tend to be manifested in measures of (1) pupil size, (2) heart rate, (3) electrical resistance of the skin, (4) breathing rate, (5) brain waves, (6) glandular products in the bloodstream, and (7) many others.

Studies of activation represent two important types of problems with respect to psychological measurement. First, it is frequently the case that incidental aspects of the experimental situation are more activating than the supposed experimental treatment. This can occur, for example, because of the sights, sounds, and odors of the laboratory rather than because of the experimental treatments. It is sometimes found that the physiological indicators of activa-tion are higher when the subject is being harnessed to the physiological measure than in subsequent periods during which he is submitted to various forms of stress. A partial solution to this problem is to investigate experimental treat-ments only after the subject has become well acquainted with the laboratory setting and after he has become accustomed to the equipment required to measure physiological processes. This frequently requires seeing the subject on more than one occasion, using the first occasion to let him adjust to the experimental setting.

A second problem of psychological measurement concerns *habituation*, a phenomenon that was discussed previously in this chapter with respect to studies of classical conditioning. All indicators of activation tend to diminish throughout an experimental session. This is particularly true in the situation where the same type of stimulation is applied repeatedly. For example, if a subject is sitting in a quiet room and a loud tone is sounded, there will be indications of strong activation. However, if the tone is sounded at one-minute intervals over the course of an hour, less and less activation will occur. The phenomenon of habituation fits the highly general principle that, by their nature, animals tend to adjust to (not be disturbed or activated by) almost any form of stimulation that is presented repeatedly.

Although habituation is an interesting phenomenon to study in its own right, it can cause problems for the measurement of experimental treatments. In a typical experiment, the interest is in determining the amount of activation resulting from memorizing lists of randomly ordered digits. The items vary from those containing only 5 digits to those containing 12 digits. It is very easy to memorize a list of 5 digits, and almost impossible for the average person to memorize a list containing 12 digits. The hypothesis is that the amount of activation is directly related to the difficulty of the items. A good measure of activation to use in this experiment would be pupil size, which is known to vary with degree of activation (Nunnally, Knott, Duchnowski, & Parker, 1967). The experimenter would make a serious mistake, however, if he presented the items in the order of least difficult to most difficult. He might not find larger pupil sizes for more difficult items because habituation had erased that result. Partial solutions to the problems of psychological measurement that occur because of habituation are to employ only a small number of trials in an experimental setting and/or to present treatments (e.g., lists of digits to be memorized) in a random order rather than from "least" to "most" with respect to the independent variable.

### Studies of blood chemistry

Whereas at first thought it might seem that the study of blood chemistry is far removed from the study of psychological processes, in some instances they are closely related. The bloodstream carries the products of glands. These glandular products stimulate various sectors of the nervous system and, in that way, influence states of activation, moods, emotions, clarity of thought processes, and many other psychological variables. Because of these important relations between blood chemistry and psychological processes, experiments have been undertaken to correlate the two types of phenomena. Such studies encounter a number of problems that are also encountered in other areas of psychological measurement.

One problem which arises is that of artifactually changing the phenomena under investigation, a problem that has been illustrated at a number of other points in this chapter. An artifactual change is one that is generated by an incidental aspect of the experimental setting rather than by the independent variable itself. This could be the case, for example, in investigating the blood correlates of anxiety. Anxiety is induced by having subjects view a gory documentary movie concerning victims of automobile accidents. Ratings and other verbal reports indicate that most people are quite disturbed by the film. The purpose of the study is to correlate the amounts of a particular product of the adrenal gland with subjective states of disturbance before, during, and after the witnessing of the movie. Samples of blood are taken at various intervals during the experimental session. Methods of chemical analysis are then used to measure amounts of the glandular product.

A major problem of measurement that would arise in such an experiment is that the taking of blood samples might be as anxiety-provoking as viewing the film. This would tend to obscure the correlations between subjective emotional states induced by the movie and the amount of the glandular substance present in the blood.

A second problem that might occur is particularly relevant to any type of investigation of the correlations between behavior and body chemistry. During the time the blood samples are taken and chemical measurements are made, the chemical composition of the samples might change drastically. Even in a test tube, a complex substance like blood evolves chemically. Measurements made after only 10 minutes from the time samples were taken might provide misleading information about the amount of the glandular substance that actually was present in the blood at particular points in the experiment.

Both of the foregoing measurement problems can be largely circumvented in the following way. First, to control for reactions to the sampling of the blood, a device can be attached to the subject which will continuously draw samples. If the device is attached a half hour before the film is shown, the subject gets accustomed to blood-sampling technique. Second, to prevent chemical changes in the blood from taking place before analyses are made, continuous measurement is made of samples by means of an electronic apparatus. This would provide a complete record of changes in the glandular substance throughout the experimental session, and because measurements are made almost simultaneously with changes in the bloodstream, there would be little opportunity for artifactual chemical changes to influence the experimental results.

## Summary

Measurement in experimental psychology concerns studies in both human beings and lower animals of learning, motivation, perception, and the physiological correlates of psychological phenomena. Whereas the topic of psychological measurement (the substance of this book) tends to be associated with studies of individual differences, the same principles apply to controlled experiments. Controlled experiments also must heed sound principles for constructing measures, ensuring reliability, controlling confounding variables, developing construct validity, overcoming technical problems of measurement, and ruling out response biases and artifacts of many kinds, as well as the many other principles of psychological measurement stated in this book.

Aside from the many particular problems of measurement that arise, the major problem of measurement in controlled experiments, as in all psychological measurement, is one of finding satisfactory empirical counterparts of psychological constructs. This is illustrated in the greatest detail in the measurement of activity in the rat, where (1) there are numerous measures that all apparently concern some type of activity, (2) the measures relate to partially different processes, and (3) the interpretation of results frequently depends upon the experimental treatments.   Psychology, like all science, is concerned with highly general statements about lawful phenomena.   The statements must be general over objects (animals in psychology), and they must be general over a variety of measures that use the same name, e.g., activity, arousal, learning rate, drive, anxiety, and intelligence.   Such generalizability is called *construct validity*; knowledge of construct validity is obtained only by patiently comparing the experimental results from different supposed measures of the same construct.

Before individual measures of a construct are compared with one another, it is necessary to control or statistically to evaluate the effects of numerous possible incidental factors in the measurement process, such as a response bias on the part of subjects regarding the reporting of "dirty" words in studies of perception and artifacts of measuring anxiety due to the responses of subjects to anxiety-inducing procedures for obtaining blood samples.   Although there are some general rules for handling such confounding influences, most of the rules can be learned only through considerable experience with particular measurement techniques.

## Suggested additional reading

Sidowski, J. B. (Ed.)   *Experimental methods and instrumentation in psychology.*   New York: McGraw-Hill, 1966.

# CHAPTER 16

Measurement
in studies
of abnormal, personality,
and social psychology

In this chapter we shall discuss some issues relating to psychological measurement in research concerned with relatively complex, real-life types of phenomena.  Studies of abnormal, personality, and social psychology will be collectively referred to as the "molar" areas of investigation, as contrasted with the more "molecular" types of investigations discussed in the previous chapter. This terminology will be employed as a handy communication device, but it should not be inferred that the types of investigations discussed in this chapter always deal with more complex units of behavior than those discussed in Chapter 15.

No effort will be made to describe the major methods of measurement employed in studies of abnormal, personality, and social psychology.  That would be a formidable task indeed.  Instead, some types of research that illustrate important principles and/or problems of psychological measurement will be discussed.

## studies of contrasted groups

In the classical experimental design for psychological research, subjects from a larger group are randomly assigned to smaller groups, each of which receives a different experimental treatment.  This would be done, for example, in an investigation of the effects of different dosage levels of a drug on reaction time.

One hundred subjects are randomly assigned to four groups, with the restriction that 25 subjects appear in each group. One group does not receive the drug, but rather is injected with a biologically neutral substance. The other three groups are injected with different dosage levels of the drug.

In the classical experimental design, extraneous differences between members of the groups should be no larger than would be expected by chance, e.g., differences in age, intelligence, weight, and all other possible confounding variables. In many experiments in the molar areas, however, it is not possible to randomly assign subjects to treatment conditions. Instead, one must work with intact groups, such as in comparing deaf with hearing subjects, criminals with noncriminals, hospitalized schizophrenics with normal persons, and Negroes with whites. If the research issues concern differences between groups of people, there is obviously no way to employ classical experimental designs. For example, it would be out of the question to randomly make half of the subjects deaf and let the remaining half retain their hearing.

Studies concerned with contrasted groups run into a variety of problems in terms of both experimental control and psychological measurement. A series of examples will illustrate the problems and some of the safeguards that can be employed.

One experiment concerns a comparison of hospitalized schizophrenics and normal persons on the extent to which judgments of perceptual illusions are affected by distracting stimuli. The Müller-Lyer illusion, discussed and illustrated in the previous chapter, has frequently been used in such investigations. Under one condition, judgments of the illusion are made in the usual way, without any distracting stimuli present. In a second condition, judgments are made when the illusory stimulus is surrounded with drawings of chairs, people, trees, and other distracting stimuli. Schizophrenics and normals are tested under both conditions. The hypothesis is that the two groups perform equally well when no distracting stimuli are present but that schizophrenics perform more poorly than normals when distractions are present.

This experiment exemplifies a number of problems in studies concerned with contrasted groups. A problem in terms of experimental control would be that of matching normal and schizophrenic subjects on possible confounding variables. If, for example, the normal subjects were college students, they would probably differ from the hospitalized schizophrenics in terms of age and general physical health, both of which might affect the experiment, regardless of the element of schizophrenia. A partial solution is to match as well as possible on age, sex, years of education, and other variables that might affect the experimental results. This would be only a partial solution because (1) it is nearly impossible to match groups on more than several variables and (2) there is always the lingering concern that some remaining confounding variable is running rampant, e.g., higher average intelligence in one group than in the other.

One problem of measurement that could arise in such an experiment concerns the testing of both groups under uniform conditions, which is the essence of measurement standardization.   If the two groups are tested in different physical environments, there is the possibility that differences in amount and quality of light would be a confounding variable.   If different persons test the two groups, there is the possibility that they would score responses slightly differently.   Even if the same examiner tests both groups, he may make subtle changes in his procedures if all the members of one group are measured before members of the other group.

A second example of a study of contrasted groups is one in which personality tests are administered to juvenile delinquents and their scores are compared with those of normal teenagers.   The juvenile delinquents are tested in a special school for wayward boys, and the normal teenagers are tested in regular high schools.   A problem of measurement could arise in this study because of different amounts of test-taking carefulness in the two groups.   Because they are generally disgruntled, the juvenile delinquents might be rather careless in giving answers, but the normal teenagers would be comparatively careful in reading and responding to the items.   Then the answers of the juvenile delinquents would be partially random, as if a mental coin had been flipped to decide whether to answer "yes" or "no" to each item. This would tend to move the average score of the delinquents toward the middle of the possible score range.   If people actually flip coins to decide each answer to 40 dichotomous items, the expectation is that 20 will be answered "yes" and 20 will be answered "no."   This artifact alone could produce highly significant differences between average scores of the two groups.

Measurement artifacts due to carelessness and confusion are probably much more rampant in psychological investigations than is realized.   In abnormal psychology, the abnormal group is frequently unhappy, confused in a general sense, and unmotivated to take psychological tests or participate in psychological experiments.   These motivational factors can result in large differences in performance which are not directly relevant to the psychological dimensions on which the abnormal group differs from the normal group.   Think, for example, how one would appear if he flipped a coin to decide whether to say "yes" or "no" to statements like the following:

1. I am wearing my father's nose.
2. I am the king of heaven.
3. There is a rabbit in my head.
4. I am glass from the waist down.

Of course everything feasible should be done to reduce carelessness and confusion, for example, by (1) impressing on all subjects the importance of paying careful attention to test materials, (2) employing very simple items, and (3) explaining tasks in sufficient detail so that confusion is minimized.   After the results are obtained, the differences between normal and abnormal groups can be compared with the differences that might be obtained as a result of carelessness in the abnormal group.  If the mean for the abnormal group is between the chance level and the mean for the normal group, there is the possibility that the results are due to carelessness and/or confusion.  If the mean for the abnormal group is further removed from the chance level than the mean for the normal group or is significantly beyond the chance level in the other direction from the mean for the normal group, logically the differences between groups could not be due to carelessness and/or confusion in the abnormal group.  Other indications of carelessness and confusion come from comparing the internal-consistency reliabilities found in the abnormal and normal groups (as with coefficient alpha, discussed in Chapter 5).  If such coefficients are significantly lower in one group than the other, this strongly suggests that one group is more careless and/or confused than the other.  As important as the foregoing and other statistics regarding the possible importance of carelessness and confusion are, they are almost never mentioned in journal articles concerning studies of contrasted groups.

A third example of a study of contrasted groups is one in which deaf children are compared with hearing children.  A measurement artifact might be introduced in any study in which written words are involved—in studies of memory for words, perceptual recognition of words, concept formation with words, and any other task in which words are prominently featured.  On the average, deaf children are markedly retarded in word knowledge as compared with hearing children.  This difference in word knowledge could produce spurious differences in experimental results regardless of any real differences between groups in abilities concerning memory, perceptual recognition, or concept formation.  For example, a deaf child might be unable to remember a particular word because he does not know the meaning of it rather than because his memory is deficient in a general sense.  This would be another example of an unwanted factor (word knowledge) in measures that are intended to tap other human attributes.

As a safeguard in the aforementioned research comparing deaf and hearing children, one could employ materials other than words (e.g., geometric forms) or only very simple words.  If anything other than very simple words is used, it would be helpful to have a special control group of hearing children, one that is matched with the deaf children on word knowledge.  To control for age, one group of hearing children would have the same average age as the deaf children; to control for word knowledge, a younger group of hearing children would be selected who had approximately the same average score on a measure of word knowledge as the deaf children.  If the deaf children differ in the same way from both groups of hearing children, some faith can be placed in the interpretation that the results are related to deafness per se rather than to the confounding factors of either age or word knowledge.

Because of the above-mentioned and many other measurement problems encountered in studies of contrasted groups, it is tempting to ask why psychologists bother to perform studies of contrasted groups. The answer is simple:
If one is interested in differences between different groups of people, as an
investigator has every right to be, there is no choice but to perform research on
contrasted groups. Otherwise, there would be no way to learn how normal
people differ in their psychological characteristics from the blind, the mentally
ill, the brain-damaged, and many other abnormal groups. In performing such
studies, however, one must employ numerous safeguards and make special
analyses of results, some of which were discussed previously. More importantly,
evidence regarding differences between contrasted groups should always be regarded as circumstantial rather than direct. Confidence in a supposed difference between groups grows as a function of numerous findings by different
investigators using various types of experimental procedures and materials on
different samples of the abnormal group and making comparisons with a variety
of normal control groups.

## studies involving deception

In many types of experiments concerning personality characteristics, either important information is withheld from subjects or outright deceptions are employed. Withholding information is ethically defensible and produces no
artifacts of measurement in most experiments. For example, in a study of
simple reaction time, the experimenter is not obligated to explain in detail the
workings of the research equipment or the theories behind the experiment. To
provide such explanations before the subject participated in the experiment
might induce unnatural responses during the experiment. As another example,
in a study of paired-associate learning, it would be unwise for the experimenter
to introduce the task by explaining in detail how the lists of word pairs were
constructed or the hypothesis being investigated. After subjects complete
experimental sessions, however, it is usually courteous and feasible to answer
questions about the experiment frankly. If subjects ask questions before participating in experimental sessions, the experimenter can say that they will be
answered later.

In contrast to the simple withholding of information until experimental
sessions are completed, in some studies elaborate deceptions are employed, for
example, in a study of the effects of "group pressure" on judgments. The subject thinks he is in a room with five other subjects, but actually the other five
people are actors who have been trained to behave in specified ways. Two lines
are projected onto a screen, and the experimenter asks the subjects to judge
which is longer. After the five actors all say that the shorter line is longer, the
subject makes his judgment. To the extent that he agrees with the actors it is
said that he is conforming to group pressure. Various treatment conditions

are employed to determine the effects of different situational variables on amount of conforming.

A second example of an experiment involving elaborate deception is one concerning the effects of different levels of stress on the performance of a test of two-hand motor coordination. An effort is made to manipulate degrees of stress by deceiving subjects regarding what is measured by the coordination task. A no-stress condition is created by telling subjects in one group that the task concerns highly specialized motor skills that are useful in daily life only for persons who will work in factory assembly lines. In a second group, a moderate level of stress is created by telling subjects that the test measures motor ability in a very general sense and is predictive of athletic ability, ability to drive automobiles, and many other abilities in which most people take pride. In a third group, a high level of stress is created by telling subjects that the task has recently been found to relate to effective functioning of large areas of the brain and that it is highly indicative of overall intelligence.

Of course there are severe ethical problems in employing elaborate deceptions such as in the foregoing illustrations. Experimenters usually try to overcome the ethical problem by having a postexperimental "dehoaxing" session, in which subjects are frankly told about the deception and why it was necessary. This is only a partial solution to the ethical problem because it cannot undo the effects of any embarrassment or anguish experienced while the experiment was in progress. Also, subjects frequently react negatively when told that they have been manipulated by deception.

Aside from the ethical issues in the use of elaborate deceptions, such deceptions frequently create problems in relation to psychological measurement. The aforementioned experiment regarding effects of stress on motor coordination illustrates some problems in the measurement of the independent variable. Supposedly the three different sets of instructions given to the three experimental groups resulted in three levels of stress. How does one know that degrees of stress are validly indexed by the three treatments? Frequently it is the case that experimenters rely on "face validity" to convince others. More direct forms of evidence would be obtained by measuring one or more physiological indicators of stress (e.g., heart rate) while the experiment is in progress and, after the motor task has been completed, by administering questionnaires regarding the experienced stress during the experiment.

Measures of independent variables created by different forms of deception require construct validation, just as all measures do. One of the major problems with experiments employing elaborate deception is that they frequently involve modes of deception that either have not been used previously in other experiments or have been used in only a small number of experiments, which means that there has been little opportunity to accrue the mass of circumstantial evidence required for construct validity. If a standard method of deception is used in numerous interrelated experiments and the overall results make good sense, one can have some faith in the deception as validly indexing the independent variable in question.   However, because "you can't fool all of the people all the time," it is difficult to standardize methods of deception that can be used year after year.

There are numerous reasons why a method of deception might not validly index an independent variable.   One reason is that subjects frequently see through the deception.   This is particularly likely to be the case if one is investigating college students or other sophisticated adults and if the deception is rather transparent, as it woud be in an experiment like the one discussed above, in which a coordination task was described as a valid measure of general intelligence.   Subjects who were submitted to that deception might be under less stress than subjects who were submitted to the more plausible deception intended to be only moderately stressful.

Even if the deception is convincing to subjects, it simply might not have the intended impact.   It might, for example, be as stressful to take a test of motor coordination in the usual way as it is under special instructions intended to create stress.   Also, some incidental aspects of the study may produce so much stress that the effects of different deceptions are obscured.   This might be the case, for example, if prior to the motor task subjects were required to fill out an inventory concerning personal matters.

Even if a deception validly indexes an independent variable in one experiment, there is a question regarding the general validity of the deception as employed by other experimenters.   Some deceptions require a considerable amount of acting skill on the part of the examiner.   This is the case in many experiments that attempt to induce different moods in different groups of subjects.   A simple example of such an experiment is one in which three groups of subjects are required to solve problems cooperatively, e.g., to assemble a complex structure with metal pipes.   In one group, the experimenter stands passively aside and makes no comments.   In a second group, he is highly critical of the subjects' speed and skill, saying, for example, "Come on now, we don't have all day."   In a third group, the experimenter is highly supportive and lavishes praise on the group.   The three different treatments are intended to affect the likes and dislikes of group members for one another and their perceptions of the personality characteristics of fellow group members.   The dependent variables are measured by postexperimental questionnaires and rating forms.

The success with which three different moods were created in the aforementioned experiment would depend to a large extent on the personality of the experimenter and his acting skill.   The group members would probably be more affected if the experimenter were a dignified professor than if he were a young, unimposing graduate student.   Because of their personality characteristics, some experimenters would irritate subjects even when praising them, and others would not severely irritate them even when being critical. Regardless of personality and general appearance, some people are simply much better at "pulling off" ruses than others are. For these reasons, many techniques of deception lack general validity of a kind that is manifested in consistent findings from laboratory to laboratory.

In any experiment where acting skill of the experimenter is important, a minimum test of the generality of results is to employ more than one experimenter. In the aforementioned experiment with three treatments, each experimenter could conduct sessions with five groups under each of the three treatment conditions. If the results were not markedly different for the two experimenters, some faith could be placed in the general validity of the method of deception.

In some experiments the deception is more directly related to the dependent variable than to the independent variable, which would be the case in an experiment concerning the extent to which amount of cheating is influenced by the importance of the outcome. Three groups of subjects are given the same examination relating to an introductory course in psychology. One group is told that the examination will have no influence on their grades and that it is being administered only for research purposes. A second group is told that the examination will be taken into consideration in assigning course grades but that it will be only a minor factor. A third group is told that the examination will be very important in the assignment of course grades. After the completed examinations are collected, copies are made. At the next class meeting, examination papers are returned along with a set of correct answers. The experimenter says that he must attend a meeting during the class hour and that he would appreciate students' grading their own papers. With the correct answers in front of them, it is easy for students to cheat by changing their answers. The amount of cheating can be measured easily by comparing the examination returned at the end of the class period with the copy made after it was administered. The dependent variable consists of the number of changed answers in the three groups of subjects. There are many other instances in which the validity of the dependent variable depends upon the success of some type of deception.

Whereas the withholding of information and the use of certain mild forms of deception will probably always be important aspects of psychological experimentation, it is questionable what place there will be for gross deception. Psychologists and some nonpsychologists are beginning to question the ethics of employing forms of deception which create anxiety or embarrassment or which require the individual to unwittingly betray things that he would rather have kept private. Aside from the ethical issues involved, experiments that employ gross deception are subject to the potential sources of invalidity discussed previously in this section.

## sample surveys

Many issues in sociology and social psychology are investigated with sample surveys, in which questions are asked either of a sample of the whole population or of some group in the population. The public is acquainted with sample surveys through the results obtained by commercial opinion-polling agencies, which are reported in many newspapers and mentioned on radio and television. The opinon polls usually deal with simple issues, like preferences for political candidates, matters of foreign policy, and controversial legislation. Sample surveys are also used in basic research in psychology and sociology. Surveys are made of opinions about child-rearing practices, prevention of crime, integration of races, medical care, and many other issues. Also, sample surveys are used extensively in market research to determine preferences among commercial products and to estimate the potential sales of new products.

In a number of places in this book it has been said that most psychological investigations are not highly dependent upon the average responses of all subjects being studied. Rather, the interest in most cases is in correlations between either individual differences on a number of measures or differences between treatment groups on one or more measures. In sample surveys, however, the average response of all subjects in the study is usually of paramount importance, and therein lies the most important problem of psychological measurement in many sample surveys. The average response of subjects as a group can be artifactually influenced in such a way as to provide misleading results. Some problems in this regard are discussed in the following sections.

### Sample size

The average response in a sample survey may be misleading because of the small number of subjects interviewed. One frequently sees in newspapers or hears on radio the results of a highly informal surveying of the opinions of only a small number of persons, e.g., 30 people questioned on a man-in-the-street radio program. Such small samples are totally inadequate for representing the opinions of people in general. The situation is made much worse by converting the results into percentages. For example, 18 out of 30 persons agree with the statement that parents are too lenient with children these days. It is then reported that 60 percent of the people interviewed feel that something is amiss with the way children are being reared. If another 30 persons had been questioned, the results might have been in the opposite direction. The sampling error attendant upon percentages obtained from any number of people can be determined by statistical methods which are discussed in most books on statistics. What is learned from applying these formulas is that there must be a bare minimum of several hundred persons before any confidence can be placed in the exact size of results. The need for a large number of subjects is particularly acute when people are nearly evenly divided on an issue. For example, most political elections are settled on the basis of no more than 55 percent of the people voting for the winning candidate. In such cases, it is typically necessary to employ a sample of several thousand persons to ensure precise results.

### Sample representativeness

In addition to having a large number of persons studied, it is necessary that the group of persons be representative of the larger group to which results will be generalized. For example, if a survey is intended to represent the opinion of all members of trade unions toward a pending item of federal legislation, the results might be misleading if all subjects were electrical workers, who might have somewhat different opinions from those of members of other trades. Then no matter how many electrical workers were studied, the results of the survey would still be misleading.

A now famous mishap will illustrate the principle that the sheer size of the sample studied is no guarantee that valid results will be obtained. The *Literary Digest* made a very bad estimate of the voting sentiment in the 1936 presidential election. The magazine predicted a Landon victory with 370 electoral votes, but Roosevelt won 523 of a possible 531 votes. This calamitous mistake drove the magazine out of business.

A look at how the *Digest* poll operated will point up some lessons regarding the needs for representative sampling. The poll was conducted entirely by mail, with 10 million ballots being sent out for the 1936 election, of which less than 2½ million were returned. Persons who reply in this way tend to form a select group, overweighted with people from the upper-income brackets and upper educational levels. People who reply to mail questionnaires usually have a more direct interest in the election than those who fail to reply. In this case it was the upper-income persons who were protesting against Roosevelt.

Worse than its dependence on mail-out ballots was the fact that the *Digest* used very poor sampling procedures. The mailing list was obtained from telephone directories and files of automobile registrations. The people in 1936 who had telephones and automobiles were, as a group, much higher on the socioeconomic scale than those who did not. At that time the lower socioeconomic groups voted heavily Democratic, and the higher socioeconomic groups voted heavily Republican. The *Digest* predicted that Roosevelt would get only 40.9 percent of the popular vote, whereas he actually got 60.2 percent.

How to obtain representative samples is not an easy matter. Theoretically, the best sample of the population in the United States would be obtained by randomly sampling a large number of persons. However, that would be nearly impossible in principle and would be prohibitively expensive in practice. For example, one of the persons so selected might live in a remote mountain village that is snowed in most of the year. Another person might be on an oil rig standing 2 miles off the coast.  Obviously, it would be extremely expensive to search such persons out for a survey.  For the foregoing and other reasons, it is necessary to employ approximate samples, ones that are purposefully constructed to represent the distributions of age, sex, education, and locality that exist in the country as a whole.  The technical problems in constructing such samples are sufficiently complex that only experts can be trusted to perform survey research.  Whole books have been written on the technical problems involved (e.g., Albig, 1956; Kish, 1965; Yates, 1949).

### Measurement bias

Even if surveys employ large, representative samples of the population under investigation, there are still numerous forms of bias that can produce misleading results.  Some of these forms of bias are inherent in the subjects themselves.  An example is a reluctance to voice undesirable opinions.  This is evidenced in a comparison which was made of responses obtained by interviewers and anonymous responses, which subjects made by filling out the questionnaire in the privacy of their own homes.  The questions concerned relations between the United States and England in the early days of World War II.  One question was as follows: "Do you think that the English will try to get us to do most of the fighting for them in this war, or do you think that they will do their fair share of the fighting?"  Whereas in the interview situation 57 percent of the sample chose the latter alternative, in the anonymous sample only 25 percent chose that alternative.  (This research was reported by Cantril, 1944.)

Other forms of response bias are inherent in the measurement methods employed in survey research.  If a statement is identified with a prominent person or popular cause, it will receive more endorsement than it otherwise would.  For example, Cantril (1944) found a significant increase in endorsement of a statement when it began, "President Roosevelt said . . ." over the percentage of endorsement it received when it was not specifically identified with Roosevelt.  A similar form of response bias occurs when a statement is connected with a widely accepted cause, for example, one that begins, "For the good of the country, do you think that we should . . . ?"  To disagree with such a statement could be interpreted by the subject as being against something that is good for the country.

Another form of response bias is introduced by interviewers.  Previously an example was given of a survey in which the presence of an interviewer produced different results from those obtained anonymously.  Here we shall consider biases due to individual differences between interviewers.  It has been found consistently that Negro interviewers obtain somewhat different responses from Negro subjects on questions concerning racial relations from those elicited by white interviewers.  More subtle forms of bias arise from the personality of the interviewer, his age, and even his own opinions. For example, in one study (Cantril, 1944) interviewers were required to respond to the same questions which they had asked subjects in a survey. On some questions it was found that interviewers recorded more subjects as agreeing with their own opinions than subjects disagreeing with their own opinions.

The above-mentioned instances of potential response biases and problems regarding adequate sampling should not lead one to the conclusion that modern surveying is a messy business. Just the opposite is true. Since scientific opinion polling started in the mid-1930s, the polls have proved to be highly accurate in most instances in sampling *present* opinions. It has been found, for example, that opinion polls conducted several days before a presidential election are highly predictive of the actual vote. The polls have been unjustly criticized because they do not predict how opinions might change. Some opinions remain stable over relatively long periods of time, e.g., opinions about the worth of the social security laws. Other opinions tend to change considerably over a period of six months or less, which is the case with opinions about candidates for political office. The polls are intended to estimate present opinions, and although in many cases the results are predictive of opinions over relatively long periods of time, such predictions are not the major purpose of most surveys.

Experts in the business of conducting sample surveys have ways of approximately overcoming the potential sources of invalidity which have been discussed. Previously it was mentioned how some of the difficulties in obtaining representative samples are overcome. There are ways of overcoming some of the forms of measurement bias discussed in this section. For example, experts are skilled at writing questions in such a way as not to bias the answers. Also, they sometimes employ different wordings of the same question. If the results are much the same for the questions worded in different ways, one can have some faith in the results. Experts who conduct sample surveys approximately control for biases arising from interviewers by employing interviewers who vary widely in terms of opinions and personal characteristics. Then any differences between responses obtained by interviewers will tend to average out in the final results.

The major lesson to be learned from the foregoing discussion of sample surveys is that such surveys can be trusted only if they are performed on a large scale by experts. No faith should be placed in surveys conducted by amateurs on small, nonrepresentative samples.

## laboratory investigations and investigations in naturalistic settings

One of the major problems of measurement in the molar areas of experimentation is that the results are frequently specific to laboratory settings and do not generalize to more naturalistic settings. When, for example, a student enrolled in a course in introductory psychology is asked to report for an experiment, he is, of course, aware that he is taking part in an experiment and that the experimenter is trying to learn something about him. Consequently, he enters the laboratory with numerous hunches about the experiment and wonders what would constitute "proper" behavior on his part. He wants to behave in a way that will reflect credit on him as an intelligent, ethical, well-adjusted individual. Also, in most cases he wants to please the experimenter, and consequently he tries to "go along with the game" insofar as he can discern the "rules." These predispositions on the part of subjects are spoken of as "laboratory effects" to contrast the results obtained from them with results obtained in real-life situations.

The foregoing problems are not very important in many investigations in the molecular areas, those discussed in the previous chapter. For example, if the individual is required to memorize lists of digits, he sees that the proper thing to do is to perform as effectively as possible. Also, no artifacts are generated by the subject's awareness that the experimenter wants to obtain the most effective performance possible. These conditions also hold in studies of perceptual judgment, concept formation, and motor coordination. Then it is reasonable to suppose that the results obtained from such investigations will generalize to real-life situations, such as memorizing a telephone number, identifying an object that appears briefly on a television screen, learning to discriminate poisonous snakes from nonpoisonous ones, and learning to type.

In contrast to most (but not all) studies of molecular topics, many (but by no means all) studies of molar topics are plagued by laboratory effects. This tends to be true particularly in studies concerned with personal adjustment, emotions, social motives, and interpersonal relationships. A number of examples will illustrate some severe problems that arise because of artificial behavior in laboratory settings.

One experiment concerns patterns of cooperation and competition in two-person games. The two subjects sit on opposite sides of a table. Each has a toy truck which can be moved on a semicircular track. If the subject can move his truck from the start zone to the goal zone, he will receive a dime. However, the two subjects share a common portion of track. If both subjects enter that portion of track, neither can reach the goal, and the rules require that after a short period of time, both trucks be returned to their starting positions. What is typically found is that after a number of trials, the subjects take turns letting each other reach the goal. Manipulated in such experiments are magnitudes of rewards given the subjects, degrees to which subjects can penalize their partners for not cooperating, and numerous other variables of interest in the study of personality and social psychology.

It should be obvious that severe problems in terms of laboratory effects are encountered in experiments like that discussed above. For example, the subjects know that their behavior is being observed by the experimenter, and for that reason they may behave rather differently from the way they would in a cooperative situation in daily life. Also, the sheer artificiality of playing with toy trucks is likely to irritate, embarrass, or bore college students to the extent that any generalizable effects of the treatment parameters are obscured.

The most extreme example of a study dominated by laboratory effects is one that the author once heard proposed to measure the interest value of magazine advertisements. The plan was to tell each subject, "Just behave naturally and look through this magazine as you would in any other situation." An experimenter on the right of the subject was to use a stopwatch to measure the amount of time he looked at each advertisement, and an experimenter on the left of the subject was to take notes regarding his facial expressions and other indications of interest. The naïve researchers were quickly dissuaded from undertaking the research because of laboratory effects that are too obvious for recitation here.

A less extreme example of an experiment in which potential laboratory effects are an issue is one in which the effects of relaxation therapy on test-taking anxiety are being investigated. Subjects are selected who rate themselves as having severe anxiety before and during course examinations. In a number of sessions, they are taught to relax many muscles of the body, which in turn results in a general mental relaxation; then they are gradually taught to relax when they form a mental image of going to and taking an examination. After the treatment is completed, subjects are asked to rate the amount of anxiety that they actually experience in taking examinations. A measure of improvement is obtained by comparing the ratings before treatment with the ratings after treatment.

The major source of laboratory effect in the aforementioned investigation is obvious. Subjects are under pressure to indicate that they have improved even if they actually have not. The experimenter has become their friend and has worked long hours trying to lower their anxiety. How can they tell him that all his efforts have been in vain? Few experimenters would be so naïve as to take the results at face value. One precaution would be to use a number of control groups, such as (1) a group of nonanxious subjects who were given the same treatment, (2) a group of anxious subjects who were taught methods of relaxation but not in conjunction with mental images relating to the taking of examinations, (3) an anxious group that was tested at two points in time but given no treatment, and (4) a group of anxious subjects who received "discussion therapy" rather than relaxation therapy. Also, before the results could be trusted, experimenters would require the use of measures of improvement that were not so easily manipulated in such a way as to please the experimenter. It has been found, for example, that the grades of students given some forms of relaxation therapy tend to improve. Also, in some experiments it is possible to obtain rather objective indices of improvement. For example, in treating stage fright, judges can rate tremor of the voice, nervous movements, and other indications of fear.

Rather than produce misleading results, the artificiality of some laboratory settings tends to obscure results that would be obtained in naturalistic settings. This tends to be the case, for example, in experiments on emotions. A typical study is one in which pupil size is used as the measure of emotionality and in which emotional states are invoked in male college students by loud sounds, threat of electric shock, and pictures of attractive nude females. Small but consistent pupillary dilation has been found in most such investigations of emotionality (Nunnally, Knott, Duchnowski, & Parker, 1967). However, the amount of pupillary dilation seems to be far smaller than that which can be observed in naturalistic settings. It is easy to induce and observe rather large momentary changes in pupil size in people. Any type of surprise or anxiety-provoking event will suffice, for example, approaching a friend with a worried look on your face and asking in a serious tone, "Has anyone told you what happened?" (It would be wise to pick a friend with a strong heart and a good sense of humor.)

In the aforementioned and other laboratory investigations of emotions, incidental aspects of the laboratory setting often induce unwanted emotions. For example, the emotional response of a male college student to the picture of a lovely nude female is partly pleasant, for obvious reasons, and partly negative because of feelings of embarrassment at viewing the picture in the presence of the experimenter. Whereas in real life the threat of an electric shock (e.g., while repairing a television set) might produce a response of fear, in the laboratory setting it partly induces bravery in male college students, and consequently there is a mixture of emotions.

There are many ways in which some types of laboratory effects can be either circumvented or overcome. They can be circumvented by performing investigations in relatively naturalistic settings, as, for example, the author and his colleagues have done in studies of the effects on visual fixation of displays in which two objects vary in terms of complexity, novelty, pleasantness, or some other characteristic. The early investigations employed an obvious laboratory setting, in which children peered into a box at pairs of pictures projected onto a screen. Near the subjects were various mechanical devices to photograph eye movements and to time the presentation of pictures. One could rightly question the extent to which the results were due to laboratory effects rather than to variables that are important in lifelike situations. Consequently, a more naturalistic environment was created. Half of a research trailer was made into a comfortable waiting room, where children sat while waiting for the experimenter to prepare materials. On the wall of the room opposite where the children were sitting were two rear projection screens, separated by about 4 feet. From the other half of the research trailer, pictures were automatically projected onto the screens for 15 seconds. A series of pairs of pictures was presented, and then the experimenter returned. The viewing behavior of the children was easily monitored through a small one-way mirror (research discussed in Faw & Nunnally, 1968).

Naturalistic settings are also used in studies of imitative behavior. At any traffic light, for example, an experimenter can note the effects of people who go against the light on persons waiting for the light to change. He will see that the tendency to imitate depends on variables such as the number of transgressors, the apparent danger from crossing, the proximity of police officers, and the social status of the transgressors.

There are many other instances in which laboratory effects could be circumvented by working in naturalistic settings. Of course it is more difficult to control extraneous variables in naturalistic settings than in laboratory settings. For example, in the aforementioned use of a waiting room to study eye fixations, children spend about half their time looking around the room rather than at either of the pictures presented. The study of imitation at traffic lights involves even more problems, such as dependence on the particular place and sample of people. Even with their problems, however, naturalistic investigations are open to far fewer questions regarding the generalization of findings to real-life situations.

Naturalistic and seminaturalistic investigations would probably be undertaken much more frequently if it were not for the time and expense involved. It is relatively easy to parade subjects into the laboratory every hour on the hour and complete an experiment within a week or two. In contrast, it is frequently much more difficult to conduct experiments in naturalistic settings because of the amount of equipment and research personnel required and because of the rarity in some investigations with which subjects are caught in the necessary situations.

Rather than circumvent laboratory effects by using naturalistic settings, the experimenter can overcome them in various ways. One way is to employ highly practiced subjects, ones who have become relatively immune to incidental factors in the laboratory environment. Then the newness of the laboratory setting will have worn off, and subjects will not be entertaining irrelevant questions about the nature and purpose of the experiment.

Another way largely to overcome laboratory effects is to use treatments that are so strong that they obscure any confounding variables induced by the laboratory setting. For example, in studies of the effects of rewards on various forms of behavior in college students, it has been customary to use rewards of no more than $2 or $3, in which case students are likely to be influenced more by the need to appear well-adjusted and intelligent than by the need to obtain the reward. However, if it is feasible to use rewards of $20, students would probably be highly motivated to obtain the rewards.

One safeguard against laboratory effects is to employ a number of treatment conditions and/or a number of dependent measures. The former would be evidenced in an experiment in which a variety of treatments are employed to test the hypothesis that pupillary response is a measure of emotionality. The latter possibility would be evidenced in an experiment in which pupillary response is used along with heart rate and electrical resistance of the skin to test the hypothesis that difficult problems in arithmetic arouse emotions. The use of more than one type of treatment and/or more than one dependent measure provides confidence that all the results are not caused by laboratory effects alone.

The practical problems of employing methods to overcome laboratory effects are essentially the same as those which arise in investigations in naturalistic settings: they both tend to be difficult, time-consuming, and expensive. However, such difficulties will have to be faced if a true science of psychology is to be developed. There is a severe limit to what can be learned about molar human processes with trivial treatments in highly artificial environments.

## Summary

Problems of experimental control and psychological measurement occur frequently in the investigation of molar human process—in studies of personality, abnormal, and social psychology. Because many investigations in these areas concern complex, real-life types of variables, they tend to pose more problems than many of the studies of molecular issues discussed in Chapter 15.

Much research in the molar areas of investigation concerns comparisons of intact groups of people, this being particularly the case in studies of abnormal groups. In terms of experimental control, one always wonders about possible confounding variables that spuriously produce differences between abnormal persons and normal persons. In terms of psychological measurement, one always wonders about differences in measurement procedures, motivation, carelessness, and confusion that might spuriously produce differences between abnormal persons and normal persons.

Many studies of molar processes have relied on complex forms of deception, which pose severe problems in generating independent variables and in measuring dependent variables. Some of the major problems are (1) transparency of the deception, (2) dependence of the deception on the acting skills and personal characteristics of the experimenter, and (3) the production of different effects on subjects from those which were intended. Not only does the use of elaborate deceptions give rise to a number of problems, but many such deceptions are also questionable on ethical grounds. Where it is ethical to employ mild forms of deception, some procedures are available for testing the effectiveness of the deception.

Sample surveys are frequently used to investigate opinions and attitudes. Some of the pitfalls in conducting such surveys are (1) inadequate sample size,

(2) unrepresentative sample, and (3) artifacts of measurement, such as the wording of questions, that can lead to misleading results. The major consideration is that survey research should be left to the experts, who have ways of handling most of the problems that arise.

Many studies of molar processes are dominated by laboratory effects. That is, their results hold only in the narrow confines of the laboratory setting and do not generalize to the natural environment. Laboratory effects are generated when (1) the subject behaves in a way in which he thinks the experimenter wants him to behave; (2) the subject is on guard to behave in an intelligent, socially desirable manner rather than as he usually behaves; and (3) incidental sources of embarrassment, anxiety, or distraction override the treatment conditions. Methods are available either for overcoming laboratory effects in laboratory settings or for performing research in naturalistic settings. Typically such methods are time-consuming and difficult, but it may be necessary to employ them in order to have truly scientific investigations of many issues in social, personality, and abnormal psychology.

Albig, W. *Modern public opinion.* New York: McGraw-Hill, 1956.

American Psychological Association. *Technical recommendations for psychological tests and diagnostic techniques.* Washington: Author, 1954.

Anastasi, A. *Psychological testing.* New York: Macmillan, 1954.

Anastasi, A. *Psychological testing.* (3rd ed.) New York: Macmillan, 1968.

Anderson, H. H., & Anderson, G. L. *An introduction to projective techniques.* Englewood Cliffs, N.J.: Prentice-Hall, 1951.

Andrew, D. M., & Paterson, D. G. *Minnesota Clerical Test: Manual.* New York: Psychological Corporation, 1946.

Barrett, H. O. An examination of certain standardized art tests to determine their relation to classroom achievement and to intelligence. *Journal of Educational Research,* 1949, 42, 398–400.

Bayley, N. *Bayley Infant Scales of Development.* New York: Psychological Corporation, 1968.

Bechtoldt, H. P. Construct validity: A critique. *American Psychologist,* 1959, 14, 619–629.

Beck, S. J. *Rorschach's test.* Vol. 1. *Basic processes.* New York: Grune & Stratton, 1944.

Beckman, A. S. Minimum intelligence levels for several occupations. *Personnel Journal,* 1930, 9, 309–313.

Bell, J. E. *Projective techniques.* New York: Longmans, 1948.

Bennett, G. K. *Hand-tool Dexterity Test: Manual.* New York: Psychological Corporation, 1947.

Bennett, G. K.   *Test of Mechanical Comprehension, Form AA: Manual.*   New York: Psychological Corporation, 1948.

Bennett, G. K.   *Test of Mechanical Comprehension, Form BB: Manual.*   New York: Psychological Corporation, 1951.

Bennett, G. K., Seashore, H. G., & Wesman, A. G.   *Differential Aptitude Tests: Manual.*   (2nd ed.) New York: Psychological Corporation, 1952.

Binet, A., & Simon, T.   Méthodes nouvelles pour le diagnostic du niveau intellectuel des anormaux.   *Année psychologie,* 1905, 11, 191–244.

Bisbee, E. U.   *Commercial Education Survey Tests: Junior and Senior Shorthand.*   Bloomington, Ill.: Public School, 1933.

Blackstone, E. G., & McLaughlin, M. W.   *Blackstone Stenographic Proficiency Tests: Stenographic Test.*   Yonkers, N.Y.: World, 1932.

Bond, E. A.   Tenth grade abilities and achievements.   *Teachers College Contributions to Education,* 1940, No. 813.

Boring, E. G.   *A history of experimental psychology.*   (Rev. ed.) New York: Appleton-Century-Crofts, 1950.

Buros, O. K. (Ed.)   *The fifth mental measurements yearbook.*   Highland Park, N.J.: Gryphon Press, 1959.

Campbell, D. T.   The indirect assessment of social attitudes.   *Psychological Bulletin,* 1950, 47, 15–38.

Campbell, D. T.   Recommendations for APA test standards regarding construct, trait, and discriminant validity.   *American Psychologist,* 1960, 15, 546–553.

Cantril, H.   *Gauging public opinion.*   Princeton, N.J.: Princeton University Press, 1944.

Carrigan, P. M.   Extraversion-introversion as a dimension of personality: A reappraisal.   *Psychological Bulletin,* 1960, 57, 329–360.

Carroll, H. A.   What do the Meier-Seashore and the McAdory Art Tests measure?   *Journal of Educational Research,* 1933, 26, 661–665.

Cattell, P.   *The measurement of intelligence of infants and young children.*   New York: Psychological Corporation, 1947.

Cattell, R. B.   *Personality and motivation structure and measurement.*   New York: Harcourt, Brace & World, 1957.

Chase, C. I.   *Elementary statistical procedures.*   New York: McGraw-Hill, 1967.

Conrad, H. S., & Jones, H. E.   A second study of familiar resemblance in intelligence: Environmental and genetic implications of parent-child and sibling correlations in the total sample.   *39th Yearbook, National Social Studies in Education,* 1940, Part 2, 97–141.

Cook, S. W., & Selltiz, C.   A multiple-indicator approach to attitude measurement.   *Psychological Bulletin,* 1964, 62, 36–55.

Coombs, C. H.   A theory of data.   *Psychological Review,* 1960, 67, 143–159.

Crawford, J. E., & Crawford, D. M.   *Small Parts Dexterity Test: Manual.*   New York: Psychological Corporation, 1949.

Cronbach, L. J.   *Essentials of psychological testing.*   New York: Harper, 1949.

Cronbach, L. J.  *Essentials of psychological testing.*  (2nd ed.) New York: Harper & Row, 1960.

Cronbach, L. J., & Meehl, P. E.  Construct validity in psychological tests. *Psychological Bulletin,* 1955, 52, 281–302.

Davis, F. B.  Item analysis in relation to educational and psychological testing. *Psychological Bulletin,* 1952, 49, 97–121.

Davis, H. (Ed.)  *Hearing and deafness.*  New York: Murray Hill Books, 1947.

Dixon, W. J., & Massey, F. J.  *Introduction to statistical analysis.*  New York: McGraw-Hill, 1951.

Drake, R. M.  The validity and reliability of tests of musical talent. *Journal of Applied Psychology,* 1933, 17, 447–458.

Drake, R. M.  *Musical Memory Test: Manual.*  Bloomington, Ill.: Public School, 1934.

Drake, R. M.  Factor analysis of music tests. *Psychological Bulletin,* 1939, 36, 608–609.

Edwards, A. L.  The relationship between the judged desirability of a trait and the probability that the trait will be endorsed. *Journal of Applied Psychology,* 1953, 37, 90–93.

Edwards, A. L.  *The social desirability variable in personality assessment and research.*  New York: Holt, 1957.  (a)

Edwards, A. L.  *Techniques of attitude scale construction.*  New York: Appleton-Century-Crofts, 1957.  (b)

Eysenck, H. J.  *Dimensions of personality.*  London: Routledge, 1947.

Eysenck, H. J.  *The structure of human personality.*  London: Methuen, 1960.

Farina, A., Arenberg, D., & Guskin, S. L.  A scale for measuring minimal social behavior. *Journal of Consulting Psychology,* 1957, 21, 265–268.

Farnsworth, D.  *The Farnsworth Dichotomous Test for Color Blindness: Manual.*  New York: Psychological Corporation, 1947.

Farnsworth, D.  *The Farnsworth-Munsell 100 Hue Test for the Examination of Color Discrimination: Manual.*  Baltimore: Munsell Color Company, 1949.

Farnsworth, P. R.  An historical, critical, and experimental study of the Seashore-Kwalwasser test battery. *Genetic Psychology Monographs,* 1931, 9, 291–293.

Farnsworth, P. R.  Rating scales for musical interests. *Journal of Psychology,* 1949, 28, 245–253.

Faw, T. T., & Nunnally, J. C.  A new methodology and finding relating to visual stimulus selection in children. *Psychonomic Science,* 1968, 12, 47–48.

Ferguson, G. A.  On learning and human ability. *Canadian Journal of Psychology,* 1954, 8, 95–112.

Fleishman, E. A., & Hempel, W. E.  Changes in factor structure of a complex psychomotor test as a function of practice. *Psychometrika,* 1954, 19, 239–252.

Freeman, E., & Zaccaria, M. A.  An illuminant-stable color-vision test, II. *Journal of the Optical Society of America,* 1948, 38, 971–976.

French, J. W.   The description of aptitude and achievement tests in terms of rotated factors.  *Psychometric Monographs,* 1951, No. 5.

Games, P., & Klare, G. R.   *Elementary statistics for the behavioral sciences.* New York: McGraw-Hill, 1967.

Gardner, R. W., & Schoen, R. A.   Differentiation and abstraction in concept formation.  *Psychological Monographs,* 1962, 76, No. 560.

Garner, W. R.   Rating scales, discriminability, and information transmission. *Psychological Review,* 1960, 67, 343–352.

Gerberich, J. R.   *Specimen objective test items: A guide to achievement test construction.*  New York: Longmans, 1956.

Gesell, A., & Amatruda, C. S.   *Gesell Developmental Schedules.*  New York: Psychological Corporation, 1949.

Ghiselli, E. E.   The validity of commonly employed occupational tests.  *University of California Publications in Psychology,* 1949, 5, 253–287.

Ghiselli, E. E., & Brown, C. W.   The effectiveness of intelligence tests in the selection of workers.  *Journal of Applied Psychology,* 1948, 32, 575–580.

Ghiselli, E. E., & Brown, C. W.   *Personnel and industrial psychology.*  (2nd ed.) New York: McGraw-Hill, 1955.

Gilliland, A. R.   *Northwestern Intelligence Tests: Test A, for Infants 4–12 Weeks Old.*  Boston: Houghton Mifflin, 1949.

Goddard, H. H.   A revision of the Binet scale.  *The Training School,* 1911, 8, 56–62.

Goodenough, F., & Van Wagenen, M. J.   *Minnesota Preschool Scale: Forms A and F.*  (Rev. ed.) Minneapolis: Educational Test Bureau, 1940.

Gough, H. G.   Minnesota Multiphasic Personality Inventory.  In A. Weider (Ed.), *Contributions toward medical psychology.*  Vol. 2.  New York: Ronald Press, 1953.

Graves, M.   *Design Judgment Test: Manual.*  New York: Psychological Corporation, 1948.

Graves, M. E.   *The art of color and design.*  (2nd ed.) New York: McGraw-Hill, 1951.

Grinker, R. R., Miller, J., Sabshin, M., Nunn, R., & Nunnally, J. C.   *The phenomena of depressions.*  New York: Hoeber-Harper, 1961.

Guilford, J. P.   *Psychometric methods.*  (2nd ed.) New York: McGraw-Hill, 1954.

Guilford, J. P.   *Personality.*  New York: McGraw-Hill, 1959.

Guilford, J. P.   Factorial angles to psychology.  *Psychological Review,* 1961, 68, 1–20.

Guilford, J. P.   *Fundamental statistics in psychology and education.*  (4th ed.) New York: McGraw-Hill, 1965.

Guilford, J. P.   *The nature of human intelligence.*  New York: McGraw-Hill, 1967.

Guilford, J. P., & Zimmerman, W. S.   *The Guilford-Zimmerman Temperament Survey: Manual.*  Beverly Hills, Calif.: Sheridan Supply Company, 1949.

Gulliksen, H.   *Theory of mental tests.*  New York: Wiley, 1950.

Gulliksen, H., & Messick, S. (Eds.) *Psychological scaling: Theory and applications*. New York: Wiley, 1960.

Hartshorne, H., May, M. A., & Shuttleworth, F. K. *Studies in the organization of character*. New York: Macmillan, 1930.

Hathaway, S. R., & McKinley, J. C. *Minnesota Multiphasic Personality Inventory: Manual for Administration and Scoring*. New York: Psychological Corporation, 1967.

Hathaway, S. R., & Meehl, P. E. *An altas for the clinical use of the MMPI*. Minneapolis: University of Minnesota Press, 1951.

Hays, W. L. *Statistics for psychologists*. New York: Holt, 1963.

Hess, E. H. Attitude and pupil size. *Scientific American*, 1965, 212, 46–65.

Highsmith, J. A. Selecting musical talent. *Journal of Applied Psychology*, 1929, 13, 486–493.

Holtzman, W. H. Personality structure. In P. R. Farnsworth, O. McNemar, & Q. McNemar (Eds.), *Annual review of psychology*. Palo Alto, Calif.: Annual Reviews, 1965. Pp. 119–156.

Holtzman, W. H., Thorpe, J. S., Swartz, J. D., & Herron, E. W. *Inkblot perception and personality: Holtzman inkblot technique*. Austin, Tex.: University of Texas Press, 1961.

Honzik, M., McFarlane, J., & Allen, L. The stability of mental test performance between two and eighteen years. *Journal of Experimental Education*, 1948, 17, 309–324.

Horn, C. C. *Horn Art Aptitude Inventory: Preliminary Form, 1944 Revision, Manual*. Rochester, N.Y.: Rochester Institute of Technology, Office of Educational Research, 1944.

Horn, C. C., & Smith, L. F. The Horn Art Aptitude Inventory. *Journal of Applied Psychology*, 1945, 29, 350–355.

Hull, C. L. *A behavior system*. New Haven, Conn.: Yale University Press, 1952.

Humphreys, L. G. The organization of human abilities. *American Psychologist*, 1962, 17, 475–483.

Jenkins, J. J., & Patterson, D. G. *Studies in individual differences*. New York: Appleton-Century-Crofts, 1961.

Kelly, E. L., & Fiske, D. W. *The prediction of performance in clinical psychology*. Ann Arbor, Mich.: University of Michigan Press, 1951.

Kendall, M. G. *Rank correlation methods*. London: Griffin, 1948.

Kent, G. H., & Rosanoff, A. J. A study of association in insanity. *American Journal of Insanity*, 1910, 67, 37–96, 317–390.

Kinter, M. *The measurement of artistic abilities*. New York: Psychological Corporation, 1933.

Kish, L. *Survey sampling*. New York: Wiley, 1965.

Klineberg, O. *Negro intelligence and selective migration*. New York: Columbia, 1935.

Klopfer, B., & Kelley, D. M. *The Rorschach technique*. Yonkers, N.Y.: World, 1942.

Knauber, A. J.   Construction and standardization of the Knauber art tests. *Education,* 1935, 56, 165–170.   (a)

Knauber, A. J.   *Knauber Art Ability Test: Examiner's Manual.*   Cincinnati, Ohio: Author, 1935.   (Distributed by Psychological Corporation.)  (b)

Kuhlmann, F.   A revision of the Binet-Simon system for measuring the intelligence of children.   *Journal of Psycho-asthenics, Monograph Supplement,* 1912, 1, 1–41.

Kwalwasser, J., & Dykema, P. W.   *Kwalwasser-Dykema Music Tests: Manual of Directions.*   New York: Carl Fischer, 1930.   (Also distributed by Stoelting.)

Larson, R. C.   Studies on Seashore's measures of musical talent.   *University of Iowa Studies, Aims Progress Research,* 1930, No. 6, 83.

Lennon, R. T.   Assumptions underlying the use of content validity.   *Educational and Psychological Measurement,* 1956, 16, 294–394.

Lewerenz, A. S.   *Tests in Fundamental Abilities of Visual Art: Manual of Directions.*   Los Angeles: California Test Bureau, 1927.

Likert, R.   A technique for the measurement of attitudes.   *Archives of Psychology,* 1932, No. 140.

Likert, R., & Quasha, W. H.   *Revised Minnesota Paper Form Board Test: Manual.*   New York: Psychological Corporation, 1948.

Lindquist, E. F.   *A first course in statistics.*   (Rev. ed.)   Boston: Houghton Mifflin, 1942.

Loevinger, J.   Objective tests as instruments of psychological theory.   *Psychological Reports,* 1957, 3, 635–694.

Lord, F. M.   The relation of the reliability of multiple-choice tests to the distribution of item difficulties.   *Psychometrika,* 1952, 17, 181–194.   (a)

Lord, F. M.   A theory of test scores.   *Psychometric Monographs,* 1952, No. 7.   (b)

Lorge, I.   The fundamental nature of measurement.   In E. F. Lindquist (Ed.), *Educational measurement.*   Washington: American Council on Education, 1951.   Ch. 14.

Lorge, I., & Thorndike, R. L.   *The Lorge-Thorndike Intelligence Tests.*   Boston: Houghton Mifflin, 1957.

Machover, K.   *Personality projection in the drawing of the human figure: A method of personality investigation.*   Springfield, Ill.: Charles C. Thomas, 1949.

Masling, J.   The influences of situational and interpersonal variables in projective testing.   *Psychological Bulletin,* 1960, 57, 65–85.

McAdory, M.   *The McAdory Art Test: Manual.*   New York: Teachers College, Bureau of Publications, 1929.

McConnell, T. R.   Locus of control, examiner presence, and source and type of reinforcement as factors in visual discrimination learning with mental retardates.   Unpublished doctoral dissertation, George Peabody College for Teachers, 1966.

McGinn, N. F., Harburg, E., Julius, S., & McLeod, J. M.   Psychological correlates of blood pressure.   *Psychological Bulletin,* 1964, 61, 209–219.

McNemar, Q. *Psychological statistics*. New York: Wiley, 1962.

Meier, N. C. *The Meier Art Tests. I. Art Judgment: Examiner's Manual*. Iowa City, Iowa: University of Iowa, Bureau of Educational Research Service, 1942.

Melton, A. W. (Ed.) *Apparatus Tests*. (*AAF Aviation Psychology Program, Research Report No. 4*.) Washington: GPO, 1947.

Messick, S., & Ross, J. (Eds.) *Measurement in personality and cognition*. New York: Wiley, 1962.

Morrow, R. S. An analysis of the relations among tests of musical, artistic, and mechanical abilities. *Journal of Psychology*, 1938, 5, 253–263.

Murray, H. A. *Thematic Apperception Test Manual*. Cambridge, Mass.: Harvard University Press, 1943.

Mursell, J. W. What about music tests? *Music Education Journal*, 1937, 24, 16–18.

Nunnally, J. C. *Tests and measurements: Assessment and prediction*. New York: McGraw-Hill, 1959.

Nunnally, J. C. *Popular conceptions of mental health: Their development and change*. New York: Holt, 1961.

Nunnally, J. C. *Educational measurement and evaluation*. New York: McGraw-Hill, 1964.

Nunnally, J. C. *Psychometric theory*. New York: McGraw-Hill, 1967.

Nunnally, J. C., Duchnowski, A. J., & Parker, R. K. Association of neutral objects with rewards: Effects on verbal evaluation, reward expectancy, and selective attention. *Journal of Personality and Social Psychology*, 1965, 1, 270–274.

Nunnally, J. C., & Hodges, W. F. Some dimensions of individual differences in word association. *Journal of Verbal Learning and Verbal Behavior*, 1965, 4, 82–88.

Nunnally, J. C., Knott, P. D., Duchnowski, A., & Parker, R. Pupillary response as a general measure of activation. *Perception & Psychophysics*, 1967, 2, 149–155.

Nunnally, J. C., Stevens, D. A., & Hall, G. F. Association of neutral objects with rewards: Effect on verbal evaluation and eye movements. *Journal of Experimental Child Psychology*, 1965, 2, 44–57.

Osgood, C. E. Studies on the generality of affective meaning systems. *American Psychologist*, 1962, 17, 10–28.

Osgood, C. E., Suci, G. J., & Tannenbaum, P. H. *The measurement of meaning*. Urbana, Ill.: University of Illinois Press, 1957.

Otis, A. S. *Otis Quick-scoring Mental Ability Tests: Manual of Directions for Alpha Test*. Yonkers, N.Y.: World, 1939. (a)

Otis, A. S. *Otis Quick-scoring Mental Ability Tests: Manual of Directions for Beta Test*. Yonkers, N.Y.: World, 1939. (b)

Peterson, D. R. Scope and generality of verbally defined personality factors. *Psychological Review*, 1965, 72, 48–59.

Pettigrew, T. F. The measurement and correlates of category width as a cognitive variable. *Journal of Personality*, 1958, 26, 532–544.

Pintner, R., Cunningham, B., & Durost, W. *Pintner-Cunningham Primary Test: Manual of Directions.* Yonkers, N.Y.: World, 1946.

Psychological Corporation. *General Clerical Test: Manual.* New York: Author, 1950.

Rapaport, D., Gill, M., & Schafer, R. *Diagnostic psychological testing.* Chicago: Year Book. Vol. I, 1945; Vol. II, 1946. (Republished in 1968 by International Universities Press, revised by R. R. Holt.)

Richardson, Bellows, Henry, and Company, Inc. *SRA Mechanical Aptitudes Manual.* Chicago: Science Research, 1950.

Roberts, J. A. F. Resemblances in intelligence between sibs selected from a complete sample of an urban population. *Proceedings of the International Genetic Congress,* 1941, 7, 252.

Rorer, L. G. The great response-style myth. *Psychological Bulletin,* 1965, 63, 129–156.

Rotter, J. B., & Rafferty, J. E. *The Rotter Incomplete Sentences Blank: Manual.* New York: Psychological Corporation, 1950.

Seashore, C. E. *Psychology of music.* New York: McGraw-Hill, 1938.

Seashore, C. E., Lewis, D., & Saetveit, J. G. *Manual of instructions and interpretations for the Seashore measures of musical talents.* (1939 revision.) Camden, N.J.: RCA Victor Division, Radio Corporation of America, 1942. (Now published and distributed by Psychological Corporation.)

Seashore, H., & Bennett, G. K. *Seashore-Bennett Stenographic Proficiency Test: Manual.* New York: Psychological Corporation, 1946.

Seashore, R. H., & Hevner, K. A time-saving device for the construction of attitude scales. *Journal of Social Psychology,* 1933, 4, 366–372.

Sidowski, J. B. (Ed.) *Experimental methods and instrumentation in psychology.* New York: McGraw-Hill, 1966.

Spearman, C. *The abilities of man.* New York: Macmillan, 1927.

Stanton, H. M. Measurement of musical talent. *University of Iowa Studies, The Psychology of Music,* 1935, 2, 140.

Steggerda, M. The McAdory Art Test applied to Navajo Indian children. *Journal of Comparative Psychology,* 1936, 22, 283–285.

Stephenson, W. *The study of behavior: Q-technique and its methodology.* Chicago: University of Chicago Press, 1953.

Stern, J. A., & McDonald, D. G. Physiological correlates of mental disease. In P. R. Farnsworth, O. McNemar, & Q. McNemar (Eds.), *Annual review of psychology.* Palo Alto, Calif.: Annual Reviews, 1965. Pp. 225–264.

Stevens, S. S. Problems and methods of psychophysics. *Psychological Bulletin,* 1958, 55, 177–196.

Stewart, N. AGCT scores of Army personnel grouped by occupations. *Occupations,* 1947, 26, 5–41.

Stromberg, E. L. *Stromberg Dexterity Test: Preliminary Manual.* New York: Psychological Corporation, 1951.

Strong, E. K. Interest scores while in college of occupations engaged in 20 years later. *Educational and Psychological Measurement,* 1951, 11, 335–348. (a)

Strong, E. K. Permanence of interest scores over 22 years. *Journal of Applied Psychology*, 1951, 35, 89–91. (b)

Strong, E. K. *Vocational Interest Blank for Men: Manual.* Stanford, Calif.: Stanford University Press, 1951. (c)

Studies in visual acuity. *Personnel Research Section Report 742,* AGO, 1948, 161.

Stutsman, R. *Mental measurement of preschool children.* Yonkers, N.Y.: World, 1931.

Taylor, C. W. (Ed.) *Research conference on the identification of creative scientific talent.* Ogden, Utah: University of Utah Press, 1961.

Taylor, J. A. A personality scale of manifest anxiety. *Journal of Abnormal and Social Psychology*, 1953, 48, 285–290.

Terman, L. M. *The measurement of intelligence.* Boston: Houghton Mifflin, 1916.

Terman, L. M., & Merrill, M. *Measuring intelligence: A guide to the administration of the new revised Stanford-Binet tests of intelligence.* Boston: Houghton Mifflin, 1937.

Terman, L. M., & Merrill, M. A. *Stanford-Binet Intelligence Scale: Manual for the Third Revision, Form L-M.* Boston: Houghton Mifflin, 1960.

Thorndike, R. L. *Personnel selection: Test and measurement techniques.* New York: Wiley, 1949.

Thorndike, R. L. Reliability. In E. F. Lindquist (Ed.), *Educational measurement.* Washington: American Council on Education, 1951. Pp. 560–620.

Thorndike, R. L., & Hagen, E. *Measurement and evaluation in psychology and education.* (2nd ed.) New York: Wiley, 1961.

Thurstone, L. L. *Examination in Clerical Work: Form A, Thurstone Employment Tests.* Yonkers, N.Y.: World, 1922.

Thurstone, L. L. A factorial study of perception. *Psychometric Monographs*, 1944, No. 4.

Thurstone, T. G. Primary mental abilities of children. *Educational and Psychological Measurement*, 1941, 1, 105–116.

Torgerson, W. *Theory and methods of scaling.* New York: Wiley, 1958.

Treisman, M., & Watts, T. R. Relation between signal detection theory and the traditional procedures for measuring sensory thresholds: Estimating $d'$ from results given by the method of constant stimuli. *Psychological Bulletin*, 1966, 66, 438–454.

Ulrich, L., & Trumbo, D. The selection interview since 1949. *Psychological Bulletin*, 1965, 63, 100–116.

Underwood, B. J., & Schulz, R. W. *Meaningfulness and verbal learning.* New York: Lippincott, 1960.

Valentine, C. W. *Intelligence tests for young children.* London: Methuen, 1945.

Walker, H. M., & Lev, J. *Elementary statistical methods.* New York: Holt, 1958.

Watson, L. A., & Tolan, T. *Hearing tests and hearing instruments.* Baltimore: Williams & Wilkins, 1949.

Wechsler, D. *Wechsler Intelligence Scale for Children: Manual.* New York: Psychological Corporation, 1949.

Wechsler, D. *Wechsler Adult Intelligence Scale: Manual.* New York: Psychological Corporation, 1955.

Wechsler, D. *Wechsler Preschool and Primary Scale of Intelligence: Manual.* New York: Psychological Corporation, 1967.

Wells, F. L. *Modified Alpha Examination, Form 9: Manual of Directions.* New York: Psychological Corporation, 1951.

Wenger, M. A. Studies of autonomic balance in Army Air Forces personnel. *Comparative Psychology Monographs,* 1948, 19, No. 101.

Wing, H. D. Tests of musical ability and appreciation: An investigation into the measurement, distribution, and development of musical capacity. *British Journal of Psychology, Monograph Supplement,* 1948, 8, No. 27.

Wittenborn, J. R. Contributions and current status of Q-methodolgy. *Psychological Bulletin,* 1961, 58, 132–142.

Wood, D. A. *Test construction: Development and interpretation of achievement tests.* Columbus, Ohio: Merrill, 1960.

Woodworth, R. S. *Personal data sheet.* Chicago: Stoelting, 1918.

Yates, F. *Sampling methods for censuses and surveys.* New York: Hafner, 1949.

# Appendix A:

## Major publishers of psychological and educational tests

American Guidance Service, Inc., Publishers Building, Circle Pines, Minn., 55014

The Bobbs-Merrill Company, Inc., 4300 West 62nd St., Indianapolis, Ind., 46206

Bureau of Educational Measurements, Kansas State Teachers College, Emporia, Kans., 66801

Bureau of Educational Research and Service, University of Iowa, Iowa City, Iowa, 52240

Bureau of Publications, Teachers College, Columbia University, New York, N.Y., 10027

California Test Bureau, Del Monte Research Park, Monterey, Calif., 93940

Consulting Psychologists Press, Inc., 577 College Ave., Palo Alto, Calif., 94306

Educational and Industrial Testing Service, P.O. Box 7234, San Diego, Calif., 92107

Educational Test Bureau, Division of American Guidance Service, Inc., 720 Washington Ave., S.E., Minneapolis, Minn., 55414

Educational Testing Service, Princeton, N.J., 08540

Educational Testing Service, Cooperative Test Division, Princeton, N.J., 08540

C. A. Gregory Co., Test Division of The Bobbs-Merrill Company, Inc., 4300 West 62nd St., Indianapolis, Ind., 46206

Harcourt, Brace & World, Inc., 757 Third Ave., New York, N.Y., 10017

Houghton Mifflin Company, 110 Tremont St., Boston, Mass., 02107

Industrial Relations Center, University of Chicago, 1225 East 60th St., Chicago, Ill., 60637

Institute for Personality and Ability Testing, 1602 Coronado Drive, Champaign, Ill., 61822

Ohio Scholarship Tests, State Department of Education, 751 Northwest Blvd., Columbus, Ohio, 43212

The Psychological Corporation, 304 East 45th St., New York, N.Y., 10017

Psychological Test Specialists, Box 1441, Missoula, Mont., 59804

Psychometric Affiliates, Brookport, Ill., 62010

Public School Publishing Company, Test Division of The Bobbs-Merrill Company, Inc., 4300 West 62nd St., Indianapolis, Ind., 46206

Scholastic Testing Service, Inc., 480 Meyer Road, Bensenville, Ill., 60106

Science Research Associates, Inc., 259 East Erie St., Chicago, Ill., 60611

Sheridan Psychological Services, P.O. Box 837, Beverly Hills, Calif., 90213

C. H. Stoelting Co., 424 North Holman Ave., Chicago, Ill., 60624

Teachers College Press, Columbia University, 525 West 120th St., New York, N.Y., 10027

University Bookstore, Purdue University, 360 State St., West Lafayette, Ind., 47906

University of London Press, Ltd., Little Paul's House, Warwick Square, London E.C.4, England

Western Psychological Services, 12035 Wilshire Blvd., Los Angeles, Calif., 90025

# Appendix B:

## Proportions of the area in various sections of the normal distribution

| | $z$ STANDARD SCORE $(x/\sigma)$ (1) | AREA BETWEEN (2) | AREA BEYOND (3) |
|---|---|---|---|
| + and − | 0.00 | 0.0000 | 1.0000 |
| | 0.05 | .0392 | .9602 |
| | 0.10 | .0796 | .9204 |
| | 0.15 | .1192 | .8808 |
| | 0.20 | .1586 | .8414 |
| + and − | 0.25 | .1974 | .8026 |
| | 0.30 | .2358 | .7642 |
| | 0.35 | .2736 | .7264 |
| | 0.40 | .3108 | .6892 |
| | 0.45 | .3472 | .6528 |
| + and − | 0.50 | .3830 | .6170 |
| | 0.55 | .4176 | .5824 |
| | 0.60 | .4514 | .5486 |
| | 0.65 | .4844 | .5156 |
| | 0.70 | .5160 | .4840 |
| + and − | 0.75 | .5468 | .4532 |
| | 0.80 | .5762 | .4238 |

| | $z$ STANDARD SCORE $(x/\sigma)$ (1) | AREA BETWEEN (2) | AREA BEYOND (3) |
|---|---|---|---|
| | 0.85 | .6046 | .3954 |
| | 0.90 | .6318 | .3682 |
| | 0.95 | .6578 | .3422 |
| + and − | 1.00 | .6826 | .3174 |
| | 1.05 | .7062 | .2938 |
| | 1.10 | .7286 | .2714 |
| | 1.15 | .7498 | .2502 |
| | 1.20 | .7698 | .2302 |
| + and − | 1.25 | .7888 | .2112 |
| | 1.30 | .8064 | .1936 |
| | 1.35 | .8230 | .1770 |
| | 1.40 | .8384 | .1616 |
| | 1.45 | .8530 | .1470 |
| + and − | 1.50 | .8664 | .1336 |
| | 1.55 | .8788 | .1212 |
| | 1.60 | .8904 | .1096 |
| | 1.65 | .9019 | .0990 |
| | 1.70 | .9108 | .0892 |
| + and − | 1.75 | .9198 | .0802 |
| | 1.80 | .9282 | .0718 |
| | 1.85 | .9356 | .0644 |
| | 1.90 | .9426 | .0574 |
| | 1.95 | .9488 | .0512 |
| + and − | 2.00 | .9544 | .0456 |
| | 2.05 | .9596 | .0404 |
| | 2.10 | .9642 | .0358 |
| | 2.15 | .9684 | .0316 |
| | 2.20 | .9722 | .0278 |
| + and − | 2.25 | .9756 | .0244 |
| | 2.30 | .9786 | .0214 |
| | 2.35 | .9812 | .0188 |
| | 2.40 | .9836 | .0164 |
| | 2.45 | .9858 | .0142 |
| + and − | 2.50 | .9876 | .0124 |
| | 2.55 | .9892 | .0108 |
| | 2.60 | .9906 | .0094 |
| | 2.65 | .9920 | .0080 |
| | 2.70 | .9930 | .0070 |
| + and − | 2.80 | .9948 | .0052 |
| | 2.90 | .9962 | .0038 |
| | 3.00 | .9973 | .0027 |
| | 3.10 | .99806 | .00194 |
| | 3.20 | .99862 | .00138 |

| | $z$<br>STANDARD<br>SCORE $(x/\sigma)$<br>(1) | AREA<br>BETWEEN<br>(2) | AREA<br>BEYOND<br>(3) |
|---|---|---|---|
| + and − | 3.40 | .99932 | .00068 |
| | 3.60 | .99968 | .00032 |
| | 3.80 | .999856 | .000144 |
| | 4.00 | .9999366 | .0000634 |
| | 4.50 | .9999932 | .0000068 |
| | 5.00 | .9999942 | .00000058 |
| | 6.00 | .999999998 | .000000002 |

* If, for example, in a normal distribution of test scores you want to estimate the number of persons who make scores between plus one standard deviation of the mean and minus one standard deviation of the mean, you would look opposite 1.00 in the first column at the proportion in the second column. There it is seen that the proportion is 0.6826, or, in other words, approximately 68 percent. This means that approximately 32 percent of the individuals make scores either greater than one standard deviation above the mean or less than one standard deviation below the mean. If you want to determine the proportions of people who lie within or beyond certain standard score units above the mean only or below the mean only, the proportions in columns 2 and 3 should be halved.

# Appendix C:

## Commercially distributed tests

### section 1: comprehensive achievement test batteries

#### California Achievement Tests, 1957 edition (with 1963 norms)

California Test Bureau
Levels:  Lower primary, grades 1–2 (110 minutes)
         Upper primary, grades 2.5–4.5 (145 minutes)
         Elementary, grades 4–6 (175 minutes)
         Junior high level, grades 7–9 (190 minutes)
         Advanced, grades 9–14 (190 minutes)

The test reports two scores in each of the three basic skill areas of reading, arithmetic, and language. Although the manual describes methods for obtaining diagnostic information about pupils, such information is based on a relatively small number of items in many cases. At the primary and elementary levels, the test provides a good coverage of the three basic skill areas. At the junior high level, the test does not provide enough information about achievement in content areas. Although items with respect to content areas are included, scores are not obtainable for different content areas. Because of the emphasis on core skills rather than content areas, the test is recommended mainly for students at the primary and elementary levels.

## Essential High School Content Battery

Harcourt, Brace & World, Inc.
Levels:  Grades 9–13
Testing time:  200–225 minutes

The battery covers four fields: mathematics, science, social studies, and English. In general, the tests appear to have been carefully designed and constructed. Although overall scores on the test should provide good indications of students' progress, some of the subtest reliabilities are rather low, and it is hazardous to seek diagnostic information from differences in scores within the test. Because of its content, the test is probably a more useful measure for students in general or college preparatory curricula than for students in technical and commercial curricula.

## Iowa Tests of Basic Skills

Houghton Mifflin Company
Levels:  Grades 3–9
Testing time:  315 minutes

This is a very thorough battery of tests.  Content areas are not covered; rather, the tests are aimed at the core skills of reading, language, arithmetic, and study skills.  The battery provides 15 scores: vocabulary (1), language (5), reading comprehension (1), study skills (4), arithmetic (3), and total score.  Reliabilities of all subtests are good.  An unusual feature is that norms are provided for the beginning, middle, and end of the school-year periods.  The manuals provide very clear instructions for administering and using the test.  Apparently the tests were very carefully designed and constructed.  Unless there is a need to test for content areas, the battery provides an excellent measure of core skills.

## The Iowa Tests of Educational Development

Science Research Associates, Inc.
Levels:  Grades 9–12
Testing time:  405–540 minutes

The battery provides 9 scores: understanding of basic social concepts, general background in the natural sciences, correctness and appropriateness of expression, ability to do quantitative thinking, ability to interpret reading materials in the social sciences, ability to interpret reading materials in the natural sciences, ability to interpret literary materials, subtotal score, and uses of sources of information.  Unquestionably the battery provides excellent measures of achievement at the secondary level. The tests were carefully designed and composed, and norms are based on large, representative samples of students. The manuals are clearly written and provide much information useful to teachers. The test publisher provides a scoring service which gives not only results for individual pupils but also statistical summaries of results from each school. The battery exemplifies achievement measurement at its best.

## Metropolitan Achievement Tests, 1959 edition

Harcourt, Brace & World, Inc.
Levels:     Primary I, grade 1.5 (115 minutes)
            Primary II, grade 2 (125 minutes)
            Elementary, grades 3–4 (177 minutes)
            Intermediate, grades 5–6 (267 minutes)
            Advanced, grades 7–9 (277 minutes)
            High school, grades 9–12 (316 minutes)

At the younger levels the test concerns primarily core skills; at higher levels tests are also included for content areas. The test can be recommended on many points including (1) careful design of content and construction of items, (2) clear and frank manuals, and (3) practicality of administration and scoring.

## Sequential Tests of Educational Progress (STEP)

Educational Testing Service, Cooperative Test Division
Levels:     Level 4, grades 4–6
            Level 3, grades 7–9
            Level 2, grades 10–12
            Level 1, grades 13–14
Testing time:   640 minutes

At each level the battery contains seven tests: (1) reading, (2) writing, (3) mathematics, (4) science, (5) social studies, (6) listening, and (7) essay. All the tests with the exception of the essay are composed of multiple-choice items. In the essay test, the student is asked to write a composition on a specified topic. The essay is scored by the classroom teacher.

The most noteworthy feature of the STEP is that the test items are aimed more at the overall goals of instruction than at the mastery of particular topics. The items concern principally how well students can use their school training to seek answers and to solve problems. Some of the items are very cleverly composed. Whereas on the one hand it can be argued that by aiming at the major end products of education, the STEP is more uniformly fair to students in different schools, on the other hand it may be hard for some schools to see how their instruction is directly related to the items. Because it emphasizes end products of education rather than obvious course content, the STEP is a significant departure from the other major comprehensive batteries.   Considerable experience will be required to determine whether this new emphasis will be widely accepted.   Aside from the nature of the item content, the STEP shares many of the features of other major achievement test batteries, including careful standardization, high reliability, and detailed reporting of norms.

## SRA Achievement Series

Science Research Associates, Inc.
Levels:     Grades 1–2  (340 minutes)
            Grades 2–4  (390 minutes)
            Grades 4–6  (445 minutes)
            Grades 6–9  (370 minutes)

The battery provides measures of vocabulary, reading comprehension, language, arithmetic, and, at the higher levels, study skills.   At the two upper levels, tests are long and provide broad coverage of material relating to core areas of instruction.   One noteworthy feature is that on the test for grades 1 to 4, part of the reading comprehension material concerns concepts essential to reading, which is much like the content found on reading-readiness tests.   The tests at each age level are somewhat more difficult than those found on other achievement test batteries.   Consequently, they will be appealing to schools that have above-average students, but they would serve rather poorly to provide diagnostic information about slow learners.   The items were apparently very carefully constructed.   Reliabilities of individual tests are good.   Because of the generally high correlations between subtests, most of the information from the test is given in one total score.   The manuals for the tests are very clear and detailed.

## Stanford Achievement Tests, 1964 revision

Harcourt, Brace & World, Inc.
Levels:     Primary I, grades 1.2–2.5  (160 minutes)
            Primary II, grades 2.5–3.9  (235 minutes)
            Intermediate I, grades 4–5.5  (230–300 minutes)
            Intermediate II, grades 5.5–6.9  (219–303 minutes)
            Advanced, grades 7–9  (201–287 minutes)

In terms of content and item type, this is one of the more conservative achievement batteries.   At all levels, spelling and arithmetic are tested, and the verbal skills are emphasized in sections on paragraph meaning, word study skills, and language.   For the younger pupils there is considerable attention to phonics; for older pupils there are many items devoted to concepts taught in general science, social studies, and advanced arithmetic classes.   All the tests are well constructed, and they have been improved during a series of revisions.   The appendix c

test manual is very good. Some may feel that the tests for content areas are too heavily oriented toward simple factual information.

## section 2: reading achievement tests

### Durrell-Sullivan Reading Capacity and Achievement Tests

Harcourt, Brace & World, Inc.
Levels:  Primary, grades 2.5–4.5
         Intermediate, grades 3–6
Testing time:   45 minutes

Five scores are obtained: (1) word meaning, (2) paragraph meaning, (3) spelling, (4) written recall, and (5) total. A noteworthy feature of the test is that part of the materials are given orally by the teacher, and the remainder is read by the student. This provides information about discrepancies between ability to comprehend oral and written language. In general this is a good test that is useful primarily for measuring overall achievement in reading but also provides some diagnostic clues about difficulties of particular students.

### Gates Basic Reading Tests

Bureau of Publications
Teachers College, Columbia University
Levels:  Grades 3.5–8
Testing time:   125 minutes

There are five subtests in the battery: (1) reading to appreciate general significance, (2) reading to understand precise directions, (3) reading to note details, (4) reading vocabulary, and (5) level of comprehension. The battery is generally well constructed and standardized. Instructions for administering and interpreting it are simple and quite clear.

### Gates Primary Reading Tests

Bureau of Publications
Teachers College, Columbia University
Levels:  Grades 1–2.5
Testing time:   8 minutes

The battery contains three types of tests: (1) word recognition, (2) sentence reading, and (3) paragraph reading. The tests are carefully constructed and highly reliable. The manual provides detailed instructions for administering and interpreting the tests and gives excellent suggestions to teachers for remedial training of students with reading difficulties.

## Iowa Silent Reading Tests, new edition

Harcourt, Brace & World, Inc.
Levels:    Elementary, grades 4–8
           Advanced, grades 9–14
Testing time:    50–60 minutes

At both levels the following scores are obtained: (1) rate of comprehension, (2) directed reading, (3) word meaning, (4) paragraph comprehension, (5) sentence meaning, and (6) location of information. The advanced battery contains a seventh test, poetry comprehension. Although in general the tests are good, they are all speeded; therefore, speed of reading and comprehension are emphasized. The tests would probably give a faulty picture of the performance of a student who reads well but slowly. Otherwise they are well constructed and standardized.

## Kelley-Greene Reading Comprehension Test

Harcourt, Brace & World, Inc.
Levels:    Grades 9–13
Testing time:    65–75 minutes

The test obtains scores for four types of reading skills: (1) selecting the central idea, (2) reading carefully and skimming for details, (3) drawing inferences from what is read, and (4) remembering details. Good norms are provided for high school levels.

## Nelson-Denny Reading Test, revised edition

Houghton Mifflin Company
Levels:    Grades 9–12
           Adult
Testing time:    35–40 minutes

The test provides four scores: (1) vocabulary, (2) paragraph comprehension, (3) reading rate, and (4) total. A noteworthy feature of the test is that it is easily administered and scored. The test is too brief to provide truly diagnostic information about reading difficulties. Its primary use is for a relatively quick appraisal of overall reading skill.

## Reading Comprehension: Cooperative English Tests, 1960 revision

Educational Testing Service, Cooperative Test Division
Levels:    Grades 9–12
           Grades 13–14
Testing time:    45 minutes

The test provides scores for (1) vocabulary, (2) speed of comprehension, (3) level of comprehension, and (4) total. Extensive research with this test demonstrates that it is a good predictor of school achievement. One of the best features of the test is that it attempts to measure subtle aspects of reading comprehension that are not measured by some other tests. This is one of the best reading achievement tests for high school students.

## section 3: tests to measure scholastic aptitude

### The American College Testing Program Examination (ACT)

American College Testing Program
Levels:   Grade 12 and junior college students preparing to transfer to four-
          year colleges
Testing time:   210 minutes

The ACT was launched in 1959 and has served as a healthy competitor to the SAT (discussed below) for use in predicting scholastic achievement at the college level. The test is administered on four Saturdays during the year (in February, April, June, and November) at participating colleges and centers established by the publisher. The test renders five scores: English usage, mathematics usage, social studies reading, natural sciences reading, and a composite score. Individual students serve as the customers of the ACT program, and hence scores are sent directly to them as well as to their high schools. The reporting service of the ACT also sends the individual's scores to three colleges which he designates at the time of application. A special feature of the reporting service is that colleges which participate in the research services of the American College Testing Program also receive predicted grade-point averages on each prospective student for each subject area tested and overall. This prediction service is efficient and has proved extremely valuable to colleges.

### College Entrance Examination Board Scholastic Aptitude Test (SAT)

Educational Testing Service
Level:   Candidates for college entrance
Testing time:   210 minutes

The SAT has come to be one of the more familiar and relied-upon tests used by colleges in selecting the most promising students from among all those who apply for admission. It continues to be the leading test for this purpose nationally, although the ACT may be used more in parts of the South and the Middle West. The SAT is administered one to five times annually (January, March, May, July, December) at centers established by the publisher. The test measures general verbal and mathematical comprehension. The verbal score is based upon antonyms, sentence completion, analogies, and reading comprehension items. The mathematical score involves word problems and data-sufficiency items. The test is very carefully constructed and has many alternative forms. Studies have found that test score gains from coaching are negligible, although two administrations effect a gain of approximately 20 points on both sections. A wealth of normative data and detailed information concerning the test is available to aid the test user. The scoring and reporting service associated with the admissions program of the CEEB is both prompt and reliable. Scores are reported to the student's high school and to three colleges or universities of his choice. He may have results forwarded to additional institutions for a small fee. A list of the candidates who select an institution as first, second, or third choice at each national test administration is sent immediately to the institution. Other features with regard to the SAT include forms for use by the handicapped and the establishment of overseas administration centers.

## Concept Mastery Test

The Psychological Corporation
Levels:   Grades 15–16
          Graduate students and applicants for executive and research positions.
Testing time:   45 minutes

This test is a by-product of Terman's extensive studies of gifted children and of those same children as adults. It is a high-level verbal test for adults and is intended to give an indication of a person's ability to deal with abstract concepts. Two types of items are employed: (1) synonym-antonym items and (2) analogies. The test has shown good validity for predicting success in university courses, but more research is needed before it can be widely used with advanced students and for predicting criteria of job success. However, it is excellent for its initial purpose of measuring at a high level and over a wide range the ability to understand verbal concepts and abstractions.

## Cooperative School and College Ability Tests (SCAT)

Educational Testing Service, Cooperative Test Division
Levels:   Grades 4–6
          Grades 6–8
          Grades 8–10
          Grades 10–12
          Grades 12–14
          Grades 15–16
Testing time:   95 minutes

At all levels the test yields three scores: (1) verbal, (2) quantitative, and (3) total. Although the total score provides most of the information obtainable from the test, if students score very differently on the verbal and quantitative portions, this indicates areas of unevenness in educational development. Generally the test is well constructed and standardized. The manual provides clear instructions for administering and interpreting the test. The major fault that some may find with the test is that it strongly emphasizes school-learned material rather than more abstract aspects of intelligence.

## Graduate Record Examinations Aptitude Test (GRE)

Educational Testing Service
Levels:   Grades 16–17
Testing time:   170 minutes

The Graduate Record Examinations have come to be used widely by colleges and universities for selecting candidates for admission to graduate school. In addition to this more obvious use, they are employed for such things as evaluating applicants for scholarships and fellowships and as a part of comprehensive examinations for undergraduate degrees. The GRE consist of (1) an aptitude test yielding verbal and quantitative scores, (2) advanced tests for 20 specialized curriculum areas, and (3) area tests covering social science, natural science, and the humanities.

There are two programs for administering the GRE: the National Program for Graduate School Selection and the Institutional Testing Program. The national program is administered five times annually (November, January, March, April, and July) at centers established by the publisher. It includes the aptitude test and one of the advanced tests selected by the candidate according to the individual college requirement. Under the institutional program, the colleges and graduate schools themselves may administer the GRE at any time except on dates when the national program is scheduled. The institutional program provides not only the aptitude and advanced tests but also the area tests, which measure general understanding of basic concepts and their application rather than the recall of specific facts.

The tests have been revised regularly and appear to be well constructed and standardized. The tests can be recommended in terms of normative data, satisfactory reliability, and generally good validity; but, as with all tests of higher-level scholastic aptitude, local studies of the predictive validity of the GRE are highly recommended.

## Miller Analogies Test

The Psychological Corporation
Level:   Candidates for graduate school
Testing time:   55 minutes

The Miller Analogies Test is a well-constructed, convenient, single-score test of high-level verbal ability. It has been used extensively for many years and subjected to a considerable amount of research. The evidence indicates that the test measures abilities which are related to general intellectual performance, and thus it has been found useful in selecting people for high-level business positions as well as in predicting graduate school grades.

The test is restricted in its distribution to prevent coaching and to protect its security, and it is administered only at licensed centers. Scoring and reporting are handled by the local center. At the time of testing, the examinee may request to have his scores reported to three institutions or companies. Scores are released to the individual as well. The brief yet comprehensive manual includes a discussion of factors which cause the test to be more effective in some situations than in others. Norms are given for 18 academic and 5 industrial groups.

## section 4: group tests of general intelligence

### California Test of Mental Maturity, 1963 revision

California Test Bureau
Levels:  Grades 4–6
        Grades 7–9
        Grades 9–12
        Grades 12–16
        Adults
Testing time:  91–93 minutes

The chief claim for validity of the CTMM is that the original test was designed to correlate with the Stanford-Binet. The test provides three main scores (language total, nonlanguage total, and overall total) and scores for each of five subtests (logical reasoning, spatial relationship, numerical reasoning, verbal concepts, and memory). This is an excellent and usable test of general intelligence and has real value for comparing an individual's verbal and nonverbal abilities. However, caution should be exercised in using scores on the individual subtests until more data are available on their validity for educational selection, prediction, and guidance at each of the age and grade levels.

### Chicago Nonverbal Examination

The Psychological Corporation
Levels:  Age six to adult
Testing time:  40 minutes

The test consists entirely of pictorial and symbolic material that requires little, if any, language usage. It can be administered either with oral instruction or, for those who have a severe language deficit, entirely by pantomime. Although tests of this type are not the best measures of general intelligence for most purposes, they have an important place with specific types of students. They are particularly useful with children who have a severe language handicap, such as the deaf and children who have recently emigrated from other countries. Also, nonlanguage tests of this type are useful with children in this country who have led culturally impoverished lives.

## Henmon-Nelson Tests of Mental Ability, revised edition

Houghton Mifflin Company
Levels:   Grades 3–6
          Grades 6–9
          Grades 9–12
          Grades 13–17
Testing time:   35–45 minutes

The test provides only one total score for grades 3 to 12 but three scores (quantitative, verbal, and total) for grades 13 to 17. Although it is a short test, it correlates well with longer tests of general intelligence and with achievement tests. The test is concerned mainly with verbal ability (as most tests of general intelligence are). Good norms are available for the test, and test reliabilities are high. The test provides a reasonably good, quick estimate of scholastic aptitude.

## Kuhlman-Anderson Intelligence Tests, 6th edition

Personnel Press, Inc.
Levels:   Kindergarten
          Grades 1–6
Testing time:   30–45 minutes

A single IQ is obtained from numerous separate subtests. Although the overall IQ has satisfactory reliability, it would be unsafe to interpret differences between subtest scores. Although little actual reading is required, the test measures mainly verbal comprehension. This is one of the best tests of general intelligence available for young children.

## Kuhlman-Anderson Intelligence Tests, 7th edition

Personnel Press, Inc.
Levels:   Grades 7–9
          Grades 9–12
Testing time:   110 minutes

This test is an extension of that used at earlier grade levels. It has many of the characteristics of the test for earlier levels, including a strong emphasis on verbal comprehension. Scores are given for (1) verbal, (2) quantitative, and (3) total. The verbal and quantitative portions correlate so highly that little information can be obtained from comparing scores on the two parts. As is true of the test for younger students, it provides a good, rapid estimate of scholastic aptitude.

## Otis Quick-scoring Mental Ability Tests

Harcourt, Brace & World, Inc.
Levels:    Grades 1.5–4
           Grades 4–9
           Grades 9–16
Testing time:    20–30 minutes

In spite of the brevity of these tests, they provide useful estimates of scholastic aptitude. The tests are almost entirely concerned with verbal comprehension. They are very easy to administer and score. The test for grades 1.5 to 4 requires no reading.

## Pintner General Ability Tests, nonlanguage series

Harcourt, Brace & World, Inc.
Levels:    Grades 4–9
Testing time:    50–60 minutes

Like other nonlanguage tests, this one requires no reading and no spoken or written language. The test is useful primarily for children with a severe language handicap.

## Pintner General Ability Tests, verbal series

Harcourt, Brace & World, Inc.
Levels:    Primary, kindergarten to grade 2
           Elementary, grades 2–4
           Intermediate, grades 4–8
           Advanced, grades 9–12 and above
Testing time:    45–55 minutes

At all levels this test has many points in common with other group measures of general intelligence, including a very heavy emphasis on verbal ability. Generally the test is well constructed and standardized.

## Progressive Matrices

H. K. Lewis and Co., Ltd. (American distributor: The Psychological Corporation)

Levels:    Standard Progressive Matrices, age six and over (60 minutes)
           Coloured Progressive Matrices, ages seven to eleven, and mental
              patients and the elderly (30 minutes)
           Advanced Progressive Matrices, age eleven and over (50 minutes)

These tests rely solely on perceptual tasks to measure intellectual functioning. The tasks or matrices consist of designs which require completion. The subject chooses his answer from among multiple-choice options. An answer which fits may (1) complete a pattern, (2) complete an analogy, (3) systematically alter a pattern, (4) introduce systematic permutations, or (5) systematically resolve figures into parts. The advanced test consists of two sets, the first of which may be used alone as a rough screening device or as a practice set. Set 2 may be used without a time limit as a "test of intellectual capacity" or with a time limit as a "test of intellectual efficiency." Although much more research is needed before the matrices should be regarded as precise measures of intelligence, they can be quite helpful as screening devices for groups where estimates of levels of intelligence need to be determined. Since the tests are easy to administer and no verbal responses are required, they should be particularly useful with individuals who have communications disorders or handicaps, such as the deaf or cerebral-palsied.

### SRA Tests of Educational Ability, 1962 edition

Science Research Associates, Inc.
Levels:    Grades 4–6 (52 minutes)
           Grades 6–9 (67 minutes)
           Grades 9–12 (45 minutes)

The test attempts to measure three different aspects of scholastic aptitude: (1) verbal, (2) reasoning, and (3) quantitative. However, not enough items are included to provide reliable measures of these three aspects, and it is much better to interpret only a total score for the three subtests. As an overall measure of general intelligence, the test should take its place with other good measures of that kind.

### Terman-McNemar Test of Mental Ability

Harcourt, Brace & World, Inc.
Levels:    Grades 7–12
Testing time:    40–45 minutes

This test has many of the characteristics of other verbal tests of intelligence. It is concerned mainly with verbal comprehension. The test was very carefully designed and constructed.

## section 5: tests for assessing creativity and reasoning

Although the tests described in this section are commercially available and hold promise for tapping abilities not measured by tests of intelligence or scholastic aptitude, they should still be considered largely experimental. More research, especially with regard to predictive validity, is needed before they should be widely used in applied settings. For the present, these tests should be confined primarily to research programs and to limited roles in educational evaluation and counseling.

## Ship Destination Test

Sheridan Psychological Services
Levels:   Grade 9 and over
Testing time:   20 minutes

This imaginative test is described to the subject in terms of conditions affecting a ship in traveling from one point to another. He is required to perform a series of easy additions and subtractions on each item. The numbers to be added or subtracted are determined by a set of rules. The rules are different for each set of three items and grow progressively more complex. Studies have shown that this test is a good measure of general reasoning ability. The manual is well constructed and provides a substantial amount of relevant data to aid in using the test.

## Southern California Tests of Divergent Production

Sheridan Psychological Services
Levels:   Varies with the individual test but generally ranging from grades 6
          to 16 and adults
Testing time:   10–30 minutes, depending on the individual test

These tests resulted from the research program carried on for many years by Guilford and his associates on the "structure of the intellect." These intriguing tests are deceptively simple but appear to have good construct validity. Other such tests in this series are still being developed and may be published over the coming years. A listing of the tests follows:

  *Alternate Uses.* Involves listing possible uses for a specified object, other than its common use.

*Christensen-Guilford Fluency Tests.* A battery measuring four types of verbal fluency (word, ideational, associational, and expressional).

*Consequences.* Items requiring the subject to list what the results might be if some unusual situation came to pass; scored in terms of ideational fluency and originality.

*Decorations.* Involves outline drawings of common objects to be decorated with as many different designs as possible and measures the "ability to add meaningful details."

*Making Objects.* Measures "figural expressional fluency" by having the subject draw specified objects using only a set of given figures.

*Match Problems.* Measures "originality in dealing with concrete visual material" and involves having a subject remove a certain number of matchsticks leaving a specified number of squares or triangles.

*Possible Jobs.* Requires the subject to list possible jobs symbolized by a given object and measures the "ability to suggest alternative deductions."

*Sketches.* Requires the subject to make as many different sketches as possible by elaborating on each of a set of identical figures.

## Torrance Tests of Creative Thinking

Personnel Press, Inc.
Levels:   Kindergarten through graduate school

These tests are divided into two batteries: (1) a verbal battery consisting of seven tasks and (2) a pictorial battery consisting of three tasks. In the verbal battery, the subject performs such activities as telling all the things that would happen if a certain improbable situation were true, making a list of unusual uses for a common object, and improving a given toy so that children will have more fun playing with it. In the pictorial battery, the activities involve drawing pictures using various shapes and lines provided by the examiner as starting points. Unusual ideas are stressed rather than artistic quality. Detailed scoring guides are provided in the manual. Scores are expressed in terms of factors labeled "fluency," "flexibility," "originality," and "elaboration."

## Watson-Glaser Critical Thinking Appraisal, 1963 revision (with 1952 norms)

Harcourt, Brace & World, Inc.
Levels:   Grades 9–16 and adults
Testing time:   50–60 minutes

Five subtests measure different aspects of critical thinking: (1) drawing inferences, (2) recognizing assumptions, (3) drawing appropriate deductions, (4) interpreting data, and (5) evaluating arguments. Some items employ content which is abstract and noncontroversial, while others involve issues of a controversial nature which typically provoke emotional and prejudiced responses from many individuals. Those interested in studying the effect of emotion or prejudice on critical thinking are advised in the manual to select for themselves the items which are likely to be pertinent to their own group. While this test can be useful for such things as selection in school and industry and evaluation of the effectiveness of instruction, the scores should be used cautiously as the test has not been standardized thoroughly enough to permit their use in any absolute way.

## section 6: interest inventories

### Brainard Occupational Preference Inventory

The Psychological Corporation
Levels:   Grades 8–12
          Adult
Testing time:   30 minutes

Covered in the inventory are six broad occupational fields: (1) commercial, (2) mechanical, (3) professional, (4) aesthetic, (5) scientific, and (6) personal service (for girls) or agriculture (for boys). The inventory is simple to administer and score. At the present time, no evidence on the validity is available.

### Kuder Preference Record—Occupational

Science Research Associates, Inc.
Levels:   Grades 9–16
          Adult
Testing time:   35 minutes

This is one of three interest inventories by Kuder. All three share the same type of test item and test format. The purpose of this inventory is to provide scores for 50 specific occupations. The average reliability of the occupational scores is only about .60, which is too low for use in counseling students. The instrument needs to be further standardized and validated for use in high school counseling programs.

### Kuder Preference Record—Personal

Science Research Associates
Levels:   Grades 9–16
          Adult
Testing time:   40–45 minutes

The purpose of this interest inventory is to measure five personal characteristics that are potentially important for occupational choice: (1) being an active participant in group activities, (2) being in familiar and stable situations, (3) dealing with abstract ideas, (4) avoiding conflict, and (5) leading and directing others.  Potentially this inventory could serve as a supplement to the occupational and vocational forms, principally the latter.  There has been neither enough research evidence about the instrument nor enough practical experience with it to enable us to know how helpful it will be in high school counseling.

## Kuder Preference Record—Vocational

Science Research Associates
Levels:    Grades 9–16
           Adults
Testing time:    40–50 minutes

For many years this has been one of the most widely used interest inventories in high school and college counseling programs.  In contrast to the occupational form, this form provides scores in nine broad vocational areas rather than for many separate occupations.  A masculinity-femininity score is also obtained. The instrument is well designed and standardized.  The ten scales each have moderately high reliability.  Although not enough evidence is available about validity, the instrument is judged to be useful by many high school and college counselors.

## Strong Vocational Interest Blank for Men, revised

Consulting Psychologist's Press
Levels:    Age seventeen and over
Testing time:    30–60 minutes

This is by far the most widely used interest inventory.  It provides scores for numerous separate occupations as well as a number of global interest scores. Considerable research has been done with the inventory.  Results show that most of the occupational scores are sufficiently reliable, that scores are predictive of occupations that students enter some years after taking the test, and that some scales differentiate between successful and unsuccessful people in occupations.  The instrument is very useful in counseling high school students and college students about future schooling and careers.

## Strong Vocational Interest Blank for Women, revised

Consulting Psychologist's Press
Levels:    Age seventeen and older
Testing time:    30–60 minutes

This inventory for women is very similar to the form for men.  It provides scores on 30 occupations.  Not nearly as much research has been done with this as has been done with the form for men.  Because of the similar methods used in constructing both instruments, it is expected that the form for women will prove to be useful in high school and college counseling.


## section 7: personality and adjustment inventories

### Bell Adjustment Inventory

Stanford University Press
Levels:   Grades 9–16
          Adult
Testing time:   25 minutes


The student form provides scores in four areas of adjustment: (1) home, (2) health, (3) social, and (4) emotional.  This inventory suffers from all the difficulties that others do.  It is dependent almost entirely on the individual's awareness of personal problems and his willingness to relate them.  This inventory is useful primarily for the rough screening of students who may need help with personal problems.  It has been used for many years in conjunction with high school counseling programs.


### California Test of Personality, 1953 revision

California Test Bureau
Levels:   Kindergarten to grade 3
          Grades 4–8
          Grades 7–10
          Grades 9–16
          Adult
Testing time: 60 minutes


This is one of the few inventories that attempt to measure personality characteristics of young children.  Scores are provided with respect to 12 personality characteristics, e.g., school relations, sense of personal worth, and withdrawing tendencies.  Also available is a total adjustment score and two subtotal scores relating, respectively, to social and personal adjustment.  Scores on the individual scales are far too unreliable for use.  Consequently, only the total adjustment scores and the two subtotal scores should be used.  Although there are some legitimate uses of personality inventories, there are so many problems in developing valid measures and so much that is still unknown about the meaning of responses to personality inventories with young children that this and other inventories should be used with extreme caution. Inventories for young children should be administered and interpreted only by well-trained counselors.

## Gordon Personal Profile

Harcourt, Brace & World, Inc.
Levels:   Grades 9–16
              Adult
Testing time:   15–20 minutes

The inventory provides five scores: (1) ascendancy, (2) responsibility, (3) emotional stability, (4) sociability, and (5) total adjustment score. Not enough research evidence and practical experience are available to enable us to say how useful the inventory will be.

## Guilford-Zimmerman Temperament Survey

Sheridan Psychological Services
Levels:   Grades 9–16
              Adult
Testing time:     50 minutes

This inventory arose from extensive factor-analytic investigations of items typically appearing on personality inventories. Scores are provided for 10 personality factors. Although generally this is a well-constructed instrument, it may provide more information than can be interpreted by counselors. Research evidence is still lacking regarding its validity. This inventory may be useful in the hands of highly trained and experienced counselors, but would probably prove difficult for less well-trained and experienced counselors to use.

## Heston Personal Adjustment Inventory

Harcourt, Brace & World, Inc.
Levels:   Grades 9–16
              Adults
Testing time:   40–55 minutes

The inventory provides six scores: (1) analytical thinking, (2) sociability, (3) home adjustment, (4) emotional stability, (5) confidence, and (6) personal relations. It was apparently well constructed and standardized.

## Minnesota Multiphasic Personality Inventory (MMPI)

The Psychological Corporation
Levels:   Age sixteen and over
Testing time:   30–90 minutes

The purpose of the inventory is to detect tendencies toward nine different forms of mental illness. The instrument is widely used by clinical psychologists and school psychologists. Considerable professional training and experience are required to interpret the results. Consequently, it is not wise to employ this inventory unless highly trained personnel are available.

## Mooney Problem Checklist, 1950 revision

The Psychological Corporation
Levels:   Grades 7–9
          Grades 9–12
          Grades 13–16
          Adult
Testing time:   20–50 minutes

This is an old and very sensible instrument. Rather than purporting to be a test, in the formal sense of the word, it is intended to be used as a screening device for students with personal problems and as an aid to counseling. The inventory consists of a long list of problems typical of those which bother some students. The items were obtained from written statements of problems by over four thousand students and from other sources. The problems concern social relations, home adjustment, health, financial difficulties, sexual problems, religious difficulties, and others. In using the checklist, it is as important to study the particular kinds of problems indicated as it is to observe the number of problems checked. Wisely used, this checklist (and the two to be described next) have an important place in school counseling programs.

## SRA Junior Inventory

Science Research Associates, Inc.
Levels:   Grades 4–8
Testing time:   About 45 minutes

The inventory is similar in item content to the Mooney Problem Checklist. Problems are sampled from five areas: (1) "about myself," (2) "about me and my school," (3) "about me and my home," (4) "getting along with other people," and (5) "things in general." The good things said about the Mooney inventory also apply to this one. It is probably the best adjustment inventory available for students in elementary school.

## SRA Youth Inventory

Science Research Associates, Inc.
Levels:   Grades 7–12
Testing time:   About 35 minutes

This is an extension of the Junior Inventory for older students. What was said about the Junior Inventory holds with equal force in regard to this form.

# Appendix D:

## Formulas relating to measurement reliability

In Chapter 5, general principles were discussed regarding the effects of measurement error on psychological investigations. Here will be presented some formulas and theoretical developments that are useful in determining measurement error and for correcting the effects of measurement error on research results.

### The domain-sampling model

The most useful model for the discussion of measurement error is that which considers any particular measure to be composed of *a random sample of items from a hypothetical domain of items*. An example would be a particular spelling test for fourth-grade students, which could be thought of as constituting a random sample of spelling words from all possible words appropriate for that age group. Another example would be the number of errors made by rats in a particular maze, in which case the errors made could be thought of as a random sample of the errors that would be made if there were an infinite number of turns in the maze and if rats were capable of traversing an infinitely long maze. Many other examples could be given of how it is reasonable to think of a particular measure as representing a sample of items from a hypothetical domain of items.

Of course, at the outset it is obvious that the model is not true to life because strictly speaking, items are almost never actually sampled randomly; rather, items are *composed* for particular measures. The model usually does, however, lead to accurate predictions in practice. First, it is stated that the purpose of any particular measurement is to estimate the measurement that would be obtained if *all* the items in the domain were employed, e.g., all the spelling words or an infinitely long maze. The score that any subject would obtain over the whole domain is spoken of as his *true score*. To the extent that any sample of items correlated highly with true scores, the sample would be highly reliable.

The model can be developed without consideration of the number of items sampled for particular measures. Each sample could contain many items or, at the lower extreme, only one item. Also, the model can be developed without concern for the type of item employed or the factorial composition of items.

### Parallel tests

The domain-sampling model discussed above offers a very general basis for developing a theory of reliability and for developing statistics needed in empirical research. The more complete theory following from the domain-sampling model is discussed in detail by Nunnally (1967). Here we shall discuss only one specific model which follows from the more general domain-sampling model, that of the model of parallel tests. The latter model is based on some restrictive assumptions about the nature of the sample tests from a domain of content. The advantage of presenting reliability theory here in terms of the model of parallel tests is that mathematical developments are much simpler to understand than those springing from the parent domain-sampling model. The same major conclusions are obtained from the more general domain-sampling model as from the special model of parallel tests (Nunnally, 1967). Two tests are parallel if (1) they have the same standard deviation, (2) they correlate the same with a set of true scores, and (3) the variance in each test which is not explainable by true scores is due to purely random error. (For some purposes, it is also useful to assume that the two tests have the same mean, but that assumption will not be necessary for developments here.)

The scores on two parallel tests can be broken down as follows:

$$x_1 = t + e_1$$
$$x_2 = t + e_2$$

where

$x_1$ = obtained deviation scores on test 1
$x_2$ = obtained deviation scores on test 2
$t$ = true scores in the domain
$e_1$ = errors on test 1
$e_2$ = errors on test 2

*these tests are given to the same person*

*— only 1 true score, same no. on both tests*

*← dealing w/ 5 diff sets of scores*

Since only the fallible scores on the two tests would actually be open to observation, the only way to learn about the true and error scores would be through the correlation of obtained scores on the two tests. Above it was assumed that the two tests correlate the same with true scores. If that correlation were known, it could then be used in a regression equation to estimate scores on the two fallible variables. From simple principles of correlation, much can be deducted about components of true and error variance.

In addition to principles incorporated in the above three basic assumptions for parallel tests, other principles can easily be deduced from the third assumption, that the portion of variance in each test not explainable by true scores is due to purely random error. First, by definition random errors tend to cancel one another, and consequently the mean of the errors on each test is expected to be zero. Second, since random errors do not correlate with one another, (1) errors on one test are expected to correlate zero with errors on the other test and (2) errors on either test are expected to correlate zero with true scores.

With this model, the following principles have been assumed or deduced:

$$\sigma_1 = \sigma_2$$
$$r_{1t} = r_{2t}$$
$$r_{te_1} = 0$$
$$r_{te_2} = 0$$
$$r_{e_1 e_2} = 0$$
$$M_{e_1} = 0$$
$$M_{e_2} = 0$$

*(handwritten annotations: error of test #1 is independent of error of test #2; says that the error is truely random (uncorrelated error); mean error)*

Since error scores are uncorrelated with true scores, it follows that

$$\sigma_1{}^2 = \sigma_t{}^2 + \sigma_{e_1}{}^2$$

and $\qquad\qquad$ (D-1)

$$\sigma_2{}^2 = \sigma_t{}^2 + \sigma_{e_2}{}^2$$

Because variances of obtained scores are equal on the two tests and variances of true scores are equal, it follows that variances of error scores are also equal.

It is important to examine the correlation between the two parallel tests, as follows:

$$r_{12} = \frac{1/N(\Sigma x_1 x_2)}{\sigma_1 \sigma_2} \qquad\qquad (D-2)$$

Since $x_1$ and $x_2$ can be expressed as the sum of true and error scores and since in the denominator the two standard deviations are equal, the correlation can be written as

$$r_{12} = \frac{1/N\, \Sigma(t + e_1)(t + e_2)}{\sigma_1{}^2}$$

$$= \frac{1/N(\Sigma t^2 + \Sigma t e_1 + \Sigma t e_2 + \Sigma e_1 e_2)}{\sigma_1{}^2}$$

$$= \frac{\sigma_t{}^2 + \sigma_{te_1} + \sigma_{te_2} + \sigma_{e_1 e_2}}{\sigma_1{}^2}$$

When the sum of cross products between any two sets of deviation scores is divided by the number of subjects, the result is referred to as a *covariance*. Thus for any two sets of test scores $x_1$ and $x_2$, $\Sigma x_1 x_2 / N$ is said to be the covariance of those two tests and is symbolized as $\sigma_{12}$. By a proper manipulation of Equation (D-2), it can be shown that $\sigma_{12}$ equals the correlation between the two measures multiplied by the product of the standard deviations of the two measures $r_{12}\sigma_1\sigma_2$. Then in any case where the correlation is known to be zero, the covariance must be zero also. In the numerator of the foregoing equation for the correlation between parallel-test forms, one of the four terms is a variance $(\sigma_t{}^2)$, and the other three terms are covariances, e.g., the covariance of errors on the two tests $\sigma_{e_1 e_2}$. Because errors are uncorrelated with true scores and uncorrelated with one another, the three covariance terms in the numerator drop out, leaving

$$r_{12} = \frac{\sigma_t{}^2}{\sigma_1{}^2} \tag{D-3}$$

Because of the importance of the correlation between two parallel-test forms, it is given the special symbol $r_{11}$ rather than the more general symbol $r_{12}$, which has been used in mathematical developments to this point. The symbol $r_{11}$ is used because theoretically one is correlating a test with itself, i.e., with a test that is parallel in all essential ways.

In a manner similar to that in which the result in Equation (D-3) is derived, many other important results about measurement reliability can be deduced from the parallel-test model and the more general domain-sampling model. The parallel-test model is important because deductions from it tend to hold for investigations of reliability by the method of alternative forms. In Chapter 5 no mention was made of assumptions regarding the statistical characteristics of alternative forms, but, rather, they were loosely defined as two similar collections of items. In most instances, a careful effort to construct alternative forms results in essentially parallel tests, ones that closely match the three assumptions for parallel tests discussed previously. Consequently, all the deductions that come from the model of parallel tests tend to hold true with actual investigations of correlations between alternative forms.

Equation (D-3) concerns a ratio (or percentage) of true-score variance to obtained-score variance. In Chapter 4 it was shown that the percentage of variance which one variable (here true scores) can explain in another variable (here obtained scores) is equal to the squared PM correlation between the two variables. Consequently, $r_{11}$ equals the squared correlation of $x_1$ with true scores. Similarly, in accordance with the assumptions of the parallel-test model, $r_{11}$ equals the squared correlation of the parallel test $(x_2)$ with true scores. Stated more formally,

$$r_{1t}{}^2 = \frac{\sigma_t{}^2}{\sigma_1{}^2} = r_{11} \tag{D-4}$$

$$r_{1t} = \sqrt{r_{11}}$$

and
$$r_{2t} = \sqrt{r_{11}}$$

The importance of the deductions in Equation (D-4) is that an estimate of the reliability coefficient $r_{11}$ leads to an estimate of the hypothetical correlation

$r_{1t}$ (or $r_{2t}$) between a set of scores actually obtained in research and a hypothetical set of error-free true scores.

## Internal-consistency reliability

In Chapter 5 it was said that the reliability of a test can be estimated from the internal consistency of the items within it. If the average correlation between items within a test is high, the internal consistency is high. If the average correlation is near zero, the internal consistency is near zero. (Correlations between items on most tests are low in an absolute sense, with average correlations above .30 being the exception.)

Because logically the best estimate of reliability is obtained by correlating alternative forms of a measure, one has a right to wonder how a good estimate of reliability can be obtained from the correlations between the items on one test. A good estimate can be obtained if the following two assumptions are correct. The first assumption is that the average correlation between items within the existing test is the same as the average correlation between items within the hypothetical alternative form. The second assumption (the one that is most frequently violated) is that the average correlation between items in the existing test is the same as the average cross-correlation between items in the existing test and items in the hypothetical test. This evidence could be obtained by actually constructing the hypothetical test and correlating each item on the existing test with each item on the hypothetical test. If the foregoing two assumptions hold, the correlation between the existing test and the hypothetical test can be deduced mathematically. (The derivation is presented in Nunnally, 1967, Ch. 6.) For a test with dichotomously scored items, the formula is as follows:

$$r_{11} = \frac{k}{k-1}\left(1 - \frac{\Sigma pq}{\sigma_x{}^2}\right) \tag{D-5}$$

where

$k$ = number of items on existing test
$\sigma_x{}^2$ = variance of total scores on test
$p$ = percentage of persons who pass each item
$q = 1 - p$

Use of Equation (D-5) is illustrated as follows. A test has 21 items; consequently, the first term on the right of the equation is 21/20 or 1.05. The $p$ values of items range from 0.30 to 0.80. Each $p$ value is multiplied by $1 - p$, and these products are summed over the 21 items. The resulting sum is 4.0. The variance of total scores is computed in the usual way. First, the number of correct answers out of 21 is determined for each person, resulting in a distribution of total test scores. The variance (squared standard deviation) is found to be 16.0. Substituting these quantities into Equation (D-5) results in a reliability ($r_{11}$) of .79.

The estimate is that, if an alternative form is constructed which approximately meets the aforementioned two assumptions, the existing test will correlate .79 with the alternative form.    Equation (D-5) is called the *Kuder-Richardson formula 20*.

Equation (D-5) takes on a slightly different appearance when the test contains multipoint items rather than dichotomously scored items.    The former would be the case, for example, if the measure consisted of the sum of ratings on 10 seven-step scales concerning attitudes toward the United Nations.    With multipoint items, the internal-consistency reliability is determined as follows:

$$r_{11} = \frac{k}{k-1}\left(1 - \frac{\Sigma \sigma_i^2}{\sigma_x^2}\right)$$    (D-6)

The only difference between Equations (D-5) and (D-6) is that in the latter, $\Sigma \sigma_i^2$ is substituted for $\Sigma_{pq}$ in the former.    In using Equation (D-6), the squared standard deviation of scores on each item is determined, and these variances are summed over items.    Actually, Equations (D-5) and (D-6) are equivalent because the variance of a dichotomously scored item equals $pq$.    Equation (D-6) is called *coefficient alpha*.

Regardless of whether or not correlations are obtained between alternative forms of a test, it is important to compute the internal-consistency reliability. In the general case this is coefficient alpha (Equation [D-6]), with Equation (D-5) being used in the case of dichotomously scored items.    It is surprising how well reliability estimated from internal consistency actually predicts the correlation of alternative forms in many instances.    In particular, this tends to be the case when (1) it is relatively easy to compose additional items for the construction of an alternative form and (2) there are no major practice effects from administration of the first form.    These conditions tend to hold, for example, with tests of arithmetic, spelling, and vocabulary and with many measures of attitudes and personality.    The foregoing conditions tend not to hold in the case where there is something tricky about the items, where if the individual catches on during the first test administration, he is likely to improve his performance markedly on administration of the alternative form.    This can occur in some of the reasoning tests concerning series completion—to take a very simple example, in completion of the following series: ababcbcd___.    Many such problems can be solved by the application of simple rules.    An individual might learn some of these rules in the process of taking the first test, which would allow him to obtain a better score on the alternative form.    If people differed from one another in the amount of such improvement, this would tend to reduce the correlation between alternative forms.

The second circumstance in which the internal-consistency reliability might provide a poor estimate of the correlation between alternative forms is that in which it is very difficult to compose numerous items that obviously relate to the same trait.    In composing items for a test, one frequently has the feeling of running out of ideas for new items even before enough items have been obtained for the original test.    Then it is even more difficult to compose items for an alternative form.    This tends to be the case in constructing measures of creativity, where items are sufficiently difficult to compose that items composed later tend to measure something different from items composed earlier.

The foregoing examples tend to be the exceptions rather than the rule. In most cases the itnernal-consistency reliability is a good estimate of the correlation between alternative forms. Since the internal-consistency reliability is only an estimate of the correlation between alternative forms, one has a right to ask, "Why not wait until the correlation between alternative forms is obtained?" There are two major reasons why this is not done. First, in some instances it is not feasible actually to construct an alternative form. This is frequently the case in large-scale factor analyses, where more than 50 tests might be employed. It is difficult enough to compose the original tests, let alone compose an alternative form for each of them. Second, the internal-consistency reliability provides evidence regarding whether or not it is worth the trouble to construct an alternative form for a test. The internal-consistency reliability is logically an upper limit to the reliability obtained from the correlation of alternative forms. (This follows from the domain-sampling model of reliability, Nunnally, 1967, Ch. 6.) Then if the internal-consistency reliability is very low, it is not worth the trouble to construct an alternative form. Rather, one would either abandon the project or attempt to construct a much more reliable test.

### Corrections for attenuation

One of the most important uses of the reliability coefficient is in estimating the extent to which obtained correlations between variables are attenuated by measurement error. The correction for attenuation is as follows:

$$\bar{r}_{12} = \frac{r_{12}}{\sqrt{r_{11}r_{22}}} \tag{D-7}$$

where

$r_{12}$ = correlation actually obtained between two tests
$r_{11}$ = reliability of first test
$r_{22}$ = reliability of second test
$\bar{r}_{12}$ = estimated correlation

In this case, $\bar{r}_{12}$ is the expected correlation if both variables were perfectly reliable. If the correction is to be made for only one of the two variables, the reliability coefficient for only that variable will appear under the radical in the denominator.

There is some controversy about when the correction for attenuation should be applied. One could argue that the correction for attenuation provides a way of fooling oneself into believing that a "better" correlation has been found than that actually evidenced in the available data. Another justifiable criticism of many uses of the correction for attenuation is that the so-called correction sometimes provides a very poor estimate of the correlation actually obtained between variables when they are made highly reliable. This can occur if a poor measure of reliability is made, in terms of principles discussed previously, and/or if the reliability coefficient is based on a relatively small number of cases (less than 300). That poor estimates are often obtained is illustrated by the fact that corrected correlations are sometimes greater than 1.00!

If, however, good estimates of reliability are available, there are some appropriate uses of the correction for attenuation. The most important use is in basic research, where the corrected correlation between two variables is an estimate of how much two traits correlate. In an investigation of the correlation between anxiety and intelligence, for example, the real question is that of how much the two traits go together. If the two measures have only modest reliability, the actual correlation will suggest that the two traits go together less than they really do.

Another important use of the correction for attenuation is in applied settings where a test is used to forecast a criterion. If, as often happens, the criterion is not highly reliable, correcting for unreliability of the criterion will result in an estimate of the real validity of the test. Here, however, it would be wrong to make the double correction for attenuation, since the issue is how well a test actually works rather than how well it would work if it were perfectly reliable. In prediction problems, the reliability of the predictor instrument places a limit on its ability to forecast a criterion, and the correction for attenuation cannot make a test more predictive than it actually is. The only use for this double correction would be in estimating the limit of predictive validity of the test as both test and criterion are made more and more reliable.

Since perfect reliability is only a handy fiction, results from applying the foregoing formula for the correction for attenuation are always hypothetical. It is more important to estimate the increase in the correlation between two variables when the reliability is increased by any particular amount. A formula for doing this is as follows:

$$\overline{r}_{12} = \frac{r_{12}\sqrt{r_{11}'r_{22}'}}{\sqrt{r_{11}r_{22}}} \tag{D-8}$$

where

$\overline{r}_{12}$ = estimated correlation between two variables if reliabilities are changed

$r_{11}'$ = changed reliability for variable 1

$r_{22}'$ = changed reliability for variable 2

The use of Equation (D-8) can be illustrated in the situation where two tests correlate .30 and each test has a reliability of .60. If the reliability of each test were increased to .90, the expected correlation between the more reliable tests would be obtained as follows:

$$\overline{r}_{12} = \frac{.3\sqrt{.9 \times .9}}{\sqrt{.6 \times .6}}$$

$$\overline{r}_{12} = .45$$

For the sake of computations, a handier version of Equation (D-8) is as follows:

$$\bar{r}_{12} = r_{12}\sqrt{\frac{r_{11}'r_{22}'}{r_{11}r_{22}}} \qquad \text{(D-9)}$$

The formula can also be used to estimate what the correlation would be if both reliabilities were *lowered*. This is useful when it is necessary to employ shortened versions of longer tests. If the reliabilities are known for both the longer tests and the shortened versions and the correlation is known between the longer tests, the reliabilities of the shortened tests can be placed in Equation (D-9) as $r_{11}'$ and $r_{22}'$, and the reliabilities of the longer tests as $r_{11}$ and $r_{22}$. Equation (D-9) applies equally well when the reliability of one test is increased and the reliability of the other is decreased. If the reliability of only one of the two variables is to be changed, Equation (D-9) becomes

$$\bar{r}_{12} = r_{12}\sqrt{\frac{r_{11}'}{r_{11}}} \qquad \text{(D-10)}$$

This version of the formula is useful in estimating how much the correlation of a predictor test with a criterion will change if the reliability of the test is either increased or decreased by particular amounts.

What should be evident from inspecting the formulas concerning corrections for attenuation is that such corrected correlations are seldom dramatically different from the actual correlations. Thus in the example above, a dramatic increase in the reliability of each test from .60 to .90 resulted in an increase in correlation from .30 to only .45. Such a difference is important, but it is much less than intuitively might be thought to occur. As another example, if the correction were made for only one variable and the reliability were increased from .60 to .80, a correlation of .30 would be expected to rise only to .35. The author once heard a colleague suggest that some low correlations found in a study probably would have been much higher if test reliabilities had been higher. The average correlation was about .15, and the average reliability was about .60. Even if the average reliability of the tests were increased to .90, the average correlation would be less than .25. The colleague had in mind an increase in average correlation to .40 or .50, which could not possibly occur.

## Confidence zones

Another use of the reliability coefficient is in establishing confidence zones for obtained scores. For any variable $x$, the standard error of measurement is

$$\sigma_{\text{meas}} = \sigma_x\sqrt{1 - r_{xx}} \qquad \text{(D-11)}$$

The standard error of measurement is the estimated standard deviation of obtained scores if any individual is given a large number of tests from a domain. It is then useful in establishing confidence zones for scores to be expected on many alternative forms of a test. It is incorrect to establish such confidence zones symmetrically about the score that a person makes on a particular test. If, for example, an individual has an IQ of 130 on a particular test and the $\sigma_{\text{meas}}$ is 5, it is incorrect to say that the 95 percent confidence zone for that person extends from 120 to 140 $(130 - 2\sigma_{\text{meas}}$ to $130 + 2\sigma_{\text{meas}})$. Even though the practice in most applied work with tests has been to center confidence zones about obtained scores, this is incorrect because obtained scores tend to be biased, high scores tending to be biased upward and low scores downward.

Before establishing confidence zones, one must obtain estimates of unbiased scores. Unbiased scores are the average scores people would obtain if they were administered all possible tests from a domain, holding constant the number of items randomly drawn for each. These are true scores, which are estimated as follows:

$$t' = r_{xx}x \tag{D-12}$$

In the previous example, the individual with an IQ of 130 would have a deviation score $x$ of 30. If the reliability were .90, his estimated true score $t'$ would be 27 in deviation-score units. Adding back the mean IQ of 100 would give an estimated true score of 127 in units of IQ. Then the correct procedure would be to set the 95 percent confidence zone as extending from two standard errors of measurement below 127 to two standard errors above 127. With a $\sigma_{\text{meas}}$ of 5, the zone would then extend from 117 to 137. If a person were administered a large number of alternative forms of the test, 95 percent of the obtained scores would be expected to fall in that zone, and the expected average of the obtained scores would be 127 (not 130).

In most applied work with tests, there is little reason for estimating true scores except for the establishment of confidence zones. Since estimated true scores correlate perfectly with obtained scores and since making practical interpretations of estimated true scores is difficult, in most applied work it is better to interpret the individual's obtained score. The estimated true score would be used only to obtain the center for a confidence zone. Thus in the example above, the individual would be said to have an IQ of 130, with the 95 percent confidence zone extending from 117 to 137. On that same test, a person with an IQ of 70 would have a 95 percent confidence zone extending from 63 to 83. Actually, such asymmetrical confidence zones have a real practical advantage: they continually remind people that scores obtained on any test tend to be biased outward on both sides of the mean.

In contrast to applied work with tests, there is seldom need in basic research to estimate true scores or establish confidence zones. In basic research the major concerns are with how much the measurement error lowers correlations and how much it increases the error components in statistical treatments. It is sometimes necessary in basic research to consider the effect of measurement error on the mean of a group of obtained scores. This would be the case, for example, if extreme groups on a measure were subjected to an experimental treatment and then either a retest were made or an alternative form were applied. The gain or loss scores for individuals, and the average gain and loss scores for the two groups, would be partly determined by regression effects from measurement error. In essence what one must do is estimate average true scores for the two groups on both tests and then see whether the average change is different for the two groups. Except for this special problem, however, in basic research there is little to be gained by estimating true scores or establishing confidence zones.

## Effect of dispersion on reliability

It should be realized that since the reliability coefficient is a correlation coefficient, the size of the reliability coefficient is directly related to the standard deviation of obtained scores for any sample of subjects. Previously it was shown that the reliability coefficient could be expressed as follows:

$$r_{xx} = 1 - \frac{\sigma_{\text{meas}}^2}{\sigma_x^2} \tag{D-13}$$

The variance of the errors of measurement is expected to be at least approximately independent of the standard deviation of obtained scores. In other words, the standard error of measurement is considered to be a fixed characteristic of any measurement tool regardless of the sample of subjects under investigation. Then it is apparent that the reliability coefficient will be larger for samples of subjects that vary more with respect to the trait being investigated, as would be the case, for example, in a study of the reliability of scores on a test used to select college freshmen. If the correlation between alternative forms is used as the measure of reliability and the correlation is computed only for persons who actually were accepted for college, the correlation will be less than it would have been if persons who were not permitted to enter college had been included in the study.

A look back at Equation (D-13) will indicate how estimates can be made of how much the reliability would change if the variance of obtained scores were either larger or smaller. If, for one sample, the variance of errors were 2.0 and the variance of obtained scores were 8.0, the reliability would be .75. If a new sample had a variance of 10.0, the variance of errors would be expected to remain at 2.0, and consequently the reliability would be .80. Thus after the standard error of measurement is found for one sample, it is easy to estimate what the reliability would be in another sample with either a larger or a smaller standard deviation of scores.

Even though it is important to keep in mind that the reliability varies with the dispersion of scores, this does not alter the direct meaning of the reliability coefficient in any particular sample of people. The reliability coefficient is the ratio of true-score variance to obtained-score variance. If that ratio is small, measurement error will attenuate correlations with other variables and will make it difficult to find significant effects with statistical treatments. If the total group of subjects in a study has a standard deviation of scores which is not much larger than the standard error of measurement, it is hopeless to investigate the variable. Approximately this condition has occurred in some studies.

For example, in some studies of creativity, investigations have been made of only those children who had IQs of at least 120. With the children preselected in this way, the standard deviation of IQs in the group being studied would not be much larger than the standard error of measurement for the measure of intelligence. Then if IQs for the preselected groups are correlated with scores on tests of creativity, the correlations obviously will be very low.

## Test length

The primary way to make tests more reliable is to make them longer. If the reliability is known for a test with any particular number of items, the following formula can be used to estimate how much the reliability would increase if the number of items were increased by any factor $k$:

$$r_{kk} = \frac{kr_{11}}{1 + (k-1)r_{11}} \tag{D-14}$$

If, for example, the reliability of a 20-item test is .70 and 40 items from the same domain are added to the test (making the final test three times as long as the original), the estimated reliability of the 60-item test will be

$$r_{kk} = \frac{3(.7)}{1 + (3-1).7} = .88$$

The only assumption in employing Equation (D-14) in this case would be that the average correlation between the 20 items in the shorter test is the same as the average correlation between the 60 items in the augmented test. The assumption would be violated if old items and new items differed systematically in content (if they were from somewhat different domains) or if they differed in reliability (if the average correlation in one set were higher than that in the other set). In spite of these potential sources of imprecision, it is surprising how accurately the effects of test length on reliability are usually estimated by Equation (D-14). This is particularly so if the shorter test contains at least 20 items. (The precision of the reliability estimate is directly related to the number of test items.)

Equation (D-14) can also be used to estimate the effects on reliability of shortening a test. In this case, $k$ is a fraction rather than a whole number, $r_{kk}$ is the estimated reliability of the shortened test, and $r_{11}$ is the reliability of the longer test. In the previous example, one could work backward from the reliability of .88 for the 60-item test and estimate the reliability of a 20-item test. Then, by placing .88 as $r_{11}$ in Equation (D-14) and making $k = \frac{1}{3}$, one recovers the original reliability of .70 for the 20-item test. For either lengthening or shortening a test, the precision of the estimate obtained from Equation (D-14) depends mainly on the number of items in the *shorter* test. To take an extreme case, one would not expect a very precise estimate if the known reliability of a 5-item test were used to estimate the reliability of a 40-item test, or vice versa.

Since Equation (D-14) shows the test reliability to be a direct function of the number of test items only, one might wonder how it can give accurate estimates where there are other sources of measurement error in tests, e.g., variation in scores over short periods of time. Actually, many such sources of error are considered by the domain-sampling model. Coefficient alpha is sensitive not only to the sampling of items but also to sources of measurement error that are present within the testing session. The alternative-form measure of reliability can be made sensitive to all sources of error, including subjectivity of scoring and variations in abilities and personality characteristics over short periods of time. If coefficient alpha is placed in Equation (D-14), the estimated coefficient alpha for a longer or shorter test takes into account the sampling of items and numerous sources of error in the testing situation. If the correlation between alternative forms is placed in Equation (D-14), the estimate takes account of variations over short periods of time and any factors that have been systematically varied for the two testings, e.g., using different scorers for the two tests. A good estimate would then be obtained of the alternative-form reliability for a longer or shorter test over the same period of time and with the same factors systematically varied. For these reasons, Equation (D-14) is not blind to sources of error other than those due to the sampling of items per se. Coefficient alpha placed in Equation (D-14) usually gives a good estimate of the coefficient alpha that will be obtained from a lengthened or shortened test. If the alternative-form reliability is placed in Equation (D-14), it will usually give a good estimate of the alternative-form reliability for a longer or shorter test. Since coefficient alpha is usually a good estimate of the alternative-form reliability, when the former is placed in Equation (D-14), it will usually give a good estimate of the correlation to be expected between alternative forms with any particular number of items.

When the estimate is of the reliability that would be obtained from doubling the length of a test, Equation (D-14) takes on the following appearance:

$$r_{kk} = \frac{2r_{11}}{1 + r_{11}} \tag{D-15}$$

An example would be in predicting the reliability of doubling the length of a test which has an initial reliability of .60. Then the numerator of the term on the right would be 1.2, and the denominator would be 1.6. The predicted reliability is then .75.

Equation (D-15) is particularly useful for estimating reliability from the correlation of split halves of a test, which is usually obtained by correlating scores on the even-numbered items with scores on the odd-numbered items. Because the correlation estimates the reliability for the half tests and not for the whole test, it is necessary to correct the correlation with Equation (D-15). The precision of reliability estimates obtained from Equation (D-15) is based on the same assumptions as those for the parent equation (D-14). Equation (D-15) is referred to as the *Spearman-Brown correction for split-half reliability*.

An inspection of Equation (D-14) shows that if the average correlation between items in a domain is positive, no matter how small, then as the number of items in a test is made larger and larger, the reliability necessarily approaches 1.00. If the average correlation is positive, the correlation between any two samples of items ($r_{11}$) is expected to be positive. If the numerator and denominator of Equation (D-14) are divided by $k$ and if $k$ is allowed to approach infinity, $r_{kk}$ approaches 1.00. At first glance this might seem to be an easy way to obtain highly reliable tests, but often in practice Equation (D-14) indicates that to reach even a moderately high reliability a huge number of items would be required. A conversion of Equation (D-14) can be used to estimate the number of items required to obtain a particular reliability:

$$k = \frac{r_{kk}(1 - r_{11})}{r_{11}(1 - r_{kk})} \qquad \text{(D-16)}$$

where

$r_{kk}$ = desired reliability
$r_{11}$ = reliability of existing test
$k$ = number of times the test would have to be lengthened to obtain reliability of $r_{kk}$

In the situation where a 20-item test has a reliability of .50, the estimated lengthening required to obtain a reliability of .80 is found as follows:

$$k = \frac{.8(1 - .5)}{.5(1 - .8)} = \frac{.4}{.1} = 4$$

Thus the estimate is that to reach a reliability of .80 an 80-item test would be required. In many cases it would be feasible to use a test of that length, but let us see what happens when a 40-item test has a reliability of only .20 and a reliability of .80 is desired:

$$k = \frac{.8(1 - .2)}{.2(1 - .8)} = \frac{.64}{.04} = 16$$

It is estimated that 640 items would be required to reach a reliability of .80. Unless the items were of a kind that could be administered very quickly, a test of that length would be impractical in most applied work and in most experiments. Thus one can see that if the average correlation between items in a domain is very low (e.g., only .05), the correlations between samples of items will not be large, and to obtain high correlations would require a prohibitively large number of items in each sample.

# Name Index

Albig, W., 503, 511
Allen, L., 301, 515
Amatruda, C. S., 296, 514
Anastasi, A., 260, 272, 309, 511
Anderson, G. L., 396, 511
Anderson, H. H., 396, 511
Andrew, D. M., 327, 511
Arenberg, D., 380, 513

Barrett, H. O., 336, 511
Bayley, N., 296, 511
Bechtoldt, H. P., 152, 511
Beck, S. J., 45, 388, 511
Beckman, A. S., 323, 511
Bell, J. E., 396, 511
Bennett, G. K., 261, 265–266, 316, 325,
 511–512, 518
Binet, A., 42, 45, 143, 234–235, 281–282,
 512
Bisbee, E. U., 328, 512
Blackstone, E. G., 328, 512
Bond, E. A., 512
Boring, E. G., 52, 512
Brown, C. W., 303, 319–322, 514
Buros, O. K., 419, 512

Campbell, D. T., 152, 421, 423, 512
Cantril, H., 503–504, 512
Carrigan, P. M., 367, 512
Carroll, H. A., 334, 512
Cattell, J. M., 41
Cattell, P., 296, 512

Cattell, R. B., 365, 385, 414, 512
Chase, C. I., 76, 512
Conrad, H. S., 300, 512
Cook, S. W., 421–423, 512
Coombs, C. H., 195, 512
Crawford, D. M., 315, 317, 512
Crawford, J. E., 315, 317, 512
Cronbach, L. J., 44, 137, 152, 272, 309,
 382, 512–513
Cunningham, B., 294, 518

Darwin, C., 39
Davis, F. B., 229, 513
Davis, H., 313, 513
Dixon, W. J., 104, 513
Drake, R. M., 330, 513
Duchnowski, A. J., 409, 507, 517
Durost, W., 294, 518
Dykema, P. W., 516

Edwards, A. L., 188, 195, 366–368, 373,
 433, 434, 460, 513
Eysenck, H. J., 366–367, 385, 406, 414,
 513

Farina, A., 380, 513
Farnsworth, D., 312, 513
Farnsworth, P. R., 330, 332, 513, 515
Faw, T. T., 508, 513
Fechner, G., 33–35, 50
Ferguson, G. A., 253, 513

# Subject Index